Irkutsk

MANCHURIA

Harbin

⊙ ULAN BATOR

Changchun

Vladivostok

MONGOLIA

Shenyang

Sea
of
Japan

N.
KOREA

GREAT WALL

Baotou

BEIJING ⊙

Dalian

S.
KOREA

Tianjin

Yellow
Sea

Lanzhou

Yanan

Taiyuan

Qingdao

JAPAN

Xian

Yellow   River

Nanjing

Shanghai

C H I N A

Hangzhou

East
China
Sea

Chengdu

River

Three
Gorges Dam

Wuhan

Yangtze

Chongqing

Changsha

Fuzhou

MATSU

TAIPEI

Guiyang

QUEMOY

Taiwan Strait

TAIWAN

GUANGDONG

Kaoshiung

PACIFIC
OCEAN

Guangzhou

Shenzhen
Hong Kong

Lang
Son

HANOI ⊙

Haiphong

HAINAN

South

THAILAND

China

LAOS   VIET

D1047236

PHILIPPINES

9 781891 620379

A GREAT WALL

SIX PRESIDENTS AND CHINA

A GREAT WALL

AN INVESTIGATIVE HISTORY

PATRICK TYLER

A CENTURY FOUNDATION BOOK

PublicAffairs • NEW YORK

Copyright © 1999 by Patrick Tyler.

Endpaper map © 1999 by Anita Karl and Jim Kemp.

Published in the United States by PublicAffairs™, a member of the Perseus Books Group.

All rights reserved.

Printed in the United States of America.

No part of this book may be reproduced in any manner whatsoever without written permission except in the case of brief quotations embodied in critical articles and reviews. For information, address PublicAffairs, 250 West 57th Street, Suite 1321, New York, NY 10107.

Book design by Jenny Dossin.

LIBRARY OF CONGRESS CATALOGING-IN-PUBLICATION DATA

Tyler, Patrick.

A great wall : six presidents and China : an investigative history / Patrick Tyler. — 1st ed.

p.   cm.

"A Century Foundation book."

Includes index.

ISBN 1-891620-37-1

1. United States—Foreign relations—China. 2. China—Foreign relations—United States. 3. United States—Foreign relations—1945–1989. 4. United States—Foreign relations—1989–

I.   Title.

E183.8.C5T93 1999

327.73051—dc21   99-27275
                                                                          CIP

FIRST EDITION

10   9   8   7   6   5   4   3   2   1

In memory of LaVesta Timberlake Knight
. . . and Lorayne Knight Tyler

CONTENTS

FOREWORD   *ix*

CAST OF CHARACTERS   *xiii*

Prologue: The Risk of War . . .   3

The Taiwan Crisis   19

The Sino-Soviet Border: 1969   45

Nixon: The Opening . . .   105

Ford: Estrangement—"I smile bitterly . . . "   181

Carter: Fulfillment—"The president has made up his mind . . . "   227

Reagan: . . . and Taiwan   287

Bush: . . . and Tiananmen   341

Clinton: The Butchers of Beijing . . .   381

Transition: . . . it begins again   417

NOTES   431

PHOTOGRAPH CREDITS   461

ACKNOWLEDGMENTS   463

INDEX   465

FOREWORD

"On her first voyage, the Columbia had solved the riddle of the China trade."

SAMUEL ELIOT MORISON

WITHOUT SLIGHTING a great historian, when one reviews U.S.-China relations in the twentieth century, it appears that very little has ever been settled for very long. And the same uncertainty—the same potential for change and surprise—seems a good bet to continue well into the new century. Under these circumstances, policymakers and the public have an especially acute need for high quality, in-depth information about the personalities, ideas, and events that form the basis of relations between the two nations. All those with an interest in these matters are well served by the sort of exceptionally thoughtful journalism represented by the work of Patrick Tyler, a distinguished reporter and former Beijing bureau chief for *The New York Times*.

In this volume, Tyler draws on his long experience in Asia and his deep understanding of Chinese politics to provide both a vivid portrait of the interaction of Washington and Beijing over the past three decades and an insightful analysis of the forces that shaped policy in both capitals. His narrative tells us a good deal about that recent history. It also is an essential starting point for anyone who wishes to understand the current agenda of bilateral relations.

China has been much in the American news these days: stories of alleged campaign finance improprieties, tales of possible nuclear espionage, reports of an errant U.S. bomb striking the Chinese embassy in Belgrade resulting in anti-American street demonstrations in many Chinese cities, and continuing coverage of conflicts over human rights issues and trade. Behind these sensational headlines, there are smaller—perhaps superficially less newsworthy—stories that may be even more significant in terms of understanding our relations with China. Chinese rockets place communications satellites in orbit for American companies; about 40,000 Chinese students pursue their studies at U.S. colleges and universities; and China enjoys a significant trade surplus with the United States.

The complex nature of our dealings with China, some of them shrouded in secrecy, makes it difficult to answer such basic questions as the following: Are relations worsening or improving? Is China an enemy, some sort of friend, or something new under the post-Cold War sun? Any attempt to answer these questions must be grounded in an understanding not simply of America's current interests in Asia but also of the abiding priorities of the Chinese leadership. In this context, Patrick Tyler's work is essential reading. He emphasizes, for example, the persistent centrality of the Taiwan issue for China's rulers. And, he makes clear that the future of that island remains a potential flashpoint that, on short notice, might undo all the constructive engagement of recent years. In fact, in Tyler's view, Washington policymakers have not always assessed these critical matters with either enough sophistication or sufficient clarity. While he maintains his journalistic objectivity, he does not pull his punches.

Since the historic reopening of relations with China during the Nixon administration, U.S.-China interaction has often been obscured by other international news of more immediate American entanglements. Since today's complex relationship is, in part, a product of those early negotiations, Tyler's book is especially useful. He reports in detail about the internal workings of Chinese politics during this critical period in the 1970s. His reporting is enhanced by his access to many of the top leaders in China and his ability to integrate their recollections effectively with the increasingly available information from the American side because of the release of numerous memoirs and monographs, as well as government records and documents, covering many of the critical meetings and issues.

While the future is uncertain and China's particular form of communism is still in power, it's clear that the former Cold War state of relations between the two nations has been relegated to the history books. It is equally clear that relations with the Asian superpower are among the most important matters in American foreign policy. In this context, Tyler's work is a welcome addition to the short shelf of useful books about the recent history of U.S.-China affairs.

The importance of Asia to American foreign policy has been a concern of The Century Foundation over the years. In the late 1970s, we supported *Island China*, a book by Ralph Clough that examines Taiwan's role in U.S.-China relations; in the late 1980s, we published Robert Manning's *Asian Policy*; in the early 1990s, Jeffrey Garten explored the economic interdependence of the United States, Japan, and Germany in *A Cold Peace*. We are now supporting works by Kenneth Pyle on U.S.-Japanese relations and their effects on creating a new order in Asia and by Selig Harrison on U.S.-Korean relations, as well as a number of broader studies of post-Cold War political relations that address economic and political issues involving Asia, Middle Asia, Europe, and the Middle East.

Patrick Tyler's close look at U.S.-China relations over the course of the past few decades adds greatly to our knowledge of foreign policymaking. The Century Foundation is pleased to have helped make this book a reality.

Richard C. Leone, President
The Century Foundation
June 1999

CAST OF CHARACTERS

Mao Zedong	Chairman of the Chinese Communist Party; died, September 1976
Zhou Enlai	Premier of the People's Republic of China; died, January 1976
Liu Shaoqi	Vice Chairman of the party; deposed by Mao, 1966
Deng Xiaoping	Secretary General of the party, 1957–1966; deposed, 1967, 1976; paramount leader, 1978–1997
Lin Biao	Marshal of the People's Liberation Army (PLA); Vice Chairman, Mao's designated heir; died in coup attempt, 1971
Chen Yi	Marshal of the PLA; mayor of Shanghai, Foreign Minister; died, 1972
Ye Jianying	Marshal of the PLA; instrumental in overthrowing the Gang of Four and returning Deng Xiaoping to power
Hua Guofeng	Mao's designated successor in 1976; displaced by Deng, 1978
Hu Yaobang	General Secretary of the Communist Party under Deng; deposed, 1987; died, April 1989
Zhao Ziyang	Premier and then General Secretary of the Communist Party after Hu Yaobang; deposed, June 1989
Qiao Guanhua	Vice Foreign Minister under Zhou Enlai; later Foreign Minister
Zhang Hanzhi	Mao's onetime English teacher; married Qiao Guanhua
Huang Hua	Chinese negotiator at Panmunjom, Korea, in 1952; rose to become Foreign Minister in the late 1970s
Huang Zhen	Ambassador to France and, later, to the United States

Qian Qichen	Foreign Minister under Deng
Nancy Tang	Interpreter for Mao, Zhou, Deng, and other senior Chinese leaders
Liu Huaqiu	Vice Foreign Minister under Deng
Ji Chaozhu	Interpreter for Zhou and Deng; later a diplomat

THE REPUBLIC OF CHINA ON TAIWAN

Chiang Kai-shek	Nationalist Party leader; fled to Taiwan, 1949; died, April 1975
Chiang Ching-kuo	Nationalist Party leader after death of Chiang Kai-shek; died, 1988
Lee Teng-hui	Vice President, then President
Frederick Chien	Vice Foreign Minister and later Foreign Minister

THE NIXON ADMINISTRATION: 1969–1974

Richard M. Nixon	President
Spiro T. Agnew	Vice President
Gerald R. Ford	Vice President
William P. Rogers	Secretary of State
Henry A. Kissinger	Assistant for National Security Affairs, Secretary of State
Melvin R. Laird	Secretary of Defense
James R. Schlesinger	CIA Director, Secretary of Defense
Richard Helms	CIA Director
H. R. Haldeman	White House Chief of Staff
George Bush	Ambassador to the United Nations; U.S. Liaison Office chief, Beijing
Elliot L. Richardson	Undersecretary of State
William G. Hyland	Kissinger assistant
Helmut Sonnenfeldt	Kissinger assistant

THE FORD ADMINISTRATION: 1974–1977

Gerald R. Ford	President
Nelson Rockefeller	Vice President
Henry A. Kissinger	Secretary of State

Brent Scowcroft   Assistant for National Security Affairs
James R. Schlesinger   Secretary of Defense
George Bush   U.S. Liaison Office chief, Beijing; CIA Director

THE CARTER ADMINISTRATION: 1977–1981

Jimmy Carter   President
Walter Mondale   Vice President
Cyrus Vance   Secretary of State
Harold Brown   Secretary of Defense
Zbigniew Brzezinski   Assistant for National Security Affairs
Richard Holbrooke   Assistant Secretary of State
Leonard Woodcock   Ambassador to China
Michel Oksenberg   National Security Council aide for China

THE REAGAN ADMINISTRATION: 1981–1989

Ronald Reagan   President
George Bush   Vice President
Alexander M. Haig Jr.   Secretary of State
George Shultz   Secretary of State
Richard V. Allen   Assistant for National Security Affairs
John Holdridge   Assistant Secretary of State
William F. Rope   Country director, China Desk, State Department
Arthur Hummel Jr.   Ambassador to China
Winston Lord   Ambassador to China

THE BUSH ADMINISTRATION: 1989–1993

George Bush   President
James A. Baker III   Secretary of State
Brent Scowcroft   Assistant for National Security Affairs
James R. Lilley   Ambassador to China; Pentagon official
J. Stapleton Roy   Ambassador to China

THE CLINTON ADMINISTRATION: 1993–2001

Bill Clinton	President
Warren Christopher	Secretary of State
Madeleine K. Albright	Secretary of State
Anthony Lake	Assistant for National Security Affairs
Samuel R. Berger	Deputy to Lake, then Assistant for National Security Affairs
Les Aspin	Secretary of Defense
William J. Perry	Secretary of Defense
General John Shalikashvili	Chairman, Joint Chiefs of Staff
Winston Lord	Assistant Secretary of State
Robert E. Rubin	National Economic Council, Secretary of Treasury
J. Stapleton Roy	Ambassador to China

A GREAT WALL

PROLOGUE:
THE RISK
OF WAR...

Chinese warplanes during exercises near Taiwan

I T APPEARS AS AN unlikely war zone.

Descending through white puffs of cloud towing their shadows across the western Pacific, the first thing one notices on the air approach to Taiwan is that the island is dominated by a central mountain range resembling the great hulk of a whale. It's as if, at the beginning of time, some mid-Cambrian squalus had lolled ashore for a nap on the leaf-shaped platform that rises out of the sea, there to expire under the luscious subtropical sun, then to rot, petrify, and, in the by-and-by of prehistory, crumble and erode. From the crevices etched by the elements in the ancient carcass, cedar and rosewood forests have risen in the fast forward of millennia, and, in the past few seconds of geologic time, inhabitants have arrived to assign a simple nomenclature to the landscape. There is Jade Mountain (higher than Mount Fuji in Japan), Snow Mountain, and the high shores of Sun Moon Lake, located at the top of the hump about where the whale's blowhole would be.

The whole of Taiwan lies 245 miles along its north-south axis and is crossed by the Tropic of Cancer in the south. Girding the circumference of the central massif is a sloping arable plain created by an eternity of rainfall whose torrents transported sand and soil in cascades down from the watershed. The plain is broader on the western side of the island than on the east, where the deep blue of the Pacific sucks the light from the sky with a vacuum of unquenchable depth. On the western side, the shallow waters glow aquamarine. A little more than 100 miles across the Taiwan Strait, mainland China fills the horizon, spreading out in all directions. If the eye pulls back, as if viewing the western Pacific from space, Taiwan becomes a barely perceptible salient in the latitudes of China's sweeping coastline, a captive of China's geography and gravitational pull.

If you are Taiwanese, one of the million or so refugees who came with Chiang Kai-shek in 1949, or part of the majority whose ancestors migrated in small fishing boats from the mainland between the seventeenth and nineteenth centuries, to stand on the western shore of Taiwan and look out across the strait is to feel the presence of the mother continent just beyond the horizon. To some it is a comfort, to others a threat. In the ideograms of the Chinese language, China's name is 中 国, or Zhongguo. The first character means "middle" and the second "country" or "kingdom," conveying the Chinese core belief that they—denizens of the Middle Kingdom—have been the center of the world for the past 5,000 years of recorded history.

Today, in the mist-shrouded mountains surrounding Taipei, the modern capital city of Taiwan, teahouses built of honey-colored timbers nestle under a sculpted filigree of tropical greenery. Buddhist temples rise like decorative stalagmites with red lacquered columns holding aloft upturned rooflines guarded by ceramic dragons.

This lush and silent topography gives way to a clanking coastal plain where 21 million Taiwanese have built one of the "tiger" economies of Asia and where, today, Taiwanese and American technicians are erecting the foundations for a future war—a war with mainland China.

It is no longer alarmist to say so.

As the century ends and the new millennium begins, America is busily preparing Taiwan for war with mainland China, and it is surprising how the relentless military buildup has engendered little debate in the United States, despite the certainty that any war between China and Taiwan would draw the United States into a defense of the island.* Taiwan's leaders stand ready to exploit the American defense commitment by ever more forcefully asserting the island's sovereign and independent status, as President Lee Teng-hui did most dramatically in July 1999 when he proclaimed Taiwan was abandoning the longstanding doctrine that there is only one China and that Taiwan is part of it, thus throwing down an open declaration of Taiwanese separatism. Few Americans understand the danger of war and the inescapable reality that America would enter such a war, which could devastate the Chinese coastline, trigger an exodus from Taiwan and send a large portion of its population fleeing to the United States. And it would wreck the Asian economies, already reeling from capital flight and a major economic contraction that began in 1997.

The risk of war was startlingly apparent in the Taiwan crisis of 1996, where this book will begin. That crisis of dangerous ballistic missile firings and American naval deployments brought the United States closer to military confrontation with mainland China than at any time since the Eisen-

---

*The Taiwan Relations Act of 1979 states, "It is the policy of the United States . . . to consider any effort to determine the future of Taiwan by other than peaceful means, including boycotts or embargoes, a threat to the peace and security of the Western Pacific area and of grave concern to the United States, [and] . . . to maintain the capacity of the United States to resist any resort to force or other forms of coercion that would jeopardize the security, or the social and economic system, of the people on Taiwan."

hower administration. And, even after the crisis subsided, the residue of Chinese indignation remained so close to the surface that it exploded again with unexpected ferocity in May 1999 when Chinese rioters assaulted the U.S. embassy in Beijing. The attack on the U.S. embassy followed the mistaken bombing by American warplanes of the Chinese embassy in Belgrade, Yugoslavia, during NATO's campaign in the Balkans.

The arms race in the Taiwan Strait developed a new and ominous momentum when cargo ships and military transports arrived at Taiwan's ports and air bases to deliver American weapons sold to the island since the late 1980s: Patriot missiles to defend the capital city, Harpoon missiles to sink opposing warships, thousands of Stinger, Sparrow, and Sidewinder missiles to shoot down enemy warplanes, 450 refurbished American tanks, 150 new American warplanes, and combat computer systems to link these systems together for waging the kind of high-tech warfare that made its debut in the Persian Gulf War. Taiwanese shipyards, equipped with American manufacturing technology, have launched (as of spring 1999) five of a projected eight new American-designed frigates of the Oliver Perry class to join six, larger Knox class destroyers leased from the U.S. Navy and equipped with over-the-horizon radar, antiair and antisubmarine sensors. Taiwanese aircraft manufacturing lines, also equipped with American technology and aided by American consultants, have stamped out the first 70 of a projected 130 "Indigenous Fighters," a smaller version of the American F-16 Falcon, the U.S. Air Force's premier interceptor. Taiwanese pilots havealso been training at Luke Air Force Base in Arizona on the real thing. (The sale of 150 F-16s to Taiwan was authorized by President George Bush in 1992.)

The buildup has been supplemented by European sales: diesel attack submarines from the Netherlands, and sixty Mirage 2000 fighter-bombers as well as Lafayette class destroyers from France. From 1990 to 1997, Taiwan ranked second to Saudi Arabia as the largest recipient of foreign arms, totaling $12 billion on contracts worth nearly $18 billion—the greatest volume by far coming from the United States.[1]

From 1996 to 1999, the commander in chief of American forces in the Pacific, Admiral Joseph W. Prueher, undertook at his headquarters at Camp H. M. Smith in Honolulu extensive contingency planning for the defense of Taiwan, perhaps as extensive as that of any of his predecessors since the 1950s, when the U.S. Seventh Fleet twice sent warships into the Taiwan Strait to prevent a mainland invasion. These contingency plans are highly classified and contain escalatory steps that bring U.S. armed forces into direct confrontation with People's Liberation Army (PLA) naval, air force, and rocket forces.

At the same time, Congress and the Clinton administration have been rushing to develop a multibillion-dollar antimissile umbrella in Northeast Asia. The missile shield ostensibly would protect American and Japanese forces from a new generation of North Korean ballistic missiles, but China was keenly aware that the antimissile system could serve as a shield against Chinese missiles, too. To China, this raised the specter of American forces gaining a first strike advantage in any potential conflict. With American forces deployed securely behind a shield, China would lose the ability to deter attacks against its own forces. Given the enormous effort and sacrifice that China put forth to become a nuclear power, Chinese military leaders view the loss of a credible deterrent missile force as a fundamental blow to their national security.

There has been little public debate about the military balance in the Taiwan Strait—about how much U.S. weaponry is enough and how much is too provocative.[2] The decisions on arms sales to Taiwan were made after secret deliberations among Pentagon and State Department bureaucrats using criteria that had never been publicly disclosed or vetted. The full measure of American military assistance to Taiwan was classified "secret," as if the American public could not be trusted to know how deeply involved the United States was becoming with Taiwan's military. During the Cold War, it is arguable that some secrecy was justified. In the 1950s, for instance, it was never disclosed that President Eisenhower had authorized the storage of American nuclear weapons in Taiwan so that they would be available for an attack on communist China and the Soviet Union. And it was a secret in 1973 when Secretary of State Henry Kissinger, meeting privately with Premier Zhou Enlai of China, relayed President Richard Nixon's promise that all American nuclear weapons would be removed from Taiwan within twelve months as a sign that the American military was disengaging from Taiwan.

But since the end of the Cold War, secrecy in America's security policy toward China and Taiwan is simply not justified. In fact, the more transparency the better. And while secrecy still surrounds U.S. relations with Taiwan, it is difficult to hide the American warplanes and warships arriving on the island, where the broad outlines of an expanding relationship are visible.

Even though the United States has accepted since 1972 that there is only one China and that Taiwan is part of it, a long history binds Americans to the preservation of a distinct Taiwan that is the master of its own destiny. For fifty years, Taiwan has been the home-in-exile of the Nationalist government of the late Generalissimo Chiang Kai-shek, whose army was routed in the communist revolution led by Mao Zedong. The generalissimo had ruled China as America's wartime ally. But the defeat of Japan in 1945 brought the onslaught of a civil war across an already devastated Chinese landscape, which Chiang's corrupt government could not administer and which his army could not control. America tried to prevent the civil war, sending General George C. Marshall in 1946 on an ill-fated mission to unite the Nationalists and Communists in a single postwar government. But when he failed, President Harry Truman washed his hands of the matter and withdrew.

In January 1949, Mao's forces marched through the gates of old Beijing, and on October 1, Mao and his military commanders climbed to the balcony of the Gate of Heavenly Peace, which guards the entrance to the Forbidden City and overlooks Tiananmen Square, and declared the founding of the People's Republic of China. At that moment, Chiang Kai-shek's Nationalist forces were in flight across the Taiwan Strait, and once landed on the island, they set up temporary quarters in squalid tent cities and began plotting a military strategy to return to the mainland. Their political strategy was to convince the United States to join them in a new onslaught against the Communists. If the generalissimo's dream was ever realistic, it was effectively shelved by the Korean War, which broke out the next summer and threw American forces into a bloody confrontation with Mao's army on the Korean peninsula.

As the Cold War set in, Taiwan was once again integrated into the American defense strategy in Asia, serving as an unsinkable aircraft carrier to contain the Chinese "menace" and, later, to support the American war effort in Vietnam. The U.S. Seventh Fleet patrolled the Taiwan Strait to assert the right of passage through that international waterway, but also to signal Beijing that American military forces would not tolerate any attack on Taiwan. More than 10,000 American troops were stationed on the island, along with a large contingent from the Central Intelligence Agency and the National Security Agency. Nearly 1,000 NSA technicians and language specialists used an extensive antenna array on Taiwan's mountain peaks to intercept military and civilian communications from all over the mainland. A huge stockpile of war matériel, including American nuclear weapons, was loaded into Taiwan's deep caves in preparation for war in Asia. CIA officers worked with Taiwanese intelligence services to parachute guerrilla forces onto the Chinese mainland, where they tried in vain to organize opposition to the Communists. Most were captured and executed.

At the end of the twentieth century, America's bonds with Chiang Kai-shek's successors in Taiwan are deeper than ever because the island has become a thriving democracy, a major trading partner with the United States, and a landscape of modern and progressive culture. Although many Americans know little about Taiwan, its leaders have spent decades cultivating important friends in the United States. By the time he ran for president in 1992, Bill Clinton had never visited mainland China, but he had made four trips to Taiwan at the head of Arkansas trade delegations. Each trip featured banquets, golf outings, entertainment, and briefings by Taiwanese leaders on Asian security from Taiwan's perspective.

For mainland China, however, bringing Taiwan back into the fold of the motherland is perhaps the most deeply felt commitment of the Communist Party leadership in Beijing and of the officer corps of the 2 million–strong PLA, who regard themselves as the guardians of the Chinese revolution and the defenders of Chinese sovereignty. Indeed, recovering Taiwan is as strong an imperative in the Chinese national consciousness as Manifest Destiny was in the American consciousness a century ago, when nationalism and commercialism combined in a burgeoning vision of an America stretching from ocean to ocean. When America was on the rise in the nineteenth century, the Chinese were suffering the humiliation of collapsing empire and the breakdown of central governance; of military lassitude so pervasive that the country was forced to surrender control over its maritime ports to Britain, France, and Germany; and of scientific inertia so paralyzing that China sat out the industrial revolution. Indeed, it was China's weakness that enabled Japan in 1895 to sunder Taiwan from the mainland, foreshadowing a century in which the Japanese army would complete the bloodiest conquest of China (1937–1945) since the Mongol invasion of the thirteenth century.

The Chinese Manifest Destiny has come to signify reasserting China's sovereignty over Tibet, Hong Kong, Macao, and Taiwan. It is not difficult for Americans to understand these sentiments, as they mirror their own notions of national sovereignty and territorial ambition. The average Chinese, of course, wants no part of war with Taiwan, or of Chinese killing Chinese. But the notion of such a war is nonetheless deeply imbedded in the political culture of the 58 million members of the Chinese Communist Party and the PLA. Recovering Taiwan has become a litmus test of national loyalty, part of the "big nation chauvinism"[3] endemic, Premier Zhou believed, to the Chinese ruling class. In any case, those with power want Taiwan back.

In 1949, the PLA under Mao was ill equipped to chase Chiang Kai-shek's forces across the Taiwan Strait, and thus Mao was denied final victory in the Chinese civil war. During the Korean War and, again, in 1958, the U.S. Seventh Fleet interposed itself between Taiwan and the mainland to thwart Mao's invasion plans. Mao ordered his troops to shell Taiwanese bunkers on the islands of Quemoy and Matsu, right up against the mainland coast; these islands were the generalissimo's most prominent stepping-stones in case a return invasion ever won U.S. support. But the shelling was symbolic and only scheduled on alternate days so the forces on each side had time to scamper to safety. Although Mao had to accept this stalemate, his determination to liberate Taiwan never flagged. He told Henry Kissinger in 1973 that it might take

100 years to win back Taiwan, and he was willing to wait because "they are a bunch of counter-revolutionaries."[4]

President Eisenhower's secretary of state, John Foster Dulles, who detested the Communists so intensely that he refused to shake hands with Zhou Enlai at the Geneva Conference of 1954, nonetheless struggled in the aftermath of Korea to keep America out of a new war with China triggered by Chiang Kai-shek's ambition to return to the mainland. As a result, Taiwan was forced, under pressure from the United States, to abandon all but a handful of the stepping-stone islands on the Chinese coast. To American military commanders, the islands were an indefensible provocation—a lightning rod for war.

At the time of his death in 1976, Mao could never have imagined the Taiwan of today, with its strong pro-independence minority, participatory democracy, and native-born Taiwanese president preaching a form of Taiwanese nationalism with grandfatherly charisma; he could not have foreseen that the U.S. Congress would become a battleground for pro-Taiwan lobbyists, human rights advocates, trade barons, and antiproliferation supporters, all seeking to influence the course of American policy on China in the aftermath of the Cold War.

Still, Mao might have relished the confrontation—and its dialectics. He believed that the key to winning wars was to make your enemy believe that you have no fear of war. China, he would say, with its vast population and its capacity to "eat bitterness," could absorb punishment better than any adversary. He once told a visitor that the warmonger image he had acquired suited his purposes, laced as it was with Mao's sober calculation—even conservatism—in military strategy. Mao understood the art of war, and, over the years, his warmonger image instilled great caution in the Soviet Union and other adversaries who contemplated attacking China.

Today, Mao's notion of fearlessness remains deeply imbedded in the Chinese military establishment. In 1979, China fought a brief border war with Vietnam. Chinese troops, fighting with antiquated weapons and uncoordinated ground tactics, and without air support, suffered tens of thousands of casualties before reaching their objective. When they did, the battered Chinese divisions turned around and marched home, having administered their "lesson"—that Beijing would not tolerate Vietnam's invasion of Cambodia or the formation of a Soviet-Vietnamese alliance on its southern flank. To China's leaders, the price paid in battle dead was necessary in the larger context of the nation's interests. China's determination to defend its national interests, as exemplified by that 1979 conflict with Vietnam, ought to sober those who argue that China cannot "afford" war.

Forty years after America's last serious crisis with Beijing over Taiwan, it may seem alarmist to speak of the risk of war, but the gathering hostility in Congress toward China and the recriminations over the American bombing of the Chinese embassy in Belgrade charted new trend lines of deterioration. For most of his second term, President Clinton carried out a largely vacuous—though photogenic—diplomacy with the People's Republic, one that suited his own domestic political requirements, but avoided the risks and compromises that would be needed to move the relationship forward. On the one hand, Clinton identified with the goals of his predecessors by embracing a policy of engagement, dialogue, and cooperation with China, but at the same time, the White House seemed flummoxed by Congress and fretful of the growing number of critics incensed about Chinese espionage in the United States, by continuing human rights abuses in China, and by a yawning trade deficit with Beijing. In advance of the 2000 presidential election season, some conservatives branded China the enemy and the centrist consensus among Democrats and Republicans that for thirty years had supported constructive relations with the People's Republic was once again on the defensive.

Beneath the gloss of superficial diplomacy, China and the United States were engaged in the preamble of war. The military and security establishments in both countries were more suspicious than ever of each other's intentions and they were acting on their suspicions. Military-to-military exchanges that had some meaning before the 1996 crisis today are perfunctory when they occur at all. War planning is on the rise while avenues of diplomacy are declining or mired in a zone of denial that all is well.

In reality, China today believes that it must gain credible military power and must show a determination to go to war if necessary in order to meet the challenge of the pro-independence politics that has flowered on Taiwan. Yet China's military forces are hopelessly outdated. At least half of its warplanes are not operational, and its navy faces "block obsolescence" as aging warships head for scrap yards.

China is not building an invasion fleet capable of crossing the Taiwan Strait in a replay of the 1944 Normandy landing. Most analysts dismiss this scenario as a futile "million-man swim." Instead, China is buying its military credibility by upgrading a portion of its armed forces for short-duration, high-tech warfare near its own shores.

Central to China's emerging military strategy are contingency plans aimed at bringing Taiwan quickly to its knees with a barrage of missiles— new and more accurate ballistic missiles and cruise missiles—that could enforce a blockade, trigger a political crisis, and cause a civilian exodus that would paralyze Taiwan's economy.

At the same time, Beijing's military planners are seeking means to deter the United States from entering the fray using "asymmetrical" tactics and weapons, those that seek to avoid the strengths of an adversary and prey on weaknesses. Missiles are a key element in China's strategy, as a weapon both against Taiwan and against American aircraft carriers.

In a 1997 report to Congress, the Defense Intelligence Agency estimated that mainland China has the capacity—though not necessarily the intention—to produce 1,000 ballistic and cruise missiles over the next decade.[5] There are indications that China is building fixed launch sites along its southeastern coast for a large missile force that could be brought to bear on Taiwan.

Each increment in the military buildup is mirrored across the strait. Taiwan believes that it must maintain a military balance against any surprise attack from the mainland as well as a strong measure of self-assurance that will allow it to eventually negotiate a mutually acceptable form of coexistence. Critical to Taiwan's strategy will be the deployment of electronic warfare systems, missile defenses, and a robust air force to destroy China's missiles, warplanes, and air defenses at the outset of any conflict. Such a strategy could not succeed without an American commitment to resupply Taiwan.

War with China is not inevitable. No side wishes it or sees it in its national interest. But the likelihood of military conflict is no longer decreasing, as it was in the decades that followed President Nixon's opening to China. The risk of war in the Taiwan Strait will continue to increase in the first decade of the twenty-first century, as mainland China presses the issue of reunification with Taiwan as the natural follow-through to the return of Hong Kong (1997) and Macao (1999) to Beijing's control.

Increasing tension will only lower the threshold for a war that could be triggered by the rise of a nationalistic Taiwanese leader who becomes so emboldened by the supply of high-tech American weapons as to proclaim permanent and separate sovereignty for the island. Or, it could be triggered by Beijing issuing an ultimatum demanding reunification, or else.

To clearly understand the increasing risk of war over Taiwan is to absorb the history of the past two centuries, especially of the period since Nixon found a formula, in the Shanghai Communiqué, to break the cycle of enmity between the United States and China, to defer the issue of Taiwan to the indefinite future, where the passage of time and the irrepressible commerce of the Chinese would knit a bridging web of connections, investment, and dialogue that, ultimately, could bring them back together in whatever form of association they could peacefully invent.

This book is about that history and the basic truths of America's relations with China from the Nixon opening to the end of the twentieth century. If Americans are to make hard choices in the years ahead about how to avoid war and accommodate the rise of China in Asia, about how best to promote peace and stability in the region and engage the Chinese on difficult questions of human rights and the proliferation of ballistic missiles and nuclear technology to unstable parts of the world, they will have to be better informed about the history of U.S.-China relations, much of which was hidden from them as it was occurring.

The most profound truths about the relationship are these.

First and foremost, the United States has reneged on the solemn promises of Presidents Nixon, Ford, Carter, and Reagan that America would show great restraint in providing limited, defensive arms to Taiwan during the transitional era that was to follow the establishment of formal diplomatic relations with Beijing in 1979. American military installations in Taiwan, erected during the Cold War, were dismantled and U.S. troops withdrawn as Washington downgraded relations with Taipei, no longer referring to Taiwan as the Republic of China, no longer pretending that the government-in-exile of Chiang Kai-shek was the legitimate government of mainland China. Instead, Washington erected a unique and unofficial relationship with Taipei that reflects America's ongoing interest in the island's security. This new relationship entailed the establishment of trade and cultural offices staffed by American diplomats on official leave from their diplomatic careers, in deference to the one-China policy that holds that Taiwan is a part of China. During the so-called transitional era, American presidents agreed to shift the emphasis away from supplying arms to Taiwan in favor of promoting the necessary dialogue and negotiation that would help reconcile mainland China and Taiwan and allow the Chinese themselves to find a formula to live together in peace as one China. America has failed to live up to these commitments.

Second, the will of the Taiwanese people was not an issue when President Nixon initiated the opening to China in 1972. It is today. The death of Chiang Kai-shek in 1975 marked the end of dictatorship in Taiwan. It awakened the latent forces of Taiwanese independence among a sizable minority on the island, an inevitable outcome among a population that had lived under Japanese occupation from 1895 to 1945 and under Chiang Kai-shek's dictatorship thereafter. In 1986, the pro-independence forces formed the Democratic Progressive Party. This awakening, along with popular revulsion against the corruption and autocratic rule of the generalissimo, forced a debate on Taiwan's future. As democratic elections have taken hold in Taiwan in the 1990s, the strength of pro-independence voters—now 20 to 30 percent of the electorate—has forced the political establishment to accommodate their views while trying not to alienate the majority of voters. That majority favors either the status quo of nonstatehood or eventual reunification with the mainland under conditions that would guarantee freedom and autonomy for the Taiwanese. For this reason, the "one-country-two-systems" guarantee for Hong Kong is an important experiment in coexistence that may, over time, cause public opinion on Taiwan to shift toward or away from reunification. However, unlike in Hong Kong, whose sovereignty was surrendered by Great Britain without consulting the 6 million residents of the former crown colony, Taiwan's democracy insists on public consultation. No majority exists for any course except maintaining the status quo. Cohabiting within that majority are ardent advocates for reunification and equally ardent proponents of independence. The craving for stability and security unites them. Any politician who presumes to lead Taiwanese democracy must reconcile the contradictions between Taiwanese nationalism and Chinese nationalism that are intertwined on the island.

Third, and inescapably, the Chinese civil war has become a permanent feature of the American political process. Americans should never forget that mainland Chinese leaders are in constant communication with Taiwan's leaders through private channels from which Americans are excluded. Public statements made by Beijing or Taipei often are attempts to gain leverage within these private negotiations. Americans should beware of the ideological battleground that these old adversaries have shifted to American soil. Taiwan's leaders recognize that whether they eventually strike a deal with mainland China or declare their independence, the island's fate will ultimately be decided by the United States, which has always been the guarantor of its security. Both Taiwan and mainland China recognize America's crucial role. For this reason, both sides endeavor to influence the American political process.

Beijing has concentrated its efforts on each successive American president, seeking continuity of the commitment to the principle of one China. Taiwan, however, has concentrated its lobbying efforts on Congress, realizing that the cultivation of even a relatively small but ideologically committed group of supporters, particularly in the Senate, could guarantee that the island's security and political interests remain at the forefront of American policy concerns in Asia. Those interests include expanding Taiwan's international image as a sovereign state, thereby strengthening its political position in negotiations with the mainland and preventing the kind of isolation that would make Taipei more vulnerable to Beijing's demands.

To further its cause, Taiwan has built a network of political support in most of the fifty American states by opening trade offices and promoting business ties with the political elite across America, especially in key states like California, Texas, Illinois, and New York. This was the vehicle through which then-governor Bill Clinton of Arkansas came to befriend Taiwan.

Like in the Arab-Israeli dispute, like in the conflict in Northern Ireland, both sides seek to manipulate American public opinion and turn congressional action to their advantage.

A final truth is this: After three decades, America's opening with China is still only beginning. During the Cold War and the first decade after it ended, the relationship between China and the United States was never defined on its own merits. China policy was always a component or a feature of some other policy. In 1972, the Nixon opening sprang from the president's urgent desire to end the war in Vietnam by undermining support for Hanoi. Nixon then played Beijing off against Moscow to improve America's advantage in setting limits on the growth of nuclear arsenals and in reducing tensions in Europe and the Middle East. Under Presidents Carter, Reagan, and Bush, China was a critical link in U.S. strategy to tie down Soviet forces in the Far East and thereby bleed the Soviet occupation of Afghanistan. The end of the Cold War provided the United States and China with a historic opportunity to lay the foundations for a new relationship in an era of Asian economic awakening, but the massacres of unarmed civilians around Tiananmen Square in June 1989 obliterated the goodwill that had been built up over the previous two decades. (Nixon told Deng Xiaoping privately in October 1989 that China and the United States would have to start all over again.) Under Bush, reconstruction seemed possible, but when Bill Clinton was elected as the first post–Cold War president, the relationship swung back and forth between confrontation and accommodation as the new president tried to fulfill political obligations to both human rights and business constituencies.

The history that follows in these pages is that of America's opening to China and of the long struggle ever since—by six presidents and a host of interested diplomats, spies, and politicians—to find a formula for coexistence, to defer the issue of Taiwan to the future, to bury the enmity of the past, and to construct the basis for a beneficial relationship between the world's most powerful nation and the world's most populous. It is a history littered with false expectations, dashed hopes, and a strong sense of betrayal on both sides, which has led many experts to assert that China and the United States will be enemies in the future. Some argue that the two countries have already become "global rivals"[6] whose national interests are in confrontation and whose security establishments have preordained a path to mutual enmity.

Every year, a large gathering of specialists on the Chinese military meet at a leafy resort in the Maryland or Virginia countryside to debate the future intentions of China's Communist Party leaders as well as the capabilities of the military forces on the mainland and on Taiwan. These specialists come from the CIA and the Defense Intelligence Agency; from think tanks and from academia. They include John Culver, the CIA's leading expert on the PLA;

Michael Swaine of the RAND Corporation; Paul Godwin of the National Defense University; Michael Pillsbury of the Office of Net Assessment at the Pentagon; James R. Lilley, former ambassador to China; and Ellis Joffe, a leading analyst from Israel. The debate has become increasingly contentious, and since the mid-1990s the group has been stalemated on these questions:

Projecting over the next two decades, will China's leaders pursue a course of economic development at home and promote peace and stability in the region? Or will China divert an increasing amount of resources to its military in order to establish Chinese domination in Asia? Will the Chinese military force Taiwan into reunification on Beijing's terms? Will it seize the oil and mineral resources of the South China Sea without regard for the competing claims of its neighbors? Will it seek to undermine American power and influence in the region? Can the PLA overcome its backwardness and acquire the military capability to dominate Asia and threaten the U.S. armed forces deployed there?

The history assembled here, based on four years of research, thousands of pages of newly declassified documents, and hundreds of interviews, suggests that almost every issue concerning China and its relations with the United States is up in the air—poised between conflict and cooperation—and under siege by the complex interaction of domestic politics and the diversity of special interests that tug and pull from all directions. It may take a more rational sorting out of national priorities in both countries before American and Chinese leaders are able to secure the framework for a more stable relationship in the coming century.

THE
TAIWAN
CRISIS

*Chinese soldiers and tanks enact a mock
assault directed at Taiwan*

T HE POSSIBILITY of a shooting war between the United States and the People's Republic of China was suddenly made real to Bill Clinton in early March 1996.

"Goddamn," the president muttered as he focused on the blunt and alarming presentation that had been prepared by the chairman of the Joint Chiefs of Staff, General John Shalikashvili, with concurrence from the secretaries of state and defense.[1]

On March 5, China announced that it would conduct ballistic missile exercises by firing surface-to-surface rockets from the mainland to "target boxes" just outside Taiwan's main commercial harbors.

Two days later, China began firing those missiles, and in that brief space of time, Clinton's ability to manage American foreign policy again came under siege.

Clinton had summoned his national security advisers to the White House to review a "matrix" of possible war scenarios and American responses. Shalikashvili, the four-star general whose easy wit and pragmatism had won recognition during the Persian Gulf War, had prepared a graphic presentation in the binder that was in front of the president. It charted the stair steps of escalation that might occur if one of the ballistic missiles from mainland China went off course and actually struck Taiwan, or if the mainland deliberately started aiming its missiles at targets on Taiwan, as some intelligence reports had suggested, or if the 150,000 troops that the People's Liberation Army had assembled just across the waterway from Taiwan decided to make a grab for one of the islands just off the Chinese coastline that Taiwan controlled, Quemoy and Matsu being the most famous.

As China escalated the pace of its military exercises in the weeks running up to the March 23 presidential elections in Taiwan, there was a real danger that events could get out of hand, and the United States had no control over the players who would be driving the escalation.

The assessment of the American intelligence community was that China's military exercises were not a prelude to invasion. Rather, China was engaged in coercion—in gunboat diplomacy. Still, the military chiefs, especially Shali, as Shalikashvili was known, wanted no one at the White House to be cavalier about real risk of an accident, surprise, or miscalculation. The general sat quietly, his hair close cut gray and chest covered with battle ribbons arrayed across the army green of his uniform. His open face had drained of its usual good humor as he sat upright, his demeanor speaking volumes about the sober assessment he had brought before the president. The joint chiefs had minced no words. They did not have high regard for the man occupying the Oval Office; they had not been consulted on the decision that had triggered the crisis—granting Taiwan's president, Lee Teng-hui,* a visa to visit the United States the previous spring—though the fact that the granting of the visa had set off a military reaction from China was enough to make the point that the chiefs should have been in the loop. Now that the consequences were at hand, the chiefs were determined to be professional in painting as clear a picture as possible, first of the risks that Clinton was facing and second of the unpleasant array of options that he would have to choose from if either side started shooting.

Clinton was sobered by what he read in Shalikashvili's binder. The risks of an accidental war were considerable. When his eyes pulled away from the general's grim accounting of what might occur, Clinton looked around the table at Warren Christopher, secretary of state, Bill Perry, secretary of defense, and Anthony Lake, his national security adviser, and told them how alarmed he was. The situation in the Taiwan Strait was a powder keg, and they were going to have to do everything they could to head off the looming catastrophe. He did not want any of the terrifying scenarios in Shali's briefing to come to pass, he said. Clinton did not have to mention that 1996 was an election year and that the specter of an unpredictable military confrontation with China—with the possibility of American casualties—was not his idea of an attractive backdrop to the coming reelection campaign. Everyone in the room remembered the wreckage the Somalia mission had turned into during their first year in office.

M OREOVER, Clinton said, someone was going to have to get the message to Lee Teng-hui to back off, because Clinton was not going to risk taking the United States to war every time the president of Taiwan wanted to attend his class reunion in upstate New York or play golf in Hawaii. Delivering this private message was to be the task of Sandy Berger, the deputy na-

*Pronounced: Lee Dung-Hway.

tional security adviser, and Peter Tarnoff, the undersecretary of state for political affairs. They were to arrange a private meeting in New York with a senior aide to the Taiwanese president and sit him down for a sober talk about
American expectations.

But neither Clinton nor his advisers that weekend addressed the larger
question—to what extent would America defend Taiwan?

In 1958, American warships escorted Taiwanese military transport ships
to within a mile of the Chinese coastline so that Taiwanese forces could off-
load munitions and supplies for their garrisons on Quemoy and Matsu. A
misguided shot from the mainland could have easily struck an American warship, triggering escalation and war.

In 1996, almost no one believed that the United States would risk war
over the defense of these outlying islands if they came under attack. All
through the 1990s, the Taiwanese military had steadily drawn down the garrisons on Quemoy and Matsu, leaving them exposed to reoccupation by the
mainland. Pentagon officials believed that holding onto Quemoy and Matsu
was an anachronism of the Cold War. The islands themselves were museum
pieces with their underground honeycombs of fortifications, pillboxes, bar-
racks, and ammo dumps, all connected by networks of tunnels. More tourists
passed through these tunnels in the 1990s than soldiers.

Still, Taiwan's armed forces were prepared to retaliate for any attack on
the territories they controlled, including the outlying islands. In private
briefings with U.S. officials in early 1996, Taiwan's military commanders had
laid out the full array of air strikes they were ready to execute against the
mainland. On maps, they pinpointed the air bases, missile bases, radar installations, and supply depots that they planned to destroy with their own
bombers and missiles.

It seemed as though a single match thrown into this tinderbox could set
off a firestorm.

Among the men advising Bill Clinton, all of them older and more seasoned in foreign policy and crisis management, there was no doubt that they
were reaping the harvest of the abrupt decision Clinton had made the previous May to allow the president of Taiwan to travel to the United States.
Lee's government had promised that the trip would be a "private visit," to
deliver a speech at Cornell University, Lee's alma mater, in Ithaca, New
York. But when Lee arrived, Cornell was decked out as though for a political
convention, and there was nothing private about the speech, which was
beamed around the world. In the speech, Lee proclaimed the sovereignty of
the Republic of China on Taiwan, to the cheers of hundreds of supporters
waving Nationalist Party flags, the symbol of Chiang Kai-shek's government-in-exile.

With the death in 1988 of Chiang Kai-shek's son, Chiang Ching-kuo, Lee became the first native-born ruler of Taiwan. With a Cheshire cat smile, courtly manners, and shrewd instincts, he straddled the politics of the island, holding on to the traditional Nationalist base while also courting the pro-independence vote. Educated in Japan and the United States, Lee had shown little interest in building new bridges to the mainland or in binding up the wounds of the Chinese civil war. Instead, he focused on the politics of separatism. And with a war chest of hundreds of millions of dollars, he had purchased diplomatic relations with more than a score of small nations willing to extend formal recognition to Taiwan (and break relations with Beijing). Whatever negotiations he carried on with the mainland were grudging, and, within his own party, he was suspected of undermining the cross-strait political dialogue at critical times.[2] Lee kept the issue of reunification at arms length by insisting that the Republic of China on Taiwan would never surrender its sovereignty or unite with the mainland while the People's Republic was under monopoly rule of the Communist Party.

In 1995, he had offered to make a $1 billion donation to the United Nations in a bid to purchase a seat for Taiwan in the UN General Assembly. Further, Lee circumvented his own government bureaucracy in hiring a Washington public relations firm to make the case in the U.S. Congress that the president of Taiwan ought to be able to visit the United States, recognizing that America was the most important venue for his message. That message was simply that Taiwan shared democratic values with America and deserved its support, wherever Lee was taking it. Every American president since Nixon had refused to allow such visits, in the belief that giving Taiwan's leader a political forum in the United States undermined the "one China" pledge and needlessly provoked Beijing. Both Clinton and his Secretary of State Christopher had upheld that standard during their first two years in office. Indeed, Christopher and his assistant secretary for East Asian affairs, Winston Lord, had repeatedly promised Chinese leaders that Lee would not be admitted.

But in May 1995, Lee Teng-hui was able to exploit the zeal of an incoming Republican Congress to turn the tide of American politics and pressure Clinton to issue the visa. All of Clinton's senior advisers had concurred with the decision—including Christopher, Perry, and Lake. They disregarded warnings from China specialists in the State Department and on the National Security Council staff. Lake even instructed his reluctant aides to reverse their negative recommendation because the president had already made up his mind.

To Clinton, the decision had been a no-brainer, and he had dominated his advisers in making it. He believed that—to the average American—it was a simple question of freedom of speech. The president of Taiwan held a doctoral degree from Cornell and had been invited by distinguished academics to return to his alma mater. Suppressing free speech made for terrible politics at any time, but it was especially risky after the Republicans had taken control of Congress. On May 2 and May 9, both houses of Congress passed nonbinding resolutions (97–1 in the Senate and 396–0 in the House) calling for Lee to be admitted. Clinton argued that if he did not cave to congressional will, he would soon be facing binding legislation and a crisis over whether to veto it.

"I don't want my first veto to be in support of the People's Republic of China," Clinton said, reflecting the political terror he felt over being put in the position of defending the regime he had so vilified during his campaign.[3]

In the aftermath of Lee's visit, the recriminations unfolded in stages. First there was silence from the mainland, then a muted reaction, then an eruption that seemed to originate in the Chinese military. Suddenly, all the organs of the Chinese Communist Party unleashed vituperative attacks on Lee in a campaign that condemned him as a separatist seeking to "split the motherland." The first Chinese ballistic missiles, six of them, were fired into the East China Sea nearly 100 miles north of Taiwan from July 21 to 26, 1995, causing the Taiwanese stock market to plunge. The State Department called in the Chinese ambassador and issued a strong protest. Embarrassed, Clinton's advisers tried to downplay the reaction.

In Beijing, the ruling politburo approved a program of military exercises—a whole symphony of mock amphibious assaults, air combat displays, and live fire drills to be conducted by the PLA over eight months, building to a crescendo in 1996 when Taiwan voters were scheduled to go the polls for the first-ever direct balloting for their president.

In December 1995, the Nationalist Party, which Lee Teng-hui headed, lost several seats in legislative elections, leaving it with its slimmest majority in history. Beijing took full credit; its muscle flexing appeared to be working. Mainland newspapers, whose content was controlled by the party, started referring to the Taiwan Strait as the "Nanjing war zone."

But the big shock did not come until the new year, with the short announcement on March 5 by the state-run New China News Agency that the PLA was going to conduct even more threatening and provocative ballistic missile exercises off China's southeastern coast from March 8 to 13. Longitude and latitude figures clattered across news tickers delineating "exclusion zones" from which all commercial shipping was warned to stay away. When the coordinates were plotted in Washington, the entire exercise looked like it might be an attack on Taiwan. The "target boxes" were no more than twenty to thirty miles off Taiwan's harbor entrances and smack in the middle of international shipping lanes, close enough for the Taiwanese to hear the sonic boom of incoming warheads descending through the atmosphere at 4,500 miles per hour.

After the announcement, the White House went into denial. There was no meeting of the National Security Council. Instead, the "principals"— Lake, Perry, Shali, and Christopher—met in the Situation Room without the president. No word came down from the Oval Office. It was as if no one imagined that the Chinese would actually begin firing the missiles. But they did, literally at the stroke of midnight on the first day they had announced for the exercises.

At 11 A.M. eastern standard time, still March 7 in Washington (Beijing is 13 hours ahead), American intelligence satellites detected the first fiery plumes of two ballistic missiles rising from mobile launchers hidden in the valleys and mountains of southeastern China. Chinese soldiers and technicians of the Second Artillery Corps, which operates the country's nuclear and conventional rocket forces, cheered the missiles into the night sky. One missile passed over the northern tip of Taiwan during its descent. On the other side of the world, White House spokesman Mike McCurry was preparing his noon briefing. Word of the launches was flashed from the National Military Command Center in the Pentagon to the Situation Room in the basement of the White House, then to McCurry.

"These missile exercises—and indeed we have some reason to believe they have occurred—we consider both provocative and reckless," McCurry said from the podium of the West Wing press room just after noon.

It was, indeed, shocking. For the first time in its history, China had lashed out with a lethal new weapon that was remarkably accurate and could threaten the vital lifelines of Taiwan's economy. No deployment of the Seventh Fleet, no aircraft carrier, no warplane could interpose itself to stop a barrage of ballistic missiles. Taiwan had no defense against them. These exercises raised the question of whether, in any future conflict, the mainland could win an air war over Taiwan without ever launching an aircraft. With accurate ballistic missiles, China could knock out the eight military airfields on Taiwan, cratering the runways and preventing the island's air force from mustering opposition to a suffocating naval blockade.

A blockade of Taiwan would threaten the interests of the United States and Japan. Clinton would be at pains not to challenge the closure of the sea-lanes around Taiwan, just as the United States was compelled to challenge Iran's attempt in 1988 to choke off the international sea-lanes in the Persian Gulf during the so-called Tanker War between Iran and Iraq. Such a challenge would require American warships to steam through the blockade zone. The rules of engagement undoubtedly would call on American commanders to attack any Chinese combatant that activated its targeting radar, signaling a preparation to fire. American forces would have to be prepared to destroy Chinese warships or coastal batteries that put American vessels at risk, just as American forces attacked and destroyed Iranian warships in 1988. The same rules of engagement that applied in the Persian Gulf would be necessary to protect U.S. forces deployed near Taiwan.

A confrontation between the United States and the People's Republic of China had the potential to undermine the Clinton presidency. The crisis struck just as the U.S. Pacific Fleet was in transition. Admiral Richard Macke had resigned over inappropriate remarks he had made relating to the September 1995 rape of a twelve-year-old Japanese schoolgirl by American sailors in Okinawa. Admiral Joseph W. Prueher, who had been named as his replacement, was in Washington for his confirmation hearing before the Senate.

General Shalikashvili called Prueher and told him that it was not too early to take some preliminary steps to mobilize for the defense of Taiwan if war broke out, but to take care not to telegraph any such moves to the Taiwanese leadership, lest they grow bolder. In great secrecy, Prueher mobilized the Pacific Fleet command staff in Honolulu to prepare for the deployment to Taiwan of a huge supply of ammunition, spare parts, and missiles, including Patriot missiles to defend Taiwan's civilian population centers from incoming Chinese rockets. These supplies would be accompanied by U.S. military advisers and logistical personnel in the event of a mainland attack.

As the Chinese were announcing the missile tests, the aircraft carrier *Independence*, anchored in Manila Bay in the Philippines, was recalling its crew from shore leave at the end of a port visit. The big flattop set sail the next morning, March 6, to transit the Luzon Strait and head north through the Philippine Sea toward the eastern flank of Taiwan. The Seventh Fleet commander, Admiral Archie Clemins, quietly gathered his forces.

Still, no one in the Pentagon could answer the question that hung in the air: If hundreds or thousands of American military personnel flooded onto Taiwan for the first time in nearly two decades, when and under what circumstances would they leave? Ever since the Shanghai Communiqué of 1972 and the establishment of formal diplomatic relations between Washington and Beijing in 1979, the United States had recognized that Taiwan was part of China and that Beijing was the sole government of the Chinese people. Any deployment of U.S. troops to Taiwan, however defensive, would be regarded by Beijing as an invasion. China would certainly claim as much at the United Nations, where Beijing holds one of the five permanent seats on the Security Council. That seat comes with veto authority, which could be wielded against the United States on a host of matters that were important to American security, such as preventing war on the Korean peninsula, holding the line against Saddam Hussein in Iraq, and keeping peace in the Balkans.

A number of advisers to Clinton, including the departing ambassador to Beijing, J. Stapleton Roy, believed that if only Clinton had been paying attention to China policy all along, he could have foreseen the congressional steamroller in support of admitting Lee Teng-hui and preempted the crisis through early consultations with Beijing. Holding a summit with Chinese president Jiang Zemin would have allowed the Clinton administration to reaffirm the one-China principle. Then he could have explained in more relaxed circumstances why it was politically necessary to admit Lee for an unofficial visit. The sequence of the visits—Jiang first as an official guest and then the Taiwanese leader as a private guest—would have inoculated Clinton against much of what ensued.

But this was the president who had little time for foreign policy. He preferred to cram for crises. In the first year of the administration, Les Aspin, Clinton's first secretary of defense, telephoned CIA director R. James Woolsey and said, "Woolz, didn't you think that when we got these jobs, we would actually meet with the president and talk about policy?"[4] Woolsey had to laugh. He assured Aspin that he was not getting invited to any White House meetings that excluded Aspin. Woolsey knew only too well Clinton's lack of focus. In the first six months of the administration, Woolsey and his intelligence officers had spent hours in the reception area outside the Oval Office, standing by to give the president his daily intelligence briefing. Clinton, more often than not, left the CIA cooling its heels for hours, frequently then canceling the briefing altogether. In September 1994, when a small Cessna aircraft with a mentally disturbed pilot crashed into the South Lawn of the White House in what appeared to be an unsuccessful assassination attempt, the joke at CIA headquarters was that the pilot was Woolsey trying to get an appointment with the president.

Lake, the national security adviser, had a similar problem of access to the president. But Lake himself also had been inattentive to China.

At the age of fifty-six, Lake had returned to Washington with the new Clinton administration bearing the quiet but nonetheless triumphal aura of a man whose adherence to principle was getting its reward. Lake had been among the small group of aides to Henry Kissinger who were disillusioned by their realization, in May 1970, that the Nixon-Kissinger approach to ending the war in Vietnam would be to escalate and expand it into Cambodia. Ever since, Lake had been trying to reconcile moral principle and national interest.[5]

Whereas Kissinger relied on the "unsentimental" approach of balancing the power of potential adversaries to improve American security, Lake believed in a foreign policy based on power *and* morality. The commingling of ideals and interests was inevitable in American society, influenced as it was by the Enlightenment. Lake considered himself a pragmatic neo-Wilsonian, not naive about the world but conscious of the moral requirements of leadership.

Kissinger's world was all about power and realism. The fate of peasants and refugees trapped in war zones, the fate of small countries that got sucked into the vortex of great-power clashes—like Cambodia—were less important than the big picture. Kissinger had learned to pay lip service to moral imperatives because it was politically expedient to do so, but he seldom acted on them. Lake, on the other hand, believed both in humanity's predisposition for virtue and in its potential for evil—an apt philosophy for the grandson of Kirsopp Lake, the British theologian who had emigrated to the United States to teach at Harvard. It was the task of governments and leaders, Lake believed, to do all they could to subdue evil, knowing that it could never be completely destroyed.

This moral dimension easily found a home in the war room of the Clinton presidential campaign in 1992, where Lake, a good draftsman and tireless punster, became indispensable in formulating attacks on George Bush's foreign policy. Although the campaign turned on domestic affairs, Clinton's advisers believed that they had to oppose Bush across the full spectrum of issues. During the campaign, Lake helped draft the Clinton slogans accusing Bush of "coddling tyrants" from Baghdad to Beijing. And in the fall of 1993, Lake consigned China to the heap of "backlash states."[6] In Kissinger's equation, the massacres at Tiananmen were an unfortunate tragedy that could not be allowed to interfere with the larger balance of power. But for Lake, China's leaders were discredited by their slaughter of unarmed civilians at Tiananmen.

So it was a great personal vindication that Tony Lake should take the post in the Clinton administration that Kissinger had held under Nixon. Unlike Kissinger, however, Lake came to the office determined not to dominate the policymaking process. Instead, he saw the job as coordinating and distilling a full range of views for the president from among all his national security advisers. This evenhanded approach lasted less than a year, after which some of those who had first praised Lake now complained that more Machiavellian instincts had emerged.

When Clinton entered the White House, he had no interest in conducting high-level dialogue with the Chinese leadership—the "butchers of Beijing," as they had been labeled. The Clinton team was more interested in putting pressure on China over human rights, weapons proliferation, and trade barriers. Winston Lord, the former Kissinger intimate and Ronald Reagan's ambassador to Beijing, was placed in charge of China policy at the State Department as assistant secretary for East Asian affairs.

Lord tutored the new administration that the Chinese would cave in to

American demands if Washington was willing to play it tough. One of the first things Lord did after he was confirmed by the Senate was to fly to Beijing, in May 1993, and tell the Chinese that Clinton was going to play a very tough hand on human rights by setting conditions for the renewal of China's most-favored-nation trade status. He told them Clinton had decided that if China did not meet the conditions for improving its human rights record, Washington would react by slapping much higher tariffs on the $25 billion to $30 billion in Chinese goods then entering the American market annually, thus wiping out China's competitive advantage and undermining its economy, along with Hong Kong's.

Clinton played the State Department's tough hand until Lloyd Bentsen (Treasury), Robert Rubin (National Economic Council), Ronald Brown (Commerce), Jeffrey Garten (Commerce), and other business advocates in the administration convinced Clinton that the American agenda with China could not be held hostage to a single issue—human rights. China was a player in Asian security, perhaps the key to convincing the North Koreans to give up their nuclear ambitions; China had a huge economy that was going to rival Japan's in a couple more decades; China had veto authority at the United Nations and could join with Russia or Europe to challenge American leadership on Iraq, on Bosnia—you name it.

Out of this chaos, Lake let it be known in December 1995 that he wanted a go at directing China policy. Christopher thought that this was a grandstand play and resisted. Lake said that he would not proceed without Christopher's assent, but still Lake began calling China experts to the White House in January 1996 and seeking their counsel, knowing that they would urge him to get involved and even to travel to China. The pressure mounted until, finally, the intelligence reports suggesting that China might be preparing for missile attacks on Taiwan brought the matter to a head. Christopher's recalcitrance to Lake's initiative appeared unreasonable, and he relented.

It was just coincidence that on Thursday, March 7, the day the launching of the first two Chinese missiles shattered everyone's complacency, a senior Chinese official arrived in Washington to conduct what Lake was calling "a new strategic dialogue" with China, a new beginning.

To protect the honor of the secretary of state, Lake had conspired to inflate the title of the arriving Chinese official, Liu Huaqiu.* Christopher did not want it to appear that Lake was conducting diplomacy outside the purview of the State Department, as Kissinger had done during his years at the White House. So Lake prevailed upon the Chinese ambassador in Washington to agree that Liu be called the "national security adviser" of the

---

*Pronounced: Leeoh Hwaa Choh.

People's Republic of China, and therefore Lake's counterpart. Never mind that China had no such position. A fig leaf was necessary.

When Liu stepped off the plane in New York, all smiles, even as the first reports of Chinese missile launches were flashing over the news wires, Lake could hardly pretend that it was going to be business as usual. At the White House, Clinton had originally planned to drop in on a meeting between Liu and Lake, but the president stayed away to show his anger. Liu protested to Lake that the missile exercises were routine, just as the ones the previous summer had been. He admonished Lake not to overreact. The Taiwan issue, he said, was an internal affair of the Chinese people, and Beijing would not tolerate any interference. Liu's toughness reflected his status as a favorite among the hard-liners in Beijing; he had ingratiated himself to Premier Li Peng, who was pushing him as China's next foreign minister.

Lake came off looking foolish in trying to stretch his hands across the waters to the Chinese the very week they were wantonly firing missiles into Asia's international shipping lanes. He invited Liu to dine that evening at the State Department. Christopher would play host and Bill Perry would be there, too. That afternoon, the three Americans met to choreograph the dinner, dividing up their message so that it could be forcefully stated and restated. Talking points were drafted from the language of the Taiwan Relations Act.

As Perry crossed the Potomac River from the Pentagon into Washington, he was under the impression that the goal of the dinner was to forcefully convey the message to Beijing that it must immediately stop firing its missiles toward Taiwan. If they were successful, Washington might be able to resolve the matter diplomatically, along the lines that Lake was planning—initiating a new strategic dialogue. But Perry discovered it was already too late for diplomacy by itself. U.S. satellites showed more than a dozen missiles on mobile launchers being readied for firing. A stray missile might set off retaliation from Taiwan, thus triggering the outbreak of a general war that could drag in the United States.

Clinton's national security advisers gathered in the elegantly appointed Madison Dining Room on the eighth floor of the State Department, near the terrace overlooking the Lincoln Memorial, radiant under evening floodlights. At the dinner table, Christopher's brow was pursed as he reiterated in the dour tones of a corporate lawyer that the missile shots were reckless and dangerous, and had to be halted at once.

Liu was far more animated than his host. He repeated that the missile exercises—and the naval and air exercises that would follow—were routine. The United States should not overreact. He reminded them how the crisis had begun, with the visa issued to Lee Teng-hui, and how the Clinton administration had broken its word. At that point, Perry had been scripted to level

Liu with a controlled outburst. But Perry, an owlish and soft-spoken scientist, even at his toughest still sounded like he was conducting a college seminar. Still, he represented the full force of the U.S. military, and his role was to lay down the ultimatum. The others at the table would then back him up.

These were *not* routine exercises, Perry said as sharply as he could, looking directly at Liu with a serious expression. They were anything *but* routine.

"You know, I am an old artillery man," he said, "and I can tell when someone is bracketing a target." He pointed out that the first missile landed to the north and second near the southern tip of Taiwan. That was bracketing—establishing the range so the missile commander could then hit any target in between.

How could that be considered routine, Perry wanted to know.

Furthermore, by firing ballistic missiles into international sea-lanes, China was not just threatening Taiwan with dangerous and reckless military acts but was also threatening the vital interests of the United States and its allies in the western Pacific. Japan received more than 60 percent of its energy supplies through those sea lanes. Japan was an American ally.

If the missile firings continued, the United States was going to respond to protect its interests. Perry told Liu that he needed to get that message back to Beijing—that very night. If the missiles did not stop, there was going to be an American response; if there was an attack on Taiwan, there would be grave consequences, he said.

Liu did not flinch. He had a reputation for bluster, and he could give as good as he got. When he was younger, he had participated in the fierce battles within the Foreign Ministry during China's Cultural Revolution. In any case, Bill Perry's "outburst" would have barely registered on his Richter scale. And, in response, Liu laid out the full menu of Chinese recriminations over the visa issue, over the sale of F-16s to Taiwan, over sanctions, and over American churlishness with regard to providing the technology that China needed for its development.

Lake and Christopher repeated their warning, and when Liu departed, he returned to the Chinese embassy on Connecticut Avenue. By morning, U.S. intelligence was able to confirm to the White House that Liu had sent a report to Beijing.

But nothing came back. American satellites saw continued preparation by the Chinese military for additional missile launches. There seemed to be no change in orders on the Chinese side. By Friday, March 8, a barely controlled panic was spreading among the Taiwanese, who rushed to the banks by the thousands to withdraw their cash or convert it into dollars. Every China Airlines flight leaving Taiwan for the United States and Canada was overbooked. People swarmed the airports trying to get a seat out.

Meanwhile, Taiwan's air and missile forces went to maximum alert in preparation for retaliation.

In Washington, Lake, Shalikashvili, Christopher, and Perry agreed that it was time to escalate. Shali, as the president's top military adviser, insisted that the planning be run out of the Joint Staff, the labyrinth at the core of the Pentagon where, in a military crisis, streams of information and resources merge through a funnel of communications, planning, and transport, all connected to the war-fighting commands of Europe, the Middle East, and the Far East.

The joint chiefs met Friday morning and reviewed their plans for the re-supply and defense of Taiwan. The USS *Independence* was on station east of Taiwan. The USS *Bunker Hill*, an Aegis class cruiser whose powerful radar could project far over the horizon, had steamed to the southern approach to the Taiwan Strait, where its crew could monitor missile launches as well as track all Chinese military activity in the area. A Los Angeles class attack submarine was helping to monitor subsurface movements in the strait with its passive sensors. A variety of other satellite and airborne sensors were brought to bear on the potential war zone by the Pacific Command.

When Shali arrived at the secretary of defense's suite on the outer ring of the Pentagon, he was confident that he had anticipated every contingency.

But Perry came on aggressively. He was visibly upset that the Chinese had ignored the warning that he had forcefully presented to Liu at dinner the previous evening. More missiles were set to fly, and each pass of U.S. reconnaissance satellites brought further evidence of Chinese mobilization. More naval and air exercises had been announced, with a new set of coordinates defining the latest "exclusion zone." When the coordinates were plotted, it looked as if China was coming perilously close to shutting down all shipping in the Taiwan Strait. Taiwan's military forces were on razor's edge.

Perry wanted to hit the Chinese hard. Sending the *Independence* out into the distant Pacific only to steam around in circles was not a strong signal. In fact, it might be interpreted as weakness. He wanted a carrier to sail right into the Taiwan Strait, right up against the exclusion zone. He wanted to let them know that the United States meant business by launching aircraft from the carrier deck right there in the strait, right in their faces.

Perry could see Shali's face collapsing in an expression of horror. The two men were friends and had learned to read each other well. Perry seemed jolted by Shali's reaction and paused. They were obviously not on the same wavelength.

Shali replied that sending an American carrier into the Taiwan Strait was asking for trouble. The risk of an accident was very high, in direct correlation with the rising emotions. If a Chinese shore battery fired a cruise missile at the carrier, the carrier's commander would have a right to defend himself by attacking the shore battery. That might also touch off a Taiwanese attack on Chinese coastal batteries. Then where would they be? At war.

But Perry was frustrated. He wanted a tougher, more aggressive response than sending the *Independence* to steam in circles out in the middle of the ocean. The Chinese had to get the message that the United States was serious.

Shali argued that the *Independence* could initially show the flag east of Taiwan; if the Chinese got more aggressive, they could then consider escalatory steps such as sending the *Bunker Hill* through the strait—even the *Independence*—but such a move should not be the first card they laid down.

Still, for Perry, it was not enough. The situation presented the classic dilemma between military symbolism and military action. The symbolism had to be strong enough to deter escalation, but not so provocative as to incite further escalation and trigger a war they wanted to avoid. Perry was seized by the former option and Shali by the latter.

What about a second carrier? Perry asked.

There was no other carrier available, Shali replied.

Perry asked about the USS *Nimitz*. Shali said that he was under Perry's own orders to keep the Persian Gulf fully covered to enforce the no-fly zone against Saddam Hussein's air force. This was the *Nimitz*'s current mission. But Perry replied that he was willing to relax the order.

Still, Shali was worried that even if they diverted the *Nimitz*, the carrier might not reach the Taiwan area by the March 23 presidential election.

For Perry, these timing considerations were not as important as the decision to mobilize a second carrier. If the Chinese saw that the United States was willing to pull an aircraft carrier out of the Persian Gulf and send it at flank speed across the Indian Ocean, they would realize that Washington took their missile launches very seriously.

Shali agreed. The second carrier would send a more powerful message, but not so provocative as to give the Chinese any pretext to react. To solve the problem of how the world would see this deployment so far out in the ocean from the Chinese shore, they agreed on a news media strategy to mobilize reporters and film crews and fly them in military transports to the deck of the *Independence*, from where their reports would affirm American resolve.

This was the logic that impelled the two-carrier deployment of March 1996, one that avoided intervention in the Taiwan Strait and one that respected the boundaries of the Chinese exclusion zones for their naval, air, and missile exercises, as long as they didn't target Taiwan.

The deployment would be devoid of any military mission, and, significantly, it would not assert freedom of navigation in the Taiwan Strait, though no one was abandoning that option altogether. Shalikashvili believed that there would be time after the crisis to send one or more American warships through the strait, to show the flag in the international waterway.

On Saturday morning, Christopher and Lord were called to Perry's office at the Pentagon for a briefing by Perry and Shali on the warship deployment plan and on plans for resupplying Taiwan if war broke out. Christopher discussed State's intended diplomatic messages to Beijing and Taipei about what the American deployment meant and what it did not mean. The messages would emphasize that America was not taking sides and that both parties should avoid acts that could trigger further escalation. Christopher planned to tell Beijing that he was calling Taiwan's national security adviser to New York for some sober talk about restraint.

When they finished at the Pentagon, they took the whole package over to the White House, where Lake presented it to Clinton. The president could see the potential for the conflict to spin out of control; for a war in the Taiwan Strait that would cause death and suffering on all sides; for American casualties and body bags coming home to a president who had evaded the draft; and for the destruction of his presidency due to his bungling the relationship that had been nurtured and handed down by his five immediate predecessors.

As he signed off on the military recommendations, Clinton said, "We've got to do everything we can to make sure none of this happens."

The next day, Christopher broke the news on a Sunday talk show that the United States had moved an aircraft carrier closer to Taiwan in case it should be needed. The following day, China conducted its fourth missile test and then announced that the tests were concluded, having launched fewer than half the missiles that it had readied for firing.

This stand-down was the first sign that the Chinese were moderating their coercive posture. They went ahead with sea exercises, but poor weather in the strait limited their scale and duration.

China's hard-line premier, Li Peng, warned American warships to stay out of the Taiwan Strait or face a "sea of fire" from PLA weaponry. The warning may have been mere bluster, delivered only after the Chinese realized that American warships had no intention of steaming through the strait. But once the warning was stated, it would have been far more provocative for the Seventh Fleet to trample on China's dignity by sending an aircraft carrier into the waterway.

Over the next two weeks, as the *Independence* steamed in circles far out at sea, hosting a series of landing parties from the American news media based in Tokyo, the *Nimitz* raced out of the Persian Gulf, trying to reach the western Pacific before the March 23 presidential elections.

The deployments did nothing to settle the war that still loomed between

America, the People's Republic, and Taiwan. But they did strip away the long-standing American doctrine of "strategic ambiguity," a bureaucratic phrase that American officials had used to evade the question of what military actions they would take if Taiwan were threatened militarily by the mainland. There was no longer any ambiguity. America was bound by law, politics, and moral imperative to act in the face of blatant coercion or unprovoked aggression. Now that this position was out in the open, the risks had escalated, along with the incentives for all sides to intensify military planning.

America had declared its intention to use force in the defense of Taiwan. The deployment of March 1996 was the first act of American coercion against China since 1958, and certainly since President Nixon opened up relations with the People's Republic in 1972. The display of American military power was seen as a victory by the Clinton administration, a demonstration of force blended with diplomacy. Bill Perry would later call it "preventative defense." But many China specialists who served under Clinton understood something different about this show of force. It deeply humiliated the new Chinese leadership and the People's Liberation Army. The significance of the confrontation would radiate out across the decades, marking, perhaps, a profound moment in which China's leaders realized that in order to fulfill their own aspirations for national unity, in order to emerge as a great power in Asia, they would have to stand up to the United States militarily, especially near their own shores.

After a month of tension, the American carriers steamed away. But many specialists in the intelligence community and elsewhere believed that Beijing's civilian and military leaders had resolved that such a humiliation would never happen again.

SHORTLY BEFORE the State Department issued the visa to Lee Teng-hui, a senior Chinese official, Wang Jisi, told an American visitor that he had just returned from a retreat for Chinese specialists on America. These specialists served as a collective advisory group to the Communist Party leadership, including Li Peng and Jiang Zemin.

"I want to tell you the consensus of this retreat," he told the visitor. "The first point was that America is in decline and, therefore, it will try to thwart China's emergence as a global power. In the opinion of the participants, the United States is the only country that poses a threat to China's national security." He then cited a litany of "evidence," which included calls in Congress to give Taiwan a forum for pro-independence activities by inviting its leaders to America, as well as public sympathy for Tibet, which was portrayed by Congress and by Hollywood as a separate country under Chinese occupation, a status the Dalai Lama did not even claim. This evidence also included the American penchant for painting an unfair portrait of China's human rights record, for treating Chinese claims over islands in the South China Sea as expansionism, and for imposing onerous conditions for China's entry into the World Trade Organization.

"You know," Wang told his visitor, "for historical reasons Japan has always been the most unpopular country for the Chinese, but I can tell you that among China's senior leaders, the United States is the most unpopular country."

. . .

So much had changed since Richard Nixon's opening to China ushered in an era of goodwill between America and the People's Republic. So much had changed since Chinese and American table tennis teams conspired to stage a match that would bring them together in Beijing; this "Ping-Pong diplomacy" captured America's imagination, as if it were another walk on the moon.

So much had changed since Nixon's journey to Beijing during the week that shook the world in February 1972, when he and his wife, Pat—she in that brilliant red coat that seemed the only speck of color in a whole country of monochromatic Mao suits—stepped out of Air Force One and headed down the stairway toward Zhou Enlai. The scene transported all of America away from the agony of Vietnam, but more, Vietnam suddenly was subsumed in a grand new strategy, and it seemed certain, for the first time, that the war would end. After all, it had been launched to contain communist China, which was bent on toppling the nations of Southeast Asia like so many dominos. But now, thunderously, Nixon and Mao were together and smiling. The image suggested that America was seizing control of its destiny, pulling itself out of the quagmire. In Saigon, the front page of one major newspaper displayed a cartoon of Nixon and Mao making love.

Everyone sensed that it was over.

A new era was beginning, an era that would be dominated by a buoyant mythology of America's relationship with China. And it would last for decades. In 1972, anyone could see that underneath the bold Nixon stroke was the realpolitik of using Beijing to undermine Hanoi, of burdening the Soviet Union with a new strategic dilemma—the fear that Beijing and Washington might ally themselves against Moscow. The split in the monolithic communist bloc had suddenly relieved Americans of the Stranglovian nightmare of global war pitting both the Soviet Union and China against the United States. It was more than relief, because in the nuclear age, America's very survival was at stake.

Because ordinary Americans were much more willing than their leaders to project morality into foreign policy, they believed that the real breakthrough in 1972 was that the Chinese had come to see the goodness of America. And goodness, the moral strength of doing the right thing, was at the core of American identity. Most Americans believed that the Chinese had been led astray, in part by the Soviet Union, in part by utopian nonsense and revolutionary excess. Historical grievances had seemed to generate rage and sustained hatred. The first targets had been landlords and Chiang Kai-shek's spies, but soon the list expanded to encompass world imperialism and foreign devils, those who had invaded and humiliated China so many times since the Opium Wars. Nixon compared the virulence of Chinese communism to "the more explosive ghetto elements of our own country." He felt their rage and it reflected his own deeper fear—one that seemed racially tinged by his "ghetto" comment—of the angry yellow horde swarming out of Asia.

Americans had been alarmed by the ferocious Chinese human-wave attacks that overran American positions in Korea. And they had been even more alarmed when China exploded its first atomic bomb in October 1964, so much so that President John F. Kennedy had sought a way to prevent it, sending W. Averell Harriman to Moscow to secretly explore the possibility of a joint attack on China's nuclear complex.[7] Four days before Kennedy's assassination, General Maxwell Taylor, the chairman of the Joint Chiefs of Staff, circulated a single copy of a top secret planning paper to each of the military service chiefs entitled "Unconventional Warfare Program BRAVO," aimed at preventing or delaying the Chinese bomb. "Nuclear development, at best, is fraught with troubles—technological, scientific, economic and industrial," Taylor told the chiefs. "If these inherent problems are intensified by a coordinated program of covert activities, there is reason to believe that the date on which the Chinese nuclear program matures may be materially deferred."[8]

But in the summer and fall of 1963, as American U-2 flights out of Taiwan recorded the construction of the shot tower where the Chinese bomb would be hoisted for detonation, Soviet Premier Nikita Khrushchev proved unwilling to risk the backlash in the socialist camp—and in the Kremlin—that would surely have followed a Soviet attack on a fellow communist state, however estranged they happened to have become through mistrust and ideological differences.

President Lyndon Johnson also was tempted. In April 1964, the National Security Council staff, under Walt W. Rostow, laid out for the president the results of a year-long study on how the United States might stop the Chinese nuclear weapons program. The only question was "when pre-emptive action against Chi-com nuclear facilities would be feasible and desirable."[9]

Johnson's top advisers—Rostow, Secretary of State Dean Rusk, Secretary of Defense Robert McNamara, and CIA director John McCone—told him in September 1964 that although they did not favor an "unprovoked" and "unilateral" attack on China's nuclear weapons facilities "at this time," they nevertheless "believe[d] that there are many possibilities for joint action with the Soviet Government if that Government is interested," including "even a possible agreement to cooperate in preventative military action."[10] Rusk was dispatched to discuss the matter with the Soviet ambassador to the United States, Anatoly F. Dobrynin, but, again, the Soviets were not ready.[11]

Most Americans feared the Orwellian vision of the future that Rusk had verbalized when he publicly warned of "a billion Chinese armed with nuclear weapons." The American strategy toward China had been one of containment—building a defensive arc around the Asian landmass by maintaining alliances with Japan, South Korea, Taiwan, the Philippines, South Vietnam, Indonesia, and Thailand.

China and the United States were in a barely arrested state of war, ever since their armies had collided on the Korean peninsula and since Mao had thrown China's defense industries in support of Ho Chi Minh's drive to unite Vietnam under socialism. Matador nuclear missiles, which could be launched from American bombers, were moved in great secrecy to Taiwan so that they would be available for use against the mainland. They were still there when Nixon went to China.

A secret war between the communist Chinese and American proxies had been waged throughout the 1950s and 1960s, and the bloodletting on both sides only added to the mutual enmity, hatred, and fear. Thousands of American-sponsored guerrillas perished in the mountainous regions of Tibet, Sichuan, and Yunnan. In Tibet, the CIA monitored the Dalai Lama's flight in 1959, when the Tibetan uprising drew a crushing military response from Beijing. In April 1955, the intelligence wars nearly claimed the life of Zhou Enlai, who later would play such a critical role in opening U.S.-China relations. A plane that was to have taken Zhou to Jakarta for the Bandung Conference was sabotaged. It crashed, killing eleven Chinese diplomats. Zhou was saved when he changed his travel plans at the last moment. Hong Kong police identified a suspect, but he fled to Taiwan.[12]

The opening to China represented a great relief from fear. Americans knew that terrible things had occurred in China during its long isolation after the Communist victory. The Communists had encouraged the peasantry to join in overthrowing the landlords, because Mao understood that shedding blood was critical to binding the masses. The virulence of Mao's revolution was confirmed by refugees fleeing to Hong Kong. They told of landowners being clubbed to death, buried alive, or dismembered. Later, Mao's Great Leap Forward had caused the deaths of tens of millions of Chinese through policy-induced famine. Even at the moment of Nixon's triumphant opening, Mao was still engaged in secret purges that resulted in the deaths of rivals and innocents alike. It was a marvel that China was ready to emerge at all. But that its leaders were also extending a hand of friendship was phenomenal. A great redemption was underway, and it was awe inspiring.[13]

All of this emotion was written on a clean slate because, by 1972, Americans had little stake in China. The isolation and trade embargoes over the preceding two decades had put the two countries, truly, on different planets. When Secretary of State John Foster Dulles refused to shake Zhou's hand at Geneva in 1954, it was a reflection that America, the preeminent global power in the wake of World War II, had constructed a world where Mao's China did not exist. Instead, America enforced the global fiction that Chiang Kai-shek was China's leader, and as a result the Nationalist government on Taiwan held China's seat at the United Nations. Mao's China had no legitimacy and Mao was caricatured as a fanatical megalomaniac. So when the opening with China occurred, it was not enough to think of it as an act of self-interested geopolitics. Pragmatism alone could not account for the gush of human emotion, the amazement at the spectacle of Mao and Nixon together in the Forbidden City. Americans were astounded that after all those years of war, after the searing vituperation of "running dog" capitalism and "godless" communism—after all of that, the Chinese did not really hate them.

China had been terra incognita for so long that the American public had forgotten much of what was there. And so Americans fell in love with Mao and with the elegant Zhou, with the Great Wall, with those amazing pandas and with chopsticks. It was said that the Great Wall was the only manmade structure that could be seen with the naked eye from space. It did not matter that this also was myth, in fact a physical impossibility. To believe it, however, was a tribute to Chinese civilization and its 5,000 years of recorded history, all of which had been denied during the Cold War. China once again, as it had in the previous century when hundreds of American missionaries built lasting bridges between the cultures, captivated the American psyche. And if Chinese Communists were no longer a threat, they must be a different order of being than once thought. One newsmagazine coined the term "cuddly communism" to describe the Chinese political theology. That was the mood.

Such was the landscape of American mythology that sprang from the opening with Beijing. As for the Nationalists, the generalissimo's political allies in America and his defenders in Congress were suddenly marginalized. Walter Judd and the Committee of One Million seemed as out of date as Bishop Fulton Sheen. They were finished; their vision repudiated. If Nixon, the ultimate conservative, the anticommunist doyen of the Republican Party, now was embracing Mao, everyone to the right of Nixon had lost credibility. Republicans whispered profoundly the new conventional wisdom that only a Nixon could have gone to China. Of course that was also a myth.

In fact, Johnson had tried to open lines of communication with Mao, if only as a desperate act to rescue his presidency from Vietnam. But the stars had been aligned against Johnson. For one thing, China was not ready for an opening to America. Mao was at the height of his purges during the Cultural Revolution. The CIA's map of China showed every major city in turmoil and the country headed for civil war. Army units were turning on other army units, and even in security organizations radical commanders were trying to overthrow their leaders, encouraged by Mao to "bombard the headquarters" and purge the party of "capitalist roaders" and "revisionists." But instead of being revitalized, the country just descended into violence and chaos. The sudden radicalism led to every manner of excess, as manifested by the floating corpses that began appearing in rivers.[14]

Johnson had no time to wait for better circumstances. In the summer of 1967, he orchestrated an authoritative probe.

During a private lunch at his Texas ranch with Max Frankel of *The New York Times*, Johnson surprised the White House correspondent. "Max, I want you to write a story." Johnson explained that he wanted to open a dialogue with China. The United States, he said, was not out to change China's government. Although conservatives would oppose him, Johnson reckoned that with his record (for toughness) on Vietnam, he was the president with the ability to stage an opening to China, and no one would dare call him an appeaser. In other words, only a Johnson could go to China.[15]

At the end of the encounter, Frankel asked how he should attribute Johnson's remarks.

"Don't quote me," Johnson said.

Frankel's dispatch—"Johnson Reviving Bid for Contacts with Red Chinese"—led the front page of *The Times* on July 11, 1967, citing authoritative White House sources.

Nixon, then living in New York, could not have missed this thunderbolt. He had just returned from a fact-finding trip through Asia that served as the basis for a long article he was writing for the journal, *Foreign Affairs*, about China policy.

The fact that Nixon later succeeded where Johnson had failed changed all perception of history. The reason for Nixon's success was not to be found in America, but in Beijing and Moscow. His advantage was not so much his skill as a statesman, though he showed great skill in exploiting the opportunity in China, but rather the convergence of geopolitical forces. The first great shift in those forces occurred in August 1968 when the Soviet military crushed the incipient rebellion in Czechoslovakia, and the Brezhnev Doctrine, with its threat to bring wayward socialist states forcibly back into line, incited Mao to turn more forcefully against Moscow. Because Mao feared that Moscow's growing power would eventually be used to dominate China and because Mao could see that America was getting out of Vietnam,* the Chinese leader had to consider reconciling with the American superpower as a countermeasure to growing Soviet pressure.

Another important factor impelled Mao. Cut off from Moscow by a decade of ideological divergence, China was falling further and further behind in technological development. The country badly needed to update its industries if the Communists were ever to succeed in building a new nation that could compete economically in the modern world. Opening up to America and the West offered a solution.

Nixon, first and foremost a political man and an opportunist, could also see the unfolding logic. Moreover, powerful Democratic voices in Congress were calling for a reevaluation of America's China policy. Preeminent China specialists like John K. Fairbank, A. Doak Barnett, Ezra F. Vogel, and Jerome A. Cohen argued that China's worst instincts could be contained without isolating the country's 700 million people. "Containment, without isolation," as Barnett had termed this approach.

Nixon sought to align his ideological rhetoric with this centrist view and wrote in his October 1967 essay in *Foreign Affairs* that "the threat [from] Red China is clear, present and repeatedly and insistently expressed. The message has not been lost on Asia's leaders. They recognize that the West, and particularly the United States, now represents not an oppressor but a protector. And they recognize the need for protection." For Nixon, that protection would come from a new Asian security alliance against China to replace the American role in Asia of providing armies to fight Communists.

"The world cannot be safe until China changes," he concluded. China had to be persuaded "that it must change: that it cannot satisfy its imperial ambitions, and that its own national interest requires a turning away from foreign adventuring and a turning inward toward the solution of its own domestic problems." And further, "Taking the long view, we simply cannot afford to leave China forever outside the family of nations, there to nurture its fantasies, cherish its hates and threaten its neighbors."

But, Nixon admonished, any short-term strategy of rushing into China's arms would be an act of political cowardice. Coming to grips "with the reality of China," he argued, "does not mean, as many would simplistically have

---

*During the 1960s, the buildup of American military forces in the Pacific in support of the war in Vietnam had seemed to Mao the prelude to an American invasion of China.

it, rushing to grant recognition to Beijing, to admit it to the United Nations and to ply it with offers of trade—all of which would serve to confirm its rulers in their present course. It does mean recognizing the present and potential danger from Communist China, and taking measures designed to meet that danger."

So it began.

THE
SINO-SOVIET
BORDER

1969

*Chinese soldiers during a "provocation"
at Damansky Island*

D AMANSKY ISLAND, USSR, March 2, 1969: Although it was nearly the end of winter, almost every dawn in this remote corner of Northeast Asia gave only weak illumination to the bleak and monotonous landscape of scrub pine forest and marshland.

Shrouded by a leaden sky, this was the domain of Senior Lieutenant Ivan Strelnikov, an officer in the border guards of the Soviet army in the Khabarovsk military region of the Soviet Far East. As commander of the outpost facing Damansky Island on the Ussuri River, 250 miles north by northeast of Vladivostok, Strelnikov lived with his small contingent of conscripts in a backwater half a world away from the center of Russian life in Moscow. Yet it was Strelnikov and his men who had begun to believe that they were playing a crucial role—indeed, perhaps, *the* crucial role—in protecting the motherland. They were the first line of defense against Chinese aggression.[1]

The Ussuri River drained the vast marshy regions between Khabarovsk and Vladivostok. In early March, its serpentine course was still in the grip of winter's rigor mortis, its channel locked in pack ice. This time of year, the ice could still support an armored personnel carrier, and so there was nothing to stop smugglers or Chinese soldiers from boldly walking across the river and violating the sovereignty of the Soviet Union.

In fact, the Chinese army, over a number of months, had undertaken a campaign of escalating provocation in the form of encroachments by armed patrols coming out of bases on the high ground of the Chinese bank, and then down to occupy the island, or out onto the ice to challenge the Soviet border.[2] The Chinese provocations had steadily intensified, as if they represented a defiant response to the Soviet invasion of Czechoslovakia the previous summer.

Damansky Island seemed an unlikely venue for confrontation—just a frozen piece of wasteland about a third of a square mile in area, just across the main branch of the river from Strelnikov's border post. The island had no economic or strategic value to either the Soviet Union or China. It was uninhabited year-round, and, during the warm summer months, thaw gave way to swamp, like much of the lowland on the Soviet side of the river. Damansky was thirty miles from the nearest Soviet city, and there was no significant military installation in the area.

Still, the Chinese were asserting their claim because the island, which they called Zhenbao Island, lay on the Chinese side of the main channel. Under international law, the center line of the channel, the *thalweg*, is the recognized demarcation of a riverine border. Moreover, Damansky Island was, topographically, part of the Chinese bank, recessed as it was in a dimple on the Chinese side. The island was barely separated from the Chinese bank by a narrow flood channel that had branched off from the Ussuri during some previous deluge.

China, for most of the previous two centuries, had done a poor job of defending its borders from encroachments. After the Opium Wars, it had given up treaty ports to Britain and France; Germany had moved into Qingdao,* and Japan had seized Taiwan. Under pressure from the czar in 1860, the Chinese ratified Russian territorial claims in the Far East, another source of humiliation for the collapsing Qing Dynasty.

Needless to say, for Senior Lieutenant Strelnikov, Damansky Island was Soviet territory and always would be. His dedication to the motherland and his ambition for higher rank were apparent in the record he had compiled for confronting every Chinese attempt to challenge the Soviet version of the border, so much so that the Chinese had branded him a "troublemaker." It was, of course, a badge of honor for Strelnikov to be so regarded by the enemy.

Chinese defiance took many forms.

Chinese patrols sometimes pulled down their pants to "moon" Soviet troops across the river. The Soviet garrisons retaliated by passing out photographs of Mao and instructing patrols to hold them aloft when any Chinese soldier assumed the mooning position. That way, the Chinese would be mooning an image of their own leader.[3]

On January 23, Strelnikov loaded his men into armored personnel carriers and drove out onto the frozen Ussuri to confront a Chinese patrol. Strelnikov demanded that the Chinese soldiers return to their bank. They refused, and a fight ensued in which both sides flailed at each other with fists and the butts of their Kalashnikovs. There were casualties, mostly bruises and gouges. But the rising tempers added to the level of residual tension. In thousands of previous border incidents, it had been rare for a blow to be struck in anger, and blood had seldom been drawn. Both sides had long been

---

*This city is known to many Westerners as Tsing Tao, famous for its beer. The spelling "Qingdao" reflects the move by the Chinese government, as well as by most scholars, from the Wade-Giles to the pinyin system of romanization. But Tsing Tao beer is still brewed in Qingdao.

under orders to practice restraint and to try to accomplish their goals through reason rather than violence.

On February 7, Strelnikov again led his men onto the ice in armored trucks and again faced down a Chinese patrol. There was no violence. But the Chinese were soon to change the rules of engagement.

On the night of March 1, the weather was still frigid. Two groups of Chinese soldiers took up positions under cover of darkness. One group infiltrated the island and the other dug in on the high ground of the Chinese bank. They wore camouflage fatigues and laid field telephone lines so they could communicate with their reinforcements.

When Strelnikov awoke on March 2, his sentries did not spot the infiltration until about 9 A.M., when a patrol of some thirty Chinese soldiers conspicuously marched down to the island. This was the bait. Strelnikov's job was to again go out onto the river and push them off. It was by now a familiar drill, but he did not act precipitously, waiting nearly two hours before he loaded his men into an armored personnel carrier.

At 11 A.M., he and six Soviet soldiers rumbled out onto the ice, lurched up onto Damansky Island, and dismounted at a spot near the column of Chinese, who began walking toward them. The Russians' rifles were still attached to the slings on their chests.

As the Chinese column approached, it became apparent that the front row of soldiers was not armed. That was the trap, for as the distance closed, the unarmed Chinese dove to the side, exposing a line of troops behind them, their guns at the ready.

The Chinese opened up at close range, the sharp explosion of gunfire shattering the morning air. Bullets tore through Strelnikov's tunic. He went down onto the ice-crusted earth, bleeding from multiple wounds.

A firefight raged for two hours. Soviet reinforcements raced forward, but the hidden reserves of Chinese troops opened fire with heavy machine guns, grenades, and mortars, whose range was so deadly accurate that the Soviets later deduced that the distances had been paced off during the night.

The Soviets called up reinforcements from two other border posts, but it was clear that they were facing a battalion-strength force, about 300 Chinese with heavy weapons. The rain of fire forced the Soviets to pull back, and only then did the Chinese break off the attack.

More than thirty Soviet soldiers lay dead, another fourteen wounded. Senior Lieutenant Strelnikov died where he fell defending Damansky Island.

.   .   .

Richard Nixon had been in office only eight weeks and was out of the country when the Damansky Island fighting erupted. The president, with his secretary of state, William P. Rogers, had embarked on a ceremonial promenade through Europe to demonstrate that he would be a foreign policy leader.

Nixon spent the day with Charles de Gaulle at Versailles and then flew to Rome for an audience with the pope. The intelligence reports from the Sino-Soviet border caught up with him as he rode on Air Force One, ensconced with Rogers and Henry Kissinger, the Harvard professor of government whom Nixon had recruited from Nelson Rockefeller's camp. Neither Rogers nor Kissinger had significant expertise on the Sino-Soviet conflict, or any particular knowledge of the history of the simmering border confrontation. The CIA also had not been able to sort out the conflicting accounts of the fighting. The Chinese blamed the Soviet patrol for opening up on their own border troops with "cannon and gunfire." In Beijing, propaganda organs called on the masses to "attack the new czars!" Thousands of Chinese marched on the Soviet embassy to denounce "Soviet revisionism." The Soviets replied by orchestrating huge crowds in Moscow who marched on the Chinese embassy, denouncing the Chinese leadership and smashing windows. Despite the lack of evidence, Nixon concluded that the Chinese had most likely started the fight since, in his view, Beijing was the more aggressive of the two powers.[4] Yet he was also fascinated by this sudden bloodletting between the communist giants. Up to now, the Sino-Soviet split had been an abstraction.

By coincidence, Nixon and de Gaulle had been discussing the tensions between Moscow and Beijing. De Gaulle was alarmed by the phenomenal growth of Soviet military power, the threat from which was the central fact of life in postwar Europe. The Soviets "are thinking in terms of a possible clash with China," he said, "and they know they can't fight the West at the same time. Thus, I believe that they may end up opting for a policy of *rapprochement* with the West."[5] Russia's traditional fear of a Western military threat would impel Moscow toward détente, he added, employing the term that would define the diplomacy of the era.

"Unless you are prepared to go to war or to break down the Berlin Wall, then there is no alternative policy that is acceptable," de Gaulle continued. "If you are not ready to make war, make peace."

Nixon agreed. He returned to the subject of China.

"In looking down the road, as I pursue my talks with the Soviets, I too might want to keep an anchor to windward with respect to China," he said. In ten years, after China had developed a large nuclear arsenal, "we will have no choice." It would be too dangerous to leave China in isolation. Therefore, it was vital, Nixon said, that the United States have more communication with China. He did not have to convince de Gaulle, who had already established diplomatic relations with Beijing.

Nixon had great respect for the French leader, whose vision spanned the century; in fact, Nixon saw himself as a kind of American de Gaulle, a leader of global vision and strategy, a stoic and fiercely independent intellect whose image was destined to be chiseled in stone. De Gaulle believed that if the Soviet Union was headed for a clash with China, there was nothing the West could, or, perhaps, should do about it. As a European leader, de Gaulle only welcomed a diversion of Soviet military attention to the Far East. But the importance of his admonition to Nixon was the clarity with which he saw the great breach opening between the Soviet Union and the People's Republic of China. With the violence at Damansky Island, the breach would open further, fracturing the monolithic communist bloc on the Asian continent. De Gaulle instinctively understood, and now Nixon understood, that an epochal change was under way.

A small group of American intelligence analysts had been arguing as much. But their views had been consistently rejected by senior policymakers who feared that the Sino-Soviet rift was no more than a family quarrel. In a highly classified study code-named Esau,[6] intelligence officers working under the legendary analyst and chief of research W. P. "Bud" Southard had been marshaling the evidence from defectors and other sources of information on Kremlin political thinking. They drew on the agency's multiyear, "all source" study of the Soviet leadership, called Caesar, and a similar study of the Chinese leadership, code-named Polo. By the time Nixon entered office, the analysts had prevailingly come to believe that the split was real and, perhaps, irreparable. Kissinger became an avid subscriber to their viewpoint If there was any intellectual resistance remaining to the reality of the Sino-Soviet rift, the bloodshed at Damansky Island blew it away. Career analysts were simply stunned. Suddenly and inexplicably, the Sino-Soviet frontier had become a war zone where blood was on the ground.

For Nixon, the big question was how this new and violent fracture would play out in Vietnam. Nothing was of greater concern than finding an exit strategy in Southeast Asia. There would be no second term if Nixon did not end the Vietnam War. In the weeks after his election, even before bringing Kissinger onto the team, Nixon had instructed Robert Ellsworth, a former congressman and his foreign policy adviser during the campaign, to get the message quickly to Moscow that Nixon would be looking for urgent assistance from the Kremlin in ending the war.

Ellsworth met in Washington's Plaza Hotel with Soviet ambassador Anatoly Dobrynin's deputy, and in late November he met with Dobrynin himself. Ellsworth explained to the Soviet diplomat that Nixon's two overarching priorities were to get the United States out of Vietnam and to begin a process of negotiating limits on the growth of nuclear arsenals. He told the Soviet envoy that Nixon not only wanted help with Vietnam, he wanted to know what the Soviets would want in return.[7]

But nothing came back from the Kremlin. On February 23, as Nixon was taking off for his promenade through Europe's capitals, the North Vietnamese launched a countrywide offensive. Nixon instructed Kissinger to telephone Dobrynin with a warning that if the offensive continued, the United States would retaliate. Nixon wanted the Soviets to take responsibility for Hanoi's actions. Moscow was, after all, North Vietnam's principal supplier of weapons and munitions. Much of that weaponry traveled by train through China, whose leaders also expressed solidarity with Ho Chi Minh, assuring Ho that China was his "reliable rear area" in the war effort. China had built an air base on its own territory for use by the North Vietnamese air force, which needed sanctuary during American bombing raids on the North. All along the rail line that connected Hanoi with China, battalions of Chinese antiaircraft forces and construction brigades fought side by side with the North Vietnamese.[8]

But as the rift between Moscow and Beijing widened, Soviet military trains began to encounter delays in China. Moscow accused China of pilfering Russian munitions. Neither Moscow nor Beijing, however, lessened their public support for Hanoi, whose liberation struggle was a touchstone of socialist solidarity in East Europe and among the socialist camp in general.

B ARELY A MONTH into the Nixon administration, Kissinger began a campaign to undermine Rogers's management of foreign policy and to establish himself as Nixon's key adviser on Vietnam, the Soviet Union, and China.[9]

Rogers had served as attorney general in the Eisenhower administration, and, although he was not an expert on international affairs, both he and Nixon believed that they could work out a system whereby Rogers would work closely with, and take direction from, the White House. Initially, Rogers did not feel threatened by Kissinger's appointment as Nixon's assistant for national security affairs. Rogers had the advantages of cabinet rank and a long-standing personal friendship with Nixon. He was also confident that he could learn the foreign policy brief and was more than willing to work with Kissinger.

But the arrangement depended on Kissinger's accepting the subservient role of invisible technocrat in charge of marshaling intelligence and options for the president. This was never to be. Nixon's failure to see that Kissinger would demand his own recognition was soon obvious, although no one in the White House had been fully prepared for Kissinger's ego-driven antics in the bureaucratic struggle that ensued. From the beginning, Kissinger, with Nixon's backing, set up the national security machinery so that the White House could dominate the foreign policy process on any issue. And Kissinger sought to minimize Rogers's role beyond even Nixon's expectations. Of all Nixon's acquisitions, Kissinger was among the most prized because he had sprung from the marrow of the eastern establishment, which had always regarded Nixon as an outsider and an ideologue. In Kissinger, Nixon had captured a mind that could help him give expression to a complex worldview that was at once conservative and pragmatic.

Kissinger had arrived in a White House staffed largely by Nixon campaign men, who looked upon him with some suspicion because Harvard's liberal ethos was anathema to them. The son of Jewish émigrés from Nazi Germany, Kissinger had come to the United States at age fifteen, and after the war, in which he served as an intelligence analyst in the army, he made a career at Harvard. In Cambridge, he soon gained a reputation as a gifted and ambitious foreign policy intellectual, and he helped establish a debating salon to which he invited national political figures to discuss America's role in the new era of nuclear weapons and superpower rivalry. It was a forum for Kissinger to display his wit and keen intelligence, and it was also the means by which he ingratiated himself with prominent politicians, Nelson Rockefeller among them.

Kissinger had a mesmerizing knack for intellectual seduction that combined blatant sycophancy with seemingly brilliant formulations of the self-evident, all conveyed with the intimacy of a suitor putting his inside knowledge and the full resources of his mind at the disposal of the object of his affection. His was truly a powerful mind of great range and analytic ability. Kissinger was also a formidable manipulator, and his skill at deception, secrecy, and bureaucratic maneuver was worthy of Georges Clemenceau, Benjamin Disraeli, or his favorite European strategist, Klemens Fürst von Metternich. With minute facial expressions, self-deprecating humor, and a scorching, satiric wit, Kissinger was endowed with an enormous social charm, and to see him focus it on men and women with political (or economic) power could be enthralling. Although his German accent was a source of insecurity, Kissinger's Germanic sentence structures infused his presentations with a judicial tone that was often mistaken for profundity when, in fact, his syntax was merely inverted or sometimes just incoherent.

By the end of the 1960s, it was clear that academia could not satisfy Kissinger's ambition, which was to enter government as a senior foreign policy adviser. And to maximize his opportunities, Kissinger, nominally in the Rockefeller camp during the 1968 campaign, secretly provided information and advice to the Nixon and Hubert Humphrey campaigns as well.[10]

After the election, Kissinger set out to ensure that the National Security Council (NSC) would be the funnel through which all policy deliberations would pass. He ordered up a prodigious number of studies to question and examine almost every aspect of American foreign policy. And from the outset, Kissinger understood that Nixon intended to open a secret negotiating channel with the Soviets, as both Jack Kennedy and Lyndon Johnson had done.

By March 1969, having quickly established his value to Nixon and having drawn the first compliments for his staff work, Kissinger laid down his first threat to resign after fomenting an exaggerated challenge to Rogers's handling of Soviet policy. The eruption followed Rogers's private meeting with the Soviet ambassador on March 8. In the confidential meeting, the secretary expressed Nixon's desire to begin negotiating an end to the Vietnam War with Soviet participation and assistance. When Kissinger saw the memorandum of the meeting, he attacked Rogers's performance, claiming that the secretary had given away an opportunity to "take a harder line" with Hanoi because the Soviets "are in trouble with China on the border."[11]

Confronting H. R. Haldeman, Nixon's chief of staff, Kissinger anguished that he could not stand idly by while Bill Rogers orchestrated the "destruction of the Saigon government." If that happened, Kissinger said solemnly, "I would have to leave."

Kissinger further wondered aloud to Haldeman why Nixon didn't bite the bullet early and name Rogers to the Supreme Court, since the secretary's self-interest was so paramount that he could not adequately serve the president. Haldeman was dumbfounded by the assault and attempted to calm the waters, but the pattern of Kissinger maneuvering against his rivals through Haldeman had been established. Such was the ethos of the early Nixon White House.

It did not take long for Rogers to figure out that Kissinger was seeking to undermine him. The secretary of state told his friends that he could detect when Kissinger was lying by the increased frequency with which he cleared his throat. It was as if he had to slow down his speech while his mind was fabricating.

WITHIN WEEKS OF Nixon's taking office, the intelligence community presented the White House with its top secret *Review of the International Situation*, a benchmark assessment of foreign policy by top government analysts. In plain language, they told the White House that the deepening strains between Moscow and Beijing would send both adversaries running to America's doorstep, and therein lay an opportunity for U.S. policy.

Each side has shown signs of concern over the possible actions of the other in the near term—Beijing because of Soviet intervention in Czechoslovakia, Moscow because of its realization that the stabilization of the internal situation in China may in the near future make the Chinese a more formidable adversary in their ideological and diplomatic competition.

Although both Beijing and Moscow have probably over dramatized their fears for maximum political impact on interested observers, we believe their contingency planning and policy decisions are influenced by suspicions in both capitals that the other fellow has something up his sleeve.[12]

The study concluded, "Given the fact that the Soviets and Chinese appear now to regard one another with more active hostility than they regard the U.S., it is possible that each will become more active in seeking to prevent the other from aligning too closely with the U.S., and to use its own relations with the U.S. as a means of checkmating the other's policies."

The opportunity for America to enhance its position by playing along in this "triangular relationship" was unmistakable. The only question was how.

Nixon knew that the China specialists in the State Department wanted the administration to take some initial, incremental steps to reduce America's level of hostility with China. On his trip through Asia in 1967, Nixon had spent a long evening on the veranda of the American ambassador to Indonesia, Marshall Green, who had argued that the war to contain China had already been won.

Green was a rarity. The son of New England industrialists, he had prepped at Groton and played football at Yale; yet, despite his eastern establishment credentials, he went out of his way to be kind to Nixon, who was despised by many of Green's peers in the foreign service. But Green and Nixon were of the same generation and shared the experience of serving in the Pacific during the war: Green as the private secretary to the American ambassador in Tokyo in the two years leading up to Pearl Harbor, and Nixon as a young naval officer in an air transport unit on Bougainville and Green Islands. The deeply insecure Nixon always remembered a kindness—as he did a slight—and Green's hospitality, coming as it did from a Democratic Party appointee, was the exception, not the rule, during Nixon's tour through Asia. But Green had another agenda: convincing Nixon, a contender for the White House, to update his view of China, and he took pride in having succeeded. If America wanted to counter the growth of Soviet power, Green said, "the road to Moscow lies through Beijing."[13] Nixon rewarded Green's insight by instructing Rogers to appoint him assistant secretary of state for East Asian affairs. Still, Nixon—once in office—seemed extremely wary about extending a hand to Beijing.

At that time, all contact with China had been limited to sterile and infrequent exchanges in Warsaw. These exchanges had begun in Geneva after the 1954 conference there on Indochina, and since then there had been 134 sessions, all of them focused on demands and recriminations over assets seized by both sides and over a handful of Americans imprisoned in China.

In August 1968, after nearly a year's hiatus and in the wake of the Soviet military intervention in Czechoslovakia, China suddenly expressed interest in reactivating the talks on the basis of "peaceful coexistence." The Brezhnev Doctrine—that Moscow would enforce discipline in the communist bloc— was a direct challenge to China as well as to any East European ruler thinking about breaking ranks. Beijing's change in tone from earlier messages was remarkable, and anyone paying close attention could see that China was concerned about Soviet aggression and that this concern was driving the Chinese to open the channels of communication with the United States, if only as a hedge.

As Nixon entered the White House, China and the United States agreed that February 20, 1969, would be the date for their next meeting in Warsaw. Yet Nixon let this early opportunity pass. The White House signaled no interest in any immediate opening to Beijing, leaving the preparations for the meeting to the State Department.

On January 27, a visibly nervous Nixon, in his maiden news conference at the White House, said it was up to the "Chinese Communist representatives" to state at the meeting "whether any changes of attitude on their part on major substantive issues may have occurred. . . . The policy of this country and this administration at this time will be to continue to oppose Communist China's admission to the United Nations." Nixon thus paid tribute to Chiang Kai-shek's continued stewardship over the China vote at the UN. It was the LBJ line.

But in private, Nixon condoned deceptive leaks intended to influence Soviet thinking. One such leak was spawned when Kissinger reported on January 31 that a Polish diplomat, lunching with a State Department official at Washington's swank Sans Souci restaurant, had probed the new administration's attitude toward China. The Polish diplomat said that China was virtually cut off from Russian and East European technology. Therefore, its only hope for rapid industrialization lay with the West, specifically the United States, whose trade and technological assistance would be crucial.[14]

After reading Kissinger's report of the conversation, Nixon instructed him to plant the idea among East Europeans that something might be going on between Washington and Beijing, but to take extreme care not to let it appear that the White House was leaking the story. "I think we should give every encouragement to the attitude that this Administration is exploring possibilities of *rapprochement* with the Chinese."[15]

Nixon's private view at the outset of his administration was that, with any luck, he might be able to entice the Chinese to open a dialogue during his second term. As an inducement to the Chinese, he was willing to undertake a number of politically safe, modest steps to ease trade and visa restrictions.[16] Moving any faster would invite political trouble. As it was, Nixon's election had been greeted by nothing but scorn from Beijing; Beijing Radio went so far as to report that during Nixon's swing through Europe, he was treated "like a rat running across the street."[17] The state-run radio also broadcast that Nixon was preparing to make a deal with the Soviet Union to divide the world into two spheres of influence.

Kissinger, for his part, saw no short-term possibility of a move toward China. On one early trip, Haldeman came out of the presidential cabin on Air Force One and sat down next to the national security adviser.

"You know," Haldeman said, "he actually, seriously intends to visit China before the end of the second term."

Smiling ever so slightly, Kissinger took off his glasses and cleaned them on his tie. He turned to Haldeman and responded, "Fat chance."[18]

So there was no Nixon overture, and the planned Warsaw talks fell apart on their own when a Chinese diplomat defected in late January 1969 by seeking political asylum at the U.S. embassy in the Netherlands.* The timing of the defection, less than a month before the scheduled talks, was unfortunate because the incident sent Beijing into paroxysms of denunciation that the United States had "deliberately engineered this grave anti-China incident" and that their diplomat had been "incited to betray his country," having been "carried off to the United States by the U.S. Central Intelligence Agency."[19] On February 18, the Chinese cancelled the Warsaw meeting.

When Nixon returned from Europe, he reflected a grim resignation on China in comments to reporters. "Looking further down the road, we could think in terms of a better understanding with Red China. But being very realistic, in view of Red China's breaking off the rather limited Warsaw talks that were planned, I do not think we should hold out any great optimism for any breakthroughs at this time."[20]

Then the military clash at Damansky Island occurred, and Dobrynin was the first to unload the Kremlin's frustrations on Nixon's doorstep.

Obviously acting under instructions from Moscow, the Soviet ambassador, in a meeting with Kissinger, railed against the atrocities that the Chinese had committed in the ambush of Strelnikov's patrol.

Soviet reporting alleged that "the wounded were shot by the Chinese from close range or stabbed with bayonets and knives. The faces of some of

---

*Liao Hoshu was no prize defector; he was even a little nutty, State Department officials said.

the casualties were distorted beyond recognition, and others had their uniforms and boots taken off by the Chinese."[21] The Soviets claimed to have found liquor bottles all over the island, indicating that the attackers had fortified themselves for the savagery. These were the kinds of gory details that Dobrynin laid before Kissinger, who was sympathetic.

But when Kissinger suggested that the border clashes were a matter between China and the Soviet Union, Dobrynin insisted that China was *everybody's* problem.[22]

This was certainly a moment of recognition for Kissinger. De Gaulle was right. Soviet paranoia over China was so deep that, in the midst of a violent rupture in the communist bloc, the Soviets were acting as though a military confrontation might lie ahead.

Three days after Kissinger's meeting with Dobrynin, Nixon, in a news conference, portrayed China as a global nuclear menace of equal concern to both the United States and the Soviet Union. In deciding to press forward with developing a limited antiballistic missile system to safeguard the continental United States* in the event of a nuclear attack, Nixon emphasized just how dangerous China had become to both superpowers.

"I would imagine that the Soviet Union would be just as reluctant as we would be to leave their country naked against a potential Chinese Communist threat. So the abandoning of the entire [ABM] system, particularly as long as the Chinese threat is there, I think neither country would look upon with much favor."[23]

This was Nixon's inner fear of China—the vision of a billion Chinese armed with nuclear weapons—and it was hardly different from the Kennedy-Johnson-Rusk view, the view that Averell Harriman had pressed on Nikita Khrushchev in the summer of 1963 and that had prompted both Washington and Moscow to believe that the two superpowers could together prevent China from joining the nuclear club.

By March, Dobrynin and his superiors in Moscow clearly understood that Nixon wanted Moscow to twist Hanoi's arm—withhold arms shipments, if necessary—to help shape a political settlement in Vietnam.

Dobrynin himself doubted Moscow's ability, or willingness, to deliver. So did the U.S. intelligence community, which made clear its belief that Nixon should expect no help from the Soviets.

To complicate Nixon's position, the Democrats opened a campaign to take China policy away from the White House and make rapprochement a Democratic issue. On March 20, Senator Edward M. Kennedy called for the withdrawal of American forces from Taiwan. "Every new Administration has

---

*The ABM system was eventually abandoned by Nixon, but three decades later it was revived as a high priority of the Clinton administration and the 106th Congress.

a new opportunity to rectify the errors of the past," Kennedy told an audience of 2,500 China specialists in New York. "If the new Administration allows this time to pass without new initiatives, if it allows inherited policies to rush unimpeded along their course, it will have wasted this opportunity."[24]

In the White House, Kennedy's assault was interpreted as the opening bell of the 1972 presidential election campaign. Kennedy attacked Nixon's decision to move forward with the ABM system and he set out his own seven-point proposal for a new China policy.

The ABM deployment "is likely to be seen in Peking as a new military provocation by the United States," Kennedy said. "From the Chinese perspective, the only utility of an American ABM system is to defend the United States against whatever feeble response Peking could muster after an American first strike against China. Virtually no experts on China expect Peking to commit aggression, in the conventional sense of forcibly occupying the territory of another country, as the Soviet Union recently occupied Czechoslovakia."

Kennedy was right. In 1969, China did not even have a missile that could reach the United States, and it would not develop one for a decade.[25] Kennedy's political challenge, however, was dangerous, for it portrayed Nixon as too inflexible to get the country on the path to peace.

Within days of Kennedy's salvo, stories leaked in Washington that Kissinger was heading up a review of China policy. Dobrynin asked him whether the stories were true, and Kissinger evaded him, saying only in their meeting on April 3 that rapprochement had always been an option under the right circumstances. Dobrynin responded that there was still time for the two superpowers to order events throughout the world, but that this window of opportunity would not last forever.[26] Dobrynin's meaning was unmistakable. It was the most pointed offer of cooperation the Soviet ambassador had yet laid down before the Nixon administration, and the president could only have been ecstatic that Moscow was probing—even soliciting.

There had been a long history of sensitive U.S.-Soviet discussions about preventing China from becoming a nuclear power. The record of these conversations was highly classified, some under the code name Cherokee, which designated the highly sensitive cable traffic from Harriman in Moscow and from elsewhere that was reserved for Kennedy's eyes only and for a few close aides. Kissinger directed William G. Hyland, a senior CIA analyst who had joined the NSC staff and who had read the sensitive records, to brief him. Kissinger wanted to know everything about the secret exchanges.

As Kissinger educated himself, the Sino-Soviet border kept erupting in violence.

It took the Soviet military two weeks to prepare its answer to the March 2 ambush on Strelnikov's patrol. The Soviets brought up tanks, heavy artillery, and a regiment-size force of 1,500 men. The Chinese reinforced their bank of the river. On the morning of March 15, a Chinese vehicle equipped with loudspeakers drove out onto the ice and warned the Soviets not to attack.

Then the artillery thundered, turning much of Damansky Island and the Chinese bank into a moonscape of craters. The Chinese withstood three Soviet armored assaults over the next nine hours. When the Soviets broke off, the Chinese complained that their artillery fire had reached seven kilometers into Chinese territory. The Soviet message was clear. For every Chinese border incursion or attack, the Soviets were going to give it back to them ten times over.

In April, Soviet Premier Alexei Kosygin tried to open the hot line between Moscow and Beijing, but a Chinese operator refused to connect him to Chairman Mao. "You are a revisionist and therefore I will not connect you," the operator said.

"Well then, will you connect me with Premier Zhou?" Kosygin asked.

But the operator again called him a revisionist and hung up.[27]

On April 11, the Soviets demanded that China send a high-level envoy to Moscow to discuss the border crisis. When no reply came, the Soviets queried the Chinese again, only to be rebuked with the response, "We will give you a reply. Please calm down a little and do not get excited."[28]

But no reply came.

On April 16 and 25, Soviet troops clashed with Chinese forces in western China on the Kazakhstan border. Radio broadcasts warned Beijing against treating the Soviet Union like a "paper tiger" because "the whole world knows that the main striking force of the Soviet armed forces is its rocket units." In any showdown, "Mao Zedong and his clique would certainly end up in utter defeat."[29]

Mao seemed to retreat in April when the Ninth National People's Congress convened in Beijing for a crucial session of Communist Party leaders called together to endorse Mao's plan to further militarize the top ranks of the party. The military had played a key role in supporting Mao's purge of civilian leaders during the Cultural Revolution, which he had launched in 1966.[30] All during the congress, Mao was at pains to demonstrate that he was not a warmonger. "I say we will not be provoked," he told the gathering, as he strengthened the military's representation on the Central Committee from 19 percent to 45 percent of its members and designated Marshal Lin Biao as his choice to succeed him as chairman.[31]

On May 2, Chinese herders in western China ran their flocks across the Soviet border. A Soviet column of tanks and armored cars rushed across the dusty plain, surrounded them, and forced them to withdraw or be shot. On

May 14, a fifteen-man Soviet patrol accosted a group of Chinese peasants planting crops on an island in the Amur River and beat them senseless with their rifle butts, then held them hostage for a week. More farmers who were violating the border near Soviet garrisons were beaten up or taken prisoner on May 20, 25, and 28.[32]

The following week, Chinese militiamen ambushed four unarmed Soviet river transport workers on the Chinese side of the Amur River, where the workers were repairing a navigational marker. One of them died in the barrage of machine-gun fire and grenade explosions. In response, Soviet patrol boats sallied forth and attacked a Chinese house on an island in the river, setting fire to it and to the surrounding forest.

The Soviet leadership was divided. Marshal Andrei Grechko, the powerful defense minister and politburo member, advocated "once and for all" getting rid of "the Chinese threat" with massive nuclear strikes on Chinese cities. Others, however, such as Marshal Nikolai Ogarkov, chief of staff of the Soviet armed forces, believed that an all-out nuclear attack on China would lead to world war.[33] There was a deeply entrenched conservative strain in the Soviet military when it came to China. After invading China, then what? How would Soviet forces extract themselves from a fight with nearly a billion Chinese? The joke among military leaders was that after a Soviet invasion of China, the glowing reports of Soviet victories would stream into Moscow, and then, after a few weeks or a few months, the Soviet high command would ring up its Far East headquarters and a Chinese voice would answer.

If there was a consensus among the Soviet leadership, it was that the Soviet Union should consider mounting a limited strike against China to cripple or eliminate Beijing's nuclear weapons industry. That industry was just beginning to produce plutonium for the warheads it was designing for the long-range missiles that would be built and deployed over the next decade.

In their debate on what to do about China, Soviet leaders wanted, first of all, to reestablish the status quo along the 4,150-mile border. To do so, Mao had to be disabused of the notion that he could poke the "Polar Bear" with impunity, as he had done at Damansky Island. To be credible, the Soviets had to look like they were prepared for war, and so the military buildup on the Chinese border accelerated. Six Soviet divisions equipped with battlefield nuclear weapons were added to the mix in 1969, two of them in the nominally sovereign state of Mongolia.[34]

On June 8, General Secretary Leonid Brezhnev publicly identified Moscow's aims as congruent with Nixon's when he advocated, in his address to the International Conference of Communist Parties, "a system of collective security in Asia." He did not elaborate on his plan, but the concept seemed identical with the one Nixon had set forth in his October 1967 *Foreign Affairs* article.* Both were unambiguously targeted at containing communist China.

In late June, Kissinger laid out for Nixon the opportunity that had presented itself, the cosmic trade that might change the course of history. He catalogued the "solid evidence" of the growing Soviet obsession "with their China problem" and suggested that the matter had reached the point where "it can be turned to our advantage, if they are in fact attempting to ensure our neutrality in their Chinese containment policy, if not our active cooperation."

Nixon sent the memo back to Kissinger with praise.

"This is our goal," he wrote in the margin.[35]

The clear implication of Kissinger's formulation and Nixon's response was that American neutrality, or even cooperation, in the event of a Soviet attack on China might be up for sale. The price: Soviet assistance in winning a dignified exit from Vietnam and obtaining greater cooperation on the entire East-West agenda—arms control, Berlin, and the Middle East. Where Kennedy and Johnson had failed due to Soviet reluctance, Nixon might now succeed—thanks to the triggering event on Damansky Island.

Nixon, in private conversations with his defense secretary, Melvin R. Laird, expressed great hopes that such a deal might take shape. If the Soviets would be willing to cut down on the supply of arms to Hanoi, the Vietnam War would come quickly to an end. The North would be totally undermined—they would be forced to accept a political settlement. If the price of peace in Vietnam was allowing the Soviets to attack the Chinese nuclear complex, Nixon told Laird that it was a trade worth considering.[36]

The ramifications of such a deal would have been immense for the global balance of power. For Nixon, the transitory political gain in Vietnam would have doubtless secured his political base for reelection, but the nuclear emasculation of China would have had unpredictable consequences. It could have led to nuclear war in Asia, a protracted conventional war, or an all-out leveling of Chinese power.

In the immediate aftermath of Kissinger's late June report suggesting a deal with Moscow, he ordered, on behalf of the president, a classified study of how the United States might mount a nuclear attack on China. No such study, focusing exclusively on China, had ever been undertaken. During the Cold War, it had always been assumed by American war planners that China

---

*Nixon argued that "The common danger from Communist China is now in the process of shifting the Asian governments' center of concern [away from Western imperialism to Chinese imperialism]. This makes it vitally in their own interest that the nations in the path of China's ambitions move quickly to establish an indigenous Asian framework for their own future security." America would provide leadership and arms. Richard Nixon, "Asia After Vietnam," *Foreign Affairs* (October 1967).

would be attacked simultaneously with the Soviet Union in a massive, World War III scenario. President Nixon was the first Cold War president to demand a separate capability to attack China independently.

In a July 14 memorandum to Rogers, Laird, and CIA director Richard Helms, Kissinger said that "the President has directed the preparation of a study" to examine "U.S. strategic nuclear capability against China"* and "a range of possible situations in which a U.S. strategic nuclear capability against China would be useful."[37] He made clear that he wanted a complete blueprint. "The study should consider possible target systems in China and U.S. capability to attack those systems. The implications for U.S. strategic force requirements, for war planning and the required command and control systems and procedures and for the definition of strategic sufficiency should be examined." Kissinger told Nixon's senior advisers to consider, for each option, "the possible effects on proliferation of nuclear weapons"; in other words, how the options might prevent China from becoming a full-fledged nuclear power by targeting its nuclear complex.[†]

But as Nixon and Kissinger positioned themselves to strike a bargain with Moscow over China, the Kremlin seemed divided about offering, or unwilling to offer, any concrete help on Vietnam. Nixon nudged the Soviets. He told Kissinger to orchestrate the visit of an important American dignitary to China—a Democrat, to distance the White House. Nixon suggested Senator Mike Mansfield, the Democratic majority leader, and he also suggested that Mansfield's request for a visa to China be made public so that it would have maximum impact. Kissinger passed the message to Mansfield, urging him to apply for a visa.

Still, nothing came back from Moscow on Vietnam. So Nixon escalated his probes. He told the State Department that he had decided on "broad foreign policy grounds" to proceed with a plan to lift restrictions on American tourists seeking to bring back curios made in China worth more than $100.

---

*At the time of this study, Admiral Thomas Moorer, the chief of naval operations and a member of the Joint Chiefs of Staff, was more than familiar with secret American planning to attack China's nuclear complex. As commander of the Seventh Fleet in the 1960s, Moorer had devised a number of contingency plans to send long-range aircraft armed with nuclear weapons up the Yangtze River valley to strike Chinese nuclear facilities around Lop Nor. These plans did not call for using U.S. strategic nuclear forces (intercontinental ballistic missiles and B-52 bombers), which were the object of Kissinger's July 1969 study.

†Kissinger asserted in a letter to the author that "we never considered cooperating with the Soviets to wipe out the Chinese nuclear capability." Members of Kissinger's staff, however, said that all options, including U.S. acquiescence and cooperation with a Soviet attack on China, were considered. Laird also said that he had clear memories of discussing this option. Kissinger refuses to discuss the classified study he and Nixon ordered to examine U.S. capability to mount a nuclear strike on China and the positive effect such a strike might have on curtailing the "proliferation of nuclear weapons." Neither Nixon nor Kissinger mentioned the study in their respective memoirs.

The announcement was made during the last week in July as Nixon departed for an around-the-world trip.[38] *The New York Times* called the plan "the first sliver of a break in the total trade embargo" against China.

Still nothing from Moscow. Nixon escalated further.

In Guam (where Apollo 11 was splashing down), Nixon, speaking extemporaneously, declared that America would no longer send troops to thwart communist insurgencies in foreign countries, a concrete signal to Moscow, Hanoi, and Beijing that the American withdrawal from Vietnam was impending. This announcement was dubbed the Guam Doctrine. Still, no response was forthcoming from Moscow.

On July 31, Rogers, speaking in Tokyo, said: "The Nixon Administration has indicated several times and in many ways that we would like to improve relations with Communist China." In Australia, he was more specific. "Communist China obviously has long been too isolated from world affairs. . . . This is one reason why we have been seeking to open up channels of communication."[39]

A Polish commentator marveled at "the continual coquetting with China by Rogers at every stop of his trip, and the lavish use of the word 'friendship.' There is no doubt that Washington has decided to take advantage of the Soviet-Chinese conflict in a more decided manner."[40]

On August 1 in Lahore, Nixon asked Pakistani president Yahya Khan to tell Beijing's leaders that he was interested in opening the lines of communication and settling differences. Later, in Romania, Nixon asked President Nicolae Ceaușescu whether he would be interested in mediating the differences between the United States and China. Aboard Air Force One, Nixon told Marshall Green, who had accompanied him, that trade might be a good incentive to draw the Chinese out, since China's trade with Moscow had collapsed.[41]

Each Nixon probe seemed a little less cautious than the previous one. He had little to lose. If the Chinese came out of their shell, he could exploit the opening for all it would be worth in undermining Hanoi. And if they didn't, the visible process of American signaling to Beijing might induce Moscow to reconsider its refusal to put pressure on Ho Chi Minh.

B Y AUGUST 1969, Nixon had concluded that the Soviets were playing him for a fool. The CIA had been right. Moscow was not going to help Nixon get out of Vietnam. And, suddenly, evidence mounted that Moscow might be going ahead with plans to attack China regardless of Washington's participation or acquiescence. The Kremlin leaders were preparing to act as if they had a free hand, just as they had in Czechoslovakia. Nixon had no leverage.

Intelligence reports from East Europe claimed that the Soviets had undertaken a drive to convince key allies to endorse a Soviet attack on China. Also, the intelligence community was intercepting increased communications activity among Soviet forces all along the Chinese border.

On August 13, in the largest-scale fighting since March, Soviet troops staged an armored attack on a remote border region in Xinjiang Province, assaulting three fortified positions that Chinese border guards had prepared during the night. The Chinese issued alarming reports that Soviet tanks had penetrated nearly two miles into Yumin County on the Chinese side, and Beijing charged that Moscow was "trying to provoke larger-scale armed conflict."

At the Defense Intelligence Agency (DIA), General Daniel O. Graham, the deputy director in charge of the agency's intelligence estimates, warned that a Soviet attack was imminent and would involve a large-scale tank and artillery assault, aerial bombardment, and nuclear missile strikes.[42] At the same time, Soviet air forces in the Far East were mobilizing at new bases in Mongolia, where the increased tempo of training flights also indicated preparations for combat operations.

The CIA was far more cautious. Its top analysts did not believe that the Soviet military command would risk an attack on China, but Director Helms and John Huizenga, a brilliant academic who served as director of the Board of National Estimates, said that they could not rule out a limited Soviet strike on China's nuclear complex.

Nixon and Kissinger could only wonder whether the Soviets were now truly prepared to go ahead on their own. Among their worst fears was that Moscow might claim that the United States had condoned an attack on China. They could, for example, invoke Nixon's statements of the previous March about the danger of the Chinese nuclear threat.

Hyland, the CIA analyst on the NSC staff, warned Kissinger that there would be no such thing as a limited attack on China, driving Kissinger further toward Graham's total war scenario.

"The Soviets are not going to attack China in some quixotic mood. If they take this drastic step, they will be fully and totally committed to pursue it to the end," Hyland wrote in an urgent memo. "They are already working up deep racial and political emotions over China and expect, at the least, sympathy and understanding for whatever actions they might take. They will almost certainly regard American gestures to China as sheer hypocrisy."[43]

Nixon now began to wonder whether a Soviet attack on China would be a disaster for the United States in general and a political disaster for the Nixon administration in particular.

If the Soviets succeeded in humiliating—even toppling—Mao, Moscow would certainly attempt to reassert the Kremlin's dominance over the communist bloc in Asia, where weakened Chinese leaders would be forced into subservience. Chinese ports might be converted into Soviet naval bases, as Khrushchev had dreamed, giving the Soviet empire greater dominion over the Pacific. These would all be grim consequences.

Nixon summoned Rogers, Laird, and Helms to the Western White House at San Clemente, California, for an NSC meeting on August 14 and told them that the United States could not afford to allow the Soviets to "smash" China. Imagine what it would mean if they succeeded. Most of the participants at the table doubted that the Soviets would take such a colossal risk, but none of them knew the details of Kissinger's secret conversations with Dobrynin, so it was impossible to gauge to what extent Kissinger had flirted with the Soviet ambassador's desire for a green light on China. And even if Kissinger's excessive charm had not been misinterpreted, the Soviets could point to American entreaties under Kennedy and Johnson to wipe out China's nuclear complex.

Over the next several weeks, Nixon and Kissinger scrambled to stop what they and their predecessors had encouraged. Rogers, Laird, and Helms were all instructed to put out the word that the United States took no position in the Sino-Soviet dispute or the border clashes, and that Washington would consider any Soviet aggression in China as a threat to peace. With great drama, Nixon and Kissinger used the NSC meeting to establish an internal government record, ex post facto, that they had opposed Soviet aggression in China all along.*

But what could Nixon do if there was an attack? America had few options. Two of the largest armies in the world were facing each other on the remote landmass of Asia, where the United States had no allies, no bases, and no means to interpose itself between these overpowering forces. If the Soviets attacked Chinese nuclear installations, there was no way to stop it. Short of an American nuclear attack on the Soviet Union—in other words, World War III—there was nothing Washington could do.

The situation continued to deteriorate.

On the morning of August 18, William L. Stearman, a State Department

---

*In his memoirs, Kissinger asserted: "From the beginning, Nixon and I were convinced—alone among senior policymakers—that the U.S. could not accept a Soviet military assault on China. We had held this view before there was contact of any sort." Kissinger, *White House Years*, p. 764. This self-serving statement is clearly contradicted by the record of Nixon's and Kissinger's other statements over the years and by their actions in June and July 1969. It is also contradicted by the recollections of Secretary Laird as well as those of key Kissinger aides. It is more accurate to say that Nixon's view that a unilateral Soviet attack on China would be risky emerged only after he had earlier considered a tradeoff: American acquiescence, or cooperation, in such an attack in return for Soviet help in Vietnam.

Soviet specialist assigned to the Vietnam Desk that summer, received a telephone call from a familiar voice. It was Boris Davydov, a second secretary at the Soviet embassy, calling to make a lunch appointment.

Stearman knew that Davydov was not an ordinary second secretary. The FBI had identified him long ago as a KGB officer, working under cover as a diplomat. This was his second tour in Washington. A trained observer like Stearman didn't need the FBI to peg Davydov's true position. KGB officers were always the best dressed and the most outgoing members of any Soviet mission; they were also the biggest spenders. They had their own cars, in contrast to regular Soviet diplomats, who were limited by the more austere budget of the Soviet Foreign Ministry.

Stearman liked Davydov, and they arranged to meet at a restaurant on Scott Circle, just north of the White House and two blocks from the Soviet embassy. Stearman ordered fish. They had just started eating when Davydov brought up the crisis with China.

"What do you think the United States would do if we took out the Chinese nuclear installations at Lop Nor?"[44]

Stearman had his fork in his hand and had just raised a bite of fish to his mouth. He lowered it back to his plate, stared across the table for a moment, and asked, "Is this for real?"

"Yes, this is a real question, I am not making a joke," Davydov said earnestly.

Stearman's mind was reeling. He realized that Davydov was undertaking this contact on instructions from his superiors and, therefore, would be reporting Stearman's reply back to Moscow.

"I think we would take an extremely grave view of that," he said, "and, on the other hand, I don't think we would in any way directly intervene in the conflict that this might generate."

Davydov absorbed this reply and seemed to be satisfied. They went on to other subjects, and when the lunch was over, Stearman raced back to the department to draft a memorandum of conversation. It was flashed to Rogers's office and to the Western White House, where Kissinger convened a crisis meeting of the NSC staff. The DIA seemed certain that an attack was coming any hour now, and America had no options to intervene.

At Beale Air Force Base in California, the 456th Bomber Wing canceled all training flights for its B-52 Stratofortresses and the K-135 tankers that would service them during an intercontinental nuclear strike. B-52 commanders assigned to implement the U.S. nuclear war plan—the Single Integrated Operating Plan, or SIOP—were ordered to "generate" their aircraft, which meant to keep them fueled and loaded with nuclear weapons, ready to launch at a moment's notice.[45] Colonel Robert S. Hopkins II was one of those commanders. He kept his crew on the runway or on home alert for weeks on end, not knowing what mission was being contemplated or who had ordered the alert. Under the SIOP, Hopkins's B-52 was assigned to targets both in China and in the Soviet Far East. His plane could carry up to four 1.2-megaton hydrogen bombs. After a time, word filtered down that the high state of readiness was precipitated by Soviet diplomatic inquiries along the lines of: How would you react if we nuked China? There was no mention of what the U.S. role would be or how the B-52s would respond—whether they would participate with, or retaliate against, the Soviet Union.

Nixon directed Helms to brief a handful of senior diplomatic correspondents in Washington to get the word out that the United States was concerned about the prospect of war. Helms told the group over lunch that the Soviet leadership was apparently trying to round up support among East European leaders for a conventional attack on China's nuclear complex.[46] Whereas the CIA had put the chances of a major Sino-Soviet clash at about 10 percent a month earlier, by the end of August the agency believed that the chances of a conventional assault with iron bombs were slightly less than 50–50.[47]

The next day, Rogers, addressing a group of interns at the State Department, said that the Nixon administration did not share the view of some Americans "who argue that it would be a good thing for the United States to let the Soviet Union and Communist China engage in a fairly sizable war."

"We don't think so," he asserted. "We think warfare anywhere is harmful to the total world community, and we think this kind of war would be injurious to all people, and we hope it doesn't occur."[48]

Then a more alarming piece of intelligence sent the White House into a higher state of alert. The National Security Agency intercepted a radio transmission indicating that the Soviet high command had ordered their air force in the Far East to "stand down," an order that could be interpreted as a final preparation for combat operations.[49]

The impact of this news on Kissinger was dramatic. The White House sent a directive to the CIA instructing the intelligence community to put aside its study of the border crisis and, instead, to analyze how the Russians would conduct a nuclear attack on China: how many cities would be hit, how much destruction would occur, and how many millions of casualties could be expected.[50]

The NSC staff—and its director, Kissinger—believed that the standdown of the Soviet air force in the Far East indicated that the Soviets might be preparing to launch an all-out attack on China with nuclear weapons. The DIA stoked these fears, reporting increased "signal traffic" from all Soviet forces.

On September 6, in the administration's most pointed public statement yet, Elliot L. Richardson, the undersecretary of state, told a meeting of political scientists in New York that the United States did not "seek to exploit for [its] own advantage, the hostility between the Soviet Union and Communist China. Ideological differences between the two Communist giants are not [a U.S.] affair." But he added, "We could not fail to be deeply concerned" in the event of "an escalation of this quarrel into a massive breach of international peace and security.

"President Nixon has concluded," Richardson continued, "that our national security would in the long run be prejudiced by associating ourselves with either side against the other. Each is highly sensitive about American efforts to improve relations with the other. We intend, nevertheless, to pursue a long term course of progressively developing better relations with both."[51]

The intensive Soviet probing continued through September and into early October, so much so that Kissinger was horrified when Dobrynin brought up the matter of a Soviet attack on China as if both men had agreed on it. The reference may have been partly cleverness on Dobrynin's part, but it may also have reflected how deeply Kissinger had gotten into bed with the Soviets in the quest for help on Vietnam. Dobrynin asked Kissinger straightforwardly whether he expected a Soviet attack on China. Kissinger was inexplicably evasive, telling the Soviet ambassador that, as a historian, he had to allow for the possibility of a Soviet attack.[52]

Nixon's and Kissinger's failure to give Dobrynin a clear, unambiguous statement of U.S. opposition to a military attack on China remains one of the most conspicuous lapses in the administration's foreign policy record during this period. Perhaps because Hyland had argued so forcefully to Kissinger that any attempt to head off Soviet military action would be regarded as "sheer hypocrisy" due to long-standing U.S. concerns about the Chinese nuclear arsenal, Kissinger and Nixon seemed unable to articulate a clear position to Dobrynin.

As late as September 29, Kissinger confided in a note to Nixon, "I am concerned about our response to these probes [from Dobrynin]. Our reactions could figure in their calculations. Second, the Soviets may be using us to generate an impression in China and the world that we are being consulted in secret and would look with equanimity on their military actions. . . . I believe we should make clear that we are not playing along with these tactics."[53] In fact, Kissinger had been doing just that during the spring and summer. It was only the belated realization that Moscow was leading Nixon on with regard to Vietnam while both stepping up propaganda and massing military forces in a huge invasion scare against China that turned the president against Moscow's scheming, which he had so enthusiastically embraced in June.

Nixon continued to say nothing publicly about the crisis between the Soviet Union and China, leaving himself maneuvering room if the Soviets were willing to come around on Vietnam. In fact, when Soviet foreign minister Andrei Gromyko came to the United States in late September for the annual meeting of the UN General Assembly, Nixon sent Kissinger a note urging him to poke the Soviet in the ribs. "I think that while Gromyko is in the country would be a very good time to have another move to China made."[54]

L IKE A BOLT from the heavens, news of Ho Chi Minh's death arrived on September 5, 1969. It was just a week after Ho had rebuffed Nixon's secret peace offer, delivered in a letter that summer. Now, Ho's death presented another opportunity. Nixon ordered a large-scale intelligence operation focused on the funeral in Hanoi, where Kosygin would represent the Soviet Union and Zhou the People's Republic.

What if Moscow and Beijing resolved their differences? What if they adjusted their Vietnam policies? Western intelligence agents were on alert for any scrap of information or gossip.

Zhou arrived in Hanoi after Kosygin but kept the Soviet leader waiting day after day for a meeting. Finally, an exasperated Kosygin left for home. U.S. intelligence, which had a satellite-based capability to track the radio signals emanating from Kosygin's airplane, tracked his flight as it crossed India and the Himalayas into central Asia. Suddenly, after a refueling stop at Dushanbe, Tajikistan, Kosygin's plane abruptly turned eastward into China and made a course for Beijing.

Alarms bells went off in Washington as Zhou and Kosygin met for four hours at Beijing's airport. Kosygin's priority was to stabilize the border crisis, but Zhou's was to press—on behalf of Mao—the unfairness of the historical border treaties between Russia and China.[55] Zhou declared that "China has no territorial pretensions toward the Soviet Union" and "recognizes the border which exists," but he brought up long-standing historical grievances. Even Vladivostok was once a Chinese city, Mao liked to say. Zhou made it clear that the Sino-Soviet rift was not over. "Chairman Mao says that polemics will continue for 10,000 more years," Zhou told Kosygin.

Kosygin warned how destructive this attitude was.

"Lies and curses do not add persuasiveness and authority to a polemic," he said, "and they only humiliate the feelings of the other people and aggravate the relations." Furthermore, Kosygin warned, disagreements between Moscow and Beijing played into the hands of "world imperialism" and weakened the socialist system and "the ranks of fighters for national and social liberation."

Kosygin left with a tacit agreement from Zhou that the two countries would resume negotiations to stabilize the border, but Mao believed that Kosygin would also be willing to discuss historical Chinese grievances.

Meanwhile, the drumbeat of Soviet threats to attack China intensified.

On September 16 in London, Victor Louis, well known as an agent of influence of the KGB, warned in a newspaper column that Russian nuclear missiles "stand aimed at the Chinese nuclear facilities" and that the Soviet high command "prefers using rockets to manpower." He added that Moscow had a "plan to launch an air attack on Lop Nor" and that "whether or not the Soviet Union will dare to attack Lop Nor, China's nuclear center, is a question of strategy, and so the world would only learn about it afterwards."[56]

The threat was so specific, and so brutal, that it was assumed to be an authoritative warning from Moscow.

WHEN MAO HAD LAUNCHED his border campaign, he had sought to protect himself from criticism at home by asking four of the most senior military men in China to advise him.[57] They were all marshals in the PLA, stalwarts of the Long March and colleagues of Mao from the revolution: Chen Yi, Nie Rongzhen, Ye Jianying, and Xu Xiangqian.

Chen Yi was foreign minister and former mayor of Shanghai, Nie Rongzhen was the father of China's nuclear weapons and ballistic missile programs, and Ye Jianying and Xu Xiangqian were heroes of the communist victory.

In the turmoil of the Cultural Revolution, all four marshals had been sent to the countryside or to factories to "learn" from the masses. Among the four, only Ye had been even partially rehabilitated, and he returned to a seat on the politburo that spring. Chen Yi had insisted that their deliberations be conducted in secret, safe from the marauding Red Guard detachments that Mao could not fully control. The marshals met twenty-three times between March and September. Cars would pick them up from their homes and drive them to the Purple Raised Pavilion in Zhongnanhai, the center of communist power in Beijing. Zhou supplied them with current intelligence. Chen led the discussions.

By mid-July, the marshals had sent an initial assessment to Zhou expressing their belief that, although the danger of war had increased, "in the foreseeable future, the chances that the American Imperialists or the Soviet Revisionists will individually or jointly launch a large-scale attack against China are not great."[58]

They conceded that the Soviets were now initiating armed incursions, building up heavily armed divisions on the border, whipping up anti-Chinese sentiment among their own population, and putting pressure on Asian countries to join a security alliance against China. But, they maintained, "if the Soviet Revisionists were truly to fight a big war against China, they would face a number of worries and difficulties."

Since China and America both saw the Soviet Union as their primary enemy, "the Soviets do not dare to have a war on two fronts against both America and China." The Soviets also understood, the marshals said, that America would only profit from such a war. Nixon, they said, "would be happy to sit on the mountaintop while the tigers fight below."

In their second report to Zhou, the marshals hedged their view. They said it was now clear that the Soviet Union had developed a plan to "launch a war of invasion against China" and that the Soviet strategic goal was to divide up the world with the other superpower and forcibly bring China into the Soviet camp. In the short run, "they have been scheming to launch a sudden attack on our nuclear installations."[59]

But the marshals—again rebelling against the empirical evidence that war was coming—contended that the Soviets "have not been able to establish the political will to do so" and that there was too much uncertainty over how they would disengage from it.

"Whether or not the Soviet revisionists invade China depends to a great extent on the attitude of the American Imperialists. Up to now, the American Imperialists have not allowed the Soviet Union to relax and, in fact, have been the greatest strategic concern for the Soviets.

"And," they continued, "the American Imperialists absolutely do not want to see the Soviets achieve a victory in any Sino-Soviet war and thereby establish a super state whose resources and manpower would exceed that of America."

It was to China's advantage, therefore, to play the two superpowers off against each other, the marshals argued. They were struck by how "anxiously" Nixon was making overtures for improved relations with China. Nixon had visited five Asian countries, they noted, demonstrating his fear that the Soviets were trying to supplant American power in Asia, and he was trying to send Senator Mansfield to make an overture to Beijing. The Soviets were equally anxious to arrange a high-level meeting with Chinese leaders, a circumstance that could be used as a China "card" against the Americans.

The marshals told Mao on September 17 that they believed China's "strategic benefit" lay in "conspicuously making use of tensions between the Americans and the Soviets" to "strengthen our position." And so they recommended that the ambassador-level talks with the Americans be resumed in Warsaw. The report went to Mao and was presented to the party hierarchy. Then Mao ordered the marshals dispersed across China, ensuring again that no collection of military leaders could coalesce to challenge his authority. "If war breaks out," Mao told them, they were to assist the local authorities and political leaders in war planning. They were to take their wives and leave their Beijing homes behind.

Before Chen left Beijing, he told Zhou privately that any new dialogue with the Americans would be a failure if they "attempt[ed] nothing and accomplish[ed] nothing."[60] He recommended a bolder course to reestablish relations with the United States, to open a dialogue with no preconditions, and to deal with the issue of Taiwan on a "step by step" basis while the overall talks on strategic issues went ahead. Chen believed that the Americans would welcome such a move. And, he argued, Asia could not move forward until China ended its isolation.

Then Mao did something extraordinary.

With a million Soviet troops at near hair-trigger readiness along the Sino-Soviet border, Mao started setting off hydrogen bombs in his western desert, including a three-megaton "city killer" dropped from a four-engine Chinese bomber so that it would burst in the air over the desert. This display of Chinese power lit up the heavens and made the earth thunder. Radioactive fallout drifted into Kazakhstan and Mongolia, where the Soviet armed forces were poised. Two tests were conducted within six days of each other.[61] China had never conducted two nuclear tests in such rapid succession, and Mao's act carried an unmistakable political message for the Soviet divisions massed across the border: Mao was willing to use his ultimate weapon against any attacker. He was practicing the art of war.

More than 2,000 years earlier, Sun Tzu, a student of Confucius, wrote the classic Chinese treatise on strategy and tactics in war. He said that "to win 100 victories in 100 battles is not the acme of skill. To subdue the enemy without fighting is the acme of skill."[62]

Just as the Soviets were threatening strikes on China's nuclear facilities, Mao had reminded the world not only that China was a nuclear power but that it had developed thermonuclear warheads many times more powerful that the Hiroshima bomb and capable of obliterating whole cities. The question that Soviet leaders had to ask themselves—if they were considering an attack on China—was whether they would be lucky enough to find and destroy all of Mao's weapons, because if they did not, they could never be sure whether the Chinese, on some dark night in the unpredictable future, might decide to lob one of those monster warheads onto Moscow—or Vladivostok, Khabarovsk, or Irkutsk. In the tradition of the ancients, Mao had fought a war without ever unleashing his army. With Kosygin's entreaty to reopen the border talks, Mao demonstrated his power and then stepped back from the brink.

On October 7, China announced that it would return to the negotiating table to try to resolve the border dispute. Of course, nothing would be settled.

F OR MARSHALL GREEN, the discovery that Nixon was interested in trying to improve communications with Beijing was a great advance. Green, like most foreign service officers, had spent a decade struggling against former Secretary of State Dean Rusk's intransigence on China. Now, he hoped, he was going to participate in formulating a policy that he truly believed in.[63]

In October, Green laid out for the White House in a memorandum the steps they should take next.[64] He pointed out that the Pentagon, "for budgetary reasons," wanted to cancel the patrols by U.S. Navy destroyers assigned to the Taiwan Strait. The patrols first started with the outbreak of the Korean War, and they represented the American commitment to Taiwanese security. By reassigning the destroyers, the Pentagon could make better use of its forces, and the Seventh Fleet could still show the flag in the strait by occasionally sending ships through the waterway.

"We recommend that we attempt to use the opportunity presented by the withdrawal of the two Taiwan Strait Patrol vessels to improve the atmosphere" for another round of talks "in Warsaw or elsewhere," Green wrote. "We would then time a renewed approach to Peking through Warsaw to allow our proposal for new talks to be read in the context of whatever symbolic significance Beijing may read into the Taiwan Strait ship move." He added, "this may provide the needed push."

Undersecretary of State Richardson agreed, and they passed the recommendation to the White House.

On October 10, Pakistan's air marshal, Sher Ali Khan, visited Washington. Nixon directed Kissinger to act on the State Department's recommendation and relay to the Pakistani that the Taiwan Strait patrol was being cancelled and that U.S. transits of the strait would be reduced to fifteen per month. If Khan informed the Chinese of Nixon's decision, it would send a constructive signal of American good faith, Kissinger told him. Nixon wanted to do more, however. On the margin of a Kissinger memo, Nixon wrote, "K—also open trade possibilities."[65]

Green already had prepared a list of trade options. In addition, Green pointed out, the Vietnam War had bloated the level of U.S. military personnel on Taiwan. "We should consider removing these forces as soon as they are not actually required for Vietnam purposes."

At the same time, Walter J. Stoessel Jr., the American ambassador to Warsaw, returned to Washington for consultations. Nixon told the veteran diplomat that he should seek an opportunity to bump into the Chinese chargé d'affaires in Warsaw and convey to him Nixon's wish to discuss an improvement in relations.

After Stoessel returned to Poland, he discovered that it was no easy matter to "orchestrate" a chance meeting with China's top diplomat in Warsaw.

Then, in the first week of December, Stoessel made contact—at a Yugoslav fashion show at Warsaw's Palace of Culture. It was a Friday night; after the show Stoessel spotted the diminutive Chinese chargé, Lei Yang, and pursued him down a hallway. Lei looked over his shoulder, recognized Stoessel, and kept walking, ignoring the ambassador's greeting in Polish. Stoessel told Lei's interpreter that he would like to "greet" the Chinese chargé.[66]

"I don't know, you must wait," the interpreter said.

Lei was now headed out the door and down the steps to the parking lot.

Stoessel realized that the Chinese diplomat was not going to stop, so he paused on the steps and spoke again to the interpreter.

"I was recently in Washington and saw President Nixon. He told me he would like to have serious, concrete talks with the Chinese."

The interpreter looked up at Stoessel, who was poised above him on the steps, and simply replied, "Good, I will report that."

It took only two days for a message to come back.

One of the young diplomats working under Stoessel in Warsaw, Thomas Simons, was called at home the following Sunday by a similarly junior Chinese diplomat and invited to the Chinese embassy. There, the Chinese handed Simons a copy of a letter from Lei Yang. It stated that two Americans who had been seized when their yacht strayed into Chinese waters in February 1969 were being released.[67] The American diplomats were pleased by the obvious gesture, but they had been hoping for a different kind of breakthrough.

Simons consulted Stoessel by telephone, and then the young diplomat returned to the Chinese embassy and pressed more pointedly for a specific response, saying that Stoessel's proposal for "serious," concrete talks was . . . "serious"!

It seemed possible that the release of the two yachtsmen was an interim gesture authorized by Zhou Enlai while Mao was considering his next move. Zhou was cautious because there was still no consensus in Beijing whether to open a dialogue with America. Some Chinese leaders argued that Nixon should first withdraw U.S. troops from Taiwan. In their minds, the reduction of U.S. naval patrols through the Taiwan Strait was not enough.

The Chinese embassy in Warsaw invited Stoessel to visit on December 11, at which time he formally proposed the resumption of the ambassador-level talks that could move the agenda forward. "We believe China has an important role in Asia, and that in the last analysis Asian decisions must be taken by Asian nations themselves, a process in which China should take part."[68]

A new dialogue did begin.

In January, Stoessel said that Nixon was prepared to send a "special representative" to Beijing or invite a Chinese envoy to Washington. He assured the Chinese that his administration did not seek to impose its views concerning Taiwan on either Beijing or Taipei. "Our only concern is that this issue not be resolved by force of arms." In this spirit, he added, "we will also not support and in fact will oppose any offensive military action from Taiwan against the mainland."

The United States was not seeking to "encircle" China as a prelude to an attack. Stoessel said that the "limited United States military presence on Taiwan is not a threat to the security of your Government, and it is our hope that as peace and stability in Asia grow we can reduce those facilities on Taiwan that we now have."[69]

The Chinese obviously were impressed, and the 135th and 136th rounds of the U.S.-China dialogue were conducted on January 20 and February 20, 1970, between Stoessel and Lei.

During the February session, Lei said, "If the U.S. government wishes to send a representative of ministerial rank or a special envoy of the U.S. president to Beijing for further exploration of questions of fundamental principle between China and the United States, the Chinese government will be willing to receive him."[70]

The breakthrough on China was at hand. Nixon's wish had been granted —a dialogue with no preconditions. But the news seemed to paralyze him. How would the public react? What would Congress do? The China initiative had progressed beyond all expectations, too quickly in fact, and, facing the greatest opportunity of his political career, Nixon froze in consideration of the potential backlash in the Republican Party. Rogers was alarmed over the upcoming visit to Washington of Taiwan's premier, Chiang Ching-kuo.[71] How would it look to stage a breakthrough with China while America's ally from Taiwan was visiting Washington?

Both Rogers and Green wanted Nixon to explore, in yet another round of Warsaw talks, what exactly the Chinese wanted from any opening to the United States. Rogers warned that a U.S.-China summit "would be a major international event, receiving the widest public attention and with widespread and substantial international and domestic political effects. It is one of the few things that the Chinese want from us just now."[72]

Rogers's caution reflected Nixon's own concerns. And Green worried that the Chinese could easily turn a special emissary's trip into a propaganda show. The State Department asked the White House whether the United States should extract some concession from Beijing as the price of sending a senior presidential envoy to China.

But what the State Department didn't know was that the White House had been in secret contact with the Chinese through the Pakistanis since the previous summer. In fact, just days after Stoessel's breakthrough in Warsaw,

Pakistan's ambassador to Washington told Kissinger that Zhou Enlai had sent a sensitive message to Nixon urging the United States to ensure that China was not portrayed as approaching the United States out of weakness or fear of the Soviet Union; if that were the case, then normalization would not go forward. Zhou also communicated to Nixon that the prospects for gradually improving relations were favorable, since "the possibility of expansion of the Vietnam War is seen as having lessened" and "a war between China and the U.S. is seen now as a very remote possibility."[73]

Had Kissinger shared these communications with Rogers or Green, their apprehensions about the risk of sending an envoy to Beijing surely would have dissipated. But Kissinger undermined them by keeping them in ignorance. With his proprietary knowledge, Kissinger was able to argue that China was genuinely ready to open a dialogue with the United States. The "effect on Hanoi" of a presidential mission to Beijing "alone would be traumatic" to the North Vietnamese war effort, Kissinger argued.[74] Nixon agreed. Indeed, he had earlier tried to send Mansfield for that very reason. But now, the only question was when to make a larger move.

Nixon had confided nothing about the China opening with the generalissimo. Taiwan's friends in the United States had helped Nixon get elected by raising money for his campaign. What would the generalissimo and his friends in Congress do if Nixon suddenly announced that he was sending an envoy to Beijing?

When Chiang Ching-kuo arrived in Washington in April 1970, Kissinger asked him privately what Taiwan's reaction would be if the United States decided to move its "ambassador-level" talks with the Chinese Communists from Warsaw to either Washington or Beijing. At the White House banquet in Chiang's honor that evening, Nixon assured him that any talks with Beijing would be "exploratory" and would not affect the American commitment to Taiwan.

Chiang expressed concern, but he also was angling to get something tangible out of his visit. It was imperative, he told Nixon, that the Asian countries on the rim of China establish a system of collective defense with American support.[75] He cleverly presented Nixon with the very proposal that Nixon himself had earlier set forth for collective security in Asia. Of course, the Taiwanese version of a new anticommunist alliance would include Taiwan, thus keeping alive the Nationalist hope for a return to the mainland. But Nixon evaded the issue, instead encouraging Chiang to discuss his security needs with the Pentagon. Then he tried to reassure the Taiwanese leader. "The United States will always honor its treaty obligations and, to use a colloquial expression, I will never sell you down the river,"[76] he promised.

The next day in New York, an assassin's bullet almost felled Chiang as he walked across Park Avenue from the Hotel Pierre to deliver a speech at the Plaza Hotel.[77] The White House could not fail to take note of the outpouring of sympathy and concern from prominent Americans and members of Congress. Whether that support was deep enough to block the opening to China, Nixon could only guess. But it was clear that any move toward Beijing would have to be carefully protected. Secrecy would be essential.

Rogers and Green were thinking in the opposite direction. They recommended that Nixon brief the governments of Japan and Taiwan on the Warsaw talks because these governments "have already begun to feel that we are not being altogether candid with them."[78] The Japanese and Taiwanese were right.

In April 1970, Nixon decided to cut the State Department out of his "China operation," a decision prompted by his realization that the politics of "selling out" Taiwan, a charge that would certainly be leveled against him, was explosive, especially for a first-term president still mired in Vietnam. Nixon summoned General Vernon A. Walters and gave him a letter for the Chinese leadership expressing that he wanted to reopen the talks with Beijing in complete secrecy, without the knowledge of the State Department. Walters, who was serving as the American military attaché in Paris, was to deliver the letter to the Chinese ambassador to France without informing the American ambassador. Walters was authorized to say that Nixon was willing to send Kissinger to Paris to meet privately with the Chinese and make arrangements. Nixon's paramount concern was a Republican revolt in Washington. But Kissinger, in enforcing the new secrecy, relied on the justification that he was protecting the White House from State's inability to conduct sub-rosa diplomacy.*

In any case, Nixon's decision to invade Cambodia pulled the legs out from under the China initiative. Since Lei Yang's momentous invitation of February 20, Nixon had temporized all the way to April 28, the day the Chinese canceled the next Warsaw meeting because of Cambodia. The setback internationally was not as wrenching as the consequences at home. College campuses erupted and, at Kent State University in Ohio, four unarmed students were killed when National Guard troops opened fire on a demonstration. Kissinger's staff rebelled against the escalation in Southeast Asia that their

---

*Kissinger constructed an argument claiming that the State Department could not be trusted to keep such diplomacy secret, but in fact State had orchestrated the earlier Stoessel contact in an expert and disciplined manner. The record suggests that once State achieved the breakthrough in Warsaw, however, Nixon feared that arranging a presidential visit to China could not be kept secret if *any* large group of government officials was involved. Indeed, much of the White House staff, including many of Kissinger's NSC staff members, were cut out of the subsequent secret diplomacy.

boss was advocating. Tony Lake, Roger Morris, and William Watts all re-signed.*

Their departure allowed for the ascendance of Colonel Alexander Haig, who became Kissinger's deputy, and Winston Lord, who became his special assistant. Lord was only thirty-two, the son of Oswald B. Lord, a New York textile industrialist, and Mary Pillsbury Lord, an heir to the Pillsbury food fortune. Lord was a child of New York society and Park Avenue privilege. His mother was also an avid political fund-raiser for the Republican Party; she served on the UN Commission on Human Rights and was an alternate delegate to the General Assembly.

Winston Lord had emerged from the same rarefied cloister of Yale as Marshall Green had a generation earlier. Lord's good manners and quizzical demeanor—his old-money sense of bemusement at life—never fully masked his ambition, always visible in the tension around the edge of his eyes and in the hooded aspect of his brow.

At graduate school at Tufts University outside Boston, Lord had met and married Bette Bao, the beautiful and gifted daughter of Chinese refugees from Shanghai, who, in 1946, during the civil war, had fled their home and had rebuilt a life in Taiwan as loyalists to Chiang Kai-shek.

Lord was an expert note taker, draftsman, and speech writer and a good sounding board, but not as seasoned a political thinker as Larry Eagleburger or as bureaucratically adept as Al Haig, both of whom were closer to Kissinger. But Lord was someone who could introduce Kissinger, the inse-cure Jewish immigrant, to New York's social and financial establishment, of which the Lords and the Pillsburys were an integral part. Kissinger was fond of saying that the best thing Morton Halperin had ever done for him was to introduce him to Winston. It was a way of putting Halperin down after he had resigned in the battle over who would become Kissinger's deputy.

Lord suffered all of Kissinger's pettiness. Energetic and self-effacing, he was a particularly skilled briefer, able to identify and lay out different options while simultaneously parsing their diplomatic, legal, and political conse-quences. It was not apparent until years later, when Lord was appointed to a managerial position in the State Department, that he was terrible at making decisions. After all the options were laid out for him, Lord's favorite response was that he was "agnostic" about which way to go.

Lord's youth rendered him completely unthreatening to Kissinger and, therefore, the indispensable aide on whom Kissinger could pour his frequent rages, his anxieties, and his ideas in complete confidence. And Lord idolized

*Morton H. Halperin had already left, frustrated by Kissinger's duplicity in dealing with his own staff. Halperin had expected to manage Vietnam policy on the NSC staff as Kissinger's deputy.

Kissinger. Even after the Cambodian invasion, even after Lord discovered that Kissinger had ordered his phone wiretapped, Lord told friends that he would not quit the NSC staff because Kissinger was a genius. Bette Bao shared this conviction. Lord's devotion was also founded on the expectation that Kissinger would help him along the path to his own career goal of one day becoming secretary of state.

NIXON HAD TRIED TO soften the blow of the Cambodian invasion, but this did not prevent Mao from going on a rampage. Nixon had tried to preempt any strong reaction with a message to Mao saying that, despite the incursion, "the United States has no aggressive intentions in Indochina."[79] The Chinese leader ignored him. In late May, Mao called on the "people of the world" to "unite and defeat the U.S. aggressors and all their running dogs." He said that American imperialism "looks like a huge monster," but "is in essence a paper tiger, now in the throes of its deathbed struggle. In the world of today, who actually fears whom?"

"While massacring the people in other countries, United States imperialism is slaughtering the white and black people in its own country," Mao exhorted a mass rally in the center of Beijing. "Nixon's fascist atrocities have kindled the raging flames of the revolutionary mass movement in the United States." China, Mao said, would support a world revolution against America.[80]

Nixon went into a rage. He told Kissinger that he wanted to send a deployment of U.S. warships to China's coast in a show of force "that will look belligerent."

"I want them to know we are not playing this chicken game," Nixon said. Kissinger tried to palliate, saying that Mao's words were all bluster. They were not personally abusive to Nixon. But Nixon raged on. What was the phrase "fascist atrocities" if not personally abusive? Nixon said he didn't want any analysis. "I want you to call Moorer," he said, referring to the chairman of the Joint Chiefs of Staff. "Tell him that it's an order from the commander in chief—there's no recourse. I want them there in 24 hours."[81]

It was a vintage Nixon rant, the kind that would pass. But it was also true that Nixon never understood Mao. He found it impossible to believe that Mao on the one hand wanted a dialogue and on the other was willing to exhort revolutionary forces to attack the United States. Mao of course was simply trying to demonstrate to Nixon that he could not expect China to roll over while U.S. forces ravaged Cambodia. Didn't Nixon see the humiliation this brought on the Chinese? Hadn't Zhou warned the White House that China could not be made to look weak in opening to the United States? The Cambodia invasion was an affront to China's dignity.

Nixon didn't care. The period of the Cambodian invasion coincided with his obsession over the movie *Patton*. He watched it over and over, sometimes late into the evening, and his aides felt that he was bonding with the Patton icon—tough and brutal on the battlefield, as Nixon was in Vietnam and, now, Cambodia.

But it seemed that Mao was not finished. In July 1970, American intelligence intercepted Chinese military communications indicating that Chinese units on the southern coast near Vietnam had been ordered to shoot down an American electronic eavesdropping plane flying a mission in that area. On July 2, the PLA scrambled two MIG-19s to destroy an American C-130 as it flew a routine mission scooping up Chinese radio signals.[82] The U.S. plane quickly retreated to safety, but Nixon was stunned by Mao's brazenness. China was trying to do what North Korea had done in April 1969, when North Korean MIGs shot down an American reconnaissance plane. The incident nearly touched off a war because Nixon had ordered—and then reconsidered—air strikes against a North Korean air base.

Kissinger explained away Mao's actions by saying that he was under pressure from "radicals." The White House renewed its overtures to Beijing. Rogers, in Japan during July 1970, said publicly that China was the key to the future of Indochina and that a settlement in Vietnam could be worked out "very quickly" if Beijing were willing to make an effort.[83] At the same time, the Romanian vice president told the American ambassador to Bucharest, Leonard Meeker, that Mao was still interested in resuming a dialogue with America.[84]

A week later, in a humanitarian gesture, China released a Roman Catholic bishop, James Edward Walsh, who had been arrested in 1958 and imprisoned for espionage.* At the end of the month, Nixon reciprocated, allowing an Italian company to sell eighty large dump trucks to China. The sale required American approval because the engines were General Motors diesels licensed to the Italian firm.

In August, Nixon lifted the restriction on American oil companies, whose depots had been barred from fueling cargo ships bound to or from China. As Nixon went back to "plying" the Chinese with trade, Mao opened his own channel to the Americans. He invited Edgar Snow, an American journalist who had been his friend for thirty-five years, to come to Beijing on October 1, 1970, and participate in the twenty-first anniversary of the founding of the People's Republic.

---

*Walsh's release was bittersweet. Ailing, he was carried on a stretcher across the border to Hong Kong. A medical examination confirmed why the Chinese were so anxious to unburden themselves. Walsh had incurable cancer and died within months. The Chinese reported that another American captive, Hugh Redmond, sentenced to life imprisonment in Shanghai in 1954 for espionage, had committed suicide three months earlier.

A stalwart of early American journalism in China, Snow had fallen into disrepute for his romantic treatment of the communist revolution. As a young man, Snow had left Kansas City to see the world and, in China, took up the pen as war was gathering in Asia. In June 1936, he trekked across China to reach the headquarters of the "Red Bandits." No journalist had penetrated the cordon Chiang Kai-shek's army had thrown up to seal off the communist stronghold, but the thirty-one-year-old Snow managed to slip through. With a letter of introduction from Song Ching-ling, the wife of China's liberating intellect, Sun Yat-sen, Snow marched into the guerrilla headquarters.

He found Mao in Baoan,

> a gaunt, Lincolnesque figure, above average height for a Chinese, some-what stooped, with a head of thick black hair grown very long, and with large, searching eyes, a high bridged nose and prominent cheekbone. ... Undeniably one felt a certain force of destiny in Mao. It was nothing quick or flashy, but a kind of solid, elemental vitality. One felt that what-ever there was extraordinary in this man grew out of the uncanny degree to which he synthesized and expressed the urgent demands of millions of Chinese, and especially the peasantry. If their "demands" and the move-ment which was pressing them forward were the dynamics which could re-generate China, then in that deeply historical sense, Mao Zedong might possibly become a very great man.[85]

Snow spent four months interviewing Mao and his commanders, who had just completed the Long March, a 6,000-mile flight from the generalissimo's army. At Baoan and Yenan, they dug caves into the soft loess hillsides and plotted the next phase of their campaign. Snow captured the fervor of their revolution in his book *Red Star over China*. But after the Communist victory, the Korean War, and the McCarthy trials, Snow was pilloried as a commu-nist dupe and sympathizer.

If his journalism was flawed, it was because his approach to China was uniquely American, full of optimism, naïveté, and goodwill for the Chinese.* And Snow was a romantic. Now, three decades later, Snow was back in Bei-jing, standing next to Mao atop the Gate of Heavenly Peace. Afterward, Zhou personally supervised the airbrushing of the photo to remove Snow's wife, Lois, and others, so as to emphasize Mao's gesture to America.

*The eminent China scholar John K. Fairbank paid tribute to Snow's reporting, writing in 1961 that *Red Star over China* "gave the first connected history of Mao and his colleagues and where they had come from" and that it also "gave a prospect of the future," an indication of the revolutionary "trend" that was to sweep the country like Mao's proverbial "prairie fire."

The New China News Agency dispatched the photo worldwide. Mao assumed that this image would be understood by Washington. Mao also was certain that Snow either worked for or had close contact with the CIA,[86] and he assumed that everything he said to Snow, including his greeting to the American people, would be reported back immediately. But it was all lost on the Nixon White House. Nixon's attention was absorbed by the task of securing his first superpower summit in Moscow, and Dobrynin was diddling him again.

Then, suddenly, on October 13, after twenty months of secret negotiations, China reestablished full diplomatic relations with Canada. The breakthrough incensed Nixon. Pierre Elliot Trudeau, the Canadian prime minister, had given no advance warning. Nixon hated to be trumped by anyone, and now he began to see Mao's game: Mao might invite other Western leaders to Beijing as a way to put pressure on Nixon. Canada made a clean break with Taiwan, severing formal diplomatic ties, a deal that Mao could now insist that Washington follow.

Nixon redoubled his efforts.

At the end of October, President Khan of Pakistan was in the United States for the annual session of the UN General Assembly, and Nixon asked him to come to Washington for a private talk on China. The Pakistani leader would be traveling to Beijing the following month. Nixon asked Khan to convey his view that a rapprochement between China and the United States was "essential." Nixon said that he was willing to send an emissary to see Mao, but strict secrecy was absolutely necessary.[87]

Zhou received Khan on November 13, but there was no immediate report on how the meeting had gone. There was only silence and, with it, frustration.

China's press agency announced that Snow had interviewed Zhou on November 5. Still, nothing came back through diplomatic or intelligence channels. On the night of December 17, Snow was in his room at the Beijing Hotel, going over notes of his travels through China. He worked well past midnight, and then found that he could not sleep. At 5 A.M. he took a sleeping pill and had just collapsed into slumber when Mao's interpreter, Nancy Tang, knocked on the door. She told Lois Snow to tell her husband: "Somebody wants to see you!"

Snow arose in a fog and struggled to a faucet to splash cold water on his face.

"Chairman Mao said to come as you are," Tang said. "No formality, come for breakfast."

The car took Snow through the Western Gate of Zhongnanhai, the mammoth walled compound adjoining the Forbidden City. Its name translates simply as "south-central lake," for the serpentine body of water around which low buildings and gardens are arranged in what was once the playground of emperors. In the communist period, Zhongnanhai became the seat of government, as the revolutionary leaders took over the buildings on its grounds and constructed many more along the perimeter of the high vermilion walls that hide them from Beijing's population.

Mao's quarters were in the southwest corner of the compound. Snow was driven to a rear entrance and was greeted by four officers in Mao's military guard. Tang confided that two of them were generals. The large room into which he was taken was a library, and the shelves were filled with Chinese titles, although Snow noticed some English ones as well. Mao was sitting on a large divan wearing a bathrobe and covered with a blanket. He apologized to Snow for hosting him in bedclothes, but he said he had a cold.

Snow had one, too, so they commiserated.

"I get a cold each winter," Mao said. "The doctors are no good. They cannot find a cure."[88]

They were back together again. Snow, paunchy at sixty-five, and Mao, rotund at seventy-seven; Mao was going on about his mortality by saying that he had "an invitation from God." Nancy Tang interpreted Mao's Chinese, accented by the palate of his native Hunan.

Snow said that people in the West were taking large doses of vitamin C to fight colds.

"I'll try it," Mao said. "If it poisons me, you'll be responsible. If it cures me, you'll be responsible for that."

The banter went on. Mao chided Snow for not coming to China in 1965. "I would have let you come earlier to see the Great Proletarian Cultural Revolution, to see the 'all around civil war,'" Mao said, referring to Western press accounts of the chaos. He had learned to say "all-around civil war" in English.

"There was fighting everywhere, and everywhere they [the Red Guards] split into two factions [in] every factory, every school, every province and every county, and the same with every ministry. There were two factions in the foreign ministry, too," Mao explained.

"But it wouldn't do if you didn't have this," he continued. "First, there were counterrevolutionaries, and second, there were capitalist roaders." Capitalist "roaders" were those who took the capitalist road instead of the socialist road, and thereby undermined the revolution.

"It was utter chaos!" Mao exclaimed; "But it turned out to be a good thing; those people were exposed, otherwise, who would know what they were?"

It was an amazing moment. Mao was giving his version of the bloody civil strife. Of course, he imparted a great purpose to his enterprise. He claimed to Snow that the Cultural Revolution had exposed Liu Shaoqi* as a secret capitalist. Liu had been Mao's colleague since the 1920s and was his putative successor until the downfall.

Liu was "struggled" viciously and died in detention. He was nothing but a "reactionary who wormed his way into the Party," Mao told Snow.

Snow had not come to Beijing to dwell on China's frozen relations with the United States, but Mao brought it up anyway, talking about Snow's interview with an Italian magazine and his assertion that Mao had been transformed into a godlike figure due to the "cult of personality" he himself encouraged.

"It is you Americans who go in much for the personality cult!" he said. "Your capital is named after George Washington." Snow nodded. "And each state has at least one town named Washington. What a nuisance," Mao exclaimed. "There is always the need to be worshipped." All American presidents had this need, he added.

Then he veered to a new subject.

"I don't like the Democratic Party," Mao said. "I like Nixon in power. Why? Because he is more deceitful. He is also stronger and resorts to more tough tactics, though also some soft ones. If he wants to come to Beijing, you may bring him a message, tell him to come in secret and not to make it known to the public. He can just get on a plane and come. It doesn't matter whether or not the talks will be successful. Why continue such a stalemate?"

Snow was astounded, but had learned with Mao to not react too demonstrably.

Breakfast was brought in, toast and coffee and four small glasses of mao-tai, the fiery white liquor that was the libation of hospitality. Mao and Snow raised their glasses and toasted each other's "long life."

Mao mused further about Nixon.

"It is not possible for a President to go abroad secretly. If he came to China, he would certainly trumpet loudly about it, saying that his purpose was to win over China so as to fix the Soviet Union."

Referring to Nixon, Mao said, "He has been sending messages through various channels for quite some time, saying he wants to send a representative here, and we have said, 'Yes, we would [receive him] . . . ,' but then he doesn't do anything about it. We haven't published the messages, because the secret is to be kept. He is not interested in the Warsaw talks in Poland, and wants to talk face to face with us. That is why I say that if Nixon is willing to come I would be willing to talk with him, and it would be all right whether or

*Pronounced: Leeoh Show [sounds like cow] Chee.

not it be successful, whether or not we quarrel, and whether he comes as a tourist or as President for talks."

Snow may have been too dazzled—or groggy—to fully comprehend Mao's message.

"Can it be understood in this way: It is not practical now, but considered ideal?"

Mao interjected a joke, then continued. "That was proposed by Nixon himself, and there are documents to prove it. He said that he would like to have face-to-face talks with us either in Beijing or Washington, that the foreign office should have no knowledge of it, that is, this must not be done through the State Department. Very mysterious indeed. He said that it mustn't be made public, that it was highly confidential."

Mao vaguely smiled. "What is he up to?"

Mao paused. When he spoke again, it was as if a critical factor had just then come to him.

"When are his next elections?" he asked Snow.

"1972," Snow replied.

"I think he might send someone here in the first half of 1972, but he himself would not come. If they come for talks, that would be the time. He loathes to give up Taiwan. And Chiang Kai-shek hasn't died yet."

Snow had fallen so far from grace in American journalistic circles that when he returned to his self-imposed exile in Switzerland, he could not find a mainstream American publisher for his account of the extraordinary conversations he had had in Beijing. He had foolishly hobbled his efforts by offering to keep most of what Mao had told him off the record. From Geneva, Snow sent his story to *The New York Times* and to *Life* magazine. "Lack of space," said one rejection notice.[89]

At the White House, there was intense interest in Snow's encounter with the Chinese leadership, but Kissinger, too, was leery of Snow and his liberal reputation. Allen Whiting, a Kennedy- and Johnson-era diplomat now returned to teaching at the University of Michigan, called Kissinger's office and offered to privately debrief Snow to determine what was on the chairman's mind. But Whiting was rebuffed.

Finally, the CIA dispatched an officer from the clandestine service to contact Snow, who agreed to meet the undercover man in Geneva. But during the meeting, Snow revealed nothing of his conversation with Mao, or particularly about Mao's invitation to Nixon.[90]

THE FINAL MONTHS OF 1970 were a low point for the president. Nothing was working for him, and he had come to believe that he would never obtain leverage over Hanoi unless he further escalated the war. He had not been able to negotiate a breakthrough agreement with Moscow or Beijing. The Soviets were stalling on the date for a summit (Gromyko had told Nixon on October 22 that Moscow was not ready). When Kissinger asked Dobrynin if the White House would have an answer by October 30, the Soviet ambassador replied that the Kremlin believed this date was still "premature."[91]

Meanwhile, in China, Mao was not responding to any of Nixon's signals. Even Edgar Snow could get Mao's attention, but the president of the United States, it seemed, could not.

Out in the larger world, Moscow seemed to have all the political momentum. Chancellor Willy Brandt's rise to power in West Germany was ushering in a more conciliatory German foreign policy toward the Soviet Union. Brandt's first moves had been to recognize the communist government in East Germany and sign a treaty of nonaggression with Moscow. Then, American reconnaissance flights over Cuba showed the construction of naval port facilities at Cienfuegos Bay. A Soviet support ship for nuclear submarines was crossing the Atlantic toward Cuba. A CIA report "confirmed the construction of a probable submarine deployment base."[92] The Soviets were trying to extend the patrol areas of their ballistic missile submarines by giving them access to port facilities in Cuba.* And, in the Middle East, the Soviets were backing Syria and the Palestine Liberation Organization in their confrontation with Jordan over the PLO presence there.

Soviet specialists on the NSC staff pointed out to Kissinger that Moscow was acting with a new boldness, in part because of the Soviet success in securing a more permanent division of Germany but also because Nixon remained mired in Vietnam. Kremlin leaders could also see that despite Nixon's efforts, his overtures to China had apparently failed.[93]

Nixon felt that he was still getting "diddled."

Then, on December 9, Kissinger walked into the Oval Office with a long-awaited message from Zhou Enlai. The message had come all the way from Pakistan by courier because Yahya Khan did not trust cables. The message said, "In order to discuss the subject of the vacation of Chinese territories called Taiwan, a special envoy of President Nixon's will be most welcome in Beijing."[94]

Nixon worried that it was a trap. Perhaps Rogers and Green had been

---

*The confrontation ended when Moscow agreed that its ballistic missile submarines would not call on Cuban ports.

right. The Chinese intended to embarrass Nixon by staging a propaganda show about Taiwan the moment his special envoy arrived. Nixon could simply not afford to expose himself to political attack[95] on the Taiwan question when he was facing reelection.*

Nixon did not trust Communists, least of all Mao. After all, Mao was still holding American prisoners, whom he had promised to release years ago. And so Zhou's secret message lay on Nixon's desk for a week while the president brooded. Presidential inaction always devastated Kissinger, and in December 1970 he already was agonizing about whether he should return to Harvard. He told Haldeman that he didn't want to stay if he was going to be ignored by the president, even temporarily. Haldeman by now well understood Kissinger's feints. He was not about to leave, but still Haldeman lathered him with reassurance that he was *the* indispensable aide.[96]

Nixon finally agreed to send a "non document" back to the Chinese, one that would carry no trace of U.S. government marking and certainly no signature. Hopefully, this communication would smoke out the Chinese. Any meeting in Beijing could not be limited to the subject of Taiwan, it said, but would have to encompass "the broad range of issues which lie between" the People's Republic and the United States. It also added a sweetener: The withdrawal of American military forces from Taiwan would not be a difficult problem to resolve.[97] Then, to ensure that both the Chinese and the Soviets received the message, Nixon instructed Kissinger to send it through both the Pakistani and the Romanian channels to Beijing. Since it was just words on blank paper, Nixon had complete deniability.

Meanwhile, the Democrats—sensing Nixon's paralysis—tried again to take the China issue away from him. Senator George S. McGovern announced his candidacy for the presidency in late January 1971, and his first policy address called for recognizing communist China and giving Beijing the China seat in the United Nations.[98] McGovern called on Americans to abandon the "fogs and myths" that "for the last 20 years have befuddled our attitudes and our actions toward mainland China." He called on Nixon to shelve his plans to build an antiballistic missile system "designed to nullify the budding Chinese deterrent force"; he further argued that Nixon should open up trade with China, giving Beijing the same privileges to buy and sell in the American market that Moscow enjoyed. Lois Snow was in the audience as McGovern spoke in Stockton, California. Afterward, she sent a mes-

---

*That fall at the United Nations, Beijing's allies in Africa and elsewhere in the developing world reached another milestone in their drive to seat China and expel Taiwan. For the first time, a majority (of 51–49) voted to consider the question, but China's allies needed a two-thirds majority to take the next step of seating Beijing. Once again, they failed, but everyone could see that the time was coming when Taiwan, and America, would lose out.

sage to the senator saying that her husband had something important he wanted to tell him and would soon be in touch.*

Nixon meanwhile was walking a tight rope, trying to prevent a spring offensive in Vietnam while also struggling to keep the China initiative alive. In early 1971, the United States launched a major military strike against Hanoi's supply lines, this time along the Ho Chi Minh trail in Laos. To inoculate himself against another Mao tirade, Nixon issued a public statement saying, "This action is not directed against Communist China. It is directed against the North Vietnamese who are pointed toward South Vietnam and toward Cambodia. Consequently, I do not believe that the Communist Chinese have any reason to interpret this as a threat against them or any reason therefore to react to it."[99]

Still, Beijing blasted him for "spreading the flames of war to the door of China." The *People's Daily* denounced him personally. "Nixon has indeed fully laid bare his ferocious features, and reached the zenith in arrogance."[100]

One evening in February, a restless Nixon telephoned speechwriter William Safire at home. The president was wrestling with the voluminous "State of the World" speech prepared by Kissinger and the NSC staff. Nixon was worried that it would have no impact. "Is there a 'lead' in it?" he asked Safire, using a newspaperman's term for whether the speech would garner a headline. "That's the one thing Henry doesn't understand."

"Maybe if you extended a hand to Red China," Safire replied. But Nixon cut him off.

"No, we have other fish to fry," he said, and rang off, his way of avoiding having to take Safire into his confidence on such a sensitive subject.[101]

In fact, China was Nixon's lead. The headline that emerged from the speech was that Nixon referred to Red China for the first time by its official name: the People's Republic of China. Nixon thus gave "face" to Mao before the whole world. In a sense, he was also officially recognizing Beijing's legitimacy and its legal status as the government of 720 million Chinese.

"We are prepared to establish a dialogue with Beijing," Nixon's report said. "We cannot accept its ideological precepts or the notion that Communist China must exercise hegemony over Asia. But neither do we wish to impose on China an international position that denies its legitimate national interests." Nixon added that in the coming year, he would "carefully examine what further steps we might take to create broader opportunities for contacts between the Chinese and American peoples."

Nixon was getting such positive domestic feedback from his overtures to

---

*Snow was planning to reveal to McGovern what he had thus far kept from Nixon, that Mao was ready to open a dialogue. But Snow then discovered that he had contracted pancreatic cancer, and he was unable to travel.

China that he decided to test the waters further. The administration lifted passport restrictions on travel to China and, a month later, relaxed the twenty-year-old trade embargo against Beijing, an act that was heralded around the world.[102] The White House, one account stated, had concluded that "much of the emotion and domestic political peril have been drained out of the issue of relations with Communist China and that the time is ripe for new initiatives." Each time the White House would leak information about a new initiative, McGovern and the Democrats would scramble to get back out in front of the issue.

At the same time, the president protected his conservative flank, secretly sending veteran diplomat Robert Murphy to Taipei to sound out Chiang Kai-shek on a plan that would allow Beijing to take the China seat in the United Nations while simultaneously preserving a seat for Taiwan in the General Assembly. This was the "Dual Representation" formula. Murphy suggested that it might even be possible for Taiwan to hold onto its seat on the Security Council if it cooperated with the United States.* The generalissimo could see the inevitable erosion of Taiwan's position, so he played the best hand he could. He told Murphy that he would be willing to go along provided the United States did not sponsor Beijing's admittance. As Murphy prepared to depart, the Nationalist leader reminded him that President Kennedy had once pledged to use America's veto at the UN to preserve Free China's seat. The implication was: Would Nixon, the conservative, do the same? Murphy did not reply.[103]

Then came Ping-Pong. China's participation in international sporting events had suffered a long hiatus. During the Cultural Revolution, Beijing's radicals shunned world competitions. But in the spring of 1971, as the thirty-first World Table Tennis Championship in Nagoya, Japan, approached, China's National Committee on Sports petitioned Zhou for permission to send a Chinese team. Zhou wrote to Mao for approval, and Mao agreed to participation.[104]

The sixty-member team flew to Nagoya full of political zeal. They refused to play the South Vietnamese and Cambodian teams because they did not represent "legitimate" governments.[105] But to the Americans, the Chinese showed special warmth. When Glenn Cowan, a nineteen-year-old player from Santa Monica, California, asked the Chinese players for a ride to an oyster farm famous for its pearls, the Chinese team captain, Zhuang Zedong, welcomed him. The next day, Cowan gave Zhuang a T-shirt, and Zhuang reciprocated with a hand-painted Chinese handkerchief. The Americans said

*This notion was dubious and Murphy certainly understood as much. If China came into the United Nations, it could accept no other seat but the one reserved for China on the Security Council.

that they would love to visit China, and, soon, the Chinese were frantically calling home for permission to make it happen.

In Beijing, Zhou feared that Mao was not ready. He recommended delaying any consideration of the players' request. At first Mao was also against the proposal, but at midnight on April 6, he told his nurse to summon Wang Hairong, his grandniece and also his eyes and ears in the Foreign Ministry, where she was chief of protocol. Mao instructed her to send word to Japan— invite the Americans.[106]

The visit was a sensation beyond all expectation. The coverage in the American press went on for a month and only added to the sense that a big change was coming in China policy. Nixon was giddy, and he took to asking visitors to the White House, "Have you learned to play Ping-Pong yet?"

Nixon was truly amazed at how the story jumped off the sports pages and onto the front page. He marveled at the suddenness of the spectacle: the buoyant public reaction, the flood of goodwill. And Nixon, ever the political calculator, understood that this positive energy might be channeled to overcome the negative politics of dumping Taiwan. The magic of young athletes, unburdened by decades of bile, discovering each other's culture, demonstrated how ready America was.

Zhou also exploited the excitement. He received the American table tennis team at the Great Hall of the People on April 14. "You have opened a new chapter in the relations of the American and Chinese people," he said. "I am confident that this beginning again of our friendship will certainly meet with majority support of our two peoples." The young Americans were enraptured. They invited the Chinese team to visit America. Zhou accepted.

Three days later, in Washington, Nixon kicked back at a Saturday afternoon "gab" session with Kissinger and Haldeman, bragging that he had already accomplished more with China than any of his predecessors. And look at the impact the flirtation with China was having on the Soviets, Nixon pointed out.[107] There was more maneuvering room now. Now we don't have our backs against the wall with Moscow, he added.

Kissinger flattered Nixon: What made Nixon so "formidable" in his dealings with the Communists, Kissinger said, was Nixon's determination to turn their theory of protracted war against them in Vietnam and Cambodia.[108] (Kissinger missed few opportunities to stoke Nixon's Patton complex.)

Haldeman brought them back to earth. Senator Mansfield was asking for presidential intervention with the Chinese. His application for a visa the previous summer had gotten nowhere. But now the White House turned on him. Things had changed. Now, Nixon's men feared that Mansfield and the Democrats would steal the thunder from a breakthrough on China.

"The Democrats are all going to jump on this," Haldeman warned, saying that it would be better to send a Republican, if anyone. Nixon agreed. Days later, Kissinger sent a secret message through the Romanians asking the Chinese to freeze the Mansfield visa request.

Kissinger didn't even want the Chinese table tennis team to come to the United States. Now that there was a chance to send a secret American envoy to China—and Kissinger knew that he was likely to be that envoy—he didn't want a bunch of Ping-Pong players diluting the glory of first contact. Nixon was also cautious, admonishing that they had to avoid making too much hay about China. Don't want to stick our necks out too far, he said. After all, these were Communists and they just might pull the rug out.

Then, the next day, Vice President Spiro T. Agnew shot off his mouth and nearly undermined the secret preparations. Agnew had called nine reporters to his room after midnight during the Republican Governor's Conference in Williamsburg, Virginia. In a rambling session, he sneered at how the Chinese Communists were scoring a great propaganda triumph out of Ping-Pong diplomacy. He chided the press for portraying the Chinese as a nation of contented proletarians living in their tidy little apartments. If the U.S. government tried to put American welfare recipients into such apartments, he scoffed, the press would call it "oppression" of the poor.[109]

Agnew's outburst revealed right-wing outrage over the flirtation with Red China. At the White House, Nixon just shook his head. Agnew's first mistake, he said, was drinking with reporters. But more fundamentally, Nixon elaborated, Agnew's comments showed that he did not understand the "big picture." The whole Chinese operation, Nixon explained to Haldeman, was about the *Russian Game*—using the thaw with China to shake up the Russians.[110]

But the episode confirmed that Nixon had to shore up his right flank. John Connally, the former Texas governor whom Nixon had recruited as treasury secretary, advised him to take a "principled" position on the China question at the United Nations as a way to hold the conservatives in line. If the White House lost the fight over the China seat, Nixon needed to look as if he had gone down fighting.

Nixon agreed, and to that end, he had asked his old running mate, Henry Cabot Lodge, to head a fifty-member bipartisan presidential commission on the United Nations. On April 26, 1971, Nixon and Lodge announced from the White House the commission's finding that the United States should seek the admission of Communist China to the UN but at the same time seek to prevent the expulsion of Taiwan. It was a two-China solution, on the one hand surrendering to the will of the majority of nations while on the other trying to maintain a beachhead for the generalissimo.[111] Nixon assured the conservatives that he would put up a fight.

With the right wing thus appeased, Nixon was ready to stage the China breakthrough, except there was no word from Beijing. Every diplomatic initiative—Chinese *and* Soviet—seemed stalled.

Dobrynin returned to Washington from Moscow in the spring of 1971 with word that the Kremlin was holding back on key concessions for the Strategic Arms Limitations Treaty, or SALT I as it came to be known. In late April, Kissinger threw up his hands in exasperation. He was going to flee to Palm Springs, California, for a vacation when Pakistan's Ambassador Hilaly asked for an urgent meeting.

Just after 6 P.M. on April 27, Hilaly arrived at the White House and handed Kissinger a two-page handwritten document entitled "Message from Premier Zhou Enlai," which partly read as follows:

> At present, contacts between the People's Republic of China and the United States are being reviewed. However, if the relations between China and the U.S. are to be restored fundamentally, the U.S. must withdraw all its armed forces from China's Taiwan and Taiwan Straits area.
>
> A solution to this critical question can be found only through direct discussions between high-level responsible persons of the two countries. Therefore, the Chinese government reaffirms its willingness to receive publicly in Beijing a special envoy of the President of the United States (for instance, Mr. Kissinger) or the U.S. Secretary of State or even the President of the United States himself for a direct meeting and discussions.[112]

Nixon was still worried that the situation might blow up. For one thing, he did not want Kissinger going to Beijing. Such an historic entrance should be reserved for the president. He also worried about the phrase "publicly in Beijing." A public spectacle, as opposed to a secret mission, would give the conservatives time to mobilize. After the Agnew incident, the Republican right smelled dissension in the administration. There had to be total secrecy, and, still, Nixon was not sure.

The president started talking about sending veteran diplomat and Vietnam negotiator David K. E. Bruce or perhaps Henry Cabot Lodge—or even Rogers or Nelson Rockefeller. But Kissinger pleaded. He would go to Beijing in total secrecy, he promised, and do nothing but prepare for the president's trip. Nixon's triumph, he argued, would be heralded around the world. Nixon brooded for two weeks. At the last minute, on May 10, he sent a reply through the Pakistanis, telling Haldeman that he still wanted "some dramatic involvement" for the president.[113]*

*In the midst of this ferment, it only helped Kissinger that Rogers had soiled himself in London, where, in an interview with British television, he was asked whether better relations with China might worsen America's relations with the Soviet Union. "Why shouldn't we try to get

Drama was the key word because, as Nixon told Haldeman and Kissinger on June 2, the naked political reality was that he had to "make the big plays now"[114] in order to get reelected. Major negotiations—SALT, China, Vietnam—simply could not be left to percolate on Kissinger's preferred drawn-out schedule. Nixon was venting his frustration, but he was also trying to light fires under his staff. He told his aides that day that if he could not get a SALT breakthrough, if he could not get a summit in Moscow, if he could not get a settlement in Vietnam—even though some of these outcomes were likely, if not certain in the short term—then he simply had to shoot for a China trip in the fall. And Kissinger would have to make it happen.

.   .   .

Henry Kissinger's secret trip to China from July 9 to 11, 1971, marked the end of a political epoch for both China and the United States.

For Nixon, the opening was an affirmation that he could escape the sclerotic politics of the Republican right wing and lead the party from the center. What sweet redemption for Nixon, the onetime commie-baiter and enforcer of the Eisenhower orthodoxy on Red China, to seize the initiative. What sweet revenge to repudiate the Democratic paralysis on China during the Kennedy-Johnson years, and what sweet victory to declare, not that the domino theory had been wrong, but that America had *won* the larger war of preventing the communist domination of Asia, making it safe to leave Vietnam and parley with Beijing.

The cover story for Kissinger's secret passage to China would be that he was on a "fact-finding" trip through Asia. But Nixon seemed imbued with his own impetuous valor, and his barely controlled excitement was almost their undoing. During an evening cruise on the Potomac aboard the presidential yacht *Sequoia*, Nixon turned to one of his political aides, Charles Colson, and asked, "Do you think, Chuck, you'll get me an SST to fly to China?" When Kissinger's face contorted in panic, Nixon replied, "Relax, relax. If those liberals on your staff, Henry, don't stop giving everything to *The New York Times*, I won't be going anywhere."[115]

Kissinger's China trip was just weeks away when, in mid-June, *The New York Times* began publication of *The Pentagon Papers*, a secret history of U.S. decisionmaking in the Vietnam War. A frenzy of recriminations erupted over

---

along better with both the Soviet Union and Communist China?" he had replied. "Now, if incidentally, that irritates one or the other, that just happens to be a dividend, but it's not our policy." Of course he was only repeating what Nixon had said many times in private, but Nixon meant to convey that this "dividend" was never to be mentioned publicly. On the flight to San Clemente, Nixon told Haig that he preferred to be portrayed "like an iceberg." You only see the tip, what's on the surface, but the real power is beneath the surface.

the hemorrhage. The leak particularly threatened Kissinger's position, due to his long-standing relationship with Daniel Ellsberg, the RAND Corporation analyst who figured as the source of the leak to *The Times*. But more, Kissinger feared that the China mission was also in danger of leaking. If it did, that would only make Kissinger the target of right-wing attack. A particularly poisonous leak might even undermine Kissinger's relationship with the Soviets, solidifying Rogers's position immeasurably.

One story leaked to *The Times* suggested that Nixon intended to send Kissinger to China as early as 1972. Kissinger was sure that Rogers was the source, as part of a State Department plot to ruin the trip and set Kissinger up as a target. Every leak sent Kissinger climbing the walls. Nixon sent orders through Haldeman to get Henry "calmed down." There was nothing to do but play out the string.

The message that made it possible for Kissinger to actually go to China came on June 2. It announced that Zhou "has reported with much pleasure to Chairman Mao Zedong that President Nixon is prepared to accept his suggestion to visit Beijing for direct conversations with the leaders of the People's Republic of China." The Chinese agreed that both sides could raise "principal issues of concern."[116] But Zhou made it clear from the Chinese perspective that "the first question to be settled is the crucial issue between China and the United States": namely, "the withdrawal of all U.S. armed forces from Taiwan and the Taiwan Strait area."

Zhou acknowledged that Kissinger's trip would not be publicized, but he added, "it may be hard to keep the visit secret." The Chinese were suspicious. They could not understand why, if Nixon was going to make a public journey to China, his emissary should come in secret. But the White House curtly replied to Zhou that "Strict secrecy of his trip is essential."

With victory in sight, Nixon obsessed about his own role. He wanted Kissinger to get an agreement from Zhou that no Democrat, no Mansfield or Kennedy or McGovern, would be invited to China before Nixon. He told Kissinger to try to meet Zhou in a city other than Beijing, so Nixon's entrance there would be all the more astounding.

Kissinger evaded these demands. He knew that Nixon could be turned around as long as he felt reassured, and Kissinger was a perceptive student of Nixon's moods. But mostly he resorted to flattery: When Nixon said that the China opening was the greatest diplomatic watershed since the end of World War II, Kissinger interjected that he considered it the most important event since the American Civil War as far as its overall effect on the nation was concerned. Nixon could only agree.[117]

Once Kissinger was in the air, on his way across the Pacific, he assumed that great sense of control that accrues to any envoy once launched. He ignored Nixon's last-minute admonitions to change the site of the meeting and to make sure there were no names in the communiqué except Nixon's and Mao's.

As Kissinger's windowless air force plane arched westward, the anxieties of Washington followed like a long tail. Haig reported by cable that the Russians had again pushed off the date for a Nixon-Brezhnev summit. Kissinger knew that if they were lucky, they would be able to repay the Soviet "favor" by announcing a U.S.-China summit. That would bring Brezhnev back to their doorstep.

Next came word that a *New York Times* columnist, James "Scotty" Reston, had obtained a visa to visit China and interview Zhou Enlai. Nixon wanted him stopped.[118] There was no way *The Times* was going to spoil this trip by getting there first. But there was nothing Kissinger could do. He figured that the Chinese would delay Reston.*

Before sunrise on July 9, Kissinger and a small group of aides and secret service agents boarded a Pakistani Airways Boeing 707. Although they had arrived at the airport in an assortment of vehicles and disguises, a Pakistani journalist named M. F. H. Beg, who occasionally filed stories to *The Daily Telegraph* in London, spotted Kissinger and asked an airport official where his plane was going. China, was the reply. Beg instantly telephoned London with the news, but the editors there didn't believe him.

With the exception of Rogers, the State Department was in the dark about the Kissinger mission. Marshall Green was in the middle of a staff meeting when news reports of Kissinger's sudden attack of stomach trouble came across the ticker. The reports stated that Kissinger planned to repair to a mountain resort outside Islamabad for two days of rest. Green looked around the table and exclaimed to his staff that no one with Delhi Belly—as South Asian digestive trouble was called—would travel the bumpy roads of Pakistan up to the mountains.

"I'll bet he's gone to China," Green blurted out. Then he clamped his hand over his mouth and looked around the room.

"Stay right here," he said.

Green ran up to Rogers's office and told the secretary what he had just realized—and what he had just said to his staff.

"Is it true?" Green asked.

"Yes," said Rogers. "Now swear them all to secrecy."[119]

A four-member delegation from the Chinese Foreign Ministry was on the Pakistani jetliner when Kissinger stepped aboard. The Americans carried thick black binders stuffed with briefing papers on every conceivable issue

---

*He was right. The Chinese delayed Reston in Guangzhou, and, by the time he and his wife arrived in Beijing by train, Kissinger had slipped out of the country back to Pakistan.

that Kissinger might be called upon to discuss. The binders all carried the code name Polo, which Kissinger had borrowed from the CIA's secret history of the Chinese leadership.

Kissinger's party flew across the 2,500-mile expanse of western China in six hours, landing in Beijing around noon. The aging and bespectacled Marshal Ye Jianying, who had been among the small group of military leaders who had studied the border crisis for Mao, greeted them. Like everyone in China, it seemed, he wore a Mao suit. With him was Huang Hua, the fierce young foreign service officer who in 1953 had blistered American negotiators at the Panmunjom armistice talks in Korea. Older now, his shock of black hair thinning, he fixed Kissinger with a smile as Ji Chaozhu, the interpreter, translated the formalities. Ji was tall and fine featured and spoke a crisp American English learned growing up in New York, where his father had been an editor at the *Chinese Overseas Daily* in the 1940s. Ji had studied at Harvard before the family returned to China to join Mao's revolution, but he had no stomach for political struggle and intrigue and so stayed as close as he could to his protector, Zhou Enlai.

The Americans were whisked through the streets of Beijing in curtained limousines to Diaoyutai.* On the way in from the airport, Huang Hua, riding with John H. Holdridge, the towering diplomat who served as a China expert on the NSC staff, brought up John Foster Dulles and his famous snub of Zhou at Geneva in 1954. Holdridge thought that Huang might be seeking some reassurance, as if Kissinger might also refuse to shake hands with Zhou. Of course there would be a handshake, he said soothingly.

The Americans were not oblivious to the power struggles that wracked Beijing. The politburo was still dominated by radicals, and Zhou himself was under attack. Nancy Tang, who along with Ji Chaozhu served as the principal interpreter for Mao and Zhou, reported to Mao on Zhou's every statement.[120]

Zhou's enemies were legion among the radicals, but chief among them were Jiang Qing, Mao's wife, and, perhaps, Marshal Lin Biao, now vice chairman of the party and Mao's designated heir. In each communication to the White House that spring, Zhou had taken care to state that he was speaking for Chairman Mao and Vice Chairman Lin. But during Kissinger's visit, Lin's name was dropped from the salutations. This omission was a missed clue.

Diaoyutai is an enclosed compound on the western side of the city, where elegant residences constructed as Western-style villas (Kissinger's resembled an English mansion) are arranged along a chain of small lakes surrounded by lush lawns and gardens. The lakes are connected by narrow channels that flow under ornate, humpback bridges. Although Kissinger did not know it, in

---

*Diaoyutai means "fishing pavilion"; the compound was so named when it served as a recreational area for the imperial household.

a neighboring villa the North Korean dictator Kim Il-Sung, on his own state visit to China, was ensconced.

Four hours after Kissinger's arrival, Zhou entered his villa.

Chinese photographers bathed the foyer in white light as Zhou and Kissinger shook hands.

"According to our custom, we first invite our guests to speak," Zhou said, and soon the American and Chinese delegations were arranged on either side of a green felt table in the guesthouse conference hall. Looking across at Kissinger's ostentatious briefing book, Zhou said, "Besides, you have already prepared a thick book."[121] Embarrassed, Kissinger noticed that Zhou had only a single sheet of paper in front of him with a few handwritten notes.

Kissinger was in awe of Zhou, whose darting eyes missed nothing and whose lean physique was a study in controlled tension. Even in a Mao suit, Zhou looked elegant. Far more experienced in the art of diplomacy than Kissinger, Zhou had already lived several lives, first as a revolutionary, then as nation builder, and, now, as a statesman. His contemporaries had included Stalin, Nehru, Churchill, and de Gaulle. When Kissinger arrived in Beijing at the age of forty-eight, with visible insecurities and a scant two years of on-the-job training in statecraft, Zhou had already been practicing the art for a quarter-century. To Kissinger, he sat there as a kind of oriental Metternich, a brilliant mandarin who had helped shape post-war Asia.

Kissinger sputtered about the historic occasion, pedantically reciting the history that had led up to the meeting. Then, with a flourish, he said, "Many visitors have come to this beautiful, and to us, mysterious land . . . "

"You will not find it mysterious," said Zhou. "When you have become familiar with it, it will not be as mysterious as before."[122]

Kissinger got down to business. He said that Nixon was prepared to meet with Mao and to assure him that the United States would never collude with the Soviet Union against China, and that if the Soviets sought to draw Washington into any agreements that affected China's interests, Kissinger would report them to the Chinese. Kissinger's whole approach was to play on Chinese fears of attack from the Soviet Union. It was in China's interest to move closer to the United States, Kissinger implied, and for the two countries to cooperate in restraining their common adversary. To dramatize the threat, Kissinger offered Zhou a full intelligence briefing on the array of Soviet forces along the Chinese border. Zhou accepted.

Then Kissinger broached the delicate question of Taiwan.

"We will reduce our forces as relations improve between the People's Republic and the United States," he said. As for the political status of Taiwan, Kissinger confirmed that the United States did not seek two Chinas, or a one-China, one-Taiwan solution. Nor did it seek an independent Taiwan.

Holdridge, speaking for a whole generation of China specialists in the State Department, had pressed Kissinger to make these pledges early in his presentation because they would demonstrate to the Chinese an American commitment to a new era. Zhou's response was instantaneous.

"Good," he said. "These talks may now proceed."[123]

These private declarations were a nod to reality, but they also marked the repudiation of the long-standing American policy that the status of Taiwan was "yet to be determined." American leaders since Eisenhower had understood that, for Taiwan, there was no going back to the mainland, even though a generation of politicians, up to and including Nixon, had helped to keep the dream alive. Now, Nixon was declaring—albeit secretly—that America recognized that the dream was over.

He went even further.

Kissinger promised Zhou that Nixon would never support a military attack on the mainland from Taiwan and was prepared to withdraw two-thirds of American forces from the island at the end of the Vietnam War. Kissinger's presentation suggested a political realignment in Asia, one focused on keeping the Soviet Union out. Had these declarations been made public at the time, they would have been applauded in much of the United States, but they also would have called down a storm in Nixon's own party. The fact that they were uttered in secret reflected Nixon's unwillingness to confront his conservative wing openly. Instead, he would try to ride the wave of popular goodwill on China over the heads of his opponents.

Kissinger told Zhou that Nixon would be willing to formally recognize Beijing during his second term. This was a promise that was based on no planning or political preparation in the United States, but that simply arose from Nixon's self-assurance that a powerful mandate in the 1972 elections would give him the authority to act.

When Kissinger completed his opening statement, he had been speaking, with translation, for over an hour. Now, it was Zhou's turn. Chinese statecraft seldom evinced gratitude to a foreigner, but Mao and Zhou were deeply grateful for what Nixon had thus far done. He was finally recognizing the legitimacy of the communist revolution in China. He was prepared to demolish the fiction that the world existed without the 720 million people on the Chinese mainland. As Zhou said, "From the beginning, he [Nixon] took the attitude he was willing to come to Beijing to meet us." For the Chinese, the new era would have to be built on a solid foundation.

"The first question is that of equality," said Zhou; "in other words, the principle of reciprocity. All things must be done in a reciprocal manner." History had not yet been made, Zhou continued. "You mentioned that the meeting today is an historic occasion. Of course, a still greater historic occasion would be if President Nixon comes to China and meets Chairman Mao Zedong. That would be an historic occasion," especially, Zhou added, "if we could solve problems.[124]

"The question of Taiwan," he continued, was one on "which we cannot but blame your government. If this crucial question is not solved, then the whole question" of U.S.-China relations "will be difficult to solve."[125] To normalize relations, Zhou said, the United States would have to recognize Beijing as the legitimate government of China and Taiwan as a Chinese province. Washington would also have to withdraw all military forces and installations from Taiwan and the Taiwan Strait area by a fixed deadline.

Despite Kissinger's statement, Zhou was unconvinced that Nixon would have the political will to come to Beijing and officially recognize the People's Republic. "I see the necessity for a period of time" during which to accomplish the formal establishment of diplomatic relations, he said. "But the time that is left for President Nixon is limited. And as a close associate of his, you must be quite clear about this point."

Kissinger deflected the inquiry with humor.

"What is the Prime Minister's estimate of the time left to President Nixon?"

Zhou replied straightforwardly that there were two possibilities.

"The first is one-and-a-half years; and the second, if he is reelected, five-and-a-half years. This would take us to the 200th anniversary of your country."

Kissinger continue to evade the pointedly stated terms of recognition, and Zhou admonished him. "When your President comes to discuss matters with Chairman Mao Zedong, the conclusion could be drawn that he [Nixon] will answer that question."[126] Even a rebuke from Zhou had the feel of velvet.

O N THE SECOND DAY of the visit, after Kissinger and his party had returned from a leisurely tour of the imperial palaces of the Forbidden City, Zhou startled him with a verbal assault. He accused America of weakness in the face of Indian aggression in South Asia; he attacked the American "occupation" of Taiwan; he defended Hanoi's "just struggle" for national liberation. America "had stretched out [its] hands too far" with imperialist ambitions, he said, adding that given the vast differences in their views, was there really any point in a presidential visit?[127]

This was Mao's strategy, a deliberate attempt to unnerve the Americans, to test their sincerity by fomenting a sense of conflict and struggle. But more, it revealed Mao's domination of the Chinese leadership in a way that Kissinger would never fully comprehend.

Kissinger was dumfounded, blindsided by the sudden reversal of tactics.

He implored Zhou not to press events too quickly because the politics of restoring relations between the United States and China was difficult. It was Nixon's wish, Kissinger said, that mainland China be seated by a majority vote in the General Assembly and that Taiwan then be expelled by a two-thirds vote. Of course America would have to oppose Taiwan's expulsion, but Kissinger willfully shared Nixon's private strategy, sensing that Zhou would appreciate reassurance.

With the outburst, Zhou had effectively conducted reconnaissance on the American position. He had provoked Kissinger to reveal a greater level of intimacy about Nixon's intentions.

Zhou achieved the same result with Vietnam. "We need time," Kissinger said, "between the military withdrawal in Indochina and the political evolution" in Saigon—a decent interval to protect Nixon from the charge of selling out an ally. In Taiwan also, Kissinger believed that a staged withdrawal was possible, but it would have to be associated with a clear renunciation of the use of force against Taiwan on the part of China. In this sense, the Taiwan problem mirrored the Vietnam problem: how to withdraw military support for a friendly government that was going to have to come to terms with a stronger communist rival.

"We are prepared," Kissinger told Zhou, "when the President visits, to discuss and sign an agreement for the mutual renouncing of force between our two countries such as you proposed in 1955."

To Zhou this seemed like a ploy.

"You know that this question must be linked to the Taiwan question and the question of China's internal affairs. Once these questions are brought into shape, then this question will be easier to deal with." Zhou's answer was a convoluted way of saying that China could not renounce the use of force against Taiwan until the issue of reunification had been settled.

"We hope very much that the Taiwan issue will be solved peacefully," Kissinger replied, somewhat plaintively.

"We are doing our best to do so," Zhou said, making no commitment.[128]

Finally, there was Nixon's insistence that no other American political figures visit China publicly before he did. Zhou had taken the question to Mao, who seemed prepared to indulge Nixon, knowing that it might help the Chinese get what they wanted from the meeting. For that reason, Zhou seemed to accentuate the burden of Kissinger's request.

"A lot of [Democratic] politicians we have not invited to come here. I have a great pile of letters from them on my desk asking for invitations, which I have not answered."

"What you have done is greatly appreciated by President Nixon," Kissinger replied.

"This is done under the instruction and wisdom of Chairman Mao,"[129] Zhou replied.

The message was clear. Nixon's debt was to Mao.

O NE OF THE MOST challenging aspects of Kissinger's secret journey was to put on paper a brief statement that effectively described its purpose pose—arranging the first summit between the leaders of two countries that had been in a state of war for two decades—and to do so in a manner in which neither side appeared to be a supplicant.

The first Chinese draft, presented by Huang Hua after midnight on the second day of Kissinger's visit, suggested that Nixon had asked to see Mao, that Nixon was seeking to come to China for the purpose of discussing the American withdrawal from Taiwan as a prelude to the normalization of relations between Washington and Beijing.

It was enough to make Kissinger gasp.

The Chinese wanted some reference to Taiwan in the brief statement, but Kissinger persuaded them that even a mention of Taiwan would drag the import of the historic event from the strategic to the parochial. In the end, the announcement consisted of three short paragraphs, most of it self-evident: Zhou and Kissinger had held talks from July 9 to 11. Zhou had invited Nixon to China. Nixon had accepted and, when he traveled to Beijing, the leaders of the two countries would "seek the normalization of relations" and "exchange views on questions of concern to the two sides."

Kissinger was happy with the outcome, even more so because his name was prominently mentioned in the statement. He could tell Nixon that there was no way to avoid this inclusion.

As he flew back to Islamabad and then on to Europe and across the Atlantic and the United States to Nixon's Casa Pacifica, Kissinger drafted his report to the president, in which he boasted: "We have laid the groundwork for you and Mao to turn a page in history." But with new insights gleaned in only forty-eight hours of contact with the Chinese leadership, Kissinger also had been brought back to earth, and he warned Nixon of the "profound differences" and "years of isolation" that "yawn between us and the Chinese."

"My assessment of these people," he continued, "is that they are deeply ideological, close to fanatic in the intensity of their beliefs. At the same time they display an inward security that allows them, within the framework of their principles, to be meticulous and reliable in dealing with others."[130]

Taiwan was going to be a core issue, he warned. The consequences, if rapprochement failed, were clear: "They will prove implacable foes" once again.

A few weeks later, Scotty Reston of *The New York Times* met with Zhou and told the Chinese leader that Nixon could not muster the boldness to break relations with Taiwan or to end the killing in Vietnam. Reston had already written that Nixon lacked the courage to bite the bullet in Vietnam as de Gaulle had bitten the bullet in Algeria. De Gaulle had admitted, "I was wrong," therefore "I [must] stop it, and I move to change it now."

Reston publicly expressed his concern that Nixon would mishandle the opportunities that were before him. Surprisingly, Zhou acknowledged that he had the same concern.

"I agree with your estimate of the character of President Nixon,"[131] Zhou said during their interview in Beijing. Perhaps Zhou understood that Nixon would read the remark, intended as it was to reinforce the challenge that China expected the United States to bite the bullet in Vietnam, and also in Taiwan.

NIXON:
THE
OPENING...

Mao Zedong and Richard Nixon

F ROM THE MOMENT Kissinger cabled "Eureka" to the White House as his plane lifted off from Pakistan, Nixon was drenched both with exhilaration and the dark neuroses that beset him at times of triumph.

"When Henry gets back, he'll be the mystery man of the age," he told Haldeman, who was to ensure that the White House built a wall around Kissinger; there were to be no background briefings for the press.[1] That would kill the whole thing, Nixon said.

Kissinger's helicopter landed at San Clemente just after 7 A.M. on Tuesday, July 13, 1971. Nixon was waiting in a golf cart. He drove a beaming Kissinger back to the residence for a two-hour breakfast. They had two days to prepare for the announcement.

Secretary Rogers, now also in San Clemente, counseled that Nixon had to clearly explain to the American people that his act had not been a reckless one, that the United States had an "orderly" leadership and that the reason for all the secrecy had been the pursuit of peace. Rogers said that it was also important to make clear what had *not* been done in China: that no agreements had been reached and no secret deals made; no promises and no concessions.[2] But in fact, the United States *had* privately offered profound commitments on Taiwan, which would be politically explosive if made public. Rogers had not read the transcript of Kissinger's conversations with Zhou. He never would.

Kissinger argued that Nixon should say nothing about what had transpired in Beijing. Owing to the "delicacy of the situation," the administration should make no comment, but Rogers countered that Nixon's credibility with America's allies in Asia and the Pacific would depend on his reassurance that he was not making deals behind their backs and that American policy toward Japan, Taiwan, Thailand, Indonesia, the Philippines, and a host of other nations was not going to change.[3]

Rogers lost the battle, not only for disclosure but also over who would give the background briefing to the press. Kissinger promised to ensure that Nixon got the credit, and he would limit disclosure of what he had discussed with Zhou.

On Thursday, July 15, at 7:45 P.M. Pacific time, Nixon took the stage at NBC's Burbank, California, studios for a seven-minute address to the nation. He had insisted upon walking onto the set after the cameras had already gone live. It was more dramatic, he told Haldeman. He looked into the camera and told millions of curious Americans that he had requested television time to bring them news of "a major development in our efforts to build a lasting peace in the world."

"As I have pointed out on a number of occasions over the past three years, there can be no stable peace and enduring peace without the participation of the People's Republic of China," he said, then reading the short statement announcing his forthcoming trip.

Nixon said that a new relationship would "not come at the expense of our old friends. It is not directed against any other nation." Rather, he hoped, it would be a "journey for peace."

The world paused, speechless.

O F   COURSE, had the geopolitical chips fallen differently, Nixon that evening might have been announcing a joint U.S.-Soviet air strike on China's nuclear installations, or a joint U.S.-Soviet accord to end the Vietnam War. Instead, he had spotted an opportunity to go another way, to create an opening he had never imagined would appear so suddenly. He had outflanked his Democratic challengers and diverted the country's attention from Vietnam. If Nixon's dissembling left the public with an imperfect understanding of the China initiative, it was due to the sensitive politics of Taiwan. In time, a separate mythology would fill the vacuum.

It was self-evident that the opening to China was also directed at the Soviet Union and Vietnam. With some glee, Kissinger, still in California, rose early on July 15 to speak with Dobrynin, who had to be driven to the White House to use a scrambled phone line. Kissinger said all the right things about how the China opening was not directed at Moscow; about how anxious the administration was to move ahead on arms control, on security in Europe and the Middle East. The clear implication was that Moscow was paying a price for "diddling" Nixon over setting the date for a summit.[4]

In San Clemente, musing with Haldeman, Nixon marveled at the twists of history. He had been one of Chiang Kai-shek's staunchest supporters, he had stood up for America's "friends" in Korea and South Vietnam, but now he was going to be the president who led the country in the other direction.[5] Nixon wondered how that would look.*

The Nixon administration's first contact with the Chinese leadership in July 1971 also changed the nature of global diplomacy this way: Over the course of the next two decades, never again would an important international decision be made in Moscow, Beijing, or Washington without the leaders of those capitals factoring in the consequences for all three.[6] Of course, the triangle had always been there, but its geopolitical significance had lain dormant until the violent articulation of the Brezhnev Doctrine in Czechoslovakia and the eruptions on the Sino-Soviet border caused both communist powers to lay new lines to Washington, principally to outflank the other.

The notion that the China card, or the American card, or the Soviet card—depending on one's perspective—could be played by a single political Svengali in any of the three capitals was naive. Each set of leaders had to ride the tiger, as the Chinese liked to say, and each had to search for advantage from the complex forces at play to orchestrate the best outcome for themselves. The advantage held by the two communist states was that they could devise their strategies within leadership circles that had something the Americans did not—longevity. Unburdened by elections, leaders in the Kremlin and of the Forbidden City had been in power for decades, whereas Nixon and Kissinger were strutting a transitory pageant across the world stage. This was both a strength and a weakness. The communists powers didn't have to worry about being voted out of office, but they did have to worry that the next American president might not be as friendly as the current one. Moscow and Beijing would have to learn how to play the cycle of American politics, how to search in each administration for an interlocutor who shared their worldview and who had the president's ear.

If there was a weakness in the triangle, it was that the United States was far less threatened by China than it was by the Soviet Union, whose nuclear arsenal was second only to America's and whose leaders were literally pouring money into an increasingly threatening navy and a frightful forest of missiles. China's great virtue was that it complicated Moscow's strategic position merely by remaining outside the Soviet camp. It tied down enormous Soviet forces in the Far East and perpetuated Moscow's nightmare of having

---

*On October 10, 1971, Nixon sent Ronald Reagan to meet personally with Chiang Kai-shek and reassure him that the United States would not sell him down the river. Reagan delivered a letter to Chiang and later told a public audience, "We will weaken no cherished associations; we will break no promises. Our defense commitment remains in full force and we will continue to support the full participation of the Republic of China in the international community." Nixon convinced Reagan to be his emissary by making the case that the China opening was all about tying down the Soviet Union. Reagan supported him even as other conservatives bolted.

to fight a two-front war against NATO forces in the west and China in the east.

When Kissinger returned to Washington, he called in Dobrynin and told him, disingenuously, that very little had been discussed in Beijing concerning the Soviet Union. But, he added, there had been an "elaborate" discussion of the war in Southeast Asia. Kissinger said that both the United States and China faced considerable difficulties in Asia, but the two powers felt that they could "neutralize" the region and prevent "any outside interference after a settlement there." This was one way of saying that Washington and Beijing intended to keep the Soviets out of the Pacific.

Kissinger said that he would leave it to "the Soviet government's discretion" to use his information as best it could in discussions with Hanoi,[7] as if Dobrynin could run to Hanoi and tell Ho Chi Minh's successors that the game was up. Kissinger's hubris was only repaid with greater humiliation on the battlefield, made possible by the continued flow of Soviet weapons to Hanoi.

Yet the China play generated immediate dividends. Dobrynin delivered a date for a Nixon-Brezhnev summit, and Russian negotiators suddenly came to agreement over Western access to Berlin,[8] quieting another crisis point between the superpowers.

IN THE MAO ERA, China had frequently shocked the world with its massive upheavals and revolutionary zeal. But it was especially shocking when, in September 1971, word reached the West—a month after Kissinger's secret trip—that a major plot had been uncovered to assassinate Mao. A group of plotters had fled China by airplane toward the Soviet Union only to crash and die on the desolate steppes of Mongolia. Only incomplete shards of intelligence could be gathered about the plot. Some time during the summer, Mao's security detachment believed that it had discovered a plan to blow up the chairman's train.[9]

It was as if a curtain had fallen. Rumor was the only currency. By early October, The New York Times was still reporting that "worldwide speculation" over the "events in China" covered the full range of possibilities, including that Mao was dead and a succession struggle was in progress. "Western analysts" were quoted as saying that portraits of Marshal Lin Biao, the defense minister and Mao's designated heir, had apparently been removed from some official buildings. That was the only hint.

There were no public announcements or explanations until months later. But ordinary Chinese knew that a significant struggle was under way when the government suddenly canceled the traditional October 1 parade marking the founding of the People's Republic. Garrison forces, heavily armed and with extra ammo clips slung on their chests, were out on the streets of Beijing.

When the truth finally emerged, the accusation that Lin Biao had been the coup leader was shocking. Lin was a titan of the PLA, the liberator of Manchuria during the Chinese civil war; had had been leader of the Chinese "volunteers" in Korea two decades earlier. He was a national hero, and, more than anyone, he had encouraged the cult of personality around Mao, compiling the "little red book" of Chairman Mao's quotations that was ubiquitous in China. It was Lin's support that had enabled Mao to topple the "capitalist roaders"—Liu Shaoqi and Deng Xiaoping—and it was the army that had contained the civil strife during the worst period of the Cultural Revolution. As a result, the National People's Congress had confirmed Lin's position as the sole vice chairman of the party, and his status as Mao's heir was written into the new Chinese constitution.

But Mao was a great balancer. He knew that increasing military control threatened his own supremacy and, therefore, Mao's growing disaffection with Lin was believed by many to be inevitable. But hard information was elusive. Lin had mounted no public challenge to Mao's policies, and some analysts would come to question whether Lin could have been behind any coup. But at the time, in part based on Mao's private statements, Western intelligence agencies surmised that Lin, along with radical forces in the party, opposed Mao's opening to America because it would take China further away from the Soviet Union, whose technology was the foundation of China's industry and military.

The crash site only generated more unanswered questions.* Meanwhile, the entire Chinese air force, where Lin's son and alleged coconspirator, Lin Liguo, had been in command, was grounded for a month. Civilian flights also were grounded, and a purge of top military officers took place.[10]

Kissinger understood that something momentous was occurring, and he scrambled for experts to determine what it was. Just before he took off for China on October 16, he called in James Shen, Taiwan's ambassador to the United States, and pumped him for anything that Taipei's intelligence services might have learned. Shen expressed his belief that Lin had not died in

---

*A longtime CIA specialist on China asserted that the results of the Soviet forensic investigation of the crash were later obtained by U.S. intelligence. The Soviet investigation indicated that none of the crash victims were over fifty years of age. Lin Biao was sixty-four. This bolstered speculation that Lin had been killed elsewhere. But a CIA specialist on the Soviet Union said that Soviet officials had confided that Lin Biao's remains had in fact been found at the crash site. Kissinger revealed to the Chinese in July 1973 that Brezhnev had offered to share the Soviet "investigative report" of the Lin Biao affair with the Americans. It is not known whether Brezhnev actually turned over the document.

the crash but was being held under arrest pending trial and secret execution, if that had not already occurred.[11] Shen was also convinced that the Lin Biao incident had been triggered by Mao's overture to America. Even a partial break with Moscow was not popular in the Chinese military, which had been trained and equipped by the Soviets.

As these extraordinary events unfolded, the Nixon White House pressed to keep the Beijing summit on track. Nixon needed the big play; the Chinese trip was essential to his reelection strategy, and any caution over how the coup attempt might affect the stability of the Chinese government was pushed aside. As long as Mao was willing to see him, Nixon was going to go.

The president was already thinking television, pageantry, and extravaganza. He wanted live coverage even if Washington had to take its own satellite ground station, and he wanted to be swarmed by thousands of Chinese. He wanted contact with the public so he could say to his critics that he had gone over the heads of the Communist leaders directly to the Chinese people.[12] The public-relations side of the trip dominated everything. Nixon even sent back Kissinger's briefing book, saying he wanted it boiled down; it was too complicated for the simple objective Nixon was after—the American de Gaulle goes to China.

"TV in front of the President is like alcohol in front of an alcoholic," Kissinger shouted at Dwight Chapin, the Haldeman deputy who was assigned to work with Kissinger on the advance team.[13]

Kissinger had other problems as well. As he prepared to leave for Beijing in October, this time aboard Air Force One, he discovered that the State Department was perilously close to undermining him on the China-Taiwan issue at the UN. Rogers was pulling out all the stops to preserve a seat in the General Assembly for Taiwan. George Bush, the American ambassador to the UN, was mounting a lobbying campaign to save Taiwan from expulsion. Kissinger feared that if this strategy succeeded, Zhou would see it as duplicitous[14] because Kissinger had told him it was Nixon's goal to have Taiwan thrown out.

With Ambassador Shen in his office on October 16, Kissinger told him—lied to him—saying that the fate of Taiwan would not be on the agenda and that Nixon's position was that U.S. relations with Taiwan were "non-negotiable" in Beijing. Kissinger said he was reasonably optimistic that Taiwan's seat at the United Nations would once again survive the annual challenge, and he urged Shen to advise his superiors to keep quiet as the debate at the UN unfolded. Let Beijing be the first to say no, he counseled.

Anyone listening to Kissinger who knew the truth of what he had said in Beijing and what Nixon had said about pulling the plug on Taiwan would have marveled at this performance, especially the way he urged Taiwan to keep quiet—a strategy that could only result in a swifter defeat. Shen had been a journalist as a younger man and had served for years as Chiang Kai-shek's interpreter, so he had seen every kind of diplomatic performance. As he got up to leave, Kissinger feigned sudden warmth. He said he had many friends in Taiwan and, therefore, found going to Beijing exceedingly painful. He really didn't care for the assignment but, with the situation being what it was, he had no choice but to prepare the way for the president.[15] Shen rode grimly back to Taiwan's diplomatic mission at Twin Oaks, exchanging expressions of utter astonishment in the car with one of his aides over Kissinger's theatrics, especially his profession of friendship.

As Kissinger departed for a second time to China in 1971, he had no relief from the fear that everything would unravel. As Air Force One made its way west, Al Haig relayed an update. State was pushing so hard at the UN that it seemed the American position was now that Beijing should not be seated if Taiwan was to be expelled.

"Rogers is fighting like a dog" to keep China out of the UN, Kissinger raged aboard the plane. "That's the hardest he has worked on anything in three and a half years!"[16] His words dripped with sarcasm. Rogers was only doing it "to ruin the China trip," he said.

Sitting in the presidential chair on the plane, Kissinger bristled before a small group of White House aides and advance personnel.

"Everything we are doing with Moscow" and to "end the Vietnam War" hinged on the China trip, he told them. If the China trip turned out a disaster, Nixon would have a horrible time with the Russians on his trip to Moscow. Those were the stakes.

The Chinese, he told them, would display a breathtaking hospitality, and they would do everything perfectly; there would be no technical foul-ups on their side. Ideologically, he said, they were much more committed than the communists that America was used to dealing with in East Europe. They were fiercely devout. Zhou was the most impressive of them all, a man of great moral quality, he said. The Russians were just a bunch of thugs who would plug away at any negotiation to try to pick up pennies, whereas the Chinese had a longer historical perspective.[17]

After a stop in Hawaii,* Kissinger donned a flight jacket and continued his leacture on China. If they did not handle themselves well in Beijing, they would "run the risk of looking like a bunch of clowns." Everything depended on the Chinese taking them seriously. "If they figure that we are lightweights," he said, "they will kill us."

---

*During their stop in Hawaii, Kissinger disappeared to Nelson Rockefeller's estate with Winston Lord, who had been supplied by Chapin with cash to tip the servants. When Kissinger returned, he was carrying an antique jade flower as a personal gift from Rockefeller to Zhou. Already Kissinger was bonding his interests with China beyond Nixon.

The advance party's propaganda line should reinforce Nixon's seriousness, he said. They should emphasize the political pressure the president was under as a result of his courageous opening to China, but also express confidence in his ability to get reelected. "Our whole strategy is based on a second term," Kissinger told them.

If the subject of Vietnam came up, he told them, they should say that it would be a mistake for the Chinese to take Nixon lightly. Nixon would "master" the war, and if the Chinese did not help with the settlement, "we will get it settled and we won't be responsible for the consequences."[18]

I N OCTOBER 1971, Kissinger returned to a China under martial law. Zhou only hinted at Lin Biao's betrayal, saying, "Chairman Mao has a thesis: those who hail you are not the ones who support you." How inscrutable it all was. Armed troops were visible in the streets of Beijing, and the tension was palpable.

The Americans were greeted with banners at the airport denouncing the "running dog" capitalists of the world. Zhou was apologetic. The banners, he said, were just so many "empty cannons" of propaganda.[19]

Kissinger's opening joke was that China had suffered many barbarian invasions in the past, but it had not encountered anything like a presidential advance trip. Kissinger had first told the Chinese to expect a presidential party of about forty people. Haldeman had laughed when he heard this. The Secret Service contingent alone would be larger than that. Kissinger tried to break the ice by quipping that if the Chinese were not careful, the advance team would have every phone in China connected to the White House switchboard.

A little revenge was also on Kissinger's agenda. He told Zhou that Nixon wanted to keep Rogers out of the substantive meetings during the summit, and so a face-saving sideshow had to be arranged to keep him busy in separate talks on technical issues with second- and third-tier Chinese leaders.[20]

The climax of Nixon's "journey for peace" was to be a joint U.S.-China statement heralding a new era of normalizing relations. Kissinger laid before Zhou the closely guarded American draft. It was full of pomp and history and was pointedly anti-Soviet. But Kissinger had forgotten that for Beijing, rapprochement had to yield some victory on Taiwan. And although the status of Taiwan could be deferred, Mao wanted the Americans to ratify the Communist dominion over all of China—to acknowledge Beijing's primacy, its legitimacy, and, therefore, its victory over Chiang Kai-shek. Zhou referred to an old Chinese saying: The person who ties the knot must untie it. China was looking to America to untie the knot of Taiwan.

On the second day of his visit, Kissinger gently replied on the Taiwan issue.

"We recognize that the People's Republic considers the subject of Taiwan an internal issue," he said, "and we will not challenge that. But to the degree that the People's Republic can, on its own, in the exercise of its own sovereignty, declare its willingness to settle it by peaceful means, our actions will be easier. But whether you do or not," he added, "we will continue in the direction which I indicated."[21] That direction was the reduction of U.S. forces on Taiwan, which he had already promised in July.

Why Kissinger started this negotiation by surrendering his leverage is not clear, except that it fit in with his abstract notion of geopolitics; in his worldview, only the dominant players counted, and it was absurd to consider Taipei a major player. Therefore, the only task for Kissinger was to construct an exit strategy along the path of least political resistance.

Zhou responded curtly to Kissinger's probe. "I had told you," he said, "that we will try to bring about a peaceful settlement."

But Kissinger persisted.

"Our attempt will be to bring about a solution within a framework of one China and by peaceful means," he said. "When Taiwan and China become one again by peaceful means," then the United States could terminate the Mutual Defense Treaty it had signed with the island. Kissinger assured Zhou that the treaty "is not a permanent feature of our foreign policy. . . . To be very frank with the Prime Minister, what we would like most and what we would encourage is a peaceful negotiation after which all the military relationships would be at an end."

Zhou, perhaps doubting whether America could completely walk away from Taiwan, asked: "Assistance or relationships?"

"After there is a political settlement between Taiwan and mainland China, yes," Kissinger replied. "We will not insist on maintaining an American presence or military installations on Taiwan after unification of China by peaceful negotiation has been achieved. And in those conditions we will be prepared to abrogate [the defense treaty] formally. If there is no peaceful settlement, which is the second contingency, then it's easier for us to withdraw our military presence in stages, which I indicated to the Prime Minister."[22]

"I understand," Zhou replied.

They adjourned for a banquet of roasted "Peking" duck, and late that evening, Zhou presented a draft of a joint communiqué that shocked Kissinger because it read like a revolutionary manifesto. Perhaps Zhou had wanted—or had been instructed by Mao—to throw down an opening hand that would please the radicals looking over his shoulder. In any case, the document was structured so that both sides could state their views and differences, and then it set forth the Chinese position with vehemence.

"Revolution," it declared, had become "the irreversible trend of history. . . . People's revolutionary struggles are just." It referred to racial injustice and pledged that China would remain the "reliable rear area" for Hanoi's insurgents and for all Indo-Chinese peoples "fighting to the end for the attainment of their goal."

Kissinger imagined how Nixon would react if he brought home such a draft. But he also recognized that the format of the joint communiqué could work. He told Zhou that the American side would draft its part of the communiqué, but he argued that the two sides had to express agreement on some fundamental points, otherwise why were they even claiming to be embarking on a new era? The communiqué had to evoke the spirit of the occasion.

Borrowing from State Department background papers, Kissinger and his aides then drafted the American contribution to this two-sided communiqué and redrafted the harsh Chinese language in hopes that Zhou would accept the editing.

Zhou read it slowly. He asked if Nixon would indeed state "that the U.S. acknowledges that all Chinese on either side of the Taiwan Strait maintain there is but one China."

Yes, Kissinger affirmed.[23]

"Then," Zhou continued, "You should also say that the U.S. would encourage the Chinese to solve this internal matter by themselves through peaceful negotiations."

"We are saying almost that," Kissinger replied.

By 8:10 in the morning on October 26, less than a hour before Kissinger's plane was to depart from Beijing, they reached an agreement on the draft communiqué, and Kissinger felt great elation.

But back in New York, where it was still Monday evening, October 25, a much larger event was occurring, as the UN General Assembly voted 76–35—with 17 abstentions—to seat the People's Republic of China and expel the Republic of China on Taiwan. The Taiwanese ambassador rose stoically and led his delegation out of the hall. Bush sat, looking dejected, having failed to save the Taiwan seat.

For the Chinese, Rogers's handling of the UN vote turned out to be irrelevant, because they saw what all the world could see—that the votes were there for the historic reversal. And Nixon was able to have it both ways. He denounced the undignified hooting and hollering by Beijing's supporters in the General Assembly, and got credit from conservatives for shouldering defeat with dignity. And he was also able to take some credit for China's entry, because it coincided with his own opening to Beijing.

But on Kissinger's plane, elation turned to apprehension as he feared that he would be blamed by conservatives for losing Taiwan's seat, that he would be blamed for the Nationalists' being thrown out of the UN.[24] Just by being in Beijing, Kissinger had undermined Bush's floor fight, people would say. Bush, who had been given the task of selling tickets on the *Titanic* in a bid to save Taiwan's seat, complained privately that he was saying one thing in New York while Kissinger was saying another in Beijing.[25] On Air Force One, Kissinger, Lord, Chapin, and the other White House aides concluded that they should skulk quietly back into Washington and delay their report to the president, since Nixon might get angry, even irrational, if a conservative backlash erupted over Taiwan.[26]

In fact, the right wing did erupt. California governor Ronald Reagan telephoned the White House and exhorted Nixon to go on television and denounce the UN—to say that America intended to ignore future UN votes.

Nixon persuaded Attorney General John Mitchell to get on the phone and try to calm Reagan down, and they thought they had succeeded until Rogers announced publicly that Washington accepted the UN vote and—though the administration "deeply regretted" Taiwan's losing its seat—did not intend to retaliate by withdrawing funding from the international body. That set Reagan off again. He called Mitchell, fuming. The president, he said, should recall its ambassador from the UN and make a strong statement threatening to pull the plug on funding for the organization. That would get their attention. The White House discovered that the conservative leadership, including Senators James Buckley of New York and Barry Goldwater of Arizona and columnist William F. Buckley Jr., were conspiring to mount a campaign to reverse the expulsion of Taiwan.[27]

As soon as Kissinger landed at Andrews Air Force Base, Nixon ordered him to start working the phones to talk Reagan and the other conservatives down. The incipient revolt could not be allowed to gain momentum, Nixon said. He did not want Reagan off the reservation, because California was key to the reelection strategy. They had to ride it through.

WITH MORE PERSONAL stroking from the White House, Nixon had just gotten the right wing back in line when war broke out between India and Pakistan. The Soviets were backing India. China was backing Pakistan. Nixon's visit to Beijing was only weeks away.

The origins of the crisis are well known. With the partition of the Asian subcontinent after World War II, India found itself girded on two sides by East and West Pakistan. India resisted this encirclement in a series of border wars. Meanwhile, Pakistan's internal strains were formidable due to a strong nationalist movement in the East. In early 1971, a full-scale rebellion broke out in East Pakistan, and President Yahya Khan responded by sending a

40,000-man army to crush it. In the middle of Khan's military drive, a devastating cyclone roared out of the Bay of Bengal and killed hundreds of thousands of East Pakistanis, leaving millions more homeless. The failure of the government to respond adequately to the catastrophe only fueled the rebellion.

On November 1, Indian army units crossed into East Pakistan, and the Soviet Union began to airlift additional weapons and ammunition to New Delhi.[28] On November 22, Indira Gandhi's forces began their attack on the Pakistani army. At noon that day, Kissinger burst into Haldeman's office to say that radio and television stations were already reporting the attack, but that the intelligence community had not been able to confirm it.[29] Diplomats were barred from traveling to the war zone. But it was soon apparent that Pakistan's army was doomed.

Due to his brutal tactics, Khan had few sympathizers in the international community. But for India, the crisis presented a golden opportunity to split Pakistan into weaker components. Indeed, Gandhi had all the pretext she needed to act. By November, millions of East Pakistanis in wretched conditions had fled into India, having been flushed from their homes by either the Pakistani army or the cyclone. The exodus put a great burden on India and caused deep resentment.

At its core, the crisis did not have a geostrategic dimension, only a regional one, but that did not stop the White House from inflating it for its own purposes and risking a military confrontation with the Soviet Union, all in an effort to curry favor with the Chinese leadership. As Kissinger put it to Nixon: "We really don't have any choice. We can't allow a friend of ours and China's to get screwed in a conflict with a friend of Russia's."[30]

And, of all the players, China was in the weakest position. Mao had decapitated his military leadership to clean out the nest of coup plotters. With Chen Yi and the other marshals of the PLA dispersed across China and the Cultural Revolution still simmering, Beijing could not afford to play in troubled waters on the subcontinent without risking humiliation.[31]

But Kissinger was making his own big play. He activated the NSC crisis machinery, bringing to the White House key officials from State, Defense, and the CIA. From the outset, this group counseled Nixon to take an even-handed approach to the crisis, one that avoiding tilting toward either India or Pakistan. But Kissinger rejected this advice—indeed, he ridiculed it.[32] At the State Department, Marshall Green and others suspected that Nixon and Kissinger were so beholden to the Pakistanis for assisting them with the opening to China that they had turned a blind eye to Yahya Khan's repression.

But that was only part of it.

On Tuesday evening, November 26, Kissinger, Bush, Haig, and Lord drove south through Manhattan to the Lower East Side where, in a seedy apartment building, the CIA maintained one of its safe houses. It was a place where spies could meet or where a foreign diplomat could be lured into a compromising position. There was no doorman.

They were meeting Huang Hua, who had just been appointed Chinese ambassador to the United Nations. He arrived in an embassy car and stepped out into the chilly night in a overcoat. At the run-down apartment building, Huang flashed his steely smile at Kissinger and shook his hand. Once they settled upstairs, he listened as Kissinger explained the meeting's urgency and the need for secrecy.

"It is in our mutual interest that we don't appear to be cooperating visibly," Kissinger said.[33] Nixon, he told the Chinese envoy, was sympathetic to Pakistan's plight: "We would not accept military aggression by India against Pakistan." Gandhi had been warned that if she launched an attack, she would face a cutoff of American aid.

Kissinger already knew the Chinese position. Beijing was backing its ally, Pakistan, and did not want to see an independent Bangladesh in East Pakistan. That would reward "Indian aggression," in China's view; it represented interference in the internal affairs of Pakistan. The subtext was that the United States should take a hard line against New Delhi and Moscow. China wanted the Americans to stand up to Soviet intervention on the subcontinent.

Kissinger was angling for something more.

"It is the President's wish that we not move too far away from you on this issue,"[34] he said. He seemed carried away with a solicitous air, an exaggerated sense of collusion, telling Huang that Bush's presence in the room meant that: "For these purposes, Mr. Bush works directly for me [and not the secretary of state or the president]. No one in the Government except the people in this room know about this channel. If others know, I will let you know, so there will be no confusion when you are talking to someone. No matter what others say, there are only these people and Commander Howe and, of course, the President who know about this." (Commander Jonathan T. Howe was the White House military aide whom Kissinger was using to pass sensitive intelligence to the Chinese about the Soviet Union and, now, about India.[35])

Huang asked for Kissinger's assessment of the "present situation" on the battlefield in East Pakistan. Kissinger motioned to Lord, who pulled out the latest CIA intelligence reports and spread a CIA map out on the table.

"This violates every security rule," Kissinger said to the Chinese. Directing Huang to the map, Kissinger showed him in detail the lines of the Indian assault on the Pakistani army.

"The major attack is through Jessore," Kissinger said, indicating the location on the map.

Haig added, "The report is that there are as many as two divisions supported by armor."[36]

They went on in this manner for a while, Haig filling in the details of Indian deployments and showing the Chinese ambassador where they were on the map. Kissinger offered to send copies of new CIA reports directly to Huang in sealed envelopes any time he wanted an update on the battlefield situation. Then he disclosed another piece of intelligence that he thought would be more useful to the Chinese.

"We were told—I'm not sure it's right—that they have taken their two mountain divisions from your frontier and moved them down" nearer to East Pakistan.

In other words, the Indian border with China might be naked.

This was the first step in Kissinger's attempt to induce China to consider an attack on India's frontier, an act that certainly would have touched off a general war in the region and driven the superpowers toward a serious confrontation.

It is impossible to understand Kissinger's manic state without taking into account his struggles within the administration; in December 1971, he was again trying to force the removal of Rogers by threatening to resign. The secret July trip to China had made Kissinger something of a superstar. By December, he had given his first televised press conference. But without cabinet rank, Kissinger was never indispensable. His meltdown came the morning after an NBC special entitled "A Day in the Life of the President," in which Nixon allowed the filming of his crisis management discussions. During one such filming, over dinner, Nixon called on Rogers and other members of his cabinet to discuss foreign affairs, but failed to call on Kissinger.* The morning after the special aired on television, Kissinger walked into Haldeman's office and announced that he had decided to resign. He would make a public resignation statement, then go on the China trip with Nixon and leave quietly the following June.

No way, Haldeman said. If he resigned, he could not go to China with the president.[37] He would have to leave the administration immediately.

Kissinger froze, looking a little stunned. He quickly changed his tack. Of course he would not leave the president in the lurch. He would consider the matter further, he told Haldeman. But Kissinger continued to orchestrate a drumbeat of dissatisfaction, using Haig to spread word of his anger, and Haig dutifully told colleagues that it was all he could do "to hold Henry together"

---

*It was known within Nixon's inner circle that the president was shopping for a new secretary of state. Kissinger was anxious to raise his own profile in competition with more weighty political figures under consideration such as Treasury secretary John Connally.

as he privately trashed the president for playing him off against Rogers, to the ultimate benefit of Rogers.[38]

Any crisis that pulled Nixon and Kissinger closer together served Kissinger's bureaucratic interests, and for Kissinger, the India-Pakistan crisis became a superpower confrontation that threatened the very existence of China, and could very well scuttle Nixon's historic journey to Beijing. For Kissinger, the conflict in East Pakistan could be exploited to get Nixon's attention again. And, in the face of Chinese anxieties over Soviet adventurism and Gandhi's project to mop up the subcontinent, Nixon was eager to appear responsive. In August 1971, Moscow and New Delhi had signed a treaty of friendship, providing a new supplier of weapons for Gandhi. For Nixon, now that Moscow had agreed to a summit meeting in 1972, there was little risk in playing a tough hand on the subcontinent, since it was clear that both superpowers wanted to avoid a full-blown confrontation. Nixon would get credit in Beijing for standing up to Moscow, he would be applauded by conservatives in the United States, and the Soviets would see that he would be no pushover at the summit. And so Nixon ordered a naval armada into the Indian Ocean.

On December 7, the UN General Assembly called on India and Pakistan to enter an immediate cease-fire and to withdraw troops from each other's territory, but Indian forces stayed on the attack. Three days later, Kissinger was back in New York at another CIA safe house, this time a townhouse on the fashionable Upper East Side. With Bush also present, Kissinger buoyantly welcomed Huang Hua, and once they were seated in the parlor, he set the conspiratorial tone by saying, "Incidentally, just so everyone knows exactly what we do, we tell you about our conversations with the Soviets; we do not tell the Soviets about our conversations with you. In fact, we don't tell our own colleagues that I see you. George Bush is the only person outside the White House who knows I come here."[39]

Kissinger then catalogued the American pressure on India. Loans had been canceled or frozen, along with $14 million in military sales. Also, Nixon had called in the visiting Soviet minister of agriculture and told him: "Pakistan is a friend of the United States and . . . if India were to continue its attacks and launch an attack against West Pakistan, it could lead to the U.S.-Soviet confrontation."

Nixon was barred by law from selling arms to Pakistan, Kissinger told Huang, "and we are barred by law from permitting friendly countries which have American equipment to give their equipment to Pakistan." But he then confided: "We have told Jordan, Iran and Saudi Arabia, and we will tell Turkey" that "if they decide that their national security requires shipment of American arms to Pakistan, we are obliged to protest, but we will understand. We will not protest with great intensity. And we will make up to them in next year's budget whatever difficulties they have."[40] He seemed to relish telling the Chinese how willing the White House was to flaunt American law.

Kissinger produced a new map, showing the Chinese ambassador how the United States was "moving a number of naval ships in the West Pacific toward the Indian Ocean." Leading the deployment was the aircraft carrier *Enterprise*, accompanied by four destroyers, a helicopter carrier, and two destroyer escorts. This armada of seven warships was impressive. Then Kissinger drew Huang's attention to the Soviet naval contingent that had entered the Indian Ocean.

"They are no match for the U.S. ships," Kissinger said dismissively.

"I now come to a matter of some sensitivity," he said. "We have received a report that one of your personnel in a European country, in a conversation with another European, expressed uncertainty about the Soviet dispositions on your borders and a desire for information about them." The Chinese ambassador said nothing. United States intelligence agencies, Kissinger continued, do not collect "tactical" intelligence on the Sino-Soviet border. "We have only information about the general disposition, and we collect it at irregular intervals by satellite. But we would be prepared through whatever sources you wish, to give you whatever information we have about the disposition of Soviet forces.*

"Secondly, the President wants you to know," Kissinger continued, "that it's, of course, up to the People's Republic to decide its own course of action in this situation, but if the People's Republic were to consider the situation on the Indian Subcontinent a threat to its security, and if it took measures to protect its security, the U.S. would oppose efforts of others to interfere with the People's Republic."[41]

Now the inducement to move against India was clear. With this comment, which Kissinger had carefully rehearsed with Nixon, Kissinger was making what must have sounded to the Chinese ambassador like a strategic commitment on behalf of the United States to defend China should it come under attack by the Soviet Union following a Chinese move against India.[42]

Huang's assistant took down Kissinger's statement, and Kissinger then proceeded to explain that the U.S. naval armada would clear the Strait of Malacca that very weekend and be in position for any possible confrontation. "I must tell you one other thing," Kissinger said with some drama. "We have an intelligence report according to which Mrs. Gandhi told her cabinet that

---

*Kissinger's talking points for the meeting indicate that U.S. intelligence, indeed, was at a disadvantage. The "next satellite readout" was expected on January 4, and the next launch of a high-resolution satellite was scheduled for December 21, with a return on about December 31. By then, the crisis would be over.

she wants to destroy the Pakistani army and air force and annex this part of Kashmir, Azad Kashmir," he said, pointing to the map, "and then to offer a cease fire—this is what we believe must be prevented."[43]

Huang grew more animated. "The Soviet Union and India," he said, "now are progressing along on an extremely dangerous track—this is a step to encircle China."

"There is no question about that," Kissinger replied. "Both of us must continue to bring pressure on India and the Soviet Union."

Kissinger was certain that China was going to act, but Nixon was leaving for the Azores to meet the new French leader, Georges Pompidou, and Kissinger had to accompany him. So Haig was designated as the secret courier to fly back to New York that Sunday, December 12, to hear Beijing's decision.* Suddenly, that morning, word came over the hot line from Moscow that the Indians had given assurances to the Soviets that they had no intention of attacking West Pakistan. In fact, "they were most anxious to find a solution."

When Kissinger saw the text, he sent a coded message to Haig, instructing him to withhold the most critical part of the message from the Chinese. "Listen first to other side's proposal," he dictated, and do "not reveal content of Soviet approach. We will try to get them [India] to move to cease fire if Chinese agree."[44] By his instructions, Kissinger undoubtedly was hoping that China would still commit its military forces by moving against the Indian border in a coordinated strategy with the United States, in effect creating a U.S.-China alliance. In any event, it would draw Beijing closer to the United States at a time when Nixon and Kissinger still had high hopes that China could be induced to reconsider its support for Hanoi in the Vietnam conflict.

Kissinger's inducement to the Chinese, based on duplicity and his own failure to disclose a critical diplomatic retreat by India when that information was so relevant to Beijing's calculations, revealed how desperate the White House was to incite China into taking a confrontational military stand against India and the Soviet Union. But it also revealed how unreliable an ally Kissinger could be.

And he was wrong about China's intentions.

"The Chinese side has carefully studied the opinions put forward by Dr. Henry Kissinger last time," Huang told Haig during their next meeting. China had decided to work for a diplomatic solution at the UN. It would not move its troops.[45] Thus, as U.S. and Soviet forces steamed toward the Bay of

---

*Even if China had been inclined to mobilize its military and move troops to the mountainous border region, the routes into India were subject to sudden closings by snow. In addition, any CIA or DIA analyst could have informed Kissinger that the PLA had serious mobility problems and was not up to the task of a rapid mobilization of forces, especially in the harsh environment of the Tibetan plateau.

Bengal for a meaningless naval minuet while the fighting raged on land more than 1,000 miles away, China's leaders balked at joining the dangerous game that Kissinger was urging them to play.[46]

In the art of war, it is always preferable to maneuver so that one's rivals fight among themselves and thus weaken each other. Mao saw no reason to enter the fray. Instead of moving his army, he instructed his ambassador at the United Nations to verbally attack the "weak" and "vacillating" response by the rest of the world to India's aggression. And Mao certainly was not willing to buy into Kissinger's offer of strategic protection. Anyone could see that the United States was in no position to protect China's northern flank from Soviet retaliation. How could an aircraft carrier and a few destroyers in the Bay of Bengal pose any threat to the million Soviet troops arrayed along the Sino-Soviet frontier half a continent away? With his extravagant and unrealizable offers, Kissinger surely incited the Chinese to carefully question American credibility.[47]

In any case, the episode was a humiliation for Nixon and Kissinger. Having set up the equation that they could not afford to allow a friend of the Chinese and the Americans (Pakistan) to get "screwed" by a friend of the Russians (India), they failed to have any impact on Gandhi's actions in East Pakistan. And, having fought their own bureaucracy to garner support for Pakistan in an alliance with China, Nixon and Kissinger were left like brides at the altar waiting for China to act. When a cease-fire finally took effect, West Pakistan's army limped home. East Pakistan emerged as independent Bangladesh, and India's hegemony over South Asia was significantly enhanced.

If anyone besides Gandhi was the winner in this regional power struggle, it was Brezhnev. He not only backed the winning horse at minimum expense, but he could also argue that his investment in the military buildup along China's northern border had paid off by preventing Mao from acting against India.[48]

The importance of the crisis, however, extended far beyond the transitory headlines that it produced. Americans had scarcely paid attention. But within the Nixon administration, Kissinger had argued that the very survival of China was at stake. Nixon had agreed, and in a secret message to Zhou he said, "It is the U.S. view that recent events in South Asia involve sobering conclusions. The governments of the People's Republic of China and the United States should not again find themselves in a position where hostile global aims can be furthered through the use of proxy countries."[49]

The threat to China from Soviet forces on the northern Chinese border also became a touchstone of American policy in the Kissinger era, for as long as Kissinger could postulate such a danger, he could inoculate himself and the White House from right-wing attacks on his China policy. The Soviet threat to China rationalized for the Goldwaters and the Reagans why Nixon had to move closer to the Reds in Beijing. And the Soviet threat to China made it possible for Nixon and Kissinger to argue in Beijing that China's leaders should not make excessive demands regarding Taiwan.

Almost none of this machination was apparent to the American public. A notable press leak to columnist Jack Anderson at the time disclosed excerpts from an NSC meeting showing Nixon "tilting" toward Pakistan,[50] despite the State Department's public posture of evenhandedness. But the contemporary accounts missed the larger game of courting China to undermine Hanoi. The courtship was more evident when Kissinger blocked the release of a documentary film about the persecution of Tibetans and the flight of the Dalai Lama. The film had been prepared by the United States Information Agency and was set to be distributed to 120 U.S. diplomatic missions around the world. The White House suddenly stepped in and killed it, citing concern that it might irritate China.[51] Nothing could be allowed to jeopardize Nixon's journey.

N IXON WAS DOWN TO two choices on Vietnam. In White House lingo, these were: *Get tough* or *bug out.*

In January, Nixon sent Haig to China, ostensibly to complete the technical preparations for the upcoming presidential trip. But Haig was also tasked with the mission of impressing on the Chinese leadership how much effort Nixon had made—publicly and privately—to end the Vietnam War honorably. He had proposed cease-fires, prisoner exchanges, and new elections in South Vietnam in which all parties could participate.[52] But Hanoi had been intransigent, and Nixon had ordered a Christmas bombing blitz over North Vietnam, trying desperately to head off a spring offensive by the North in an election year.[53]

Now Haig also carried the extremely sensitive message that the United States was not wedded to the Saigon regime, even though Washington was staunchly supporting the government of Nguyen Van Thieu in public.

In meetings with Zhou and Foreign Minister Ji Pengfei on January 3–4, Haig said that Nixon needed China's help in getting a settlement in Vietnam. Haig warned that it was in China's interest to do so. Soviet expansionism represented a dangerous encirclement of China, and the United States was willing to oppose any aggression against China in the fight against Soviet domination in the region. All Nixon asked in return was help in convincing Hanoi to come to acceptable terms. Haig even said that the United

States was willing to orchestrate the toppling of the South Vietnamese president if that was what it would take to get a deal on the table.*

On January 25, Nixon began his own political offensive in the United States, revealing to a national television audience his secret efforts to end the war.

The next day, Kissinger sent a secret message to Zhou reiterating all the points in Nixon's speech and suggesting that the Chinese use their "good offices" to moderate Hanoi's demands,[54] which included an unconditional withdrawal of American forces and the removal of the "puppet" Thieu regime in Saigon.

But Zhou had heard all of this already from Haig, and so the Chinese leader sent Kissinger an acerbic reply. China, he said, supported Hanoi. Period. China rejected the suggestion that it should "exert pressure on the Vietnamese side on behalf of the United States."[55]

But enticements continued to flow from the White House.

On February 6, two weeks before Nixon was to depart for Beijing, Kissinger sent another message to the Chinese offering to fly immediately to the Chinese capital, where the North Vietnamese official Le Duc Tho was visiting Chinese leaders prior to Nixon's arrival. Kissinger offered to discuss a settlement "with generosity and justice."[56]

When there was no immediate reply, the White House approved upgrading China's trade privileges. Still, Beijing remained a wall of granite: "China supports Vietnam and will definitely not meddle in U.S.-Vietnamese negotiations," another message said.[57]

As Nixon's departure date drew near, the White House also worried about Taiwan. Kissinger called in Ambassador Shen and told him that the president wanted the Taiwanese government to withhold all official comments on the Nixon trip until after the president had returned and had a chance to brief everyone. Nothing would please Beijing more, Kissinger said, than to see Washington and Taipei exchange unfriendly remarks. Then Kissinger, as if confiding one of the utmost secrets of the government, said that the trip had an urgent geostrategic dimension. Relations between Moscow and Beijing were in such a drastic downward spiral that a Soviet military attack on mainland China "cannot be ruled out even now."[58]

That was Kissinger's message—the issue was bigger than Taiwan. Taiwan should keep quiet. Nixon would never sell them out.

---

*Haig recounted his presentation to Ji Pengfei in a private briefing to Chapin and John Scali of the White House staff; the briefing is recorded in Chapin's eighty-page diary of the trip. Since Haig's presentation was carefully prepared and reviewed in the White House, this private message, if delivered as Haig described it to his colleagues, reveals Nixon's determination to get a breakthrough at almost any cost and as early as possible in the presidential campaign season. The briefing also reveals that Nixon's closest aides were saying in private what they were denying publicly: that America was prepared to jettison its allies in Saigon in order to get a deal to end the war.

O N A CLEAR WINTER'S MORNING in February 1972, Richard Nixon and his wife, Pat, boarded Air Force One for their journey to the People's Republic of China. The nation's attention was riveted on their departure, as if they were leaving for the moon. Indeed, the moon had seen more official visits by Americans—and more television time—than China.[59]

No American president had ever visited China. Only a handful of Americans had ventured onto the mainland during the previous two decades. The cultural divide between the two countries was planetary, greater than geography could explain. Closed for so long to the West, China was all mystery and myth, a nation where the "masses" seemed as numerous as ants and lived a fierce and revolutionary life behind the towering iron curtain that rose on the western shore of the Pacific. Now Nixon, who had made a political career of whipping up American sentiment against communists, was departing like some jet-borne Columbus going out beyond the great barrier.[60] Max Frankel of *The New York Times*, among the 250 reporters traveling with the presidential party, wrote, "The very idea of the thing—after Korea and Vietnam and 'Who Lost China?'—accounts for the sense of history."*

Messages flooded the White House wishing Nixon well, and the president confided in Haldeman and Kissinger that Americans were hopelessly naive, willing to pay almost any price for peace. But Nixon also knew that public naïveté could help them sell the opening.[61]

Air Force One, its fuel tanks brimming, took up most of the runway at Andrews Air Force Base before heaving itself into the morning sky. On board, Nixon's aides set up a color television on Kissinger's small conference table. They were watching their own takeoff—live. Some were taking home movies of the TV screen, and when Kissinger saw the spectacle, he wondered aloud what it would be like to watch his own crash.[62]

Late that first night, Nixon came out of his cabin and chatted with Chapin, who complimented him on the "profile shot" of his departure with Mrs. Nixon. As Nixon accepted Chapin's flattery, Kissinger was on the satellite phone to Haig, directing him to "call off the next strike." Chapin realized that there had been contingency plans for a bombing raid in Vietnam or Cambodia. Nixon was showing caution. He told Kissinger that they would have to be ready for a North Vietnamese offensive. Hanoi would spoil the trip if it could.

*One correspondent who would not make the trip was Edgar Snow, who died on February 15, 1972. When Mao and Zhou heard that Snow was suffering from cancer in January, they sent a seven-member medical team to his home in Switzerland to administer to him until his death. Snow was to have covered Nixon's trip for *Life* magazine. Mao, Zhou, and Song Ching-ling, the widow of Sun Yat-sen, all sent personal letters of condolence to Snow's widow, Lois Wheeler Snow. Nixon also sent a letter expressing his sorrow, but Mrs. Snow could not bring herself to answer it. See Lois Wheeler Snow, *A Death with Dignity* (New York: Random House, 1974).

When Kissinger hung up the satellite phone, he looked up at Nixon.

"Mr. President, it's all right, it's canceled."[63]

Nixon, a tinge of cynicism in his voice, asked how successful the last raid had been.

"Very successful," Kissinger replied.

"I'll bet they told you they got every gun," Nixon sneered.

Air Force One flew from Hawaii to Guam and from Guam to Shanghai. The White House took care to avoid stopovers that might offend the Chinese politically, such as Okinawa, where American military forces are based, or Hong Kong, the "sovereign" British colony wrenched from China in the nineteenth century.

On the final leg from Guam to Shanghai to Beijing, Nixon called Haldeman and Kissinger up to the presidential cabin to reinforce the point that no one was to leave the plane until he had gone down the steps solo to meet Zhou. That would be the key image of the whole trip, and it had to go flawlessly.

Just before 11:30 A.M. on February 21, Air Force One taxied up to the tiny stone terminal at Beijing's airport. The windswept tarmac was virtually empty. The winter sun was low in the sky, barely above the line of naked poplar trees that girded the airport. A Secret Service agent stepped into the aisle of the plane and blocked the path behind the president as Haldeman, Kissinger, Rogers, Green, Lord, and dozens of White House aides craned their necks to see Nixon's back as he turned and stepped out into the daylight.[64] From atop the jetway, he surveyed the modest welcoming party—a dozen Chinese Foreign Ministry officials led by Zhou. Two flags, one Chinese and one American, flew over the reception area as a 500-member band played "The Star-Spangled Banner."

Nixon descended and Pat followed in her brilliant red coat. At the bottom of the ramp, Zhou, frail, hatless, and bundled in a topcoat, awaited. As Nixon descended, Zhou began to clap. Nixon clapped, too, and then stretched out his hand to the Chinese premier. Zhou's avian eyes locked onto Nixon's and he seized the outstretched hand. Their lips were moving but it was the image—not the words—that flashed around the world. The leaders of the United States and the People's Republic had joined their hands, ending an epoch, beginning a new one, however undefined. Something was over. Something was beginning.

The arrival ceremony was over in minutes. Nixon reviewed the honor guard, and then he and Zhou stepped into a limousine and led the entourage on the hour-long ride down the two-lane road into the city, across Tiananmen Square, past Zhongnanhai, where Mao was hidden behind the vermilion walls, and on to the beautiful mansions at Diaoyutai.

L ITTLE DID NIXON KNOW, but Mao was desperately ill.
The deterioration started when Marshal Chen Yi died on January 6, during Haig's visit, although Haig was never aware of the drama. On the day of the funeral, Mao had risen at 1 P.M. and told his nurses that he was leaving for Baobaoshan Cemetery to greet the family and attend the service.[65] It was a frigid day, and he was dressed only in his bathrobe when his guards brought his car around. The doctors had called ahead and pleaded that someone turn up the heat in the funeral hall, but there was no heat. When Mao returned to his study later in the day, he was shivering with cold and fatigue. Angry at his own frailty, he snapped at his doctors and refused to take his medication.

On January 18, a nurse came running out of Mao's study shouting that she could find no pulse on the chairman and that his breathing was labored. When they finally got an electrocardiograph strapped onto him, it revealed that Mao was in a state of congestive heart failure, that his brain and vital organs were not getting enough blood, that his body was swollen with edema, and that a serious lung infection had set in that could finish him off any day. Li Zhisui, Mao's longtime doctor, feared that the chairman would die and implored Zhou to intervene.

Mao's wife, the rabid political infighter Jiang Qing, burst in on this medical crisis and started a commotion by calling the medical team a "ring of spies." She convened a politburo meeting to denounce them for undermining the chairman's health.

Marshal Ye Jianying stepped in at that point. He told the medical staff to stay at the ready. "The chairman does not want treatment now. He is angry," Ye told the quaking doctors. "But when he gets over that, he will need your help."

The prospect of Nixon's arrival, however, seemed to motivate Mao to recover. On the afternoon of February 1, Mao sent for Dr. Li and asked, "Do you think there is any hope? Would you still be able to help me recover?" Li was ecstatic, but on the first day of Mao's recovery, after he had been shot full of antibiotics and other medications, his throat swelled up and he was seized by a choking fit and collapsed. The doctors revived him, but it was going to take weeks of therapy just to render him functional for a state visit. Day by day, Mao practiced standing up and sitting down so that his legs would be strong enough to support himself when the Americans arrived.

Zhou was to be Nixon's official host and would preside at the high-level meetings, but on the day of Nixon's arrival, Mao was beside himself with anticipation. He awoke early. He got his first shave and haircut in five months. An attendant put scented tonic on his hair, and he arranged himself on his sofa as aides came in with reports of Nixon's landing in Shanghai and each increment of his flight to Beijing. When Mao learned that Nixon's plane had landed in the capital, he asked his nurse to tell Zhou that he wanted to see Nixon immediately. Zhou had hosted tea for Nixon at the guesthouse and was allowing the American visitors an hour's rest when Mao called and urged Zhou again to bring Nixon straightaway to Zhongnanhai.

Nixon was just out of the shower and putting on fresh clothes in the master suite when Kissinger rushed in and said that Zhou was downstairs. The invitation was for Nixon, Kissinger, and one note taker.[66] Kissinger brought Lord to fill that role.

They were escorted into Mao's study. Nixon was struck by the plainness of it—just shelves filled with books, many of them opened and strewn about or piled on the horizontal surfaces. The simplicity magnified the sense that they had reached the inner sanctum of a dynastic figure—"this colossus," in Kissinger's mind. Just as Edgar Snow's imagination had been set to flight by Mao's presence in 1938, so Nixon and Kissinger were affected.*

The visitors could not see the emergency medical equipment tucked behind the furniture and potted plants. Zhou said that the chairman had been suffering from bronchitis for about a month. Nixon made a careful mental note of this comment.

"I can't talk very well," said Mao after a weak handshake.

Nixon said that he had come because it was in the interest of the United States that he do so.

Then, offhandedly, he added, "You read a great deal."[67]

Mao ignored the observation.

"Yesterday in the airplane, you put forward a very difficult problem for us. You said that what it is required to talk about are philosophic problems." Mao was referring to Nixon's remark to Qiao Guanhua on the flight from Shanghai to Beijing. Nixon had told the deputy foreign minister that he considered Mao a man with whom philosophical discourse was possible. It was an innocuous remark, but Mao used it to establish a self-effacing tone at the outset.

"I said that because I have read the Chairman's poems and speeches, and I knew he was a professional philosopher."

The Chinese laughed in enjoyment of this, and Mao seemed delighted. He motioned at Kissinger and asked, "He is a doctor of philosophy?"

Nixon—already forewarned by Haldeman that Kissinger was upset by some belittling "quips" that the president had made earlier to Zhou— replied: "He is a doctor of brains."

---

*As Kissinger recorded in his memoir, "Mao just stood there, surrounded by books, tall and powerfully built for a Chinese. He fixed the visitor with a smile both penetrating and slightly mocking, warning by his bearing that there was no point in seeking to deceive this specialist in the foibles and duplicity of man. I have met no one, with the possible exception of Charles de Gaulle, who so distilled raw, concentrated willpower." All this for the eighty-year-old Mao, bloated by edema and propped up by his nurse.

"I used to assign the Chairman's collective writings to my classes at Harvard," Kissinger said.

"Those writings of mine aren't anything. There is nothing instructive that I wrote," said Mao. His words were mumbled and slurred, and Nancy Tang, the interpreter, turned them, miraculously it seemed, into sentences in English.

Nixon, joining Kissinger in flattery, said, "The Chairman's writings moved a nation and have changed the world."[68]

"I haven't been able to change it," Mao said, refusing to accept their praise. "I've only been able to change a few places in the vicinity of Beijing."

Then Mao veered mischievously to the present.

"Our common old friend, Generalissimo Chiang Kai-shek doesn't approve of this. He calls us 'Communist bandits.'"

After more banter, Mao said, "Let us speak the truth. As for the Democratic Party, if they come into office again, we cannot avoid contacting them."

This seemed to be Mao's way of broaching the question of Nixon's longevity on the political stage.

"We understand," said Nixon. "We will hope that we don't give you that problem."

Mao shifted the subject around again, as if his mind were searching for the best way to proceed.

"I voted for you during your election," Mao said.

"When the Chairman says he voted for me, he voted for the lesser of two evils," Nixon replied.

"I like rightists. People say you are rightists, that the Republican Party is to the right, that Prime Minister Heath is to the right," Mao said.

"And General de Gaulle," Nixon added, savoring Mao's point, which was his own.

"I am comparatively happy when these people of the right come to power," Mao said.[69]

Nixon agreed, adding, "I think the important thing to note is that in America, at least at this time, those on the right can do what those on the left talk about."

"There is another point, Mr. President," Kissinger interjected. "Those on the left are pro-Soviet and would not encourage a move toward the People's Republic, and in fact criticize you on those grounds."[70] Kissinger's partisan smear might have seemed out of place, except that Mao used it to mention the coup attempt.

"Exactly," Mao agreed. "In our country also there was a reactionary group which is opposed to our contact with you. The result was that they got on an airplane and fled abroad."

Zhou, not sure that Nixon and Kissinger understood Mao's meaning, interjected, "Maybe you know this?"

Mao went on, referring again to the coup attempt.

"The U.S. intelligence reports are comparatively accurate," he said. "As for the Soviet Union, they finally went to dig out the corpses, but they didn't say anything about it." In case Nixon was missing the subject, Zhou prompted him: "In Outer Mongolia," where the Soviets had examined the wreckage of the plane that had carried members of Lin Biao's family and, perhaps, Lin himself.

But Nixon seemed oblivious. He prattled on about how the American Left was pro-Soviet.

Nixon said that he hoped he and Mao could talk about Taiwan, Vietnam, Korea, Japan—all of Asia—and the future of U.S.-Soviet relations. "Because only if we see the whole picture of the world and the great forces that move the world will we be able to make the right decisions about the immediate and urgent problems that always completely dominate our vision."

This was Nixon's way of saying that Vietnam was dominating the American agenda.

"For example, Mr. Chairman, is it interesting to note that most nations would approve of this meeting, but the Soviets disapprove," Nixon said. "So we must examine why, and determine how our policies should develop to deal with the whole world, as well as with the immediate problems such as Korea, Vietnam and, of course, Taiwan.[71]

"We, for example, must ask ourselves—again in the confines of this room—why the Soviets have more forces on the border facing you than on the border facing Western Europe," Nixon continued. His statement was a serious exaggeration. CIA estimates at the time reported that only about one-quarter of the Soviet forces were deployed against China, with the remainder ranged against Europe and the United States.[72]

But Nixon was selling the threat.

"The Prime Minister," he said, "has pointed out that the United States reaches out its hands [as an "imperialist" nation] and that the Soviet Union reaches out its hands. The question is: which danger does the People's Republic face? Is it the danger of American aggression, or Soviet aggression?"

Mao gave the answer Nixon had hoped for. "The question of aggression from the United States or aggression from China is relatively small," he said. "Therefore, the situation between our two countries is strange." Mao continued, for twenty-two years, "our ideas have never met," and now, just ten months "since we began playing Ping-Pong," much had happened. Mao confessed that for two years—even though he had received all of Nixon's "signals"—he had blocked any Chinese opening to America. "We stuck with our stand that without settling major issues [such as Taiwan] there was no reason to talk about the smaller issues. I myself persisted in that position." Mao then added, "Later on, I saw you were right, and we played Ping-Pong."[73]

In the midst of it all, Mao reached over and took Nixon's hand and held it for a long minute. Nixon just glowed.

"Do you have anything to say, Doctor?" Mao asked, turning to Kissinger.

"Mr. Chairman, the world situation has also changed dramatically during that period. We've had to learn a great deal. We thought all Socialist-Communist states were the same phenomenon. We didn't understand until the President came into office the different nature of revolution in China and the way revolution had developed in other Socialist states."

Nixon seemed not completely in agreement with Kissinger's flattery of Chinese communism. And so he addressed Mao again. "We know China doesn't threaten the territory of the United States," he said. "I know you know the United States has no territorial designs on China. We know China doesn't want to dominate the United States. We believe you too realize the United States doesn't want to dominate the world. Therefore we can find common ground, despite our differences, to build a world structure in which both can be safe to develop in our own ways on our own roads. That cannot be said about some other nations in the world."

Then Nixon seemed to get a little too caught up in the moment.

"I would like to say in a personal sense—and this to you, Mr. Prime Minister," he said, turning to Zhou, "you do not know me. Since you do not know me, you shouldn't trust me. You will find I never say something I cannot do. And I always will do more than I can say. On this basis I want to have frank talks with the Chairman and, of course, with the Prime Minister."

Nixon spoke in a manner that revealed his inherent contradictions, on the one hand reminding the Chinese that he was in Beijing as a self-interested political figure while on the other offering himself in the communion of secret friendship, based on the tenuous notion that he would always "do more than I can say."[74] It was his iceberg metaphor again.

Mao, pointing at Kissinger, said, "Seize the hour and seize the day," meaning that he and Zhou should go to work. Then he leaned back, again waxing philosophical: "I think that generally speaking, people like me sound a lot of big cannons."

Zhou laughed deferentially as Mao parroted the rhetoric of the day. "Things like, 'The whole world should unite and defeat Imperialism, Revisionism and all reactionaries, and establish Socialism.'"

"Like me," Nixon said. "And bandits."

"It is all right to talk well and also all right if there are no agreements," Mao said, "because what use is there if we stand in a deadlock?" Mao's real meaning was so hard to discern.

U P UNTIL THE MEETING with Mao, there had been a rumble in the press corps that something was amiss. The bleak airport arrival, followed by a motorcade through deserted streets, added up to a mediocre reception.[75] It certainly did not feel like a breakthrough. This was not how de Gaulle would have landed in China. But the news of Nixon meeting Mao hit the makeshift press center like a prairie squall. One minute, Press Secretary Ron Ziegler was fending off negativism, and the next his voice shot up an octave with all the excitement. It was as if God had stretched out his hand and conferred celestial meaning on the event. For Nixon, the summit with Mao instantly put the whole China trip on a higher plain. It was the highlight of the week. No matter what was achieved on the diplomatic front, Nixon had gotten the image he wanted—the first meeting ever with Mao by an American leader, embarked on a quest for peace.

That evening, Nixon and Zhou rose as solitary figures above the sea of Chinese and American faces in the Great Hall of the People and raised their glasses to friendship. Nixon was soaring.

On the second day of the visit, the president seemed worried about Rogers, and, in the presidential suite that morning, he drafted a long, handwritten note on yellow legal paper to his secretary of state entrusting him with a special task. It was very important, Nixon said, for Rogers and his aides to be on the lookout for the "comers" among the Chinese leaders, because, after all, Mao and Zhou were on their last legs and there would be a new regime to deal with in the future. Even though that regime "might be against us," usually there were some sympathetic people in the bureaucracy who could be spotted and cultivated. Rogers and the boys at State should make contact with them and establish some kind of rapport.[76]

It was almost touching the way Nixon was trying to make it up to Rogers for cutting him out of the meeting with Mao, but it was a charade. The damage had been done, the press corps was on fire with speculation, and the humiliation of Rogers became the emblem of Nixon's lack of regard for the overall institution of the State Department and for the man he had chosen to run it.

The surface choreography of the president and Mrs. Nixon taking in the Great Wall and the other tourist sights dominated each day's reportage, but behind closed doors, Nixon worked on Zhou Enlai, affirming to the Chinese leader that America would play the role of counterweight to the growing Soviet power. He admonished Zhou that China should not feel threatened by American military forces in the Pacific because they were there to enforce peace and stability. And besides, if America were to withdraw, Moscow would fill the vacuum. Looking at Zhou across the broad negotiating table, Nixon said that he realized he sounded like an old cold warrior, "But it is the world as I see it, and when I analyze it, it is what brings us, China and America, together."[77]

But Zhou did not dwell on points of agreement, rather on points of contention. Vietnam, he said, was the "most pressing question," an issue that "the whole world is watching." Betraying a familiarity with the American political scene, Zhou pointed out that the Democrats in Washington already were belittling Nixon for rushing to China to try to settle Vietnam. "Of course, this is not possible. We are not in a position to settle it," Zhou said.[78]

Nixon said that he had "no illusions" about being able to settle the war in Beijing, but, of course, he had hopes. And to make his case, he argued that the only party to gain from the continuation of the war was the Soviet Union.[79] "They want us tied down because they want to get more and more influence in North Vietnam as a result," Nixon said. "From all the intelligence we get, they may even be egging on the North Vietnamese to hold out and not settle."

That may be true, Zhou allowed, but the later the American withdrawal, the more painful it would be. He reminded Nixon that de Gaulle had cut the knot in Algeria, even though it cost him politically. And, he added, "Our position is that so long as you are continuing your Vietnamization, Laoization and Cambodianization policy, and as long as they keep fighting, we can do nothing but to continue to support them [Hanoi]."[80] Nixon saw that there was no daylight between Beijing and Hanoi.

That was the way they left it.

Nixon shifted to Taiwan, reiterating his plan to withdraw two-thirds of U.S. military personnel there. "We will support any peaceful resolution of the Taiwan issue that can be worked out," he said, "and the reduction of the remaining third of our military presence on Taiwan will go forward as progress is made on the peaceful resolution of the problem."[81]

But for Beijing, making a commitment to "peaceful resolution" was a huge problem, as Zhou explained.

"You want a peaceful liberation [for Taiwan]," he said. But so did Beijing, and Zhou said that the Chinese leadership was committed to "strive for peaceful liberation."

"This is a matter for both sides," Zhou continued. "We want this." However, he added, "What will we do if they [the Taiwanese leaders] don't want it?"[82] What if Taiwan didn't agree to reunification? It was a fundamental question, and if Beijing couldn't answer it, then Beijing was not the sovereign power. How could Beijing credibly enforce its sovereign claim to Taiwan without a credible threat of force? Even if Beijing committed to a peaceful resolution, the threat would always have to be in the background.

Zhou professed that Beijing did not want war, but to give up the threat of force would cripple the mainland's sovereign claim and encourage Taiwan toward separatism. Zhou's presentation made it clear that no American could answer these questions for the Chinese. Kissinger had said that it would take ten years to solve the Taiwan question. "I can't wait ten years," Zhou told Nixon. If China accepted a time limit, "it would be equivalent to accepting interference in our internal affairs, so we have not accepted that. We are not asking you to remove Chiang Kai-shek. We will take care of that ourselves."

"Peacefully?" Nixon asked.

"Yes, we have self-confidence,"[83] Zhou replied. "We have already waited over twenty years—I am very frank here—and we can wait a few more years. I can go a step further. Even when Taiwan comes back to the motherland, we will not establish any nuclear bases there."

O N THE EVENING OF February 22, Nixon's entourage was treated to a cultural spectacular, *The Red Detachment of Women*, at the people's auditorium. It was combination ballet and rock opera in which the "running dogs of capitalism" are defeated by communist heroes. Mao's wife, Jiang Qing, had supervised its production, and Nixon, seated next to her that evening, praised the ballet effusively. He understood from U.S. intelligence that "Madame Mao" was behind the efforts to topple Zhou and that her radicalism induced such fear among Chinese leaders that she was regarded as a kind of vampire.

And, looking at her severe features, it was not hard to see why. Jiang Qing wore a style of horn-rimmed spectacles that rendered her face particularly stringent. The prominent widow's peak didn't help. A sour visage was framed by short black hair combed strait back to accentuate the pallid landscape of jowls that pulled the corners of her mouth into a perpetual frown. As a young woman, she had been a pixie beauty, an actress from Shanghai who became a camp follower of the Communist leaders when they were holed up in the caves of Yenan. She had danced with Mao and he had married her. Now she wielded power like a chainsaw, and only Mao could control her, although he too often seemed reluctant to do it.

Just a month earlier, when Mao was still refusing to take his medication and seemed ready to throw in the towel, Jiang Qing had been present in the chairman's study when he had turned to Zhou and said, "My health is too poor. I don't think I can make it. Everything depends on you now."[84] Mao's unmistakable pronouncement on the question of succession had shocked everyone in the room and, for Jiang Qing, it had also painted the bull's-eye more prominently on Zhou's back.

So the president was on his guard. In his mind, the safest course was to flatter her, hence Nixon's incessant praise for the propaganda display that was masquerading as art.

"It is good to know that you find it acceptable," she said, "but tell me how you would go about improving it."[85]

Nixon could only feign ignorance.

They watched for some time in silence, and then in the middle of the ballet, Jiang Qing turned abruptly to the president and asked, "Why did you not come to China before now?"[86]

The president was too flummoxed to reply.

When the show was over, Haldeman looked over to see Nixon standing and applauding as if he had just seen a great performance of Verdi or Puccini. It worried Haldeman because the image was going out live to the United States, where Americans might be horrified to see their president applaud such an anti-American spectacle. The conservatives already were gathering in rebellion, including those who had accompanied the presidential party to China. Nixon had picked Patrick Buchanan, the most conservative of the White House speechwriters, to staff the trip, in part because the appointment looked good with the right.[87] But after they landed in Beijing, Buchanan became deeply concerned about the imagery that Nixon was beaming back home from the communist capital, and he worked himself up into a contentious state. Worse, Rose Mary Woods, Nixon's longtime personal secretary—a serious conservative herself and very protective of Pat—had joined the Buchanan sulk. Nixon also had been forced to reject several of Buchanan's trenchant drafts, most importantly the draft he had written for the toast to Zhou Enlai at the Great Hall.

In fact, Buchanan did not object to the China trip per se. He understood why Nixon had made the journey: The United States was in a weakened condition, and Nixon had to approach the lesser of two evils in the communist camp.[88] But by the time he reached Beijing, Buchanan had developed serious second thoughts. Here America was fighting a war in Vietnam, he reasoned. American boys were still dying, and the president was telling the American people that it was still necessary for them to continue resisting Asian communism. How was Nixon going to reconcile this position with the fact that he had jetted off to Beijing to hobnob with the most ruthless Asian Communists of them all? The great risk, Buchanan thought, was that Nixon was going to undermine national morale and the psychological basis of support for further resistance in Vietnam.

Buchanan thought that he could influence events by drafting tougher language for Nixon. But it was clear almost from the moment they arrived that he would fail. Nixon and Kissinger had taken Buchanan's draft of the Zhou toast and rewritten it to such a degree that, when Buchanan heard it, he thought they had gone too far. There was too much euphoria, too much bonhomie with the commies. Haldeman and a few other members of the staff were having twinges of the same reaction, worried that Nixon was overdoing it. Haldeman was glad when he saw Kissinger editing Nixon's drafts, excising flourishes that would offend the conservatives, though few conservatives would have been happy to have Kissinger as their editor. And Buchanan was headed for a meltdown.

The tension within the Nixon entourage only got worse as the joint communiqué emerged. The language agreed on the previous October was no longer satisfactory to either side. Kissinger struggled over the text with Qiao Guanhua, the courtly vice foreign minister. The Chinese wanted a stronger statement about the American military withdrawal from Taiwan. Then Rogers submitted language that the State Department wanted, including a "guarantee" that China would use only peaceful means in any effort to reincorporate Taiwan so the agreement could be defended in Congress. And so Qiao and Kissinger chiseled and weaseled day after day in negotiating sessions.

Friday morning, February 25, was Nixon's last day in Beijing, and the deadline for the communiqué if it was to be issued Sunday night from Shanghai.* At the end of the morning session, Qiao broke the news that there would be no second meeting between Nixon and Mao. The reason could have been Mao's health, or it could have been Mao's feeling that he was not getting a firm enough commitment from Nixon to withdraw American forces from Taiwan. In any case, the Chinese leader stayed aloof, and Nixon, too, seemed to have lost interest in another meeting.

All during the week, Rogers had tried to carve a larger role for the State Department in the communiqué negotiations, but Nixon kept Rogers and Green away from it. Rogers did not get his hands on the document until the Nixon entourage arrived in Hangzhou and only after Kissinger and Qiao had finished their negotiations, at 3 A.M. on Saturday; after which the Chinese politburo met and approved the text.

At Hangzhou, a beautiful lake resort near Shanghai, Rogers and Green had adjoining suites, and they sat together—two patricians without portfolio—and went line by line over Kissinger and Qiao's handiwork. After a few minutes of studying the lengthy document, Green looked up and said, "Mr.

---

*The document had to be read and approved by Mao and a meeting of the politburo called to ratify it.

Secretary, there is a serious problem."[89] Green rose, his face manifesting intensity under his swept-back red hair. He explained that there was a paragraph in the communiqué that reaffirmed all American treaties and security commitments in Asia, including the treaties with Japan, South Korea, and the Philippines as well as the Australia–New Zealand security pact. But the document omitted the Mutual Defense Treaty of 1955 with Taiwan, entered into by President Dwight Eisenhower and ratified by the Senate. The treaty was the foundation of the American commitment to Chiang Kai-shek and the American commitment to defend the island from attack. Green said that the Republican right wing would savage the communiqué for such an omission and that Chiang Kai-shek would howl. The omission was potentially as serious as Dean Acheson's, Green said, reminding Rogers of how Harry Truman's secretary of state in 1950 had carelessly proclaimed the boundary of the American "defensive perimeter" in Asia, leaving out South Korea. North Korea attacked weeks later.

"My God, you're right," Rogers murmured.

Marshall Green's discovery of a fundamental flaw in the communiqué energized Rogers to try to rescue Nixon and thereby exact a measure of revenge for himself and the State Department against Kissinger. Nixon was mortified, suddenly concerned that everything would fall apart; meanwhile, Kissinger defended himself not by attacking the substance of Rogers's intervention but by calling the secretary's loyalty into question: How could he make such a noisy objection that might leak to the press and blight the entire Nixon journey?

It was already Saturday evening, and Nixon didn't want a rebellion. An untimely leak *would* kill their efforts in China by setting off the conservatives. Kissinger stoked the flames of Nixon's anger because it deflected attention from his own error. Soon, he had Nixon storming around his elegant guesthouse in his underwear, ranting against the bureaucracy, not just because there was a gaping hole in the communiqué—there was—but because the State Department people seemed to be telling everyone about the flawed document and lining up in opposition to it.

Green had no idea that Rogers had gotten word of the flaw to the president. He had gone to the evening banquet in a funk, believing that Rogers's call to the president had been intercepted by Haldeman. Ron Ziegler saw the scowl on Green's face and asked, "What the hell is wrong with you, Marshall?" There in the banquet hall, Green confided everything; Ziegler immediately recognized the impending disaster and called Haldeman.

At two o'clock in the morning, Green was awakened by loud knocking on his door. It was John Scali, a former ABC news reporter and now Nixon's press adviser.

"All hell has broken loose over this and it is because of you,"[90] he said, asking Green to tell him everything.

Meanwhile, Nixon dispatched Kissinger at 10 P.M. Saturday to explain to Qiao that the American side needed to make some minor changes. Since Kissinger had made the mistake, he would have to fix it. When a puzzled Qiao walked into the guesthouse, Kissinger told him with a straight face that in order for the communiqué to find support at home, the State Department had to feel that it had participated. This argument only brought further puzzlement to Qiao's face. With a preemptory tone, Qiao said that the negotiations had concluded many hours ago after both sides had made many concessions. Further, the Chinese politburo had approved the text on Friday night after it had been completed in Beijing and after Kissinger had assured him that Nixon accepted it. Qiao had no authority to reopen the negotiations. Kissinger persisted, however, and Qiao departed to get instructions from Zhou.

When he returned, Qiao told Kissinger that the Chinese side would not agree to any changes in the Taiwan section of the communiqué, but was willing to consider other minor changes. They were not about to allow Kissinger to insert a reference to the Mutual Defense Treaty between the United States and Taiwan, and so Kissinger suggested taking out the whole section that cataloged America's security commitments in Asia. It was a shame, because Nixon had wanted to remind and reassure America's allies of those commitments. At 1:40 A.M., the revised and excised communiqué was completed. Instead of showing any gratitude to Rogers, Nixon seemed angry that State had taken advantage of the situation. Rogers protested that he was not trying to undercut the document. He would support it 100 percent.

On Sunday morning, groggily, the Nixon party gathered on the tarmac in Hangzhou for the flight to Shanghai. There, Green ran into Kissinger, who was in a surly mood. He glowered at Green and said, "What are you doing poor-mouthing my communiqué?"

Green merely regarded him with contempt. After all, as a young foreign service officer Green had served with Douglas MacArthur, George Marshall, and Dean Rusk in rebuilding postwar Asia when Kissinger was still in college. Green had helped draft America's security commitments in Asia, and yet Kissinger had discarded and abused him as though he were some worthless bureaucrat. Still the restrained Yankee diplomat, Green nevertheless indulged himself in the pleasure of that moment on the tarmac.

"Well there is a very serious flaw in it, Henry," Green said, "and I just want to spare the president the agony of what will happen if we don't correct it."[91]

But Kissinger was full of recriminations. "But you have been talking to John Scali and he has no right to be involved in this thing."

Green gave it right back to him.

John Scali was the president's press adviser, Green pointed out, and the problem with the communiqué was very distinctly a public relations problem. At the time Green had spoken to Scali, there was no way of knowing whether Rogers had gotten through to the president. Besides, Green added, just to test Kissinger's memory of the Constitution, the secretary of state and the assistant secretary did have a role in foreign policy, whether Kissinger liked it or not. Green restrained the urge to say more. And as they stood there, nearly toe to toe, Kissinger suddenly changed his tone and said, "Marshall, you must brief the press with me."

But Green said that that would depend on whether the communiqué had been amended and whether the president wanted him to brief the press. Kissinger then assured him that the flap was over—Nixon and Zhou would initial a revised communiqué in Shanghai—and hurried off.

In Shanghai, Green's greatest contribution at the press conference was providing Qiao Guanhua's name*—a name that Kissinger could never pronounce or even remember.[92] Kissinger, on the other hand, was able to plant a question with a *Los Angeles Times* correspondent, David Kraslow, who asked why there was no reference in the communiqué to the continuing American security commitment to Taiwan.[93] Kissinger, not surprisingly, deftly handled the question, saying, "The particular issue which Mr. Kraslow raised is, of course, an extraordinarily difficult one to discuss on the territory of a country with which we do not maintain formal diplomatic relations and for which this particular issue is a matter of profound principle." There was no question, he said, that the security commitment to Taiwan remained in force, and the proof of it was that the president had only recently reaffirmed it in his annual Foreign Policy Report to Congress. "Nothing has changed on that position,"[94] he concluded.

The bomb was defused.

T HE JOINT COMMUNIQUÉ between the People's Republic of China and the United States of America issued in Shanghai on February 27, 1972, became known as the Shanghai Communiqué, the basic instrument on which an entirely new relationship was built. Its four "principles of international relations" stated that:

- Progress toward the normalization of relations between China and the United States is in the interest of all countries.

*Pronounced: Chow Gwaan-hwaah.

- Both wish to reduce the danger of international military conflict.

- Neither should seek hegemony in the Asia-Pacific region and each is opposed to effort by any other country or group of countries to establish hegemony.

- Neither is prepared to negotiate on behalf of any third party or to enter into agreements or understandings with the other directed at other states.

On Taiwan, it was clear that the United States had come closer to recognizing Beijing's position than ever before.

The Chinese side reaffirmed its position: The Taiwan question is the crucial question obstructing the normalization of relations between China and the United States; the Government of the People's Republic of China is the sole legal government of China; Taiwan is a province of China which has long been returned to the motherland; the liberation of Taiwan is China's internal affair in which no other country has the right to interfere; all U.S. forces and military installations must be withdrawn from Taiwan. The Chinese government firmly opposes any activities which aim at the creation of "one China, one Taiwan," "one China, two governments," "two Chinas," and "independent Taiwan," or advocate that "the status of Taiwan remains to be determined."

The U.S. side declared:

The U.S. acknowledges that all Chinese on either side of the Taiwan Strait maintain there is but one China and that Taiwan is a part of China. The U.S. Government does not challenge that position. It reaffirms its interest in a peaceful settlement of the Taiwan question by the Chinese themselves. With this prospect in mind, it affirms the ultimate objective of the withdrawal of all U.S. forces and military installations from Taiwan. In the meantime, it will progressively reduce its forces and military installations on Taiwan as the tension in the area diminishes.

When Buchanan saw the text of the communiqué, he was stunned and angry. It seemed to him that the United States had formally recognized the People's Republic as the legitimate government of all China and pulled the rug out from under Chiang Kai-shek's Republic of China on Taiwan.[95] Support for Taiwan was a touchstone of the Republicans' conservative wing.

When the presidential party reached Shanghai, Buchanan refused to attend Kissinger's press conference. That night, as the staff assembled for the final banquet hosted by Zhou to celebrate the signing of the joint communiqué, Buchanan was closeted with Rose Woods; they were reinforcing each other's anger over the "sellout."

It was Dwight Chapin who first realized that Woods had not come down from her room to leave for the banquet. He used a house phone to call upstairs, and Buchanan answered. Chapin told them to hurry. A few minutes later, the president came down and got into his car, but Woods and Buchanan still had not appeared. Finally, a door burst open in the lobby and Woods pushed her way through.

"Don't rush me," she said as she swept past Chapin. "As long as we have sold out to these bastards, it doesn't make any difference."[96]

At the banquet, Zhou went from table to table toasting the president's staff, and when he came to Woods, those who knew how upset she was just held their breath. Zhou said, "gan bei!" (bottoms up!); she glared at him and knocked back the fiery mao-tai.

From the moment Nixon was airborne back to the United States, he began erecting firebreaks against the expected conservative backlash. The press summaries showed a mostly positive reaction, with the exception of *The Washington Post*, whose coverage suggested a sellout of Taiwan. Kissinger walked toward the tail of Air Force One to find Buchanan, who was hunkered darkly in a rear seat, drinking. Kissinger sat down next to him. "Show me what is wrong with this," he said, a copy of the communiqué in his hand.

Buchanan unloaded on him. It represented de facto recognition of the communist state. It was a betrayal of the Republic of China on Taiwan. Kissinger tried to address his objections, but Buchanan just kept stubbornly repeating them until Kissinger retreated. Later in the flight, Kissinger came back again, this time standing above Buchanan, trying to charm him with a little Kissinger levity. "Where were you and your right-wing friends when we needed you?" Kissinger asked, referring to an earlier foreign policy battle.

Buchanan rose up out of his chair, bringing his face to within inches of Kissinger's, and yelled, "Bullshit!"[97]

Kissinger walked away, and that was the last time they spoke during the trip home. During a refueling stop in Anchorage, Kissinger telephoned Haig and told him to get hold of Shen, the Taiwanese ambassador. Kissinger hoped that the Taiwanese media would not go off half-cocked. Haig called the envoy and passed on Kissinger's message as well as a pledge that Kissinger would ask the president to reiterate the U.S. commitment to the defense of Taiwan in case of an attack from the mainland.[98]

But Kissinger delivered a more profound message when he met with Shen on March 1. He told the Taiwanese envoy that it was obvious that Mao and Zhou would be dead within five years, possibly ushering in an era of chaos and upheaval on the mainland. Nixon had said as much in his note to Rogers. For this reason, Kissinger said, the Taipei government must be kept alive. He didn't think the Communists would try to invade the island before 1976, but Taiwan must remain viable.

What should the generalissimo do, Shen asked?

"Nothing," Kissinger replied. "Just sit tight."[99]

Shen then left Washington, returning to Taiwan for consultations. He found the aged generalissimo brooding in the presidential palace, pacing the floors in a traditional Chinese long gown. Chiang fixed his trusted aide with a look of authority and determination and said, "Henceforth, we must rely on ourselves more than ever before and we must work harder than ever before."[100]

Contrary to Kissinger's hopes, Taiwan denounced the Shanghai Communiqué, stating that any agreement with the Communists "is tantamount to inviting wolves into one's home."[101] William Buckley, the conservative columnist, also broke with Nixon, declaring his support for Representative John Ashbrook of Ohio, who was leading a quixotic right-wing attempt to block Nixon's reelection. Buckley appeared with Ashbrook in New Hampshire to declare, "I have lost interest in Mr. Nixon. I no longer have reason to suppose Mr. Nixon is an effective leader of this country in a troubled period. He has come back with a communiqué which in my judgment undermines the whole moral basis of the treaty we painfully stitched together" in 1955 "which kept the enemy at bay."[102]

It wasn't just Buckley. In the immediate aftermath of Nixon's return from Beijing, Washington itself was all a quarrel over what he had accomplished. But all of the bickering did not obscure the fact that Nixon's journey to China proved to be his finest hour as president. For all his ulterior motives— the nakedly political "big play," the hoped-for benefits in Vietnam—Nixon had gotten on a plane and flown to the heart of the enemy capital and, without any apology, had engaged Chairman Mao in a discussion that ended the isolation of the People's Republic and ended America's isolation from China. Nixon had confided in Zhou that, when he was serving in the Eisenhower administration, his views had been no different than those of John Foster Dulles. "But the world has changed since then," he said, "and the relationship between the People's Republic and the United States must change too."[103] And once the isolation was broken, neither America nor China showed any interest in going back. Nixon's journey, as complex as its motivations were, had cut through one of the great knots of international politics of the twentieth century, and many recognized that it would stand as an act of farsighted diplomacy—Nixon's diplomacy, in which Kissinger was the instrument, and not the other way around as Kissinger would later assert.

Nixon's opening brought the final acts of Mao's revolution onto the world stage at a time when that revolution had almost exhausted itself. Spent of its energy, its collapse was coming. The Chinese sensed it and anticipated it, and they hoped that the collapse would lead to a more constructive era. Zhou had said to Kissinger that the very size of China drove the nation inward and created a tendency toward "nationalistic sentiments and big-nation chauvinism." If China succumbed to this tendency, he said, "then one will cease to learn from others; one will seal oneself in and believe one is the best or will cease to learn from the strong points of others."[104]

The world had also changed with the rise in the Soviet Union of Leonid Brezhnev, who was establishing himself as first among equals in the troika of leaders that had pushed Nikita Khrushchev from power in 1964. Not an intellectual like Premier Alexei Kosygin, Brezhnev was rough-hewn, a product of the system and a bureaucratic brute who fought for the interests of the military-industrial sector that had supported his rise to power. His victory in the Kremlin ensured that the Soviet Union, instead of cutting its defense budget, as Khrushchev had sought, would expand the juggernaut of spending to support a military build-up across the board. And it was Brezhnev's policy in particular to finance a Soviet military buildup in the Far East—he called it a "gun on the table" to deter Mao—because the rise of China as a military power threatened the eastern frontier of the Soviet empire. Military expansion would fuel Soviet ambitions to rival the United States as a global military and political power, able to compete for influence on any continent as well as impose discipline within the socialist camp.

K ISSINGER HAD BEEN RIGHT—the successful trip to Beijing ensured that Nixon's first summit with the Soviet leader would also go well. The two leaders signed the first-ever agreement on controlling the growth of nuclear weapons, the Strategic Arms Limitations Treaty (SALT I), which set upper limits on the nuclear missiles of both sides. The Soviets obviously had felt the pressure of the China opening. Proof was found in one U.S. intelligence report that spring that captured Kosygin complaining to a Danish leader, "Is everyone ganging up on us?"[105]

But setting China aside, the Soviet Union had achieved major goals of its own by 1972, most prominently in central Europe, where Moscow had sought to extend the division of Germany into the indefinite future so that country would never again threaten the Soviet Union. The Quadripartite

Agreement on Berlin of 1971, along with new accords with West Germany and Poland, had achieved that objective. Then, with the completion of the SALT I agreement, the Soviets had firmly established the principle that America would not seek to dominate the postwar world with superior numbers of nuclear forces.

To China, however, these were false dividends. Détente was a trap, Mao believed. In Beijing's view, negotiating arms control accords with Moscow was foolhardy. The Soviet system was immutably expansionist, and negotiations with Moscow only dulled the sense of real danger that existed.[106] That danger took a new form when Moscow put forward the Agreement on the Prevention of Nuclear War, which called for the superpowers to renounce any attack on each other's territory and required them to collude against any third power that was deemed a menace to the bipolar world order. In Moscow's view, that third power was China.[107]

From the beginning, the agreement was a wolf in sheep's clothing, and, to Beijing, it would throw up a veil behind which the two superpowers could conspire against any third country that they believed threatened their interests. Under the artifice, Moscow could invent any pretext—claiming, for example, that its security was threatened by a particular political or military development in China—to launch an attack. Nixon and Kissinger also saw the trap, but Brezhnev was adamant. He made the agreement the centerpiece of the Soviet agenda. In this sense, if Nixon wanted to do business with Moscow, the price would be negotiating an accord along the lines of the one Brezhnev had tabled, the terms of which were quite similar to the very initiatives Washington had pressed in the Kennedy and Johnson years—with the aim of preventing the rise of China. Nixon had once been attracted to the concept, but no longer. Only now, Brezhnev was trying to take it a step further. The general secretary pointedly told Nixon that the Chinese leadership was out to sow discord in the world and to exploit the tensions between the Soviet Union and the United States.[108]

After the Moscow summit, Kissinger flew to Beijing, but there was little he could do to ease the suspicion that Washington was colluding with Moscow. Huang Hua already had read a formal note to Kissinger saying that the People's Republic considered it "impermissible"[109] for the United States and Soviet Union to enter into a nuclear agreement that so blatantly divided up the world between them. Kissinger pressed Zhou to make a visit to the United States to balance the imagery of America's relations with Moscow and Beijing, but Zhou demurred. How could he come to Washington and risk bumping into Chiang Kai-shek's ambassador?

But there was another reason for the sudden Chinese reticence.

Unknown to Kissinger, the Chinese leadership was distracted by its health crises. Kang Sheng, among the most radical and conspiratorial of the polit-buro members, had been diagnosed with bladder cancer.[110] Mao refused per-mission for Kang to undergo surgery; he did not believe in treating cancer. It was hopeless, he would say. Better to enjoy what time one had left and get some work done. But coming just six months after Marshal Chen Yi had died from colon cancer, Kang's diagnosis prompted a series of chest X rays and urine screenings for the leaders.

Mao came up clean. But the doctors found cancer cells in Zhou's urine and advised exploratory surgery. Again, however, Mao refused. Much later, when reports of Zhou's cancer began to circulate, Kissinger would hark back to a conversation he had had with Zhou during the Nixon visit. Zhou had asked, "Do you have a way of curing cancer?"[111] and then talked about his own mor-tality. He cited a poem by Chairman Mao called "Ode to a Plum Blossom," whose message was that those who begin great tasks may not be around to see them completed. The plum blossom, when it reaches full bloom, Zhou explained, is nearest the moment of its death.

A NOTHER KIND OF CANCER was growing on the Nixon presidency. Early in the morning on June 17, 1972, five operatives financed by and connected to the Nixon campaign organization were arrested for break-ing into the Democratic National Committee headquarters at the Watergate complex in Washington. There was a surreal quality to the dualism of the Nixon administration, where public grand strategy and high purpose coex-isted with a shadowy underworld of secret "plumbers" and political assassins. The afternoon before the burglary, Nixon delivered an extraordinary monologue to his cabinet on the realpolitik of his foreign policy. Bob Dole, the Republi-can national chairman, was there, soaking up Nixon's pearls for the expected struggle over the platform at the upcoming convention in San Diego.

"Too many people in the media," Nixon said, had praised the Russia and China trips "for the wrong reasons."[112]

"People want to believe the best about the world, and about other peo-ple," he continued. "They don't want to believe the truth that nations are motivated by self-interest, and not by love and understanding. This does not mean that understanding is not good—but this won't change the Mexican position on salinity of the Colorado River, and it changes the Communists even less."

The reason the Soviets and the Chinese had both separately moved closer to the United States to begin a dialogue, Nixon continued, "is not because we or they finally reached the conclusion that we had been mistaken. It was because at this juncture in history there were very fundamental shifts in the world balance of power that made it imperative that they look elsewhere, and useful to us to have better relations with them.

"Put yourself in the position of the Chinese leaders—with 800 million people. On one border they see the Russians, with more men there than against Western Europe. To the south, there is India. The Chinese have contempt for the Indians after the 1962 [border] war. But it gives them pause to see what India could do with the support of the Soviets against China's friend, Pakistan. To the northeast, they see Japan. . . . Japan is now the third, and will soon be the second economic power in the world, and they could well develop nuclear weapons soon on the industrial base that they have.[113]

"Mao and Zhou make no decisions on a personal basis," Nixon continued. "They do it only on cold calculation, which is true of most world leaders. So if you were the Chinese, you would welcome better relations with the United States—a nation that because of its interests might restrain some of China's neighbors." As for using the "China card," Nixon said, "Did we go to China to play against the Soviets, and vice versa? We have to say no. If we ever said yes, they'd have to react the other way."

For their part, "The Soviets are no more interested in peace as an end in itself than the fascists were," he said. "They prefer it. Their people don't want war. But as for the leaders—their goals, while not as violently expressed as the Chinese, have not changed. They still want communism to spread to other countries, by subversion perhaps. They play it down. No Soviet soldier has been lost since World War II. But because they have avoided a military confrontation with the United States, this does not mean that the Soviet leaders have abandoned their ultimate goal—the victory of communism in other areas of the world.

"These clowns who write for the media don't understand this,"[114] Nixon repeated, laying down the talking points for the campaign—straight from the American de Gaulle—and just hours before the Watergate break-in.

VIETNAM REMAINED THE backdrop for Nixon's reelection effort, and during the fall campaign, Kissinger peppered Beijing with secret cables seeking last-minute help to buttress his public assertion that peace was "at hand" in Vietnam.

Then, after Nixon's landslide victory over George McGovern, and in the period running up to the Vietnam peace accord signed in Paris on January 17, 1973, Nixon pounded North Vietnam with B-52 strikes while Kissinger pushed the new relationship with the Chinese to the brink. In New York, Kissinger told the Chinese deputy foreign minister, Qiao Guanhua, that if

Le Duc Tho and the North Vietnamese leaders were farsighted, they would take the package that was on the table, "otherwise, the United States will bomb."[115] Kissinger warned China again on January 3 that "a breakdown [in the peace negotiations] would weaken the U.S. ability to respond to the Soviet strategic rocket buildup," further exposing "China, as well as the United States, to Soviet pressures."[116]

Zhou could not have been more blunt in his response. After endless rebuffs, he sent his final word on Vietnam to Kissinger on January 6. "Mao takes satisfaction" in the development of U.S.-China relations, Zhou said through diplomatic channels. "But if the Vietnam War continues, progress is bound to be affected." It all boiled down to this, Zhou said. "Dr. Kissinger will be welcome to visit China after the Vietnam War is over."[117] Not before. So it was to everyone's great relief that Kissinger, on January 14, informed Beijing that Nixon would suspend all military actions against North Vietnam on January 15, and the peace accord would be signed in Paris two days later.

The victory brought the usual struggle over who was to get the credit, and Kissinger infuriated Nixon by claiming in an interview with the Italian journalist Oriana Fallaci that he, Kissinger, had "done it alone."[118] In retaliation, Nixon refused Kissinger permission to travel to China until after the inauguration,[119] and, had it not been for the signing of the Vietnam peace accord, Nixon may well have taken the opportunity to fire him. But the quickly spreading Watergate brushfire made that impossible. The reality was that Nixon needed Kissinger.

The settlement in Vietnam brought a conspicuous improvement in Kissinger's reception in Beijing in February 1973.[120] His plane was not shunted off to a far corner of the airfield. The Chinese pulled back the curtains of his limousine for the ride into the city so ordinary Chinese could readily see that Ji-xing-ge—the transliteration of Kissinger's name in Chinese—had arrived.

Kissinger found Beijing in full mobilization for war. Swarms of workers were ripping up the streets to build air-raid shelters and dig tunnels. PLA soldiers were everywhere, in the city and in the countryside. The military mobilization seemed to confirm the intelligence reports indicating a major redeployment of PLA divisions from the south of the country to the north in order to meet the threat on the Soviet border. Mao was preparing for a "people's war," breaking down army divisions into small groups to be deployed in villages on the North China plain and throughout Manchuria.[121] But in the aftermath of the Lin Biao coup attempt, the whole scheme also served as a great diversion for the army and the masses.

Despite the warmer reception, Mao had incited the Chinese leadership against America, at least rhetorically, so there was also a new tone of belligerency. Zhou accused Kissinger of trying to "get at the Soviets by standing on China's shoulders"[122]—in other words, of playing the China card to leverage arms control deals and other agreements out of Moscow. Zhou spoke the words, but they came from Mao. The Americans and Europeans, Zhou said, were seeking to avoid war by turning Moscow toward the East. Hadn't America and Britain done the same thing with Hitler, sending him East against Russia to spare Europe?

After Zhou bluntly stated China's misgivings about U.S. intentions, the chairman summoned Kissinger around midnight on February 17.

"In the West you always historically had a policy, for example, in both world wars you always began by pushing Germany to fight against Russia,"[123] Mao said, sparring with Kissinger. Mao was in good form, smoking a cigar and offering one to Kissinger and to his note taker, Lord.

"What I wanted to ask," Mao said, "is whether or not you are now pushing West Germany to make peace with Russia and then push Russia eastward. I suspect the whole of the West has such an idea, that is to push Russia eastward, mainly against us and also Japan." Mao employed a metaphor: "Europe and you would think that it would be a fine thing if the dirty water would flow toward China."

Kissinger protested: "If the Soviet Union overruns China, this would dislocate the security of all other countries and will lead to our own isolation."[124]

"How would that be?" Mao asked, incredulously. It was more obvious to him that America, bogged down for so long in Vietnam, would love to return the favor to the Soviet Union.

"And then you can let them get bogged down in China for half a year, or one, or two, or three, or four years," Mao mused. "And then you can poke your finger at the Soviet back. And your slogan will be for peace, that is, you must bring down Socialist Imperialism for the sake of peace." Then America might turn on China, Mao said.

"Mr. Chairman, it is really very important that we understand each other's motives. We will never knowingly cooperate in an attack on China," Kissinger responded.

"No, that's not so," Mao said. "Your aim in doing so would be to bring the Soviet Union down."[125]

As the weakest of the three parties, China, Mao feared, might be sacrificed in any alliance or coalition to defeat the Soviet Union. America might be the lesser of two evils from China's perspective, but that did not mean that an alliance with America was risk free, as Kissinger's actions during the India-Pakistan crisis had shown.

"I once had a discussion with a foreign friend," Mao said. "I said we should draw a horizontal line—the United States—Japan—Pakistan—Iran—Turkey and Europe." This axis was Mao's idea of an unspoken alliance to contain the Soviet Union.

"We have a very similar conception," said Kissinger, and he explained that Nixon had just dispatched Richard Helms, the former CIA director, to be ambassador to Iran with a special mission. "We sent Helms to Iran to take care of Turkey, Iran, Pakistan, and the Persian Gulf. We needed a reliable man in that spot who understands the more complex matters that are needed to be done."

Once Nixon had all these capabilities in place, Kissinger said, "we will act very decisively and without regard to public opinion. So if a real danger develops or hegemonial intentions become active, we will certainly resist them wherever they appear. And as the President said to the Chairman—in our own interests, not as a kindness to anyone else."[126]

"Those are honest words," Mao said.

"Yes, we both face the same danger," Kissinger replied. "We may have to use different methods some times, but for the same objectives."

"That would be good," said Mao. "So long as the objectives are the same, we would not harm you, nor would you harm us. And we can work together to commonly deal with the bastard!"[127] (Mao's term for the Soviets). "It is all right to quarrel and bicker, but fundamental cooperation is needed."

Kissinger agreed. "Even if we sometimes criticize each other, we will coordinate our actions with you, and we would never participate in a policy to isolate you."

It was the most profound conversation Mao had undertaken with a westerner in years. His decision to play the triangular game in opposing Moscow demonstrated his understanding that he, too, had to ride the tiger to protect China's fate from being determined by the superpowers. Mao and Kissinger knew that China was essentially defenseless against a massive assault by the Soviet Union. For Nixon and Kissinger, it was nothing short of stunning how suddenly the triangle had formed, how active it had become, and how all three powers now understood how dangerous it was *not* to play.

What Kissinger did not understand at the time was that Mao expected America to act on its own. China was weak, and therefore Mao wanted America to take the lead, to rally Europe, Japan, Turkey, and Iran against the Soviets. China would continue to be Mao's China, firing "empty cannons" against imperialists and revisionists alike.

D URING THE LONG, SECRET discussions of February 1973, Zhou Enlai accepted a State Department proposal that the two sides establish unofficial embassies in each other's capitals. They would call the missions "liaison
offices," staffed by diplomats who would have diplomatic immunity and
speak on behalf of their respective governments.

The opening of Chinese and American liaison offices in the spring of 1973
proved to be one of the most important milestones of U.S.-China relations
during this era. It was one thing to have Kissinger commuting as a kind of
global carpetbagger between Washington and Beijing, but it was quite another to set up a permanent mission staffed by diplomats and U.S. Marine
guards[128] on Chinese soil for the first time since 1950. With the establishment of these missions, the two countries crossed a threshold that seemed irreversible in all but the most dire circumstances. Also, the diplomatic
foundations being laid sent a clear message to Chiang Kai-shek on what the
future had in store for Taipei.

The unofficial embassies were instrumental in laying the groundwork for
restoring trade between China and the United States, facilitating the diplomatic machinery, and multiplying channels of communication. If China was
to get back on the road to modernization, its 850 million people would have
to abandon the dogma of self-reliance in order to acquire the American,
Japanese, and European technology that was the key to the country's development.

At the outset of the 1970s, few Chinese villages had electrical power.
China's automobile and truck industries were based on the technology of the
1930s. The country's rail network was less developed than the U.S. rail system had been at the time of the American Civil War.[129] There was no civilian
aircraft industry capable of building a passenger jet; when Nixon went to
China, the Ministry of Aviation took the first crucial step in inaugurating an
air transport sector by purchasing ten Boeing 707s from the Seattle aircraft
manufacturer.[130] Also in early 1973, Mao approved a State Planning Commission proposal to spend $4.3 billion in precious hard currency on complete
sets of industrial manufacturing equipment from the West.[131] But modernization remained a perilous proposition in China. The radicals, still out to
overthrow Zhou, condemned him for every retreat from the traditional policy of self-reliance.

With boundless patience, Zhou seemed never to tire of the struggle. His
cancer had by now been confirmed by additional tests, forcing Mao to cast
about for a suitable leader who could step into Zhou's shoes. Deng Xiaoping
had always been an option, but Mao mistrusted Deng's revolutionary commitment, believing him to be a closet "capitalist roader." Purged in 1967

along with so many other senior leaders and banished from the capital, Deng together with his family made the long train ride back to Beijing in March 1973. They came from Nanchang, the provincial capital of Jiangxi in south-central China, where Deng and his wife, Zhuo Lin, had lived in internal exile working in a tractor factory.[132]

Deng had the stature of Napoleon, about five feet tall, but that estimate, as one observer said, "is surely an exaggeration."[133] Still, as far as Mao was concerned, Deng had the heart of a lion and had proved it in debates with Khrushchev when the Sino-Soviet schism first erupted in the late 1950s. Deng had joined the Communist Party in the 1920s, like Mao and Zhou, but he was a decade younger and, therefore, had looked up to the top leaders as a Chinese does to an elder brother. Although he was of the founding generation of the revolution, Deng was always an apprentice to power—the adjutant in someone else's command.[134]

In Paris, where he had worked in the Chinese underground with Zhou, Deng had earned the nickname "Doctor of Mimeography," because—far from being the intellectual of the movement—he was an energetic staffer, reproducing manifestos and then enforcing them with great zeal. As an ideological foot soldier under Zhou and the others, Deng had shared their victories and defeats. He suffered on the Long March, surviving a bout of typhoid and riding a donkey when he was too weak to walk. As political commissar under Marshal Liu Bocheng, he commanded an army in the field, learning what it meant to kill and to face death in battle. The experience steeled him with a sense of what was possible in politics and war—and what was not.

Like Zhou, who had traveled to France as a young man, Deng had seen the world. In fact, his politics reflected his formative struggle as a young and persecuted foreign worker in France, sent there by his father to help bring science and technology back to China. His strongest bond was his fierce loyalty to the party, which he saw as the best hope for building a new China. Indeed, the party was Deng's family more than his wife and children, to whom he remained something of a mystery.

Born in Sichuan Province, Deng came from that stock of rural Chinese who speak seldom, play their cards close to the chest, and practice a relentless pragmatism. It was Deng who had infuriated Mao by popularizing the aphorism: "It doesn't matter if the cat is black or white, as long as it catches the mouse." Of course, to Mao, the color of the cat was everything—it was the difference between capitalism and socialism!

Deng's heresy cost him dearly when Mao lashed out during the Cultural Revolution and purged the party's "capitalist roaders." Mao accused Deng of treating him as if he were some kind of "dead ancestor" during the years Deng had served as the party's secretary general. Deng was labeled the second-worst capitalist roader in China, after Liu Shaoqi, Mao's putative heir until his downfall. In 1967, Deng was sacked from his position as secretary general. His whole family suffered, especially his eldest son, Deng Pufang, who jumped out of a fourth-floor window at Beijing University in a desperate attempt to evade his Red Guard torturers. The fall broke his back and left him a paraplegic.[135]

.   .   .

All James Roderick Lilley could think about when he heard that the United States was going to open a liaison office in Beijing was how he could position himself to become the first CIA station chief in the People's Republic of China. Among the old boys in the clandestine service, Lilley was distinguished by having been born in China, where his father marketed gasoline and lube oils for the Socony-Vacuum Oil Company, the precursor of the Mobil Corporation. Lilley spent his first seven years living among the Chinese in the seaside enclave of Qingdao, with its German architecture and excellent beer. The family left in 1935, but China had made a lifelong imprint.

Lilley's older brother, Frank, returned to China to serve as an army artillery officer under General Joseph Stilwell during World War II. Frank had been the family's big achiever to that time, but he fell into a depression after the war and took his own life in May 1946. Like Frank, Jim Lilley attended Exeter, and he then went on to major in Russian studies at Yale, where the faculty network nudged him toward a career in the newly formed CIA. Soon after the Korean War broke out, Lilley, with the agency, was back in Asia, along with one of his Yale schoolmates from the class of 1951, John T. Downey. They were stationed at bases in Japan and South Korea. Downey's operation worked with indigenous Chinese agents, the so-called third force the CIA hoped to build to overthrow the Communists. Lilley's base ran agents recruited on Taiwan from among Chiang Kai-shek's forces. During the Korean conflict, both bases sent agents behind enemy lines in Manchuria to report on the strength and movements of Mao's forces. The infiltrations used nighttime parachute drops, and agents were later extracted with small, twin-engine C-47 aircraft, each fitted with a nose scoop and rope sling contraption that jerked an agent off the ground without the plane's landing and then reeled him in through the rear cargo door.

It was on such a mission that Jack Downey and Richard Fecteau had been captured on November 29, 1952. They had received a distress call from one of their agents behind enemy lines. Quickly, they boarded a C-47 and flew to the prearranged pickup site, but a trap awaited them. When the C-47 dropped down out of the sky to the pickup zone, gunfire erupted. Dozens of Chinese soldiers shot out the cockpit, killing the pilot and copilot. Downey and Fecteau were captured and put in leg irons. Under interrogation, the officers told their captors most of what they knew about CIA operations in Manchuria. They were then tried and convicted for espionage. Fecteau drew a twenty-year sentence and Downey got life. The U.S. government officially claimed that the pair were army civilians whose plane had drifted off course. Secretary of State John Foster Dulles refused to admit they were CIA officers.

Lilley did not take the news of his friend's capture easily. In his own unit, no CIA officer was allowed to violate Chinese territory for an agent pickup. Such an operation was too risky. Still, Lilley admired Downey's and Fecteau's valor because, like them, he was an activist by nature. More soldier than intellectual, Lilley came of age in the operations side of the CIA, where clever opportunism and tactics were everything and where the goal was to conduct multilayered operations against the communist bloc. The analytic side of Lilley's nature would develop much later, but he always seemed more comfortable in the role of an operative, and through the 1950s and 1960s he saw duty all over Asia.

When Lilley was assigned to the Hong Kong station in 1969, he was able to apprentice under two of the CIA's star performers in the field, Bill Wells and Ted Shackley. Wells had mentored a generation of spies. He spoke Chinese and read Chinese history, and to Lilley it seemed that the vigor of the CIA's intellectual side was on display when Wells would have journalistic giants like Joe Alsop over for dinner and, afterward, over good brandy and Cuban cigars, engage in long, energetic debates about war and politics.

Vietnam so dominated the CIA's agenda that when Lilley mentioned to Shackley that it seemed possible there might be a war further north between China and Russia in 1969, Shackley had replied, "I wonder how that will affect Vietnam."

The Hong Kong station worked with the British to run agents into China and then share the take. And, on the technical side, it wasn't that difficult to intercept the primitive communications of the mainland. The Hong Kong and Taiwan stations had been able to easily track the unfolding civil conflict of the Cultural Revolution because Red Guards throughout China reported to their central organizations in provincial capitals or in Beijing using the country's extremely porous telephone system.

In Hong Kong itself, British intelligence occasionally penetrated the local branch of the New China News Agency, which served as Beijing's diplomatic representation in Hong Kong. When important internal speeches or edicts came down from Mao or Zhou, the British or the Americans often intercepted them and put them into their system so Washington and London could stay current on what Chinese leaders were telling the cadres who carried out day-to-day diplomacy abroad.

After a year in Hong Kong, Lilley returned to Washington in 1970; he was working in the China Operations Division at CIA headquarters in Langley, Virginia, when Nixon's big diplomatic breakthroughs occurred. The prospect of a liaison office assignment in China animated Lilley to go straight to William Colby, who was then the CIA's director general, and make the case that the agency had to have a person in Beijing and that that person had to be Jim Lilley. Colby sent Lilley to James R. Schlesinger, who had replaced Helms as CIA director. Schlesinger was interested in asserting CIA's bureaucratic interests, and with Lilley sitting in front of him, he told his secretary to get Kissinger on the line.

Schlesinger's face could have been chiseled for a Roman tribune, all forehead over powerful jaw, with a tassel of graying hair imperiously out of place. He almost never smiled and spoke with a measured baritone, exuding an aura of arrogance and excessive intellectualism. Beneath this Rushmore was a more complicated man, a bird-watcher with a sense of humor and mischief, but Schlesinger, pipe in hand, was seldom out of character squinting through his granite facade at a room full of bureaucrats.

"I've got a guy sitting in my office," said Schlesinger as the Germanic grumble of Kissinger's voice came over the speaker. "He was born in China, and I want him in Beijing."

Kissinger made it clear that he would make the decision, but there was no reason to antagonize Schlesinger, one of Nixon's favorite budget cutters and bureaucratic house cleaners.

Luckily for Lilley, the State Department's objection to his appointment—more bureaucratic than substantive—was probably the key to his getting the job, because Kissinger enjoyed trumping the bureaucracy—especially that of the State Department. Kissinger argued that he had gotten personal approval from Mao to place a CIA man in Beijing. What Mao had said during his meeting with Kissinger on February 17, 1973, was: "Let us not speak false words or engage in trickery. We don't steal your documents. You can deliberately leave them somewhere and try us out. Nor do we engage in eavesdropping and bugging. There is no use in those small tricks."[136] This was the basis for Kissinger's assertion that he had an "agreement with Mao" that the two sides would not spy on each other.* Kissinger pledged to the Chinese that no

---

*The agreement lasted until the Carter administration, when CIA director Stansfield Turner placed the first undercover CIA officers in China.

CIA officer would be allowed to enter China without prior notification to the Chinese.* Lilley was to be "declared" to the Chinese as the CIA station chief, an open approach the CIA had never taken in communist countries. This was a practice reserved for allies. The Chinese also were invited to send their own "station chief" to Washington. And they did.

Kissinger told Lilley that Nixon personally would have to interview him for the job and insisted that Lilley fly out to San Clemente. Shackley, who was then chief of the agency's Far East Division, insisted on accompanying Lilley. Kissinger refused, but Shackley went anyway. That was Shackley. When they got to San Clemente, it would become clear that Nixon was not personally involved in the matter. The whole charade was Kissinger's way of putting on airs. Instead of finding Nixon at the Western White House, Lilley found himself facing Kissinger and General Brent Scowcroft, Kissinger's deputy.

"You are going to China," Kissinger said, "but you have got to understand one thing: I don't want you screwing around in your CIA business. I don't want you recruiting any shitty little militia men. You are there as my representative and you will do what you are told."

Lilley just said, "Yes, sir." He was ecstatic to be going.

One of Kissinger's brightest aides on China, Richard Solomon, had confided to Lilley that Kissinger, deep down, believed that America had to deal with the Chinese now, because if they ever got strong, they would be impossible to deal with. This was the Nixon view, and Lilley came to agree with it.

When he got to Beijing, Lilley wasted no time in bending Kissinger's orders by scouting the city for "dead drops" and signal points that could be used when the station started running agents. Lilley set up the first limousine watches to monitor high-level meetings at the Great Hall and at Zhongnanhai. Eventually, sophisticated electronic equipment was brought in by diplomatic pouch and then assembled on the liaison office roof to monitor Chinese aircraft movements and intercept military and civilian communications. The liaison office would soon be able to predict when a Central Committee meeting had been called by all the flights coming in from the provinces.

David K. E. Bruce, the patrician elder of the American foreign service and first chief of the Beijing liaison office, encouraged Lilley to work the diplomatic circuit, because in those days, the Poles, the Romanians, the Pakistanis,

---

*Once, when a CIA technician was called to Beijing from Manila to install communications equipment at the liaison office, the State Department and liaison office officials neglected to inform the Chinese. The Chinese said nothing officially, but in the *People's Daily*, a small item announced that several American visitors had arrived in Beijing. Each of their names was transliterated into Chinese. The Chinese characters chosen for the CIA technician also carried a separate meaning: *He Who Deceives*. "They just wanted to let us know that they knew," said one American diplomat.

and the Tanzanians all had great lines into the Chinese leadership, and there was plenty of intelligence to be gathered through normal political contacts.

Despite his "agreement" with Mao, Kissinger was willing to approve a number of esoteric intelligence operations against the Chinese, most of them involving eavesdropping and bugging. Kissinger's apparent manner with the mainland Chinese reminded Lilley of Taipei station chief Ray Cline's approach to the Nationalists on Taiwan: you embrace them, you make all the right statements about building strong and genuine relations, and all the while you run espionage operations "right up their ass." These were national interests, after all.

Lilley got to China right after Downey, his old classmate, was finally released from prison under a secret agreement in which Nixon admitted what Eisenhower had refused to admit—that Downey and Fecteau were CIA officers on an espionage mission behind Chinese lines when they were captured. Zhou, in a private message to Kissinger, had insisted on honesty. Nixon's public admission of Downey and Fecteau's true identity, tucked inconspicuously into an answer to a reporter's question during a presidential news conference, had cleared the way in 1973. Zhou suggested that an illness in Downey's family would also help and, suddenly, Downey's mother was reported to have fallen ill. On March 13, Downey emerged from twenty-one years of captivity, gray and slightly balding, at the age of forty-two.

When Kissinger returned to Washington from Beijing in early 1973, Mao's rebuke—that Nixon was trying to stand on China's shoulders to make a superpower deal with Moscow—hung in the air. And Beijing's disenchantment could only get worse as Brezhnev was preparing to come to America that June to complete the Agreement on the Prevention of Nuclear War. There were no way to avoid entering some kind of agreement, Kissinger had explained to the Chinese. But Beijing denounced the whole idea as "claptrap" and "utterly unacceptable."[137]

Anxious to reassure the Chinese, Nixon sent a letter to Mao on March 16, 1973, with an extraordinary pledge. The letter, which has never been made public, stated that the territorial integrity of China was a "fundamental element"[138] of American foreign policy and that the "viability and independence of China" was a requirement for world peace. The language suggested an American commitment to come to China's defense militarily if it was attacked. And yet no word of this pledge was ever transmitted to Congress or distributed outside the White House.

Within a month of receiving the letter, the Chinese asked Kissinger to explain its "implication."

"The implication of this remark to Chairman Mao is for its own purpose and without any reciprocity on the part of the People's Republic," Kissinger said to Huang Hua during an April 1973 meeting in New York. "The United States would consider any threat to the integrity of the PRC as incompatible with its own interests and with the interests of world peace. This is as an American decision and without a request for reciprocity."[139]

Nixon's motivation for making this unilateral pledge was not clear until early May, when Kissinger arrived in Moscow. Nixon obviously hoped that the pledge would alleviate China's anger over the Agreement on the Prevention of Nuclear War. To the Chinese, this agreement was superpower "collusion." Although Nixon felt that Kissinger could water down the agreement so that it could never be used as a pretext to attack China, the very fact that such an agreement even existed threatened the Chinese.

Kissinger arrived in Moscow ready to whittle away at the agreement's language, but he did not stay long in the Russian capital. It was early spring, and the Soviet leader whisked Kissinger away to the politburo's exclusive hunting preserve at Zavidovo, a cluster of Russian villas, or dachas, that served as a private playground for the Kremlin bosses. There was a huge indoor swimming pool, a lake for boating, and a sprawling hunting preserve. Brezhnev suited Kissinger up for a boar hunt so they could bond and negotiate over beer, cold cuts, and the slaughter of wild game.[140] The hunting blinds were deep in the forest, well up in the trees. Dusk fell quickly into evening and Brezhnev started talking about China. His brother had worked in China as an engineer during the 1950s, he said, and had come back with tales about the backwardness of the culture, about people urinating on train platforms. Brezhnev's loathing for the Chinese seemed to Kissinger to have racial origins.

"Cannibals," Brezhnev called them. "Flesh eaters!"[141]

"Something has to be done about China," Brezhnev continued. Now they have nuclear weapons, and in a decade or so they would have a substantial arsenal of nuclear weapons. The Soviet Union and the United States had a joint responsibility to prevent China from becoming a big nuclear power, he argued.[142]

"Do you consider China an ally?" Brezhnev asked Kissinger.

"No, we don't consider it an ally—we consider it a friend," Kissinger said.

"Well, you can have any friends you want, but you and we should be partners,"[143] the Soviet leader replied. Moscow could not stand by as China armed itself, he continued, and if China got military assistance from the United States, that would lead to war.[144] Brezhnev didn't have to remind Kissinger that there was a long record of American proposals to eliminate the Chinese nuclear threat or that it was hypocrisy for the United States to oppose the containment of China's growing power. Kissinger had very little room to maneuver. He had to acknowledge that the emergence of China could be a problem, but he temporized by talking about the importance of settling disputes peacefully.

The next day, Kissinger and Dobrynin made a quick round-trip flight from Zavidovo to Moscow so that Kissinger could use the embassy's secure communications line. During the flight, Dobrynin said that Brezhnev's remarks in the hunting blind had been "serious" and not "social."[145] The Soviet ambassador also wanted to know if there was a formal agreement between the United States and China. Kissinger replied that no agreements existed, but that in any event Washington would be guided by national interest.

On May 4 at Zavidovo, Brezhnev made his formal presentation for a tough version of the agreement based on what the Soviets characterized as a shared responsibility between the superpowers to enforce a stable world order and a shared view of China as a threat to that stability. "We should not pass over in silence," Brezhnev said, looking across the table at Kissinger and his aides, "the fact that there do exist in the world other nuclear powers as well, and there have to be such points in the agreement to show them it would be wrong to play with nuclear war."[146]

During the negotiating sessions, the Soviets proposed that the United States and the Soviet Union agree never to use nuclear weapons against each other's territory. That would leave Moscow free to use nuclear weapons elsewhere, while binding the United States not to retaliate against Soviet territory for a Soviet nuclear attack on China.

Brezhnev was not a gifted diplomat but he knew what he wanted out of the negotiations, and as a result he was prone to browbeating and crude humor. During a break in one negotiating session with Kissinger's team, Brezhnev followed Hal Sonnenfeldt into the men's room, and while Sonnenfeldt stood at the urinal, Brezhnev grabbed his briefcase stuffed with top secret documents and ran out, setting off a frantic chase by the startled aide and American security officers to retrieve it.[147]

Back at the negotiating table, Kissinger continued to whittle at the text of the agreement in an attempt to neuter any content that could be used against China or other countries. Point by point, he deconstructed the collusionary elements, reading at times instructions from Nixon that sent Brezhnev into furious bouts of anger. But although American resistance succeeded in diluting the dangerous elements of the accord, Beijing remained unhappy.

Kissinger was not sure that he had done an adequate job at Zavidovo. He sent word to the Chinese that Nixon was prepared to make a "joint declaration" with China, publicly or privately, saying that neither side would sign agreements affecting the interests of the other without prior consultation.[148] But the Chinese were not going to let Nixon have it both ways. Hadn't Kissinger just completed negotiating the draft of an agreement with Moscow that affected China's interests?

At the White House, Nixon and Kissinger convinced themselves that Brezhnev's ultimate aim was to create the circumstances in which he could legally bring military force to bear against China, and so they fretted about the relentless Soviet buildup on the Chinese border. Soviet nuclear missile batteries had been moved to within a few miles of the border.

"We must look at our contingency planning[149] for the event of Soviet military action against China,"[150] Kissinger told Nixon. The question of what China would do in the event of a Soviet attack remained a mystery. Mao always said that the Chinese army was ready to revert to "guerrilla war and protracted war." But Kissinger had challenged Mao's logic. "But if they use bombs and do not send armies?"

Mao never had a good answer. "What should we do?" the chairman had asked. "Perhaps you can organize a committee to study the problem."[151]

WITH POMP AND CEREMONY, Leonid Brezhnev arrived in the United States in June 1973 for a visit that marked the culmination of his own rise to power. But during a long conversation with Nixon in San Clemente, the Soviet leader bluntly stated his suspicion that the United States and China were constructing a secret military agreement, perhaps even a mutual defense treaty.[152] It could have been espionage or just strong Soviet deduction, but Brezhnev seemed to have some inkling of the overtures Nixon had been making to Beijing. Perhaps a Soviet spy in Beijing had informed Moscow about the intelligence Kissinger was sharing regarding Soviet military deployments in the Far East.

Without commenting on the Soviet suspicions, Nixon protested that he did not share Brezhnev's concerns about the Chinese. It would be twenty years before China had a nuclear arsenal substantial enough to threaten the Soviet Union, he said. Brezhnev disagreed, and Nixon asked him for the Soviet estimate regarding China's nuclear weapons capabilities. Brezhnev held up both hands, extending all ten fingers. "In ten years, they will have weapons equal to what we have now," he said. "We will be further advanced by then, but we must bring home to them that this cannot go on. In 1963, during our Party Congress, I remember how Mao said: 'Let 400 million Chinese die [and] 300 million will be left.' Such is the psychology of this man."[153]

Brezhnev proposed that Moscow and Washington begin exchanging intelligence on China's nuclear program. Couldn't Nixon see through the Chinese strategy? Brezhnev asked. Mao wanted to be the one to sit on the mountaintop and watch the tigers fight. Nixon waved him off, but the Soviet leader would not be rebuffed. He said that if military arrangements were made between the United States and China, it would lead to the most serious consequences. Moscow would take drastic measures.[154] Brezhnev asked for an assurance that the United States would not enter into a military alliance with China, and Nixon gave a vaguely positive response, but he hedged about what he might do in the future.[155]

During the week that Brezhnev was in the United States, Nixon and Kissinger regularly summoned China's new envoy to Washington, Huang Zhen,* a senior military officer turned diplomat. They briefed him each day on what was being discussed behind closed doors with the Soviets. And when Nixon and Brezhnev flew to the Western White House in San Clemente, China's envoy flew behind them. Huang Zhen was taciturn and cautious by nature; his chief value as a diplomat was his prompt and scrupulous reportage back to Zhou. Huang would sit soldier-straight in his Mao suit, his brush cut showing the salt and pepper of age, placidly taking in Kissinger's long monologues. Then he would return to the Chinese mission and transcribe them into clipped and straightforward messages, as a field commander would report from the front.

In California, Kissinger told Huang Zhen that the president "considered our discussions with the Soviets quite ominous." It was crucial, Kissinger argued, to make a maximum effort "to deter attack on China." To that end, Kissinger said, "I have set up a very secret group of four or five of the best officers I can find to see what the U.S. could do if such an event occurred. This will never be publicly known. I tell it to you in the strictest confidence. The group is only being formed this week. I talked to the Chairman of the Joint Chiefs of Staff about it when he was here this week."[156]

The central question being considered by these secret contingency planners boiled down to this: If Brezhnev decided to risk an all-out attack on China, was there anything the United States could or should do? Obviously, if America entered the fray, it would risk an annihilating global war. If America stood by and did nothing, Moscow might turn China into a vassal state through military coercion. Then the United States would be facing an enemy with immense power and size. Both possibilities were remote, but the fact that they could be credibly postulated created the potential for leverage in the triangle.

With the nation diverted by a summer of Senate Watergate hearings,

*Pronounced: Hwaang Jen.

Kissinger pressed Defense secretary Melvin Laird to assign a small group of nuclear war planners to examine worst-case scenarios and determine what Nixon's options might be in a Sino-Soviet war. All of them turned out to be nightmarish, as shown by the following case study:[157]

> As a result of threats by the PRC to attack Vladivostok ... with nuclear weapons, the USSR makes a massive effort to eliminate the PRC nuclear capability. After attacking delivery sites [silos and caves] with nuclear weapons, Soviet airborne troops capture certain nuclear weapons development and production facilities, start ground link-up operation from Mongolia and Central Asia, and threaten an invasion of Manchuria.
>
> Partly due to their remoteness, the PRC forces in certain areas appear to be ready to collapse. At the same time the USSR offers to cease hostilities in return for certain concessions which would assure a strong Soviet position in Asia. At this time, the PRC requests U.S. assistance.[158]

The war planners considered an emergency airlift of American nuclear artillery shells and battlefield nuclear missiles to Chinese forces, but rejected it "because these options would either require too much training time for PRC forces or too many U.S. forces in the combat area." They also considered using intercontinental ballistic missiles (ICBMs) fired from the United States at attacking Soviet forces, but this "was rejected as too risky" because the missiles would have to overfly the Soviet Union to reach their targets. Detecting such missile launches, the Soviets might believe that their territory was under attack and fire their own ICBMs at the United States. Ultimately, the war planners recommended, the president would have to rely upon B-52s launched from Guam and American tactical bombers that could be ferried into China loaded with nuclear weapons. From Chinese airfields, the U.S. bombers could then launch nuclear attacks on Soviet forces.[159]

These nuclear contingency plans were among the most closely guarded of the Cold War, but they raised the immediate question for Nixon and Kissinger of whether or how to broach them to Beijing. It was clear that China would never put itself under the American nuclear umbrella, just as it was clear that America could never offer China such protection without provoking war with the Soviet Union. Still, as Brezhnev pressed Washington for a free hand against China, as the war in Southeast Asia dragged on even without direct American participation, and as Watergate began to hobble the administration, Nixon and Kissinger searched for the means to ingratiate themselves to the Chinese leadership.

One way was to help Mao realize his goals for military modernization. In the summer of 1973, Kissinger revealed to the Chinese that the Nixon administration had privately communicated to the British and French that the United States would not oppose the sale modern of jet engine manufacturing technology and nuclear reactor technology to Beijing.* "Under existing regulations we have to oppose this," Kissinger told Huang Zhen, because China, like the Soviet Union, was not eligible to buy certain high-tech systems, including those that could be converted to military use. "But we have worked out a procedure with the British," Kissinger assured the envoy, "where they will go ahead anyway."[160] The French would follow.

Yet China remained mistrustful. After Brezhnev left the United States on June 14 with his superpower agreement signed and sealed, Beijing delivered a formal note to the White House accusing the United States of complicity in a Soviet propaganda campaign. Kissinger was helping Moscow to project a "posture of peace" and to "arouse a false sense of security in the world, which would lead Europe to feebleness and demoralization instead of strength." The Chinese acknowledged that it was "Kissinger's firm belief that this movement will serve to gain time and that the Soviet Union can be enmeshed by peace and commitments. But we believe that this precisely meets Soviet needs, making it easier for the Soviet Union to mask its expansionism, attack soft spots and take them one by one."[161]

That summer, Zhou told David Bruce that China believed the United States would side with Moscow if a war broke out.[162] "That is absurd," Kissinger protested to Huang Zhen. But it was Mao's view, and Mao's view was all-controlling.

Thus, the assault on the Nixon-Kissinger policy of détente with the Russians, already gathering momentum in the United States, was mirrored in Beijing. Within the administration, Schlesinger, now installed by Nixon as secretary of defense, questioned whether tying up Moscow with the Lilliputian threads of arms control agreements would really do anything to improve American security. This was also Mao's argument.

Kissinger's focus on the threat of war and the danger to China could not be separated from the siege mentality at the White House. Nixon would call Kissinger in a rage about the demands being made by the Senate Watergate Committee. He had already had been forced to sacrifice Haldeman and John Ehrlichman, his top White House aides.

"I mean I cut off two arms," Nixon told Kissinger on July 12. "Who the

---

*American technology for nuclear reactor and jet engine production had been licensed to Britain and France by Westinghouse, General Electric, and other industry giants, and under the licensing agreements such technology could not be reexported to third countries without U.S. government approval. Further regulations prohibited the reexport of such technology to communist countries.

hell else would have done such a thing—who ever has done that before? I cut off two arms and they went after the body."[163]

Kissinger was always a sympathetic ear.

"When you consider the meritorious things you have done for the country," Kissinger commiserated, "the treasonable actions that these people have condoned . . . "

"They are treason," Nixon replied, admonishing Kissinger to "keep fighting."

M EANWHILE, the Chinese leadership convened its Tenth Party Congress, and, over four days in August 1973, Mao crafted a finely balanced slate of radicals and moderates to sit on the Central Committee and the politburo. Neither Mao's wife, Jiang Qing, nor the poisonous propagandist, Yao Wenyuan, got seats on the inner Standing Committee of the politburo. With the radicals in the wings, Deng Xiaoping returned to full-time work as vice premier, a sign that the moderates were still holding sway, if barely.

As the Party Congress met, Kissinger pressed for a return trip to Beijing, and it seemed certain that he was planning to seek a more overt military relationship with Beijing despite Brezhnev's warnings earlier that summer. He first pressed for an August meeting* and was dumfounded—even indignant—when the Chinese refused to allow him to come. Kissinger blamed everything on Congress and the bombing halt in Cambodia forced by the Democratic majority in the Senate. In a series of diplomatic messages, he pressed Zhou for a meeting in October.

"In view of the great danger which [Kissinger] foresees, it is increasingly important for the United States and the People's Republic of China to synchronize their policies,"[164] one message to Zhou said. Still, the Chinese ignored him.

Kissinger was sworn in as secretary of state on September 22, 1973. Rogers had finally surrendered the job, returning to a wealthy law practice.

---

*Kissinger's concern about his personal image was evident on July 11, when he sent General Scowcroft to see Han Xu, the number two Chinese official in Washington, to admonish him that Kissinger, as the "sole architect" of normalization with China, could not afford to be embarrassed over the Cambodian issue, demanding that the Chinese tell Kissinger in advance what he could expect to bring back from Beijing on Cambodia before he would agree to go. The Chinese canceled his trip. Kissinger later acknowledged his error, saying, "Insolence is the defense of the weak."

A NEW CIA National Intelligence Estimate on the Soviet Union challenged the underpinning for détente by arguing that Moscow was trying to garner all of the economic and political advantages of dialogue while simultaneously moving ahead at full speed with a buildup of its strategic nuclear forces and a modernization of its conventional forces. The CIA document, which reflected the intellectual legacy of Schlesinger, portrayed a much more aggressive Soviet leadership seeking to take advantage of American retrenchment in order to make additional gains wherever it could.[165]

Meanwhile, Nixon was in trouble. The Senate Watergate Hearings had gone on for 325 hours on television, 20 percent of which was John Dean's testimony implicating Nixon in a cover-up. The White House's secret taping system was exposed. And in late October, Nixon fired the Watergate special prosecutor, Archibald Cox, causing the mutiny and resignation of Attorney General Elliot L. Richardson, who had himself refused Nixon's order to fire Cox.

In early October, Brezhnev took advantage of Nixon's chaotic domestic circumstances and activated seven divisions of Soviet airborne troops, preparing to insert them as a "peacekeeping" force between the Egyptian and Israeli armies then engaged in the Yom Kippur War. The Soviets bluntly told the White House that they preferred to act jointly with the United States but would act unilaterally if Nixon did not join them. With the support of Schlesinger, Admiral Thomas Moorer, and Kissinger, Nixon ordered an alert of U.S. nuclear and conventional forces worldwide, an action that the Soviets immediately detected. They promptly canceled their airlift. The incident proved that the Agreement on the Prevention of Nuclear War was entirely ineffective as an instrument requiring the superpowers to consult in a crisis. The Chinese had been right. The Soviets would not be bound by a piece of paper. Brezhnev had been prepared to act unilaterally, and it was only the threat of nuclear confrontation with the United States that backed him down.

Kissinger had convinced himself that the Chinese were so alarmed about the Soviet threat that they would gladly defer the issue of Taiwan until the very end of Nixon's second term. But as the Watergate investigation deepened, the Chinese began to wonder whether Nixon would survive. They also could see that Taiwan's friends in Congress and the Pentagon were making plans to upgrade the island's armed forces, indicating that as long as U.S.-China relations remained in limbo, the pro-Taiwan lobby would continue to maneuver to undermine the China opening.

In early October, Qiao Guanhua told Kissinger that the Chinese leadership was not content to let normalization sit on the back burner. "We wish normalization could be accomplished faster,"[166] he said. But Nixon was in no position to act. Breaking with Taiwan, withdrawing troops, tearing up the Mutual Defense Treaty, and establishing relations with Beijing—none of this was a "big play" to Nixon. It was a huge risk.

When Nixon sent Kissinger to Beijing in November, the administration was in political free fall. The Chinese relationship was poised to move forward, but Nixon no longer had the political capital to take it further. Of all people, Mao seemed to understand this best.

Kissinger arrived in the Chinese capital with a whole set of new inducements that would have led to spectacular headlines in the United States if Mao had accepted them. The first proposal was for the United States and China to establish diplomatic relations *even though* Washington still maintained diplomatic and military ties to Taiwan. The Shanghai Communiqué could be rewritten to allow dual recognition, with the understanding that a one-China solution was still the goal. It was effectively a two-China policy, although Kissinger insisted that there would be some kind of understanding that it was not.

Kissinger sought to soften up Zhou with what became known as the "five assurances": (1) that the United States would conform strictly to the Shanghai Communiqué, which affirms that there is only one China; (2) that the United States would not support any independence movement on Taiwan and would oppose a two-China policy; (3) that the United States would oppose any attempt by a third country to move into Taiwan as America pulled out; (4) that the United States would support any peaceful resolution of the Taiwan problem; and (5) that the United States would discourage any military moves from Taiwan against the mainland.[167]

Kissinger then pledged that the United States would remove all U-2 spy planes from Taiwan by the end of 1974; Nixon would also order the removal of all nuclear weapons from the island. And the United States would redeploy the two squadrons of U.S. Air Force F-4 Phantom jets stationed on Taiwan. "This will reduce our presence on Taiwan to communications and logistics,"[168] Kissinger reported to Zhou.*

"It is also our intention, which we have mentioned to you and which the President reconfirmed to you, to complete the full normalization of the relations between China and the United States during this term of office, before the middle of 1976," he added.

It was only after this long prelude of concessions that Kissinger slipped in the reference to his two-China plan. "If at any point the Chinese thought the

---

*Kissinger neglected to specifically inform Zhou in this conversation that among the "communications and logistics" forces remaining were 900 employees of the National Security Agency, whose mission was to target communications and military signals on the mainland.

formulation of the Shanghai Communiqué, or an adaptation, would provide some way to have diplomatic relations," he said, the United States would be prepared to "intensify the relationship."

After their meeting, Zhou and his aides reported to Mao.

Nancy Tang, the interpreter, guessed at Kissinger's meaning: He was talking about establishing relations with the People's Republic of China while refusing to break relations with the Republic of China on Taiwan. With Nixon's presidency in jeopardy, Mao could only regard such a plan with suspicion. If China took such a step, what if the next president also was unwilling to break relations with Taiwan? And the next?

On the second day, Kissinger and Zhou were no more than ten minutes into their session when Zhou mentioned that he had reported the previous day's conversation to Chairman Mao and that "there was one point that I did not explain very much because I did not entirely understand. Yesterday you mentioned that you would like to find some wording similar to the Shanghai Communiqué or slightly altered that would be able to promote the development of our relations."

"My comment," Kissinger said, "was in reference to the establishment of formal diplomatic relations." Kissinger continued that if the United States were to keep its pledge and follow the "Japan formula" of breaking relations with Taiwan and recognizing Beijing as the sole government of China, the process would surely take until 1976. "However, if we could find a formula which is more flexible, as long as we understand that we will end up there, we are prepared to establish diplomatic relations sooner."[169]

Kissinger's indirection was puzzling to Zhou.

"Yesterday you mentioned that you also reaffirmed that you would not support the idea of two Chinas," Zhou said. "Under this condition, what kind of flexible formula have you in mind? Perhaps you have worked out a good idea."

"No, I have not actually yet worked out a good idea," Kissinger replied. "I have in mind something like the Shanghai Communiqué which would make clear that the establishment of diplomatic relations does not mean giving up the principle of one China."

Zhou was clearly astounded at Kissinger's lack of forthrightness, since he clearly *was* proposing a two-China policy, the very thing China had rejected in the UN debate in 1971, the very thing China had rejected during the Shanghai Communiqué negotiations.

Zhou, looking at Nancy Tang, said, "She had made a good guess of what you meant. When we were with the Chairman, I dared not explain the statement, but she dared to make an explanation of the statement."[170]

Kissinger finally spoke plainly, only after it was clear that his proposal had landed with such shocking impact.

"As I understand it, Mr. Prime Minister, your problem in having diplomatic relations while we have relations with Taiwan is that it might give rise to a two-China policy which we have agreed not to support. What we should search for is a formula for consideration that makes clear that that principle is not being abandoned; that there is only one China by either side."

"She has guessed very correctly what you think," Zhou said again, dwelling on the most superficial aspect of the profound realization that Kissinger, after all, was not committed to completing the normalization process, that Nixon did not feel strongly enough—or was not willing—to bite the bullet. Kissinger was grasping for a painless formula, one that Beijing might be induced to swallow so he could return to Washington with a triumph at the very time that Nixon so desperately needed one.

But there was another factor in Kissinger's calculations. Zhou and Mao were truly on their last legs, and China, after Mao, could face another descent into chaos, possibly giving the Nationalists on Taiwan another chance. Nixon and Kissinger already had delivered the message to Chiang Kai-shek to "sit tight." Nothing was spelled out, but the implication was clear: America was keeping open its options. Of course, the China opening was part of the Nixon-Kissinger legacy. Indeed, it was the most positive achievement of an administration that was now under siege for alleged high crimes. Both hoped that it would succeed and, for that reason, both hoped that Mao and Zhou would compromise their principles enough to establish formal, diplomatic relations with the United States without forcing Washington to break with Taiwan. Neither Nixon nor Kissinger was anxious, or even willing, to confront the politics of Taiwan.

Nixon and Kissinger understood that America's interests were not wedded to Mao if his legacy was overthrown. Would Washington want to back a post-Mao regime headed by his wife and the Gang of Four? Who would control China's nuclear weapons? And how would Washington hold off Moscow if China, with nuclear weapons, fell apart into factions of warring radicals? There might have to be joint action by the superpowers. In any case, a thousand permutations could come to pass that might improve the generalissimo's position.

Zhou asked if they could take a fifteen-minute break. During this intermission, one of Kissinger's aides walked into a bathroom and found two orderlies injecting Zhou with a syringe.[171] This scene only reinforced the overall image of decline.

After the break, the Chinese broached another unpleasant discovery. "We

hear you intend to assist Taiwan in building an airplane assembly factory,"
Zhou said, "and we would like to know what form it would take—rented,
leased, a gift, sold on credit . . . "

"You asked me that . . ." Kissinger started to reply.

"Of course," Zhou interrupted, "there is no question the material would
come from you, the United States."

"You asked me that the last time," Kissinger replied. "I may say now, Mr.
Prime Minister, it is for an airplane of short range. It cannot reach the mainland. It is a defensive airplane, and a means of avoiding our having to sell
longer range airplanes to Taiwan."

When Zhou returned to the subject the next day, he corrected Kissinger's
assertion that the plane was defensive and could not reach the mainland.
Actually, Zhou said, the plane had a fighting radius of 108 miles, and with
refueling and bomb racks, it could carry out bombing missions on the mainland.*

Kissinger had to admit that the Nixon administration had approved the
signing of a contract between the Northrop Corporation and Taiwan's Defense Ministry to build an assembly line for production of 100 F-5E fighters
on Taiwan over a five-year period.

Zhou then asked Kissinger if the United States would forgo the fighter
production agreement. "It would be good if it could be delayed . . . for another five years,"[172] he said.

Instead of responding to Zhou's request, Kissinger resorted to assurances
that he could never hope to enforce. "We have no plans on this project beyond
1978," he said. "You have our assurance they will not be allowed to attack the
mainland. . . . If they do, they will lose American support completely."

Zhou stated the obvious. "If they ever try to do that, they will do it unilaterally."

On the night of Tuesday, November 13, Kissinger and Zhou banqueted at
the Great Hall until late in the evening and then, with Marshal Ye Jianying,
repaired to a small conference room where Kissinger laid down proposals for
a secret military alliance with China, the very thing Brezhnev had warned
against. First, he spelled out what America would be prepared to do in the
event of a war with the Soviet Union.

"If the war should be prolonged," Kissinger said, "we could be helpful by
supplying equipment and other services."[173] But the more immediate proposal was to help China improve its "warning time" in advance of a Soviet attack.

---

*The next day, Kissinger countered by saying that the plane, the Northrop F-5E, could not carry
an external fuel tank and a full bomb load at the same time. They left the matter there.

To help in this manner, Washington could utilize "a very good system of satellites which gives us early warning. The problem is to get that information to you rapidly. We would be prepared to establish a hot line between our satellites and Beijing by which we could transmit information to you in a matter of minutes."[174]

Kissinger said that in order to disguise the early warning system, China and the United States would announce that they had only established a hot line for telephone communications, just as Washington had with Moscow and Japan. "Yours would be of a special nature but that would not be generally known. This would enable you to move your bombers and, if possible, you could move your missiles if you knew that an attack was coming. We could also give you the technology for certain kinds of radars but you would have to build them yourselves," he added.

Zhou came out of the meeting after midnight looking visibly agitated. His longtime aide and friend, Qiao Guanhua, asked him if it had been an important meeting.

"Yes," he replied. "I must speak with the Chairman."

But Zhou did not have direct access to Mao. In order to see the chairman, he had to go through the "liaison" staff of nurses, bodyguards, and various female attendants. Zhou could not always get through when decisions had to be made. With half of the politburo members from the radical faction, each decision Zhou proposed was placed under a magnifying glass.

Zhou's effort to see Mao that night failed; he later told colleagues that the "liaison women" would not let him enter.[175] Without having had a chance to consult with Mao, Zhou met again the next morning with Kissinger and confided that China had also made a careful study of its vulnerability to Soviet attack. He had hinted at this study the previous February when he had told Kissinger, "China must be prepared to resist a Soviet attack for several years, both for its own self-confidence and to hold out long enough to elicit support from the rest of the world." Now Zhou returned to that theme. Because Soviet forces were poised to strike swiftly and massively across the border, "We must envisage that there will be a period when we will have to be fighting alone and that will be the basic military concept," he told Kissinger. He further implied that he supported Kissinger's plan for America to provide assistance.

Zhou continued: "We are not going to go into detail now, but we have put forward such a proposition. And under those circumstances, if as you envisaged it would be possible for you to cooperate with warnings, that would be intelligence of great assistance. And, of course, there are also communications networks. But this must be done in a manner so that no one feels we are allies."[176]

When Mao got a full accounting of what had transpired in the meetings with Kissinger, he called a politburo meeting and criticized Zhou for daring, without first consulting Mao, to touch on matters that could be construed as an alliance against the Soviet Union.[177] Zhou protested that he had tried to reach Mao, but the "liaison women" disputed his testimony.

A number of senior Chinese near the inner circle felt that Mao's indictment of Zhou in front of the politburo in late 1973 was the beginning of the end for the premier. And his political decline was in proportion to his physical decline. He would carry on as premier, but Mao had turned on him in a personal way, even endorsing the campaign of the radicals to "Criticize Lin Biao, Criticize Confucius." As in every Chinese campaign, there was a code, and Confucius was Zhou.

Mao's frustration with Kissinger's attempts to bend the relationship to Nixon's political advantage hardened into disappointment and suspicion. Before Kissinger left the Chinese capital, Mao also decided it was time to lay down the law on Taiwan.

On the evening of November 12, with Kissinger again seated in the chairman's private residence, Mao said that there was only one way on Taiwan. "So long as you sever the diplomatic relations with Taiwan, then it is possible for our two countries to solve the issue of diplomatic relations. That is to say like we did with Japan," he said. "As for the question of our relations with Taiwan, that is quite complex. I do not believe in a peaceful transition."[178]

Mao turned to Ji Pengfei, the chubby and ineffectual foreign minister, and asked, "Do you believe in it?"

Zhou said something in Chinese to Mao, but because Kissinger almost never brought a Chinese-language specialist to these meetings, he had no idea of the degree of tension. In any case, Mao's remark undermined everything Zhou had been saying to Kissinger for two years about the Chinese determination to recover Taiwan by peaceful means.

Mao turned back to Kissinger.

"They are a bunch of counterrevolutionaries," he said, referring to the Nationalists on Taiwan. "How could they cooperate with us? I say that we can do without Taiwan for the time being, and let it come after 100 years. Do not take matters of this world so rapidly. Why is there need to be in such great haste? It is only such an island with a population of a dozen or so million."

"They now have 16 million," Zhou gently corrected.

"As for your relations with us, I think they need not take 100 years," Mao said. "But that is to be decided by you. We will not rush you. If you feel the need, we can do it. If you feel it cannot be done now, then we can postpone it to a later date."

Mao characterized Watergate as just another "fart in the wind"[179] and said he hoped that Nixon would survive it.

Yet, for all of Mao's personal warmth, Kissinger keenly felt the narrow confines of the box that Mao had constructed around him. Mao's formulation was relentlessly simple: It called on the United States to trust that Beijing would handle the Taiwan problem well. Mao, after all, understood that the Seventh Fleet had enforced the peace in the Taiwan Strait since the 1950s and would continue to do so. Any strategy that Mao developed to entice Taiwan over the long haul to reunite with the mainland would have to take that into account. Perhaps that is why he gave himself so much time—100 years.

China's leaders believed that they could never give up the threat of force to preserve the union of China. Sovereignty demanded it. Lincoln had done the same, they liked to point out.

"From our point of view we want diplomatic relations with the People's Republic," Kissinger replied after Mao's commandment. "Our difficulty is that we cannot immediately sever relations with Taiwan, for various reasons, all of them having to do with our domestic situation. I told the Prime Minister that we hope that by 1976, during 1976, to complete the process, so the question is whether we can find some formula that enables us to have diplomatic relations, and the utility of it would be symbolic strengthening of our ties," even though "the Liaison Offices perform very usefully."

But Mao was not going to go down the two-China road.

"It can do to continue as now," Mao said, "because you still need Taiwan."[180]

Kissinger felt the taunt in Mao's words.

"It isn't a question of needing it; it is a question of practical possibilities."

Mao just laughed and said, "That's the same—we are in no hurry."

When Kissinger persisted, Mao cut him off again.

"We have established diplomatic relations with the Soviet Union and also with India, but our relations with them are not as good as our relations with you. So this issue is not an important one. The issue of the overall international situation is an important one."

This was Mao's most important point. Taiwan could wait a little longer, and there could be no intervening compromise, no half measures. But countering Soviet power had become a paramount concern.

"They have to deal with so many adversaries," Mao said in reference to the Soviets. "They bully the weak and are afraid of the tough."

Kissinger bragged that he was willing to be "brutal" in resisting the Soviets, even going to war if necessary.

"I also think it would be better not to go to war," Mao said. "I'm not in favor of that either, though I am well known as a war monger. If you and the Soviet Union fight a war, I would also think that would not be very good. If you are going to fight, it would be better to use conventional weapons, and leave nuclear weapons in the stockpile, and not touch them."[181]

Kissinger never truly understood what happened in November 1973, and he would never learn of the damage that had been done to Zhou as a result of their collaborative discussion of a secret military alliance, which Kissinger was anxious to construct but which Mao inherently mistrusted. Mao had shut Kissinger down.[182] Nevertheless, the secretary remained hopeful that the Chinese would pick up his offer for a hot line, for satellite links, for communication networks, and for war planning coordination, but the Chinese quietly demurred each time these proposals were mentioned.

The rejection caused Kissinger to lament the decline of Zhou's power, as mysterious as it was, for it was Zhou whom Kissinger had most admired, seeing in him the qualities of an oriental Metternich, whose worldview showed great intellectual subtlety and whose diplomacy showed the skill of a leader seeking to play off the adversaries arrayed against him. Yet Kissinger's sentimental view of Zhou caused him to misjudge Mao's enormous power over every decision made in Beijing.

After Kissinger left Beijing, Mao reviewed the record of Zhou's talks with him and pronounced Zhou guilty of not taking a firm enough stand on Taiwan. Zhou's line to Kissinger that China would seek to liberate Taiwan by peaceful means was wrong, Mao told him. "It can only be attacked."[183] Zhou's weaknesses in dealing with the Americans came dangerously close to "rightist capitulationism," Mao declared. At the end of the month, Zhou was called before another politburo meeting and criticized again, this time for a "rightist error" in dealing with the United States. The radicals, many of whom had been invited to the session even though they were not politburo members, were buoyed by the humbling of the premier.

In the face of all this, Kissinger reported to the White House that his trip to Beijing had been a "positive success on all planes."[184] Nowhere in his thirteen-page memo to the president did Kissinger mention the rebuke he had suffered from Mao for backsliding on the principle of one China. Indeed, when Zhou—under Mao's instructions—inserted a sentence in the joint statement at the end of Kissinger's visit that "the normalization of relations between China and the United States can be realized only on the basis of confirming the principle of one China," Kissinger characterized it to Nixon as a "breakthrough proposed by Zhou on Taiwan" instead of as what it was— a firebreak against any further attempts by Kissinger to dress up a two-China policy in a one-China frock.

Conspicuously, Kissinger never referred to his two-China feint, even though it was his habit to explain to Nixon exactly what he had said to the Chinese in carrying out his instructions. It seems plausible that Kissinger had gone beyond his instructions, for no candid report to the president could have failed to record Zhou's shock at Kissinger's proposal, a shock so profound that Zhou had not "dared" to guess at Kissinger's meaning when reporting to Mao.

The headlines written about the November 1973 Kissinger visit to China declared that he had scored a significant success. The "senior administration official" who briefed reporters traveling with Kissinger* said, shortly after Kissinger arrived in Tokyo on November 14, that there was now hope for "a definite movement to normalization."[185] In truth, of course, no such hope existed, and Kissinger's public statements only added to the Chinese sense that he and Nixon had resorted to duplicity, or that at least they were failing to live up to the promise of the Shanghai Communiqué.

Kissinger had promised Zhou that within "weeks" he would formulate a new proposal on how the United States and China could establish formal diplomatic relations under the one-China principle, but he never fulfilled that promise. Indeed, for nearly six months Kissinger virtually ignored China, refusing to reply to a number of memorandums from his staff suggesting ideas on how to go forward. It wasn't that he was too busy disengaging the Arab and Israeli armies in the Middle East. He seemed genuinely paralyzed by Mao's terms, by Watergate, and by his own reservations over whether it was politically possible for Nixon to break with Taiwan.

By the end of May 1974, three of Kissinger's top aides on China—Solomon, Lord, and Arthur Hummel Jr.—wrote to him saying, "Our China policy is drifting without a clear sense of how we will move toward normalization, or indeed what the shape of a future normalized relationship with the PRC will look like—particularly as it affects Taiwan."[186]

But Kissinger, paralyzed by a collapsing presidency and a hostile Congress, continued to ignore them.

The effect of Mao's disenchantment with the United States was soon apparent. China cut off low-level talks on solving claims for properties seized before 1949. At the same time, China's cooperation with the U.S. liaison office in Beijing suddenly sagged. Meetings were canceled. The off-duty rowdiness of the U.S. Marine guards assigned to the liaison office was increasingly criticized. American diplomats and their families, cramped in temporary

---

*This official was Kissinger; he had established the ground rule for the reporters who traveled on his plane that any remarks quoted or paraphrased be attributed to a "senior administration official" and not to Kissinger by name.

quarters at hotels month after month, were delayed in being assigned permanent apartments. Meanwhile, the Chinese Foreign Ministry recalled Huang Zhen from Washington in November, and there was no word on when he would return.

In February, Kissinger recommended that Nixon nominate a senior diplomat, Leonard Unger, to be the new ambassador to the Republic of China on Taiwan. The appointment was made, and it caught Beijing completely by surprise, being read as an ominous sign of the flagging American commitment to normalization. If Kissinger had been thinking about how to move forward on normalization, he might have recommended that Nixon not fill the ambassadorial post in Taipei. Unger's appointment followed the State Department's decision, approved by Kissinger, to go ahead with plans to expand Taiwan's representation in America to twelve consulates in addition to the embassy in Washington. And this was followed by a decision to begin the construction of a new U.S. embassy building in Taipei as well as a new ambassador's residence.

Beijing's suspicions deepened.

Such was the state of the virtually suspended relations between the United States and China in April 1974 when Deng Xiaoping came to America for the first time. As vice premier and a member of the politburo, Deng was the highest-ranking mainland Chinese official to visit the United States since 1949. Yet very little was known about him beyond general observations that he had been a "tough, energetic political administrator"[187] in the 1950s and 1960s.

It was also known that Deng was "hostile to the Russians"[188] and had proved so when Mao had sent him to Moscow in the early 1960s to slug it out with Khrushchev over ideology, technology, and socialist alignment.

At Kissinger's invitation, Deng and his entourage arrived at the Waldorf Astoria Hotel in New York on April 14 at eight o'clock sharp for dinner. They rode the elevator to Kissinger's suite on the thirty-fifth floor, and, during three hours of conversation, Kissinger sought to charm Deng while evading the question of Taiwan. Late in the evening, a quizzical look came across Deng's face as he asked, "What is to be done on the Taiwan question?"

Kissinger had to admit that he had done nothing. "We have not worked out all our thinking yet, but we are willing to listen to any ideas you have."

Given the history of the issue, Kissinger's words must have sounded like an affront, and Qiao Guanhua took an apparent cue to speak up.

"The essential meaning is as Chairman Mao told you. The normalization of our relations can only be on the basis of the Japanese pattern. No other pattern is possible. So, I might also mention that, with regard to the present relations between our two countries, my view is that our relationship should go forward. It should not go backward."[189] Qiao Guanhua added that he had already said as much to Ambassador Bruce in Beijing.

"I am aware of what you said to him," Kissinger replied. "We keep this very much in mind."

Deng wanted the last word.

"With regard to this question, there are two points. The first point is that we hope we can solve this question relatively quickly. But, the second point is that we are not in a hurry on this question. These points have also been mentioned to you by Chairman Mao."[190] The exchange was perfectly revealing of the Chinese approach—which sought to envelope the Nixon administration with politeness on the Taiwan question, but which at the same time attempted to convey how urgently the Chinese wanted to move to fulfill the expectations of the Shanghai Communiqué. The Chinese approach also revealed how intensely Beijing felt that Nixon's willingness to bite the bullet on Taiwan was connected to the destiny of U.S.-China relations. But all during this period, Kissinger chose to ignore the Taiwan issue, instead constructing a view of a China that emphasized how Beijing was principally seeking global reassurance from America and how Beijing's fear of Soviet aggression would continue to relegate Taiwan to the status of a subordinate issue, where Kissinger preferred that it remain. He had, in fact, developed his own grave doubts as to whether normalization was really possible. It was as if China and the United States were playing on the same checkerboard but with entirely different rules.

O N THE SHORE OF THE Black Sea, in the Crimea, the green lawn and well-tended gardens of Brezhnev's villa made for a lush panorama that swept down from the main house to the line of the sea wall. There, in Khrushchev's time, a pool had been constructed, and, nearby, an outcropping of rock had been molded to create a grotto in which one could sit and contemplate the sea.

On June 30, 1974, Brezhnev and Nixon sat in the grotto alone, with a single Russian interpreter, for nearly an hour.[191] Kissinger was pacing near the pool, chewing his nails with unusual ferocity. He was livid that Brezhnev had maneuvered Nixon into a one-one-one meeting. Given that the Judiciary Committee of the House of Representatives was almost certain to approve the articles of impeachment, it was particularly mischievous. Kissinger could imagine the headline: "Nixon Tries to Make Secret Deal with Russians to Save Presidency."

The two superpowers were close to another breakthrough on arms control, this time with an agreement that would cast a broader net over the whole range of strategic weapons and their delivery systems; it would freeze the massive expansion of arsenals and technology that was under way. But because Nixon was so weakened politically, he had not been able to bring the bureaucracy together behind a single proposal. Schlesinger, the defense secretary, had broken with the administration over Moscow's advantage in land-based ICBMs. These monstrous missiles would soon would be enhanced with multiple warheads. Paul Nitze, a silver-haired defense intellectual who had sounded hawkish alarms over the growth of Soviet power to both Eisenhower and Johnson, resigned from Nixon's SALT negotiating team. Opposition to SALT was merging with Watergate-induced cynicism— the widespread belief that Nixon would cut a deal, any deal, with Brezhnev and then rush home and announce that, as a matter of national security, he was too important to be impeached.

As Kissinger paced, the wreckage of the Nixon administration plagued him. He knew that if they couldn't get a deal that would sell at home, it was best not to bring one back at all, and it didn't seem likely that Nixon would be able to sell even the most favorable of deals. Hal Sonnenfeldt, the European expert on the NSC staff who considered himself Kissinger's Kissinger, could see the fury and anxiety in his boss's face. He tried to loosen Kissinger up by reminding him of the Treaty of Bjorko. In 1904, Czar Nicholas and Kaiser Wilhelm met on a ship and engaged in a nostalgic conversation about their common grandfather. Nicky and Willy, as Sonnenfeldt liked to tell it, in their dotage, fell into each other's arms and signed a treaty of alliance that contravened the solemn commitments of their respective governments. No sooner did they return home to their respective capitals than their foreign ministers promptly canceled the treaty, and that was the end of that.

It was only after Nixon emerged from the grotto that Kissinger discovered what Brezhnev had been after—China, again. Brezhnev had tried to draw the weakened American president into a "treaty of friendship and cooperation" in which the two superpowers would have sworn to come to each other's aide in the event of an attack by a third country—in other words, he was pressing another superpower cabal against Beijing, though he was ever coy about specifying the target.

The implication of Brezhnev's presentation was that if Nixon was willing to go along with him on the treaty, they could complete SALT II, and that, Brezhnev assumed, might be sufficient to save the Nixon presidency.[192]

Afterward, Nixon explained the whole conversation to Kissinger as the two men walked along the sea wall. If Nixon was tempted, he did not show it. He was in pain from the phlebitis that had inflamed his legs, and he was enveloped in the gloom of the impeachment proceedings back in Washington.

Brezhnev had reached out a self-interested hand to help him, but for the price of giving Moscow the freedom to destroy Mao's power.

Because Nixon resisted, the SALT negotiations foundered on Soviet intransigence. Moscow was not going to complete the treaty without an answer on China. Nixon walked away from it. On the powerboat ride that afternoon, with Brezhnev at the helm and full of himself, Nixon sat alone in deep contemplation and pain.

FORD:

ESTRANGEMENT

"I SMILE BITTERLY ...."

Mao Zedong and Gerald Ford

O N AUGUST 9, 1974, just before noon in Washington and just before midnight in Beijing, a communications clerk in the White House Situation Room encoded and then dispatched a top secret cable to Ambassador David Bruce in the Chinese capital over a CIA circuit known as the Voyager channel.

The encrypted signal, bypassing the State Department altogether, bounced off a military satellite and brought a teletype machine to life in the radio shed on the roof of the U.S. liaison office in Beijing. A code clerk tore off the message and rushed it to the ambassador's quarters.

Bruce: Please deliver immediately the following personal message from President Ford to Chairman Mao. Dear Mr. Chairman: As one of my first acts as President of the United States, I wish to reaffirm the basic continuity of American foreign policy in general and our policy toward the PRC in particular. My Administration will pursue the same basic approach to the international situation that has been carried out under President Nixon. I share the perspectives on the basic forces at work in the world that he and Secretary Kissinger have set forth. The U.S. will maintain the strength and resolve needed to conduct a strong international role. We will take the necessary steps to preserve world stability. Our relationship with the PRC will remain a cardinal element of American foreign policy; we will continue to see a strong, independent China as being in our national interest. These views have solid, bi-partisan backing in the U.S.[1]

Needless to say, Kissinger would stay on.

Ford pledged to the Chinese that he would dispatch his secretary of state to Beijing before the end of the year, because "There will be no higher priority during my tenure as President than accelerating the normalization process that our two countries have embarked on after two decades of separation."

American foreign policy seemed reinvigorated. Nixon's departure had opened a new era of opportunity to move forward.

Ford's high-flown commitment to China's Communist Party leaders was emblematic of a White House suffused with a cautious new optimism that the nation was coming out of the grip of Nixon's long strangulation. In Ford, the nation saw a decent and pragmatic man, one whose centrism was bound up in the careful, consensus-seeking style that he had pursued as the Republican leader in the House of Representatives.

On the day Ford was sworn in, Kissinger summoned Huang Zhen, the Chinese envoy in Washington.

"President Ford will have the broadest base of political support in this country which has existed for a long time,"[2] Kissinger said. The message to the Chinese was that a window was opening for the completion of the process Nixon had begun. But under what terms? Kissinger did not say.

Huang was ushered into the Oval Office; he was greeted by Ford, who pledged to strengthen the relationship. Again, the rhetoric was lofty, but Huang made it clear that there was only one way to proceed.

"We will appreciate your carrying out the Shanghai Communiqué," he said cordially.

Within five days of that meeting, Kissinger placed on Ford's desk a thirteen-page plan of action. Ford should try to strike a deal while Mao and Zhou were still alive,[3] Kissinger advised.

"Mao's health is precarious and so is Zhou's, and it appears that our best course is to take advantage of their continued presence on the scene as leaders, and to discuss in concrete terms what we have in mind,"[4] Kissinger told Ford. But neither Kissinger nor Ford was willing to take the risk of breaking with Taiwan without an ironclad guarantee that Beijing would *not* use the withdrawal of American forces as a pretext to conquer the island militarily.

The State Department's lawyers concluded that the Mutual Defense Treaty with Taiwan would be legally defunct after Washington broke relations with Taipei, and thus the United States would no longer have a legal basis to intervene in a conflict over Taiwan. Kissinger told Ford that "Taiwan's security" would "probably have to rest chiefly on declarations."[5]

"The most important of such declarations will be that of the PRC, and it will be important for us to obtain for public use the strongest formulation possible of their intention to solve the Taiwan issue by peaceful means," he continued. "In return, we could say that our Defense Treaty with Taiwan is moot—without formally abrogating it—since we have every expectation that no armed attack will occur.

"The PRC might be induced to state," Kissinger continued, "that peaceful reunification is their goal providing Taiwan or outside forces do not make that goal impossible, thus deterring a declaration of independence." Finally, Kissinger concluded, "We could add to our statement that if our assumption that there will be no armed attacks on Taiwan prove incorrect, we will have to reconsider our stance on this issue."[6]

G ERALD FORD HAD SPENT A CAREER espousing the basic Republican po-
sition on China, which centered on open hostility toward Mao and Chinese communism, condemnation of the human rights abuses that were rampant under Mao's totalitarian regime, and support for Chiang Kai-shek's Free China. No one had been more surprised than Ford when Dick Nixon, as Ford called him, had announced that he was going to China in 1972. Ford had worried that Nixon's undertaking was too dangerous. Gradually, how-ever, he became convinced that it was a skillful maneuver based on a far-sighted vision—China was going to be a force in the Pacific in the future, so it was best to establish some kind of contact with its leaders.[7]

After Nixon returned from Beijing in 1972, Ford and Hale Boggs, the Democratic leader in the House of Representatives, traveled to the Chinese capital to have a look for themselves. They did not get to see Mao, but Zhou invited them for dinner at the Great Hall, and, after endless courses of Chi-nese delicacies, Zhou rose and escorted Betty Ford and Lindy Boggs to the door.

"You ladies have had a hard time, and I know you have plans for a long day tomorrow," he said. After sending them on their way, Zhou returned to the dinner table and explained to the two senior members of Congress how China hoped the United States would continue to keep its military forces deployed around the world as a counterweight to the Soviet Union.[8] Ford was amazed by Zhou's sophistication and by the depth of his anti-Sovietism. When Ford asked whether, in Zhou's opinion, the Soviet Union would cut its defense spending if the United States did, Zhou replied, "Never, never, never . . . "

The Chinese leader was, the future vice president and president thought, a man that America could do business with. Nevertheless, Ford had come to believe that such a course was fraught with danger due to the deep well of support for Taiwan in Congress. Indeed, Ford had been part of that support.

Now, as president, Ford looked at the world, and at the expectations placed on him in Nixon's wake, and he saw a bewildering complexity of is-sues. He knew that he was not going to be a foreign policy president, as Nixon had been. It was a mistake to compete with that legacy. So Ford, in the most magnanimous way, told his friends that he felt grateful and lucky to have Kissinger stay on to help him sort things out. Ford was a solid golf-course Republican who felt that he knew one thing extremely well—Congress. He was willing to take some risks in foreign policy—with Kissinger to guide him—but he was never going to stray far from the centrist wisdom of his old colleagues in the House and Senate leadership. And that's how he looked at China and the task of completing what Nixon had started—moving closer to Beijing was something worth doing, indeed it was the right thing to do, but there was no rush. Only after the ground was carefully prepared would Ford, in consultation with Congress, move ahead.

For Ford there was a more pressing priority on the domestic front. On September 8, 1974, he granted a full pardon to Richard Nixon and thus triggered a political storm in Congress over whether Nixon and Ford had conspired to spare Nixon the indignity of prosecution. The pardon and the uproar it set off made it impossible for Ford to undertake a high-risk foreign policy venture during his first six months in office.

But Ford, like Nixon, also saw the China opening for its value as a political prize and a public relations sensation that might be orchestrated in advance of the 1976 presidential election. So Ford dispatched Kissinger that fall to see if he could lay the groundwork with Mao and Zhou for a deal on Taiwan, a deal they might be able to sell to the congressional leadership during late 1975 or early 1976.

Instead of making it easier, however, China made it harder.

In early September, Senator J. William Fulbright, chairman of the Senate Foreign Relations Committee, took his own congressional delegation to Beijing. Over dinner with Qiao Guanhua, still vice foreign minister, Senator Hiram L. Fong of Hawaii asked why Taiwan and the mainland couldn't simply sit down and negotiate their differences. After all, the senator said, both sides maintained that there was only one China.

It came as quite a shock when Qiao replied that the "basic attitude of the Chinese government" was that "peaceful reunification is an impossibility."[9] Up until that time, the only American who understood Mao's dictum—that Taiwan could not be recovered by peaceful means—was Kissinger. Representative Clement J. Zablocki, chairman of the House Foreign Affairs Committee, could hardly believe his ears.

"But what is the alternative to a peaceful solution?" he asked.

Qiao was steely.

"It is simple logic. The opposite of a peaceful solution is a non-peaceful solution. Any solution is either one or the other. If it is not peaceful, it will be otherwise."[10]

Zablocki was incredulous.

"But isn't this somewhat contradictory?" he asked. "After all, China is supposed to support peace."

"There is no contradiction," said Qiao. Since 1955, he explained, "The American side has always tried to get us to commit ourselves to a peaceful solution of this problem. We have always refused to do so for the simple reason that this is an internal affair. As a result, some people in America, many people in fact, have said that China does not want peace. But the Chinese view of this problem is quite different. We see the Taiwan question as the last phase of our civil war which has continued for many decades. Consequently, the Chinese government is not in a hurry over Taiwan. We are prepared to wait even for 100 years."[11]

The senators also heard, during their audience with Deng Xiaoping, that the Chinese leadership had begun to ridicule the Kissinger line that China faced an imminent threat of Soviet attack.* Deng said that he had heard endlessly "from American visitors that the Soviets will launch an all-out attack at such and such a time. Last autumn, we heard that the attack would come before the rivers froze. Our view was that this was very unlikely. The winter passed. Next we heard that the Soviets would attack us when the ice melted in March. Well, the thaw came, but not the attack. And now once again from very good sources we hear that the Soviets will attack us before the freeze in October. This once again seems to us very unlikely. But, as it is in the future, we can only wait and see."[12]

When Kissinger read the exchanges, he knew that his credibility was under assault in Beijing. And Mao's words about prospective violence against Taiwan were now becoming the mantra of the Chinese bureaucracy. How on earth could anyone craft a normalization agreement under the threat of violence?

Kissinger got his first chance to take his own measure of the Chinese leadership a few weeks later, when Qiao came to New York for the annual UN General Assembly session. In his speech to the UN, Qiao attacked "imperialism" and "revisionism" with vehemence, and it seemed to Kissinger and his aides that China wanted it both ways—it wanted the United States to provide a counterweight to Soviet expansionism, leaving Beijing free to organize a "third force" of nations in opposition to the United States.[13] This scenario was not an attractive basis for a relationship.

---

*Sometime during the 1970s, the Chinese leadership began to acquire deeper insights into U.S. government assessments of Chinese security, the Soviet military threat, and a host of other issues, through the services of Larry Wu-Tai Chin, an agent in Beijing's intelligence service who worked under cover as a translator at the CIA. With clearance to read sensitive documents, Chin photocopied many of them and delivered their contents to Beijing, until his espionage was detected with the help of a defector in late 1985. It is entirely possible that the Chinese leadership learned from Chin's spying that the CIA's judgment during the 1970s was that the Soviet Union would not risk an attack on China because Moscow could not predict the outcome or consequences of a protracted war against the Chinese. The intelligence assessment during these years was that the Soviet buildup in the Far East was focused on protecting Soviet interests throughout Asia, principally against Japan and U.S. forces in the Pacific.

Qiao arrived at Kissinger's suite at the Waldorf Towers, where he found the secretary of state flanked by George Bush and a cast of State Department officials including Phil Habib, Art Hummel, and Richard Solomon. Bush was replacing David Bruce in Beijing, in part because Bush, who had been serving as Republican national chairman, was trying to get as far as he could from Watergate. Not that he had been involved in the scandal, but it nevertheless swirled all around him because of his position. This appointment to Beijing as chief of the U.S. liaison office did not require Senate confirmation, so Bush would be spared an embarrassing inquisition; it was the fastest escape route from the poisonous atmosphere in Washington. Kissinger praised Bush as "one of our best men—a good friend—also a presidential candidate."[14]

Qiao was accompanied by his new wife, Zhang Hanzhi, who had the beauty of a country girl and the intellect of a scholar. She was the daughter of one of Mao's oldest friends, and, because of her skill as a linguist, she had served for a time as Mao's English teacher. As such, she had been pulled into the orbit of Jiang Qing, Mao's radical wife, who sought to befriend and manipulate any woman who had access to Mao. The marriage of Qiao Guanhua and Zhang Hanzhi seemed, in fact, to be based from the beginning on both love and politics. Qiao, bespectacled, fluent in German, highly educated in Western philosophy and Chinese dynastic history, was one of Zhou's closest confidantes. Madame Zhang, on the other hand, was an acolyte of the radicals. Mao had personally encouraged the match after Qiao's first wife died. Some observers saw the union as a kind of survival strategy—keeping a foot in each rival camp.[15]

Kissinger's banquet was the usual world tour, an artful display of Metternichian conceits in which Kissinger described how he and Ford, in contravention to the will of Congress, were organizing anti-Soviet forces around the globe through third-party arms sales and covert CIA operations. As always, he took pleasure in denigrating the Democrats, the bureaucracy, and any rival whose name happened to come up. Toward the end of the evening, Qiao and Kissinger exchanged toasts. Qiao used his salutation to remind Kissinger what Mao had said the last time they met—that normalization could only occur after a complete break with Taiwan.

"Let us return to the topic of your toast," Kissinger responded. "We think late 1975 or early 1976 would be a relatively good time for the completion of the process."[16] In exchange for advancing the schedule, Kissinger implied that China would have to make some concessions.

"Our conditions are not the same as Japan's," Kissinger said. "The history of our relations with Taiwan is not the same, our internal situation is more complicated, and our legal requirements are complex. We want to move so that our public opinion does not have a bad feeling about our relations with

China." Kissinger added that it was "important that we not be seen as throwing our friends away."[17]

Qiao patiently reminded him of Mao's well-known views on the subject.

"The question, then," said Kissinger, "is whether our difficulties are ripe for overcoming. We see several problems. First, what sort of office we will maintain in Taipei after normalization. One obvious possibility is a liaison office there. Another possibility is a consulate. But we have a second problem which is more difficult. The defense relationship. We clearly cannot have a defense relationship with a part of a country—at least we are not aware that you can."

Kissinger suddenly excused himself to take a call from the president, which he, of course, announced to the table. When he returned, he started to speak with the words, "We obviously can't . . . ," and then thought better of it.

"Our problem," he started over, "is how to present a new relationship with you where we have not just abandoned people whom we have had a relationship with."[18] Kissinger added that it was not in their mutual interest to create opposition by stirring up the Taiwan lobby. If Beijing could not show some flexibility, Kissinger said, "then it is best to defer for a while."

Qiao gave him no hope that he would find any flexibility in Beijing.

The next morning, Kissinger's staff pointed out that the United States was in a difficult diplomatic squeeze. Nixon, Kissinger, and Ford all had pledged to complete the normalization process by 1976 at the latest. The clock was ticking. Beijing had laid down immutable terms, and the ball was in Washington's court to fulfill the expectations of the Shanghai Communiqué.[19]

Within a week of his disappointing encounter with Qiao, Kissinger ordered a major study by U.S. intelligence agencies of whether mainland China had the capability to retake Taiwan by military force and of the likelihood of such an attack during the coming three to five years.[20]

After weeks of analysis, the agencies concluded that the costs would be high, but the odds favored the mainland. Even with Soviet troops on its northern border, China could deploy up to 2,200 combat aircraft and 850,000 soldiers for operations against Taiwan. Beijing would have to accept massive losses, but its superior numbers of aircraft would grind down Taiwan's defenses in a matter of days, giving Beijing the advantage of air superiority over Taiwan and the Taiwan Strait.[21]

After achieving air superiority, the PLA could launch an invasion force of up to 100,000 men using 30 amphibious ships and about 500 smaller landing craft. These forces would have to land against heavily defended shores, but with air superiority, the PLA would prevail.

The CIA and Pentagon analysts found no evidence that the mainland was actually planning such an attack, but they concluded that in three to five years, as the PLA acquired more advanced air-to-air missiles, Beijing would be in a better position to strike.

As a result, they said, "over the next three to five years, the political and psychological importance of the U.S. supply of weapons" to Taiwan "will be greater than the objective military importance of the weapons themselves."[22]

There was an additional factor that might force Beijing's hand. Chiang Kai-shek was secretly trying to obtain nuclear capability. "Henceforth, we must rely on ourselves," he had said in the wake of Nixon's opening to the mainland. Now, the generalissimo and his son, Chiang Ching-kuo, were obviously seeking to formulate a survival strategy for the Nationalists. If they could build or acquire a nuclear weapon, Beijing would have to think twice before trying to conquer the island.

The intelligence warnings first landed on Kissinger's desk during the chaos of 1974. The CIA had been operating a spy inside Taiwan's primary research and development laboratory, the Zhongshan Institute, since the 1960s. There, Taiwanese scientists, most of them educated in the United States, were preparing to extract weapons-grade plutonium from the nuclear fuel of a research reactor supplied by Canada. Separately, they were working on the design of a ballistic missile that could deliver a warhead against mainland targets. It fell to a rather meek-looking diplomat, William H. Gleysteen Jr., the second-ranking American envoy in Taipei, to pay a visit on Chiang Ching-kuo and raise the matter. Gleysteen demanded that Taiwan shut down the nuclear program or face a cutoff of American assistance, including sales of nuclear technology for Taiwan's electric power industry. Chiang never admitted anything. But the CIA mole inside the research institute reported that the program was curtailed and plans postponed as Taiwan reconsidered how best to deter an invasion from the mainland. The research base and the team of physicists, however, remained intact.

To the Taiwanese, it must have seemed onerous for the United States to make such constricting demands while at the same time refusing to engage in any long-term planning for the defense of Taiwan. But from Ford's perspective, if China attacked the island, congressional support for a U.S. military intervention was not at all a sure thing. Congress had, after all, shut down the bombing of Khmer Rouge targets in Cambodia during the summer of 1973. And the Senate contested every request to resupply the Saigon government with munitions.

It seemed a grim scenario. But missing from Kissinger's analysis was any attempt to assess whether Mao would actually risk a military confrontation with the United States. Attacking Taiwan would undermine the very strategic realignment he had undertaken. Of course if Taiwan declared independence, Beijing would be compelled to act. But that was not likely under

Nationalist leaders who were all born on the mainland and wanted nothing more than to return some day. To them, declaring independence would be treasonous. Furthermore, the mere mobilization of a PLA invasion force would incite a strong political reaction in the United States and give any president time to galvanize public support for preventive action. The greatest uncertainty for Beijing was always the American Seventh Fleet, which was the most potent military force in the region. When Truman had sent American warships into the Taiwan Strait in 1950, Mao had abandoned his invasion plans. Eisenhower had done so again in 1958. It would probably be the same in 1974. But Kissinger had a dark premonition that once American forces withdrew from Taiwan, Mao would find it irresistible to attack the island. Then America would be in the "preposterous" position of going to war with China over actions it was taking on its own territory.[23]

The psychology of war and deterrence in the Taiwan Strait was never thoroughly explored by Ford or Kissinger. To them, it was Vietnam all over again. They simply were not willing to take the risk. And so Kissinger resolved that if he could not get an assurance of "peaceful transition" from Mao, he would not lead Ford into an unpredictable wilderness.

B Y JULY 1974, Mao's health had deteriorated to the point where he could scarcely see a finger in front of his face, and his speech was so slurred that even Nancy Tang, the most expert of interpreters, had to give him a notepad to write out the characters for what he was trying to say. The right side of Mao's body was increasingly paralyzed; this development, together with his slurred speech, led to speculation among his doctors that he had suffered a stroke.[24] Imelda Marcos, the First Lady of the Philippines, emerged from an audience with Mao and passed along to American officials a "graphic portrayal of a Mao far into his decline—attended by nurses, drooling, and reeking of medicinal balm and decaying gums."[25] When Mao consented to examination by a team of Chinese specialists, they concluded that the chairman was suffering from a rare degenerative disease known in the United States as Lou Gehrig's disease, which attacks nerve cells that control the muscles of the throat, tongue, diaphragm, and the right side of the body. Mao's vision was ravaged by cataracts. He was also suffering from coronary and pulmonary heart disease, a festering lung infection, and a shortage of oxygen in his blood.

The physicians did not believe that Mao could last more than two years longer.[26]

When Zhou, also hospitalized, heard of the diagnosis, he asked the doctors if there was a cure. They informed him that there was none.

"So the case is terminal," he said.

There was a long silence as none of the doctors could bring himself to speak of the chairman's mortality.

"Then you must use the available time to find a way to deal with the problem. If you really cannot cure the disease, then at least you should try to prolong the Chairman's life."[27]

In his final days, Mao was a man obsessed—about his political legacy, the fate of the revolution, the threat from the superpowers, and the recovery of Taiwan. Meanwhile, the conspiracy of the radicals deepened, and Mao continued to encourage the rivalries among them—using one faction to check the power of the other. This was a sign of his own uncertainty. Mao had elevated Deng to be the principal vice premier and set him to work managing the tatters of the Chinese economy. By now, Deng was party vice chairman and chief of staff of the army, second in command to Mao on the Central Military Commission. Mao told the party leadership that Deng was a person of extraordinary ability, and to the radicals he explained that Deng's experience gave him superior political wisdom, even if he had rightist tendencies. But Deng's position was far from secure.

With the radicals, every battle was Armageddon. They knew that they needed to win only one major battle to win the war, and so they let a thousand defeats roll over them. When Deng proposed that China purchase foreign cargo ships to boost the country's maritime transport capacity, the radicals shrieked that he was selling out the domestic industry, which was centered in Shanghai, a radical stronghold. On each policy issue, swords were drawn, and Zhou would have to climb out of his hospital bed, or dispatch Deng, to request an audience with the chairman to explain the sound and underlying logic of the decision. Mao most often sided with the moderates.

In early 1974, Jiang Qing drew up a political manifesto condemning "Lin Biao and the Confucius-Mencius Way"—another veiled attack on Zhou—and Mao approved the report, urging the party's cadres to study her work. Thus encouraged, she took the next step of calling a mass rally in Beijing to launch a political movement based on her work. Standing above the crown, she and her allies from Qinghua University, often regarded as China's M.I.T., delivered speeches attacking "rightists" in the leadership, including Zhou and Marshal Ye Jianying. Zhou surprised everyone by attending the rally. He apologized to the masses for not calling the rally sooner and led the crowd in chanting, "Learn from Comrade Jiang Qing!"[28] This was Zhou at his most abstruse, identifying with his attackers, riding the wave of radical dialectics not just as a survival strategy but as a means of playing out the string of radical politics until Mao himself saw the danger that events might spin out of control again.[29]

After the rally, Mao criticized his wife at a politburo meeting for "unilateralism," because she had not sought permission to hold the rally. Marshal Ye accused her of trying to grab power. In March 1974, Mao wrote his wife a letter, saying, "It would be better for us not to see each other. For years I have advised you about many things, but you have ignored most of it. So what use is there for us to see each other? I am 81 years old and seriously ill, but you show hardly any concern. You now enjoy many privileges, but after my death, what are you going to do? You are also like those people who do not discuss major policies with me but report to me every day on trivial matters. Think about it."[30]

That same month, Jiang Qing attacked Deng for going to the UN General Assembly session in New York. Mao had to rebuke her again. "That Comrade Deng Xiaoping should leave the country is my idea," he said. "Take care to be prudent. Do not oppose my suggestions."

At a politburo meeting in July, Mao put greater distance between himself and his wife, telling the leadership that "she doesn't represent me, she represents herself. With her, one divides into two. One part is good, one part is not very good." He warned her not to form a "four person small faction" in Shanghai. She did anyway, and it soon became known as the Gang of Four.[31]

After the politburo meeting, the ailing Mao fled the capital for a trip to Wuhan in central China. His doctors were terrified that they would not have access to emergency facilities there. But the chairman held himself together, brooding at a guesthouse near the banks of the Yangtze River for two months, occasionally meeting visitors. Then he moved by train to Changsha in his native Hunan Province.

Mao refused to accept his mortality. In Changsha, he announced that he was going to swim. There was something admirable about the determination of the eighty-one-year-old chairman, even as his doctors feared that so much as a mouthful of water might drown him.[32] But no one dared stop Mao.

The chairman's descent into the pool dissolved quickly into a collapse that left him gasping for breath. Mao tried two more times to swim during the last half of 1974, and then gave up for good.

KISSINGER SWEPT INTO Beijing in November 1974 with his largest-ever entourage. His wife, Nancy, and his two children were on the plane, as well as Donald Rumsfeld, perhaps the most politically ambitious of Ford's White House aides. George Bush met them, having just taken up his duties as head of the liaison office in Beijing. Kissinger gathered them all around him so they could bear witness to what Kissinger hoped would be a breakthrough in Beijing.[33]

He had just accompanied Ford to Vladivostok for the president's first summit with Brezhnev, and the ailing Soviet leader had moved the superpowers to the brink of a new strategic arms accord, making the concessions he had withheld from Nixon. It was a promising new start, although it was immediately attacked by Senator Henry "Scoop" Jackson and other conservatives. Only after he had arrived in China did Kissinger realize that it had been foolish to have accepted Vladivostok as the venue for the Ford-Brezhnev summit. The Pacific seaport, forty miles from the Chinese frontier, had once been part of China's domain in East Asia. The Chinese refused to call the city Vladivostok, which means "Power of the East" in Russian. Holding the U.S.-Soviet summit there had—to the Chinese—reinforced the notion that Washington accepted Soviet power in the Far East.[34] Not surprisingly, instead of a breakthrough, Kissinger, in China, faced one disappointment after another.

First, Zhou was again in the hospital. U.S. intelligence had gotten a stronger clue about his ailment the previous summer when Senator Jackson briefly visited Zhou's hospital bed and surmised that he was suffering from prostate cancer. Kissinger was allowed a thirty-minute visit to the premier's hospital suite, where he got a whiff of urine. This led to speculation among the Americans that Zhou might have a kidney disease or cancer of the bladder.*

Zhou's frail state made it clear that he would not likely return to prominence, and this was a profound disappointment for Kissinger. To make matters worse, Deng Xiaoping appeared as Kissinger's new interlocutor. Of all the Chinese leaders, Deng seemed to incite the most visceral reaction in Kissinger. This was not the oriental Metternich that he had seen in Zhou. There was none of the grace, sophistication, or charm. Deng sat across the negotiating table like a grumpy little Buddha, too self-conscious to engage in frivolous conversation and too imbued with the words of Mao to show any flexibility. Deng could be tough, pugnacious even, and he seemed wholly unimpressed by Kissinger. In the middle of a subtle diplomatic presentation, Deng was prone to clear his throat like a peasant, hawking up a big wad of phlegm and leaning over to loudly expectorate in the spittoon that was never far from his chair. Kissinger, in private, took to calling him "that nasty little man."[35]

When Kissinger and his delegation made its entrance along the red carpet laid in the Great Hall, Deng sat them down in a horseshoe of armchairs and then invited American photographers and reporters to record the first few minutes of the session.

*Zhou was suffering from three independent malignancies in his bladder, lung, and colon, according to Li Zhisui, Mao's physician.

"It probably would be good if one day we would be able to exchange views in Washington,"[36] Deng took the opportunity to say.

It was a subtle reminder that the relationship had not progressed far enough to make that possible, but Kissinger, ever hoping to spin the press positively, replied: "I think we can do that very soon." But then he acted as if China were to blame. "Your foreign minister always refuses my invitations."

"It is difficult for him to come now," Deng said coolly. "What will he do if he meets the Chiang Kai-shek ambassador in Washington?"

At that point, the news reporters and cameramen were escorted from the room, but Deng had planted the headline that China was impatient with the pace of normalization.

And Deng shortly returned to the point.

"Outside there are many opinions in the world and a lot of talk saying that our relations have chilled and our speed has slowed down. But in the essence I believe that both sides hold that the progress of our relations has been normal.

"But we should also say it is not correct to say that there is no ground whatsoever for such talk," Deng continued. "It is only natural that there should be some speculation and talk when you send a [new] ambassador to Taiwan, and when they [the Taiwanese] increase the number of their consulates in the United States."[37] It was time for America to "move forward," Deng said.

Kissinger pleaded with Deng for a more accommodating posture on Taiwan, but Deng was impassive and replied that they would go into greater detail when they met in a small group later in the day. But then, before they adjourned, and in front of Kissinger's entourage, Deng said, "But I must first fire a cannon."

"At me?" Kissinger asked.

"On this issue, as we see it, you owe us a debt,"[38] Deng said.

Neither Mao nor Zhou had ever been so blunt, although Deng was unquestionably speaking on orders from Mao. For four years, the United States—Nixon and Kissinger—had reaped the benefits of the opening to China. They had used the China card to help wring concessions from Moscow. But what real concessions had Nixon and Kissinger and, now, Ford made to China? The U.S. military drawdown on Taiwan was not a concession—it was inevitable with the end of the Vietnam War. And, since 1972, neither the Nixon administration nor the Ford administration had made any serious attempt to prepare Congress or the American public for the kind of normalization that Canada, Japan, West Germany, and other countries had already completed with Beijing. Instead, Kissinger had promised Taiwan's ambassador in Washington that Beijing would not be recognized as the sole legal government of China. He had told members of the Senate that the Mutual Defense Treaty with Taiwan was secure and that America would continue to ensure that Taiwan had the means to defend itself. In other words, he had tried to have it both ways. Now Deng was laying a political invoice on the table. Kissinger owed the Chinese a debt for all that the Nixon administration, and Nixon and Kissinger personally, had benefited from the opening to China. And the debt also arose from the promise of the Shanghai Communiqué, the promise to complete the process that they had begun.

When Deng and Kissinger met again, late in the afternoon of November 26, Deng brought so many aides with him that it prompted Kissinger to say, "They outnumber us today." Deng responded confidently, "I don't think you will ever outnumber us because we have 800 million."[39]

Kissinger moved to his own defense. The United States, he said, had led the world with its opening to China. This by itself had created momentum that had helped China shift the orientation of the international community away from Chiang Kai-shek and toward Beijing as the center of Chinese authority. It was American political momentum that had rallied Beijing's supporters at the United Nations and enabled Beijing to take China's seat on the Security Council a year earlier than anyone expected; it was America that had encouraged Japan and other countries to establish relations with Beijing. But now that it was time for the United States to act, Washington had some special considerations. "There is a rather substantial group in the United States that historically has been pro-Taiwan," Kissinger said. "Together, with your cooperation, we have been able to neutralize the pro-Taiwan element." It was in neither side's interest, Kissinger emphasized, "to have emerge a senator or a senatorial group which does to Sino-American relations what Senator Jackson* has attempted to do to U.S.-Soviet relations.

"I am speaking frankly to you," Kissinger continued, "so that we understand each other exactly." He then laid out the first cut of his proposal. The United States would "substantially" follow the Japanese model, except that it would like to keep a liaison office in Taiwan while opening an embassy in Beijing. "With respect to the presence of troops on Taiwan," he said, "we are prepared to remove all our troops from Taiwan."[40] He suggested a schedule of reducing the remaining detachment of 3,000 by half by the summer of 1976, with the last troops to be removed by the end of 1977. That would push any risk of a mainland move against Taiwan to Ford's second term, which Kissinger may have thought more manageable. Kissinger said that the Ford administration would not be able to enter into such an agreement until

---

*Jackson had become the most prominent critic of the policy of détente. A Democrat, he had joined with Republicans in challenging the merit of the SALT process and worked to highlight the growth of Soviet military power and Soviet violations of earlier accords.

late 1975, "but we want to come to an understanding about it now, that this is what would happen.

"Now, that leaves the last problem, which is our defense relationship with Taiwan," Kissinger said. "And this is a problem to which, in all frankness, we have not come up with a good answer."

He explained, as he had told Qiao in New York, that "we need a formula that enables us to say that at least for some period of time, there are assurances of peaceful reintegration that can be reviewed after some interval in order to avoid the difficulties which I have described.

"If we can, this would mean that we would have accepted Beijing as the government. We would have withdrawn our recognition from Taiwan, we would have broken diplomatic relations with Taiwan. We would have withdrawn our troops from Taiwan. All that would remain is that we would have some relation to peaceful reintegration," Kissinger said, adding, "we need a transition period for our public opinion in which this process can be accomplished without an excessive domestic strain.[41]

"To us the question of the defense commitment," he added, "is primarily a question of the way it can be presented politically. It is not a question of maintaining it for an indefinite period of time."

Deng listened impassively, and when Kissinger seemed to pause after the translation, he asked, "Is that all?"

It was not clear whether Deng understood the tangle of nuances Kissinger had placed before him. In any case, Deng argued that since the United States had formulated the defense treaty as an act of law, "naturally, you can also do away with it."

"That is also true," Kissinger explained. "Our point is not that it could not be done, our point is that for reasons I have explained to you, it is not expedient to do—the act of recognition in itself will change the nature of that arrangement because you cannot have a defense treaty with a part of a country."

Now Deng seemed to understand. But he was no more flexible than before. China would not stand for a liaison office in Taipei. That was too much recognition, he added, and could lead to a "one-China, one-Taiwan" state of separatism. As for the defense treaty with Taiwan, it "must be done away with."[42]

Kissinger tried to protest. "The defense treaty can have no international status after the normalization of relations."

"But still it has a substantial meaning,"[43] Deng replied. He could see what anyone could see. Kissinger wanted it all—relations with Beijing *and* a defense treaty with Taiwan. "It still looks as if you need Taiwan."

That line: "You still need Taiwan." It was Mao's taunt, and it always infuriated Kissinger.

"No, we do not need Taiwan," he insisted. "That is not the issue. That would be a mistake in understanding the problem. What we would like to achieve is the disassociation from Taiwan in steps, in the manner we have done until now. There is no doubt that the status of Taiwan has been undermined by the process which we have followed."[44]

But Deng just dug in his heels.

"The Taiwan question should be left with us Chinese to solve among ourselves. As to what means we will use to solve the Taiwan question, I believe Chairman Mao Zedong made it very clear in his talk."

"Chairman Mao," Kissinger replied, "made two statements. One was that he believed that the question would ultimately have to be solved by force. But he also stated that China could wait for 100 years to bring this about, if I understood him correctly."

"It is true, he did say that. Of course, the number '100 years' is a symbolic one," Deng replied.

"We want to avoid a situation where the United States signs a document which leads to a military solution shortly after normalization,"[45] Kissinger said.

But Deng would give him no satisfaction on the point. He resorted to sending for the transcript of Mao's remarks of a year earlier and reading aloud from it.

Unable to get a word in edgewise, Kissinger retreated. He said that he was willing to give up the idea of maintaining a consulate or liaison office in Taiwan. If that was the case, Kissinger argued, it all came down to one issue— "How can we avoid the impression that we have simply jettisoned people with whom we have been associated . . . how can we have a period of time to give this process a chance to work."

Instead of taking the bait, Deng delivered a salvo from Mao.

"As I have said before, some people have been saying the relations between our two countries have been cooling down." Therefore, "the Chinese government wishes to extend a formal invitation to the Secretary of Defense of the United States, Mr. Schlesinger, to visit China. We think this would be a good answer to all these opinions which are going on in the world."[46]

It was as if Deng had kicked Kissinger in the stomach.

For anyone following the politics of the Ford administration, it was clear that Schlesinger had mounted a challenge to détente; that he, like Senator Jackson, believed that Moscow's massive buildup of conventional and nuclear forces required an adjustment in American strategy; that Nixon's "era of negotiation" was proving insufficient to deter Soviet expansion. By playing the Schlesinger card, the Chinese signaled their repudiation of the Kissinger line and of his preoccupation with making deals with Brezhnev.

Now, hearing Schlesinger's name, Kissinger sputtered that such an invitation would be a reckless act. "It will produce a Politburo meeting in the Kremlin," he said.

"We don't mind," Deng replied. "Actually, it is our wish that they have a Politburo meeting there. But we really extend this invitation in all seriousness."

With breathtaking speed, Kissinger launched a preemptive strike against the invitation. Once his session with Deng had ended, he used a CIA communications link to the White House to send his deputy, Brent Scowcroft, an "eyes only" report to be passed to Ford. In the second-to-last paragraph of a three-page memo, Kissinger raised and then repudiated the Schlesinger invitation.

"This [invitation], I believe, would have very severe repercussions in the USSR. I shall turn it off today and try to turn it into an invitation to you. I shall offer them any other cabinet member. If they agree, there will be no way to keep it out of the final communiqué,"[47] Kissinger said.

It was becoming transparent that Kissinger—seeing that no diplomatic breakthrough would be possible on the November trip—would use the announcement of a Ford visit to China to claim some success for his high-profile mission. But in simply trading away the currency of Ford's agreement to such a state visit, Kissinger sacrificed his leverage—Ford's acceptance—and failed to even explore the implication of Deng's remark that the question of Taiwan might be addressed on a follow-up visit. If Kissinger—as in 1971—had tabled a draft communiqué on a normalization accord that included a commitment by the United States to break relations with Taiwan and to recognize Beijing as the sole government of the Chinese people in a transition that provided for a peaceful reunification process with Taiwan, he would at least have discovered if there was any further give after Mao had had the opportunity to examine the text.

Instead, once Deng agreed to invite Ford, Kissinger seemed to lose all interest in negotiation. He expressed a sense of *anything-but-Schlesinger*. For Kissinger, empty summitry was enough.

On his final day in Beijing, Kissinger frenetically worked to get the Chinese to quickly sign off on the joint statement announcing that President Ford would visit Beijing the following year. Ford had scheduled an evening news conference that weekend, and Kissinger seemed driven by his desire to make headlines in Washington.

Knowing that the Americans had given themselves an artificial deadline, Deng took advantage of it. He summoned Kissinger and told him that there could be no compromise on what the Chinese were calling the "three principles" of normalization: (1) breaking relations with Taiwan; (2) withdrawing all U.S. forces from Taiwan; and (3) "abolishing" the mutual defense treaty.

Kissinger immediately agreed. "The principles are accepted," he said. "In all of them, the only practical problem we have is how to implement it."[48]

Deng admonished Kissinger to think through the American position on Taiwan "clearly" and to solve it "briskly" so that it could be "written off at once."

"I understand," Kissinger replied, "and I believe it can be solved in connection with these three principles." He then praised Deng for his generosity, self-restraint, and wisdom.

There was no attempt to push the negotiations further.

Kissinger, his wife, his children, and his entourage flew off to Suzhou, famous for its gardens, in hopes that Mao would appear. Qiao Guanhua accompanied Kissinger to Suzhou, but the Chinese were extremely secretive regarding Mao's whereabouts, even as Mao continued to meet with other foreign leaders, including Prime Minister Eric Williams of Trinidad and Tobago and Salem Robaya Ali, the South Yemeni leader. Kissinger was left to dawdle in an elegant guesthouse among the gardens, where he could only chew his nails and inveigh against Deng. After a day of waiting, he left for home disappointed. On a stop in Tokyo, Kissinger told reporters traveling on his plane that the Chinese had not pressed him to move forward on establishing full diplomatic relations.

But privately, Kissinger began to think there was no possibility of normalizing relations with China before the 1976 elections, if ever.[49]

THE CHINESE BEGAN TO bring pressure on Ford to complete the normalization process immediately after Kissinger left the country. U.S. intelligence and Western embassies in Beijing and Hong Kong reported a coordinated campaign by Chinese diplomats to call on the United States to live up to the Nixon promise.[50] It seemed that, for the first time, the Chinese were taking their diplomacy outside the channel controlled by Kissinger, an indication of how little they trusted him. The Chinese had seen how Kissinger manipulated public opinion. And so they began to light a backfire against the Kissinger line.

Qiao hosted Senate majority leader Mike Mansfield in Beijing that winter, and when Mansfield returned to Washington, he gave a highly critical report to the Senate regarding Nixon's and, now, Ford's delay in achieving normalization. Kissinger got so upset that he called in Han Xu, the senior Chinese diplomat present in Washington. Speaking for Kissinger, the tough-talking assistant secretary, Phil Habib, told the Chinese that their pressure campaign "complicates the process of ensuring public support for what needs to be done."[51] But what needed to be done was normalization, and Kissinger had abandoned that. His hypersensitivity had more to do with criticisms that were aimed at him personally.

Kissinger was not the only senior member of the administration who had walked away from normalization. In January 1975, after only a few months on the job in Beijing, George Bush—more focused on presidential politics in America than anything else—warned in a top secret back-channel cable to Kissinger that the issue of Taiwan "should not be solved in a manner" that added to Ford's "political worries" or threatened "his conservative, convention-going support." Against all evidence to the contrary, Bush said that "there is no pressure here in Beijing" to break American military and diplomatic ties with Taiwan. "The President must not be postured as having 'sold out' Taiwan," he added. And, most importantly, "The people Ford needs at the GOP convention would accept downgrading Taiwan to less than embassy status, but would not accept sell-out." He didn't specify what that meant.

The subject matter of Bush's cable was well beyond his brief as the head of the U.S. liaison office in Beijing, but as a Republican from the liberal wing of the party, his opposition to breaking with Taiwan signaled to Ford that neither conservatives nor liberals in the party favored a high-risk venture in the unstable political climate that followed Watergate and the Nixon pardon. Bush may also have feared that a conservative backlash would endanger his own presidential fortunes.

· · ·

In April 1975, the Saigon government fell under a fresh onslaught from the North. The fall of Phnom Penh in Cambodia quickly followed. The U.S.-backed government of Lon Nol collapsed before the hardened forces of the Khmer Rouge, whose leader, Pol Pot, ushered in a brutal campaign of rural collectivization and politically motivated slaughter.

In Beijing there was satisfaction, not with the carnage but with the knowledge that U.S. involvement in Indochina had come to an end. But instead of relations between Beijing and Washington improving, tensions remained high over Taiwan. A mainland singing troupe invited to the United States in the spring of 1975 insisted on performing a song about the "liberation of Taiwan."[52] The State Department maintained that cultural exchanges could not be used as vehicles for "blatant" political content, and the visit was canceled.

Also that spring, when the American military cargo ship *Mayaguez* was seized by Cambodian forces, Kissinger tried to use the Chinese to pass messages to the new Cambodian government, with which Washington had no relations. The Chinese envoy in Washington, Huang Zhen, refused, saying, "this is your problem,"[53] forcing the loss of precious time as the request was passed through other diplomatic channels to Beijing. The taciturn Huang was under great pressure to enforce the more aggressive foreign policy stance coming from Beijing, and so he took every opportunity to tweak Kissinger about the fallacy of détente or about American decline in the face of Soviet expansionism.[54] National security wiretaps also captured Huang telling Iranian and other foreign diplomats* that there was a split within the Ford administration, that Ford was giving more responsibility in foreign affairs to his close advisers outside the State Department, particularly Rumsfeld and Robert Hartmann. One intelligence intercept reported that Han Xu, a high-ranking Chinese diplomat, "spent considerable time with the Iranians discussing purported differences in approach to national security issues between [Kissinger] and Secretary of Defense Schlesinger. The Chinese official emphasized that the Pentagon is not very optimistic about détente, a position which the Chinese appreciate."[55]

The mere fact that Kissinger's staff highlighted such intelligence was another indication of Kissinger's preoccupation with personal bureaucratic interests.

Chiang Kai-shek died during the first week of April, ravaged by age and the bitter realization that he would never return to the mainland. Power on Taiwan had already passed to his son, who was much more popular among the native Taiwanese population, many of whom had seen the old man as an uncaring dictator. But the real impact of Chiang's death was felt in the United States, where conservatives rallied for his memorial, exploiting the imagery of his steadfastness as an ally—the man who had stood with America, first against Japanese imperialism and then against communism. And they used this imagery to attack Ford and America's retreat from its principles.

Senator Barry Goldwater led a large American delegation to the generalissimo's funeral.

"If they want to change our relationship with Taipei," Goldwater told *Washington Post* correspondent Lou Cannon, "as I told the President and as I told Kissinger, they've got a hell of a fight on their hands."[56]

The White House did not help its own cause. Ford initially designated Secretary of Agriculture Earl Butz to represent the United States at the generalissimo's funeral. Conservatives roared over the slight, and Ford added Vice President Nelson Rockefeller to the delegation at the last minute, but the damage had been done. Goldwater warned Ford that if he refused to visit Taipei on his trip to China in the fall, the conservatives would attack.

---

*Each morning, the intelligence community provided to the office of the National Security Adviser transcripts of intercepted communications from the embassies, consulates, and UN missions of countries whose diplomatic communications were of interest to the president and his aides.

With the 1976 presidential primaries less that a year away, Ronald Reagan cast a growing shadow across the political landscape, and the pressure of a challenge from the right compelled Ford during a press conference in May to "reaffirm" America's "commitments to Taiwan."[57]

Normalization was the furthest thing from his mind.

When Ford formally announced his candidacy in the summer of 1975, his political advisers were deeply concerned that Kissinger had become a liability for his pro-détente stance. They may have respected Kissinger's intellect, but they resented his penchant for undercutting Ford on the domestic front. They blamed Kissinger for condescending to Ford in public, casting him in the role of pupil; they blamed him for his habit of giving speeches two or three days before Ford—on the same subject that Ford intended to cover. Kissinger himself seemed to be running for office, or running to keep his approval ratings higher than Ford's. At the State Department, Lord, nominally the director of the Office of Policy Planning, was serving as Kissinger's speechwriter as the secretary crisscrossed the country in a public speaking campaign. All this grandstanding prompted Reagan to start referring to the "Kissinger-Ford" campaign.

Furthermore, some of Ford's aides disliked Kissinger's parlor games even less than Nixon's top aides had. To make matters worse, Kissinger blindsided them by walling them off from the planning for the Helsinki Conference on Security and Cooperation in Europe, in which Moscow achieved its goal of cementing the borders of East Europe. Conservatives attacked the conference as Western capitulation, and they blamed Ford for sealing the fate of millions of East Europeans living under oppression. Both Reagan and Senator Jackson had admonished Ford not to go to Helsinki, but Kissinger had counseled that Ford had no choice but to stand with European leaders who were committed to drawing Moscow into a meaningful structure of European security. The Soviet writer and dissident Aleksandr I. Solzhenitsyn sneered that Ford "will shortly be leaving for Europe to sign the betrayal of Eastern Europe, to acknowledge officially its slavery, forever." Solzhenitsyn then came to Washington, and conservatives demanded that Ford meet with him; the White House, however, couldn't schedule the visit, and Kissinger was ultimately blamed for this "snub" of the Nobel laureate.

Ford's advisers were furious when the White House was leveled by this criticism. Had Kissinger not been so secretive, had he brought Ford's political aides into the loop, they complained, Ford could have done more to sell the strong points of the Helsinki accords, including what was perhaps the most significant breakthrough of the Cold War, the establishment of the principle of universal adherence to human rights.[58]

Reagan's shadow only grew larger with each Ford misstep. In his first for-

eign policy speech in June, Reagan ridiculed détente and Ford's pursuit of relations with "Red China" at the expense of Taiwan. He voiced his agreement
with Senator Goldwater that if the president was going to visit Beijing, he
also ought to visit Taipei.[59] Goldwater threatened to switch his allegiance to
Reagan if Ford did not cancel his China trip altogether. The Arizona senator
admonished Ford to change the focus of his policy "away from communism
and toward freedom in the Far East."[60]

The Chinese were anything but neutral as they watched the American debate. That summer, the *People's Daily* accused the United States of lapsing
into "strategic passivity." The allegation sent Kissinger to the ceiling. No
one would take America seriously if that view were allowed to hold, he said.

But then the Angolan civil war provided Ford and Kissinger with a chance
to demonstrate to the Chinese—and to the world—that Washington still was
willing to act, that the United States was *not* strategically passive, that it was
still willing to commit military force against Soviet expansion.

In early 1975, Portugal's leftist government declared that it was giving up
its African colonies, including Angola, where Lisbon hoped to pave the way
for takeover by the Angolan communists under Agostinho Neto.[61] Two other
political movements—based, like Neto's, on tribal affiliations—were vying
for power. National elections were set for November 1, 1975.

China had long cultivated close relations with the black African states,
many of whose leaders were steeped in Maoist revolutionary thought and liberation politics. In early 1974, Beijing had been the first major power to develop a relationship with Neto and his Popular Movement for the Liberation
of Angola, or MPLA. But Beijing later switched its allegiance after Neto became enamored of Moscow.

Instead, China cultivated both of Neto's rivals: the National Front for the
Liberation of Angola, or FNLA, and the National Union for the Total Independence of Angola, or UNITA.

In May 1974, China dispatched about 100 military advisers to Zaire,
where they trained some 5,000 FNLA fighters under Holden Roberto, their
leader. Beijing also provided weapons, including tanks and artillery, for
Roberto's fighters. In addition, China provided smaller amounts of assistance
to UNITA and its leader, Jonas Savimbi.

In January 1975, when the independence timetable was set, the FNLA
mounted a military campaign, and by March they had reached the outskirts
of the Angolan capital, Luanda. Fierce skirmishing with the MPLA garrison
there followed.

At the same time, Savimbi's UNITA forces closed in on Luanda from the
south, and Neto, seeing his army surrounded, sent urgent pleas for assistance
to Fidel Castro in Cuba and to Moscow. Castro, acting on his own, dis-

patched hundreds of Cuban combat troops to Luanda. They were followed over subsequent months by a massive Soviet airlift of tanks, artillery, and munitions. Soviet and Cuban military advisers directed Neto's first counteroffensive, which drove the FNLA and UNITA forces away from the capital. The Kremlin not only favored Neto and the communists in Luanda but also felt a need to respond to China's backing of the two insurgent forces.[62] The United States was barely in the game, but Kissinger would soon reinterpret this Sino-Soviet clash as a direct challenge to American global leadership.

In early 1975, Ford had approved a $300,000 political contribution to Roberto's FNLA, but no military funding. Kissinger convinced Ford that Washington could not ignore the massive infusion of Soviet and Cuban military aid. To do so would be to risk even deeper recriminations over America's "strategic passivity." Kissinger's formulation was little different from that of 1971, when India had dismembered Pakistan. At that time, he said that the United States could not afford to stand by while a friend of China's was getting screwed by a friend of Moscow's. Kissinger believed that Ford needed to get involved in this African civil war—not necessarily to win, but for America to be taken seriously again, especially by China and the Soviet Union. If the United States did not respond to the Soviet challenge in Angola, the Soviets might not feel compelled to compromise on the final provisions of the SALT II agreement, Kissinger reasoned. And Mao would only scorn Ford for his inaction, if he agreed to meet with him at all, during the president's trip to China.

As the MPLA counteroffensive drove Roberto's and Savimbi's forces out of the capital, Kissinger marshaled and Ford approved a $48 million program of covert CIA support for the FNLA and several million more for UNITA. The American intervention was unpopular within the government. The assistant secretary for African affairs, Nathaniel Davis, resigned after warning Kissinger that he was dealing the United States into a losing hand. "The worst possible outcome would be a test of will and strength which we lose," Davis said. The CIA complained that the operation was too small to prevail and too large to keep secret. And what was the American interest in the fight? some asked. Still, the first planeload of CIA arms left the United States by military transport on July 29, and the weapons reached the combatants through Zaire and South Africa.

Few African civil wars had ever triggered such intense mobilizations. By November, Soviet air and sea transports had landed 4,000 Cuban soldiers and a formidable arsenal of heavy weapons to preserve the MPLA hold over the capital.

All of this groundwork had been laid when Scowcroft, in July 1975, cabled Bush in Beijing with the news that Kissinger was making the final preparations for Ford's visit to China and was considering the "possibility of partial steps that the president might take short of a fully normalized relationship with the PRC which would sustain the momentum of our relationship, but which would not require a break in formal relations with Taiwan."[63]

That September, Kissinger told Qiao Guanhua in New York that "We cannot complete the process"[64] during Ford's state visit to Beijing. "It is domestically impossible." Still, Kissinger was hoping for some kind of positive spin. Ford, and Kissinger, needed a success.

Kissinger asked Qiao whether Ford and Deng could sign a communiqué that would give the appearance of progress in the relationship.

"On this question, my mind is blank," said Qiao. Kissinger pressed and pressed over dinner at his suite at the Waldorf, but Qiao repeated his earlier reply, that his mind was blank.

"That in itself is an historic event,"[65] Kissinger quipped, and gave up.

Kissinger was only weeks away from leading Ford on the president's first trip to China, and it had again become an unknown country. He had no idea what to expect, and he feared the worst, a public snub or criticism that would make headlines and embarrass the President. Kissinger therefore had decided to make an advance trip to Beijing in October to prepare the way, but the Chinese were less cooperative than they have ever been. It was a way of showing displeasure.

At Andrews Air Force Base, the tension level on board Kissinger's grounded plane was palpable. The Chinese had held up final approval for Kissinger to enter China until the last minute by delaying their formal permission for the secretary's plane to land.[66] Sitting on the runway at Andrews was an excruciating embarrassment, and when permission finally came through, Kissinger seemed ruined for the journey. Once they landed in Beijing, Kissinger tried to play an opening card. While he and Qiao Guanhua were driving in from the airport, Kissinger said that he had a very sensitive intelligence-sharing proposal that he wanted to present to Deng in a restricted meeting. U.S. reconnaissance satellites had detected a huge area of construction in the Semipalatinsk region of the Soviet Union. The CIA was calling the site PNUT,* an acronym for "possible nuclear underground test" facility. Kissinger wished to propose that the United States and China establish a joint seismic and electronic intelligence base in China's western mountains at a site that overlooked the Semipalatinsk region. Such a base could also improve China's ability to monitor Soviet military forces and detect a Soviet attack in advance.

But as soon as they sat down for formal talks the next day, Deng rejected

---

*The acronym was pronounced "peanut."

the offer. "If what you want to discuss in a restricted group is what you mentioned to the Foreign Minister in the car," Deng said, referring to Kissinger's offer, "then as Chairman Mao has made our position very clear to you in his discussions before, especially in the visit in 1973, it is our view that perhaps such restrictive talks will not be necessary."[67]

It was another rejection of the "tacit alliance." Moreover, Deng was on to Kissinger's game of deliberately exaggerating the Soviet threat to China's borders—a snare designed to create Chinese dependency. The rejection left Kissinger even more on the defensive, and he was forced to spend a great deal of time trying to explain to Deng why détente was not a policy of weakness. Kissinger's defense on the first day of his visit went on for an hour, at the end of which Deng asked, again in his deadpan manner, "Are you finished?"

Kissinger tried a joke, but it fell flat. Instead of responding, Deng adjourned their session and sent Kissinger off for another tour of the Forbidden City. When the American party returned late in the afternoon, Deng delivered a blistering and contemptuous review of the Ford-Kissinger policy.

Kissinger, he said, was no better than Neville Chamberlain: blind to a Hitlerean threat and then trying to redirect the threat toward the East. Deng invoked and exalted the spirit of Nixon. Those were the days when the common aim was to "fix the Polar Bear."[68] But then détente came along. "In 1972, after you reached the SALT agreement, the Soviet Union drastically quickened their pace in the development of nuclear arms," Deng said. "Their pace was quicker than the United States. When the Agreement on the Prevention of Nuclear War was reached between your two countries, the strategic balance had reached an equilibrium. In November last year when we met, after the Vladivostok meeting, the Doctor informed us that the number of Soviet missiles had not yet reached the ceiling, and this morning you told us that the number of Soviet missiles had exceeded the ceiling."[69]

"In terms of total military strength," Deng continued, "the Soviet Union has a greater military strength than the United States and the European countries put together. But the Soviet Union has two big weaknesses: one, they lack food grains; the second is that their industrial equipment and technology is backward." As a result, "when war breaks out, the Soviet Union cannot hold out long.

"Therefore," Deng said, "we do not understand why the United States and the West have used their strong points to make up for the Soviet weaknesses." In Helsinki, Deng continued, the European "Insecurity" Conference, as he called it, had the smell of Munich in 1938, where the weak Europeans put on their blindfolds. "We have a Chinese saying: even a donkey can be made to push the millstone around and around if you blindfold it,"[70] Deng said.

When the translator finished putting all of Deng's statements into English, the tension in the room was almost overpowering. There was a long, difficult pause, as if it took the Americans a few moments to absorb Deng's disturbing words and then to overcome the momentary disbelief that he could have said such a thing. Kissinger was speechless, fighting for control of his emotions. He asked Deng if they could take a break. His aides felt the volcanic rumble as he stalked out of the room. Equating Kissinger with Chamberlain. No one had ever been so insulting.

After composing himself, Kissinger returned.

"I must say I listened to the vice premier's presentation with some sadness. I had thought, obviously incorrectly, that some of the public statements, which I had heard, were said for public effect. But this is obviously not the case.

"If there is not a common strategic perception," Kissinger continued, "then one wonders what exactly the basis of our policy is. If you seriously think that we are trying to push the Soviet Union to attack the East, then we are in grave danger of frittering away all our efforts—with yourself and everyone else."[71]

Kissinger tried to turn the tables on Deng. It was China, he said, that had failed to act in the India-Pakistan crisis of 1971. The United States moved a naval armada into the Bay of Bengal and thought that China would move troops to the Indian border, but it did not.

"President Nixon and I decided that if you moved, and if the Soviet Union brought pressure on you, we would resist and assist you, even though you had not asked us to. We did that out of our conviction of the national interest.

"Since I have been in Washington," Kissinger continued, "We have gone to a confrontation with the Soviet Union three times: once over a nuclear submarine base in Cuba; once over the Syrian invasion of Jordan; once over the question of the alert in the Middle East in 1973 and—no, four times— once on the question of access to Berlin. We did all these things on our own, without knowing what any other country, much less China, would do."[72]

Deng remained impassive.

"The vice premier referred to the spirit of Munich. I have studied that period and lived through it, as a victim, so I know it rather well. The Munich policy was conducted by governments who denied that there was a danger, and who attempted to avoid their problems by denying that they existed. The current United States policy, as we have attempted to tell you, has no illusions about the danger, but it attempts to find the most effective means of resistance given the realities we face," Kissinger said. "A country that spends $110 billion a year for defense cannot be said to be pursuing the spirit of Munich." It was the United States that organized the defense of Europe through

NATO, Kissinger reminded Deng. "If the Soviet Union should stretch out its hands, we will be brutal in our response, no matter where it occurs—and we won't ask people whether they share our assessment when we resist.[73]

"And we do not separate the fronts into East and West," he continued. "If the Soviet Union feels strong enough to attack in either the West or East, the policy will already have failed. The Soviet Union must not be in a position where if feels strong enough to attack at all."

As for which superpower was stronger, Kissinger commented that there was much nonsense in the press about the issue. "Numbers are not so important anyway, as each American missile can carry more warheads. We have been ahead by a ratio of six or seven to one. Moreover, since the Soviets like big things which take room, they have about 85 to 90 percent of their forces on land, where they are vulnerable because the accuracy of our forces is improved. Less than 20 percent of our forces are on land, and they are less vulnerable. So it is not true that in the strategic balance we are behind.

"In 1960 President Kennedy was elected by speaking of the missile gap, even though the Soviet Union had only thirty missiles, each of which took ten hours to get ready to fire, and we had 1,200 airplanes [with nuclear weapons]. Ever since then, it has been the secret dream of every American presidential candidate to run on a missile gap campaign, so we are in danger of this issue erupting every four years.

"So our policy is quite clear, and in pursuing it we have not asked anything from China." Kissinger said further that China had asked nothing of the United States. "We do not object to your public posture. We do object when you direct it against us, when you accuse us of betraying our allies and endangering the security of the world by deliberately promoting war and standing on the sidelines, when in fact we are doing actual things to prevent a war and preserve the world equilibrium."[74]

Kissinger said that if Deng thought the United States "was engaged in petty tactical maneuvers," then that was a pity for both sides. "We don't need theater," he said, "and we don't need you to divert Soviet energies—that would be a total misconception and it might lead to the same catastrophe as in the 1930s."

Deng made no response to the substance of Kissinger's rebuttal.

"It is quite late," he said. "Shall we go on tomorrow afternoon?"

It was an extraordinary encounter—first, Deng siding with Kissinger's domestic critics with a withering assault on the administration's policy toward the Soviet Union. Then, an indignant Kissinger delivering his defense, partly rational but partly sanctimonious in the Kissinger way. Beneath the armor of his indignation, Kissinger knew best of all that he *had* engaged in "theater" and "tactical maneuvers" in conducting relations with China; of course the

United States had profited by having China divert Soviet energies and by tying down more than forty Soviet divisions in the East. And of course Kissinger's vaunted commitment to a strong and independent China was just words—and the Chinese knew better than to rely on them. After all the bombast, what really did Kissinger mean when he said that he and Nixon would have "resisted" a Soviet attack on China during the India-Pakistan crisis of 1971, that they would have "assisted" Chinese forces? Surely he did not mean that an American aircraft carrier in the Bay of Bengal could have stopped all those Soviet divisions from bursting out of their bases in Mongolia and Kazakhstan and onto the northern plain of China thousands of miles to the north? Surely Kissinger did not mean that he and Nixon would have escalated an Asian border war to global conflict by deploying American B-52s and nuclear weapons?

Mao and Deng had indeed provoked Kissinger with the tirade about Chamberlain; they, too, were engaged in "theater," trying to exhort the United States out of what they saw as strategic passivity. That was in their interest. They were playing the American card against Moscow by preying on American insecurities about its own image in the world.

F ROM THE GREAT HALL of the People to Mao's study at Zhongnanhai is just a two-minute drive down the Avenue of Eternal Peace, past the giant stone lions that guard the New China Gate and down a willow-lined avenue that winds around a lake to the chairman's compound. It had been two years since any American had seen Mao, and his state of deterioration was shocking. He stood with great difficulty to greet the Americans. His face was slack, his mouth open, and his speech impossibly slurred.

"You know I have various ailments all over me. I am going to heaven soon," Mao said.

"Not soon," Kissinger replied politely.

"Soon," Mao said. "I have already received an invitation from God."75

"I hope you won't accept it for a long while," Kissinger persisted.

"I accept the orders of the Doctor," Mao said, in deference to his guest.

But after these pleasantries, Mao made it clear that it was he who had been standing behind the curtain of Deng's assault.

"So you have quarreled with him," Mao said pointing to Deng.

"Only about the means for a common objective," Kissinger replied.

"Yesterday, during your quarrel with the Vice Premier, you said the U.S. asked nothing of China and China asked nothing of the U.S. As I see it, this is partially right and partially wrong. The small issue is Taiwan, the big issue is the world."

Suddenly, Mao's face contorted in a spasm of coughing, and a nurse rushed into the study to steady him,[76] but he waved her off.

"If neither side had anything to ask from the other, why would you be coming to Beijing?" Mao asked. "Why would we want to receive you and the president?"

"We come to Beijing because we have a common opponent and because we think your perception of the world situation is the clearest of any country we deal with and with which we agree on some—many points."

"Those words are not reliable," said Mao, "because according to your priorities the first is the Soviet Union, the second is Europe, and the third is Japan."

Kissinger tried to correct him. "The Soviet Union is a great danger for us, but not a high priority."

But Mao was quarrelsome. "That is not correct. It is a superpower, there are only two superpowers in the world. We are backward. We see what you are doing is leaping to Moscow by way of our shoulders,[77] and these shoulders are now useless."

"We have nothing to gain in Moscow," Kissinger said.

"But you can gain Taiwan in China."

"But we will settle that between us."

"In a hundred years," Mao grunted.

"It won't take a hundred years," Kissinger protested. "Much less."

"It's better for it to be in your hands," Mao said. "And if you were to send it back to me now, I would not want it, because it's not wantable. There are a huge bunch of counterrevolutionaries there."

Mao was repeating himself. After a little more banter, the chairman pointed toward the heavens and said, "And when I go to heaven to see God, I'll tell him it's better to have Taiwan under the care of the United States now."

"He'll be very astonished to hear that from the Chairman," Kissinger said.

"No, because God blesses you, not us. God does not like us," Mao said, waving his hands in resignation, "because I am a militant warlord, also a Communist. That's why he doesn't like me. He likes you." Mao pointed to Kissinger, Bush, and Lord, who was taking notes. "He likes you and you and you."

"I have never had the pleasure of meeting him, so I am not sure," Kissinger said, at a loss again on how to deal with Mao's mysticism.

"I'm sure. I am eighty-two years old now. How old are you?"

"Fifty-one," Kissinger said.

Mao pointed to Deng and said, "He's seventy-one," and then made another sweeping gesture with his hands. "And after we're all dead, myself, him, Zhou Enlai, and Ye Jianying, you will still be alive. See? We old ones will not do. We are not going to make it."[78]

Kissinger finally found his tongue, and he began to flatter Mao. Kissinger said that Mao's exposition on the state of the world had left a "profound" impression on him. He even apologized for America's distraction with Watergate. "We've had a difficult period because of the resignation of President Nixon, and we've had to do more maneuvering than we would have liked," he explained.

Mao said that maneuvering was "allowable" in some instances. Yet he was still puzzled by the American scandal.

"It was inexcusable," said Kissinger. "Inexcusable."

Nancy Tang, the interpreter, asked Kissinger to explain.

"It was inexcusable to conduct it in that manner. It was a minor event that was played into a national and international tragedy by a group of very short-sighted people. President Nixon was a good president."

Mao nodded in agreement.

"I am still in very frequent contact with him," Kissinger said.

"Please convey my regards to Mr. Nixon," Mao replied, and Kissinger promised to call Nixon as soon as he returned to Washington.

"Dunkirk,"[79] Mao said suddenly.

He was back to attacking the American strategy of "retreat" in Europe.

"When the wind and rain are coming, the swallows are busy," Mao continued. There was nothing a busy swallow (referring to Kissinger) could do to prevent the arrival of the Soviet storm in Europe.

"We have 7,000 nuclear weapons in Europe and they are not there to be captured," Kissinger said.

"But there are a considerable portion of Americans who do not believe you'll use them," Mao said. "They do not believe Americans will be willing to die for Europe."

Mao shifted.

"Please give my regards to your secretary of defense," he added. "We want to invite him here for the Soviets to see, but you are too miserly. The United States is so rich, but on this you are so miserly."

"He will not come with the president. Maybe later," Kissinger said.

"We would like to invite him to pay a visit to the Northeast of our country, Mongolia and Xinjiang. He perhaps will not go, nor would you have the courage."[80]

"I would go," said Kissinger. He again broached his offer to provide military aide to the Chinese to improve security on the northern border. But Mao was not interested.

"As for military aspects, we should not discuss that now. Such matters should wait until the war breaks out before we consider them."

"Yes, but you should know that we would be prepared to consider them," Kissinger said.

Mao was too weak to get up and walk Kissinger to the door. But he motioned that their discussion was over.

Kissinger was shaken by the experience. Back at his villa, he collapsed in a chair.

Mao had become some kind of "monster," he told his aides.

"He is holding himself together by sheer will power," Kissinger said. "He has a bad case of Parkinson's disease and can barely stand up. He mumbles so badly that the interpreters have trouble hearing him. Yet there he is. He's a monster!"[81]

The next day, Kissinger asked the Chinese when they would be ready to go over the communiqué for Ford's trip, but they told him it was still being "translated." The Chinese had gone into a stall. Deng told Kissinger that Ford's visit would have to stand on its own without a communiqué. Yet Kissinger pressed for something. What about a statement that accelerated trade relations? What about establishing a hot line, or a branch liaison office in Los Angeles or San Francisco? Deng rejected these ideas. Such progress, he said, could only be made between countries with established diplomatic relations. If Ford was not prepared to break with Taiwan, there was no point.

After midnight on the eve of Kissinger's departure, Qiao Guanhua delivered a draft communiqué that reeked of radical defiance: "The factors for both revolution and war are increasing. . . . Nations want liberation and the people want revolution. . . . The peoples of the Third World countries have won a series of significant victories in their struggle against colonialism, imperialism, and hegemonism. The contention between the superpowers for world hegemony has become ever more intense. There is no lasting peace in the world. There definitely does not exist an irreversible process of détente; instead, the danger of a new world war is mounting. . . . People of all countries must get prepared against war."[82]

Kissinger was livid. This was not the way the representative of the president of the United States should be treated. The document was "completely unacceptable," Kissinger said, and Ford would not come to China without an acceptable communiqué.[83] But Qiao held firm, calling Kissinger's bluff. It was no great matter to the Chinese if there was no communiqué.

Kissinger's plane was due to leave in just a few hours, and so he suggested that once back in Washington, he would redraft the communiqué and send it to Qiao through diplomatic channels. By the time Qiao left Kissinger's villa at 2:30 A.M., there was a sense on both sides that the relationship had been reduced to sparring over empty words.

On the way back to the United States, Kissinger sent a message to Ford advising him that they should be prepared to cancel the trip unless the Chinese were willing to put something on paper that could signify the trip's success.[84]

Kissinger arrived home just in time for the Halloween Massacre.

Ford fired Schlesinger, whom he had never liked, replacing him with Rumsfeld. Kissinger was relieved of his dual role in foreign policy. He retained his cabinet seat as secretary of state, but Ford elevated Scowcroft to be national security adviser and to provide what he hoped would be better communication with his political advisers. Bush was offered the CIA director's job, from which William Colby had been fired. Bush had hoped for a better offer, and so had his wife, but he was nonetheless happy to return to Washington to be closer to the theater of presidential politics.

In Beijing, Deng was facing his own political siege.

From his sickbed, Mao launched a campaign of criticism against Deng's domestic policies, and Deng's power subsequently declined further, although he remained in charge of foreign policy. It appeared that Jiang Qing and the radicals not only were out to have him removed from office, but wanted him imprisoned or even executed. As Mao's health continued to deteriorate, his channels of information were filtered by a favored nephew, Mao Yuanxin, now constantly at his side. In times of intensified internal struggle, all politics tended to veer toward the radical camp. Everyone feared the wrath of Mao, and so the safest course was to heave the hard line on all issues.*

For weeks, the Chinese refused to allow Ford's advance team to come to Beijing. When it finally arrived in late November, there were only a few days left to make the elaborate preparations necessary for a presidential visit. Kissinger surrendered to the Chinese on the communiqué. The secretary of state was reduced to offering a perfunctory "announcement" of the Ford visit. It was so embarrassing in its brevity and lack of substance that it was later abandoned.[85]

Then, on November 19, Reagan telephoned Ford to say that he was going to seek the Republican nomination for president. The China trip was not the sole reason, but it was certainly part of the reason, for the Reagan challenge. Ford was angry and crestfallen.[86] He had seen it coming, but he had also

---

*Qiao Guanhua summoned George Bush on November 4, 1975, and told him bluntly: "In the past twenty-six years, in the absence of diplomatic relations with the United States, the Chinese people have led a life much better than in any period in China's history. It can be said with certainty that further delay in the establishment of diplomatic relations between China and the United States will not cause the sky to fall, and the 800 million Chinese people will continue to enjoy their happy life."

hoped to rally the party around himself so the Republicans could concentrate their energies on holding the White House.

As he prepared to leave for China, Ford's in-box continued to bring alarming news. Out of the blue, the CIA warned that China's leadership had begun a five-year preparation for the invasion of Taiwan. In a top secret document, the agency referred to reliable, clandestine reports indicating that Luo Ruiqing, a PLA marshal who had once been purged but was now rehabilitated, had been placed in charge of long-range military planning for the "liberation" of the island.* The CIA interpreted this to mean that "China plans to invade Taiwan within five years, and they explicitly link the five-year time frame to the 1980 U.S. Presidential elections."[87]

Ford knew that such planning did not necessarily mean that an invasion would be carried out, but it almost didn't matter. The CIA assessment reinforced Mao's statements and those of Deng and Qiao—they put the United States on notice that after the withdrawal of American forces from Taiwan, China might resort to military force to retake Taiwan. Ford had to wonder how any president could break with Taiwan under these circumstances.

GERALD AND BETTY FORD arrived in China in December 1975 with all the ceremony that had attended Richard Nixon's visit in 1972. The timing was roughly the same, just in advance of the presidential election season, but up until the moment of the Fords' departure, some in the White House felt that the president should not be making the trip. If the president was not going to normalize relations with China, then why was he going at all, at a time when an economic crisis was gripping the country? (Ford brought along his budget director, James T. Lynn, to help deflect domestic criticism. While in China, the president intended to spend four hours each day reviewing domestic spending programs that he would submit to Congress in January.)

Air Force One arrived at Beijing's airport in the afternoon, and the presidential party was whisked in the elegant antiquity of Red Flag limousines to the same guest villa at Diaoyutai where Nixon had stayed. The Avenue of Eternal Peace was a corridor of American and Chinese flags. To Ford's surprise, Deng Yingchao, the wife of Zhou Enlai, was there in the garden to greet the entourage. Zhou was near death in a military hospital not far away, but no one betrayed a hint of his condition to the Americans.[88]

The White House had done everything it could to lower expectations for the trip, and so on the first evening, when Deng hosted the Fords and their daughter, Susan, for the welcoming banquet at the Great Hall, there was

*These "reliable," clandestine reports proved utterly wrong.

some anxiety about his toast, which would be broadcast live to the United States, where Americans were just getting up to eat breakfast and turn on the morning news shows. Deng chose the moment after the meal's fifth course (white Chinese cabbage with chestnuts) to stand and welcome the Fords, but in no time he was talking about the threat of Soviet hegemony.

"Today it is the country which most zealously preaches peace that is the most dangerous source of war," he said. "Rhetoric about 'détente' cannot cover up the stark reality of the growing danger of war."[89] Hegemonism, Deng said, "is weak by nature—it bullies the soft and fears the tough."

Relieved that Deng said nothing in public about Chamberlain or the "spirit of Munich," Ford stood to deliver his rebuttal. "The world confronts us all with dangers, but it also offers opportunities," he said. "The current situation requires strength, vigilance, and firmness. But we will also continue our efforts to achieve a more peaceful world even as we remain determined to resist any actions that threaten the independence and well being of others."

The next morning, Deng was far more gracious to Ford than he had been with Kissinger. But he brought up his World War II analogy and the parallels between the 1970s and the 1930s. Then, like now, Deng said, there were two approaches—one represented by Chamberlain and the other by Churchill. At that time, Deng pointed out, Hitler was not as strong militarily as the Soviets under Stalin already had become. Then Deng told a parable from the Chinese classic the *Romance of the Three Kingdoms* as a way to reinforce Mao's point about the danger posed by the Soviet Union.

"Seventeen hundred years ago in China there were three kingdoms," he said.[90] "The king of one of the three kingdoms was the Martial Emperor of Wei, and his name was Tsao Tsao. He was a great military man, a great statesman, and a great man of letters. During this war of confusion between the three kingdoms," Deng continued, "there was a general named Liu Pu who was the most outstanding and most courageous. During the war he was defeated and surrendered to Tsao Tsao." But after his surrender, Liu Pu suggested to Tsao Tsao, "With your wisdom and leadership and my bravery in battle, we could conquer the world. May I lead the forces?" But Tsao Tsao's advisers were deeply suspicious about Liu Pu's true loyalty, and they expressed their doubts in this manner: "Liu Pu is like an eagle, which when it is hungry will work for you, but when it is well fed, it will fly away."

Deng then made his point. "When you have fed the Soviet Union until it is full, it might not only fly away, but it might fly back to take a peck at you."[91]

They all laughed, but Ford took the point, insisting that the United States was "not overly eager" to feed the Soviet "eagle" with grain and financial credits.

Ford and his family were visiting the Temple of Heaven when Mao summoned them. Up until that moment, no one had been sure whether Mao would personally greet Ford. There was a preemptory quality to the summons, forcing the president to rush back to his villa and change, as if he were a suitor called before the emperor.

Mao stood with the help of a nurse, and all anyone could notice was how animated he became when his eyes fell on the blonde-haired Susan Ford, who was sixteen. The chairman sparkled and he dallied an extra few moments in greeting her[92] before moving on to the paunchy adults. Ford was anxious to make a good impression on Mao as a tough and resolute American leader whom the chairman could take seriously. That was the Kissinger line. Mao asked what Ford and Deng had discussed.

"We discussed the problems we have with the Soviet Union and the need to have parallel actions . . . [and] the need for your country and mine to work in parallel to achieve what is good for both of us."[93]

"We do not have much ability," Mao grunted, and then scribbled on a notepad, "We can only fire such empty cannons."

"I do not believe that, Mr. Chairman," Ford said.

"With regard to cursing, we have some ability in that respect," Mao said with a twinkle.

"We can too," Ford said, trying to keep up.

"And you also? Then we shall reach an agreement," the chairman said with mock satisfaction.

"We can also use force against a country which causes much trouble, "[94] Ford said, with a little too much machismo.

The conversation seemed destined to remain on this perfunctory plane until Ford brought up the subject of Angola.

"I am in favor of driving the Soviet Union out," Mao said, more energetically.

"If we both make an effort, we can," said Ford, delighted to find Mao responsive.

For the first time, Deng spoke up, addressing Mao in Chinese, which was lost on the Americans.

"The complicating factor here is that of South Africa," Deng said. South Africa's apartheid government had thrown its weight behind Savimbi's UNITA forces. In October, a South African armored column had crossed the border into Angola and was now fighting alongside Savimbi.

"This has offended the whole of black Africa," Deng added.

"But they are fighting to keep the Soviet Union from expanding," said Ford, defending the South African involvement, "and we think that is admirable."

"Do you mean you admire South Africa?" Deng asked.

"No," said Ford, but he added, "they have taken a strong stance against the Soviet Union. And they are doing that totally on their own, without any stimulation by the United States."*

Deng was still incredulous. "In Angola?"[95]

"South Africa is against the MPLA," Ford said pointedly, implying that anyone who was against the Soviet-backed MPLA was on the right side.

For nearly a half hour, Mao, Deng, Ford, and Kissinger discussed the politics and tactics of how to fight the Russians and Cubans in Africa. They exchanged assessments and political intelligence and made requests for covert action. Kissinger suggested that the United States would provide weapons if the Chinese would help train the rebels in guerrilla warfare tactics. Deng suggested that the United States pressure South Africa to withdraw for the sake of black African unity. And Ford revealed that "just before I left Washington, I approved another $35 million" to further equip the forces opposed to the MPLA.

"Good," said Mao, and then let the Chinese photographers into the room for the farewell.

The next day, Kissinger told Deng, "We are prepared to push South Africa out as soon as an alternative military force can be created."[96]

Ford praised China's actions. "You have been effective," he said, and then he asked Deng to commit to a joint strategy in Angola.

"Will you move in the north if we move in the south?" Ford asked.

"But you should give greater help in the north too," Deng added. "As far as I know, you have many ways to help, also through third countries."

"We have and will," said Ford.

"Good."

Never had China and the United States come so close to direct cooperation in a covert war on a distant continent. Where Nixon and Kissinger had failed so many times to draw the Chinese into a deeper level of cooperation, the blatancy of the Soviet-Cuban airlift had combined with alarm in African capitals to create the conditions for genuine collaboration between China and the United States. Ford's frankness and earnest persistence had drawn the Chinese leaders into an unforeseen bargain to work against Soviet-backed forces in Angola.

The high note of the Angola cooperation momentarily took much of the pressure off the Taiwan dispute, which Deng brought up on the last day if

---

*This statement was not fully candid, since the CIA station in Pretoria had been beefed up specifically to coordinate the air, ground, and maritime transports of weapons to the FNLA and UNITA, which could only be done by coordinating with the South African military and secret services. See Stockwell, *In Search of Enemies*, pp. 162–165.

only to reinforce the notion that, although Taiwan was subordinate to the larger issues of the Cold War, it was nonetheless critical.

"We have understood Mr. President's point; that is, that during the time of the election it will not be possible to make any new moves. As for our side, we have told the Doctor many times that we are very patient. And in our relations we have always put the international aspect first and the Taiwan issue second."[97]

Ford could only be thankful that the Chinese were willing to let him off the hook.

"We are very grateful that you are understanding of the domestic political situation in the United States," he said.

Deng was obliged, however, to reiterate to Ford what China ultimately expected of him—breaking with Taiwan and abrogating the defense treaty. And Ford, just to make sure that Deng understood what *he* expected, added, "We would certainly anticipate that any solution would be by peaceful means as far as your government and Taiwan are concerned. We can't just cast aside old friends. It would have to be a peaceful solution, which I understand is the understanding President Nixon made at that time."

Deng did not let this statement pass.

"To put it frankly, we do not believe in peaceful transition. Because there is a huge bunch of counterrevolutionaries over there, and the question of what method we will take to solve our internal problem is something that we believe belongs to the internal affairs of China, to be decided by China herself.

"Chairman Mao mentioned 5 years, 10 years, 20 years, 100 years," Deng said, as how long it might take. He pointed out that Kissinger always like to stress the 100-year figure, and that drew a laugh around the table.[98]

"You can argue that 100 years is a peaceful transition," said Ford, adding to the laughter.

"But I think it is clear that the Chairman's meaning was that even in 100 years, a peaceful transition would be impossible," Deng said.

.   .   .

Ford had scarcely arrived back in Washington when, on December 13, the whole story of the secret CIA campaign in Angola was spilled to the press. The consequences could not have been worse for the strong new bond Ford believed he had forged in Beijing. He stood by helplessly as the Senate cut off all U.S. funding for the rebel groups. The CIA was ordered to disengage. The ranking Chinese official in Washington, Han Xu, sent the message that "The situation in Angola only proves our position that appeasement will whet the Soviet appetite for expansionism."[99]

The decline of the Republican era that began with Nixon, paralleled the collapse of the Mao era in China. Zhou died on January 8, 1976. His death incited new concerns about the Chinese succession. Although Deng delivered the eulogy at Zhou's funeral, he remained under attack by the radicals. In February 1976, the Central Committee, at Mao's behest, named the plump and reliable former party secretary of Hunan, Hua Guofeng, acting premier, and many of Deng's duties were reassigned as the campaign against him intensified.

In the United States, following the humiliation over Angola, Ford abandoned foreign policy and waded into the presidential primary campaign. But Mao could not resist meddling in American politics by inviting Richard Nixon to make his first trip abroad since his resignation. Nixon accepted, and Ford was stunned by the news. Scowcroft, the most mild mannered of security advisers, swore.

Nixon had given no warning. In fact, in a telephone call to Ford in January, he had given his assurance that he would stay out of sight during 1976 to minimize his association with the president.[100] The Nixon pardon still clung to the Ford White House like skunk weed. Now, Nixon's face would return to the front pages just as Ford was out on the hustings trying to get elected as his own man. Why Nixon would want to raise his own profile at such a moment was a question that plagued the Ford camp.

Of course, Ronald Reagan seized the initiative.

"In place of a determined and confident America the Chinese bargained with four years ago," Reagan told a crowd of retirees in Port Charlotte, Florida, "they see in Washington today a timid, vacillating, and divided leadership.[101]

"Under the circumstances, it is not surprising that the Chinese, in their frustration, would send a jet for Richard Nixon." The question was not whether Nixon should have gone, Reagan said, but "whether Mr. Ford is viewed by the Chinese as a man capable of dealing effectively with the Soviet Union."

In the Ford campaign, all references to "détente" were dropped by March, and James A. Baker III, then Ford's undersecretary of commerce, told a group of Republican fund-raisers in Oklahoma City that if Ford won the election, he couldn't imagine that Henry Kissinger would be in the administration.[102]

Nixon's visit notwithstanding, the Chinese were increasingly absorbed with their own succession struggle.

One hundred days after Zhou's death, tens of thousands of Beijing students and workers flooded Tiananmen Square to lay wreathes in his honor at the foot of the Monument to the Martyrs, the marble obelisk that stands on a terraced platform near the center of the square. This outpouring of Beijingers registered an obvious political message: the repudiation of radicalism. Horrified by the mob, Mao's wife rushed to the chairman's sickbed and emerged minutes later to declare the demonstration a "counterrevolutionary rebellion" directed by Deng Xiaoping. With Deng already weakened, Jiang Qing and her radical cohorts—the Gang of Four*—made their move. Public security forces cleared the square, arresting hundreds of "counterrevolutionaries." Deng was stripped of his remaining titles and placed under house arrest.

Mao suffered his first heart attack on May 11.[103] The episode affected only a small area of heart tissue and so did not completely incapacitate the chairman, but it did further embolden the radicals. One of the Gang of Four, Zhang Chunqiao,† met in July with a visiting American congressional delegation headed by Senator Hugh Scott and blew their hair back with his vehemence. Scott was shaken by the encounter, especially since he had hand-carried a letter from Ford about the importance of ensuring a peaceful transition on Taiwan. But Zhang dismissed all talk of peace. He said that Taiwan's future would be settled "with bayonets" and that the PLA was at that moment preparing for the liberation of Taiwan.[104]

A report of his diatribe reached the White House about the same time as Nixon's "eyes only" account of his talk with the new premier, Hua Guofeng. Again, the military option seemed to figure prominently in Beijing's thinking. "In the final analysis," Hua told Nixon, "if it is necessary, we will have to liberate Taiwan by war."[105]

To add to this air of belligerence, the Chinese navy launched a series of large-scale exercises in the Taiwan Strait. And as Mao's second heart attack struck on June 26, affecting a larger area of his heart, the Chinese politburo became a den of long knives in anticipation of the struggle that would follow Mao's death.

No one in the White House needed the CIA, or anyone else, to conclude that things were getting pretty scary in Beijing.

YET NO ONE WAS READY for what happened at 3:42 A.M. on July 28. The plains east of Beijing heaved again and again with such enormous energy that nearly every house in and around the city of Tangshan, population 1 million, collapsed under its force, burying the occupants. In twenty seconds, the third most destructive earthquake in 2,000 years of recorded history killed 242,000 people and injured another 160,000.

*The "gang" consisted of Jiang Qing, Yao Wenyuan, Zhang Chunqiao, and Wang Hongwen.
†Pronounced: Jaang Chwuun-chow.

Seven thousand families were completely exterminated, every member dead in the rubble. Survivors crawled from collapsed houses in darkness and silence. A light drizzle fell over a landscape of destruction.

"It was silent for a few seconds, and then you began to hear the shouts and the cries," said Liu Chuanzhen, who was pulled from her collapsed house that morning.[106]

For thousands of years, the Chinese believed that their emperors had an intimate relationship with the heavens. They associated the coming of great natural phenomena, like comets, floods, and earthquakes, with dynastic changes. As Mao lay dying, after Zhou had expired in January and after Zhu De, the PLA commander during the revolution, had died on July 6, the Chinese knew that this was a sign.

From Tangshan, a single coal miner set out in a dilapidated army jeep to cover the 105 miles to Beijing. It took him half a day to reach the New China Gate of Zhongnanhai, where he told the guard that he had come to report to the leaders on the devastation. The radicals treated the rescue operation like another political movement. Their slogan was "Resist the Earthquake and Rescue Ourselves." Foreigners were forbidden to travel to the area, and the government of Hua Guofeng rejected offers of aid from international relief agencies.

In Washington, seismic monitoring confirmed that a monstrous quake had struck. The first estimates of the death toll were numbing, perhaps a half million or more. This gargantuan temblor could be interpreted as a paradigm for political collapse. A third heart attack leveled Mao on September 2.[107] Gasping for breath, he hung on, a great, wasted hulk of a revolutionary. But at ten minutes past midnight on September 9, his heart stopped. The chairman was gone.

The Chinese looked blankly into their future with a mixture of wonderment, fear, and an unnerving, unquenchable curiosity about what was to come. The masses, whom Mao had galvanized into an indomitable force in Chinese history, had been cut adrift by the loss of the Great Helmsman. In the late summer heat, countless millions of listless Chinese slept outdoors and wandered the streets in search of answers. They made the pilgrimage to the Great Hall, where Mao lay in state, his once mighty stature now supine in a new and strange revelation—repose, an emperor in slumber. There was no certainty that he would not again awaken, for Mao was a god, and no one could be sure that his invincible willpower would not, in the end, conquer death itself.

James Schlesinger, fired by Ford but favored by Mao, was in the midst of his long-delayed visit to China when the chairman expired. He attended the funeral as the unofficial representative of the United States.[108] Mao's body was embalmed but, due to the heat and inadequate technique, only with great difficulty. The politburo laid plans for permanent preservation of the corpse and the construction of a mausoleum on Tiananmen Square.

In Beijing, much of the population was still living in tents and makeshift shelters because of Tangshan aftershocks that were still rattling the city's buildings, but behind the scenes, intense scheming had begun among the rivals for power. In Shanghai, the Gang of Four was rumored to be forming a militia that would race to Beijing and seize control of Zhongnanhai. But the Beijing leadership quickly organized the forces needed for a countercoup. Marshal Ye Jianying and the head of Mao's palace guard, Wang Dongxing, persuaded Hua Guofeng to strike preemptively, and, when he agreed, the military men laid the trap.

At the politburo meeting of October 6, Wang's guards arrested Zhang Chunqiao and Wang Hongwen as they walked into the meeting room. Yao Wenyuan and Mao's wife, Jiang Qing, were seized in their quarters, along with a number of their cohorts. The palace coup, together with the passing of Zhou and Mao in the same year, marked not just a change of leadership, but a new era. But with Hua Guofeng at the helm, it was difficult to estimate what kind of transition lay ahead and what kind of leadership would eventually emerge.

B Y COINCIDENCE, Qiao Guanhua, now China's foreign minister, was in New York.

On the night of October 8, just two days after the Gang of Four were arrested, Qiao hosted Kissinger at the Chinese mission. This would be their final meeting, though neither imagined it at the time. It was a feast of bitterness.

Qiao had just delivered one of his most searing assaults on American "appeasement" in a speech to the UN General Assembly. Kissinger was agog at Qiao's churlish and insolent attack, which only added to his funk. Ford was losing ground to Jimmy Carter, and Kissinger had become something of a punching bag in the campaign.

Less diplomatic than usual, he lectured Qiao on the flawed logic of the Chinese attack on America. "If the Foreign Minister will permit me," he said. "As I understand it, you said in your speech that when the U.S. negotiates with the Soviets, it is engaging in appeasement and pushing the Soviets toward China. But when the United States resists the Soviets, it is engaging in a rivalry of the superpowers against which all mankind should unite. Under those conditions, we are playing under rules where we cannot possibly win."[109]

All through the evening, they quarreled in this manner, Kissinger complaining about the unfairness of China's criticism, Qiao attacking him no matter what he said.

"I was almost alone in the U.S. over Angola,"[110] Kissinger asserted indignantly. "I forced the U.S. to do something about Angola. By December 1, we were on the verge of assembling a force which, when deployed, would have exhausted the Cubans. Several countries were involved. On December 8, President Ford called in Ambassador Dobrynin and told him to stop arms shipments to Angola. A few days later, the Soviets did stop shipments. Then, on December 19, Congress voted to cut off all money for Angola, and there was no prospect for our using force. On December 24, the Soviets resumed armed shipments. When the time came for me to go to Moscow in January, the only thing left for me to use was a bluff and I tried it. It didn't work. Since then I have made violent attacks on the Soviets. In Angola, we were defeated by our own people. I know this is of no consolation to you. But I wanted to explain."

"Our view is that the Soviets, through Helsinki, see your weakness," said Qiao, baiting Kissinger.

"Really Mr. Foreign Minister, I don't want to be impolite, but I don't agree. We are not weak. Rather, we are temporarily weak until after our elections. We have gone through a period of temporary weakness when the forces which overthrew Nixon have been dominant in this country. But that will end on November 2."

"I don't want to be impolite," replied Qiao. "The Soviets, through Helsinki, have come to feel that the West is anxious to reach agreement." Munich thinking, Qiao called it.

"But we don't have Munich-like thinking," Kissinger said, barely able to contain his anger. "Frankly, we find it insulting. At Munich, the allies sacrificed others. We have not."[111]

"There is not much change in the trend of appeasement," Qiao needled.

"Repeating twice something we find insulting doesn't make it true," Kissinger said, his indignation threatening to boil over.

They circled round and round the same point, picking at each other's scabs like a couple of old crows. Qiao shifted from one grievance to another. Why had the United States supported Taiwan's entry in the 1976 Olympics as the Republic of China, Qiao asked?

"If you must know the truth, because of the Republican convention," Kissinger replied.

"And then we have Governor Scranton's remarks about welcoming Taiwan into the UN," Qiao said, pulling out a transcript of Meet the Press from October 3, where Scranton had said that he would be "glad to have" Taiwan back in the UN.

"Ridiculous, outrageous!"[112] protested Kissinger. "Perhaps you can't believe me when I say I didn't know about this until you told me just now."

"This reflects a trend," said Qiao.

"Yes, in public opinion," Kissinger had to admit.

"Not only in your society, but in your government, too," Qiao added.

Kissinger did not deny it. He simply said that Scranton was a friend. "He is a fine man. I have no idea why he said what he did."

"I smile bitterly," Qiao replied.

Kissinger returned to Washington and gathered his senior China aides. It was a few days before the presidential election, and he poured out to them his long-held pessimism about China.

"It is not possible to normalize," he told Habib, Hummel, Gleysteen, and Lord, strewn dejectedly on their chairs around the secretary's office. "What price makes normalization worthwhile?"

Gleysteen tried to puncture the gloom. "But we can try."

Kissinger would not hear it. Even if Mao had agreed to guarantee a peaceful transition on Taiwan as the price for diplomatic relations with Washington, "it would be a fraud," he said. What would the United States do if China attacked Taiwan? "Go to war?"[113]

Kissinger continued: "If Taiwan is recognized by us as part of China, then it may become irresistible for them. Our saying we wanted a peaceful solution has no force. It is Chinese territory. What are we going to do about it? For us to go to war with a recognized country where we have an ambassador over a part of what we would recognize as their country would be preposterous!"

Kissinger's men, those who had long understood his doubts, were not surprised. Some attempted to argue with him, but he was adamant. Only a "bleeding heart" liberal, he said, would be foolish enough to take the risk of establishing relations with China. He most certainly would not.

"I never believed that normalization is possible,"[114] Kissinger said.

CARTER:

FULFILLMENT

"THE PRESIDENT

HAS MADE UP

HIS MIND . . . "

Deng Xiaoping and Jimmy Carter

I N THE EARLY MONTHS OF 1949, the war in the Pacific was over, but
China was still roiling with civil strife. Chinese Nationalists were fighting Chinese Communists for control of an already devastated countryside. Jimmy Carter, then a young submarine officer whose diesel-powered
vessel was patrolling the coast of China, could barely comprehend the enormity of what was unfolding before him. China had long been a source of fas-
cination for Carter, ever since he had read the letters of his missionary
uncle—the amazing dispatches of a southern Baptist preacher bringing
Christ to Cathay.

Now, at long last, he was seeing it for himself in port calls from Hong
Kong to Qingdao, the once beautiful city of German architecture and good
beer. Between fleet exercises, the young Carter raced ashore to see the sights,
and he observed firsthand signs that the Nationalist army of Chiang Kai-shek
was disintegrating before the onslaught of Communist forces, already in
control of Beijing.[1]

These were the last days of old China, where the tawdriness and decay
were visible in the bars and opium dens of ancient ports, and where thousands of years of Chinese tradition were soon to be wiped clean.

Qingdao was just 300 miles southeast of Beijing on the Yellow Sea coast,
and from the waterfront at night Carter saw the campfires of Mao's army in
the hills above the city as he scurried with his shipmates to buy silk and hand-
carved ivory mementos from the desperate vendors.[2] The streets of the port
city had fallen into chaos. Shops were boarded up. The Nationalists were retreating southward and, as they did, Carter saw them using bayonets to impress old men and boys into their doomed ranks.

Over the next three decades, Carter, like most Americans, lost contact
with China. But the Nixon opening, and Carter's own political awakening,
had brought it back.

By the time he ran for president, Carter had adopted the Democratic position on China—the position of Mike Mansfield, J. William Fulbright, and

Edward M. Kennedy—that the process of normalization, begun under Nixon and stalled under Ford, should be completed. Carter understood that Taiwan was a political problem that had to be solved, but he was willing to lead the country to a new state of relations, one that reflected the reality of modern China.

There was never any doubt in Carter's mind that he would be the president who took the final difficult step, and he said as much when he outlined his foreign policy goals for those who would serve under him.[3]

No one imagined, however, that when the China breakthrough came, it would come as a result of all-out civil war within the Carter administration; that Carter's achievement on China would rise from a destructive collision of personalities and from the irreconcilable worldviews of his secretary of state and national security adviser, whose poisonous competition would add to the perception that Carter had lost control of his presidency and of his own political destiny.

A CHANGE OF administrations in Washington, especially where one party throws out the other, rises like a thunderstorm over a picnic. Panic is the dominant feature. Thousands of political appointees, who may have been in power for up to eight years, scramble for the exits, and for jobs in the private sector. Thousands of new political appointees sweep into town with one eye on the new era and the other looking under every rock for unpleasant surprises. Honesty in government is an abstraction. And all contact with the outgoing administration is conducted as if a gun were on the table.

This was especially true of the transition between Ford and Carter, because Carter had run an outsider's campaign against Washington, against the moral betrayal of Watergate and the Nixon-Ford-Kissinger legacy of secret deals and secret wars. The populist streak in the Carter campaign resisted any association with the eastern establishment. During the transition, Hamilton Jordan, among Carter's closest aides, said publicly, "If, after the inauguration, you find a Cy Vance as secretary of state and Zbigniew Brzezinski as head of National Security, then I would say we failed. And I'd quit."

But the ethos of the campaign quickly gave way to the self-validation of administration-building, where star quality overruled populist ideals. For Carter, both Cyrus Vance and Zbigniew Brzezinski had star quality, as did James Schlesinger (Energy), Harold Brown (Defense), W. Michael Blumenthal (Treasury), and Griffin Bell (attorney general).

In truth, the Carter campaign had made great use of the eastern establishment, many of whose sons and daughters volunteered to help the former

Georgia governor get elected. Tony Lake joined the campaign's foreign policy staff, making his first return to politics since quitting Kissinger's staff in 1970 over the invasion of Cambodia. Richard Holbrooke, the thirty-five-year-old managing editor of the journal, *Foreign Policy*, became Carter's foreign policy coordinator, having switched allegiance after the failed primary campaign of Sargent Shriver.

Whereas Lake was jocular, wry, and affable, Holbrooke was strung for pizzicato and wore his ambition like a vicuña coat. His nervous energy, like his wild hair, seemed to have no boundaries. He carried on conversations with visitors while taking phone calls and watching television, all the while urging the visitor to keep talking—he swore he was listening. For all the distractions of his personality, Holbrooke was also intensely bright and had a great appetite for the policymaking process of government. His desire to become secretary of state oozed from his pores, and this obsession was accepted by his friends: "That's Dick," they would say.

Like Lake, Holbrooke was of the Vietnam generation. He had served as a special assistant to Ambassadors Maxwell Taylor and Henry Cabot Lodge, and, between 1967 and 1969, he wrote one volume of *The Pentagon Papers*, the secret history of American involvement in Indochina, while also serving as a member of the American delegation to the Paris Peace Talks on Vietnam, headed by Averell Harriman and, later, by Lodge.

And so it had been Holbrooke who was chosen by Harriman in the summer of 1976 to arrange an introduction to candidate Carter. Harriman was in his eighties but was still serving as a Democratic Party sage, one of the few remaining from the war generation of Roosevelt and Truman. Harriman had never really imagined that Carter could become president. In the middle of the primaries, R. W. Apple Jr. of *The New York Times* started going on at a Harriman dinner party about how Carter might actually succeed. Harriman snorted in Johnny Apple's direction and, with all of the pomposity that was allowed him, said, "That's ridiculous, I have never met him."[4]

So a meeting was arranged in the parlor of Washington physician Peter Bourne. Holbrooke[5] provided the introductions.

It was Harriman whom Jack Kennedy had selected to open the sensitive conversations with Khrushchev to explore a joint strike against the Chinese nuclear program. Nearly fifteen years later, seated with the candidate in Bourne's parlor, Harriman was not so much concerned with Carter's China policy as he was with his policy toward the Soviet Union, but China was always part of the equation.

He believed that there would be a fight for Carter's soul over the best approach to the Soviet Union: Was it a malevolent empire playing America for

a fool in the disarmament game while building up a massive military establishment, or was it a misunderstood and vastly overrated giant struggling
against fatal economic weaknesses and insecure frontiers?

Harriman believed the latter. He told Carter that there was a great psy-
chosis in America. People were whipping up hysteria about the Soviet threat,
talking about a Soviet first strike on the United States as if that were rationally probable, which, of course, it was not. One had only to look at Brezhnev's speeches to see that the Soviet leadership clearly understood that
nuclear war would ultimately destroy the attacker as well as the victim.[6]

A new obsession had entered the American debate, Harriman argued, that
the United States must match every Soviet advance. That was ridiculous, he
said. Every year, the Pentagon came up with a new technology—multiple
warheads, cruise missiles—and this only frightened the Soviets further. Indeed, Harriman believed that the United States was so far ahead of the Russians scientifically that even if Moscow undertook a drastic act of aggression,
the United States would still have plenty of time to react and recover.

"We can afford to wait and see what they do," Harriman emphasized, and
it might even be time to consider an offer of unilateral American restraint,
particularly in the development of new weapons systems, as long as the Russians showed parallel restraint.

Harriman believed he had gotten through to Carter that day. But the veteran diplomat also believed that Carter, as a conservative Democrat, was
susceptible to the powerful polemic of the hawks in both parties—Senators
Henry Jackson and Barry Goldwater, Jim Schlesinger and Ronald Reagan—
who were promoting an alarming view of Soviet adventurism and expanding
military might. The fact that Carter's closest foreign policy adviser was
Zbigniew Brzezinski was enough to incite fear in Harriman's circle that the
hawks were going to dominate the Carter camp.[7] Brzezinski, a Polish academic whose family emigrated to Canada because of the Nazi onslaught in Europe, was a well-established hard-liner on the Soviet Union at Columbia
University.

In a way, Brzezinski felt that he had invented Jimmy Carter. As director of
the Trilateral Commission in the early 1970s, Brzezinski had recruited and
tutored Carter at a time when the organization had been looking for a progressive Democratic governor sympathetic to the commission's worldview—
that close cooperation between the United States, western Europe, and
Japan was the most effective bulwark against Soviet expansion.[8] Carter found
Brzezinski charming and brilliant, willing to freely share his highly developed insights about Europe, the Soviet Union, the Middle East, and Asia. By
1975, Brzezinski and Dean Rusk, a fellow Georgian, were Carter's principal
advisers on foreign policy.

From his perch at Columbia, where his friends called him Zbig ("Zzz-big"), Brzezinski had advocated military cooperation with China as a way to further contain the Soviet threat.* But Harriman and the traditional Soviet specialists, like Marshall Shulman, were encouraging one of their own, Cyrus Vance, to join the Carter campaign, in part as a counterweight to the hard-liners. In all of these maneuvers, Holbrooke, a protégé of Rusk, Vance, and Harriman, served as facilitator, as note taker for Harriman's conversations with Carter, and as Harriman's eyes and ears in the Carter camp.

The night of Carter's victory, Vance and Brzezinski and their wives gathered at Holbrooke's apartment in New York,[9] neutral territory for the competing clans, where they watched the returns come in until after midnight; they parted cordially, wondering who would get the upper hand as Carter's strategist. During the weeks that followed, as the president-elect grappled with forming his cabinet, Harriman led an effort to open a secret channel directly between Carter and the Soviet leadership, cutting Brzezinski out of the loop. Harriman's intervention seemed a preemptive strike to ensure that the management of Soviet policy (and, therefore, China policy) remained in what the traditional Soviet specialists considered safe hands. They believed that the worst manifestation of triangular diplomacy—the game that Nixon and Kissinger had begun—would be to play the China card to pressure Moscow, capitalizing on the Soviet fear of encirclement. That could only lead to miscalculation, or war. Harriman and Vance did not want to confront the So-

---

*By the 1970s, Brzezinski, like a number of analysts in the government and in academia, believed that the split between the Soviet Union and China was the most profound strategic event of the Cold War era. (A decade earlier, Brzezinski had argued that the Sino-Soviet dispute was only a "family quarrel.") These analysts also believed that the United States should exploit the split as a means to further complicate Soviet strategic planning in the face of a prospective two-front war. Beginning in 1973, Michael Pillsbury, a young academic and later an analyst at the RAND Corporation, began discussing the possibility of U.S.-China military cooperation with the Chinese defense attaché assigned to Beijing's UN mission in New York. Pillsbury became an advocate of military relations with the Chinese and, in 1975, published in *Foreign Policy* a proposal to supply the Chinese with defensive weapons that would improve the security of their border with the Soviet Union. Aides to Kissinger said that the secretary "hit the ceiling" over the Pillsbury article because it threatened to reveal his own secret overtures to sell military equipment to China in order to enhance China's "warning time" in the event of a Soviet attack. Pillsbury's published writings also complicated Kissinger's negotiations with the Soviet Union, whose leaders already suspected military cooperation between China and the United States. In 1974, Morton I. Abramowitz, then a Defense Department official, authored a study recommending the opening of military ties with China. His boss, James Schlesinger was intrigued, but soon discovered Kissinger's opposition to the Pentagon's involvement in China policy. Although Kissinger failed to draw the Chinese into a quasi-alliance, he continued to offer the Chinese access to sophisticated types of American computers. In 1974 and 1975, Nixon and Ford approved a Kissinger plan to secretly encourage British and French sales of high-technology equipment to China, including technology licensed from American manufacturers. Subsequently, the British signed a $160 million contract to provide China with a production line for the Spey-Rolls-Royce jet engine, which was the power plant of America's workhorse F-4 Phantom fighter-bomber. Kissinger did not disclose his actions to State Department officials in charge of China policy, who learned of the engine sale through intelligence channels.

viet Union as much as they wanted to engage Moscow in an extended process of arms reduction and diplomatic cooperation to defuse conflicts in the Third World.

Three weeks after the election, Harriman returned to the United States from Moscow,[10] where he had seen Brezhnev and delivered, with Carter's blessing, a private, conciliatory message on behalf of the new administration. Then the Soviet ambassador in Washington, Anatoly Dobrynin, took the extraordinary step of flying to Harriman's home at Hobe Sound, Florida, with a personal reply from the Soviet leader. The Soviets, it seemed, were likewise trying to open a private channel to Carter.

Arrangements were hastily made. With Dobrynin's reply in hand, Harriman called Holbrooke to Hobe Sound. Together, they drafted a Carter response to the Soviet leader. Then they flew to Plains, Georgia, by chartered jet to confer with the president-elect.[11]

Brzezinski was out of the circuit, and a whispering campaign was initiated against him, no doubt by the Harriman circle: Brzezinski was too divisive, too much like Kissinger.

At the end of November, Holbrooke got the opportunity he had been waiting for. The switchboard in Plains alerted him that a call from the president-elect would be coming through. Carter was on the line because he was canvassing all of his foreign policy advisers on his cabinet choices. Holbrooke wholeheartedly endorsed Vance for State, Brown for Defense, Blumenthal for Treasury, and Ted Sorensen, Jack Kennedy's speechwriter and confidant, for CIA director.

When Holbrooke finished, Carter said, "Okay, but you haven't said anything about Zbig, or the NSC job or yourself."[12]

Holbrooke replied that he was willing to serve wherever the president needed him.

Carter's question was still hanging there: "What about Zbig and the NSC?"

Holbrooke dared not say everything he was thinking—that Brzezinski, an erstwhile Kissinger rival, would try to compete with the Kissinger legacy as a foreign policy czar, running the world from the West Wing of the White House and undermining the State Department's role. He dare not say that Brzezinski, whose ego stood like a pompadour over his sharp features, would encourage Carter to put his own imprint on foreign policy, but underneath it would be Brzezinski's imprint.

Holbrooke gathered his courage.

Zbig was very talented, he told Carter, and Zbig had done a lot for the campaign, but he couldn't see how Zbig and Vance were going to make a solid, coherent team. Their worldviews were too far apart.

Holbrooke tried to stick the knife in with as much delicacy as possible. But as he spoke, he could feel the chill coming over the phone line. It was almost as if he could see Carter's eyes narrowing. Holbrooke suddenly realized that he had misjudged Carter's receptivity. The silence lasted an eternity, and then, bloodlessly, Carter thanked him for his advice and rang off.[13]

Carter never initiated another conversation with Holbrooke. Their relationship was over. Holbrooke would be offered the job of assistant secretary of state for Asia under Vance. It was a good job. It was the job that Harriman had held under Rusk. But by challenging the president's team when it was already clear that Carter wanted Brzezinski, Holbrooke had declared opposition to Carter's judgment.

When Brzezinski's appointment was announced, Holbrooke also understood that if the new national security adviser ever found out how he had spoken against him, there would be hell to pay.

Like Nixon and Ford before him, Carter came to Washington with the overarching goal of reducing the danger of nuclear annihilation, and he focused his attention on the Soviet leadership. The Carter team assumed that China could be taken for granted, that normalization was something to shoot for after a new Soviet arms deal was locked up. That was Vance's view, in any case.

Then syndicated columnist Joe Kraft wrote on the morning of February 27, 1977, that Nixon and Kissinger had made a secret deal with the Chinese to complete normalization during Nixon's second term.[14] Kraft also reported that the chief Chinese envoy in Washington, Huang Zhen, had made a point of asking Carter, when the two men met for the first time on February 8, whether the new president was aware of this pledge.

Carter was not.

Vance had agreed to appear on CBS's talk show *Face the Nation* that Sunday, his public debut as the new administration's foreign policy spokesman. He was doing fine until Don Oberdorfer of *The Washington Post* asked him if he was satisfied that he had a full record of the Nixon-Kissinger era, especially in light of Joe Kraft's column that morning. A hooded expression came over Vance. He said that he had been getting the "fullest cooperation"[15] from Kissinger. "With respect to the specific issue on which you asked your question, if there are any papers which we do not have, I am sure we will be able to get those papers," Vance elaborated.

Oberdorfer, a gentlemanly Georgian, was nonetheless persistent.

"If Secretary Kissinger's cooperation was so good, why does the Administration have to be looking at this point to see if there was some understanding you don't know about?"

Stricken by his own ignorance, Vance lamely retreated.

"There are an awful lot of papers. We have only been there for five weeks, and we are, you know, in the process of reviewing many different subjects to complete our work; and I simply, myself, haven't had a chance to go through all these papers yet."

When Vance got back to the State Department, he told his staff, "I don't ever want to have to answer that question that way again."

A crash investigation into the record of U.S.-China relations began.

MICHEL OKSENBERG, a gregarious China scholar from the University of Michigan, was thrown into this assignment by Brzezinski. Oksenberg had just arrived from Ann Arbor to coordinate China policy for the National Security Council. He knew little of government and even less about the role of the NSC. When he landed at Washington's National Airport to start his career in government, a CIA China analyst named Charles Newhauser picked him up.

"Welcome to the club," Newhauser said dryly, as if being a Washington insider came with a secret handshake.

On his first day in the Old Executive Office Building adjoining the White House, Oksenberg stared at his telephone, wondering whom he should be calling. Then he got his orders to work with Holbrooke to reconstruct the Nixon-Kissinger record on China. But where were the files? Kissinger and Scowcroft had ordered "empty safes" for the incoming Democrats; everything that was not carted off to presidential libraries, or to Kissinger's private archive at the Rockefeller estate, was dispersed in the hinterland of the bureaucracy or shredded.

Holbrooke and Oksenberg had first met in Plains just after the election, when a large group of foreign policy specialists were summoned to meet the president-elect. On the sidelines, Oksenberg also learned of the apprehensions that Holbrooke and Lake harbored about Brzezinski.

In January, after Oksenberg had arrived in Washington to begin working for the new administration, Holbrooke invited him to breakfast. They were both in favor of normalization with China, that was obvious, Holbrooke said. That meant that they were going to work closely on a great enterprise.

"I want to make one commitment with you—one promise," Holbrooke said. "We will not keep secrets from each other.[16] We will tell each other everything we know so that there is no rivalry between us."

Oksenberg, still full of idealism, thought that this was an excellent idea. And when Holbrooke said, "Let's shake on it," Oksenberg immediately reached across the breakfast table and took his hand.

By the end of February, Oksenberg and Holbrooke had discovered that only a partial record of the U.S.-China dialogue existed in government files. Important chunks were missing. What kind of government, they asked, carries on eight years of sensitive diplomacy without ensuring that the next administration has a full record? Each administration was guilty of negligence in this regard—the Kennedy family had carted off JFK's papers and audiotapes; Johnson had done the same. But this practice seemed particularly damaging to the continuity of government policy. Nixon's presidential papers were the subject of a custody fight between the Nixon estate, the Watergate prosecutors, and the National Archives. Nixon's lawyers initially refused to make any of his papers available to the Carter White House, but then they relented. Oksenberg flew to Ann Arbor, where Ford's documents were stored. With Ford's permission, he hand-carried back to Washington a sealed envelope that contained, among other things, a transcript of Ford's last conversation with Chairman Mao, in which Ford had committed the United States to breaking relations with Taiwan under the "Japan formula."[17]

For days, Oksenberg and Holbrooke poured over the extraordinary record of the previous eight years of U.S.-China relations. For an academic, it was like reading Lincoln's secret diary. Oksenberg was in awe of the breadth of the dialogue. He was so excited, he compiled long extracts that Carter could read for himself. He was certain that Carter would see how profound a meeting of minds had occurred.

He was wrong.

Carter was struck by Kissinger's fawning.[18] "Why he just kissed their ass,"[19] the president told his aides, calling Kissinger's performances in private sessions with the Chinese leaders "despicable!" He was offended by Kissinger's style of denigrating Democrats in these conversations as "pro-Soviet" dupes. Kissinger had made fun of Mike Mansfield, George McGovern, and even Cy Vance. He had trashed the CIA, the Pentagon, and Jim Schlesinger and had characterized Nixon's Watergate crimes as inconsequential, asserting that Nixon was a good president who had been "overthrown."

Still, all of the secret understandings were there, and Oksenberg considered them perfectly defensible. He drafted a memo to Brzezinski recommending that the president authorize the secretary of state, at the first opportunity, to reaffirm the Nixon-Ford assurances. Brzezinski took the memo, added his own cover note, and sent it to the president for approval.

Carter checked the "approved" box.

The explosion went off when the memo reached the State Department. Vance was outraged. He lectured Brzezinski on the protocol of how foreign policy was going to be made while he was secretary of state. He admonished Brzezinski not to make policy recommendations to the president without clearing them first through him. Washington was already brimming with rumors that Brzezinski was angling for a dominant role in foreign policy, just as Kissinger had done. Right after the inauguration, Holbrooke, Lake, and Peter Tarnoff, Vance's chief of staff, had warned the new secretary that Brzezinski was rigging the system so he could dominate it. The very first presidential directive issued by Carter had laid out the procedures for interagency coordination in making and managing foreign policy. Brzezinski positioned the NSC at the center of the process, just as Kissinger had done.

The national security adviser was the first person in the Oval Office every morning; he would give the president a worldwide briefing. At first, this briefing was listed on Carter's schedule as the daily intelligence brief. But when the CIA director, Stansfield Turner, asserted that he should be in charge of delivering any intelligence briefing, Brzezinski changed the next day's schedule to read: "the president's national security briefing."[20]

Vance's biggest problem was that Jimmy Carter liked Brzezinski immensely and relied on him to spin out a broad range of options and analyses—even jokes and wild ideas—that Carter found helpful in forming his own judgments. Carter did not agree with Brzezinski's sometimes outlandish proposals, but he liked the range. Vance had no similar daily forum with the president. But more, Vance was too much the Wall Street lawyer, too much the restrained Presbyterian elder to connect with Carter in the same way. It was clear that Carter felt more comfortable with a brilliant rogue like Brzezinski, and Vance would never be that—too much Yankee rectitude.

One had only to look at the young aides around the president—Hamilton Jordan, Jody Powell, and Gerald Rafshoon—to see that Carter was imbued with that southern gene that conflicted church-going virtue with an appreciation for mischief.

At the end of each day, Vance sent Carter an "evening notes" memorandum on foreign policy developments and decisions that were in progress or that needed to be made. But it soon became apparent that Brzezinski was exploiting the magical morning hour, when the president was in his most activist mood.

It soon began to happen that notes floated over to the State Department saying, "The President has decided this . . . "; "The President wants this . . . "; "The President thinks this . . ." And Vance would have to decide: Do I agree? . . . Should I try to catch up? . . . Better turn this around. Or he would just throw up his hands.

Sitting around Vance's conference table, Lake, Holbrooke, Tarnoff, and Hodding Carter, the State Department's press spokesman, tried to convince the secretary that the department was getting euchred by Brzezinski, but Vance would just slam his hand down on the table and end the conversation.

He could manage Brzezinski, he would say. They had their differences, but he was sure they could work together. This was *not* going to be a replay of the Kissinger-Rogers relationship, and he was not going to indulge the competitive obsessions of his aides.

Giving China a set of detailed assurances was premature, Vance said. State was not ready for a China initiative. He demanded that the Oksenberg memorandum be withdrawn and that all copies of the original memo be collected and shredded.*

.　　.　　.

Jack Kennedy had tried to make an ambassador out of Leonard Woodcock in 1961, by offering him first Pakistan and then Taiwan, but both times Woodcock had turned him down. In 1977, however, with his retirement as president of the United Auto Workers (UAW), Woodcock was ready to succumb to a new political calling.

Woodcock was never the prototypical union boss, but he possessed considerable political instincts. He had a long face, straight out of Dickens, and big horn-rimmed glasses that perched on a long nose, as if he *meant* to defy handsomeness. More the parish priest than labor tough, Woodcock exuded a brand of guileless midwestern idealism, but, of course, he had all the guile of any political kingmaker. He liked to humble his eastern friends by reminding them of the enormous political power that resided in the more benighted parts of the country, parts they seldom visited.

Truth be told, Woodcock had always hoped that he would serve in the administration of a Kennedy before the end of his life, and he had placed great hopes in Senator Ted Kennedy, feeling that Ted had the spark that could mobilize the country and, more importantly, that Ted had the agenda of working-class Americans—national health insurance, higher minimum wage, and greater employment opportunity.

Carter's debt to Woodcock arose from the Michigan primary,[21] where Carter was in a do-or-die face-off there and in two other states whose primaries fell on the same day. Woodcock threw all his energies into turning out UAW members to vote for Carter, even as the AFL-CIO put its organizational muscle behind Morris Udall's candidacy. When the votes were tallied, Carter lost to Senator Frank Church in Nebraska, and he was trounced in Maryland by Jerry Brown. But in Michigan, Carter emerged the winner by 14,000 votes. Everyone in Michigan politics knew that Woodcock was the reason.

The next morning, Carter was on the phone.

"I know what happened yesterday, and I know who I owe it to."

---

*All but one copy was destroyed. Oksenberg squirreled it away for Carter's presidential archive.

Carter said that he would forever after be indebted to Woodcock, and, after the election, Woodcock's name was on every list for prospective appointments in the new administration.

Then the Harriman committee, which was making ambassadorial recommendations, came up with China. The job as head of the U.S. liaison office in Beijing opened up with the departure of Ford's last appointee, Thomas Gates, who had been secretary of defense in the Eisenhower administration and was an old navy buddy of Ford's. China was not yet an ambassadorship because diplomatic relations did not exist. But whoever got the job would hold ambassador rank in the State Department. Woodcock had just begun to mull it over when Harriman sent word through Holbrooke that China would be the last great challenge of Woodcock's life, and he could not possibly turn it down.

Woodcock was not just an ordinary American voyeur of the events that had convulsed China in the twentieth century. He was a longtime student of the socialist movement and an early fan of Edgar Snow's reporting from China. In the 1930s—though few people knew it—Woodcock had been a card-carrying member of the American Socialist Party. He even rose to become a member of its executive committee in 1940, the year he walked out on Norman Thomas over support for the coming war (Woodcock's faction backed Roosevelt).

The young Woodcock was fascinated with China and with the struggle of Mao Zedong and his guerrilla army, simultaneously waging war against the invading Japanese and the Nationalists, who were trying to exterminate his movement. Writing for the *Socialist Call* in the late 1930s, Woodcock penned a tribute to Mao and the valor of the Long March.

Even though decades had intervened, Woodcock stayed current on China. And, in 1972, he was among the first to applaud Nixon's journey.

Now, he saw a culmination under Carter.

Gates returned to Washington that spring and said to Woodcock, "I hear you have the reputation as a great negotiator. Well, I just want to tell you there is nothing to negotiate. The deal is there, lying on the table. All you have to do is pick it up."

WHETHER IT WAS POLICY toward China or the Soviet Union, there was nothing auspicious about Carter's first year in office. Far from engaging the Soviets in a constructive new dialogue, Carter and Vance stepped back from the nearly completed Ford-Brezhnev agreement on strategic arms reduction. Instead, Carter tabled a proposal calling for far more sweeping reductions.

Brezhnev was outraged at the repudiation of his investment in six years of negotiation and compromise. Moreover, Carter's tough new emphasis on human rights,[22] including his public correspondence with the dissident physicist Andrei Sakharov, inflamed the atmosphere between Moscow and the new administration. Vance's first diplomatic mission to the Soviet Union, in March, dissolved into recriminations over Carter's "interference" in Soviet affairs, and by summer, the whole relationship had turned into a sweaty diplomatic scrum.

None of this was helped by the fact that Brzezinski, even more than Kissinger, saw a Soviet challenge in every Third World flare-up. When mercenaries based in Angola staged a raid into Zaire against rebel bases that had at one time been supported by China and the United States, Brzezinski argued that it was a direct Soviet challenge to American interests that warranted an American response. The Chinese saw it the same way. "If America does nothing, it will only boost Soviet expansionism and America will get hurt," Huang Zhen warned Vance on April 11.[23]

But Vance believed that it was a trap to allow the Chinese to goad the United States into confrontation with Moscow over every regional dispute.

Carter sided with Vance, largely because the new president came into office detesting the whole Kissingerean ethos of playing off China and the Soviet Union. Carter believed that he could deal with Moscow and Beijing separately, on the specific merits of each relationship. And where the politics of the campaign drove him to seek a better arms control deal than Ford had negotiated with the Soviets, the same politics drove him toward a better deal on China—the deal that Kissinger could not close. Once in office, however, Carter faced the same obstacles: principally, how to break with Taiwan while ensuring a peaceful transition.

Due to the early focus on Moscow, a blueprint for Carter's China policy did not begin to develop until April.[24] By then, the Chinese were already showing impatience. "There is no sign in sight at this point that the United States has made up its mind to discuss normalizing relations between the two countries,"[25] an unnamed senior Chinese official complained in an interview with *The Washington Post*.

When Presidential Review Memorandum No. 24 was completed in June 1977, it stated what was already self-evident—that it was in America's interest to complete the normalization task along the lines of the Japan formula—a clean break in relations, abrogation of the Mutual Defense Treaty, and withdrawal of U.S. troops. But the Carter policy would also try to ensure that Taiwan's security would not be endangered. And Brzezinski added an anti-Soviet angle, pushing for the sale of high-technology equipment to China, including "dual use" items that could have military applications.

These were the goals, but for Carter the sequence of events was everything. Vance believed that the arms control agenda with the Soviet Union should come first. In July, Carter startled Woodcock by asking him how *he* thought the administration ought to proceed. Woodcock had assumed that Carter would have had it all figured out by then. At the end of the month, Carter called his advisers to the Oval Office.[26] He was going to send Vance out to Beijing to tell the Chinese of his intention to complete the normalization deal and to get a feel for Chinese terms and expectations.

Everybody assumed that Carter was going to stick to the Vance script— that the deal with China should come *after* the United States got back on track in negotiations with Moscow. But Vice President Walter Mondale reminded Carter that history had saddled the Democrats with "losing" China after World War II. If, for instance, China swung back into the Soviet orbit, another generation of recriminations might be laid at the doorstep of the Democratic Party. Mondale's argument was not intended to challenge the sequence, it was just a reminder of the stakes.

So it was a considerable surprise to everyone in the room when Carter abruptly turned to Vance and said, "Cy, lay it all out on the line" in Beijing. If the Chinese were ready for normalization, so was Carter. "I've never gained anything from procrastinating. Describe our full position."[27] By that, Carter meant that he needed some political cover on the issue of Taiwan, some commitment to a peaceful transition and an understanding that the United States would continue to sell defensive arms to Taiwan after breaking the Mutual Defense Treaty.

Carter said that he believed he could win support for a new China policy from the American people. He was willing to take on the political responsibility of doing so.

No one was as rattled by Carter's decision as Vance. He knew that he was headed for a tough negotiation in China, but suddenly the mission had been transformed. The bar was now set very high.*

Vance was due to leave for China on August 20, but out of the blue, on August 10, Ellsworth Bunker and Sol Linowitz, Carter's Panama Canal negotiators, reported that they had locked up a treaty providing for the canal zone to revert to local control and sovereignty. It would be ready for signing in September. A major battle now loomed over ratification in the Senate. Carter would need sixty-seven votes, and he could not afford to alienate anyone,[28]

*In June, Vance had tried to signal the Chinese that they would have to be flexible. The Carter administration expected the Chinese to compromise on Taiwan. China's answer came quickly. Vice Premier Li Xiannian, an old revolutionary leader returned to prominence after Mao's death, told an American visitor, Admiral (Ret.) Elmo Zumwalt, a few days later, "As to when and in what way the Chinese people are to liberate their sacred territory of Taiwan, that is entirely China's internal affair, which brooks no interference."

including the Republican conservatives who would see a China initiative as a sellout of Taiwan.

Still, Carter was unwilling to abandon his China plan. He called Vance and Brzezinski to Camp David on August 17 to go over, line by line, the draft communiqué that Vance would be authorized to put before the Chinese.[29] It called for the establishment of full diplomatic relations with Beijing and a clean break with Taiwan. But as they worked over the document at the presidential retreat, in Maryland's Catoctin Mountains, Senator Goldwater released a public statement arguing that it "would dishonor America" to break relations with Taiwan at a time when 800 million Chinese were living without "basic human rights."

Goldwater publicly warned Carter that he would be risking "impeachment"[30] if he tried to break the Mutual Defense Treaty with Taiwan. The Goldwater statements put a chill over the whole enterprise.

WHEN WOODCOCK ARRIVED IN Beijing in the summer of 1977, a new power struggle was beginning. During August, hundreds of thousands of Beijingers flooded the streets to express their joy at Deng Xiaoping's reemergence more than a year after he had been purged. Intelligence indicated that a tense negotiation had been under way for months between Deng—still under house arrest—and various intermediaries, who shuttled back and forth to the politburo, where the terms for Deng's return to the ruling circle were under debate.

With strong backing from the military, Deng demanded that all of the titles he had held before the Gang of Four overthrew him in April 1976 be restored.[31] Deng's principal backer was Marshal Ye Jianying, who had led the coup against the Gang of Four. Hua Guofeng, Mao's heir, was less enthusiastic.

The power struggle in the Chinese leadership was a rumble in a dark alley for the American diplomats stationed in Beijing. No one was sure who the good guys were—or whether there were *any* good guys—but it was well known that Deng was anti-Soviet.

In the basement of the cramped U.S. liaison office, technicians had constructed a small, soundproof room for secure conversations. Woodcock gathered his staff of diplomats.

"Hello. I am Leonard Woodcock. Don't stand, I am not that kind of person."

He told them that he had little experience with diplomatic work, but that he had been selected by the president for what he considered a political task, normalizing relations with China, a policy that he strongly supported.

"Before I came out,"[32] Woodcock confided, "I read the record of the Kissinger negotiations."

"While I am here," he said, there would never be the same kind of shameful denigration of American institutions and American leaders that Kissinger had engaged in during his years of diplomacy behind the veil.

Vance arrived on August 21, 1977, the last day of the Eleventh Party Congress. A huge crowd, more than a million people, surged into the streets of Beijing just as Vance's motorcade was coming in from the airport. Of course, the crowds had nothing to do with his arrival; rather, the Communist Party machinery had turned out the huge numbers to cheer the new leadership slate of Hua Guofeng and Deng Xiaoping.

Vance's visit turned out to be a disappointment to both sides. His first encounter was with Huang Hua, who had been called back from the United Nations to become foreign minister. Now twenty-five years older than the doctrinaire firebrand who had bullied American negotiators at Panmunjom, Korea, Huang still seemed more comfortable when he was hectoring an adversary, and he treated Vance to a verbal lashing over America's failure to meet the Soviet challenge. He asked Vance bluntly whether the United States was going to maintain the world balance of power. Considering that he was facing a new American secretary of state, his tone was surprisingly sulphurous.

"We think the United States is afraid of the Soviets," Huang taunted, adding that the "superpower rivalry is about to lead to a world war."[33]

Vance recoiled. In his view, Huang was indulging in the crude Chinese instinct to incite one superpower against the other. But it was clear that the Chinese had already lumped Vance in the "Chamberlain" camp of "appeasers" who preferred negotiation and engagement with the Soviets instead of resolute strength or, if needed, confrontation.

When Vance said that the United States was prepared to discuss normalization of relations with China, Huang was impassive, listening to Vance's generalizations. The two men never got beyond a sterile recitation of their divergent worldviews. To the members of his own delegation, Vance seemed uncomfortable. He read his talking points from note cards and seemed unable to look up often enough to make sincere eye contact. Even if he had, Huang Hua was a grumpy dance partner in any negotiation—he was relentless and inflexible.

At the end of the day, the American party retreated to the guesthouses of Diaoyutai. Vance gathered Woodcock, Holbrooke, Oksenberg, and Phil Habib for a walk. They strolled through the gardens to get away from any intruding microphones and over the same humpbacked bridge that Kissinger had once paced with his aides.

Vance told them that the next day they were going to meet with Deng. The secretary assumed that it would be the key meeting of their trip, and so, he said, he had to make some decisions about what to do with the draft communiqué in his pocket.

The Chinese leadership, Vance surmised, had clearly rejected the signal that there would have to be flexibility on both sides in order to move forward. Even though he had the president's authority to lay the draft communiqué on the table, Vance said that he had decided against it. Instead, he was going to explore positions that had been tabled in the past.

No one argued with his decision. Among the group standing on the bridge, Holbrooke and Woodcock knew that Vance had never intended to table the draft communiqué. In the days before Vance's arrival, an advance team had delivered a sealed note to Woodcock from Holbrooke. It read, "Contrary to our expectations, the proposal that the Secretary is bringing to present to the Chinese will include a continuing official presence on the island of Taiwan after normalization." Woodcock saw that Vance was carrying on a charade with the Chinese, and he could only guess that Carter, for some reason, was not ready.*

The next afternoon, seated across from Deng at the Great Hall, just as Vance was in the middle of exploring a fallback position, such as keeping a U.S. consulate or liaison office on Taiwan, Deng interrupted him.

"No!" the Chinese leader said sharply.

Nancy Tang, who was translating, said something to Deng in Chinese, but he didn't need to be prompted. "This is a retreat from the position of Ford in 1975," Deng said, his face showing his irritation. He reminded Vance of Ford's commitment to normalize along the lines of the Japan formula. China would not accept a so-called liaison office on Taiwan, Deng said. That would just be an embassy without a flag. It would promote the image of two Chinas, or one China and one Taiwan. It was completely unacceptable, he said.[34]

Vance plodded through three days of meetings and banquets, betraying the stiffness and formality of a diplomat uncomfortable with his circumstances. Deng, too, just emerging from political banishment, was wary and punctilious in enforcing Mao's long-standing dictum on Taiwan. He could do no less.

As Vance was leaving China, a newspaper story leaked in Washington claiming that the White House was pleased with Vance's talks in Beijing and that the Chinese had shown new "flexibility" on normalization. Vance

---

*In the middle of Vance's trip, Brzezinski drafted a cable for Carter's signature instructing Vance to take advantage of any opportunity that developed to normalize relations with China. But Carter killed it, telling Brzezinski that after talking with Mondale again, he felt that a China initiative would jeopardize ratification of the Panama Canal treaties in the Senate.

erupted with anger. Someone was trying to sabotage the whole trip by provoking the Chinese. It was a pernicious leak, and everyone on Vance's plane
suspected Brzezinski. Vance fired off a cable to Woodcock, instructing him to
rush to the Chinese Foreign Ministry and discredit the story,[35] but it was too
late.

The Chinese decided they had to respond.

Deng chose the visit of Arthur O. Sulzberger and Katharine Graham,
publishers of *The New York Times* and *The Washington Post*, respectively, to fire
his cannon. The publishers had come in a delegation headed by Keith Fuller,
managing editor of the Associated Press, and they were delighted to find
themselves ushered into an audience with the mysterious and powerful new
Chinese leader.

Deng came right to the point. The American secretary of state's visit to
China had been a failure, he told them, because Vance had backtracked on
the commitment of the Ford administration. That was unacceptable to
China, Deng added.

Woodcock had not been included in the session, but he was anxious to
glean any bit of intelligence. He invited the press barons to a reception at his
residence. By prior agreement, the publishers stayed mum about Deng's
blast, but in the middle of the reception, they thought better of it.

"Mr. Ambassador," Fuller asked, "did Secretary Vance propose to the Chinese the establishment of a liaison office in Taiwan as a result of normalization of relations with the PRC?"

Reflexively, Woodcock replied, "No, he didn't."

"That's strange," Fuller said, adding that Deng had just told them in their
meeting at the Great Hall that the Vance mission had been unsuccessful for
that very reason.

Woodcock tried to soften the blow, but Deng's rebuke was crystal clear. It
hit the newspapers the next day.[36]

IN LATE SEPTEMBER, Woodcock returned to the United States to accompany Vance to the UN General Assembly meeting in New York, where
they would again meet Huang Hua. Over a formal dinner, Vance told Huang
that the United States had gotten Deng's message. The Carter administration, he said, was reviewing its policy on normalization and would soon come
up with a new formula.

A few days later, Vance called his China staff together and asked for suggestions.

Woodcock surprised them by advancing the view that there was no way
the United States could negotiate a guarantee from the Chinese that they

would not use force against Taiwan. That was already clear from the record. The Chinese considered Taiwan an internal Chinese affair, a matter of sovereignty. How could the United States negotiate a guarantee on how China would recover sovereign territory? That would be like asking Abraham Lincoln to promise England that he would not use force to recover the Confederacy. It just wasn't going to happen.

Woodcock believed that the president had the constitutional right to conduct foreign policy, and that included recognizing whatever government he saw fit. But in order to ensure the security of the people of Taiwan, the president ought to be prepared to do whatever he needed to protect Taiwan from invasion, including selling defensive arms to the island. He could reserve this right without putting it on the negotiating table.

Vance had listened without commenting. Holbrooke declared the birth of the "Woodcock Formula." His tone was half joking, half serious. When they broke up, Vance assured Woodcock that instructions would be ready for him to take back to China by the following Monday, October 3.

But Monday came and went. Then three weeks went by. Still nothing from Vance. Woodcock would call Bill Gleysteen, Holbrooke's deputy, and Gleysteen would say, "We are having more trouble than we thought," or "It's taking longer than we thought."[37]

Then Phil Habib, who had made the transition from Kissinger's staff to Vance's, telephoned Woodcock and told him that he would have to return to Beijing without instructions. They would follow later, he said. Woodcock suspected that Vance was filibustering, unwilling to move on China. He puzzled over the reason. During his stay in Washington, Woodcock had gotten his first whiff of the debate over the sequencing of Soviet and China policy. He wondered whether that was the issue. In any case, Woodcock told Habib that he would not go back to China without first seeing the president.

Habib was startled and then became angry. But Woodcock held his ground.

"If I am to go back without instructions, then I am going to insist that I ask to see the President."

Habib quickly shifted his ground.

"Of course you'll see the Secretary before you see the President, won't you?"

Invoking his presidential connection worked. At the end of October, Woodcock finally got a piece of paper from the secretary of state, but it was not an outline on how to proceed with normalization. Rather, it was a clarification. The Carter administration, it said, was aware of the Ford commitments on Taiwan and would not insist on maintaining a liaison office there.

When Woodcock returned to Beijing and delivered the note to Huang

Hua on November 14, the Chinese foreign minister looked at him as if to say, "All this time, and this is it?"

THE WEATHER IN Washington was balmy in early November, and so when Brzezinski and two of his aides emerged from a luncheon at the International Club, Brzezinski suggested that they walk back to the White House.

He was in an expansive mood, instructing Oksenberg how to navigate the sidewalks of a big city, how to watch the traffic and the street lights so as to pace one's advance toward each intersection to catch the green light. It was typical Zbig: irrepressible presumption.

Their luncheon guest had been Lee Kuan Yew, the Singapore leader who was creating one of the tiger economies of Southeast Asia with transparent, laissez-faire business policies under an authoritarian political regime. At the luncheon, Lee had been quite insistent that America's approach to China was wrong.

"Why don't you normalize relations with China?" he had prodded Brzezinski. The whole of Asia expected the Carter administration to make the move. Indeed, Asia wanted it. With the death of Mao, it was time to draw the Chinese out of their isolation, and Deng Xiaoping was the right leader at the right time.

As Brzezinski, Oksenberg, and Michael Armacost, the senior NSC policy coordinator for Asia, strolled along the sidewalk on H Street, Oksenberg changed the subject from street lights back to China.

"You know," he said, "Lee Kuan Yew was right."[38]

Brzezinski did not respond directly. Instead, he blurted out a question: "Do you think you could get me an invitation to China?"

"Jesus, Zbig," a startled Oksenberg replied, "of course I could. They would love to have you."

But Oksenberg wondered if Brzezinski had the president's permission to make such a drastic encroachment on the State Department's turf.

"No problem," Brzezinski grinned. "Just get it."

Oksenberg wasted no time. He arranged a lunch with a Chinese diplomat and advertised Brzezinski's interest.

A few days later, Huang Zhen strolled into the Roosevelt Room of the White House escorted by the vice president, who was hosting a farewell luncheon for the retiring Chinese diplomat. There, in front of Vance and his aides, Huang loudly declared that Brzezinski was most welcome in Beijing—"I am extending an invitation for you to come."

It was as if a dead animal had been thrown on the table. Vance's face was frozen; Habib and Holbrooke were wide-eyed in disbelief.

Brzezinski was gracious and accepted the invitation, as if it were a routine matter. As soon as lunch was over, Oksenberg's telephone rang. It was Habib calling from a car phone, probably Vance's. They had not waited to get back to the State Department to register their indignation.

"What the hell have you been doing?" Habib demanded.

"I don't know anything about this whatsoever," Oksenberg protested.

Habib's call was followed by a Vance call to Brzezinski and a Holbrooke call to Oksenberg.

Holbrooke was yelling over the phone. "Have you been playing games?"[39]

Oksenberg played dumb. He wondered whether his boss had enough presidential backing to pull this off, because it essentially meant taking China policy away from the State Department. Over the next several months, Brzezinski would use that magical hour he had with the president at the beginning of each day to gently press his case.

B Y THE END OF 1977, the Carter administration was already a demolition of colliding interests. The president was trying to pull U.S. troops out of South Korea; he was threatening to pull U.S. forces out of the Philippines as well if President Ferdinand Marcos did not improve his human rights record. Japan policy was drifting between neglect and preemption, and Thailand's overtures for assistance against the Khmer Rouge were being ignored.

On China, Carter seemed torn between Vance, who wanted to go slowly to protect the Soviet relationship, and Brzezinski, who wanted to move faster to pressure the Soviets.

Into this vacuum sailed Ted Kennedy. In a speech that once again advertised his presidential aspirations, Kennedy called on Carter to break relations with Taiwan and get on with it.[40] Then Kennedy flew off to Beijing, where the Chinese leadership warmly received him and Woodcock hosted a reception for him.

Cut off from the rivalries of Washington, Woodcock had come to his own conclusion that it was time to build a fire under his friend Jimmy Carter. With mock bravado, he told his staff in Beijing that he was going to go back and "throw down the gauntlet" before the president.[41]

And so on the last day of January 1978, Woodcock arrived in Washington, where he had been invited to address a UAW leadership meeting at the Shoreham Hotel. Also just returned from China, Kennedy was there as the featured speaker. When Woodcock got up to give his remarks, he decided to say what was on his mind. American policy toward China was "founded on an obvious absurdity,"[42] he said. Since the end of World War II, the United States had recognized the Nationalist government on the island of Taiwan as representing all of China. By continuing to do so thirty years later, the United States was still participating in the Chinese civil war. In the six years since President Nixon had "opened the door" to China, he continued, "sixty-seven other nations have walked through that door—including virtually all our allies.

"I am positive this nation can find the necessary courage to take the obvious step," Woodcock went on. "I strongly believe it is necessary for the peace of this world for there to be a normal relationship between the United States and China."

The press reaction was immediate. Woodcock's "absurdity" comment was all over television that night and on the front pages the next morning. The gauntlet had been thrown down—perhaps too forcefully, Woodcock worried. When the telephone rang in his hotel room early the next morning, Woodcock knew it would be Vance's office. And when Woodcock reached the State Department, dark clouds enveloped the secretary's face. Vance spoke deliberately, as though he were pronouncing a sentence.

It wasn't that he objected so much with what Woodcock had said, Vance explained, but the timing was terrible. The president was in a fight for his life on the Panama Canal treaties, and Vance worried that Woodcock had handed the opposition another club with which to pummel the administration.[43]

Vance showed Woodcock the draft statement the department planned to put out at the noon press briefing. It said that Woodcock had been speaking without clearance. His remarks amounted to a personal assessment. Woodcock nodded his concurrence.

Vance then turned to another subject. There was some talk in the administration about organizing another high-level visit to Beijing. Vance said that it would be helpful if Woodcock would take the position, especially if he saw the president, that there should be no further cabinet-level visits to China. Anxious to set things right with Vance, Woodcock readily agreed. It wasn't until later in the day that he understood that Vance was trying to shoot down Brzezinski's planned visit.

At the White House, Brzezinski pulled Woodcock into his confidence about that same topic, his mission to China. Woodcock temporized, still heavily influenced by the State Department's view that Brzezinski was a snake, a cut-rate Kissinger who acted behind State's back without regard to institutional courtesies or civilized procedures. But Woodcock could also now see how divided the Carter camp had become. Even the State Department—Vance and Holbrooke—was trying to prevent him from seeing the president by not forwarding his request for an appointment.

Woodcock picked up the phone and called Carter's appointments secretary. That's all it took to get on the president's schedule for February 7. Then Holbrooke was on the line saying that the department was a little irritated that Woodcock had gone outside proper channels. Woodcock just smiled.

Holbrooke said that the department would prefer that Vance or himself attend Woodcock's meeting with the president.

It was a private meeting, Woodcock insisted.* The last thing he wanted was company.

J IMMY CARTER SEEMED completely serene to Woodcock, who was amazed that this president, so besieged by politics and the crises of high office, could project such an aura of supreme self-confidence. For a midwesterner, there was something awe inspiring about the mind and the manners of the South, and Carter, with those luminous eyes that floated like mercury above a keyboard smile, was, if anything, a great specimen of the South.

"I read in the newspaper all the things you said about China," Carter said.

Woodcock braced himself for a reprimand.

"And I agree with you."[44]

Carter's serenity, it seemed, stemmed in part from the turning tide in the Senate. It was beginning to look as if the Panama Canal treaties would be ratified. The president could now look forward to the end of the year, when a window would open after the midterm congressional elections, a window that would allow him to complete a new strategic arms accord with Moscow and establish diplomatic relations with China. These were Carter's big plays, and his political advisers were urging him to pursue both goals in parallel. That would improve the chances to land one or the other—or both—in the run-up to the presidential campaign season.

But Carter still had his personnel problems. All during February and much of March, Vance thought that he had contained Brzezinski's ambition to go to China. Carter stalled on making any decisions about China, keeping his eye on the Senate debate over the canal treaties. He even snapped at Brzezinski to stop pestering him about it. Victory on the treaties came in March, giving Carter a political boost and the freedom to act. Harriman was just back from Moscow with news that Brezhnev was ready to move forward on arms control negotiations. That gave Carter the pretext for a Solomon-like decision—sending Vance to Moscow and Brzezinski to Beijing. Vance was crestfallen. He thought that he had convinced Carter to send Mondale to China.

*Woodcock wanted to tell Carter that, at the tender age of sixty-five, he had fallen in love with the Beijing liaison office's nurse, Sharon Tuohy, and that he wanted the president's blessing to marry her. Carter carefully took down her name so he could write her a personal letter.

I N EARLY MAY, Brzezinski told Carter in blunt terms what was ahead.
"To establish diplomatic relations with Beijing, we will have to close
down our official representation on Taiwan, terminate the Mutual Defense
Treaty with Taiwan, and withdraw our remaining military personnel and installations." With concurrence from Vance and Brown, he recommended a
formula under which the United States would "make a unilateral statement
indicating the importance of a peaceful settlement of the Taiwan question by
the Chinese themselves." Then, Washington and Beijing would "issue a joint
communiqué establishing diplomatic relations, in which we would recognize
the PRC as the sole legal government of China."[45]

Brzezinski wrote his own instructions for Carter's approval. The most difficult task, he said, would be to win acceptance for the American requirement
that the transition on Taiwan be peaceful and that the United States reserve
for itself the right to provide arms to Taiwan as it saw fit.[46] Both Carter and
Brzezinski knew from the Kissinger record that Deng was a tough negotiator. They had accepted Woodcock's view that they could not negotiate a Chinese guarantee on peaceful transition for Taiwan, and they opted for the
notion of the American side making a "unilateral" statement of peaceful transition. But they would insist that China not contradict such a statement. That
way, China could say that it had preserved its sovereign right to use force if
all else failed, and Washington could say that it maintained a continuing interest in Taiwan's security, leaving ambiguous whether U.S. military power
would back up that interest.

Although Vance had insisted that Holbrooke and Gleysteen accompany
Brzezinski to China, Brzezinski would not even allow them to read the talking points he was preparing for his meetings with Chinese leaders. Brzezinski's access to the president gave him extraordinary license, and he used it to
humiliate the State Department, especially Holbrooke. As they were preparing for the trip, Holbrooke tried to expand the number of State Department
officials involved in the planning, and Brzezinski retaliated with a screaming
telephone assault at 6:30 in the morning, threatening to throw Holbrooke off
the plane. A shaken Holbrooke complained afterward that he had been subjected "to the most humiliating treatment."

"I have never heard such a vile, profane man," he told Oksenberg. "Zbig
yelled at me over the phone so loud that it woke up my wife!"

J UST DAYS BEFORE THE departure, Oksenberg summoned Gleysteen to
the White House and offered to show him Carter's instructions, but
only if Gleysteen swore not to reveal the contents to Holbrooke or Vance.
But then Holbrooke discovered that he had been cut from the roster of aides

who would accompany Brzezinski to the most important meeting in Beijing—Brzezinski's session with Deng. Appalled, but also unwilling to directly confront Brzezinski, Holbrooke sent secret instructions to Woodcock to fly to Tokyo and meet the Brzezinski delegation as it made its way toward China.

Woodcock had no idea what was going on. When he arrived in Tokyo, Holbrooke pulled him aside and told him what Brzezinski had done. It seemed unthinkable to Woodcock that the assistant secretary of state in charge of Asia would be excluded from the key meeting in Beijing.

Would Woodcock speak up for him? Holbrooke asked.

At dinner that evening with Brzezinski and his wife, Woodcock furrowed his brow and wondered aloud whether the Chinese would understand why the State Department was not represented at the critical meeting with Deng.

"You represent the State Department don't you?"[47] Brzezinski asked.

"Frankly," Woodcock replied, "I don't think of myself as representing the State Department. I think of myself as representing the President."

Brzezinski laughed and, without saying so, seemed to understand now that Woodcock was fronting for Holbrooke. He held his ground. No one could challenge Brzezinski at this late hour without going to the president, and no one had the stomach for that, certainly not Holbrooke. Woodcock told Holbrooke he had tried his best, but failed.

The next day, during Brzezinski's tour of the Forbidden City, Gleysteen—also fronting for Holbrooke—made a final plea, saying, "Zbig, this is totally wrong, you are destroying the processes of government, you have to have Holbrooke in the meeting."

But Brzezinski just turned and said, over his shoulder, "Screw you. I'm not going to."[48]

B RZEZINSKI ENTERED THE Great Hall of the People in early May 1978, triumphant that he was now poised to finish the task that Kissinger had failed to complete. He had outmaneuvered Vance in China, and, in the running debate over how to deal with the Soviet Union, he was gaining ground. To graphically present his analysis of the Soviet threat, Brzezinski had drawn a line across the world map from Angola to Ethiopia to the Middle East and to South Asia. He described it as an "arc of crisis" arising from relentless Soviet challenges to the West. The CIA was coming to a similar conclusion, arguing that Moscow had found a useful new working model for intervention in Third World conflicts—the airlift of Cuban troops armed with Soviet weapons to overpower indigenous forces.

Vance and the Soviet specialists in the State Department disputed

Brzezinski's analysis, arguing that the hostilities in Angola and the Horn of Africa were essentially local conflicts that should not be escalated into super-power confrontations. But the advantage was shifting to the cocky national security adviser. The Chinese, not surprisingly, embraced Brzezinski's view of the world. Deng was happy to greet a fellow hard-liner.

Brzezinski told Deng that America would continue to play a global leader-ship role. Carter intended to build up NATO forces in Europe and hold the line against Soviet expansion in the Middle East. And regarding normaliza-tion with China, he said, Carter was ready to act. The president wanted to start secret negotiations immediately, with an eye toward completing a nor-malization agreement by the end of the year.

Deng agreed that it was past time for America to act. "The question re-mains how to make up one's mind. President Ford stated that if he were re-elected he would move to full normalization according to the three conditions without any reservation. We were very happy at that time with the oral commitment of President Ford.[49]

"Subsequently," Deng continued, "President Ford was not reelected, and of course the new Administration has a right to reconsider this question."

The United States, Brzezinski replied, had "certain domestic problems" and "certain historical legacies" that would have to be overcome. "These are complex, difficult, and in some respects very emotional issues," he said. "That is why we will have to find some formula which allows us to express our hope and our expectation regarding the peaceful resolution of the Tai-wan issue, though we recognize that this is your own domestic affair."

Then, as Brzezinski broached this most sensitive issue, he descended into what could only be called mumbo jumbo.

America wanted to be known as trustworthy, he said. The American pres-ence in the Far East—though reduced by continuing withdrawals from Tai-wan—should continue in a manner that was not destabilizing, so that the situation could not be exploited by the Soviet Union—the mutual adversary. And then he said, "This consideration must be borne in mind when resolving the issue of normalization[50] and when defining the full range of relations dur-ing the historically transitional period of our relationship with the people of Taiwan."*

*In his memoir, *Power and Principle*, Brzezinski asserts that he "made it plain to Deng that our security commitment to Taiwan would continue even after normalization," during the "historically transi-tional era," a phrase he says was "deliberately vague." However, no evidence from the record has emerged to support his claim that he carried out his instructions to speak plainly about the Taiwan arms sales question. Others who were in the room or have read the transcript of this session do not support Brzezinski's claim that he spoke of any American security commitment to Taiwan extend-ing beyond normalization, or that he insisted on the American "condition" of continued arms sales to Taiwan, as set forth in his instructions. In his report to the president, Brzezinski acknowledged that

Even if Deng spoke English, he could not have understood the sentence. But this brief and highly ambiguous statement was as close as Brzezinski ever got to explaining how Carter intended to accomplish normalization by reserving an American right to sell limited amounts of defensive weapons to Taiwan.

Nevertheless, Deng accepted the proposal that Woodcock and Huang Hua begin meeting in secret to discuss normalization. At the same time, he indicated that he did not have high expectations.

"I think that is all on this question," Deng said. "We look forward to the day when President Carter makes up his mind. Let's shift the subject."

"I have told you before, President Carter has made up his mind," Brzezinski injected.

"So much the better,"[51] Deng replied evenly.

B RZEZINSKI'S VISIT WAS A success largely because Deng saw in him a man with whom China could do business, a strategist close to the president who shared China's self-interested view of the Soviet threat. Brzezinski was not afraid to talk about confronting "hegemony" or hectoring "our mutual adversary"—the Polar Bear. During his visit to the Great Wall, Brzezinski challenged his Chinese hosts to a race. "If we get to the top first, you go in and oppose the Russians in Ethiopia. If you get there first, we go in and oppose the Russians in Ethiopia."[52] Vance was mortified when he read Brzezinski's remarks in *The Washington Post*.

Despite the flap, Brzezinski sensed the connection he had made with Deng, and Deng accepted an invitation to dine at Brzezinski's home if the Chinese leader ever visited America. Brimming with self-satisfaction, Brzezinski skated past his wife and Sharon Woodcock during breakfast one morning with his hand poised high in the air as if he were a waiter carrying a tray.

"I have Richard Holbrooke's head on my platter and I am going to serve it to the Chinese,"[53] he crooned.

Holbrooke was a continuous target of scorn. Muska Brzezinski, Zbig's wife, criticized Holbrooke for coming to a state dinner looking disheveled. And someone, it could only have been Brzezinski, ensured that Holbrooke's

---

"we did not talk about arms sales directly." Brzezinski argues that when he told Deng that an insecure Taiwan might turn to the Soviet Union after normalization, he meant it to be an indirect reference to continued American arms sales to the island, but the connection seems to have existed only in Brzezinski's mind. In any case, it was lost on Deng, who responded, as he had in the past, that China was not worried about the Soviets moving into Taiwan, in part because Taiwan would continue to maintain trade relations with the United States, Japan, and European countries.

car brought up the rear of every motorcade. It got so bad that Holbrooke would get out and run forward to ask Woodcock if he could ride with him.

Brzezinski did not want Vance or anyone else at the State Department to see the transcripts of his talks with Deng before he had had a chance to brief Carter, so Oksenberg was instructed during the flight back to Washington to keep Holbrooke in the dark.

"He is not to see them," Brzezinski insisted.

Oksenberg tried to compromise, allowing Gleysteen to read the transcripts, but Holbrooke then lost his temper. Raging down the aisle of the air force plane, he grabbed Oksenberg by the collar and accused him of violating the pledge they had made to each other at the outset of the administration.

"If you don't give me those memcons [memo of conversation] after we get back, I will destroy you!" Holbrooke yelled.

Oksenberg seized Holbrooke in the same manner and, with the two men locked as if in combat, he yelled back, "If I give you those memcons after we get back and you violate our trust, I will destroy *you*."

The two men stared fiercely at each other, but neither wanted to take the personal confrontation over the cliff. Holbrooke disengaged and asked indignantly, "Are you trying to threaten me?"[54]

B RZEZINSKI'S TRIP TO China ruined Carter's meeting with Soviet foreign minister Andrei Gromyko at the end of May. The frosty encounter reinforced Vance's growing concern that it was a mistake to play the China card in the midst of the final, delicate stages of arms control negotiations with Moscow. But Carter insisted to Vance that he was not playing a China card. He was determined to establish relations with China on its own merits and, at the same time, he very much wanted a SALT II agreement with the Soviets to get the arms race under control.

All of Carter's aides agreed that an end-of-year window was the right timing to bring both negotiations to a climax. But Vance was still maneuvering to stage the Soviet breakthrough first, while Brzezinski seemed determined to upstage him.

The schedule saddled Woodcock with a nearly impossible negotiating strategy: He was to take up the issues of normalization one by one, without ever laying down the full American position. And, starting in July 1978, Woodcock dutifully sliced the baloney, serving up each bit to a cantankerous Huang Hua, who could see that the Americans were stretching out the negotiations until the congressional elections were over.

That autumn, Carter became preoccupied with his drive to bring Menachem Begin and Anwar Sadat together to craft a peace plan that would return the Sinai Peninsula to Egypt and ensure greater security for Israel. A breakthrough came on September 17, and a buoyant Carter came down from Camp David more determined than ever to push forward on all other fronts. Beijing had sent a new envoy to Washington, Chai Zemin,* who had arrived in August. Carter called him to the White House for introductions, but also to pump up the momentum.

Oksenberg flagged for Carter the sensitive issues that had not yet been broached in Woodcock's secret negotiations. So, with Chai seated before him, Carter went right to the heart of the matter. The Chinese leadership, he said, would have to understand one thing—no American president could complete the normalization deal without ensuring the security of Taiwan. It was essential that America continue to sell limited amounts of defensive military equipment to Taiwan after normalization.[55] Chai took it all in and, afterward, Carter's aides congratulated him on a brilliant delivery. When the president took on an issue, everyone had cover, and Oksenberg was delighted that Carter had spelled out so clearly what Brzezinski had left so vague in May.

NEVERTHELESS, just two weeks later, Huang Hua delivered a shocking reply.

On October 2, Vance was again in New York for the UN General Assembly meeting. It was Huang's turn to host the annual dinner for the American secretary.

When they settled at the Chinese mission on the West Side of Manhattan, Vance took forever to broach the most delicate subject, and when he did, Huang pounced. The government of the People's Republic found it absolutely unacceptable for any residual security relationship to carry on between Washington and Taipei after normalization. China rejected Carter's suggestion that American arms sales to Taiwan continue after the Mutual Defense Treaty was canceled. Huang warned that if Carter insisted on such a condition, the whole normalization deal was in jeopardy, and they might as well call off the talks.[56]

Woodcock, who had flown back to the United States just to join Vance for this dinner, listened to the heat and fire of Huang's presentation. What a grim evening, he thought. He was more convinced than ever that the arms sales issue could not be put on the table.

When the transcript of Huang's remarks reached the White House the next day, Brzezinski could see that they were looking at a stalemate.

Woodcock stayed on in Washington that fall. He and Huang Hua had

*Pronounced: Chai (sounds like "eye") Zzz-meen.

nothing really to negotiate until Carter and Vance figured out how to confront the remaining issues, especially arms sales to Taiwan.

Vance had recruited the former Republican attorney general Herbert Brownell to bless the State Department's plan to terminate the Mutual Defense Treaty without going to Congress for approval. Brownell asserted that Carter did not need to go to Congress if he terminated the treaty under its one-year cancellation clause. Barry Goldwater and other conservatives might challenge the action, but they would be unsuccessful, Brownell believed.

With the end of the year in sight, Carter called his China strategists together on October 11. Brzezinski maneuvered to keep Vance out of the meeting, which was billed as a private discussion between the President and Woodcock.* But of course Brzezinski joined them.

Carter wanted some hard-nosed assessments on the China front. Was there a stalemate or could they get an agreement done by January 1?

Woodcock believed that an agreement was possible. He had believed it from the moment he went to China. He also believed that American public opinion would support it and that Congress would follow. Woodcock outlined the remaining issues. Deng already understood—from Carter's forceful statement to Chai in September—that the United States was going to do what it felt it had to do, which was sell defensive arms to Taiwan after normalization. Deng had to oppose it. That's why Huang Hua had been so vehement. So there was no need to respond to Huang's outburst or even bring it up again. Woodcock could not "negotiate" a right to sell arms to a portion of a sovereign country.[57]

The key would be to table a draft communiqué on normalization and see if the Chinese took the bait. If Deng was willing to go ahead, even though the document was silent on the arms sales question, it would mean that Beijing understood: The United States would continue to provide for Taiwan's security, discreetly.

Carter told Brzezinski that he wanted a communiqué drafted immediately so Woodcock could take it back to Beijing and present it. They were going ahead. Carter would fill in Vance later.

Back in China, Woodcock delivered the draft communiqué to Huang on November 2.[58] It said that the United States and the People's Republic agreed to establish full diplomatic relations and that Beijing was the sole government of China. It carried a proposed date of January 1, 1979.

---

*Vietnam had signaled earlier in 1978 that it was ready to engage in normalization talks with the Carter administration without preconditions or demands for reparations. Brzezinski saw the Vietnam gambit as a diversion to throw the China initiative off the rails. Tension between Beijing and Hanoi was escalating as Hanoi moved closer to Moscow and as Beijing feared "encirclement." Carter wanted Woodcock's appraisal, which was the same as Brzezinski's—the timing was wrong.

Huang said nothing. The Chinese government would reply in due course, he replied, and that was it.

In November and December 1978, Deng Xiaoping made a bid to consolidate his power with a breathtaking display of political maneuvering at the top of the Chinese Communist Party.

When Deng first emerged from exile, his admonishment to the Chinese people and the Communist Party leadership was "Seek truth from facts," a line borrowed from Mao, but one that Deng employed as a repudiation of the years of turmoil and chaos. Deng wanted to move the country forward, returning to the platform of the Four Modernizations—industry, agriculture, science and technology, and national defense. To accomplish this, he promoted like-minded reformers to key party positions—Hu Yaobang chief among them.

In the streets of Beijing, the Chinese were pouring out their grievances against Mao, the Gang of Four, and the Cultural Revolution in big-character posters they pasted up on a stretch of wall just west of Zhongnanhai and the Forbidden City. Beijingers called it Democracy Wall.

On November 16, Deng and Hu went to Beijing University and Qinghua University to publicly embrace the goals of the democracy movement. "Democracy has to be institutionalized and written into law, so as to make sure that institutions and laws do not change whenever the leadership changes, or whenever the leaders change their views or shift the focus of their attention," Deng said.[59]

In comparison, Deng's rival, Hua Guofeng, seemed little more than an empty Mao suit. That year he had pushed up targets for steel production three times beyond China's capacity. His exhortations reminded too many people of the Great Leap Forward, when Mao's crazy policies, especially on steel production, had undermined agriculture, calling down ruin and starvation that killed an estimated 20 to 30 million Chinese.

Deng pressed the politburo with plans for genuine reform. With Deng's support, Chen Yun, the party's leading economic thinker, called for the rehabilitation of sixty-one party elders purged by Mao during the Cultural Revolution, including Peng Zhen, the former Beijing mayor, and Yang Shangkun, Deng's former deputy. Five days later, on November 15, the *Guangming Daily* newspaper[60] announced the party's decision to reverse the verdict on the Tiananmen incident of 1976, which Deng's enemies had used to purge him. It had not been a counterrevolutionary rebellion after all, but a patriotic expression, the party now decreed.

As the momentum strengthened behind Deng's leadership, an ill wind of Soviet-Vietnamese cooperation gathered ominously in Southeast Asia.

On November 4, Moscow and Hanoi signed a treaty of friendship and co-operation. The meaning was clear: Hanoi was making a bid to extend its domination over the region. Vietnamese troops already were massing on the Cambodian border. Deng charged that Moscow was building a "military alliance" on China's southern flank, and China began its own mobilization.

On November 18, in a meeting with Japanese parliamentarians, Deng said that he was looking forward to restoring relations with America. When the time came, he added, it could be done in "two seconds,"[61] and then he could visit the United States.

Oksenberg was in Ann Arbor at the annual Michigan–Ohio State football game when he saw a translation of Deng's remarks, and he picked up the nearest telephone and dialed the White House operator. When Brzezinski came on the line, Oksenberg sputtered in makeshift code, since they were on an open line and everything about the negotiations was top secret.

"The little one is ready to travel," he said cryptically.

WASHINGTON WAS FILLED with rumors that a breakthrough was imminent in the strategic arms talks with the Soviet Union. And within the government, Brzezinski and Vance were still locked in an intensifying competition. As Vance stoked his negotiators in Geneva to get a final agreement on strategic arms, Brzezinski pressed China's top diplomat in Washington to get the message to Deng that he should seize the moment, because Moscow was trying to outflank China in Vietnam as well as in Washington by concluding the arms control deal. That deal, Brzezinski warned Beijing, would pave the way for a visit to Washington by Brezhnev.

Brzezinski thus cleverly played on China's fear of slipping behind in the power triangle and urged Deng to act on normalization.

But Moscow was playing its hand with the same energy. Woodcock had been amazed when the Soviet ambassador to China, Vasily Tolstikov, during a diplomatic reception in Beijing that fall made a big show of rushing across a crowded room to greet him; clutching the American's arm, the Russian then walked him to a private corner and spoke to him in hushed tones. Woodcock almost laughed, because Tolstikov was babbling about the weather and other inconsequential matters, but his display was intended to incite gossip in the Beijing diplomatic corps about Soviet-American "collaboration."

Deng waged his own campaign. He received the American columnists Rowland Evans and Robert Novak on November 28 and told them that normalization of relations between China and the United States would do more for American security than any number of arms control treaties signed with Moscow.

Still, Woodcock was nervous. It was nearly December and the Chinese had not set the date for their next negotiating session. It had been nearly a month since he had handed the draft communiqué to Huang Hua, who was since reported to have taken ill. Woodcock had to consider whether it was a "political" illness; perhaps an indication of a political struggle in the Chinese leadership.

In early December, Woodcock was finally summoned to the Foreign Ministry by Han Nianlong, a vice minister. For the purposes of meeting, Han was given the title "acting foreign minister," so there would be no sense that the Chinese were downgrading the negotiations.

Han presented a counterdraft of the communiqué. This Chinese version also carried the date January 1. The two sides were now locked into a schedule to complete the normalization agreement by the end of the month.

Han also delivered a key Chinese concession on Taiwan. If the United States made a public statement that it expected a peaceful transition on the island, the Chinese would not contradict it. The Woodcock Formula was succeeding.

When Woodcock got up to leave, Han said, almost casually, "Deng Xiaoping will see you soon."

Back in Washington, the news of Woodcock's session sent Brzezinski into a frenzy to stay ahead of Vance and the SALT negotiating team in Geneva.

When Woodcock reported that he would see Deng on December 12, Brzezinski called Chai Zemin to the White House, ostensibly to update him on American foreign policy developments around the world, including information on the Middle East, SALT, and the mounting revolution in Iran. Chai's appointment was not placed on Brzezinski's official calendar, and the Chinese envoy, who had always come in the front gate of the White House, instead was met by Oksenberg at the West Gate to keep him away from the press or any State Department spy who might be wandering about.

Brzezinski quickly reviewed the international scene and then said he would like to go off the record, which only accentuated the importance of what he was about to say, since they were already meeting in secret.

President Carter, Brzezinski said, was going to extend an invitation to Chairman Hua or Vice Premier Deng to visit the United States as soon as the normalization negotiations were concluded.

"Now I want to speak to you as a friend,"[62] he said. A SALT agreement was very near, and there was a good possibility that Leonid Brezhnev would visit Washington in January. Brzezinski said he hoped that events would unfold in such a way as to enable Deng to come to the United States before Brezhnev.

Oksenberg just sat there in awe, wondering whether Brzezinski was freelancing without the president's knowledge. If Carter put him up to it, it was all the more amazing for what it revealed about the president's subterfuge against his own secretary of state.

IN BEIJING, the Great Hall of the People was astir in December 1978 with a new economic revolution, one that was being engineered by Deng and the legion of reform-minded leaders who were flooding back from internal exile now that Mao was safely in his tomb.

They had plans for agriculture, for industry, for education, and for a new political order within the party based on more debate and an end to the destructive political purges that had characterized the Mao years. Deng laid out his new agenda to the Third Plenum of the Eleventh Communist Party Central Committee, an assemblage of nearly 200 top leaders from every province. The first set of economic reforms would empower Chinese peasants to sell a portion of their own agricultural output for profit after they delivered a quota of grain to the state. After three decades of rigid commune discipline, after years of political indoctrination that had sought to exterminate the market instinct among the Chinese, after endless attacks on "capitalist" farmers who dared to raise vegetables as sideline crops or engage in poultry production against the socialist ethic of communal production—this was truly a revolutionary concept.

Deng and the reformers launched a new program to unleash private initiative in the countryside, allowing rural markets to form, thus touching off an economic revolution for 800 million Chinese peasants. Deng was no economist. His program was simple, yet profound. All that had been needed was the spark. The Chinese, like the prairie fire, would do the rest.

Woodcock—closer in proximity than any other American to the anvil where Deng was hammering these foundations—was blinded to them by the party's secrecy. And when Woodcock entered the Great Hall on December 12 to meet the still-mysterious vice premier who spoke with a thick Sichuan accent, the American envoy had little understanding of the economic revolution that was being plotted in other parts of the same building.

Woodcock was in the company of his new deputy, J. Stapleton Roy, who had grown up in China as the son of Presbyterian missionaries. Everyone called him Stape, and he spoke Chinese as if it were his first tongue. As Deng strolled in to greet the Americans, he projected such an air of confidence that his guests surmised that Hua Guofeng might soon be another dead ancestor in the Chinese leadership circle.

Woodcock expressed the hope that the long negotiations on normalization were almost done. He gave Deng a single sheet of paper, the latest draft of the proposed communiqué, and he told the vice premier that in order to avoid a fight in Congress, the administration would have to terminate the Mutual Defense Treaty by Article 10, which provided for one year's notice by either party.

Deng interrupted him. He had been forewarned about the American proposal. Brzezinski had laid it out to Chai in Washington the day before, and that had given the Chinese time to think about their own negotiating strategy.

During the one-year period that the treaty was still in effect,[63] Deng asked, would the United States agree that there would be "no new commitments" of arms sales to Taiwan? Deng hastened to add that any weapons already in the pipeline could be delivered—he didn't care about that. But he wanted arms sales to end.

Woodcock said that he would relay the proposal back to Washington, but Deng was not finished. He wanted Woodcock to understand why the arms sales issue was so important—how arms sales, in his view, injected a destructive psychology between the mainland and Taiwan. Deng was anticipating. He was planning to unveil, the following month, a reunification offer to Taiwan. It would guarantee nearly total autonomy. Taiwan could keep its own political and economic system—even its own military—but under the banner of one China, with national sovereignty residing in Beijing. The concept would come to be called "one country, two systems."

Arms sales to Taiwan introduced a significant psychological factor that undermined reunification, Deng told Woodcock. Such sales would stand between Beijing and Taipei. To sell any kind of arms to Taiwan, Deng said, would only make Chiang Ching-kuo's "tail feathers grow ten thousand meters high!" He would be impossible to deal with, and that would increase the risk of conflict.

Woodcock didn't dare engage Deng's point. He just listened. Woodcock was not going to lay the president's position on arms sales out there on the table again, as Carter had in September. That would be a deal breaker. Woodcock was sure he was doing the right thing.

Deng looked at the draft communiqué—one page and in English—and called his interpreter, a young woman named Shi Yanhua,* to look over his shoulder and sight-translate for him. She stooped to Deng's level as he dictated his proposed changes, making his decisions on the spot, without consulting any other Chinese official.

*Pronounced: Shur Yan-hwaah.

Back at the liaison office, Woodcock and Roy drafted their cables throughout the afternoon so they would reach the White House by dawn on the same day.*

I N WASHINGTON, it was hours before dawn. Oksenberg had stayed at the White House until 1 A.M. in the vain hope that Woodcock might have dashed off a quick summary of the meeting with Deng. But nothing came over the CIA circuits. Oksenberg instructed the communications clerk in the Situation Room to call him—no, wake him—as soon as the cables came in from Beijing.

At 5:30 A.M., Oksenberg rolled over in bed and looked at the clock. He reached for the telephone on the nightstand and called the Situation Room.

"Have you gotten the message?"

"No message yet," the clerk said.

He waited an hour, and then called again. Still no cable.

Oksenberg drove to the White House with a gathering sense of dread.[64] It was already nighttime in Beijing, and the meeting with Deng had been at ten o'clock that morning in the Chinese capital. What was going on?

He arrived at the Situation Room at 8:30 A.M. The clerks looked at him, deadpan. "No message."

When Oksenberg got to his office, Harry Thayer, the China desk officer from State, was already on the line conducting reconnaissance for Holbrooke. What had come in from Beijing? Then Holbrooke himself called. What was going on?

Finally, Oksenberg called Brzezinski.

"Zbig, we still don't have a message from Beijing. I can't understand this."

Brzezinski betrayed nothing.

"Come over right away," he said.

Oksenberg walked into Brzezinski's office, and, before he could say anything, Brzezinski announced that the cables from Woodcock had come in the middle of the night. He had instructed the Situation Room clerks not to show them to Oksenberg, or to anyone else.

"The deal has been made," he said. "Normalization is going to occur. The President wants to announce it Friday evening and I want you to draft a statement that the President will read on television."[65]

Oksenberg's head was spinning.

Brzezinski handed him the cables. They had been marked up by Brzezinski and then by Carter. As he read, Oksenberg felt a twinge of concern. The

*Washington is thirteen hours behind Beijing in winter.

transcript of Woodcock's session with Deng and Woodcock's personal report on the meeting revealed several outstanding items. It was clear they were almost done, but another negotiating session was needed to clean up the details of the communiqué. Oksenberg wondered what had been said between Brzezinski and the president.

Carter wanted to announce normalization on Friday—it was now Tuesday morning, and the communiqué had not even been agreed to by the two sides. What was the rush? It had to be Vance and SALT. The secretary was in the Middle East and, in Geneva, the arms control negotiators were on the threshold of a new agreement. Brzezinski knew that Vance opposed announcing any China deal before SALT was wrapped up. But Carter had obviously taken sides. He was going with Brzezinski. They would use the China announcement, just as Kissinger had in 1971, to build a fire under Brezhnev.

Brzezinski ordered Oksenberg to tell no one at State that the China deal was done and would be announced that Friday. But Oksenberg could not draft everything that needed to be drafted by 5 P.M. He called Roger Sullivan on the China Desk.

"Roger, you have got to get sick and go home. Then, you have got to come over here right away."[66]

For the rest of the day, Oksenberg and Sullivan worked in the Old Executive Office Building next to the White House as Oksenberg took call after call from Holbrooke and Thayer. Under orders from Brzezinski, he lied to them time after time.

Because Vance was out of town, Deputy Secretary Warren Christopher was running the State Department. Holbrooke called him and shared his suspicion that something was going on at the White House. Christopher reached Brzezinski, who asked him to come over late in the afternoon. Christopher left the building without telling Holbrooke, who finally went home, exasperated.

At the White House, after Christopher had read everything, he asked Brzezinski, "When will Dick Holbrooke learn about this?"

Brzezinski, savoring the moment, replied, "Well, maybe Friday evening," when all of America would see it on television.

Christopher said that he didn't want to lose an assistant secretary, and that was the risk if they kept him in the dark. But Brzezinski was unmoved. He didn't think that the president wanted Holbrooke in on it. Holbrooke was a leaker, and he was dating Diane Sawyer, the CBS journalist, and that made him a security risk.

In his lawyerly way, Christopher told Brzezinski that he just couldn't cut the assistant secretary of state responsible for China out of China policy. Besides, Christopher needed him. If it would help, Christopher said, "I will take the responsibility. I will vouch for Dick."[67]

The phone rang about 10:30 P.M. at Holbrooke's house. He was already in bed.

"I am sitting here in Zbig's office and we've got a message from Beijing. Would you like to come down and see it?" Christopher asked. Holbrooke dressed in an instant and drove to the White House.

Brzezinski was smirking as Holbrooke read Woodcock's account of the session with Deng. Then he read the messages that Brzezinski proposed to send back to Beijing.

He read over Deng's "no new commitments" proposal on arms sales and Brzezinski's draft reply accepting Deng's formulation. Holbrooke could see that nothing in the communiqué or its accompanying documents showed that the Chinese either understood or *agreed* that the United States reserved the right to sell defensive weapons to Taiwan. At the same time, the United States was agreeing to make "no new commitments" in arms sales during the one-year period. The ambiguity virtually leapt off the page.

Holbrooke looked up and said, "Zbig, Chris, if you send that message out, we're never going to be able to get Congress to approve what we have done." There had to be an explicit statement that the United States reserved the right to sell arms to Taiwan, or Congress would simply revolt, Holbrooke explained. After all, he was the person who was going to have to sell the package on Capitol Hill and he was alarmed at what was about to happen. But Brzezinski just waved him off.

Having failed to change anything, Christopher and Holbrooke left the White House and headed to Georgetown. Over a drink at Nathan's, a favorite watering hole for Carter aides, they commiserated. Had Christopher told Vance what was going on? Holbrooke asked.

No, Christopher replied. He still wasn't sure himself what was going on. The only thing that was certain was that Brzezinski was running rampant over the department.[68]

The overnight cables were late in arriving in Beijing, and Woodcock was startled by his instructions. He was to seek an immediate audience with Deng and tell him that the United States, upon review of the record of Deng's session the previous day, considered that the negotiation had essentially reached a conclusion, and, therefore, the president wanted to advance the announcement of a normalization agreement from January 1 to December 15, at 9 P.M. Washington time, which would be 10 A.M. on December 16 in Beijing. That was in seventy-two hours.

Deng seemed puzzled when Woodcock reached the Great Hall for an audience that had been arranged in great haste. The vice premier was still waiting for an answer to his "no new commitments" proposal on arms sales, and about the minor changes he had proposed in the communiqué. Why the hurry, Deng wanted to know?

The president was afraid that the normalization decision would leak, Woodcock explained. He wanted to be the first one to announce it to the American people so that the opponents of normalization could not tear it apart before all the facts were known.

How would it be done? Deng asked.

Woodcock didn't know, but he said that there would probably be an address by the president or a press conference that would go out to the nation on radio and television.

Deng thought for a moment, then agreed. He also accepted Carter's invitation to come to the United States, another indication that his influence had eclipsed Hua Guofeng's.

Everything seemed to be falling into place. Woodcock returned to Deng at 9 P.M. Thursday night with the approved American language for the communiqué. Washington was willing to pledge that there would be "no new commitments" of arms sales to Taiwan during the final year of the defense treaty.

B RZEZINSKI HAD DISREGARDED Holbrooke's concerns, but another potential landmine just as suddenly appeared.

On December 14, Chai Zemin came to the White House for a meeting with Brzezinski to discuss the sequence of cabinet-level visits to China after diplomatic relations had been established. Everyone in the administration wanted a piece of China, it seemed. As Chai was getting up to leave, Brzezinski asked him if he had been informed of the latest developments in Beijing. Chai said that everything appeared to be moving extremely well, especially since the United States had agreed to end arms sales to Taiwan.[69]

Brzezinski tried not to show his surprise and quickly begged to differ. This was not the case at all, he said. What the two sides had agreed to was a one-year moratorium, during which weapons sales already in the pipeline could be delivered. After the one year was up, limited sales of defensive arms would resume, Brzezinski clarified.

Chai looked quite surprised. That was definitely not his understanding of what had been agreed to, he said.

Suddenly, Brzezinski was facing a debacle. First, Holbrooke had asserted that the agreement was flawed. Now, the Chinese were stating that their interpretation of "no new commitments" amounted to an American agreement to end arms sales to Taiwan altogether.

In a remarkable way, this was a replay of 1972, when Kissinger had cut the State Department out of the Shanghai Communiqué negotiations only to have Marshall Green spot a fatal flaw and force an embarrassing eleventh-hour scramble to reopen the negotiation. Brzezinski also had cut the State Department out of the process, and again the White House faced an embarrassing eleventh-hour crisis. Congress would savage any agreement that was vague or equivocal on the critical question of Taiwan's security. And everyone knew that Brzezinski had had exclusive control over the negotiations. Any debacle over the normalization agreement would be a very personal disaster for Brzezinski.

The first thing that Brzezinski did was cable Woodcock asking whether he was certain that the Chinese understood Carter's determination to continue limited sales of defensive arms to Taiwan. Woodcock may have thought that this was Brzezinski trying to cover his backside at the last minute, but he wasn't going to let anyone's weak knees get the better of him.

Woodcock and Roy made the case to the White House that any careful reading of the record would show that it was "implicit" that arms sales could continue after the one-year termination period had ended. But their argument didn't calm the storm in Washington.

Carter made it clear to Brzezinski there was only one thing to do. Deng would have to understand that the deal could not be made unless the president was able to reassure Congress that American security assistance to Taiwan would continue. It would be limited and defensive, but Carter had to reserve that right, and Congress had to *know* that he had reserved that right.

In Beijing, more than five hours after Woodcock received the White House's cable seeking clarification on the arms sales question, a second cable arrived. Woodcock's heart sank.[70] It instructed him to seek an immediate meeting with Deng Xiaoping to ensure that the Chinese leader both understood and agreed that the United States reserved the right to sell defensive arms to Taiwan.

Good grief, Woodcock thought.

They were fifteen hours away from the joint announcement that the United States and China were reestablishing diplomatic relations. The communiqué was all locked up. And now Woodcock had to go in and state explicitly that the United States intended to do the very thing that the Chinese had made clear they would never accept.

Woodcock and Roy fought their gloom as they climbed the steps of the Great Hall at 4 P.M. on December 15. Deng was waiting for them. Woodcock laid it out, making clear that he was under instructions. Did Deng understand and did he agree that the United States reserved the right to continue selling arms to Taiwan?

The look that came over Deng's face foreshadowed the imminent explosion. He then slammed the arm of his chair.

"We do not agree![71] We will absolutely never agree, and we absolutely oppose . . ." Deng simply unloaded. This was impossible! It could not be allowed!

Woodcock and Roy shrunk into the cushions of their chairs as Deng thundered. They both believed that he was calling off the whole deal. Everything was going down the drain.

Deng went on. If America was going to continue to sell arms to Taiwan, why would Chiang Ching-kuo ever come to the negotiating table? And if he never came to the negotiating table, that meant that Beijing would *have* to use force to recover Taiwan. How could that be in the interest of the United States? How could the United States say that it was in favor of a peaceful resolution of the Taiwan question while it was arming Taiwan so extensively that the Nationalist leaders would turn away from negotiation with the mainland for good? That, too, would lead to war.

Deng went on for some time, his anger still fulminating from the logic he was trying to impress on the Americans. And when he was done, he looked across at Woodcock and asked what he thought they should do.

At this point, Woodcock was beyond his instructions. He said to Deng that it was essential to get normalization behind them, because then everything would change. A transitional era would open up in which they could solve the problems left over from history. The transitional era would change the relationship not only between the United States and China but between China and Taiwan, because Washington would recognize Beijing as the sole government of the Chinese people.

Woodcock kept repeating the point about how much would change after normalization and how much easier it would be to solve problems.

They had been talking—and yelling—for an hour. And when Woodcock finished, Deng stared at him for a moment, shrugged, and threw up his hands, uttering a single word: "Hao." *Okay*.[72]

The Chinese leader said that he reserved the right to return to the subject of arms sales, and he then added a request that he hoped would limit the damage from what he was being forced to accept at the eleventh hour. If the United States made any future arms sales to Taiwan, he wanted an assurance that such sales would be made secretly.

Woodcock said that he would send Deng's request back to Washington immediately. Then Deng got up and left the room.

As they walked silently out of the Great Hall, down the steps, and toward Woodcock's black Marathon Checker* with its fender flags, Roy startled

---

*The liaison office in Beijing did not warrant a Lincoln or a Cadillac under State Department guidelines. A Marathon Checker is a boxy sedan used by many cab companies.

Woodcock by saying, "I don't think they'll buy it." He meant Washington. He meant the formulation that normalization would go ahead with the Taiwan issue left hanging out there, unresolved.

Woodcock glowered at his deputy and thought to himself that Roy's mind always went straight for the worst possible outcome, or that he had suddenly gone weak-kneed and bureaucratic, and did not see that in moments like this, politics transcended everything. If both Carter and Deng were ready to normalize, normalization was going to happen, and the wisest course for a political facilitator—and Woodcock was that—was to make it happen.

The White House had no choice but to accept the formulation that Woodcock had invented on the spot—the two countries would establish diplomatic relations while leaving unresolved the dispute over future American arms sales to Taiwan.

When Brzezinski got to his office on the morning of December 15, Woodcock's cable was on his desk.[73] He marveled at Woodcock's acrobatics and hoped that it would be enough. In any case, he immediately adopted the new position and took it to Carter.

At 8:45 A.M., Chai Zemin was sitting in front of Brzezinski, not at all sure whether the deal was on or off. The president was going on television in twelve hours. Brzezinski explained to the Chinese envoy what had happened in Beijing and that Deng had requested that any future arms sales to Taiwan be made secretly.

Brzezinski was going to have to disappoint Deng again. It was impossible for the Carter administration to agree to "secret"[74] arms sales to Taiwan, Brzezinski said. It was impractical, too. It would never fly on the Hill. And, in any case, Taiwan would make them public, and Washington would have no control over that.

But the U.S. government would be discreet, Brzezinski assured him. The White House would not volunteer public information about such sales. "If asked," he said, the U.S. government would say that the sale of selected, defensive arms after the expiration of the Mutual Defense Treaty would continue in a way that did not endanger the prospects for peace in the region. And, also "if asked," the U.S. government would take note of Beijing's continuing opposition to arms sales but would add that, nonetheless, the two sides had agreed to go forward with normalization.

Brzezinski urged Chai to ensure that Deng was quickly informed of this position so as to avoid any public controversy just as normalization was about to be announced. Carter was set to go before the nation that evening. Brzezinski was imploring the Chinese to accept the deal as it stood, as imperfect and conflicted as it was.

Deng made them sweat all day. Everyone knew that if the Chinese pulled out of the agreement, the recriminations would be endless. Brzezinski would be history, Vance and Holbrooke would make sure of that. But when no reply had come by airtime, they knew that Deng had swallowed their bitter pill.

And Carter went before the cameras and stunned the world, as Nixon had.

He told the nation that the establishment of formal diplomatic relations with the People's Republic of China was not aimed at any third party. But in the joint communiqué, as the whole world could see—most particularly Brezhnev—Washington and Beijing had dedicated themselves to opposing hegemony, which had been Mao's code word, and then Kissinger's, for the Soviet Union.

The Soviets were offended. Brezhnev turned down Carter's invitation to visit Washington, and the SALT II accord, which was completed that very week, arrived like a newborn whose parents had fled the nursery.

I⊤ FELL TO Warren Christopher to fly to Taiwan and break the news in person to Chiang Kai-shek's son.

Songshan Military Air Base, in downtown Taipei, is a sprawl of hangars astride a single runway at the foot of Yang Mingshan, the mist-shrouded mountain that rises on the northern tip of Taiwan. Christopher and eleven American officials descended from their plane on December 27 and filed into a reception hall.[75]

Frederick Chien, the vice foreign minister, was there to greet them. The government of the Republic of China on Taiwan was seething over how little notice it had received before Carter's announcement. Brzezinski had insisted on only two hours' notice. Almost no one thought that was fair. But by the time he relented, it was already the day of the announcement, and Holbrooke could not find his ambassador in Taipei, Leonard Unger, who had gone to a Christmas party. When they reached him, it was late in the evening, and by the time Unger got through to Chiang Ching-kuo's aides, the president of the Republic of China had gone to bed.

At 2 A.M., awakened and somber in his nightgown, the generalissimo's son and heir received Unger and the crushing news. After Unger left, it was said that he wept.

Christopher was not expecting unmitigated warmth from the Taiwanese. He had not relished going there, and he had in fact cut short his own Christmas holiday in California. His mission was to tell Chiang that the United States was going to maintain a full range of cultural and economic relations with Taipei and was going to take a continuing interest in Taiwan's security, including the sale of weapons.

In the Songshan terminal, Fred Chien stepped up to the microphones before the state-controlled news media and started talking about the "disastrous damage wrought by this mistake," how the United States had "unilaterally yielded to Chinese Communist terms."

He turned to Christopher. "During your stay in Taipei, you will gain a clear understanding of the position of our government and the feelings of our people,"[76] he told him.

It sounded to Christopher like a threat. They walked out to the line of cars, and Christopher joined Unger in the ambassador's Cadillac. As soon as the cars cleared the gates of the air base, a crowd of 10,000 angry Taiwanese swarmed around them in the narrow street. The motorcade stopped. Unger's car was stuck behind a television truck that was blocking his path.

The crowd was screaming.

"Carter is a liar!"

"Jimmy, you bastard!"

Christopher heard thudding sounds and realized that the ambassador's car was being pelted with rocks, eggs, and tomatoes. Unger was shouting at the driver. A loud crashing noise startled them, and Christopher turned to see blood on Unger's face; the ambassador was no longer wearing his glasses. Another window burst from the force of a rock, and the screams of the crowd now filled the car, drowning out Unger's shouts. A long bamboo pole was thrust into the back seat, and Christopher pushed himself backward to avoid getting hit. He was covered with shattered glass, and his dark suit was a smear of raw egg and garbage. He squinted into the din for signs that the demonstration was orchestrated, that it was under some kind of control, in which case they could just endure it. If the mob was not under control, Christopher feared that they might be killed.

The crowd pounded and then began to rock Unger's car. Christopher watched as the windshield wipers were ripped away and as a policeman helplessly flung himself on the hood of the car, as if that were going to protect them. It seemed an eternity before they began to move. The mob was still hurling projectiles at them, running alongside the car as it crawled forward.

Placards danced above the crowd.

"Carter Sells Peanuts, Also Friends" and "Free China Will Never Fall."

Miraculously, the driver found an opportunity to swing around the truck, and they sped away. Unger told the driver that they were not going to the hotel but up the winding road to the mountain where the ambassador's summer residence was located. No one expected them to go there.

When they reached the safety of the house, Christopher was trembling. Soon, Vance was on the phone. The whole incident had been beamed around the world on television. The president would be happy to call him home, Vance said, if that was what he wanted. But Christopher did not want to leave if the Taiwanese authorities could ensure the safety of the delegation.

The next morning, Christopher was scheduled to meet Chiang Ching-kuo at the Foreign Ministry, but embassy security personnel reported that the building was surrounded by 20,000 demonstrators, many of them dumping bags of peanuts on the street and stomping on them, yelling "This is Carter!" A cab driver set himself on fire and was rushed to a hospital.

Christopher still had received no assurance that the delegation would not be assaulted again. His meeting was moved to the Grand Hotel on the north end of the city. When he walked in, there was Chiang, acting as if nothing had happened. Yes, he said, Taiwan would ensure the safety of the delegation. The words seemed to come grudgingly. Christopher then delivered his message from Carter. But, by then, the message, too, was devoid of any warmth.

O N JANUARY 1, 1979, the United States severed diplomatic relations with Taiwan and established formal ties with the People's Republic of China.

Barry Goldwater accused Carter of "lying, thumbing his nose at the Constitution and the U.S. Congress, and selling out Taiwan." He took the president to court, alleging that any treaty ratified by the Senate could not be terminated unilaterally by the president.*

Taiwan took advantage of the two weeks between the announcement of normalization and the establishment of relations to transfer title to its real estate in Washington, including Twin Oaks, its elegant Chinese embassy property. Beijing protested, but the transaction was legal.

Ronald Reagan decried Carter's act as a "betrayal" and made a campaign trip to Taiwan. Even George Bush, who already was portraying himself as a leader with strategic vision on China, attacked Carter's decision as a sellout of Taiwan's security, one that "diminished American credibility in the world" and "darkened the prospects for peace."77

"For President Carter, who professes a strong belief in Christian ethics, it should be a tormenting thought that by his hand, the United States has put an entire people adrift in a cruel, hostile sea—and for scarcely any purpose," Bush wrote in a commentary in *The Washington Post*.

The White House received reports that Kissinger, too, was attacking the agreement in private because it lacked a clear guarantee for Taiwan's security. Brzezinski sent word to his rival and predecessor that there were plenty of details in the secret record from the Kissinger years that Carter had not revealed.78 The threat worked.

Of all the Republican leaders who knew the history of the U.S.-China negotiating record, only President Ford publicly supported Carter.

When Congress came back to town, the pro-Taiwan forces mobilized.

---

*Goldwater's suit did not prevail, as the administration's claim that it had lawfully terminated the treaty under its own provisions was upheld by the courts.

During February and March, they rewrote the Taiwan Enabling Act, the bill that Carter sent to Congress to formalize the downgraded relationship between Taipei and Washington. Congress renamed it the Taiwan Relations Act and wrote into law a security commitment to Taiwan nearly as strong as that contained in the Mutual Defense Treaty that had been cancelled.

"It is the policy of the United States," the rewritten bill stated, that "diplomatic relations with the People's Republic of China rests upon the expectation that the future of Taiwan will be determined by peaceful means," and that "any effort to determine the future of Taiwan by other than peaceful means, including by boycotts or embargoes," would be considered "a threat to the peace and security of the Western Pacific and of grave concern to the United States."

The act also required the president to "provide Taiwan with arms of a defensive character" and in times of crisis to "make available to Taiwan such defense articles and defense services in such quantity as may be necessary to enable Taiwan to maintain a sufficient self-defense capability."

Deng felt betrayed.[79] The two sides had agreed to normalize, and to leave the issue of arms sales to Taiwan unresolved for future negotiation. Now Congress was resolving it unilaterally.

Carter considered vetoing the Taiwan Relations Act. He feared that Deng might pull out of normalization. But the votes in Congress that passed the Taiwan Relations Act were so overwhelming, 339–50 in the House and 85–4 in the Senate, that a presidential veto would have been impossible to sustain.

Carter signed the bill into law on April 10 and told the Chinese that he had broad latitude to interpret it, and would do so in the spirit of the normalization agreement.

Given the irreconcilable positions over arms sales to Taiwan, it is, perhaps, hard to imagine that normalization could have succeeded in any more orderly a fashion. If Vance had directed the final hours of the negotiations, insisting with lawyerly precision on America's *right* to sell arms to Taiwan, normalization might never have occurred. The virtue of the diplomatic mudslide that occurred, ladled as it was with Brzezinski's subterfuge and Woodcock's remarkable instinct to hold things together through inventive—even contorted—improvisations, was that it allowed both parties to assert that they had not compromised their principles.

But deferral is both a gift and a curse.

For the Chinese, neither the misunderstandings nor the betrayal were great enough to undermine Deng's strategic realignment, moving China closer to America than it had ever been under communist rule. With his army marching toward the Vietnamese border, it is virtually certain that Deng's thinking was dominated by strategic concerns, not only his country's need to complicate Moscow's calculations but also his personal need to assume full command of the PLA.

For Carter, the culmination of the China opening was a great political and diplomatic prize, a powerful validation of his presidency and of the foreign policy goals he had set for himself. The glory of this big foreign policy success had been timed for maximum political impact in advance of his reelection campaign.

The revolt in Congress notwithstanding, Carter, like Nixon, understood that the opening to China was a crusade of farsighted diplomacy that, for many Americans, transcended politics. It was a fulfillment and a redemption. And Carter staged it with that same sense of drama and surprise that Nixon evoked so skillfully when he orchestrated his journey to China in 1972.

For both presidents, the surge of public approval overwhelmed the opposition.

THE JANUARY 1979 arrival of Deng Xiaoping in America was a spectacle that exceeded even Nixon's standards. There was Carter, the southern governor, and Deng, the revolutionary, parading across the South Lawn of the White House to the thunder of a twenty-one-gun salute. That night they walked across the stage at the Kennedy Center, hand in hand, while the band played "Getting to Know You." Deng walked the halls of Congress and toured the new East Wing of the National Gallery of Art.

It was as breathtaking as it was kitsch. Hollywood producer George Stevens and Gerald Rafshoon, Carter's media adviser, choreographed the extravaganza. But Deng had come with his own native instincts for public relations. He played the role of the simple old man from Sichuan, beaming back all the admiration that Americans showered on him. He even kissed the children who sang Chinese songs to him from the stage of the Kennedy Center. When Republican Senator Paul Laxalt, a close ally of Ronald Reagan, saw Deng's performance that night, he told Carter, "You've got us beat," because there was no way to vote against little children singing.[80]

At the White House, Deng warned that war was coming, and the only way to prevent it was to unite. Like-minded countries, including China, the United States, Japan, and the states of western Europe, working together, could "fix" the Polar Bear until his energies were spent. Peace in the world could not be preserved unless the United States played its leading role and unless China was willing to cooperate against their common enemy. This was Deng at full power, stepping out from behind Mao's shadow to risk a fuller engagement with the American superpower.

China, he said, needed a long period of peace to build its economy and modernize the country after decades of turmoil. The Chinese wanted all the American technology they could get.

Seated at the massive cabinet table across from Carter, Mondale, Vance, Brzezinski, and a dozen other members of the administration, Deng's legs didn't quite reach the floor.

"Has your Congress passed a law that I cannot smoke?"[81] Deng asked.

When Carter raised the issue of free emigration from communist countries, Deng leaned forward, spreading his arms, and said to Carter, "Fine. How many do you want? Ten million?"[82]

In the late afternoon, Deng asked for a private meeting with Carter. The White House bustled with preparations for the state dinner in Deng's honor. Carter walked down the hallway with the Chinese leader, who was scarcely taller than the president's daughter, Amy. This revolutionary figure, who had fought in brutal wars, who had stood with peasants as they bloodied landlords in the Communist uprising, now pattered across the regal blue carpeting of the West Wing like some Yoda from a distant galaxy. To Carter, Deng was a marvel.

Mondale, Vance, and Brzezinski arranged themselves around the president in the Oval Office. Deng, calm and businesslike, brought Huang Hua, Fang Yi, and Ji Chaozhu, the interpreter. China, he said, felt compelled to spoil Soviet plans to dominate Southeast Asia through its alliance with Vietnam, which was now like a Cuba on China's southern flank. "We consider it necessary to put a restraint on the wild ambitions of the Vietnamese and to give them an appropriate, limited lesson,"[83] he said, and by "limited" he meant limited in scope and duration. Deng did not use the word "invasion," but he didn't have to. All the men in the room were aware of the intelligence reports of Chinese divisions mobilizing on the Vietnamese border. Deng was going to start a border war to send a political message to Hanoi and Moscow.

Deng admitted that it was possible that the Soviet Union might react to a Chinese strike against Vietnam. If the Soviets sent aid, Deng said, it would not have any effect because the operation would not last that long. If the Soviets staged incursions on the northern Chinese border, it wouldn't matter.

"We have had 5,000 border incidents over the years," Deng said. A few more were tolerable. If the Soviets sent troops into China, the PLA would wage a people's war, drawing them in deep and then attacking. And if Moscow ordered nuclear weapons to be used again against China, Deng said, "We have nuclear weapons too."[84] China would be able to destroy a few large Soviet cities, he said.

Carter was sobered by Deng's bloodless accounting of these possibilities.

The next morning, Deng and Carter met again in a small group, and Carter read from notes that summarized his personal reservations about the invasion of Vietnam. Carter had carefully considered what he wanted to tell the Chinese leader. He had to protect the administration politically. He had to be able to tell Congress and the Soviets that he had not conspired with Deng or exhorted China to invade Vietnam. The Soviets would see collusion no matter what he did.

In any case, Carter was sympathetic to the Chinese. Vietnam was invading another country with Soviet assistance, and hundreds of thousands of ethnic Chinese were being thrown out of their homes in Vietnam. Refugees were streaming into southern China, or onto the sea in boats. Carter had concluded that the best thing he could do was oppose the invasion—make the obvious case against it—and then let the Chinese do what they felt was in their interest.

After Carter had said his piece, Deng said that he wanted to speak candidly about Taiwan.[85]

The United States and Japan could make a great contribution to peace, he said, if they would urge Taiwan's leaders to negotiate reunification with the mainland. Don't make Chiang Ching-kuo and his clique of Nationalists feel that they have nothing to fear by continuing to arm them, Deng said. China would only be forced to resort to nonpeaceful means if that were the case.

Deng reiterated that he was absolutely opposed to the sale of any weapons to Taiwan, and he hoped that Carter would be extremely prudent in that regard. The mainland would only resort to force, he said, if Taiwan refused over a long period to negotiate or if the Soviets tried to forge an alliance with Taiwan after the Americans left.

B EFORE DENG LEFT Washington to begin his tour of America, Carter and Brzezinski arranged one more private discussion. Brzezinski explained that the United States had been cooperating with the shah of Iran to spy on the Soviet Union in central Asia and the Far East.

Deng looked puzzled. This was news to him.

From the mountains in northern Iran, it had been possible to erect electronic listening posts whose antennae could collect much of the communications traffic and military signals in the central Asian region of the Soviet Union. These signals included not only the telemetry of Soviet strategic missile tests but also communications about troop movements, radar signals from Soviet air defense forces, and the like. The stations used state-of-the-art technology and powerful computers to record and sort every bit of radio frequency emanating from the target area.

The problem now, Brzezinski said, was the Iranian revolution.[86] The CIA had been forced to close or destroy the bases in Iran, which had gone by the codename Tacksman.

Since Deng thought that arms control agreements with the Soviets were a waste of time, Brzezinski did not dwell on the administration's central concern—that without an the ability to intercept Soviet missile test telemetry, the United States could not verify Soviet compliance with the SALT II treaty. Instead, Brzezinski emphasized that a joint U.S.-China listening base in China's Far West would be an act of tangible cooperation against the Polar Bear. Its code name would be Chestnut.

Deng liked the idea. Whatever reservations Mao had had about forging a more concrete alliance with the United States, Deng was willing to shake them off in the belief that this approach would improve the prospects for wholesale technology transfer—the key to China's modernization. He said that he would consider the proposal, and then he left Washington to barnstorm America.

In Houston at the Astrodome, Deng impishly wore a ten-gallon hat for the rodeo. Television cameras captured his face peering out the window of a stagecoach, from which he beamed his affection for Americans and their cowboy culture. Of course, it was all scripted, but Deng carried it off with an aplomb that few had expected from the "nasty little man."

The only real tension on the trip was caused by an assassination scare that was never publicized. China's Ministry of State Security reported to the White House that it had information that Taiwan's security services would stage an attempt on Deng's life.* For this reason, Deng's advance team initially refused an invitation for Deng to visit the gravesite of Martin Luther King Jr. in Atlanta. The site was out in the open and would expose Deng to a sniper's bullet. However, Woodcock worried that Deng's refusal would be misunderstood. He whispered to the Chinese leader directly how important it was to Carter that Deng make the pilgrimage to the gravesite. Deng did not hesitate. Of course he would go.

---

*The secret service had no way to evaluate this report, but security was a significant if unpublicized factor during Deng's stay. Several disturbances were staged by a tiny fringe group of Chinese "revolutionary Marxists." But the White House was most concerned about Taiwan, especially after the violence directed against Warren Christopher on December 27. Carter grew so concerned that Taiwan intelligence operatives in the United States would disrupt normalization that he instructed Attorney General Griffin Bell to place Taiwan on the "criteria list," a secret ranking of countries that carry on friendly relations with the United States but that for intelligence purposes are treated as enemies due to their undercover activities in the United States. A country's inclusion on the criteria list authorizes the FBI to use more aggressive bugging and surveillance operations against that country's embassies, consulates, diplomats, and spies.

CARTER WAS IN Mexico City, in the middle of a state dinner with Mexican president José López Portillo, when word came that war was imminent. Brzezinski was called out of the room.

It was Oksenberg on the line from Washington. The Chinese wanted an urgent meeting at 9 A.M. the next morning with Brzezinski or Vance. It was agreed that Oksenberg would stand in for Brzezinski,[87] but he was not to inform the State Department. Oksenberg disobeyed and called Holbrooke. This was no time to be silly, he thought. A midlevel Chinese diplomat came to the White House at 9 A.M. the next morning and read a note.

The Chinese leadership, the envoy read, had considered President Carter's points, but due to the deterioration of conditions on the frontier with Vietnam, Beijing was compelled to go ahead. The PLA would undertake "self-defense measures" of a limited duration.

None of this information was passed on to the CIA, whose analysts began to wonder, given the size of the Chinese invading force, whether Deng planned go all the way to Hanoi.

Soon, the hot line in the basement of the White House came alive with an indignant message from Brezhnev, asking, "is it a mere coincidence" that two weeks after Deng met Carter in Washington, China had embarked on a military aggression against a Soviet ally?

Vance, too, began to develop second thoughts about the Chinese attack. He had initially agreed that the United States should stay neutral. But as the days wore on and the alarm over Chinese intentions grew, Vance began to press Carter to take punitive measures against China, first by canceling the upcoming trip of U.S. Treasury Secretary Michael Blumenthal to Beijing.

But Carter continued to sympathize with the Chinese, believing that Deng's goals were indeed limited.[88] Deng sought to inoculate himself against international criticism by drawing a comparison that Americans could relate to. "We cannot tolerate the Cubans to go swashbuckling unchecked in Africa, the Middle East, and other areas," he said, "nor can we tolerate the Cubans of the Orient [the Vietnamese] to go swashbuckling unchecked in Laos, Cambodia, or even China's border areas. I think the people of the world should not tolerate such actions."[89]

Carter held to a balanced stance, calling for Vietnam to withdraw from Cambodia and for China to withdraw from Vietnam.

China sent 85,000 troops against Vietnam's northern defenses in an attack that began on February 17. The bloody infantry assault unfolded in mountainous terrain. The Vietnamese defenders were well armed, well fortified, and battle hardened after three decades of war against the French and the Americans.

Chinese forces attacked along a broad front intended to keep Hanoi guessing about the principal axis of advance. Thousands of PLA soldiers fell on the first day. The Chinese air force tried to provide close air support for the attacking infantry, but a number of its planes were shot out of the sky by friendly fire.[90] After a few days, the Chinese air force refused to fly near its own troops.

PLA units that had been mobilized from different parts of China found that their weapons and ammunition were not interchangeable. The Chinese army had become a collection of autonomous entities that did not know how to fight together. Still, their commanders pushed them forward against the Vietnamese. The army had been instructed to take the city of Lang Son, no matter what.

To take Lang Son, an invader had to breach the mountain barrier between Vietnam and China; afterward, nothing stood between the invading army and Hanoi. That was the message that Deng and the PLA leaders were sending to the Vietnamese—that Beijing could conquer Vietnam if necessary and topple the government in Hanoi. It was a warning for the Vietnamese to abandon their alliance with the Soviet Union.

Carter was determined not to be excessively apologetic to Moscow. The Soviets were exploiting the Iranian revolution and stoking anti-Americanism all over the world. Inclined to play a tougher hand, he told Dobrynin on February 27 that the superpowers should be restrained. But Carter was concerned about escalation, and he asked Dobrynin to pass along to Brezhnev his assurance that there were no secret agreements between the United States and China. The United States, he said, had not been informed in advance about Chinese preparations to attack Vietnam.[91] He said that as soon as reports had reached Washington of a Chinese buildup on Vietnam's border, he had strongly warned the Chinese leader against military action. And, Carter added, he had demanded a quick withdrawal of Chinese troops after the attack. There was no collusion, he assured Dobrynin.*

The day after Dobrynin met with Carter, Soviet foreign minister Gromyko pointedly warned China to call off the invasion. "The Soviet Union decisively demands that the Beijing leadership stop its aggression against the Socialist Republic of Vietnam before it is too late—I repeat, before it is too late." And Brezhnev weighed in with an ominous verbal assault a few days later, saying that China constituted the most serious threat to peace in the world.[92]

---

*Carter's diplomatic dissembling suggests that he already was deeply invested in Brzezinski's drive to play the China card against Moscow, which required that the White House deny that it was doing so not only to Brezhnev but also to the secretary of state. Obviously, the White House had been informed in advance of China's invasion plan; in addition, Carter was actively seeking a secret agreement with Beijing to undertake a joint intelligence operation against the Soviet Union.

The question was, would the Soviet Union act? Arguably, Moscow was ob-ligated to do so. Under Article VI of the Friendship Treaty signed by Moscow and Hanoi the previous November, the two sides had agreed to initiate ur-gent consultations in the event of an attack on either party, with the goal of removing the threat. Brezhnev made clear that Moscow took its obligation seriously, saying, "Nobody should have any doubts: The Soviet Union is true to the treaty of friendship and cooperation binding our two countries together."

A government statement issued after Brezhnev's speech on March 2 warned, "The Chinese aggressors must know that the more crimes they commit, the more severe will be the retribution for them."[93] But Soviet mili-tary communications, and Soviet forces, showed no change in status. Still, tens of thousands of Chinese civilians, fearing an imminent Soviet attack, fled the northwestern border region.

Although Deng had denied any concern that Soviet forces on China's northern border would retaliate, Brzezinski ordered a higher level of U.S. in-telligence monitoring of the border. He was not the only one watching. After Chinese troops had crossed into Vietnam, KGB communications lit up the radio spectrum all along the border with China, indicating an intelligence alert.

Brzezinski called the Chinese ambassador, Chai Zemin, to the White House almost every night during the Chinese invasion and briefed him on U.S. monitoring of Soviet forces in the Far East.* During one late-night ses-sion, Brzezinski handed Chai a piece of paper.

"I thought you ought to know," Brzezinski said. "I cannot give you any in-terpretation of this, but, again, I thought you ought to know."

The intercepted message indicated that the Moscow high command had asked all meteorological stations along the Sino-Soviet border to report the weather forecast over China for the following day.

"That's all," Brzezinski said, not knowing whether it was a prelude to at-tack or simply a routine request.

Was Brzezinski trying to provoke the Chinese into mobilizing for war? Or was he just playing delivery boy for every fragment of information that was snatched out of the ether by a spy satellite? It made for a strange alliance—one man at the White House, without the knowledge of the State Depart-ment, Pentagon, or CIA, passing out dollops of raw intelligence to the Chinese ambassador.

The PLA captured Lang Son on March 9. With the Vietnamese in flight, the Chinese invaders ceased fire. Then, they turned around and marched home. Their mission had been accomplished. Estimates of Chinese casual-

*Brzezinski asserts that Chai's nightly visits to the White House were known to Carter, who asserts that he does not recall the clandestine visits.

ties went as high as 30,000. Deng had administered a very costly lesson to the Vietnamese.

T*ime* magazine named Deng "Man of the Year" in 1979, predicting that Deng would be to Hua Guofeng what Zhou Enlai had been to Mao. No one predicted that Deng was preparing to push Hua Guofeng aside altogether. Deng was by no means all-powerful; he had to push his moderate reform agenda through a complex leadership structure where family connections, party seniority, military service, and institutional loyalties empowered many constituencies. Deng could act decisively, especially when these constituencies were lined up behind him. But as Deng pushed the reform agenda forward, the outcry from those party stalwarts whose interests or sensibilities had been offended led to periods of retrenchment. This gave rise to the pendulum swings so characteristic of Chinese politics.

In climbing back to power, Deng identified with the grievances of the Chinese people. He and Hu Yaobang called for greater democracy and rule of law. They praised the young firebrands who were pouring out their aspirations for freedom on the Democracy Wall. But after the crucial party meetings in the winter of 1978–1979 ended and Deng had consolidated his power, the Chinese leader cracked down. He told the party elders that the pendulum had swung too far; the attacks on the party from the grass roots were too severe.

A number of pro-democracy activists did not sense the danger, or did not care. One in particular kept targeting Deng, pointing out that Deng had been all too eager to invoke democracy as he struggled to regain power, but as soon as he got to the top, he turned his back on his promises. This critic argued that Deng was becoming a dictator, just like every other Chinese leader before him.

His name was Wei Jingsheng, a former Red Guard and an electrician at the Beijing Zoo. In December, Wei had published an essay, "The Fifth Modernization,"[94] arguing that it was not enough for China to develop in agriculture, industry, science and technology, and national defense. Without democracy, the Fifth Modernization, China could not truly evolve.

Wei and other writers, Xu Wenli and Ren Wanding in particular, drafted powerful and articulate essays against the party and Deng's emergent leadership.

"The people must maintain vigilance against Deng Xiaoping's metamorphosis into a dictator," Wei warned in the journal *Exploration*. Deng promptly arrested the journal's founder, Fu Yuehua.

Responding to the arrest, the defiant essayists announced that they "would like to know if it is legal or not for a vice premier and a vice chairman to announce the arrest of people rather than for the courts and the people's representative organs to do so."

In February, Wei denounced China's invasion of Vietnam. The *People's Daily* lashed the Democracy Wall essayists as "anarchists." Wei himself was arrested on March 29. Six months later, he was sentenced to fifteen years in prison and placed in solitary confinement.

The secret transcript of Wei's trial found its way clandestinely to another pro-democracy journal, the *April Fifth Forum,* and the editor, Liu Qing, published Wei's defiant rejection of the charges and his tribute to the unfulfilled promises of China's Constitution. Liu was then arrested himself and also sentenced to fifteen years in prison.

From the U.S. embassy in Beijing, Woodcock watched the Wei trial unfold. On the last day of arguments, the panel of Chinese judges decided to adjourn and postpone their verdict for one day, but that did not stop the state news agency, apparently missing its cue, from issuing its report that Wei had been found guilty,[95] proving that the trial's outcome had been preordained by party leaders. Even with this blatant proof of the sham, the State Department and the American embassy remained silent.

Woodcock, too, was silent, and later he would regret that he had not spoken out.

On March 30, Deng stood before the Communist Party's "Theory Conference," in which the party's intellectual elite set out to overthrow Maosim and condemn the Democracy Wall activists. "In the China of today, we can never dispense with leadership by the party," he said. The party had made "many errors, but each time the errors were corrected by relying on the party organization, not by discarding it."

Taking away the leadership of the party would "inevitably lead to the unchecked spread of ultrademocracy and anarchism, to the complete disruption of political stability and unity, and to the total failure of our modernization program."

With these words, Deng put democracy aside. In China, democracy could only exist in the Leninist mode of "democratic centralism," which simply meant the will of the politburo.

Deng's speech became the emblem and the rationale for the state's opposition to broad-based political reform and provided the basis for the persecution of those who promoted genuine democracy and human rights. But although Carter had publicly lauded the human rights campaigns of Soviet dissidents and publicly corresponded with Andrei Sakharov, the White House was conspicuously silent as Deng mopped up the Democracy Wall campaign in China. Patricia M. Derian, Carter's assistant secretary of state for human rights, agitated within the administration for Carter to take a stand.[96] But Holbrooke and Oksenberg restrained her. There were bigger issues of geostrategy involved, they argued.

In fact, human rights was never going to dominate China policy in the Carter administration because China policy was driven by the exigencies of the Cold War. The Soviet invasion of Afghanistan triggered Carter's decision in December 1979 to sell "nonlethal" military equipment to China. Later, Secretary of Defense Harold Brown dispatched his engineering deputy, William J. Perry, to determine how the United States could assist in China's industrial modernization in both the military and civilian sectors.

Deng told a visiting congressional delegation in April that he would dare to buy high-performance jet fighters from the United States if Carter dared to sell them. But Vance held the line, telling Brzezinski and Brown that the day the United States started selling weapons to China, the Carter administration would have one fewer cabinet member.

Still, Carter watched with frustration as the Soviet navy moved into Cam Ranh Bay, Vietnam—the sprawling naval facility built with American tax dollars. Not only had the Soviet fleet gained a warm-water port in the region, but Soviet intelligence set up an electronic surveillance base that sucked in communications from the entire region.

Consolation came when the CIA got the final go-ahead for the Chestnut program during Mondale's trip to China in August 1979. Deng surprised Mondale by saying, "We would have given you an answer earlier, but we had some problems on our side. Now they are resolved."[97] Some Chinese military leaders apparently had objected to the CIA's insistence that the listening posts be permanent. That smacked of American "bases" on Chinese soil. When news of the dispute reached the White House, Brzezinski had said, "Tell the Chinese that we don't want them on a permanent basis. Tell them we want them on a continuous basis." That seemed to solve it.

Between August and December 1979, the Pentagon and the CIA airlifted the equipment for the Chestnut monitoring stations by military transport. When the first C-141 Starlifter arrived in Beijing, the Chinese air traffic controller directed the cargo plane to park next to an Aeroflot passenger jet from the Soviet Union. The Chinese wanted the Soviets to see that military cooperation between the United States and China was under way.[98]

The CIA set up a school in Beijing to teach Chinese military intelligence technicians how to use the equipment, how to change the rolls of magnetic tape that recorded everything that moved on the radio spectrum for analysis back in Beijing and Washington. The monitoring stations were then flown to the Mountains of Heaven northwest of Urumqi, Xinjiang Province, where antennae were installed and camouflaged. From those magnificent heights, the stations commanded an unobstructed view of the Semipalatinsk region of the Soviet Union. Their sensitive antennae could monitor military communications from central Asia to the Far East, as well as air traffic, radar signals from Soviet air defenses, and KGB communications; they could also detect any change in the alert status of Soviet nuclear forces. The signals emitted from any ballistic missile fired out over the central Asian test range would be an easy target. Also, with these bases, China increased its warning time in the event of attack, and that alone made the project a huge advance in Chinese security.

In fact, the Chestnut program far exceeded anything that Mao would have allowed in the Nixon and Ford years. Mao certainly would have opposed a joint venture with the CIA, although Deng's decision was basically an extension of Mao's anti-Sovietism. For certain, Deng was escalating—striking Vietnam, normalizing with America, working with the CIA—and all on terms that Mao might have questioned, although Mao would have agreed with the underlying motives.

Carter was also escalating. The brutal Soviet move into Afghanistan shocked and angered the president, and he organized what eventually became a large-scale covert war against Soviet occupation forces. The Chinese agreed to sell weapons to the CIA-led alliance of Egyptian, Saudi, and Pakistani intelligence services arming Afghan "freedom fighters."

After Vance resigned in April 1980, over the failed military raid to rescue American hostages in Iran, the hard line enjoyed unchallenged ascendancy at the White House. U.S.-China relations tilted more and more toward the military arena.

Woodcock was struck during William Perry's September 1980 visit to Beijing as the head of a large Pentagon delegation how openly the Pentagon spoke of growing military cooperation between the two countries. And in a lengthy, handwritten letter intended for the new secretary of state, former Senator Edmund Muskie, Woodcock wondered where the relationship was going, and how Japan and the rest of Asia would regard the headlong rush to arm China. Woodcock was not declaring any opposition to American policy, he was just becoming a little alarmed. The Carter administration was collapsing under the strain of the Iran hostage crisis and Ronald Reagan's domestic political assault, and no one was really thinking about the long term.

Someone, Woodcock believed, ought to be standing back and asking some questions about where it all was going.

REAGAN:
...AND TAIWAN

Alexander Haig, Ronald Reagan, and
Zhao Ziyang at the Opening Session of
the Economic Summit in Cancun, Mexico

E VER SINCE Nixon's breakthrough eight years earlier, Ronald Reagan had gone along with the idea that in order to confront the Russians and tie down all those Soviet divisions in the Far East, it was necessary to seek improved relations with the Chinese Communists in Beijing.

But that did not mean Reagan, now running for president, had to like it.

After the opening in 1972, Reagan told fellow conservatives that Nixon had taken him into his confidence on the *real* logic behind his thunderbolt of diplomacy. Both he and Nixon were constrained from speaking about it publicly, he said, because doing so would "blow the whole diplomatic game plan."[1]

"It is true the president dressed this visit up in all of the proper diplomatic, peaceful co-existence, forgive-and-forget trappings that are so much a part of the great international game," Reagan told M. Stanton Evans, head of the American Conservative Union, in a private letter. But the surface diplomacy should not mislead conservatives, Reagan advised, because Nixon was pursuing a "hard-headed" policy against the Communists. He explained how:

American public opinion will no longer tolerate wars of the Vietnam type because they no longer feel a threat—thanks to the liberal press—from Communism, and they cannot interpret those wars as being really in the defense of freedom and our own country. So the president, knowing the disaffection between China and Russia, visits China, butters up the warlords, and lets them be, because they have nothing to fear from us. Russia, therefore, has to keep its 140 divisions [sic] on the Chinese border; hostility between the two is increased; and we buy a little time and elbow room in a plain, simple strategic move a million miles removed from the soft appeasement of previous Democratic administrations.[2]

This view mollified many conservatives, and possibly persuaded them that Nixon would never take the next step.

But when Jimmy Carter broke relations with Taiwan in 1979, Reagan dumped Carter's act onto the bonfire of conservative rage over the sellout of American friends and allies. American leaders, especially Democratic ones, in Reagan's view, had neglected or abandoned too many of the traditional alliances on which American security was based. Reagan was going to rebuild them.

In the case of Taiwan, Reagan considered himself a true friend of the Nationalist Chinese and a personal friend of the late Chiang Kai-shek and his family. Taiwan's leaders had returned Reagan's loyalty with financial support for his political organization by retaining Michael Deaver and Peter Hannaford, whose public relations firm also represented Reagan.

Within the Reagan camp, there was no stronger supporter of Taiwan's cause than Richard V. Allen, the silver-haired impresario of the Republican Right.[3] Allen was one of Reagan's foreign policy advisers, the same job he had held in the Nixon campaign of 1968. Then, Allen had been a messenger between Nixon and Kissinger, and he was quickly pushed aside by Kissinger once Nixon was in office.[4] This time around, he fought off all competitors for the key White House job of assistant to the president for national security affairs.

During the 1980 presidential primary campaign, Reagan threw the most incendiary grenades of any candidate at Carter's China policy, saying that if he was elected, a Reagan administration would reestablish formal diplomatic relations with Taiwan, which he continued to call the Republic of China.[5]

In May, Reagan moderated his rhetoric somewhat, saying that he would upgrade the "unofficial" American Institute in Taiwan to the status of "an official liaison office."[6] He said that he wanted to return to an arrangement where Taiwan maintained government-to-government relations with Washington.

Each Reagan statement sent the Chinese leadership in Beijing into paroxysms of denunciation. For Beijing and Taipei, the symbolism of diplomatic representation was a war zone. If Beijing was the sole government of the Chinese people, no country could have government-to-government relations with Taiwan. Woodcock would try to calm Beijing down by pointing out that a lot of wild statements are made in American political campaigns, and, besides, there was no need to take Reagan that seriously since Carter, at that time, still had a good chance of getting reelected.[7]

After Reagan secured the Republican nomination, his political advisers, Allen among them, understood that to defeat Carter, Reagan would have to reposition himself nearer to the Republican mainstream. In early August, he proposed a plan to adjust Reagan's stance on China, telling the candidate that "we are getting killed" on the issue because Reagan had exposed himself to the charge that he was undermining the bipartisan consensus on China that extended from Nixon to Carter.

"We are going to get hit with this on every single campaign stop unless we do something about it," Allen argued, and he then suggested that Reagan dispatch his running mate, George Bush, on a mission to China designed to contain the damage and allow the candidate to distance himself from the extreme statements he had made in the primary campaign.

Bush was an ideal choice because, as the new face on the ticket, he was a clean slate on China. And, as the former head of the U.S. liaison office in Beijing, Bush was also a friendlier face to the Chinese. Allen was confident that a Bush mission would allow the campaign to eliminate the negatives of the China issue and "confuse the hell out of our critics,"[8] as he boasted.

Reagan instructed Bush to deliver a stern message to the Chinese. They would have to understand that Ronald Reagan would not abandon an old friend in order to gain a new one. He was willing to back away from the idea of reestablishing diplomatic relations with Taiwan, but, in other ways, Reagan said, he was going to demonstrate American friendship to Taipei.

For his part, Bush was heartened to get a high-profile assignment. If anything, it reinforced the image that Bush provided the essential centrist balance to an otherwise ideological ticket. Bush recruited Jim Lilley to accompany him on the trip.*

In the afterglow of the convention, Reagan gave Bush a public send-off from Los Angeles. During a photo opportunity, a reporter asked Bush whether the Republican ticket still favored government-to-government relations with Taiwan. Bush demurred, saying, "Well, I'll leave that to the governor. It's his policy."

Then Reagan stepped in it, again.

He said that his policy would be to maintain full diplomatic relations with Beijing, but at the same time, he would transform the "unofficial" American Institute in Taiwan into an operation of the U.S. government.[9]

Bush just stood there in disbelief, and after the press conference was over, he turned to Lilley and told him to get on the telephone with the Chinese embassy in Washington. He was to implore the Chinese ambassador to ask Beijing not to condemn Reagan's statement because that would cast a pall over the mission. Bush hoped that the Chinese would let it pass.[10]

---

*During Lilley's tenure as CIA station chief under Bush in Beijing, his diplomatic cover was revealed by journalists in the United States seeking to expose CIA officers working overseas. Lilley left the clandestine service for the Directorate of Intelligence, where he served as national intelligence officer for East Asia.

By the time the Bush party arrived in China, it was not even clear whether they would meet any senior Chinese official. Sitting in elegant isolation at Diaoyutai, Bush sent word to the American embassy that Stapleton Roy should come across town and brief the delegation on current events in China, making clear that the invitation was for Roy and not for Woodcock, since Woodcock was seen exclusively as a Carter partisan.

After Bush passed a day in briefings and sightseeing, Deng agreed to receive him, and the next day, Bush, Allen, and Lilley climbed the steps to the Great Hall. It was Allen's first exposure to the Chinese leadership. When Deng walked out to greet them, Allen allowed Deng to take him by the arm, and, with Bush on his other side, the three men entered the brightly lit room decorated with Chinese paintings and sprays of flowers. They arranged themselves in the familiar horseshoe configuration of arm chairs. A spittoon demarcated Deng's seat.

Allen feigned politeness toward Deng, but he was thinking, "Look at this little fucker. I am *under*whelmed."[11]

Bush had the opposite impression. He was a great admirer of what Deng was trying to do for China. He was effusive with praise, and exuded warmth on the renewal of their long friendship. He gingerly—too gingerly in Allen's view—worked through his talking points, emphasizing Reagan's commitment to improve relations with Beijing and insisting that Reagan was not trying to turn back the clock on Taiwan. Still, Bush explained, Reagan felt strongly about his old friends on Taiwan.

Allen prompted with a word here and there, but in the end, he felt that he needed to nail down Bush's presentation with greater force, so he told Deng that although the People's Republic and the United States could work together to contain the Soviet threat, Beijing was going to have to get used to a higher profile for Taiwan in the circle of American friends.[12] And by the way, Allen added, Reagan would appreciate it if the Chinese would knock off their vitriolic attacks on his campaign positions.

Deng's indignation filled the room.

Allen did not understand—or did not care to understand—the raw nerve of Deng's grievance in the wake of the Carter normalization process. Eighteen months earlier, Deng had gone along with Brzezinski's eleventh-hour stampede on the issue of arms sales to Taiwan by leaving it as an unresolved issue. At the time, Deng felt that he had no choice if he was to strengthen his hand at home over the Chinese military, discipline Vietnam, and stand up to Brezhnev. So Deng had gone along, but he had pointedly reserved the right to raise the issue of arms sales to Taiwan again.

The "unresolved" issue had then been stampeded further—indeed, it had been unilaterally resolved—by Congress with the passage of the Taiwan Relations Act, which Carter signed into law only after making a pledge to Deng that any president had wide flexibility in interpreting the law, and that Carter would do so in a manner consistent with the normalization agreement.

But Allen did not want to listen to Deng's grievances. Allen was no "old friend" of China, as Bush styled himself; he was just trying to save Reagan's campaign from a corrosive issue that would not go away. Allen, like Kissinger,[13] believed that the People's Republic, in opening to the United States, was motivated by fear of the Soviet Union. Therefore, Washington could extract a price from Beijing for the strategic and military benefits it was reaping by moving into the American orbit. The price, as far as Allen was concerned, was tolerance for Reagan's friendship with Taiwan and a higher profile for the relationship between Washington and Taipei. Allen assumed that Beijing could be forced to compromise its "principles" over Taiwan. It was just a question of leverage.

The meeting already was going south when, in a stroke of bad timing, a Chinese aide came into the room and delivered a piece of paper. Deng read for an instant and then looked up at Bush.

"Who is Ke-Lai-Ne?" he asked, transliterating the English name.

Lilley thought, "Oh my god, it's Cline."

Why, Deng asked, was someone named Ray Cline[14] making statements that the Reagan administration would reestablish diplomatic relations with Taiwan?

Bush had to backpedal again. Cline, the former CIA station chief in Taiwan, was a Bush campaign adviser who had joined the Reagan team only to become a mouthpiece for Taiwan. All Bush could do was tell Deng that Cline did not speak for Reagan—or himself.

But there was no containing the damage. To Deng, Reagan and Bush did not seem capable of enforcing any discipline on the ideologues who surrounded them. Bush left the Great Hall and went straight to the American embassy, where he tried to put the best face on things by holding a press conference.

The vice presidential candidate explained that Reagan would follow the letter of the Taiwan Relations Act, which prohibited official relations with Taiwan. A reporter asked if Reagan wanted to change the law, and Bush said, "Well, I don't want to speak for the man," and he turned to Allen, thinking that he might want to address the question. But Allen just stared straight ahead, forcing Bush to turn back to the questioner and respond, lamely, that he didn't think Reagan intended to do so.

Within hours, a New China News Agency report rebuked Reagan for promoting a two-China policy.[15] Summing up all of the candidate's statements, the report raised the question, "What other interpretation can there be?"

Woodcock had watched it all with a sense of alarm. It was apparent that a struggle was under way within the Reagan camp over China, and it had gotten to the point where normalization itself seemed vulnerable—even reversible. Woodcock wondered whether he should do something about it. He had a sinking feeling that the Carter administration, with its China policy, was—well, sinking.

As Bush's plane raced back across the Pacific to rendezvous with Reagan, Allen and Lilley drafted a new China policy statement for the campaign, hoping they could still take the issue off the table and prevent Carter from hammering them in the fall.

They found Reagan in his suite at the Marriott Airport Hotel in Los Angeles on Sunday night, August 24. Reagan was pleased that his message had been delivered to the Chinese, but he was not at all happy with the draft statement that Allen had handed him. To Allen and Lilley, it was a reasonable reaffirmation of the one-China policy. But to Reagan, it read like surrender, like he was backing off everything he had said about upgrading relations with Taiwan.

"I am not going to give this statement," he said.

Ed Meese and Lyn Nofziger, both longtime Reagan loyalists who were directing the campaign, urged Reagan to go along with the statement. But Reagan protested that it went against the grain of his commitment to the Nationalists, "who stood with us against Communism."[16]

Reagan took a legal pad and wrote out that Taiwan was America's friend, and America would always stand by its friends; we stand against Communism. . . . I am willing to go to Beijing, but the Chinese must understand where we come from as Americans.

Reagan read these phrases aloud and looked up at the others in the room.

"If you say that, you will have a war with China," Lilley said flippantly.

They went round and round. It was not an intellectual argument, more an emotional and ideological one.

"Governor," Allen kept saying, "If you read this statement, Taiwan will not come up again in this campaign."

With Meese and the others urging him to adjust his position, Reagan filibustered until the last moment, when the press corps filed into the hotel the next day to hear the candidate's report on Bush's mission.

"Do you really want me to say this?" Reagan asked, looking into the furrows and jowls of Ed Meese's face.

"I think you should, Governor," he replied. "I think this is the way to go."

Reagan was shaking his head. They were all sitting in a small anteroom off the press conference hall. Reagan started telling jokes. Then Bush told a joke. Then Reagan looked again at Meese.

"You're sure you really want me to say this?"

"Yes governor. It would be the best thing for the campaign."[17]

Finally, the hour arrived, and Reagan, followed by Bush, went before the cameras.

George Bush had explained his position in detail to the Chinese leadership, Reagan said, and they now understood it clearly. The Reagan-Bush team, he added, would abide by the Carter normalization agreement.

But Reagan was not finished. He cocked his head in that way that conveyed that he had really chewed over the problem, because he felt strongly about it. He said that even though he still thought it was a mistake for the American government to have abandoned the idea of keeping a liaison office with official status in Taiwan, that would have to be water under the bridge.

Then he added, "I would not pretend, as Carter does, that the relationship we now have with Taiwan, enacted by our Congress, is not official."

Moreover, he continued, "I will eliminate the petty practices of the Carter Administration which are inappropriate and demeaning to our Chinese friends on Taiwan. For example, it is absurd and not required by the act that our representatives are not permitted to meet with Taiwanese officials in their offices and ours."

Reagan said he recognized that the People's Republic was not pleased with the Taiwan Relations Act and that senior Chinese officials had made their dissatisfaction known to Bush, as they had to Carter. "But it is the law of our land,"[18] Reagan said, and they would have to live with that.

Reagan's declaration sounded a deepening knell of betrayal to Beijing. For all of Deng's faith in Carter's reassurances, a Republican candidate was now saying that if he was elected, he would unilaterally scale back America's commitment. And the candidate was from the party of Nixon.

Woodcock was appalled by Reagan's performance; everything about his tone indicated that he was going to turn back the clock. And so the ambassador once again took matters into his own hands. The embassy hastily organized a press conference.

"The normalization of relations with China has been pursued through three Administrations, both Republican and Democratic," Woodcock told the press corps in Beijing. "To endanger the carefully crafted relationship between the People's Republic and the United States, which is progressing so well and to mutual benefit, is to run the risk of gravely weakening the American international position at a dangerous time."[19]

It was always an extraordinary act for an ambassador to inject himself into a presidential campaign. But Woodcock had calculated that no one was likely to do anything about it. The White House was delighted, but said nothing, letting Woodcock's statement speak for itself. If it did not help to defeat Reagan, it did not matter. Woodcock wouldn't be serving as ambassador to China in a Reagan administration anyway.

In the end, Woodcock's assault failed to land a serious blow. With Reagan wrapping himself in the Taiwan Relations Act—the law of the land—it was difficult to criticize him as reckless.

T HAT WINTER, the Reagan administration burst into Washington with a muscular, conservative agenda that called for building up America's defenses, reinvigorating the country's alliances, and challenging the Soviet Union in every theater of competition.

Reagan drafted Alexander M. Haig Jr. as his secretary of state, bringing the tough Cold War general back to Washington to give concrete expression to Reagan's determination to confront the Soviet Union with a military man's ardor. Although Reagan didn't immediately realize it, he had chosen the person who most strongly believed that China was the key to a global American strategy to contain the Soviet empire and that some kind of alliance with China was a strategic imperative.

Haig felt that Reagan's rise to power signaled the demise of the enervating Vietnam syndrome that had sapped American self-confidence. The Soviet invasion of Afghanistan, the Soviet-Cuban interventions in Angola and Ethiopia, and Vietnam's Soviet-assisted occupation of Cambodia had sobered the political climate, making a new geopolitical activism possible for a strong American president.

Haig could see that Reagan's power over the electorate stemmed from his ability to project native optimism and self-confidence that also bespoke American strength. But from the outset, Reagan's vision of precisely where he would take the country was as inchoate as it was buoyant and regenerative. His thinking seemed a jumble of cherished and even conflicting ideological notions and loyalties. He was not a man who could articulate a systematic worldview. He ruled by instinct and anecdote. Like Nixon, Haig had little regard for Reagan's intellect, but believed that as Reagan's secretary of state, he could give expression to the new president's anti-Soviet instincts.[20]

Haig, whose views had been shaped by Nixon and Kissinger, wanted to move quickly to transform the tacit alliance between China and the United States developed during the Carter years into a "strategic association,"[21] a term that he invented, because creating an "alliance" with a communist country was an idea that would not sell. Still, Haig was determined to militarize the relationship by offering China sophisticated American weapons that could be deployed along the 4,150-mile Sino-Soviet border.

Unfortunately for Haig, however, Reagan's views on China were rooted in a bygone era. Reagan's political rise coincided with the struggle of Free China to regain the mainland, and he deeply admired the Nationalist leaders who had stood with America against communism and who still harbored the dream that they might someday return to the mainland.

But for Haig, the Chinese civil war was over. Chiang Kai-shek had lost, and Haig knew as well as anyone the feudal nature of Chiang's legacy. As a young staff officer in Tokyo, Haig had participated in a survey of Taiwan's military capabilities in 1950. His lasting memory was that of a poorly equipped army living in squalor and stench on the outskirts of Taipei and run under a command structure that had more in common with Genghis Khan[22] than with any modern force.

Haig, like Kissinger, believed that America's strategic interests were on the mainland. But Reagan confused sentimentalism with national interest, and, of course, the Taiwan lobby had skillfully learned to push his buttons.

A S PART OF THE education of Ronald Reagan, Haig arranged in the opening weeks of the administration for the president to learn the secrets of the intelligence alliance between Washington and Beijing.

William Casey, the new CIA director and longtime Reagan friend, unveiled the Chestnut program, which had given the CIA an important new window on the Soviet Far East. Casey also dramatized for Reagan China's secret cooperation in providing arms to the guerrillas fighting Soviet occupation in Afghanistan. Reagan was impressed and was more than willing to continue, even increase, the level of strategic cooperation with China against Soviet tyranny.

The next step in Reagan's education was a presidential meeting with a sophisticated Chinese Communist, someone who might break the stereotype implanted in Reagan's mind. With the connivance of his China specialists, Haig chose Ji Chaozhu,* a Harvard-educated interpreter who had been promoted to a diplomatic position in the Chinese Foreign Ministry.

Ji was articulate, thoughtful, and sensible, and he provided American diplomats with insights into how the Chinese leadership perceived Washington. He wore horn-rimmed glasses and scrunched up his face like an academic searching for the right word, one of many small mannerisms that made him seem more "one of us" than "one of them." Ji had been a longtime aide to Zhou Enlai and Chen Yi. His father, along with Nancy Tang's father, had

*Pronounced: Jee Chow-Jew.

edited a Chinese newspaper in New York before World War II, and because of that Ji himself had crossed the cultural barrier—that great wall—that stood between the Chinese leadership and any American president.

The meeting was an inspired idea, except that no one had considered that Chai Zemin,[23] the curmudgeonly ambassador, would insist on coming along.

On the American side, things also went awry.

The intimate meeting that Haig had envisioned—just the president, Haig, and Ji—quickly became a full house. Meese decided that he had to be there, then Mike Deaver had to be there, then Jim Baker had to be there, then Allen had to be there, and of course, Bush had to be there.

When the "intimate chat" finally occurred on March 19, it was neither intimate nor friendly. Ji was relegated to the role of interpreting the ambassador's lecture about America's broken commitments. Haig could see that Reagan was taken aback. The Chinese ambassador came on like a tough commie sent over from central casting.

When it was over and the Chinese had been escorted out, Reagan just shook his head. "I always thought they were sons of bitches,"[24] he said.

O NLY A FEW DAYS after this encounter, in the spring of 1981, the administration paused while the president recovered from the gunshot wound he received in a failed assassination attempt.* But as soon as Reagan recovered, Haig convinced him to take a step that no previous president had dared to take.

On June 6, Reagan issued a secret directive adopting a plan to offer China a "strategic association" against the Soviet Union. Never had China achieved such a prominent position in America's global military strategy.

And, within this association, the United States would begin to sell lethal, offensive weapons to the People's Republic of China.[25]

Haig had in mind a whole array of frontline weapons, including antitank and air defense systems, which would make China a much more formidable adversary to the forty-five Soviet divisions that were arrayed against it by the early 1980s. And Haig hoped that by daring to sell arms to China, he would relieve the pressure mounting from Beijing to repeal the Taiwan Relations Act and stop the flow of American arms to Taiwan.

Brezhnev had once warned Nixon that arming China would lead to war, but Haig, with Reagan's backing, was prepared to brazenly cross the red lines of the past. Haig flew off to Beijing to tell Deng that he was going to make

*Reagan was wounded on March 30, 1981, by John W. Hinckley Jr.

good on all the unfulfilled American commitments. He not only would dare to sell arms, he also would liberalize U.S. export controls on dual-use technology, which China needed for its modernization drive.

But instead of finding unreserved enthusiasm among China's leaders, Haig encountered suspicion and wariness about the Reagan administration. They were determined to resolve the Taiwan arms question.

Of all of Reagan's aides, the Chinese wanted Haig to come to Beijing, because they had identified him among Reagan's close advisers as the strongest advocate for China as central to the American security strategy. And having thus identified Haig as an advocate, they hit him as hard as they could with their dissatisfaction.

Huang Hua was perfect for the task. When he greeted Haig on June 15, the acerbic foreign minister said that a new strategic partnership between the United States and China could not proceed without an understanding on Taiwan and firm action to end arms sales to the island within a fixed period of time. Such sales were an affront to China's sovereignty, as was the Taiwan Relations Act, which was an "inappropriate" basis for U.S.-China relations. One billion Chinese people "can't be bribed," Huang scolded. One billion Chinese "would not compromise their principles."[26]

Huang invited Haig to recall how poisonously Lincoln had regarded the sale of British weapons to the Confederacy during the American Civil War. American weapons sales to Taiwan, Huang said, were regarded similarly. Their continuation would represent a grave threat to the further development of relations between China and the United States.

The next day, Haig returned to the Great Hall, where Deng warned that a "cloud" had settled over their relationship. Taiwan arms sales were "an interference in our internal affairs and cannot be tolerated." If they could not find a solution to the this issue, Deng said that he would not be able to face the Chinese people.

Haig countered by arguing that the Chinese leadership should not "drive Taiwan into a state of desperation"[27] by insisting on a complete cutoff of the weapons trade, since this provided the island with a modest measure of security. Haig mentioned the very sensitive nuclear question.

"Taiwan authorities could easily explore a Soviet option or, even more dangerously, attempt development of a separate nuclear capability," warned Haig. "These dangers we must avoid."[28]

Deng did not disagree. China, he said, had been tolerant, but there was a limit, and if the interference in China's internal affairs went too far, relations would come to a standstill or even go backward. Haig's aides speculated that Deng's warning against going "too far" was related to the rumors in Washington that the Reagan administration was preparing to sell Taiwan an advanced fighter jet known as the FX.*

In any case, the stakes were now clear. Haig could not build a strategic alliance with China without addressing the issue that the Carter normalization had failed to resolve and that Congress had complicated by passing the Taiwan Relations Act. And there was no apparent formula to do so. The question for Haig was whether Deng was looking for a compromise.

Deng's decision to go forward or backward with the United States would depend on his assessment of what Reagan had to offer in the way of U.S. technology and modern weaponry.[29] This, at least, was the view of the CIA specialists reading all the signals emanating from Beijing. If Washington was truly going to free up technology for China's dilapidated industries and begin selling weapons, then Deng could move ahead, provided he had some additional assurances of restraint over Taiwan.

As if to confirm this analysis, Geng Biao, the Chinese defense minister and one of the elders of the PLA, told Haig that the Chinese military was anxious to engage in coproduction of military equipment with the United States. Haig, the old general said, should work to strengthen China "so it poses a great threat to the Soviets."[30] There was nothing subtle about his appeal.

I N THE POLITICS OF diplomacy, field commanders who are trying to shape events do not always adhere to the letter of their instructions, and Haig certainly fell into that category. He had been instructed to keep Reagan's decision to sell arms to China secret for two months. The White House wanted time to consult with Japan and other Asian allies and to soften the blow on Taiwan. Reagan's presidential directive, signed after a meeting of the National Security Council on June 4, had specified that the president's decision would be made public in August when China's vice chief of staff, General Liu Huaqing, was scheduled to visit Washington. Then China's arms purchases could begin.

But secrecy was not in Haig's interest. There was already a great deal of discomfort in the Pentagon and the White House that Haig was taking this "strategic association" notion too far, that it did not make sense to sell billions of dollars in sophisticated weapons to "Red China." Besides, China was a poor

*The "X" simply indicated that the exact model of aircraft had not yet been designated; it could be one of several advanced fighter types, such as General Dynamics' F-16, which was the most capable interceptor in the U.S. Air Force. Or, it could be Northrop's F-5G, a slightly less capable fighter, but with a powerful General Electric engine. Northrop had sunk $250 million into the development of the F-5G and desperately needed the Taiwanese market, because General Dynamics had taken the lion's share of world markets with the F-16.

country. How could it pay? Haig discarded these arguments. He was out to sell arms and thereby cement the relationship. The money could be found.

Winning the policy fight was the big issue for Haig, but as long as Reagan's decision remained secret it could be reversed by any coalition of rivals, some of whom opposed arms sales to China. Haig wanted the policy decision out in the open—he wanted there to be no question that the United States had turned a strategic corner and that Reagan was seeking an active partnership with Beijing against Moscow. That would create momentum in the bureaucracy and get the pipeline moving.

On his last day in Beijing, Haig called a news conference. When repeatedly asked if the United States was about to begin selling arms to China, he dodged the question; but his efforts were useless, since his aides had earlier leaked details of the White House policy decision to *New York Times* and *Wall Street Journal* correspondents covering his trip. In any case, Haig eventually confirmed the change in policy;[31] the news rocketed through Asia, blindsiding the Japanese and provoking a wounded outburst from Taiwan, whose leaders warned that Beijing could not be trusted in any form of alliance.

Haig's disclosure sent Jim Lilley (then an aide to Allen on the NSC staff) and Richard Armitage (an aide to Defense Secretary Caspar Weinberger), both in Beijing with Haig, scrambling back to the American embassy to report the secretary's breach of Reagan's directive. That same day, Reagan appeared before a news conference and took the opportunity to bring Haig down a notch.

Haig got no warning that the president was going to zing him by reaffirming the Taiwan Relations Act while he was still dealing with the Chinese in Beijing. Reagan said that arms sales to China were a normal part of trying to improve relations with Beijing, but that his administration would continue to live up to the provisions of the Taiwan Relations Act, including the continued sale of weapons to the Nationalist Chinese on Taiwan.

The next morning, when Haig was on the tarmac preparing to board his jet, the Chinese sent out a senior diplomat, Zhang Wenjin, to confront him with a sheet of paper.[32] It was the text of Reagan's remarks. The reporters covering Haig's trip could see the foreign ministry official gesturing emphatically to Haig.

It was anything but a warm send-off by a "strategic associate."

IT MAY HAVE BEEN inevitable that Haig would become a lightning rod in an administration torn by so much conflicting ideology and political ambition.

George Bush and James A. Baker III, the White House chief of staff, saw Haig as a rival to a future Bush presidency.[33] And Baker had his own ambition to become secretary of state. Weinberger chafed at Haig's attempts to pre-empt the prerogatives of the Pentagon, and some of Weinberger's aides, such as Richard Perle, formerly on Senator Henry Jackson's staff, mistrusted Haig's tilt toward the Communists in Beijing. Reagan's political advisers, particularly Deaver,[34] and his wife Nancy regarded Haig's profile as the self-proclaimed "vicar of foreign policy" as too outsized and, therefore, in competition with the president's.

There was, indeed, something outsized about Al Haig. It seemed altogether possible that he had been born standing in that arms-akimbo pose that most conveyed his sense of self-assured activism as a military and political leader, a posture he had learned to emulate during his assignment as a young army officer at the headquarters staff of General Douglas MacArthur.

When Haig first arrived at the White House in 1969, he was a forty-five-year-old colonel[35] who had served a tour as a decorated infantry commander in Vietnam and held a series of key staff jobs that had immersed him in the national security apparatus of the Kennedy and Johnson administrations. His exceptional bureaucratic skills had brought him to Kissinger's attention.

Haig's first job in the Nixon White House was assembling and distilling the overnight intelligence report for the president's morning briefing by Kissinger. But soon Haig was the indispensable aide, outmaneuvering Kissinger's other assistants and coming to dominate the national security adviser's basement domain in the Nixon White House.

After a year, even Nixon had noticed that "Haig's always down there while Henry's off having dinner in Georgetown."

Haig had lost his father at the age of nine, and his attachments to the war heroes and political titans he served over the years often became deep and emotional. His charm was successful because it was filial, given without reservation to the men who fathered his career. In the darkest hours of crushing schedules and staff tensions, Haig would often regale his colleagues by telling outlandish tales of loyalty under duress. "You haven't seen anything," he would say, and then he would recount how he almost drowned during an amphibious landing in Korea holding his general's sleeping bag aloft as he walked with his head still beneath the waves to get ashore,[36] or how Major General Edward M. Almond, MacArthur's chief of staff, had sent Haig back to the front lines to blow up the mosaic tile bath that the general had enjoyed at his forward command post. (Haig had supervised the construction of the tiled bath and decorated the general's inner sanctum with pots of flowers.)

"What the hell is wrong with you, Haig?" the general had roared. "Go back and blow it up—no stinking Chinese general"[37] was going to get a bath "in *my* bathtub."*

One of the seminal moments of Haig's professional army life came when he was sitting outside the war council of Truman's Joint Chiefs of Staff, who had flown to Tokyo in 1950 to review MacArthur's plan to roll back the North Korean offensive with an amphibious landing at Inchon followed by a pincer movement against Seoul. After the chiefs laid out all their reservations about the bold plan, it seemed to Haig, listening outside the door, that MacArthur had no support in the room. But instead of folding up his tents, the old general put down his pipe and said, "Gentlemen, we will land at Inchon on September 15 or you will have a new Supreme Commander in the Far East."[38]

Haig had seen it as a supreme act of moral courage, but he had also seen how none of the chiefs dared to pick up the gauntlet after MacArthur had thrown it down. It was one part righteousness, one part poker, and Haig would remember that, too.

As Nixon's last chief of staff, Haig had played the role of political undertaker, which ruined him for a high-level job in the Ford administration. After a tour as supreme allied commander in Europe, he retired to the private sector and was considering his own run for the presidency when Reagan swept the field.

Haig accepted Reagan's offer to become secretary of state, but privately he consulted Nixon, with whom he spoke almost every week. Nixon counseled him to insist on frequent and personal access to the president. The first week of the administration, Haig sent a memo to Reagan suggesting that he set aside an hour each week for a foreign policy discussion with his secretary of state. There was no reply.[39]

In fact, the rivalries among Reagan's top aides were such that, from the beginning, whenever Haig arrived at the White House for a meeting with the president, Baker, Bush, Meese, Deaver, or Allen were likely to file into the Oval Office behind him to monitor the secretary and protect their own bureaucratic interests.

---

*Haig has told this story differently over the years. Roger Morris, who served with Haig under Kissinger in 1969–1970, recounted in his 1977 memoir, *Uncertain Greatness: Henry Kissinger and American Foreign Policy* (New York : Harper & Row, 1977), that Haig told of throwing the grenade to deny any "stinking Chinese general" a bath. But Haig, in his 1992 memoir, *Inner Circles*, said that the bath was destroyed to deny any "damn Russian general" its pleasures. The adjustment may have reflected Haig's sensitivities in 1992, when his private consulting firm served corporations doing business in China. As for the historical truth, in December 1950, during the American retreat from the Yalu River region, there were no Russian generals reported to be among the attacking Chinese forces, which were under the command of Chinese Marshal Lin Biao.

R EAGAN HAD PUT Anna Chennault, the doyenne of the Taiwan lobby, on the Reagan-Bush Inaugural Committee. She was the widow of General Claire Chennault, who had organized the Flying Tigers in the China theater of World War II. In January 1981, stories suddenly appeared in the Taiwanese press that three prominent Taiwanese officials were coming to Washington as official guests to attend the Reagan inauguration.

Beijing's ambassador, Chai Zemin, telephoned Lilley and said that he wanted to host Bush and Allen for dinner at the Chinese Embassy.[40] It would be an evening of "old friends," the ambassador said, graciously setting the snare.

The inauguration was only days away when Bush and Allen arrived by limousine, and the dinner went well, but afterward Chai pulled them into a side room with only a Chinese interpreter. Allen flagged Lilley to join them because Lilley spoke some Chinese.

Chai put on his stern diplomatic face. If any Taiwanese government official was allowed to attend Reagan's inauguration, it would be a great insult to Beijing and it would hurt the feelings of 900 million Chinese, he said. China would refuse to attend. He hoped that any invitations to Taiwanese officials would be rescinded.

The ambassador, reading from notes, was not done. He started in on the Taiwan Relations Act, calling it an illegal interference in China's internal affairs. He reminded Allen that the United States had recognized Beijing as the sole government of China. This went on for several minutes, and it was clear that Chai had been instructed to put China's dissatisfaction on the record.

Allen felt his blood rising. He had shown great politeness, he felt, in attending the ambassador's dinner. But he had no respect for Chai or his Communist bosses in Beijing. Allen was thinking, "Enough with this frigging diatribe. This is high-level abuse, and abuse of the relationship and abuse of being a good host."

The president's national security adviser was suddenly holding up his hands in a strange "T" formation.

"Time out, Mr. Ambassador," Allen said.

"What means 'Time out'?" Chai asked with a quizzical expression.

"Stop, stop, stop all of this," Allen said emphatically.

"But I am not finished,"[41] Chai responded.

Bush sat frozen, that characteristically friendly, puzzled look on his face.

"I would like to thank you for a nice evening, Mr. Ambassador," Allen said, "It has been wonderful, but the Vice President elect and I have to go, we have other . . . "

"I am not finished," Chai again protested.

"But we are finished listening," Allen said, "and I would like to say something that was said to your leadership in Beijing: Don't shout at us! The inauguration of the President of the United States is a private event. We have no control over it whatsoever."

And then Allen turned to Bush. "Mr. Vice President, let's go."

Bush, mortified, left with Allen, but as soon as he was clear of Reagan's hotheaded security adviser, Bush turned to Lilley and said, "Take care of this goddamned thing."[42]

It was clear that Allen's hand was behind Anna Chennault's effort to use the inauguration to boost Taiwan and resist the new emphasis on mainland China.[43] When Haig found out about the invitations and Allen's support for them, he dressed Allen down in front of Reagan. Of course the Taiwanese leadership sensed a friendlier atmosphere with Reagan in the White House, Haig said, and of course Taiwan would seek symbolic gains and increased access to administration officials to score points against Beijing. But this could not be permitted, Haig scolded, because it would undermine the unofficial status of Taiwan and provoke a breach in relations with China at a time when the United States wanted to forge a strategic alliance against Moscow.[44]

The Chinese, Haig continued, were serious people who talked straight and did not bluff. Haig used his heel so forcefully on Allen that the cocky White House aide never again took the secretary on frontally without first marshaling powerful allies to protect himself.

It fell to Lilley and John Holdridge, a former Kissinger assistant, to defuse the crisis over the invitations. They told Chennault how displeased the White House was by the controversy. Holdridge, using an open telephone line so that the Taiwanese intelligence services would hear him, called Charles Cross, the unofficial U.S. representative in Taipei, and told him how much the attendance of Taiwanese officials would disrupt U.S.-China relations and how much Reagan hoped the problem could be somehow taken care of.

All they could do was hope that the megaphone diplomacy would work.

In the final days before Reagan's swearing in, Ambassador Chai pressed for a guarantee that he would encounter no Taiwanese officials anywhere near the Capitol, where the oaths of office were to be administered. But the Taiwanese had not responded. Then, with only hours to go, reports started coming in: The governor of Taiwan, one of the invitees, discovered that he had urgent business at home and canceled his travel plans to Washington. The mayor of Taipei, another invitee, followed suit.

But the secretary general of the ruling Nationalist Party, Chiang Yan-shih, already had arrived in the United States. Lilley and Holdridge were at a loss. What face-saving ruse could they devise to uninvite the old gentleman? Luckily, Chiang spared them any further embarrassment. He checked into a hospital in suburban Virginia, sending his regrets that he could not attend the inauguration because he had come down with the "flu."*

The crisis was over, if only briefly.†

IN TIMES OF ADVERSITY, Haig was famous for standing over his staff and bellowing like a tank commander to let everyone know that things were not going the way he wanted.

And in August 1981, those staff members who knew Haig best could see that Vesuvius was about to blow during Holdridge's long-winded explanation of why the list of weapons that Haig wanted to sell to China had not yet been approved. Haig's senior staff encamped in his conference room on the seventh floor of the State Department as Holdridge explained that the Pentagon was throwing up obstacles to most of the sophisticated weapons systems that Haig wanted at the top of the list.

For Haig, time was short. General Liu Huaqing, the chief arms buyer in the Chinese military, was due to arrive in Washington at the end of August. Beijing, however, was holding up his trip pending clarification over whether Washington intended to sell Taiwan an advanced fighter, the so-called FX.[45]

At least in Haig's mind, the assumption was that if the United States was willing to sell top-of-the-line U.S. weapons to Beijing, Deng might be persuaded to accept the sale of the new airplane to Taiwan. But the Pentagon was undermining Haig, and Holdridge had not been bull moose enough to force a positive decision out of Weinberger's bureaucracy.

Holdridge was as tall as a redwood and had the gift of patience and eloquence when dealing with Congress, but as the assistant secretary of state for East Asian affairs he was lacking that essential bureaucratic skill that Haig treasured most—how to put a spear in your adversary's chest to get something done. Holdridge was smart without being cunning, and so he was losing ground to the Pentagon. But in fairness to Holdridge, no one could have pried loose the kinds of state-of-the-art weapons he was trying extract from the Pentagon without personal backing from the president as well as from Weinberger. Holdridge had support from neither. All he had was a policy decision by the White House to sell arms to China. It was up to the Pentagon to sort out which ones.

Haig had chosen Holdridge because they had worked together under

---

*To show his gratitude, Holdridge visited Chiang in his hospital room and conveyed the administration's warm greetings and wishes for a speedy recovery.
†After the inauguration, Michael Deaver met with Taiwanese officials at his White House office. Allen followed suit, announcing to the State Department that Reagan had reversed the Carter administration's ban on such visits by Taiwanese dignitaries. Haig reined these decisions in somewhat by drafting stringent guidelines for such meetings.

Kissinger in the Nixon White House and because they both shared a devotion to the China opening; after all, they had been there at the inception of this global realignment. They were both West Pointers and on a certain level they talked the same language. But Haig could see that Holdridge was getting outflanked by Richard Perle, Richard Armitage, and the other Weinberger terriers who seemed to fear that every weapon or high-technology system sold to China would end up in Moscow.

Haig thought that such fears were nonsense. He wanted to sell the Chinese navy a top-of-the-line torpedo for its submarine force, but Holdridge reported that these were reserved for NATO countries and Japan.

Haig wanted to sell the Chinese army the latest armored personnel carrier, but the Pentagon would only go along with an older model. It was the same story with TOW antitank missiles and Hawk air defense missiles.

Holdridge was ticking off these defeats when Haig came out of his chair, spewing chunks of magma.

"John, get it through your thick head—we are going to sell arms to the People's Republic of China in September so that we can sell arms to Taiwan in January—so get off your ass!"[46]

I N THAT MOMENT, Haig crystallized his strategy. He was going to sell the most advanced weapons and technology he could to Beijing, hoping that this would allow Deng to claim success, while at the same time selling an advanced fighter jet to Taiwan. In doing so, Haig hoped to satisfy the pro-Taiwan ideologues in the White House and bail out the Northrop Corporation, the most likely FX supplier.

In reality, the sale of a single weapons system—in this case, 100 or more high-performance fighters—would not change the balance of power in the Taiwan Strait, but it would take on enormous symbolic significance in the wake of the normalization agreement. It would be proof that the Mutual Defense Treaty had been, in effect, replaced by the Taiwan Relations Act. A fighter jet sale would magnify Taiwan's image, demonstrating that the island had survived normalization with its separate and sovereign status intact, that it could not be muscled by the mainland into any reunification deal. The sale of fighter aircraft to Taiwan was particularly sensitive since, in the 1958 skirmishes, Taiwanese pilots flying F-86 Sabrejets had humiliated the mainland air force, shooting many of Mao's MIG-17s out of the sky.

When Bill Rope heard about the fighter deal, he thought that Haig was headed for disaster.

William F. Rope was a forty-year-old career foreign service officer and, under Holdridge, was the head of the China Desk in the East Asia Bureau.

Like everyone else in the bureau, he could see the evidence all over Washington—in the press and in the statements of defense industry lobbyists—that Northrop and Taiwan already had White House support for a new fighter. Tom Jones, Northrop's chairman, was Reagan's friend and political supporter,* not to mention that Northrop employed thousands of workers in Reagan's home state of California. Northrop had been coproducing the F-5E fighter in Taiwan since 1973, when Nixon and Kissinger approved the first 100-plane deal. Jimmy Carter had extended the production run by another 100 planes as a way to head off Taiwan's request for a more sophisticated aircraft.

Rumors already had reached the State Department that Allen, confident of success, had passed the message via back channels to Taiwan's leaders that he could guarantee they were going to get a new fighter. Reagan was for it. And it appeared that Allen was leaking an FX story every few days indicating in one way or another that Taiwan's prospects were excellent.[47]

Although Allen was clearly in the tank for Taiwan, Lilley proposed that the administration nonetheless make a professional case for the sale of the fighter. Allen agreed to order up an examination by the intelligence community[48] of whether Taiwan needed an advanced fighter and, if so, what effect such a sale would have on the political fortunes of Deng Xiaoping.

The Defense Intelligence Agency (DIA) took the lead on studying the fighter question, and the CIA took the lead on assessing its impact on Deng. As the studies got under way in secrecy, Jones made a lobbying call on Haig and told him that Jimmy Carter had all but promised Northrop that it would be able to sell the F-5G to Taiwan. Jones was a world-class salesman, and Northrop was a national asset as a leading defense contractor (already at work on the B-2 stealth bomber), so there was great sympathy in the government for Northrop's bid. But Haig told him that there was no record of any government promise to Northrop. Still, Haig said, he was doing what he could.

The staff around Haig could sense that he was trying to accommodate both the White House and Northrop, but when Rope heard about it, he became alarmed that an FX sale would break the back of the U.S.-China relationship. Earlier that year, China had expelled the Dutch ambassador and called its own ambassador home from the Netherlands after the Dutch sold a

---

*Haig would later assert that Reagan personally directed the Pentagon to procure planes from Northrop to create a squadron of mock Russian intruders for training American pilots. After the president issued this instruction, Haig followed him back to the Oval Office and advised him that it was both unseemly and illegal for a president to direct the procurement of weapons from a particular company instead of following the usual government bidding process.

pair of sophisticated diesel-electric submarines to Taiwan. Deng would not be able to withstand the criticism for having so misjudged American fidelity to its pledge to limit arms sales to the island. He would be forced to downgrade relations, and no one was considering the consequences of that.

Rope's feelings only reflected the mood on the China Desk and among a number of specialists both inside and outside the government. Rope's deputy, Scott Hallford, told his colleagues that fall: "You have heard of the Sino-Soviet split. Well, we are about to witness the Sino-U.S. split."

With so many FX stories in the press, the Chinese began their own investigation.

Bill Rope was not a go-along-get-along bureaucrat. Ambitious and tenacious, he seemed perfectly willing to throw a spear at any rival to advance his own bureaucratic cause. After Yale and a navy tour in the western Pacific, he became a China specialist because he was convinced that China was central to the two disasters that had befallen the United States in Asia in the postwar era—Korea and Vietnam.

Rope had been a young China watcher at the U.S. consulate in Hong Kong when Nixon pulled off the opening. He was perfectly positioned to go straight to Beijing as the youngest diplomat selected to staff the newly opened U.S. liaison office in 1973. There, he joined Holdridge and got to know Lilley, who saw Rope, barely thirty at the time, as a little too starry-eyed about the People's Republic.

Of course, Rope was infected by the enormity of China. Seeing the country in those last crazy years of Mao, observing the consequences of the Cultural Revolution, Rope felt that he understood the trauma inflicted on the Chinese. His deepest impression was that America would have to help China if it was to modernize. A renegade China was a danger, but a modernizing China could be a constructive force in the region.

Helping China would be difficult because the cultural differences were vast. Rope was struck by how hard it was for Chinese leaders, even progressive Chinese leaders, to act as rationally as Americans would have liked them to act. Their doctrinaire rigidity and fitful styles of negotiating were a consequence of the turbulence within the Communist Party leadership, where all bureaucrats, especially those dealing with foreigners, lived under hair-trigger scrutiny; where the slightest breach of discipline could bring down years of recrimination and persecution. And much of the persecution was arbitrary. That was why Chinese diplomats often took what seemed to Westerners irrational positions—they were often just playing it safe or playing for time as they waited for the political winds to shift in Beijing.

In 1981, the Chinese leadership was still dominated by the revolutionary clan that had sat both as government and war council around Mao, often suffering his abuse. Now, however, the council was a collective of aging warriors to whom nation building was still a mystery. They had copied much from the Soviets in the 1950s, but collectivism and the straightjacket of a command economy worked no better in China than it did in the Soviet Union. Rope, like his elders among the China specialists, saw Deng's emergence and the boldness of his reforms as the most positive developments yet in China's modern history. But reform remained fragile. The pendulum swung back and forth between the reformers and the hard-liners, and Deng, at times, struggled to keep his initiatives moving.

At the end of August, Haig formally notified the Chinese that he had a significant list of U.S. weapons that the United States was willing to sell to China. Haig was anxious for Deng to send Liu Huaqing[49] to Washington to start negotiations. But it was apparent to the Chinese that top-of-the-line weapons were not on the list, whereas Taiwan still stood to win the prize of a new fighter jet. So they canceled General Liu's trip, fearing that their own purchase of American weaponry might provide the pretext for Washington to announce the FX sale to Taiwan. Such an announcement would surely provoke a crisis for Deng.

At the end of August, Deng granted an interview to a Hong Kong newspaper and stately gruffly that if Washington forced China to "act according to the will of the United States," then Beijing was prepared to see "relations retrogress."[50]

Haig tried to sooth the Chinese. On September 22 in New York, he told Zhang Wenjin, the vice foreign minister, that the FX was merely a "drawing-board concept" that did not exist as an airplane. Haig admonished Zhang that he should ignore the rumors swirling around Washington about an advanced fighter for Taiwan.[51] But in the privacy of his office, Haig confided to his aides that he was going to try to satisfy the White House and give Taiwan the plane it wanted.

On September 30, the aging Marshal Ye Jianying, speaking for Deng and the entire Communist Party leadership, unveiled Beijing's nine-point plan offering Taiwan "substantial autonomy under the sovereignty of the People's Republic."[52] Taiwan would be able to maintain independent social, economic, and cultural relations with other countries as well as a free market economy, private property rights, and its own military. Ye was thus formalizing the offer that Deng had promoted immediately after normalization in 1979. The timing was conspicuous, and Rope suspected that the Chinese were attempting—by making a public commitment to peaceful reconciliation with Taiwan—to give Haig and Reagan a rationale *not* to sell the FX.

In truth, the Reagan administration never understood or even tried to understand how earnestly Deng was trying to find a formula that would open a political dialogue with Taiwan's Nationalist leaders, one that could lead to reconciliation. And the Reagan team never appreciated how much their campaign to sell advanced weapons to Taiwan threatened to undermine Beijing's legitimate diplomatic efforts to end the Chinese civil war. There was no hint of military intimidation in Deng's offer; in fact, the situation was just the opposite. In the more than two years since normalization, all of Kissinger's fears and all of the intelligence community's estimates that the mainland might mobilize an invasion force to send against Taiwan had proven wrong.

IN EARLY OCTOBER, Richard Holbrooke, out of government and living in New York, invited Zhang Wenjin for a night at the theater. *Evita* was the Broadway spectacle of the season. That evening, Holbrooke recounted for the Chinese diplomat the history of the Carter administration's deliberations over Taiwan's request to purchase an advanced fighter. In late 1980, Carter had decided against selling Northrop's high-powered, long-range F-5G fighter to Taiwan, preferring instead to extend the coproduction agreement for the more modest F-5E, the same plane that had been rolling off the Taiwanese production line since Nixon and Kissinger first authorized the deal in 1973. Holbrooke's explanation of the Carter decision reinforced Chinese convictions that the U.S. government already had committed itself to *not* selling Taiwan an advanced fighter.

Holbrooke suggested that Zhang go to Washington and find out for himself what was going on.

On October 3, Haig was out of pocket, so Zhang was ushered into the State Department to see William Clark. Known as Judge Clark because of his service on the California Supreme Court, Clark was among Reagan's oldest friends and closest political advisers. He had been gently imposed on Haig as deputy secretary of state, and Haig had willingly accepted him, thinking that Clark would make a useful conduit to Reagan. Of course, the arrangement worked both ways: Clark was also a set of White House ears in Haig's inner circle.[53]

Rope sat on the sidelines and took notes while Zhang delivered the simple message that the aircraft issue had become dangerous for U.S.-China relations. The Chinese diplomat told Clark that the status quo—continuing the coproduction of the F-5E in Taiwan—might be tolerable to Beijing. "But I know if you sell the FX, it will be very bad," Zhang said.

Clark was affable and convincing. He told Zhang that Reagan was not a rash person and wanted good relations with Beijing. Reagan would make the right decision, Clark said, and he urged Zhang to be patient.

Zhang was under instructions to try to educate Reagan's aides about how Beijing saw the arms sales question. China, he said, was looking to open lines of communication with Taiwan, to begin a genuine reconciliation. Marshal Ye Jianying's nine points, Zhang said, were a profound development. "This is a long-term policy that will not change," he emphasized.

Rope left the meeting and raced back to the China Desk. It seemed to him that all the elements were in place for a deal to solve the FX crisis. He began to put his ideas on paper for Haig.

The president would be going to Cancún, Mexico, for the North-South Summit and a sideline meeting with Chinese premier Zhao Ziyang.* Rope argued, in his notes, that Reagan should take the opportunity to tell Zhao that the United States had decided against selling an advanced fighter to Tai-wan. At the same time, as a face-saving gesture to Taiwan, Northrop could make marginal improvements to the current F-5E, such as adding a "heads up" display for the pilot, a feature that was now standard issue on top-of-the-line fighters. Rope's confidence was boosted by the DIA report that had be-gun to circulate in the intelligence community. Taiwan did not *need* an advanced fighter, the agency had concluded. The current generation F-5E was an adequate interceptor for the island's defense, and it was still superior to any plane in the mainland's air force.

The CIA added its own analysis of the politics of the fighter jet issue. The agency argued that the sale of an advanced fighter to Taiwan would cause se-rious political problems for Deng and could lead to a rupture in U.S.-China relations.

When Haig read Rope's memo, he bristled that the China Desk was trying to undermine him.

In the first week of October, 1981, Haig called Walter Stoessel, now the undersecretary of state for political affairs, and James Buckley, the depart-ment's legal counselor, as well as Holdridge and Rope into his office for a dressing down. Holdridge and Rope felt like they were on the carpet.

Haig's face was a thundercloud.

He had a perfectly good solution, he said, and was going to proceed with it. Northrop could design a more advanced fighter for Taiwan, but the State Department, in explaining the transaction to Beijing, could simply call the new plane a variation of the current fighter. The engineers could give the F-5E a single powerful engine from General Electric and call it the F-5E/T ("T" for Taiwan). They could even throw in the latest cockpit technology. It

*Pronounced: Jow (sounds like cow) Zzz-yaang.

would have all the hardware and capability of the FX, but no one would know the difference.

Holdridge and the others did not speak, so Rope felt he had to.

"If we do that," he said, "we are going to get caught."[54]

"No we won't," Haig said.

"Yes we will," countered Rope. "They will see through it."

"No they won't," steamed Haig. "They won't be able to tell the difference."

"Yes they will," Rope said. "They can get a picture of it in *Jane's*," referring to the universal guide to worldwide military equipment.

"No they won't," Haig disparaged.

"Yes they will and if they don't, they have friends who will help them see through it," Rope persisted.

"Who?" Haig asked.

"Holbrooke for one," Rope said, not knowing whether Haig was aware that the former assistant secretary had tutored Zhang Wenjin on the history of the fighter jet decision in the Carter administration.

Haig's aides knew that they could speak their mind in these private sessions without fear that the secretary would throw them in the stockade, and so Rope warned him that by trying to disguise an advanced fighter, "you are ratcheting this thing up as tight as you can get it," and that was increasing the risk that it would all blow up in their faces. But Haig just glowered and stood his ground. That was the way it was going to be, he said.

When they got back to the East Asia Bureau, Rope told Holdridge that they would have to turn Haig around, but Holdridge was too much the good soldier. Once the boss made up his mind, he believed, you saluted and carried out your orders, and, besides, Holdridge himself seemed to believe that a little sleight of hand in upgrading Taiwan's air force was worth a try.

Rope started shopping for allies. He found one in Rick Burt, Haig's director for political-military affairs. Burt had missed the FX meeting, and, after reading a report on what had transpired, he requested another meeting to reconsider the notion of disguising the FX. But it was just a repeat of the same heated exchange, with Burt and Rope challenging their boss and Haig standing firm. Finally, when Burt realized that it was hopeless, he looked evenly at Haig across the conference table and said, "Well Mr. Secretary, we are here because we have to give you the reasons we are against this decision, but you have not told us what your reason is for supporting it. What is your reason?"

Haig lowered his head and peered at Burt over the rims of his reading glasses, as if to ask with incredulity: *Were you born yesterday?* But Burt's face was blank in response, forcing Haig to address the question.

"You know," the secretary said.

"No, we don't," Burt replied.

Haig looked around the room as if it might be bugged. He raised his right forearm and rubbed his thumb against his forefingers in a gesture indicating that money was involved.[55] Something between a smirk and a frown appeared on his face.

Everyone in the room understood. It was all about money, all about saving Northrop, all about bailing out the president's friend. There may also have been an ideological component for some people in the White House like Allen, but Haig was admitting that, first and foremost, the deal was about money.

IN LATE OCTOBER, Reagan attended the North-South Summit in Cancún, where the new president would have his first face-to-face meeting with Zhao Ziyang, the reformist Chinese premier and Deng protégé.

Zhao was younger than Reagan and inexperienced in international diplomacy, so he came on a little stiffly, making his boilerplate arguments that China wanted a long-term relationship with the United States to counter the Polar Bear. The words brought a smile to Reagan's face. Zhao then repeated Deng's admonition of the "shadow" over U.S.-China relations caused by arms sales to Taiwan.

"We have made a generous proposal to Taiwan," Zhao said, referring to the nine-point reunification offer proposed by Marshal Ye. "They can retain their social system, economic and cultural relations with foreign countries, their property system, and their military. Leaders on the island can take up national posts and we propose negotiations on an equal basis."[56]

Zhao, too, tried to get through to Reagan on the critical issue of how arms sales to Taiwan interfered with reconciliation, but Reagan was fidgeting. The meeting had gone overtime, and Deaver and Baker both were clearing their throats and looking at their watches.

Reagan only wanted to point out that he did not intend to abandon his old friends on Taiwan; he assured Zhao that the Taiwanese were not afraid of their fellow Chinese across the Taiwan Straits—what they were afraid of was communism.

Because of the time constraint, Zhao had to pull up short. He said that there was another important message that the Chinese government wanted to convey, but that he would leave it for his foreign minister, Huang Hua, to deliver, and the two leaders then parted.

Haig was now prepared to perform his Houdini act in which he would pave the way for an advanced fighter jet sale to Taiwan by telling the Chinese that there would be no such thing. Careful talking points had been drafted. Haig would start out by telling Huang Hua that the United States had decided not to sell the FX to Taiwan. That deal was dead. Then Haig would explain that coproduction of the current F-5E would continue. Of course, there would be modifications to the F-5E design, and, in time, the two engines of the F-5E would disappear and become a single engine (effectively transforming the plane into an advanced fighter identical to the FX). And with this bit of magic, Haig hoped it would be over. Problem solved.

But Haig never got a chance to deliver the talking points. On Friday night, October 23, after Reagan had already left Mexico, the Chinese foreign minister walked into Haig's suite and presented him with a formal diplomatic note that landed like a stomach punch. In it, the Chinese demanded for the first time that the United States end all arms sales to Taiwan. They could be phased out over time, the note said, but Washington must set a fixed date for them to end. "Between now and that date," the note said, the level of U.S. arms sales were not to exceed the levels proposed by the Carter administration and were to be reduced year by year, completely ending on the termination date. The note further said that these terms represented "the maximum extent of Chinese tolerance."⁵⁷

The People's Republic, Huang said, wanted to enter immediate negotiations to set the date. If Washington refused, China would downgrade its relations with the United States and call its ambassador home. Huang said that he hoped Haig would have a reply within a week, because he was planning to travel to Washington and wanted to meet with Reagan to deliver the same message.

Haig felt like he had been mugged. This ultimatum was the voice of Deng, and he could sense the gravity of it. When Haig got back to Washington Saturday morning and assembled his staff, it was clear that the FX deal was dead. To go ahead in the face of the ultimatum would be betting the farm. An advanced fighter was not worth the risk, especially with the intelligence community preparing to announce that Taiwan didn't even need the new planes. Haig's well-laid campaign had turned into a pile of corpses. Rope and the others in the room could read the frustration on his face.

"What do we do about this disaster?" Haig asked as he flung the ultimatum at Holdridge and Rope.

They all agreed that they could not set a cutoff date for arms sales to Taiwan, but as Rope read the document it occurred to him that its actual demand was for a negotiation to construct a new modus vivendi on arms sales to Taiwan. This would not be impossible to accommodate, as long as the resulting agreement would allow Taiwan to receive an adequate supply of defensive arms. Both sides would have to compromise.

Rope pointed out to Haig that the level of arms sales to Taiwan in the last year of the Carter administration was exceptionally high, $835 million,* and that the secretary could realistically tell the Chinese that the Reagan administration intended to stay within those levels.

When Huang was ushered into the secretary's suite at 10 A.M. the next day, Haig told him that Reagan could not accept a deadline for ending arms sales to Taiwan, although such sales would continue to be "sensitive" and "restrained"[58] and limited to defensive weapons. But, Haig added, the United States did not expect to exceed, "in qualitative or quantitative terms," the level of arms sales in recent years.† Then Haig, sending a clear signal, added that the "FX issue will be dealt with in this context."

Haig did not say so directly, but the sale of any new airplane to Taiwan would meet the test of not exceeding the "quality" of previous sales. By implication, that ruled out the FX.

Later that day, Haig walked Huang Hua into the Oval Office to meet with Reagan, reasonably confident that the basis for compromise and negotiation had been laid. But he was shocked to hear the Chinese foreign minister suddenly threaten the president with an even tougher demand.

China, Huang said, not only wanted a date on which arms sales to Taiwan would stop, but in addition, if the United States sold any weapons to Taiwan while the two sides were negotiating this question, it would have the most serious effect on U.S.-China relations, and Washington would "be responsible for the consequences."

Reagan gave a startled look and uttered some reassurances as Haig hurried the meeting to a close, furious that Huang had run the risk of provoking the president. What if Reagan had reared up and said, "No one threatens me . . . "? He might have approved the FX on the spot. Then where would they be?

Art Hummel, who had replaced Woodcock as ambassador to China and was with Haig in the Oval Office, returned to the State Department spreading the word about the new ultimatum. Soon, all the China hands were angry at Huang for ambushing the president. Over the lunch hour, they drafted some bare-knuckled remarks that Haig could use in reply and sent them up to the secretary's suite on the seventh floor.

---

*In 1982 dollars.
†Haig had invented this formulation the day before as he, Holdridge, and Rope had debated what to tell Huang Hua.

Haig then summoned Huang back to the State Department and staged an explosion of his famous temper.

"You have caused us to doubt your good faith," he told Huang, thumping the conference table between them. "No president," he said, could set a cutoff date for arms sales. "You cause us to wonder whether you really want a solution."[59]

Huang, a man who had raised the delivery of bluster to an art, seemed rattled by Haig's outburst and backed off, telling the secretary that he had not expected him to react so strongly. Huang almost never gave concessions, but Haig's anger impelled him to resort to some measure of sincerity.

The Communist Party leadership, Huang said, had adopted a long-term, peaceful policy toward Taiwan, but for reasons of sovereignty could never announce this publicly or give the United States a specific pledge that it had done so.

IT WAS BEIJING'S custom under Mao and now Deng to use a multitude of channels to convey dissatisfaction. And to a parade of American visitors who passed through Beijing that fall, Deng complained that China was getting nothing out of the relationship with Washington. He told Donald Regan, Reagan's treasury secretary, that China was still waiting for the computer that Kissinger had promised eight years earlier to facilitate the implementation of a new census. "Frankly, we have been very patient," Deng said, but there was a limit.

A few days later, Deng told Walter Mondale, the former vice president: "The U.S. has never sold China any advanced technology and seems to look at the People's Republic as a hostile force, not a partner."[60] A foreign ministry official added in another conversation that few Chinese could see any benefit from the relationship with the United States, which had offered so much hope for China's modernization.

In fairness to Haig, the State Department had cleared a backlog of nearly 1,200 export license applications submitted by American firms seeking to sell their products to China. There had been fewer than fifty denials. But it was also true that the Pentagon had exercised one veto after another on technology transfer applications. In denying the export of computers to China, department heads at the Pentagon argued that they were not satisfied that such technology would not be diverted to the Soviet Union or otherwise used against American interests.[61]

With Huang safely out of town, Haig brought his senior staff back together. The only concrete idea that emerged was to take advantage of the tenth anniversary of the Shanghai Communiqué—coming up in February 1982—to issue a joint statement in which Washington and Beijing could perhaps spell out a set of principles governing arms sales to Taiwan. The document could invoke the positive imagery of ten years of relations, restating the common goal of peace in Asia and opposition to hegemony. And this would provide the rationale for some concessions. Rope was the first to suggest that they could agree to gradually reduce arms sales *provided* the Chinese agreed to pursue a peaceful policy toward Taiwan.

Haig agreed, not knowing whether Reagan would buy it.

At Thanksgiving, Rope and his deputy, Scott Hallford, drafted a presidential decision memorandum authorizing the State Department to enter into negotiations for a third major communiqué with the People's Republic of China.

To justify a reduction in arms sales, Rope and Hallford suggested that Reagan single out Marshal Ye's nine-point reunification offer to Taiwan as tangible evidence that China was pursuing a constructive and peaceful course, which Beijing had now characterized as its "long-term policy."[62]

Haig approved the draft and sent it to the White House at the beginning of December 1981 with his own recommendation that the president sign it. He got a boost from the Joint Chiefs of Staff, who, in a letter to Reagan, concurred that Taiwan did not need an advanced fighter; the joint chiefs also agreed that going ahead with an FX sale would risk relations between Washington and Beijing.

WHEN HAIG'S MEMO reached Reagan, the White House was in turmoil. On November 13, a scandal erupted involving Richard Allen's acceptance of, and failure to report, $1,000 in cash from a Japanese magazine that had interviewed Nancy Reagan. Allen valiantly defended himself, but he was forced to take a leave of absence on November 19. It was soon clear that his ethical lapse in not reporting cash that ended up in his office safe had so sullied his standing in the White House that the Reagans, by their silence, made it clear they wanted him to go. Allen's exile removed a major obstacle from Haig's path.

It also helped that a crisis in Poland was building into a potential confrontation with the Soviet Union—no time to be needlessly antagonizing China—and so it fell to Art Hummel, the new ambassador in Beijing, to try to get a negotiation going.

Hummel was a sixty-one-year-old career diplomat who had been born to missionary parents in China. Under the care of a Chinese nanny, he learned to speak Chinese before he spoke English. His family actually had its own rickshaw driver, and his childhood memories included gauzy scenes of the mountains of Shanxi Province and the dusty alleys of Beijing in the 1920s. The Hummels fled China in 1928 when Chiang Kai-shek's army, then known for abusing foreigners, was mopping up the warlords in what would be called the Northern Expedition. Hummel's father returned the family to Washington, and young Arthur grew up in the suburb of Chevy Chase, Maryland. He returned to China in 1940 only to be interned by the Japanese occupation army and forced to sit out most of the war in a civilian quarantine camp. In 1944, he escaped to join a nearby guerrilla force loyal to Chiang Kai-shek. Just by chance he missed joining the Communists, whose forces were much more prevalent in the anti-Japanese campaign that was under way along the Yellow River southeast of Beijing.

Hummel spent the balance of the war in frequent flight from Japanese patrols and well-organized Communist irregulars. In this crazy, three-cornered war zone, Hummel, due to his fluent Chinese, was the designated intermediary for communications between interned Americans and the U.S. military command in Chungking.* It was a brutal period in which prisoners were routinely tortured or buried alive, and Hummel would carry through life a deep impression of the Chinese capacity for deception in the art of war, their quest for advantage, and their use of leverage—of whatever was at hand—to prevail. These impressions didn't diminish his affection or admiration for Chinese culture, but they imbued him with the wisdom that the best soldiers bring back from war: a sense of balance and proportion, whether in negotiating the terms of everyday life or relations between great powers, and the ability to discern what is truly important and what is not.

Hummel had been a valuable source of levelheaded analysis for Kissinger during the Ford years and had invested great hopes in becoming the first American ambassador to the People's Republic, only to be trumped by Carter's decision to send a political appointee, Leonard Woodcock. Under Reagan, Hummel finally got his chance. Only now, Haig had handed him the thankless job of trying to negotiate in the face of a Chinese ultimatum.

The talks quickly broke down in recriminations over the continuing supply of military spare parts—announced in December 1981—to Taiwan. Haig had calculated that the Chinese would not drag relations over a cliff over the spare parts issue, but the Chinese reaction was vehement.

Rope was too much the activist to let events drift, and he and Hallford hatched a plan to have Haig and Weinberger write a joint letter to Reagan endorsing the joint chiefs' conclusion that Taiwan did not need a new airplane. Their memo went straight upstairs, but it was followed by thunder

*Now spelled Chongqing.

rumbling back down from the seventh floor. Soon, Holdridge, Burt, Thomas Shoesmith (the deputy assistant secretary), and Rope were ordered to stand by for a summons to the secretary's office. When the call came, it was after 5 P.M., and Haig was fuming like a raging bull. Rope wondered if the secretary had fortified himself with a martini or two.

"Have you all lost your senses?" he yelled in greeting to his China aides. "I don't believe we are working in the same building. Are you working for that short little bastard across the river or are you working for me?"[63]

No one spoke, then they all tried to calm him down, but he would not be mollified.

There was to be no joint letter with Weinberger, Haig said. He was not going to let Cap in on China policy. When Burt returned to his own staff to brief them on what the secretary had said, he was restrained. "The secretary," he said, "was indulging his more self-destructive side."

R EAGAN SAT ON THE draft decision memo until the first week of January 1982, when he agreed to convene his National Security Council to decide the fate of the FX.

Whatever anguish Reagan was suffering by having to disappoint his old friends on Taiwan, this was no time to explode relations with mainland China. And the crisis in Poland was bringing the administration into sharper focus. Strategic unity was necessary to face down the Soviet challenge in East Europe.

On January 6, Rope got a message from the seventh floor to draft, on a crash basis, a presidential decision memorandum setting out the pros and cons of continuing the F-5E coproduction on Taiwan versus selling the more advanced single-engine F-5G that the Carter administration had refused to provide.

The next day, Haig's limousine rolled down the street to the White House, and, when it returned, he stepped out looking cocksure. But Haig insisted that Reagan had not reached a final decision and would not do so until the weekend up at Camp David. Then he mobilized the whole East Asia Bureau. How soon could Holdridge and a team of diplomats be in Beijing? Haig said that he needed them on the ground by Monday, January 11, to report the presidential decision to the Chinese leadership. And he wanted to know how soon Jim Lilley, who had just been appointed by Reagan as the unofficial U.S. representative in Taiwan, would arrive in Taipei, where, presumably, his first act would be to break the bad news.[64]

The Chinese got one day's notice. Holdridge and Rope scrambled to assemble a six-member team of diplomats. John Davies, director of the East

European office at the State Department, was added to the group so Holdridge could discuss the threat of Soviet intervention in Poland and possible strategies for a coordinated response by China and the United States. Armitage was added from the Pentagon. They flew to Beijing over the weekend and arrived in the Chinese capital well after dark on Sunday, January 10.

The Chinese official who greeted them was puzzled when Holdridge said that he couldn't yet explain the purpose of his mission, but he nonetheless wanted a meeting with a high-level foreign ministry official the following day, when he would explain everything.

Haig's instructions, cabled to the embassy, did not arrive until early Monday morning in Beijing. Haig confirmed that Reagan had decided to kill the FX. He would continue the F-5E line and agree to negotiate limitations on future arms sales.

It had taken six months to turn the FX decision around. Whether in backing the FX Reagan had been motivated by a desire to make a political gesture to his friends in Taipei or by a desire to bail out Northrop, or both, the president finally recognized that it was not worth risking a rupture in U.S.-China relations, especially when Soviet tank divisions were menacing Poland and, by extension, all of East Europe.

The FX crisis had also revealed the evolution of Haig's relationship with Beijing. In his first months in office, the secretary's own hubris had convinced him that he could reap the benefits of "strategic association," as Kissinger had, without paying the hard currency of restraint in arms sales to Taiwan. Indeed, he had been prepared to resort to trickery and deceit in trying to pass off an advanced warplane in the guise of the F-5E. If this scheme had been exposed, it would have revealed the cynicism at the top of the Reagan administration and cast Haig as someone willing to mock the intelligence of the Chinese leadership.

THERE WAS NO celebration when the Chinese heard the news. Instead, the Holdridge mission was treated to a drubbing. Why was Washington going forward with the sale of military spare parts to Taiwan, they demanded? They complained of "bad faith" and asked for public assurances that no weapons would be included in the spare parts deal.

It wasn't until the welcoming banquet that evening that the Chinese showed some gratification that the FX crisis was behind them. But the good feelings were short-lived. After Holdridge explained how the State Department was going to announce the abandonment of the FX, while also confirming the continuation of F-5E coproduction on Taiwan, another storm of recriminations burst forth. This sounded like an announcement to sell more arms, the Chinese argued. It would violate Huang Hua's ultimatum that no arms sales could go forward until the whole question had been settled.

Zhang Wenjin, the vice foreign minister hosting the banquet, warned Holdridge that the announcement could lead to a breakdown in relations. It was already approaching midnight in Beijing, nearly noon in Washington, when Holdridge and Rope raced back to the ambassador's residence so they could get the State Department spokesman, Alan Romberg, on the phone before his noon briefing for the Washington press corps.

The only phone extension in Hummel's residence was in the bedroom, and so Betty Lou Hummel, flustered and in her nightgown, quickly made room for the midnight encampment of diplomats, who proceeded to coach the spokesman, twelve time zones behind them, on how to focus his comments.[65] The emphasis had to be on the cancellation of the FX, they told him. And, as a fig leaf for the Chinese, he was to say that Taiwan's needs could be met with additional F-5Es, but the exact numbers, details, and timing had yet to be worked out. Romberg pulled it off.

The next day, Holdridge told Zhang Wenjin, "You have to understand, this is not a decision to sell, this is a decision *not* to sell."[66]

The Chinese now understood that they could get no more. Zhang looked across the table at Holdridge and smiled. "Coming from you, Ambassador Holdridge," he said, "we accept that."*

H AIG NOW WANTED TO USE the anniversary of the Shanghai Communiqué as a decision-forcing mechanism to nail down a new understanding on arms sales. But when the Chinese submitted their version of a new communiqué, it again called for a complete cutoff.

Haig sent a letter to Zhao Ziyang urging the Chinese leadership to take advantage of the upcoming anniversary to reaffirm the bedrock principle of one China and perhaps to find a formula for addressing the arms sales question. But there was silence from Beijing.

China specialists at the CIA and in the State Department's intelligence bureau warned that a breakdown in U.S.-China relations was imminent. Deng's critics among the party elders were flogging what they saw as the perversion of the normalization commitments Carter had made. Then, in March, in one of the last diplomatic initiatives of his life, Leonid Brezhnev flew to Tashkent in central Asia and made a conciliatory speech confirming that the Brezhnev Doctrine, in effect, had never been intended as a threat of force against China for leaving Moscow's orbit. In Beijing, the government announced the

---

*Holdridge had served as U.S. ambassador to Singapore.

resumption of Russian studies programs in the school system, an obvious pressure ploy aimed at Washington. When Rope saw this news item in the Chinese press, he passed it on to Haig, who was trying to explain to a frustrated Reagan why the arms pipeline to Taiwan was still frozen with nearly a year's worth of deliveries backed up.

The February 28 anniversary came and went with no agreement. Reagan and Premier Zhao exchanged perfunctory letters that masked the underlying turmoil.

In early April, Reagan decided to write a letter directly to Deng and forthrightly express his desire to reach a compromise on the arms question and then move the relationship forward. The president continued to believe that China's Communist leaders understood and even respected the United States for refusing to abandon its longtime friends and allies on Taiwan. And when Haig expressed his own doubts, Reagan simply said that he was going to sell military parts to Taiwan whether Beijing liked it or not.[67] If the Communists wanted to negotiate some understanding about future arms sales, that would be fine, Reagan added, but if they did not, then that was fine, too.

Haig warned Reagan that they would be flirting with disaster, that the Democrats would pounce on any collapse of relations and accuse the Republicans of "losing" China, just as the Democrats themselves had been accused of the same blunder in 1949. Haig's lecturing, and the implication that if China policy foundered Haig might resign, always made Reagan uncomfortable. But he would not be railroaded. He would explain his policy in the letters; he genuinely believed that he could get through to the Chinese, but if he couldn't, then he would offer to send Bush to Beijing to help straighten things out.

When Haig returned to the State Department, he told his senior staff that Bush was going to China. "Let George do it," Haig said, with a touch of sarcasm. He knew that Bush would be sailing into the same storm.

Notification of the spare parts sale went to Congress on April 13, and the Chinese retaliated by canceling Weinberger's first visit to China.[68] When Bush arrived in Beijing, he was greeted with the familiar theme: "He who ties the knot should untie it."

Deng greeted the vice president on May 8, and a few minutes into their meeting, the Chinese leader suggested that the two "old friends" first have a private meeting of about fifteen minutes, alone. Bush took Hummel and left Holdridge behind. Deng brought a single interpreter.* The fifteen-minute meeting turned into an hour-long conversation in which Deng made much of Bush being an "old friend," even apologizing for the rough treatment he had given Bush during his August 1980 mission with Allen.

---

*Deng, who spoke with a thick Sichuan accent, always assumed that Hummel understood every word he said. But Hummel needed the interpreter as much as Bush.

Bush warmed to the intimacy, but faithfully conveyed what he saw as the limits of Reagan's flexibility. The administration would have to decide by August whether to close down the F-5E production line in Taiwan or renew the contract. If the production line were closed, then Taiwan would initiate a new campaign for an advanced fighter, and Congress would get involved again. Deng seemed to understand this logic.

Bush was not armed with any concessions, but he was able to inject a new and conciliatory element into the discussion. The letters Bush brought from Reagan had been polished by Haig's speechwriter, Harvey Sicherman, and they were sprinkled with phrases like "There is only one China" and "We will not let our unofficial relations with the people of Taiwan undermine our commitment" to the principle of one China. Bush told Deng that Reagan's refusal to accept a cutoff date for arms sales to Taiwan did not mean that anyone in the administration foresaw selling arms to Taiwan forever.

Deng seized on the statement and said that the two sides should negotiate the form and the wording of an American commitment. In fact, even before Bush left Beijing, Chinese Foreign Ministry officials who had done little but attack the U.S. position for months suddenly were considering possible new formulations, such as "phasing out" arms sales over a fixed period of time.

The Bush-Deng meeting had broken the spell of imminent collapse.

B ACK IN WASHINGTON, Haig's relationship with Reagan had reached the limits of tolerance for both men. The final clash took place over the Soviet gas pipeline to Europe, a massive energy project that would link Moscow's economic interests with European security. Haig wanted Reagan to support the pipeline as an issue of American solidarity with Europe. But Reagan sided with the harder line coming from the Pentagon and the NSC. Haig, more isolated than ever, threw down each of his arguments like a gauntlet.

"I don't have much passion with people who threaten to resign if they don't get their way," the president confided to Baker, who took his own satisfaction from Haig's decision to resign.[69]

Reagan asked Haig to stay on until he could get someone else confirmed, and Haig agreed.[70] Then Reagan called George Shultz and offered him the job. Shultz came racing back from London on the Concorde,[71] leaving behind his job as president of Bechtel, the global construction giant.

Beijing was jolted by the news of Haig's sacking. The clash over China policy had been a prominent factor in the long deterioration of Haig's relations with the president. By the time Haig made his exit, the Republican conservatives were threatening revolt over Reagan's treatment of Taiwan. There were rumblings that Reagan had been "captured" by Haig and the other "liberals" in the administration. Senator Strom Thurmond of South Carolina was preparing to circulate a letter calling on the president to sell an updated fighter to Taiwan, and Senator Barry Goldwater told Reagan that he was "profoundly disturbed by the mounting evidence that we do not intend to honor our commitments" to Taiwan.[72]

In his final days in office, Haig tried to persuade Reagan to accept a general commitment to phasing out arms sales to Taiwan. Haig and his China aides had become convinced that the United States should make some further bow in the direction of Beijing's "principled position" on arms sales, if only to create a stronger incentive for China to commit to peaceful reunification with Taiwan. Haig was not proposing the announcement of a cutoff date, just a statement that the United States looked forward to the day when arms sales could end.

On June 29, Haig put the recommendation in writing to Reagan, giving the president two options. Reagan refused the first, which suggested that arms sales could end. He was adamant that he was not going to make any statement that could be interpreted as a commitment to do so. Instead, he chose Haig's second option, which was to gradually reduce arms sales to Taiwan as long as there was peace.

Haig could not stand to part without the last word, and so he told Reagan that if the decision to waffle on arms sales triggered a major crisis in U.S.-China relations, then he would personally lead the parade to publicly condemn the president.

Then Haig was gone.

On July 13, Hummel finally handed a new Reagan letter to Deng along with a draft communiqué governing U.S. arms sales to Taiwan. In the letter, Reagan told Deng that the United States had reached its bottom line. He proposed that Deng accept it and that they then move the relationship forward with an exchange of high-level visits by Shultz and Zhao Ziyang.

Five days later, the Chinese negotiators in Beijing dropped the key demand that the United States end all arms sales by a fixed date and agreed instead to the more accommodating position that a gradual reduction in arms sales was a sufficient basis to reach an agreement. Deng had made his decision. He had most of the elements he needed to quell the uproar in his own party. Arms sales to Taiwan were now locked into a program of gradual reduction, and Washington now accepted the gravity of the issue. Beijing would have to keep the pressure on, but to Deng it looked like a significant victory—and the best deal he could get.

In Washington, Reagan called a large group of pro-Taiwan congressmen to the White House on July 28 and spelled out the commitments he was going to make to reduce arms sales to Taiwan. But he wanted them to know that the United States was going to extend the coproduction of the F-5E on the island.

Hummel's work was finished on August 17. The U.S.-China Joint Communiqué on United States Arms Sales to Taiwan was issued in Beijing and Washington simultaneously.

China went further than ever before in stating that its overtures for reunification "represented a further effort" under a "fundamental policy to strive for a peaceful solution to the Taiwan question."

And the United States could claim that, due to China's clear statement of peaceful intentions toward Taiwan, there were now "favorable conditions for the settlement of U.S.-China differences over the question of United States arms sales to Taiwan." Specifically,

> The United States government states that it does not seek to carry out a long-term policy of arms sales to Taiwan, that its arms sales to Taiwan will not exceed, either in qualitative or quantitative terms, the level of those supplied in recent years since the establishment of diplomatic relations between the United States and China, and that it intends to reduce gradually its sales of arms to Taiwan, leading over a period of time to final resolution.[73]

Afterward, Deng called Hummel to the Great Hall of the People and told him bluntly that China expected a reduction of arms sales to Taiwan by more than a dollar a year.[74] It was an attempt at humor, but Hummel understood his meaning.

.   .   .

The August 1982 communiqué addressed the last of the unresolved issues of normalization between the United States and the People's Republic. It provided a framework for Beijing to tolerate something that it could not completely halt, and it gave the United States a long-term formula for gradual reduction that would nevertheless guarantee Taiwan's security. And, most importantly, it reinforced the peaceful pursuit of reconciliation between the mainland and Taiwan.

But at the same time, the new document did nothing to relieve the basic contradiction between American law (the Taiwan Relations Act) and American policy as expressed in the three communiqués that now governed U.S.-

China relations. Whereas the act required a permanent security commitment to Taiwan based on arms sales and military balance in the Taiwan Strait, the communiqués looked forward to gradually declining arms sales leading to a "final resolution." Politically, the United States was committed to the "transitional era" that would inevitably lead to Beijing's recovering its sovereignty over Taiwan, but Congress made no similar commitment or investment in extricating the United States from the civil war. The law of the land was still the maintenance of a military standoff, therefore putting Taiwan in effective control of the process.

In the days and weeks after the communiqué was signed, Reagan and his senior aides were reported to have reassured conservative members of Congress that the document was not binding, that it was merely a statement of U.S. policy that could be revised. The administration was still committed to the Taiwan Relations Act. And the gradual reduction of arms sales to Taiwan could be reversed if Beijing abandoned its peaceful approach to the island.

Of course, the Chinese attacked these interpretations as duplicitous; Reagan's pacifying statements to the conservatives served to deepen suspicions that his administration would not keep its word. To some extent, their assessment was true.

Beginning in 1983, the Reagan administration concluded that the August communiqué did nothing to limit the transfer of advanced defense technology and defense services—as opposed to weapons—to Taiwan. Therefore they developed a program to exploit this loophole by transferring manufacturing technology to Taiwan that would allow the island's defense industries to eventually design and build advanced combat aircraft, air defense systems, naval frigates, and scores of other military systems on their own.[75] The rationale was that by building up Taiwan's own industrial base, Washington could eventually remove itself from Taiwan's defense program altogether, while also reducing direct arms sales. In reality, however, the program expanded the American entanglement in the island's defense.

MEANWHILE IN CHINA, a larger reassessment was under way. Brezhnev's overtures were taken seriously by Deng, whose impeccable anti-Soviet credentials made it politically possible for him to explore a thaw. In the fall of 1982, the Chinese Foreign Ministry sent a bright, Moscow-educated diplomat, Qian Qichen,* to open a marathon seventeen-day dialogue with Soviet Vice Foreign Minister Leonid F. Ilichev. On the surface,

*Pronounced: Chee-an Chee-chen.

China maintained that no rapprochement could occur until Soviet troops withdrew from the Chinese border and from other contested territories from Afghanistan to Cambodia. Still, Qian's presence in Moscow signaled that the two adversaries were undertaking a full review of their contentious relations with an eye toward initiating a new era.

Beyond these talks with the Soviet Union, China was beginning to reassess the strategic environment that had impelled Mao to move closer to Washington in the first place. The danger of world war, some argued, was receding.

On September 1, 1982, during the Twelfth Party Congress, Hu Yaobang, the new general secretary under Deng, said that Beijing would pursue a policy of "peaceful coexistence"[76] with all communist countries, including the Soviet Union. In another sign that China was reevaluating its tilt toward the United States, Hu said that Chinese foreign policy was independent from "any big power or group of powers."

Then, when Brezhnev died in November 1982, Deng sent Huang Hua to represent China at the funeral; during his visit, Huang continued the new Sino-Soviet dialogue by meeting at length with Andrei Gromyko, the Soviet foreign minister.

While these signs of thaw glistened in the East, Deng told a Japanese visitor that the United States was proving to be an "untrustworthy" partner[77] whose policy changed with each new president.* There was talk that China was pursuing a policy of "equidistance" from the superpowers. And, as Europe and Japan offered to transfer critically needed technology to China with favorable financing, Deng and the party leadership began to realize that they could maneuver on a broader landscape.

At the same time, the long truce between China and the United States on the espionage front ended. Kissinger's promise to Mao to keep American spies out of China had lasted until the Carter administration, when CIA director Stansfield Turner won approval to insert the first undercover officers in China to try to improve American understanding of the forces at work in China's society, leadership, and military. Beijing's counterintelligence soon detected the change in policy, and Deng responded in kind, using the increasing exchange of scientists and academics to set up the first Chinese espionage operations in the United States, most of them geared toward the

---

*Richard Nixon gave a magazine interview on the tenth anniversary of his 1972 journey to China and issued what could have only been read as a rebuke by the White House: "Some people here in the U.S. took the attitude that they could do anything they wanted with regard to Taiwan, and that forced the Chinese leaders to demonstrate that Beijing can't be taken for granted, that China has other places to turn to." Admonishing the Reagan White House, he added, "Let's keep the problem on the back burner and not go off on new arms sales at least so long as Beijing continues down the path of peacefully resolving the issue."

acquisition of military and industrial technologies that China could not acquire legally.

China's intelligence services, the Ministry of State Security and the Second Department of the PLA General Staff, set up front companies in Hong Kong, Singapore, and the United States to purchase weapons and high-technology equipment that was otherwise off-limits.

Chinese scientists, including physicists from the country's nuclear weapons programs, began making their first contacts with American scientists, and throughout the 1980s an extensive and beneficial exchange program developed. But salted among the Chinese delegations who visited American corporations, universities, and even nuclear weapons laboratories, specifically those at Livermore, California, and Los Alamos, New Mexico, were intelligence officers seeking to acquire the latest technology, and solve the knotty problems of physics and engineering that would allow China to improve its antiquated arsenal of weapons. The Chinese were particularly interested in updating their long-range ballistic missiles, on which they had mounted huge thermonuclear warheads. China was in the nuclear club, but barely. The country's strategic doctrine, therefore, was geared toward ensuring that if China were ever attacked with nuclear weapons, whoever was left in charge in Beijing would be able to retaliate by dropping at least one huge warhead on at least one of its adversary's cities.

GEORGE SHULTZ arrived at the State Department with little regard for the geostrategic view of his predecessors. He purged the department's senior staff of many Haig appointees, sending Holdridge off as ambassador to Indonesia. Paul D. Wolfowitz, Holdridge's replacement, banished Rope from the East Asia Bureau. Wolfowitz ordered an internal review of the negotiations that had led up to the August communiqué; in a tone that seemed to some both partisan and ideological, the review pronounced Haig and his China team guilty of allowing themselves to be railroaded by an excessive desire to accommodate Beijing.

In temperament and style, Shultz proved a much better student of the Reagan White House than Haig, although Shultz's path was preordained to be smoother because neither Baker nor Bush saw him as a rival. Shultz quickly aligned himself with the White House view that Haig had gone overboard in treating China as the strategic linchpin of American policy. He had overindulged a psychology that called for making concessions to Beijing.

Shultz agreed that China was an important player, but he adopted the view that it was a mistake to ever tell this to the Chinese.[78] They would just use it as leverage. Haig's inflation of China's importance had only escalated Beijing's demands on the Taiwan question. Shultz's assessment was, of course, a misreading of history, but it had the virtue of positioning the new secretary more comfortably in the administration, especially now that the most contentious issue, that of arms sales to Taiwan, had been settled.

For all the self-satisfaction that Shultz and his team took in getting China back into "perspective," as they saw it, China's dialogue with Moscow in the fall of 1982 foretold another profound shift in the continental plates, and the U.S. intelligence community was suddenly alive with warnings that China's disenchantment with America might be driving Beijing to consider rapprochement with Moscow. These warnings, more than anything, forced Shultz to make his first trip to Beijing to see if he could arrest the process.

Shultz traveled to the Chinese capital with a set of conflicting messages. On the one hand, he advocated the view that China was just a big, poor, backward Asian giant that was decades away from becoming a global power and was not nearly as important to American interests in Asia as Japan. On the other hand, Shultz had to be mindful that China was central to American war planning should a conflict break out with the Soviet Union. By the 1980s, in all of the basic planning documents that fed into U.S. military strategy, China's armed forces were a key ingredient in holding down the Soviets in the Far East while America "swung" its Pacific forces to Europe—the most likely arena of World War III.

Irrespective of such planning, China was also still a full partner in supplying weapons to the Afghan guerrillas in their war against Soviet occupation. And Beijing was working closely with Thailand and the United States to drive the Vietnamese out of Cambodia.

Shultz's effective downgrading of the China relationship prompted Zbigniew Brzezinski to complain that the Reagan administration was presiding over "quiet decay."[79] Leslie H. Gelb of *The New York Times* pointed out what was embarrassingly obvious about Reagan's foreign policy. "Over the last two years, the Reagan team has gone from the extreme of thinking of Beijing as a major diplomatic counterweight to Moscow almost to the other extreme of simply seeing China as a struggling Asian giant lagging far behind Japan."[80]

Which was it? It was clear that Reagan, for all the buoyant optimism that he had brought to the Oval Office, was unable or unwilling to take U.S.-China relations beyond the simplistic notion he had cribbed from Nixon—"buttering up the warlords." Even that he did disingenuously, moving the center of gravity of American attention back to Taiwan.

Shultz's first trip to China in early 1983 proved to be a review of a relationship that did not add up to much, and the residue of dissatisfaction over the Taiwan settlement hung over every conversation. In laying out Shultz's goals for the trip, Wolfowitz crafted one of those sentences of pure bureaucratic mush that conveys how little substance might be behind a policy: "The purpose of your trip is to arrest drift, put our relations on a more stable footing, and impart renewed momentum that will enable us, gradually, to revive important aspects of the relationship that have languished while promoting steady expansion in most, if not all, areas."[81]

Shultz offered China no "strategic association," as Haig had, but he nonetheless insisted that Soviet aggression and expansionism was still the most compelling threat to regional security. Yet with Brezhnev dead and the new Soviet leader, Yuri Andropov, inclined even more favorably toward rapprochement with Beijing, Chinese leaders seemed less willing to join in any fresh attack on Soviet "hegemony." The new foreign minister, Wu Xueqian, told Shultz that China was not a "card" to be played and that it was not seeking equidistance from the superpowers. China seemed to be moving toward some middle ground that had not yet been defined.

Shultz told Defense Minister Zhang Aiping that the Reagan administration was still willing to sell weapons to China,[82] as Haig had pledged in June 1981, despite the fact that Chinese interest had flagged considerably. Premier Zhao would tell Weinberger later that year that it was "inconceivable for a big nation like China to bring about its modernization of defense by buying military equipment from foreign countries."[83] He was right. The U.S. government had undertaken a number of studies, which had concluded that it would cost $60 billion or more to outfit the Chinese military with just the basics of modern weapons systems. China would never develop if it spent its precious resources on American weapons.

Meanwhile, in Moscow, senior officials told Western journalists that the "silly policy" of the Reagan administration—placing so much emphasis on Taiwan—had taught China a lesson about the fickle and unreliable nature of American politics. By early 1983, high-ranking Soviet officials claimed that they had reached "substantial détente" with Beijing, which would ultimately lead to a settlement of differences between the longtime communist rivals.*

Not only did Shultz have little to offer the Chinese, but part of his mission was to send Beijing a warning: U.S. intelligence reports indicated that Chinese scientists were assisting in Pakistan's secret effort to develop nuclear weapons in the wake of India's "peaceful" nuclear explosion in 1974.

But to the Chinese, Washington's sudden concern about nuclear proliferation seemed hypocritical to say the least. Less than a decade earlier, American officials had encouraged Pakistan to deter Indian aggression. Indeed,

---

*In March 1983, Leslie H. Gelb quoted a high-ranking Soviet official as saying, "The United States started out well with China and now you are losing. The pinnacle of American-Chinese relations was in 1980, and there will not be another such pinnacle. At first, China thought of the United States as a strategic partner. Now, China believes the Soviet Union will not attack China."

hadn't Kissinger bragged about circumventing Congress to funnel military assistance to Pakistan? Kissinger and his assistant, Winston Lord, had even joked—in front of Chinese leaders—that the best way to contain India's ambitions was to arm Pakistan and Bangladesh with nuclear weapons. Now that China was secretly doing just that, American indignation seemed a contradiction.

Shultz was certainly ignorant of the Kissinger legacy and, therefore, could not have understood how absurd it sounded to the Chinese when he told them, in his dour tone, that the United States would *never* be able to sell China civilian nuclear reactor technology unless it addressed Washington's proliferation concerns.

Shultz returned to the United States relieved only that he had gotten through a tough visit without causing a major explosion.

The State Department meanwhile announced that it would sell nearly $800 million in weapons to Taiwan in 1983 and about $760 million worth in 1984. Under a formula worked out by Lawrence Eagleburger, now the undersecretary of state for political affairs, the United States had set a goal of reducing arms sales by $20 million a year from a base of $835 million, with allowance for fluctuations. Accounting for inflation, the State Department estimated that arms sales to Taiwan could thus continue for forty years or more.

By the end of Reagan's first term, there was a strong sense of self-satisfaction at the top of the administration that the president's team was playing an appropriately tough hand with Beijing while still getting the benefits of cooperation against the Soviet Union. At the same time, on the Taiwan front, they were moving forward with building a foundation for a defense-oriented industrial base on the island.

ZHANG WENJIN, the graying diplomat and now Chinese ambassador to Washington, called on Vice President Bush in May 1983 and told him that Beijing had resigned itself to a long and contentious diplomatic battle with the United States over Taiwan, which he called "an issue left over from history." Given that U.S.-China relations with respect to the island would be unavoidably stormy, he continued, the two countries had to find other ways to build trust and confidence, and the best place to do that was in the area of technology.

From the Chinese perspective, this was perhaps the gentlest way Beijing could communicate that it no longer saw an urgent need to remain a tacit ally of America in the global containment of the Soviet Union. China could see what the world could see—that Moscow was overextended. But for China, now much more open to the rest of the world, the business of modernization still loomed as a huge and unfulfilled task. Beijing still harbored hopes that Washington would open the technology gates and help modernize the country's hopelessly outdated industries. Because Bush was an oilman and wanted to help, he was already pushing new partnerships involving his friends in the petroleum business that would transfer oil and gas technology to China's energy sector.

And so the relationship was moving into a new phase, one more mature— some would say more cynical—with regard to each side's fidelity to its commitments. Although China and the United States were still carrying on extensive joint covert operations against Moscow, the rise of their espionage activities against each other betokened a more normal state of affairs for two large countries with both common and divergent interests.

For these reasons, every dispute relating to Taiwan, trade, and technology transfer erupted at greater volume. The Chinese vigorously protested the American decision to grant political asylum to a Chinese tennis star, Hu Na, and they denounced the U.S. court system for issuing a $40 million default judgment against China in a class action suit by Americans who had invested in Huguang Railway bonds in 1911. When Shultz told Deng that he should have hired a lawyer, the Chinese leader exploded. Likewise, in the Hu Na case, Chinese officials all the way up to Deng loudly objected when, after the young tennis player bolted from her handlers while in the United States, the Reagan White House debated whether to grant her asylum or simply let her remain in the country as a student. Even Hummel was outraged at the ideological tinge of Shultz's decision to grant Hu Na political asylum after Deng had personally conveyed a guarantee that she would never be persecuted if she chose to return.* Beijing also protested every pro-Taiwan vote in Congress and sought to prevent Taiwan from taking a seat on the Asian Development Bank board as the Republic of China. Although a compromise was worked out to save Taiwan's seat (under a different name), Reagan then approved the sale of Sparrow air-to-air missiles and Standard air defense missiles to Taiwan over boisterous Chinese objections that he was violating the agreement to diminish "qualitative and quantitative" arms shipments.

By the mid-1980s, China and the United States had established a broader agenda of routine business. Hundreds of American corporations opened representative offices in Beijing. Shultz spent the balance of his term in office working to upgrade China's status as a trade partner and opening the gates for a broad spectrum of technology sales. American news organizations

---

*Granting asylum requires a determination that the asylum seeker will be subjected to persecution if returned to the country of origin.

opened bureaus in Beijing. More than 11,000 Chinese students migrated to American universities, and academic exchanges created an enormous new intercourse between the two countries.

Under Deng, the party's general secretary,* Hu Yaobang, and the premier, Zhao Ziyang, struggled to experiment with a new economic model that looked a lot like capitalism while carrying on a vigorous debate over the utility of Marxism and Leninism in the modern era. The class of reformers, younger Chinese who wanted to rationalize the country's command economy and open up the political system to broader participation, injected new concepts of democracy, humanism, and rule of law into Communist Party deliberations.

The pendulum swung back and forth as conservatives mobilized campaigns against "bourgeois liberalization" and "spiritual pollution"; with each new swing, there were human casualties. Each of these campaigns was a struggle over ideas, but, more practically, they forced Deng to move in one direction or the other where concrete policy initiatives, such as the creation of "special economic zones" near Hong Kong and other coastal cities were at stake. In these zones, foreign corporations were allowed to set up factories that tapped China's low-cost labor market to manufacture and export goods to the world.

The relationship also matured in that a journey to Beijing became an important political backdrop for each new president.

Like his predecessors, Reagan saw that a presidential journey to China would benefit his reelection campaign, and in the spring of 1984 he led an entourage of 1,000 American officials, support staff, and news reporters to Beijing for an agenda that was dominated by photo opportunities at the Great Wall and in the ancient city of Xian.†

Reagan rebuffed Deng's request that the United States urge Taiwan's leadership to accept the mainland's invitation to sit down and discuss reunification under a formula that would leave Taiwan with almost total autonomy in all but foreign relations.

And Deng, when asked about the significance of Reagan's visit, said simply, "The most important progress is that I met the president the first time." The double entendre—that the relationship lacked any substance—was, at least, polite.

The one substantive document signed during the trip was an agreement for cooperation concerning the peaceful uses of nuclear energy, an attempt

---

*The title "party chairman" had been retired in deference to Chairman Mao.
†Xian was China's one-time Western capital where archaeologists have unearthed in modern times, thousands of astounding life-size terra-cotta warriors near the tomb of Emperor Qin Shi Huangdi (221–210 B.C.).

by Reagan, Shultz, and Weinberger to boost the fortunes of American corporate giants such as Westinghouse and General Electric and the American nuclear industry in general, while also drawing China into its first international commitment to halt the spread of nuclear weapons technology. China was forecasting that it would seek to build eight nuclear power plants by the year 2000, and the participation of U.S. companies was estimated at $25 billion.

China had joined the International Atomic Energy Agency, agreeing to place its exports of civilian reactor technology (for electric power production) under international safeguards, as most other nuclear powers had. Although Beijing had refused to sign the Nuclear Non-Proliferation Treaty on grounds that it was a superpower plot to maintain a nuclear monopoly, the White House privately signaled Beijing that if its leaders issued a statement opposing proliferation, that would be sufficient for the nuclear cooperation agreement to go forward.

When Zhao visited Washington in January 1984, he included such a statement in his toast at a White House dinner. "We do not engage in nuclear proliferation ourselves, nor do we help other countries develop nuclear weapons," Zhao said. The State Department was so anxious for Zhao's comments to receive public attention that the embassy in Beijing was asked to bang the drum. Well after midnight on January 14, Chas. W. Freeman Jr., the second-ranking American diplomat in Beijing, awakened *The Washington Post*'s Beijing correspondent with a telephone call and urged him to file a story on the "historic clarification" Zhao had made in Washington.* Freeman explained how the statement was linked to the pact that Reagan was going to offer during his state visit.

But the nuclear pact ran into immediate opposition in Congress, where skeptical senators, particularly John Glenn of Ohio and Alan Cranston of California, delved into the intelligence that showed a steady stream of Chinese assistance to Pakistan's nuclear program, including evidence that China had provided the design for one or more nuclear warheads.

When Washington hesitated, China tried to demonstrate that it had other alternatives. While Reagan was still in Beijing, the Chinese announced that the Soviet first deputy prime minister, Ivan V. Arkhipov, would visit their capital the following month to reinforce the continuing diplomatic thaw between the two countries in the wake of Yuri Andropov's death in February. Arkhipov was the highest-ranking Soviet visitor to China since the 1969 talks between Alexei Kosygin and Zhou Enlai. And in June 1984, Zhao flew off to Paris to sign a contract for the construction of a French-designed 900-

The Washington Post's Michael Weisskopf thought that Freeman's call was an extraordinary intervention, but he also recognized the importance of the Chinese statement. He filed a story that appeared the same day in Washington.

megawatt nuclear power station to provide electricity to southern Guangdong Province and Hong Kong.

This pressure may have convinced the Reagan administration, the following month, to sign off on the sale to China of two dozen Blackhawk helicopters, stripped of any weaponry but nonetheless state-of-the-art aircraft that would be employed by Chinese military commanders in western China and Tibet for transport purposes.

The death of Yuri Andropov so soon after Brezhnev, and Konstantin Chernenko's brief succession to power before he, too, succumbed to his ailments, prompted Deng to undertake the most profound strategic reassessment of his tenure, which took place in a series of leadership conferences in 1984 and 1985. Gathered in 1984 for the traditional late-summer parley at the beach resort of Beidaihe northeast of Beijing, Deng and the revolutionary elders concluded that no major world war was likely to break out in the next two decades and, therefore, it was safe for China to stand down from its high state of readiness and to reduce expenditures on its 4-million-member defense establishment.

To deter its enemies, China would deploy a small force of medium-range and intercontinental missiles with nuclear warheads that could reach targets in Japan, India, the Soviet Union, and, eventually, the West Coast of the United States. China was also developing a missile-launching submarine, which, it was hoped, might improve the security of the country's small nuclear force by putting some of its missiles at sea. A second generation of intercontinental ballistic missiles was under design, and these weapons, Deng was told by his military leaders, would provide sufficient deterrence for China as it turned its full attention to the civilian economy.

Deng met with the Central Military Commission that fall and exhorted China's military commanders, "Our national defense industry, which is well equipped and has a huge contingent of technicians, should be put to full use in every aspect of national development to help boost civilian production."[84]

In early 1985, Deng presided over a large gathering of politburo members and senior military officers in which the formal decision was made to change the state of combat readiness among China's armed forces from preparation for "early, large-scale, and nuclear war" to "peacetime construction for building up the national defense."

This series of decisions represented a momentous change of course for China and was little recognized in the West. The Chinese leadership had established a new national policy dictating that budget resources would be redirected to the civilian economy while the military would be forced to convert a portion of its massive industries to civilian production and to reduce its ranks and in other respects; in effect, to pay its own way. But Deng's decisions, so clearly made in the interest of promoting China's peaceful development, also had unintended consequences. Military factories that had once produced radars were now producing television sets, motorcycles, and washing machines. And those plants that continued to make weapons now looked for international markets for their guns, planes, and missiles. They found such markets in the Middle East, where the continuing Arab-Israeli dispute and the Iran-Iraq War had created a robust economy in weaponry.

In April 1985, the Saudi ambassador in Washington, Bandar bin Sultan, received his first invitation from China's ambassador to the United States to conduct an extraordinary transaction in secret. The Chinese leadership conveyed the message that Prince Bandar was welcome in Beijing to discuss Saudi Arabia's desire to purchase ballistic missiles that would deter both Iran and Iraq from ever firing their own missile forces at the desert kingdom.*

And soon, Chinese missile engineers were negotiating with Syria—and possibly Iran, Libya, and Pakistan—to sell a new missile with a 350-mile range, the M-9, that could be used against Israeli or American forces in the Middle East. In addition, China began shipping Silkworm missiles to Iran, whose revolutionary leaders sought to use such weaponry to dominate the shipping lanes of the Persian Gulf.

In July and September 1988, Shultz and Frank Carlucci, Weinberger's successor at Defense, undertook efforts to induce China to forgo such dangerous missile sales in return for participation in the American space-launch business. Soon after Carlucci pronounced that he was "fully satisfied" that the M-9 sales to Syria would not go forward, American corporations began the first negotiations to strap their telecommunications satellites onto Chinese rocket boosters.

Other Chinese policies began to draw critics in the United States. In the early 1980s, American academics and journalists came back from China with the first reports on Beijing's population control program, the one-child policy that was being enforced in some areas with mandatory abortions and involuntary sterilization. Senator Jesse Helms of North Carolina and others began a campaign to deny U.S. contributions to any United Nations or other international organization that carried out family planning assistance to China. And when Reagan chose Winston Lord to succeed Hummel as ambassador in Beijing, Helms took the Lord nomination hostage for months over the family planning issue.

Yet even as American conservatives challenged the repression that they

---

*In early 1986, Bandar traveled to Beijing and completed a secret $2.7 billion deal to purchase 120 Chinese-built CSS-2 ballistic missiles. With a range of 1,860 miles, the CSS-2 had been designed to carry a nuclear warhead, but it was refitted with a high-explosive conventional warhead that could be lofted into Iran or Iraq, should either of those countries ever threaten Saudi Arabia.

were discovering in Chinese society, profound sociological and political changes were simultaneously under way in China. The Communist Party under Hu Yaobang was engaged in a historic and at times acrimonious debate. Wang Ruoshui, a deputy editor of the *People's Daily*, penned eloquent essays on humanism, the most prominent of which mocked Marx's *Communist Manifesto:* "A specter, the specter of humanism (not Communism), has loomed large in China's intellectual circles." Wang demanded that the state uphold "the principle that all men are equal before the truth and the law and that a citizen's personal freedom and dignity are inviolable."

A Chinese "Enlightenment" was struggling against the old orthodoxy, and conservatives attacked Hu for tolerating it, for failing to discipline journalists, many of whom were working for major party newspapers, who had begun to probe and expose rank injustice, incompetence, and corruption in what was still a one-party state.

Corruption, which the Communists had eliminated under the totalitarian system, was also making a comeback. Party officials who controlled internal markets or the extraction of natural resources were in the catbird seat to extort payments from foreign investors seeking an entry to the Chinese market. The sons and daughters of high party officials were spotted in Hong Kong, setting up companies that could "introduce" foreign corporations to China for a percentage or a fee. These party scions soon became known as the Princelings.

By the end of 1986, Deng, fearing that political reformers were again going too far and threatening the supremacy of the party, went along with conservative demands that he reimpose ideological order. In the ensuing crackdown of early 1987, Deng and the other elders removed Hu Yaobang as general secretary and authorized the expulsion of the most powerful voices of change, Liu Binyan and Wang Ruoshui among them.

China's domestic struggles were lost to most Americans.

By the mid-1980s, Washington's grand plans to refurbish the Chinese armed forces and coproduce major weapons had been reduced to a modest program to upgrade China's F-8 fighter (based on the Soviet MIG-21) with a modern suite of radar and avionics systems. Small programs were also initiated to help China develop an antiartillery radar and to provide China's submarine fleet with a workable torpedo and an improved artillery shell. But these programs were really only a sideline to what was occurring in the civilian economy, where China was rapidly connecting to the world, not in any systematic manner but in a fission reaction, with contacts spontaneously springing from contacts and on and on.

By the end of the decade, China had become controversial in the routine manner of American domestic politics and diplomacy, where noisy disputes and congressional outrage are voiced on an array of issues, with the goal in the case of China of influencing administration policies but without questioning the strong bipartisan support for the U.S.-China relationship itself.

And as for the Chinese, they had learned to do business with a president they mistrusted, but they pinned substantial hope that he would be succeeded by George Bush, who—they believed—had a deeper appreciation for China's long-term importance, but without the right-wing obsession for the memory of Chiang Kai-shek.

BUSH:
...AND
TIANANMEN

Pro-democracy demonstrations in Beijing in 1989

J IM LILLEY CAME DOWN the ramp of the Boeing 747 at Beijing's Capital Airport on May 2, 1989, as the new U.S. ambassador to the People's Republic of China. He greeted the protocol officer from the Chinese Ministry of Foreign Affairs and breezed through the diplomatic channel at customs before hitting the terminal lobby, where he ran aground in a crush of reporters and their photon barrage.

Lilley was surprised that anyone had taken notice of his arrival, but when he heard the questions and saw that most of the reporters were from Taiwan and Hong Kong, he understood. The Asian press corps was stalking the day's news, which was dominated by the visit to Beijing by Taiwan's finance minister, Shirley Kuo. She was attending the first meeting of the Asian Development Bank board in China* and was the highest-ranking Taiwanese official to have ventured onto the mainland since Chiang Kai-shek had fled forty years earlier.

Lilley was amazed that there was not a single question about the massive student demonstrations that had been under way at Tiananmen Square since the death of Hu Yaobang on April 15; not a single question about the impending arrival of Soviet leader Mikhail Gorbachev for a summit that would bring an end to three decades of Sino-Soviet hostility, a profound new milestone after a quarter century of Sino-Soviet hostility. All the reporters wanted to know was whether Lilley was going to meet with Shirley Kuo. Would Lilley offer her asylum in the American embassy if she was arrested by the Communist authorities? Was the embassy going to handle her communications?

Lilley pushed through the crowd, replying that he was in China to represent the United States. "If I see Shirley Kuo, I will say hello to her,"[1] he said.

*Beijing had lost the battle to have Taiwan expelled from the regional bank's board but had managed to have Taiwan's status downgraded. The island no longer held its seat as the Republic of China, and the ROC flag was banned from the bank's headquarters, but Taiwan remained a full member.

No longer a spy, Lilley had returned to China as a seasoned diplomat with a long friendship and association with George Bush, the new president, whose most important priority was to make sure that the coming rapprochement between China and the Soviet Union did not occur at the expense of the United States.[2]

Bush himself had traveled to China during his first month in office, when the death of Japanese Emperor Hirohito* provided the pretext for an Asian trip. Bush and Brent Scowcroft, his national security adviser, had spent long hours with Deng and the two younger leaders he now was grooming: Zhao Ziyang, the new party general secretary and Deng's presumptive heir, and Li Peng, the new premier, a technocrat from the electric power sector—and also a favorite of the conservative party elders.

They had said everything that Bush wanted to hear and more. The arrival of Gorbachev, Deng told him, was not meant to signal the revival of the communist bloc or of any monolithic Asian alliance against the United States and Japan. Instead, Deng said, China was looking to Gorbachev to make good on his word to get all Soviet troops out of Afghanistan, to remove Soviet forces from the Chinese border, and to bring an end to the Vietnamese occupation of Cambodia.

Sitting as an old friend with his visitor in the Great Hall, Deng soothed Bush.[3] He retold the history of the Russian seizure of Chinese territories in the Far East during the previous century. He lamented the loss of 3 million more square kilometers of Chinese land to Moscow at the end of World War II and the loss of Outer Mongolia under pressure from Stalin, who wanted a buffer between the two countries.

"Those over fifty in China remember that the shape of China was like a Maple leaf," Deng said. "Now, if you look at a map, you see a huge chunk of the north cut away." Add to that, Deng continued, the "encirclement" strategy under Khrushchev and Brezhnev, whose alliances with India and Vietnam were all part of a threatening envelopment of China. "How can China not feel that the greatest threat comes from the Soviet Union?" he asked.

This had all been sweet music to Bush, and he returned to Washington determined to get Lilley confirmed expeditiously so that a new ambassador—Bush's ambassador—could carry on the strong relationship in the tradition of Nixon, under whose administration Bush had been introduced to China.

When Lilley arrived on May 2, just two weeks before Gorbachev was due in Beijing, the White House and Pentagon had agreed on a plan to steal some

*Hirohito died on January 7, and his funeral was held on February 24.

thunder from the Soviet leader's landmark journey. Under the plan, as soon as Gorbachev arrived in Beijing, Lilley would leave the Chinese capital and fly to Shanghai. There, the American ambassador and a large cast of Chinese leaders would welcome Admiral Henry H. Mauz Jr., commander of the U.S. Seventh Fleet, whose command ship, the USS *Blue Ridge*,[4] and two other American warships would sail up the Huangpu River to the famous Shanghai waterfront. With their armaments and flags in brilliant relief before the skyline of China's most populous city, the warships would disgorge their crews for several days of sightseeing and banqueting with their Chinese hosts.

Lilley called it an "in-your-face" display of the American military might that would show the Soviet leadership—and the world—that China's relationship with the United States was far more important than Moscow's new overture to Beijing was ever likely to be. The naval visit could not compete with Gorbachev's getting a twenty-one-gun salute or reviewing the guard in Beijing, but it would be an unmistakable reminder of America's proportional advantage in China's relations with the superpowers.

But apart from these well-laid plans, Lilley arrived in China to find an incipient rebellion in progress by hundreds of thousands of Chinese university students. At the highest political levels, Washington was scarcely paying attention, and the China specialists were in a state of bafflement, unable to explain the paralysis in the Chinese leadership.

Forty-eight hours after Lilley got off the plane, a massive demonstration commemorating the May Fourth Movement* overran Beijing's largest thoroughfares, paralyzing the center of the city. Lilley sallied forth in his conspicuous black Lincoln to have a look at the crowds. He marveled at their size. Why were the authorities letting it happen? he asked himself. For anyone who knew the history of the Communist Party's absolute control over the citizenry, this loss of discipline was profoundly disturbing. The chaos was all too reminiscent of the Cultural Revolution.

But for all the amazement, no one could answer with any clarity the question that Lilley had posed to his predecessor, Winston Lord, before leaving Washington: Is this a critical moment in the history of China? Or is it spring fever? The only relief Lilley took from his observations that day was in how many students waved at him when they saw the American flags fluttering from the fender stanchions of his car.

---

*On May 4, 1919, thousands of Chinese students marched in Tiananmen Square to demonstrate their patriotic fervor and their outrage over their government's failure at the end of World War I to prevent Japan from taking over from a defeated Germany the treaty ports that Germany had held along China's coastline. These were awarded to Japan under the Treaty of Versailles. The demonstrations and subsequent intellectual movement symbolized the nationalist spirit of Chinese youth and their quest for "science and democracy" in the development of China.

In a bizarre way, the poison that had developed between Lord and the White House during Lord's last months in Beijing had prevented the Bush administration from focusing on the collision of social and political forces that was occurring in China. On Bush's last day in Beijing in February 1989, the Chinese police had swooped down on Fang Lizhi, the astrophysicist and human rights campaigner, preventing him from attending a banquet that Bush was hosting for Chinese leaders at the American embassy.

The banquet was part of the protocol of any state visit, and Bush had added his personal touch, offering a Texas barbecue with a cactus motif on every table. But then Lord had gotten a little too creative and, in Bush's view, sandbagged the White House by inviting the outspoken astrophysicist without any prior consultation. Lord might have considered asking in advance whether the president wanted to risk a confrontation over inviting such a prominent critic of the regime. A separate and private meeting with Fang would have made the same statement, but Lord had sent in a cable with Fang's name prominently on the guest list, leaving it up to Bush's aides to remove it if they wished.

But it was difficult for them to do so without risking an even greater outrage from the human rights community if the story leaked. And it *would* leak, since Lord's cable had broad distribution.

Bush did not find out about the flap until he was already in Tokyo, headed for China. To him, nothing in Lord's cables had forewarned the White House of how radioactive Fang had become since January 1989, when he wrote an open letter to Deng calling for "amnesty" for all political prisoners, in particular for the release of Wei Jingsheng. To Bush, there was a way to support American human rights goals in China, but staging confrontations at banquets between political dissidents and their leaders was not it.

A phalanx of secret police had prevented Fang from reaching the embassy banquet,[5] and another phalanx of journalists recorded the drama, headlines of which dominated coverage of Bush's visit. This kind of scene was the last thing the new president had wanted.[6] When Bush and Scowcroft returned to Washington, Scowcroft called in R. W. Apple Jr. of *The New York Times* and David Hoffman of *The Washington Post* and told them that the embassy in Beijing had mishandled the episode.[7] By making public remarks, Scowcroft signaled to the Chinese that Lord was out of favor. This reinforced the Chinese government's belief that Lord and his prominent Chinese-American wife, Bette Bao, had exceeded the bounds of diplomatic conduct by courting artists and intellectuals critical of the Communist Party leadership.

When Lord read that an anonymous "senior official" was blaming him, he knew that it was Scowcroft, and he was overcome with indignation. He drafted a long cable rebuking the president's national security adviser for making Bush look weak on human rights. Lord sent the cable through the confidential CIA channel to the White House, with a copy to James Baker, Bush's new secretary of state.

When Scowcroft saw Lord's cable, he became even angrier, calling the ambassador a "bum." The White House pushed for Lilley to get to Beijing as soon as possible. Although Lord had boasted to Kissinger and others that he expected to be named to a high-level post in the Bush administration,[8] the flap over the Fang Lizhi incident ended his chances for advancement in the Bush administration.

When Hu Yaobang suddenly died of a heart attack on April 15, 1989, Lord was packing to leave. Two days later, after thousands of Beijing University students arrived at Tiananmen Square to mourn the death of a leader who had led the struggle for tolerance, accountability, and democratic reform, Lord and his wife began to see that a historic gathering of dissident forces was coalescing on university campuses. But Lord's warnings were discredited in the White House. As a lame-duck ambassador, there wasn't anything he could say that would register. Bush and Scowcroft remained self-absorbed on a high strategic plain, competing with Gorbachev for advantage in the international public relations contest over whose disarmament proposals were more genuine, over whether perestroika was an empty sensation or a profound reckoning.

Before he left Washington, Lilley sought out Lord, and over dinner Lord expressed his certainty that the demonstrations in China were a critical development, a manifestation of the deep dissatisfaction of the Chinese with their government. Lord said that disaffection now permeated the system in China—as it did in Poland—and was creating a potentially explosive situation.

Before leaving for Beijing, Lilley could find almost no one in the U.S. government who was focused on the mounting civil unrest. Among the few was Barbara Bush, who had been following events closely and was alarmed that Deng, whom she admired greatly, had not acted to stop the chaos from spreading. She asked Lilley how Deng could let this happen when the country seemed to be moving ahead. Why couldn't Deng get things under control?* Lilley told her what Lord had said, but she immediately dismissed anything coming from Lord.

As Lilley looked out from behind the bulletproof windows of his car at the

---

*The Bush administration, in its first six months, was poorly organized to foresee crisis. Scowcroft had most of the foreign policy bureaucracy distracted with a "strategic review" of the world, an exercise in paperwork that many resented because Bush had spent the previous eight years as vice president, and therefore, could be expected to be up to speed on world events. Secretary of State James Baker and his deputies assumed that the White House was overseeing the China relationship, since Bush had just returned from Beijing.

students around Tiananmen Square, at their fervor and their enthusiasm, Lord's assessment and Lilley's own instincts about the nature of China and the Chinese played on his mind. He wondered where the whole thing was going.

Over the following days and weeks, the intensity of the demonstrations grew. Students at dozens of universities around Beijing organized marches to the square under hand-painted banners criticizing their leaders; they formed a leadership council, the Provisional Students' Federation of Capital Universities. The Communist Party leadership appeared divided on how to react, and their paralysis only magnified each day's events. On the day of Hu's funeral, Beijing authorities issued an order to close the square, but by the time the police could react, more than 100,000 students had already flooded to the center of the city in defiance.

Inside the Great Hall of the People, the party elite stood in nervous commemoration of Hu Yaobang, the leader Deng had deposed because he had shown too much tolerance to those who saw the party as the real obstacle to reform. Standing in the house that Mao had built, the party elders could not escape the din rising from the square. The walls and columns resonated with the voices of China's youth. Some of them were the children of the party elders gathered inside.

"Li Peng, come out," they demanded. "Dialogue, dialogue, dialogue!"[9]

Out in the daylight, a sea of young faces held up their banners, which called Hu "The Soul of China" and which admonished the leadership that "Whoever Conducts Real Reform Will Get Our Support."

Inside the hall, as Zhao Ziyang delivered the eulogy, student leaders outside drafted petitions calling for better conditions at their schools and for press coverage of their demonstrations. They rolled their petitions into scrolls and knelt on the top step of the Great Hall, holding them high in the air in supplication to the "emperor" so that he would come out and accept them.

The student demonstrations inflamed the power struggle that had been under way for many months at the top of the Communist Party, where Zhao and his reformers were trying to fend off charges from hard-liners that their lack of discipline over the economy had incited a devastating level of inflation and rekindled the blight of corruption and other vices that the communists had eradicated under Mao.

The leadership quickly deadlocked over what the demonstrations meant and how to bring them to an end. As the crowds returned day after day, the paralysis deepened. A week after Hu's death, Zhao left for a state visit to North Korea, and, in his absence, Deng showed his impatience for the chaos in the streets. On April 26, the front page of the *People's Daily* carried Deng's message: "Take a Clear-Cut Stand Against the Instigation of Turmoil." His editorial repeated the words Deng had used to lay down the law in a speech to party officials: The student demonstrations were a "well-planned conspiracy" by "an extremely small number of people with ulterior motives," who were seeking "to poison people's minds" and "sabotage the nation's political stability and unity." Their goal was to "negate the leadership of the Communist Party and socialist system."

The paper's editors revealed that Deng had ordered his message to be published as a warning. If the government continued to "take a lenient attitude toward this turmoil and just let it go, a situation of real chaos will emerge," and "hope for reform and opening up" would be "reduced to nothing."

Deng told the party elders that if the editorial were not heeded, military force to put down the students would follow. "We are not afraid to shed a little blood, or to lose face, since this will not seriously harm China's image in the world," he said.

But Deng's intolerant condemnation only incited the students further. On the day after the editorial was published, more than 150,000 of them pushed past police barricades outside their campuses to march through the streets of the university district. The students demanded dialogue. But none was offered from the elders.

As the demonstrations passed the second week, the ad hoc student leadership group convened a large assembly at Beijing University. The demonstrators' energy was flagging, but the core leadership was anxious to keep the movement alive.

Chai Ling, a twenty-three-year-old psychology student at Beijing Normal University, was a wisp of a girl, frail and nearly always on the edge of emotion. When she spoke, her breathless sincerity gave way quickly to tears as she professed a passionate love of country and an enthusiasm for martyrdom. On the night of May 12, she and Wang Dan, a nineteen-year-old history student from Beijing University, addressed the crowd. Wang exuded commitment and sincerity, but he was laconic—even somnolent—compared to the rapture of Chai's charisma. With final exams approaching, the student leaders were searching for a way to galvanize support and escalate their pressure on the government. Everyone knew that Gorbachev was coming—and with him, the international news media. The students saw a great opportunity to stand on the world stage.

That's when Chai Ling seized on the idea of a hunger strike.

Taking the microphone, she told the students that she was prepared to die for her country, and in so doing, to reveal the "true face of the government."

A hunger strike would force the government to either "crush" the students or to listen to their pleas.

Wang Dan was sitting next to her as she spoke and as the tears began to roll down her face. He could see her power reflected in the crowd, whose voices surged in response to her cries.

"We, the children, are ready to die!"

"We, the children, are ready to use our lives to pursue truth!"

"We, the children, are ready to sacrifice ourselves!"

Mao had warned that when people were disaffected, a single match could light a prairie fire, and Chai Ling sparked new life into the movement that night. Her speech was reported by word of mouth to every campus in the capital, and an ultimatum was issued to the Communist Party leadership warning that if dialogue did not begin immediately, the students would begin a fast.

B UT ALL WASHINGTON COULD think about was Mikhail Gorbachev. Lilley could see that Washington was in the grip of the Kissinger disease— looking at everything through the prism of triangular diplomacy.

In contrast, Lilley had several immediate parochial concerns. Television news anchors Dan Rather, Tom Brokaw, Peter Jennings, and Bernard Shaw had landed in China as hundreds of thousands of Chinese students were rising in a tide of insurrection. It was one thing if the students embarrassed Gorbachev in Beijing, but now America had taken a stake in the week's events by seeking to upstage the Soviet leader in Shanghai, where demonstrations were also occurring. Lilley now had to worry whether the demonstrations there might turn ugly while hundreds of American sailors were wandering the streets of that city in splendid ignorance of the revolution that was gathering its energy.

Before leaving for Shanghai, Lilley tried to warn Qian Qichen, now foreign minister, that they—the American and Chinese leaders—were sitting on top of a volcano. Lilley felt that the Chinese did not understand the power of the American media. Any incident would become magnified. The press would pounce on it.

"They'll go after you," he warned Qian, but he meant "us." When CBS anchorman Dan Rather came on the air on the morning of May 19, he said, "What a place, what a time, what a story. It's Friday morning here and this is Tiananmen Square. Today, it's the people's square, all right. More than a million Chinese demanding democracy and freedom, and proclaiming a new revolution."

When Lilley got to Shanghai, the streets there were packed with demonstrators. The crowd was calm, but that did nothing to still Lilley's alarm that trouble could flare in an instant. As a spy, diplomat, and CIA analyst, Lilley had been studying Deng for more than a decade, and he believed that the Chinese leader was a man of the Old Testament, a revolutionary who was not afraid of bloodshed. Lilley felt that Deng was capable of exacting a full measure of revenge on the students by bringing down the wrath of the People's Liberation Army.

As all of this was happening, Lilley had instructions to accompany an old Chinese leader named Wan Li to the United States. Wan Li, one of Deng's close advisers, was a member of the politburo and chairman of the National People's Congress, China's parliament; he was also George Bush's friend and former tennis partner. Despite this distinguished company, Lilley felt like a deserter because he was forced to leave Beijing as the most important event of his diplomatic life was unfolding.

In Beijing, the Gorbachev visit was going horribly. Thousands of student hunger strikers occupied the square, with tens of thousands more supporting them. They refused to vacate. At the last minute, Gorbachev's arrival ceremony had to be moved to the airport. After the Soviet leader's motorcade got into the city, his official meetings at the Great Hall were truncated or delayed, and he was forced to use a rear entrance because the ceremonial entrance faced the square.

Meanwhile, the students had their own spies in the Great Hall.

Sympathetic Chinese officials passed word to the students that Zhao was struggling to contain hard-liners in the politburo who wanted to crack down. And Zhao himself, in a sign of desperation that he was losing the power struggle, broke party discipline by stating publicly to Gorbachev that Deng still functioned as absolute ruler even though he had given up most of his titles. Although Zhao was general secretary of the Chinese Communist Party, he confided to Gorbachev, "on most important issues, we still need Deng Xiaoping at the helm." Deng was outraged at the younger man's presumption to disclose the party's secret protocol of power.

The humiliation of the Gorbachev visit was the last straw for Deng. He rebuked Zhao's failure to act against the students. "You are the general secretary of the Communist Party, aren't you?"* Deng asked the question so bluntly that Zhao understood there would be no redemption if he did not act.

Down in Shanghai, the USS *Blue Ridge* and its escorts arrived on the wa-

---

*This rebuke was not published at the time. Zhao described the scene to his aide, Bao Tong.

terfront on May 19, but hardly anyone in the city noticed them against the backdrop of the student demonstrations that had taken over the streets, as they had in many large cities throughout China.

Lilley saw the throng and was even more deeply alarmed. U.S. intelligence was predicting an imminent martial law crackdown. The PLA was bringing troops in from Shenyang in northeastern China and from bases all around Beijing. Lilley telephoned the State Department and told the China Desk that he was not going to leave China; the biggest spontaneous uprising of the century was under way. This was not about triangular diplomacy and the global equilibrium. This was about what was happening at Tiananmen.

There was a brief protest from the State Department, but Lilley made it clear that he was making the decision. He then pulled Admiral Mauz aside and told him that he and his ships ought to leave Shanghai as soon as possible. Mauz agreed, and canceled his plans to travel to Beijing for further ceremonies.

Lilley took his wife Sally's airline ticket and flew back to the capital. As he landed in Beijing, Li Peng was on television monitors in the airport terminal declaring martial law. That could only mean that Zhao Ziyang was out. Now, Lilley feared, there could be a bloodbath.*

"Unbelievable! We all came here to cover a summit, and we walked into a revolution!" declared CNN's Bernard Shaw, as American and other international networks wired Tiananmen Square to the rest of the world.

By the time Lilley reached the embassy in Beijing, his staff had mobilized diplomats and military attachés, dispatching them by car and bicycle to the outskirts of the city to find and report on the massive movements of troops that satellite imagery showed converging on Beijing.

The senior American defense attaché, Jack Leide, a one-star army general with twelve years of experience in Asia, including a tour as an airborne rifle company commander in Vietnam, came back from Shanghai with Lilley and told his small contingent of officers to fan out, mingle with the crowds that were following the troops approaching the city, ask Chinese civilians to question the troops about their orders, and stick their heads into the military vehicles and report back the frequency numbers on the vehicles' radio sets. For

---

*In the United States, Bush seemed to be caught off guard. Hosting French president François Mitterrand at Boston University, he said, "I don't think that it would be appropriate for the president of the United States to say to the demonstrators and the students in Beijing exactly what their course of action should be." He urged the students to "stand up for what you believe in," but quickly added, "we do not exhort in a way that is going to stir up a military confrontation." Baker was equally restrained. "I don't think it is in the interest of the United States if China has major instability," he said. "It's the same as if there's major instability in the Soviet Union, it isn't in the interest of the United States, either."

more than a decade, the DIA had gathered license plate data on PLA vehicles,[10] and they could therefore identify any military unit in China by its bumper markings. Leide equipped his men with walkie-talkies smuggled in from DIA headquarters and the Pacific Fleet.*

All the data gathered in the field was funneled back through the embassy's communications channels to the National Military Command Center at the Pentagon. Frequency numbers from Chinese radios were passed on to the National Security Agency, whose satellites and listening posts around China could then tune in on Chinese military communications in hopes of determining what might come next.

But the Chinese military also seemed to be in chaos.

During the second night of martial law, Ken Allen, a young Air Force attaché, found a column of 200 troop transports and armored vehicles on the western approach to Beijing. Sometime after midnight, the soldiers suddenly loaded their ammunition clips and prepared to mount their vehicles.[11] Several young Chinese bystanders told the American attaché that orders had come down to storm Tiananmen Square at 2 A.M. Allen radioed in the message, which was flashed to the Pentagon, the first of many false alarms.

As they tried to keep up with troop movements, Lilley and his military and CIA advisers worked through the first stages of evacuation planning, including the worst-case scenario of Chinese gunfire directed against Americans, which would trigger a "forced entry" evacuation in which American airborne troops would fly into Beijing, possibly against opposition from the Chinese military, to rescue American citizens and get them out of the line of fire.

At the State Department in Washington, Baker met with Wan Li and expressed deep concern about what might happen.

Wan said that his government had no choice but to try to restore order. "Some things are unavoidable. One should not exclude the possibility of unfortunate incidents. There might be a possibility that bloodshed cannot be avoided," he said, too ominously for Baker.[12]

By the end of May, the student movement was in a state of fatigue and near collapse. The students had twice prevented Chinese troops from occupying the square, but the heady days of the hunger strike had waned. Some student leaders, like Chai Ling, were approaching nervous exhaustion, while others were trying to persuade the students to declare victory and return to their campuses. It was becoming more and more clear to the older intellectuals advising the students that hard-liners had reasserted control over the politburo and that Deng was bent on using military force—it was just a ques-

---

*US defense attachés, like all other diplomats, were prohibited from maintaining their own private radio communications inside China.

tion of when. The square itself had become a squalid and unpoliced campground, and parts of it smelled like an open sewer.

On Saturday, May 27, the student leaders met with their older advisers at the offices of the Chinese Academy of Social Sciences, a mile east of the square; after a long discussion about the goals and the risks of the movement, they voted to end the occupation and return to their campuses. Chai Ling, the most emotional and unpredictable of the group, voted with the majority.[13]

They drafted a statement that Wang Dan read as soon as they returned to the crowd. "In order to avoid an irrational confrontation with this irrational government; in order to take the initiative to create conditions for resolving this conflict through legal and democratic procedures, we propose to end for the time being our peaceful demonstrations in Tiananmen Square on May 30, the tenth day since martial law was declared. On that day, a citywide rally will be held here to celebrate the unprecedented victory of this student and people's movement." But the crowd hooted him down. Thousands of Chinese youth had just arrived from other cities. Every train brought more. They all wanted a piece of history, and that meant keeping the protest alive.

Chai Ling's deputy, Li Lu, challenged her right to make the decision to abandon the square when so many new students had come to protest. She was acting against democracy, he claimed.[14]

Supporters from Hong Kong had just delivered 27 million Hong Kong dollars (about US$4 million) in financial support. Others had donated dozens of new tents for their Valley Forge.

Chai Ling saw the boxes of cash. She felt the surge of the crowd. Suddenly, the revolution was back on. Chai Ling stepped onto the platform of the Martyrs monument and told the cheering crowd, "I am Chai Ling. I am the commander in chief of the Defend Tiananmen Headquarters. We will mobilize the Chinese all around the world to protest martial law! The government won't be able to enforce this martial law in ten days, in one year, in one hundred years!"

Lilley had a bad feeling that the attack was going to come that very weekend, and he told Washington to get ready for the onslaught. The State Department issued an urgent bulletin warning Americans not to travel to China until further notice, advising Americans already in the country to stay indoors. Lilley's hunch turned out to be another false alarm, but everyone sensed that it was close.

The morning after her triumphant speech, which would extend the student protest for another month, Chai Ling made her way across the square to the Beijing Hotel, where an American friend, Phil Cunningham, had a room.

A young language student from Lynbrook, Long Island, Cunningham was working as a freelance journalist.

"You have got to help me," Chai Ling told him. "I am on the black list. I need to escape." She gave him a piece of paper, a last will and testament, authorizing Cunningham to tell her story if she was killed. They drove to another hotel, and Cunningham set up a video camera. Chai began to speak in Chinese. Cunningham couldn't follow it all, but he got it all on tape.

"I have been feeling very sad recently,"[15] she said. "The students themselves lack democratic qualities. To be honest, from the day I called for a hunger strike I was clear that we wouldn't get any results. Certain people, certain causes are bound to fail. I've been very clear about this all along, but I've made an effort to present a staunch image, as if we were striving for victory. But deep down I knew it was futile."

Cunningham could see that she was very fragile.

"The deeper I got involved, the sadder I became. I already felt this way back in April. All along I've kept it to myself, because being a Chinese I shouldn't bad-mouth the Chinese. But I can't help saying: 'Oh, the Chinese, you are not worth my struggle! You are not worth my sacrifice!' But then I also can see that in this movement there are many people who do have a conscience, there are many decent people among the students, workers, citizens, and intellectuals.

"Our final goal is to overthrow this inhuman government, to set up a real people's government, so that the Chinese people could really stand up!" These were the words of Mao when he declared the People's Republic.

"Unless we overthrow this inhuman government, our country will have no hope! Our race will have no hope!"

She paused before continuing.

"My fellow students kept asking me, 'What should we do next? What can we accomplish?' I feel so sad, because how can I tell them that what we actually are hoping for is bloodshed,[16] the moment when the government is ready to brazenly butcher the people. Only when the square is awash with blood will the people of China open their eyes. Only then will they really be united. But how could I explain any of this to my fellow students? And what is truly despicable, is that some students and some famous and well-connected people are working hard to prevent the government from taking such measures. For the sake of their selfish interests and their private dealings they are trying to cause our movement to disintegrate and get us out of the square before the government is provoked to violence.

"If we allow the movement to collapse on its own, then the situation in China will be like this: All the enlightened people in the government will be purged. Deng Xiaoping has made it very clear that there is a small handful of people, not only in the Party and in society, but also among the students. If all these people were jailed or murdered by the government, how long would it take before the voice of democracy would be heard again? I don't know. But if the government uses violence, then we could expect a revolution.

"That's why I feel so sad, because I can't say all this to my fellow students, telling them plainly that we must use our blood and our lives to wake up the people. Of course, they will be willing. But they are still so young!"

Cunningham interjected a question: "Are you going to stay in the square yourself?"

"No," Chai Ling replied without hesitation.

"Why?"

"Because my situation is different. My name is on the government's hit list. I'm not going to be destroyed by this government. I want to live. Anyway, that's how I feel about it. I don't care if people say I am selfish. I believe that people have to continue the work I have started. A democracy movement cannot succeed with only one person."

After a moment's hesitation, she added, "I hope you don't report what I have just said for the time being, okay?"

THE DAY THE STUDENTS erected the Goddess of Democracy, a twenty-one-foot-high statue that stood as a challenge to the Communist Party, Jack Leide and Billy Huff, the CIA station chief, decided to drive across town for lunch with General Xiong Guangkai, the head of the PLA's military intelligence.

General Xiong* had been the prize CIA contact ever since the Chestnut program had brought the Chinese and American intelligence agencies together to spy on the Soviet Union with electronic listening posts in western China. Huff had jealously guarded his relationship with the general, like all station chiefs before him, but desperation over the Tiananmen stalemate was breaking down the barriers within the embassy.

As Huff, Leide, and their driver crawled through the sea of anarchy toward military intelligence headquarters, Leide surmised that it might be too late for the Chinese leadership; the genie seemed so far out of the bottle. It was hard to imagine how Deng could pull things back together. This could be the end of the regime, because it was too paralyzed—like the Shah of Iran a decade earlier—to strike out against its own people.

---

*Pronouned: Shyeeohng.

Both Americans were skeptical when General Xiong told them over lunch, "We cannot let this go on. What the students are doing is wrong." Leide could sense from Xiong's cryptic remarks that the government and army felt that they were getting backed into a corner and that their choices had narrowed. To them, it was either the survival of the Communist regime or total chaos. But would they strike? Shards of intelligence indicated that there was dissension in the military. The Thirty-eighth Army, in charge of the capital region, was reportedly unwilling to mount an assault against the students.

Huff agreed with Leide that the stakes were high, but he decided to fly out of the country that week to attend a station chiefs' meeting in Williamsburg, Virginia, explaining to Lilley that it was better for his career not to miss it.

On Saturday, June 3, new intelligence gleaned from Chinese military communications indicated that the Beijing military command was getting ready to strike. The embassy, anxious not to sound like it was crying wolf with every report, passed the fragment along to Washington without commenting on it. They should have said something, because the assault began late that evening.

Everyone had expected the attack, but still it came as a surprise. The main arteries into the center of the city were blocked by tanks and armored personnel carriers. Leide told his staff not to risk trying to penetrate the barriers. Hang back and report from a distance, he advised them.

But no one had told Jim Huskey to stay away, not that he would have listened.

James L. Huskey, six-foot-one with sandy brown hair, was a junior consular officer who had been drafted by Lilley to help cover the square, and, that evening, after a day-long vigil with a half dozen political officers from the embassy, Huskey was lingering near the northeast corner of Tiananmen. At 10:30 P.M., the loudspeakers controlled by the students came alive with an agitated voice announcing that PLA forces had been successfully turned back two miles east of the square on the Avenue of Eternal Peace. A wave of euphoria swept the crowd of 200,000.

Huskey was an unusual diplomat who had joined the service at the age of forty after spending his youth on tramp steamers bumming around the world. After earning a Ph.D. in American–East Asian relations from the University of North Carolina at Chapel Hill, Huskey had wandered through Africa and India. He had studied Chinese in Hong Kong and Taiwan. Lilley found him stamping visas in the embassy's consular section, where Huskey had drawn attention to himself by spotting visa applications from the sons and daughters of Chinese Communist Party officials. Thus tipped off, Lilley arranged to drink tea with some of these Princelings, who had to come in for a chat with the ambassador if they wanted a visa to America. In this manner, the embassy had picked up valuable gossip and made useful political contacts in the leadership circle.

But Huskey had also proved that he had good instincts for the streets: how to spot trouble, how to keep moving, and how to write a clear report about what he had observed. Huskey was already scheduled for advancement from the visa section to the political section when the crisis struck.

As Huskey ran to the Beijing Hotel to use the pay phone to report the rebuffed assault to the embassy, the students' loudspeaker declared, "Today is the beginning of democracy in China." But Huskey learned from embassy officials that the assault was far from over.[17] A large column of armored personnel carriers and trucks was approaching Tiananmen from the west. On foot, Huskey raced across the square in that direction, warning any foreign face he saw that the army was coming. The night sky was orange with the glow of burning cars and buses set alight by students seeking to block the army's advance.

Gunfire erupted in front of him. Huskey could see the column approaching. He gathered a group of American onlookers and exchange students and led them down an alley, making a long circuit through backstreets back to Tiananmen. When they reached the square, the loudspeakers declared what Huskey already knew. The army was coming in at full force from the west.

All through the night, Huskey ran back and forth on the northern boundary of the square under the Gate of Heavenly Peace and the giant portrait of Mao as PLA units bore down on the protestors, firing indiscriminately into the crowds of students and workers, who at times charged toward the gunfire to show their rage.

By 2 A.M. the square was surrounded, and a few minutes later soldiers who had pulled up at the north of the square sprayed gunfire toward the large crowd of demonstrators that lingered on the Avenue of Eternal Peace on the eastern approach to the square near the Beijing Hotel.

The air hissed with bullets. Huskey heard screams of pain as he ran for the stand of trees that lined the avenue on the north. He was conscious that people were falling around him. A man who had just shouted, "Do something! You foreigners must help us!" seemed to freeze as the bright red circle of an entry wound appeared on his forehead. He fell to the ground dead as Huskey dashed for cover.

At 5 A.M., the 3,000 students hugging each other under the Monument to the People's Heroes at the center of Tiananmen Square negotiated with an unidentified PLA infantry commander for their own safe exit. The students marched as a group through a southwest passage off the plain of Tiananmen and then made their way around to the Avenue of Eternal Peace, where they headed west toward their campuses. They walked in horror and dejection.

After an hour, just as dawn was breaking, Chinese soldiers near the retreating students opened fire again, claiming dozens more lives. At the same time, a marauding tank ran into another large group of students and bystanders, killing and maiming a dozen or more.* Some DIA analysts later conjectured that a "killing zone" had been deliberately set up to slaughter the retreating students.

All day Sunday, the reports of the massacres poured into Washington, and the Bush administration was unprepared to deal with the horrific truth that Deng had sent tanks and machine gunners against unarmed students.

By Monday morning, Bush was deluged with demands from Congress that he break diplomatic relations with Beijing, recall his ambassador, and impose the most severe sanctions he could muster. Bette Bao Lord, in an essay dictated over the telephone from Beijing, where she was serving as a consultant to Dan Rather, declared that "the legitimacy of the Communist Party has been destroyed."[18]

Nixon telephoned Bush at 8 A.M.

"Don't disrupt the relationship," Nixon counseled. "What's happened has been handled badly and is deplorable, but take a look at the long haul."[19]

Bush agreed. He told Nixon that he was not going to call Lilley home. He was going to have to impose sanctions and put the whole relationship on hold, but he would try to keep the lines of communication open.

But Bush was under severe pressure. Senator Jesse Helms on the Right and Representative Steven J. Solarz on the Left both demanded a dramatic response. Bush privately disparaged Solarz, saying, "he is the guy who wants to overthrow no matter who is involved. He is the kind of guy that was delighted about the overthrow of the Shah, not worrying about what follows on."[20]

Frustration within the administration also was building. Margaret Tutwiler, one of Baker's top political aides, interrupted the drafting of the presidential statement with a loud complaint that it did not take into account the revulsion that ordinary Americans were expressing over the images of twisted corpses of Chinese students. "You cannot *not* respond to these images on

---

*One bystander, Fang Zheng, a senior at Beijing's main sports university, lost both of his legs under the marauding tank as he tried to push several friends out of its path. After he recovered, he continued to pursue athletics even though confined to a wheelchair. In 1992, he won the championship for discus throwing in China's Special Olympics. But in 1995, when China sponsored the Asian Special Olympics, he was expelled from the national team because Communist Party officials feared that he might embarrass the regime by disclosing how he had lost his legs.

TV," she told Baker; "you have got to say something that expresses the outrage people feel and about how unacceptable this behavior is."[21]

But Bush was seized by caution. Intelligence reports made wild assertions that Li Peng had been shot and that Deng, who was eighty-four years old, might be dead. Deng had not been seen for days; U.S. intelligence had tracked him leaving the capital by special airplane to Wuhan in central China, where China's elite paratrooper units were based.[22] Some intelligence analysts believed that Deng feared for his own safety. After all, significant voices in the military questioned whether the PLA could be used against the Chinese people. Units from ten military divisions had converged on the capital. What if the commanders decided to oppose Deng? So it made sense for the Chinese leader to repair to a safe distance while they did their bloody work.

Later that day, Bush walked into the White House press room and denounced the violent crackdown, but he quickly qualified his denunciation by saying that he was not going to make "an emotional response" while so much was still uncertain. He suspended all military sales to China and all visits between American and Chinese military officials. But he stopped there. "It would be a tragedy for all if China were to pull back to its pre-1972 era of isolation and repression," he said. He would not impose economic sanctions or call his ambassador home, but he did add: "I reserve the right to take a whole new look at things if the violence escalates."

The next day in Beijing, as the city lay frozen by martial law, and with tanks and heavily armed troops at major intersections, Lilley was in the embassy cafeteria addressing a large group of American dependents, trying to reassure them about the previous day's events, when gunfire suddenly erupted outside—an explosion of high-caliber rounds that sounded to Leide, seated near Lilley, like an infantry assault. And it was incoming fire, deafening in the leafy streets of the embassy district.

Leide raced out through the embassy gates, where he saw a group of panicked wives of embassy officers running toward him with terrified children. People were cowering or running for cover as if snipers were on the rooftops. The wives told Leide that a column of Chinese armor had turned its machine guns on the diplomatic apartments that lined the broad avenue two miles east of Tiananmen. The apartments housed not only Americans but envoys and journalists from dozens of countries. Leide ran back into the embassy and told Lilley that an attack on the diplomatic quarter was under way. Wives and children were herded into the lead-lined vault that had been constructed inside the embassy to protect key personnel in the event of a terrorist attack. Leide ordered all classified material in the defense attaché's offices shredded.[23]

Lilley telephoned the Chinese Foreign Ministry, angrily telling the head of the Americas Department that troops were firing on Americans and that they had better stop. Ten U.S. embassy apartments had been hit with over 100 bullets. In one, security officer Fred Krug's wife and children had been watching television when the wall of glass that faced the street shattered from gunfire. They dived onto the floor, unhurt.

An inspection of the bullet holes suggested that some of the rounds had been fired from buildings directly across the street. Lilley's military attachés told him they believed that deliberate fire had been directed against Americans by Chinese soldiers placed in those buildings.

At almost the same time, the embassy's political officers came in with a gruesome report. A Chinese source reported that some senior military leaders wanted to scare all foreigners out of the country. The army would then clean up the student movement once and for all. *Close the door and beat the dog.* That was the expression they used.

Lilley got on the phone to Baker, who was incredulous. He didn't want to cast doubt on his ambassador, but he didn't think such reports could be true. They decided to make urgent contact with Chinese officials in Washington and Beijing. In the meantime, Baker agreed to issue the order to evacuate all American dependents in the embassy and prepare for a full evacuation of the 1,400 Americans in Beijing and 8,800 Americans living in the rest of China.

Bush tried to get a call through to Deng to find out, first, if he was alive, but mainly to get some authoritative reassurance that Americans would be protected and to express his deep concern that events were spinning out of control. But all efforts failed. The Chinese Foreign Ministry said that they were not too clear about Deng's whereabouts and therefore could not put the call through.

Over the following weeks, the crackdown rolled across the country. Reports of thousands of arrests and scores of executions flowed in from political and intelligence channels. There were no more gun attacks on Americans, and Lilley moderated his assessment of the danger to the embassy community, but by then the decision to send all dependents home had already been made.

Liu Huaqiu, the Chinese vice foreign minister, assured Lilley that there was no policy to shoot at Americans or scare them out of the country. He said that the troops had fired on the embassy apartments because they believed that a sniper was on the roof.

Lilley was seething.

"I was a private in the infantry," he told Liu. A sniper on the roof was no excuse to machine-gun an entire block of apartments up and down eleven floors.

Liu was lying and they both knew it.

Days later, a Chinese military intelligence official told one of Lilley's political officers, "What happened was most unfortunate."

That was all he said. It was the closest the Chinese government ever came to apologizing for the shooting spree against American and other foreign diplomatic residences.

In the midst of it all, Fang Lizhi and his wife, Li Shuxian, requested sanctuary at the embassy. Fang said that he feared for his safety. Lilley sent the head of his political section, Raymond Burghardt, and McKinney Russell, his public affairs officer, to talk Fang out of it, and when they succeeded, Fang returned to a nearby hotel, where he was staying with American friends.

Lilley was pleased to have avoided the siege that a Fang request for political asylum would have brought down on the embassy. Then, to his astonishment, a cable from Washington landed with the force of a rocket. It instructed Lilley to find Fang immediately, bring him back to the embassy, and offer him asylum. Washington feared recriminations in Congress and the press if Fang was arrested after being turned away by the Americans.* So Lilley got the siege after all. Fang's dash into the embassy made headlines. Heavily armed Chinese troops surrounded the embassy, challenging every entrant and searching every vehicle from front to back. Relations between America and China were openly hostile on the front lines; it was worse than at the height of the cold war. And Lilley was mad as a hornet.

Deng finally appeared on television on June 9, congratulating his military commanders for their valor and condemning the students. By now, the Tiananmen leaders—Chai Ling, Wang Dan, and Wuer Kaixi—were at the top of Deng's "most wanted" list. Thousands of Chinese youth were arrested; purges began in every institution that had supported the students or participated in the demonstrations. Vice Premier Wu Xueqian's son, a senior producer at Beijing Radio, was arrested for a broadcast that condemned the crackdown and the bloodshed. The son of State Counselor Qian Dayong was reportedly among the students killed by army gunfire. A prominent university professor, Ding Zilin, lost her son in the gunfire. Reformers in academia, the Chinese press, think tanks, and ministries were arrested or purged.

By June 20, the increasing numbers of arrests and executions (eleven Chinese already had been executed for "crimes" related to the protests in Beijing and Shanghai†) forced Bush to escalate sanctions. He banned all high-level official contacts with Beijing and suspended American support for all inter-

*Fang and his wife lived in the dental clinic behind Lilley's residence for a year, as Chinese military guards kept the embassy surrounded with armed troops, who searched every vehicle coming and going.

†The common feature of these trials resulting in executions, according to human rights mon-

national loans to China through the World Bank and the Asian Development Bank.

"They killed three guys yesterday who allegedly burned a train in Shanghai," Bush wrote in his diary, "but I hope they won't go after all the student organizers in Beijing with the same brutality."

On June 23, Bush penned a long and emotional letter to Deng that was strikingly reverential.

> I write as one who has great respect for what you personally have done for the people of China and to help your great country move forward. There is enormous irony in the fact that you who yourself have suffered several reversals in your quest to bring reform and openness to China are now facing a situation fraught with so much anxiety. . . .
>
> It is with this in mind that I write you asking for your help in preserving this relationship that we both think is very important. I have tried very hard not to inject myself into China's internal affairs. I have tried very hard not to appear to be dictating in any way to China about how it should manage its internal crisis. I am respectful of the differences in our two societies and in our two systems. . . .
>
> I simply want to assure you that we want this difficult matter resolved in a way which is satisfactory to you and does not violate our commitment to our basic principles. When there are differences between friends, as now, we must find a way to talk them out.[24]

Bush wrote that he would leave "to the history books" any final judgment on the massacres, and he asked Deng if he would receive a secret emissary from Washington. Deng, through diplomatic channels, immediately agreed. But nothing slowed the brutal wave of repression that was under way.

Deng and the party elders formally ousted Zhao Ziyang on June 24 and elevated Jiang Zemin, the Shanghai party boss, to replace him. More executions followed, with at least thirty-five people in five cities tried, convicted, and shot for acts committed during the uprising.

Bush's second round of sanctions were too late to head off Congress, where comprehensive sanctions legislation passed in the House (418–0) at the end of June and in the Senate in mid-July, forcing Bush and Baker into months of slogging negotiation to avoid a veto override.

On the evening of the House vote, Bush secretly dispatched Scowcroft and Lawrence Eagleburger, Baker's deputy, to Beijing to ask Deng for his cooperation in beginning a process of recovery and to explain to the Chinese

---

itors, was that those on trial were accused of violent acts. Yet, because there was little due process in the trial procedures, the executions further inflamed international reaction.

leader the political pressure that Bush was having to fend off as the brutality continued. Bush wanted Deng to know that American sanctions were not permanent. They were, however, politically necessary.

Scowcroft and Eagleburger flew all night in the belly of a C-141 Starlifter jet transport. They refueled in midair to avoid landing and detection. Chinese air defense controllers, when they picked up the flight as it entered Chinese airspace, had received no notice of an American military jet's arrival, and they queried their commanders whether to shoot down the intruder. President Yang Shangkun quickly intervened and cleared the plane for landing.

Deng was waiting for them on the morning of July 2. He told Scowcroft that George Bush was his friend because he had found him trustworthy over the years. But Deng said that relations were at a "dangerous state" and, despite his good relations with Bush, nothing was going to be resolved by friendship alone.

"China will persist in punishing those instigators of the rebellion and its behind-the-scenes boss in accordance with Chinese laws. China will by no means waver in its resolution of this kind. Otherwise how can the PRC continue to exist?"

Scowcroft made Bush's case that, although China's recent actions might be an internal affair, Deng nevertheless had to take into account "the reality that what you do and the way you do it will have a major impact on opinion in the United States and throughout the Western world."

But Deng was in a hard-line mode, referring to the 20 million Chinese who had died during the crucible years of the founding of the People's Republic. "With regard to concluding this unhappy episode in the relations between China and the United States," Deng added, "let me just repeat that we have to see what kind of actions the United States will take."

With that, Deng got up and left, and Scowcroft saw that Li Peng was in charge, flanked by Vice Premier Wu Xueqian and Foreign Minister Qian Qichen.

Li delivered another hard-line defense of the crackdown, arguing that no nation could stand by while its capital was besieged by demonstrators. The leadership had waited forty-eight days before acting. Reports of massacres were lies and exaggerations. Only 310 people died, and that included a number of PLA soldiers brutally killed by the students. Only 36 Beijing students died, he asserted.[25]

Then he turned to America. The United States government had suppressed protestors all through the 1960s, killing a number of them, he claimed.

In China, the demonstrators were trying to overthrow the government.

They would be punished according to law, and some would receive death sentences. He blamed the ousted Zhao for "failing to educate the youth" of China.

When Scowcroft tried to carry on the conversation at lunch, Li waved him off. "Let us talk of something else," he said.

Scowcroft and Eagleburger put their best face on it, but their mission accomplished little except to convey that Bush would try to minimize the damage. There was no attempt to engage the Chinese leadership in a concrete negotiation to discuss terms in which moderation, an end to martial law, and a suspension of executions on the part of China could be rewarded by positive actions on the part of the United States. Instead, Bush, in early July, took the first step by offering unilateral rewards as the repression continued. He approved the sale of four Boeing 757 passenger jets to China's national airline even though the cockpit navigational systems were among the civilian-military dual-use technologies that had been banned by his sanctions.

As he flew on Air Force One to Europe on July 9, Bush confessed his inability to develop any concrete approach to lifting the crisis beyond the corrosive stalemate it was mired in. He scribbled in his diary as the blue slate of the Atlantic filled his window:

> China still worries me. We see nothing that I really want China to do in order to solve the existing problem of strained relations, and I don't think any other Western country does. I think they're glad I am holding the line . . . though I am uneasy about my ability to keep this relationship on track. As long as China tries to say there was no massacre in Tiananmen Square, no lives lost except for the lives of Chinese soldiers, then the matter will not be quiet.[26]

Nothing remained quiet in that momentous year. On his trip to Europe, Bush saw the first evidence that Soviet domination of the eastern bloc was crumbling. One tumultuous uprising after another toppled communist regimes in Poland, Hungary, Czechoslovakia, and East Germany, where, in November, the Berlin Wall fell spectacularly. As the months rolled by, these breathtaking changes made Bush and Baker feel that much more unnatural in propping up Deng and the suddenly anachronistic Communists in Beijing, who might just as easily be swept away.

Congress forced the White House into protracted negotiations over sanctions against China. The House and Senate were seeking to codify penalties and threaten more serious steps if China continued on its course of repression. Bush signed one sanctions bill into law once he was satisfied that it would not restrict his presidential prerogatives. But a new uproar broke out over Bush's decision to allow Chinese military engineers to continue working in the United States on contracts with Grumman to upgrade the F-8 fighter.

When Congress passed a bill extending the visas of Chinese students in the United States so they wouldn't be forced to return home to martial law,* Bush vetoed it, saying that he could accomplish the same goal with an executive order. His critics nonetheless recoiled, accusing him of protecting the "butchers of Beijing." When Congress returned to session in January 1990, the White House had to mobilize all its forces to defeat an attempt to override the veto. The override failed in the Senate by only five votes.

Kissinger, Haig, and Nixon all traveled to China in the fall of 1989, seeking to inject themselves into the recovery process. Privately, Nixon gave Deng a bleak assessment. Tiananmen had devastated the relationship, negating much of the progress that had been made. They were going to have to start over.

Publicly, Nixon was also blunt. "Lenin wrote that facts are stubborn things," he said in a toast to Deng's longtime adjutant, President Yang Shangkun, at a formal banquet. "The fact is that many in the United States, including many friends of China, believe the crackdown was excessive and unjustified. The events of April through June damaged the respect and confidence which most Americans previously had for the leaders of China." Nixon had no particular prescription for recovery, but he was sure that it would take a long time, and as he surveyed the heavy encampment of Chinese troops still present in Beijing, even surrounding the U.S. embassy, where Fang Lizhi lived as a prisoner of sanctuary, Nixon asked, "Are martial law and political repression permanent features of life in China?"†

During Nixon's session with Deng, the Chinese leader said that the United States would have to "take the initiative in putting the past behind us, because only your country can do that." It was not possible, Deng said, for China to take the first step, "because the United States is strong and China is weak, China is the victim. Don't ever expect China to beg the United States to lift the sanctions. If they lasted 100 years, the Chinese would not do that."27

But Deng was also searching for a way back from the brink. He told Nixon that he was interested in discussing a comprehensive "settlement" of the issues that divided the two countries. Bush sent Scowcroft and Eagleburger

---

*The bill was sponsored by Representative Nancy Pelosi, Democrat of California.
†At Halloween, Lilley threw a costume party at his residence. The Chinese military guards, suspecting that the party was a cover for smuggling Fang Lizhi out of the compound, pulled the masks off party goers to make sure that their target was not among those who left that night.

back to China in December, this time publicly and with concrete proposals. Deng indicated that martial law could end, and Scowcroft laid out a roadmap of reciprocal steps that both sides could take.

But even in this more positive environment, Li Peng—anxious to burnish his image—exploited Scowcroft's presence as if to show the world that China conceded nothing while American leaders were returning to Beijing as supplicants. During an evening banquet, the Chinese premier orchestrated the arrival of a CNN camera crew just as Scowcroft raised a champagne glass to toast Li and tell him that Bush "still regards Deng as a friend forever." When he saw the camera, Scowcroft said to himself that he could either freeze and refuse to complete the toast (and end the visit with an insult), or he could go ahead with it, knowing that he would be called a toady back home.[28] He gave the toast. He also disparaged the "negative forces" in both societies that were trying to frustrate Sino-American friendship. When Baker saw the whole thing on television, he just shook his head at Scowcroft's flare for public relations.

But that was not the end of it. Days later, the Chinese spread the word among the Beijing press corps that Scowcroft and Eagleburger had been to Beijing secretly the previous summer—in clear violation of Bush's ban on high-level visits only days after he issued it. Winston Lord, who had been holding his fire for nearly a year, unleashed an assault on Scowcroft's mission in *The Washington Post*, accusing him—and, by extension, Bush—of "appearing weak to China's leaders and callous to the Chinese and American people."[29]

In his essay, Lord advocated a new foreign policy approach to China. With the Cold War over—and, with it, America's "de facto alliance" with China—it was time, Lord wrote, to address the double standard in human rights that had existed since the 1970s. American leaders had long championed the Helsinki accords and the human rights movement they spawned in the Soviet Union and East Europe, while standing silent over human rights abuses in China.

"For years, critics complained of a double standard—one for the Soviet Union and one for China," Lord wrote. "But there were two legitimate reasons for a more muted approach toward Beijing. First, Chinese society, with glaring exceptions, was generally moving in the right direction while the pre-Gorbachev Soviet Union was not. Second, China posed no threat to the United States and proved helpful on many international issues while the Soviet Union was expanding its arsenals and engaging in adventurism.[30]

"With many of these premises now overturned, it is time to shelve the double standard," Lord concluded.

The defection of Winston Lord and his attack on Bush, orchestrated as it was for maximum political effect, was emblematic of the broad spectrum of opposition that was building among liberals and conservatives alike to Bush's management of China policy in the wake of the Tiananmen massacres.

In truth, some of Bush's closest friends and advisers worried that his emotional attachment to the Chinese leaders he had known for more than a decade had clouded his judgment. He needed to express American outrage and take a firmer stand. Baker, the most politically attuned member of Bush's inner circle, found himself valiantly defending his president while orchestrating pressure on the White House to get out in front of the steamroller. In one instance, Baker announced in congressional testimony sanctions that he had recommended to the White House in what seemed like a calculated effort to force Bush to take a harder line.

Bush's sentimentalism toward Deng, his Yankee reticence in the face of the brutality unleashed against unarmed students and civilians, arose unmistakably from his prudent instincts to preserve long-term relations. But these characteristics were also evidence of a missing political gene in Bush, one that should have allowed him to identify with the outrage that Americans were feeling. Bush found it difficult to indulge his emotions for political purposes, and he misperceived how much a more emotional reaction on his part would have helped him to lead the American response. Steeled by Nixon's advice on the morning after the crackdown, Bush seized on the notion that he should remain calm—unemotional—in order to help preserve the long-term relationship with China. But, as Margaret Tutwiler had stated, Bush could not afford to *not* react to the images coming back from Beijing. It is impossible to believe that Nixon himself, if still in office, would not have tried to lead—instead of follow—the public outrage over China's actions and, in so doing, channel the emotionalism more constructively toward concrete steps to bring an end to martial law and to secure freedom for the thousands of students and workers thrown into prison. It is hard to imagine Nixon or Ford or Reagan writing the kind of maudlin letter that Bush addressed to the Chinese leader two weeks after Deng had chosen the most brutal course available to him—allowing front-line infantry forces to hose down the streets of his own capital with live ammunition. If Deng and the party elders felt threatened by the forty-eight-day paralysis of the capital, where was the effort to reimpose civil control through civil means—through nonlethal instruments such as water cannons, tear gas, and riot-trained police forces?

Bush's deep interest in not jeopardizing a long-term relationship with the People's Republic does not adequately explain his rush to exempt China from international accountability in the face of such flagrant cold-bloodedness.

There seemed little basis for Bush's assertion that a sterner condemnation and more punitive set of presidential actions would have resulted in an irreparable break in relations. Indeed, any analysis of China's national goals in 1989 would have reaffirmed that Beijing's leaders were incapable of retreating to the isolation of the Mao era. China was too far down the road to modernization and development.

Bush might have triggered a diplomatic crisis by taking a firmer stand, but such a crisis would certainly have forced the Chinese leadership to focus on the proposition that nations that defend massacres and indulge in brutal repression put at peril their ability to conduct normal intercourse with the modern world. Bush shrank from administering this lesson.

Some even defended the Chinese action, arguing, as Kissinger did publicly,* that no set of leaders could stand by while their capital was paralyzed for six weeks by young revolutionaries storming the gates of the leadership compound. Moreover, with the demonstrations spreading all over the country, the rationale went, China was in danger of descending once again into the chaos of the Cultural Revolution. But this simply was not the case. The June 1989 demonstrations were a peaceful outpouring of aspirations. There may have been Jacobin elements among the students, but it was never inevitable that a rapacious military assault was the only way to convince them to return to their campuses.

For Bush, even the prospect of calling his ambassador home for consultations, by no means an extreme act, was out of the question. Bush insisted that he needed Lilley in Beijing to keep the lines of communication open, but he then bypassed Lilley altogether in delivering the series of messages that Scowcroft and Eagleburger carried to Deng and Li Peng.

Some Chinese believed that Deng never intended the army to mangle its task of crowd control so grotesquely; members of Deng's family asserted this position. Deng himself was vigorous in his own defense: "If those people who caused the turmoil had had their way, there would have been a civil war," he told the Chinese-American physicist T. D. Lee of Columbia University, who visited Beijing that fall. "Of course, if there had been a civil war, we would have won, but who knows how many people would have died, and that would have really damaged the tendons and the bones. We had no choice but to act

---

*Kissinger, as a commentator for ABC News, argued on the evening of June 4 against imposing economic sanctions on China. Over the next several months, he rationalized Beijing's crackdown in a series of newspaper columns and media appearances. It was not until September 1989, however, that Kissinger acknowledged that he was in the midst of launching a multimillion-dollar investment syndicate, China Ventures, in which he was the managing partner and stood to gain millions in fees and profits. Kissinger's conflict of interest was disclosed by Richard Cohen of *The Washington Post* and John Fialka of *The Wall Street Journal*.

decisively. In our efforts to quell the rebellion, our principle was to do every-thing possible not to harm the people, especially students. But if we had not taken resolute measures to put it down, the consequences would have been unimaginable."[31]

Deng never admitted how many Chinese youths he sacrificed to preserve his notion of Communist Party discipline, and this refusal on his part added to the shame that history would confer on the act. Western intelligence ex-perts were unable to reconcile the different estimates, but it seems certain that hundreds of civilians, perhaps as many as 1,500, perished. Some Ameri-can intelligence officers believe that a count of 2,500 is more accurate. Tens of thousands more were scarred by recrimination and persecution. The fact that ten years after the event, the official death toll of students, workers, passersby, and soldiers remains an official secret reveals the continuing deep sensitivity of party leaders. Even if, as Li Peng asserted to Scowcroft, only 36 Beijing students died—an assertion that is undermined by many eyewitness accounts—the Tiananmen massacre stands as one of the greatest tragedies that has befallen China in the twentieth century. The senselessness of the killing nurtured a latent instinct for revenge even among those Chinese who moved on, rebuilding their lives or "diving into business" because they had no remedy for what had occurred.

In elevating Jiang Zemin to head the party, Deng picked the one regional party boss who had most firmly and ingeniously prevented widespread disor-der and minimized the violence. Under Jiang, Shanghai mayor Zhu Rongji had gone into the streets and stayed up late into the night, discussing the stu-dents' demands and identifying with their discontent.

But those who were in charge in Beijing had no such communications skills, and perhaps such skills would have been wasted anyway on a student leadership that, ultimately, indulged their valiant, if self-destructive, instinct for confrontation, even after it became woefully apparent that their failure to vacate the square would result in a military crackdown. Still, even the harsh-est indictment of the judgments made by student leaders could not justify the acts of retribution that followed. Americans could not avoid the obvious con-clusion, that the army had massacred hundreds of unarmed civilians.

On December 19, Bush made his first China-friendly gesture in the wake of the Scowcroft mission. He approved the sale of three American communi-cations satellites for launch on Chinese boosters, preempting a proposed congressional ban on high-tech trade. And he directed the Export-Import Bank to resume lending to firms doing business in China. Congressional out-rage was muted by Bush's decision to invade Panama the next day.

On January 10, China lifted the martial law decree, reopened Tiananmen

Square under heavy guard, and released nearly 600 people who had been detained during the crackdown. Still, Bush, Scowcroft, and Baker found the
Chinese leadership an impenetrable glacier. The Christmas 1989 overthrow
and execution of Nicolae and Elena Ceauşescu in Romania rattled the timbers of China's revolutionary elders. Of all the East European dictators,
Ceauşescu was seen by the Chinese as a Gibraltar of authoritarian rule. To
Deng and the others, the Romanian leader had demonstrated that if you are
tough, if you are resolute, you will prevail. And underlying Deng's fear was
the suspicion that the West—particularly the United States—was out to topple Chinese communism by encouraging democracy and human rights.

It wasn't just Romania that had Chinese leaders spooked. They looked
with astonishment at Moscow, where Gorbachev, in February, announced
that he would revise the Soviet Constitution to allow for a multiparty elec-
toral system, thereby ending the seventy-two-year monopoly on power by
the party of Lenin. Within days, China's state-run press carried a defensive
rebuttal, rejecting political pluralism.

Bush, having come to the presidency with two decades of experience
watching China struggle to emerge from the chaos of the Mao era, was
forced into a role he despised, that of managing punitive sanctions and defending himself from congressional blowbacks over each new outrage that
emanated from Beijing. Unable to articulate a new strategic basis for the relationship that was as compelling as the one that sustained it during the Cold
War, Bush fell back on the generalization that China was "important" and, by
implication, in a special category that constrained him from expressing the
outrage that many Americans—and many Chinese—felt.

In Beijing, with the hard-liners in charge of the government and security
apparatus, Foreign Minister Qian Qichen launched a diplomatic campaign
to bring China out of its isolation by seeking to negotiate an end to Western
sanctions. Beijing broadened its diplomacy in Europe and the Soviet Union
to, again, demonstrate to the United States that China had other options in
an increasingly multipolar world. In late April 1990, Li Peng flew to Moscow
and signed a ten-year agreement for trade and scientific cooperation with
Gorbachev.

Bush did what he could at home. On May 24, he extended China's most-
favored-nation trade status despite the calls of prominent Americans to cancel China's low-tariff trading privileges in the American market as
punishment for continued human rights abuses and for sales of missile and
other weapons technologies in the Middle East and South Asia. Bush justified
his decision with the argument that he had weighed "our impulse to lash out
in outrage" against "a sober assessment of our nation's long-term interests."[32]

In response, the Chinese announced that they were going to purchase $2 billion worth of Boeing passenger jets. Then, two weeks later, they agreed to allow Fang Lizhi and his wife to leave the U.S. embassy compound in Beijing and emigrate to England and, eventually, the United States.

A new form of balance-sheet diplomacy was emerging. Any positive step taken by either side had to be reciprocated. Negative steps, of course, invited like responses. The tension seemed to engender a return to the earlier era of hostility and mistrust, when Mao and Zhou had bargained with the lives of captive American spies or servicemen and exchanged them for concessions made by Nixon and Kissinger in lowering the trade embargo and easing other sanctions imposed during the Cold War. The new hostages were Chinese, many of them young heroes of the pro-democracy demonstrations.

As the Democratic majority in Congress looked ahead to the 1992 presidential election, Senate majority leader George Mitchell of Maine presided over a series of caucuses to devise a legislative strategy that would allow the Democrats to attack Bush from the high ground of human rights by daring him to veto congressionally mandated sanctions on China. One Democratic staff member who attended these sessions described the strategy as a "win-win" proposition. If the Democrats overturned a presidential veto, they would be in a position to dictate a tougher approach to China. If the Democrats failed to overturn Bush's vetoes, the president would still be forced to defend the "butchers of Beijing," causing further political erosion in the Republican administration.

As the first anniversary of the Tiananmen massacres approached, Winston Lord and Holly Burkhalter, the Washington director of Human Rights Watch, a private advocacy organization, called on Bush to use the annual renewal of China's most-favored-nation trade status to impose stiff conditions requiring improvements in human rights. In Washington's highly charged partisan atmosphere, the human rights assault on Bush's China policy was based, inescapably, on both principle and politics.

It was interrupted, only briefly, by Saddam Hussein, whose invasion of Kuwait in August 1990 unified Washington in the effort to build an international coalition to liberate the desert sheikdom. All through late 1990, Baker played the suitor to Beijing in order to guarantee that China would not veto the critical UN resolutions that authorized Operation Desert Storm. Qian Qichen said that China would never vote "yes," but he held out the promise of a Chinese abstention for a diplomatic price.

Baker offered Qian an invitation to Washington, the first since the Tiananmen massacres, but it would be limited to meetings with senior State Department officials. But Bush and Scowcroft overruled Baker. On November 30, they invited Qian to the White House, where the president made a great display of Washington and Beijing's "standing up against aggression." Bush's congressional critics protested that he was kowtowing to Qian as a reward for China's cooperation at the UN.

By the middle of 1991, the CIA had sent conclusive evidence to the White House that Chinese military industries—keen on garnering export earnings—were discussing the sale of surface-to-surface missiles to Pakistan, Syria, and Iran.[33] The Chinese were also providing air defense missiles and radars to Libya, where Muammar Qaddafi was using them to protect a large chemical weapons complex under construction in the desert.

Chinese nuclear scientists shuttled between Beijing and Pakistan's nuclear weapons laboratories at Kahuta, while other scientists had begun advising Iran's nuclear physicists.

Bush looked to Baker to work with Qian Qichen to rehabilitate relations, but Baker resisted. He had promised Qian that he would travel to China in 1991, but the months passed and Baker put the visit off, dragging his feet as human rights abuses in China continued to dominate the news. Baker had to consider that his own reputation might be tarnished by an unsuccessful encounter in Beijing. He would be the highest-ranking American to visit China since the massacres. The only thing that could inoculate him from attack was some improvement in China's behavior. In New York that fall, Qian attended the UN General Assembly session, and Baker leaned as hard as he could on the tough-minded diplomat.

"Congress is waiting to override the president," Baker told Qian, referring to the fight over whether to revoke China's most-favored-nation trade privileges. Therefore, Baker added, "I want to leave China with something on human rights and proliferation."[34] Baker wanted to talk specifics, but Qian demurred. "Any issues can be discussed, and I am sure there will be some successes," he said, refusing to make a commitment. Baker's frustration was tormenting. China for him was a cipher. The cultural and political barriers that stood between him and the Chinese foreign minister were formidable—truly a great wall. After three years of trying to break through, their personal rapport was almost nonexistent, in striking contrast to Baker's relationship with Eduard Shevardnadze, Gorbachev's foreign minister, who had the ability to reach across the divide and, without betraying national loyalty, speak with a level of candor that Baker felt was much more constructive.

Baker eventually extracted a Chinese pledge not to export M-9 missiles to Syria or the shorter-range M-11 missiles to Pakistan. Beijing also agreed to adhere to the guidelines of the Missile Technology Control Regime, the international accord signed by two dozen nations seeking to control the spread of ballistic missile technology. Significantly, China signaled for the first time that it was preparing to sign the Nuclear Non-Proliferation Treaty, indicating a profound evolution of international thinking in Beijing. These concessions allowed Baker to schedule his trip to Beijing for November 1991. But on the human rights front, the increments of forward movement seemed microscopic. Baker had pressed for an amnesty of Tiananmen protestors still in jail, but all he got was a pledge to issue more student exit visas for those completing their jail sentences. He had laid a stack of paper before Qian, a list of more than 700 names, all of them political detainees, that the State Department had compiled with the help of human rights organizations. Qian promised an accounting of their "crimes" and their sentences. He pledged to address American concerns about the use of prison labor and to allow American diplomats to visit a prison.

"It has now been two and a half years since the tragedy of Tiananmen," Baker told reporters as he prepared to leave. "Unless we were to keep U.S.-China relations in the deep freeze forever, we had to start talking." He then added, "I did not come here expecting a dramatic breakthrough."

A few weeks later, Bush lifted the six-month-old ban on high-technology exports to China, a step Baker had promised as a quid pro quo. Bush and Baker then agreed to meet with Li Peng when the Chinese premier traveled to New York for a United Nations summit.

Li was still the hard-line face of the martial law crackdown, of the internal repression and economic retrenchment, which, by early 1992, had slowed economic growth and foreign investment dramatically. Chinese reformers and Western economists alike began to worry that China's harsh post-Tiananmen government would undermine reform itself. Jiang Zemin, the party's new general secretary, was far too weak to do anything but position himself at the conservative center of this backlash. Party conservatives were on a rampage against the return of drug use in China and the rise of prostitution in the special economic zones. The party launched campaigns against "spiritual pollution," foreign "interference," and Western plots to topple Communist Party rule through "peaceful evolution" and creeping capitalism.

In a speech to the UN Security Council, Li defended the regime. "A country's human rights situation should not be judged in total disregard of its history and national conditions," he said. "It is neither appropriate nor workable that all countries measure up to the human rights criteria or models of one of a small number of countries."[35]

Finally, Deng recognized that the pendulum had swung too far.

In early 1992, as Bush headed into his campaign for reelection, Deng started up a campaign of his own, sallying forth at the age of eighty-seven, with Yang Shangkun at his side, to exhort the party leadership to speed up the pace of economic growth and push reforms forward. For two months, Deng barnstormed through southern China, rallying provincial leaders wherever he stopped. The Chinese referred to this trip as Deng's *nan xun*, or "southern tour," a Chinese term once used to denote the movement of a Chinese emperor across his realm.

Jiang Zemin and Li Peng were left behind. The top party leaders sat in Beijing stunned and speechless as they beheld Deng's willful evangelism blazing across the landscape, going over the heads of the men he had installed in power to talk directly to the Chinese people about what was important for the country's future. The *People's Daily* was paralyzed, unable to report the news without guidance from Jiang or Li, who seemed unable to decide how to react. After all, they were Deng's targets, along with Beijing's incessant obsession with petty ideological maneuvering. And, in the end, Deng's evangelism carried the same simple message that Bill Clinton would employ in his presidential campaign against Bush: "It's the economy, stupid."

Deng told the Chinese people: "To get rich is glorious!" He admonished them that in the new era, not everyone would get rich at the same time or at the same pace, but that China's opening to the outside world and its growing prosperity had allowed the country to weather the storm of June Fourth, as the Tiananmen massacres were now referred to. Reform would go on for 100 years at least, Deng assured regional leaders, and anyone who tried to overthrow reform "would be toppled." This seemed to be an explicit warning to the hard-liners.

"We must not act like women with bound feet,"[36] he told party leaders in Shenzhen, one of China's special economic zones, right across the border from Hong Kong. "Once we are sure that something should be done, we should dare to experiment and break a new path. That is the important lesson to be learned from Shenzhen." However, Deng readily admitted that he was no economist. He lived by the simple aphorisms of his native Sichuan, one of which instructed that rivers could only be crossed by feeling out the stones on the bottom. This passed for Deng's economy theory.

"Are securities and the stock market good or bad? Do they entail any dangers? Are they peculiar to capitalism? Can socialism make use of them?"

Deng, as ever, answered his own questions.

"We must try these things out. If, after one or two years of experimentation, they prove feasible, we can expand them. Otherwise we can put a stop to them and be done with it." And, he added, "If we want socialism to achieve superiority over capitalism, we should not hesitate to draw on the achievements of all cultures and to learn from other countries, including the developed capitalist countries."[37]

Deng's message served as a pretext for China's provincial leaders to ignore the narrow politics of Beijing and get the economy moving again on their own initiative. State banks ignored the limits and quotas set in Beijing and promoted an explosion of easy credit and new growth, as cities and counties and provinces funded pet projects and real estate ventures by simply creating and extending credit.

Deng was moving on, but Washington was not.

With the coming presidential political season in full view, Senator Mitchell in late February introduced legislation to impose strict conditions on the annual renewal of China's most-favored-nation trade privileges. The bill also criticized China's continued "occupation" of Tibet and its $13 billion trade surplus with the United States. Bush, true to his promise, vetoed the bill on March 3. The House voted 357–61 to override the veto, but there were not enough votes in the Senate. Bush had won, but the Democrats felt that they, too, had gained by forcing Bush to defend China's indefensible repression.

Still riding the popularity of victory in the Persian Gulf, Bush was confident that he could prevail over any Democratic challenger. Richard Nixon, in a more sober assessment, tried to warn Bush that he was liable to lose California[38] and, therefore, that he would lose the whole election if he failed to develop a strategy for carrying the South and the Midwest.

Seeing Bush's vulnerability, Taiwan's friends in the United States teamed up with General Dynamics and the Texas congressional delegation to persuade Bush that in order to carry Texas in the November elections, he ought to approve the sale of F-16 fighters to Taiwan because that would save thousands of jobs in Fort Worth. This was the advanced fighter that Taiwan had long been denied. Bush, Scowcroft, and Baker all knew that, in order to sell the F-16 to Taiwan, the president would have to violate the August 1982 communiqué on arms sales to Taiwan. They debated for weeks. Fort Worth representative Joe Barton increased the pressure by playing both sides of the fence. Rumors swirled that Barton was also talking to the Clinton campaign, telling the Democrats that whoever made the commitment to sell the F-16 to Taiwan would enhance his fortunes in the Texas presidential sweepstakes.

On July 30, General Dynamics announced that if it failed to get any new F-16 orders, it would reduce its labor force by 5,800 workers.[39] Bush still wavered because he knew what a blow his decision might be to U.S.-China relations. The China specialists at State did not have to remind Bush that in 1981 Deng had been poised to downgrade the whole relationship over Reagan's proposed sale of an advanced fighter to Taiwan.

But Taiwan was playing its hand differently this time. Intelligence reports were coming in that France was negotiating to sell sixty Mirage 2000-5 fighter-bombers to Taiwan. Now, national economic interests were also at stake.

With his own political fortunes on the line, Bush decided a month after his nomination to violate the principles of arms restraint that he, as a member of the Reagan administration, had helped to negotiate a decade earlier. Nearly all of Bush's associates understood that in order to sell 150 F-16s to Taiwan, Bush would have to violate the American commitment in the August 1982 communiqué to stay within the "quality and quantity" limits of previous years' sales.

J. Stapleton Roy, whom Bush had sent to Beijing in 1991 to succeed Lilley as ambassador, was thunderstruck when he heard what was under consideration. In Roy's mind, it was impossible to read the communiqué and conclude that the United States could sell the F-16 to Taiwan. Politics aside, Roy worried that Bush was taking a grave risk by repudiating a solemn commitment of the American government.

But others felt differently.

Lilley, who had returned to Washington to serve in the Pentagon as assistant secretary for Asian policy, worked with Douglas Paal and others in the White House to construct a set of arguments that Bush could use to sell the decision publicly. Irrespective of politics, Lilley had convinced himself that the sale was justified. Taiwan had no alternative but to purchase a newer-model aircraft because its F-5Es and older F-104s were out of date, he argued. Moreover, Taiwan's indigenous fighter would not be ready for several more years. Lilley pointed to intelligence reports that mainland China was upgrading its air force with purchases of SU-27 supersonic fighters from Russia. And, he pointed out, many Asian capitals were beginning to voice concerns about the growth of mainland China's military power. Beijing's proclamation in early 1992 that Chinese sovereignty extended as far as the Spratly Islands in the South China Sea was greeted with great alarm in Vietnam, the Philippines, Indonesia, and Malaysia, all of which claimed portions of the Spratlys and the potential oil resources there.

The contrasts to 1981 were striking.

Then, Lilley had proposed a full-blown intelligence community assessment of whether Taiwan actually needed a new fighter. But in 1992, the Bush administration already knew the answer it wanted and, therefore, took no chances on another assessment of Taiwan's needs. To turn such a study over to the intelligence community would have meant a loss of control for the White House, and so the historical professionalism that attended the evaluation of 1981 was jettisoned in favor of a more politicized evaluation in 1992.

Doubtless, Lilley's knowledge and judgment of the military balance was extensive, but the former ambassador was a partisan player still seething with personal anger over the violence and carnage of the Tiananmen massacres. From Scowcroft down, the bureaucracy was marshaled in a highly partisan manner to create the illusion of professionalism and to manufacture an "expert" assessment that Taiwan needed the F-16. Even Dick Cheney, the defense secretary, confided in his staff that the decision was going to be driven by politics, regardless of how it was rationalized in public.[40]

And in the end, the White House exceeded even the Pentagon's recommendations. Lilley had made the case for a fifty-fighter sale to Taiwan, arguing that that number of F-16s would bridge the gap in Taiwan's air defense needs. But General Dynamics and the Texas political delegation were not satisfied with a fifty-plane deal, and so the White House trebled it with no military justification at all.

Anyone in the Bush administration who knew the history of U.S.-China relations knew that the decision had been railroaded. Stape Roy told the Chinese privately that Bush regretted making the decision and hoped the Chinese would understand; Bush himself confided to his aides afterward that it had been a tough decision and that he hoped, if reelected, he could "make it up" to the Chinese.[41]

Bush allowed White House and State Department spokesmen to assert publicly that a careful and professional review had been conducted to justify the sale, but then Bush and Scowcroft called the Chinese ambassador into the Oval Office and bluntly told him the truth. "This sale of F-16s is not done for Taiwan or for you," Scowcroft told Ambassador Zhu Qizhen. "It is being done because the production line is in Texas and Texas is crucial to the President."[42]

Bush, Scowcroft, and Baker told Chinese officials privately that China would be much better off with George Bush in the White House for the next four years than Bill Clinton, whose campaign was taking on the hard edges of the human rights community, criticizing Bush's China policy in particular. In the end, Bush felt that the Chinese understood.[43]

And so the president—who had refused to even recall his ambassador after the Tiananmen massacres in the interest of protecting America's long-term relationship with the People's Republic—made a campaign appearance in Fort Worth on September 2 and announced the sale of 150 F-16s to Taiwan to a cheering crowd of General Dynamics employees. The contract would earn as much as $5.8 billion for the defense contractor.

The Chinese vented most of their anger at the French for selling the Mirage fighters to Taiwan. Beijing recalled the Chinese ambassador from Paris, cancelled agreements, and forced the closure of the French consulate in Guangzhou. Beijing held its fire against the United States in hopes that Bush would be reelected, providing the opportunity for significant political payback.

But Bush disappointed them.

CLINTON:

THE

BUTCHERS

OF BEIJING ...

Jiang Zemin and Bill Clinton

I N THE EARLY 1990S, a whole new sensation dawned over Asia—the notion of China as the next superpower.

Tiananmen still dominated the political agenda with the West, but along the Pacific Rim, where trade, industry, and markets ruled, Deng's southern tour at the outset of 1992 was read as a sign that the productive forces of the Chinese had once again been unleashed. A deluge of investment, new construction, and monetary expansion was surging into the Chinese economy, propelling economic growth forward at a dizzying pace.

The explosion of manufacturing along China's southeastern coast—textiles, plastics, toys, shoes, and electronics—was difficult to capture in any familiar metaphor that could convey the man-made diastrophism that was underway. Armies of bulldozers assaulted ancient vistas of rice paddies and mountains as Patton had assaulted the plain of Europe. Mechanized brigades engorged red-clay landscapes to make bricks; mammoth rock-crushing machines shredded promontories into aggregate gravel to be poured into the concrete foundations of factory skeletons.

Beyond Hong Kong, construction cranes poised over the horizon of Guangdong Province like a captive mantis plague, each standing erector-straight and toiling with slender arms and steel filaments to nudge skyward the windowless shells of office towers and assembly lines. To connect them all, engineers were laying an ambitious network of highways and bridges across the Pearl River Delta in a circuit that ran all the way to the container ports of Hong Kong and, from there, to the world. Out of the rich and diverse topography of coastal China was rising new plain of Chinese commerce, just as it had in Taiwan and Hong Kong in earlier decades.

Although the scale of growth was breathtaking, the assertion that China was headed for superpower status was gross exaggeration, reflecting the hyperbole of a generation of young financial managers based in Hong Kong, Singapore, Tokyo, and New York, all vying to out-envision each other in defining the new paradigm of the coming Pacific Century. Each hoped to capture a share of the enormous capital flows arriving in Asia in search of high returns in the emerging markets of the region.

China was at the center of the forecasting frenzy. There were fervent estimates that its economy would quickly surpass Japan's and then America's; there were warnings that China's new wealth would enable Beijing to purchase—at bargain prices—a high-technology military from the former Soviet Union and the defunct Warsaw Pact. Thus armed, some analysts asserted, Beijing could move to establish a new era of Chinese hegemony over Asia, as unlikely as this seemed to those China specialists who could see beyond the furious development to the enormity of what China would still have to overcome.

After leading the world in economic growth during the 1980s, the Chinese economy had gone keel-up after the Tiananmen crisis. Companies pulled out, expatriates fled, joint ventures collapsed, and capital retreated. But then Deng had sallied forth in early 1992, rebuilding the bonfires of growth in Shanghai, Shenzhen, and in the other special economic zones where China had established new manufacturing centers; growth mushroomed, and the hyperbole seemed to have no bounds.

China's growth in the first decade of Deng's reforms had been the almost invisible growth of agricultural markets, but in the 1990s, a new industrial revolution was blossoming. China was catching up to and surging past the rest of Asia, gaining on, though certainly not surpassing, Japan.* Unlike Japan's, China's economy was still a hybrid. Decaying state firms that were married to a centrally planned economy existed alongside the new growth industries and joint ventures. China's new capitalist enterprises included provincial governments, the army, municipalities, and state-owned companies whose managers were looking for strategies to sustain their communities as the old state industries began to collapse under the weight of unpayable debts, bloated workforces, and pensioners.

The hybrid had its own synergism between the public and the private, the new and the old, that no economist could effectively model or fully understand beyond generalizations that it was highly dynamic and that the new parts of China's economy were contributing half or more of the country's total economic output. But the hybrid economy was also cannibalizing and stripping the assets of the old economy, further undermining its ability to pay down the bubble of debt in the state banking system. One Western economist who had surveyed the Chinese economy for over a decade characterized new order as "rampant ad hocism."[1]

Still, compared to the desolation of Mao's time, China's growth in the

---

*At the beginning of the new millennium, Japan's economy is still three to four times that of China.

Deng era was something to behold. Ezra F. Vogel, a Harvard sociologist, wrote that China's success was "staggering."[2] Under Deng's exhortations, China's growth rate headed for a new record, 13 percent in 1992 and again in 1993, and it would stay above 10 percent for another three years.

"The largest other backward economy thus far to grow for several years at a rate close to double digits is South Korea, with a population of 40 million," Vogel wrote. "China's population is roughly thirty times as large."

More importantly, Vogel argued,

> What makes China's success so striking is the contrast to the economic failures of the European countries that abandoned communism. Many westerners, and perhaps Americans above all, were thrilled by the overthrow of the communist regimes of Eastern Europe and the Soviet Union, and repulsed by the survival of the Chinese communist regime after the Tiananmen incident. Yet many knowledgeable Chinese familiar with the recent developments in Eastern Europe are thankful that they live in China. They may not like their Communist Party, but after having seen the results of chaos in their nation over the last 200 years, they are prepared to accept a regime that provides order and allows them to escape poverty and begin to enjoy the benefits of modern industry. Their hope for greater democracy lies in the evolution of totalitarian governments that have undergone economic growth.[3]

China's leaders understood that their country could not become a superpower as that term was defined during the Cold War: a nation that projected its power globally through robust conventional and nuclear forces, using both military and economic power as leverage to expand and protect its interests through international diplomacy and, if necessary, coercion. But Beijing's opening to the world had demonstrated that China was an important regional power with global responsibilities by virtue of its seat among the five permanent members of the UN Security Council, its global trade, and its well-established diplomatic relations beyond Asia in Africa, the Middle East, Europe, and the Americas.

In their internal councils, China's leaders set their sights on joining the middle ranks of developed countries by the middle of the twenty-first century. To do this, they would have to raise the standard of living and nutrition for the hundreds of millions of Chinese who did not live in the booming coastal areas. Specifically, they would have to make formidable investments in electrical power production to electrify the country, in highway and bridge construction to open internal markets, in flood control to prevent rural disasters, and in agriculture to feed the 400 million Chinese who would be added to the country's population by 2025.

In the military realm, China's leaders aimed to gradually modernize the country's armed forces so that it could respond to conflicts on its borders and along its coastline. A key goal would be to protect China's sovereignty over Taiwan, by force if necessary, and to defend China's ambitious claim to the mineral resources of the South China Sea.

Some security analysts in the United States began to see China as a new adversary, a regional "hegemon," that was shopping for aircraft carriers and other "power projection" weapon systems and that might therefore have to be "contained" by an alliance of regional military powers, America and Japan being the most important. The Chinese defense budget began to grow in the 1990s after contracting during much of the 1980s, in part because the country's military leaders were astounded by the displays of American high-tech weaponry during the Persian Gulf War, and they realized that their own armed forces were even more backward and vulnerable than Saddam Hussein's. But China's military seemed to resist a disciplined modernization.

Even for lifelong students of China, that country's long-term development was still impossible to predict, but one thing was certain: China was going to be a player in the global economy and in Asia's security. George Bush had understood this, even if he could not articulate a vision of the future in which America's interests would intertwine with China's on a whole range of global issues. In this vacuum, no consensus existed on the future of U.S.-China relations. The impact of Tiananmen had kicked up a cloud of indignation that still circled the globe, obliterating any clear vision of how the two nations might come back together to manage the urgent issues of trade, security, and development that are likely to bind them in the new century. The massacres also galvanized a coalition of China critics in both political parties on issues that included human rights, religious freedom, and weapons proliferation as well as China's trade surplus with the United States.

Bill Clinton had charged into this breach with a tactical assault on Bush's foreign policy, backed by a group of advisors so disposed against China as to preordain the path to confrontation.

At the Democratic National Convention in New York, Clinton proclaimed a "New Covenant" for "an America that will not coddle tyrants, from Baghdad to Beijing."

That line was a brilliant debunking of the Bush presidency. It had been crafted in the Clinton campaign's war room, a product of Tony Lake's philosophy that the only way to defeat a foreign policy president is to speak out on foreign policy as often as he does and criticize everything that could be construed as a mistake.

Lake, now a college professor who had returned to politics to advise the Clinton campaign, understood that no candidate could win election on foreign policy, but a challenger could lose to a strong foreign policy president if he just rolled over and gave the impression that he didn't have any foreign policy views.[4] Lake had provided Clinton with a ready dose of morality-based criticism—that Bush had been too cozy with Saddam Hussein before the Iraqi dictator overran Kuwait; that Bush was too callous about the carnage in Bosnia, too unconcerned about the plight of Haitians and Somalis, and too paralyzed by China's butchery and repression. This hard-edged campaign rhetoric was not the thoughtful stuff of long-range policymaking. It was tactical moralism in the matrix of deconstructing Bush.

In Beijing, when Ambassador Stapleton Roy heard the "coddling tyrants" line, he had a terrible feeling that—if Clinton got elected—it would become the emblem of a new, confrontational China policy. Lumping Beijing onto the same scale of tyranny with Baghdad was over the top for Roy, and he knew that it would deeply offend the Communist Party leadership. Roy wished that someone with some wisdom in the Clinton camp would tell the candidate that, while it was okay to criticize his opponent's foreign policy, he should consider the consequences. People have to live with what candidates say.

Roy had returned to China in 1991 resigned to conducting a long campaign of post-Tiananmen damage control and rehabilitation. It was going to be a thankless task, and Roy went at it every day, admonishing young political officers that diplomacy, for them, comprised the search for opportunities to bring China out of its defensive coil after Tiananmen and to create incentives for Beijing's leaders to continue the processes of opening their economy to the outside world and of expanding the zones of freedom within Chinese society.[5] He knew that it was going to be a long, hard slog. For Roy, Tiananmen had been like a death in family. The scale of the tragedy was so huge that it would certainly take years, maybe decades, to overcome.

Yet nothing had changed in the great-power equation, Roy believed, only shifted. Whatever strategic weight China had lost as a foil to the Soviet empire in the East, it had gained as a coming economic powerhouse armed with nuclear weapons, as a vote on the United Nations Security Council, and as an influence over North Korea, whose secret nuclear weapons program, which threatened the survival of both South Korea and Japan, was the region's most immediate war risk.

Roy believed in redemption for China after Tiananmen because Deng, the pragmatist from Sichuan, trusted what Mao had never trusted in his own people—their unstoppable industry. Mao had sought to control it, to channel it for revolution; Deng's simple genius was to turn it loose. Roy, having served in Beijing under Leonard Woodcock in 1978, having watched Deng fight his way back to power, could scarcely believe how much China had changed. He could see it not only in the glittering skyscrapers, factories, and hotels that were rising out of the battered hinterlands of major cities but also in the faces and voices of the Chinese people, who were seizing a larger zone of personal freedom to open private businesses and move about the country at will. People were taking their destiny into their own hands. A private economy was sprouting, at first like blades of grass in the cracks of a sidewalk, but then suddenly like a forest whose roots were connected with the capitalists of Hong Kong, Taiwan, and Singapore, and increasingly with the greater Chinese diaspora in Vancouver, Los Angeles, San Francisco, and New York.

Roy compared all this to the devastated China of his youth. Born to missionary parents, Roy grew up during the Japanese occupation. At thirteen, the Communist advance on Nanjing forced the closure of his school, and his parents put him on a U.S. Navy destroyer that took him downriver to Shanghai. From the rooftop of the Shanghai American School, Roy and his classmates saw and felt the explosions of Nationalist army ammo dumps, which the generalissimo's forces blew before fleeing southward. They saw dive bombers screaming down out of the sky to strafe the remnants of Nationalist power.

In the spring of 1950, Roy slipped back into Nanjing to rejoin his parents, who were already living under Communist authority. From the front door of his parent's house, he watched thousands of Communist troops train for the invasion of Taiwan on the athletic fields of Nanjing University. A few months later, Roy turned fifteen and the Korean War broke out. Suddenly, the Communists turned openly hostile toward the handful of Americans hanging on in Nanjing. Roy and his brother were sent unaccompanied by train to Hong Kong for the passage back to America. His parents were placed under house arrest, accused of being "imperialist spies"; his father was convicted in a public trial and expelled in the spring of 1951.

Leaving China was the bittersweet culmination of a great youthful adventure for Roy. Immediately after graduating from Princeton, he joined the foreign service with a determination to make a career in the secular realm of diplomacy, to which he brought a missionary's zeal. The foreign service sent Roy to Moscow, Thailand, and Singapore. Between these assignments, he honed his political skills in Washington as a senior official in the East Asia Bureau, as an intelligence analyst, and as James Baker's executive secretary during the Bush years. But Roy's connection with China was the central element of his life, and when he returned there as ambassador, he found that the basic truths of China had not changed. The Chinese were still a nation of confounding contradictions. They were capable of both terrible brutality and great benevolence. In war and diplomacy alike, they respected power but seldom took a step without knowing what the outcome would be. They clung tenaciously to their principles, and their fierce independence made them seem, at times, very American. Getting the Chinese to change their position could take a long time.

Clinton's "butchers of Beijing" slogan had entered the lexicon of the political debate at a time when Roy was doing everything he could to convince the Chinese leadership to follow Bush's roadmap to recovery—further easing the repression, releasing more dissidents from jail, controlling the export of dangerous weapons from Chinese military companies. In return, Washington would be willing to lift sanctions and increase the flow of technology.

As he watched the campaign, Roy recoiled at what he considered the extreme superficiality of the political debate. He wondered why Clinton seemed so willing to stray into the realm of excessive moralism when the American tradition was to strike a reasonable balance between moralism and national interest. He didn't understand why Bush was unable to articulate for Americans any deeper understanding of China and its transformation from a totalitarian communist state to something that already was more open and constructive. Roy was never surprised by human rights atrocities in China. The country's security system rewarded thuggery, but that would gradually change, too. And while thuggery and brutality offended American moral precepts, that did not change the reality that the United States needed to maintain a stable and constructive relationship with China—especially if Americans wanted China to succeed as a country that shared its goals for peace, prosperity, and stability in Asia. That meant American presidents had to deal with reversals and brutality in China—not by applauding them, but within a relationship that kep the lines of communication open. Within such a relationship, China would realize that the path to economic development was paved by the rule of law and by respect for human rights.

In this sense, Roy defined one pole of the human rights debate. It was really a question of what should come first, of where to place the emphasis: respect for human rights or the imperative of development. Deng had made his position crystal clear in 1979 when he jailed Wei Jingsheng and crushed the Democracy Wall movement. Building the economy—China's modernization—came before everything. After economic development had reached a certain stage, the party and only the party, Deng believed, could then begin experimenting with political reforms.

But there was another point of view that argued that basic human rights cannot be deferred: If governments cannot keep a contract to protect the human rights of their own people, they cannot be trusted to keep contracts in business and trade. Full economic development in any large society is bound to fail without the guarantees of personal liberty, due process, and the rule of law. Deng had equated democracy with the chaos of the Cultural Revolution and the Tiananmen uprising, and his distortion betrayed the fear of all authoritarian rulers: that they would be the first casualty of a people free to choose.

The Helsinki accords of 1975 had spawned the first international human rights movement in history, and it had been instrumental in undermining the communist systems of East Europe and the Soviet Union. By the 1990s, the growth and influence of human rights organizations was a new reality in post–Cold War politics and diplomacy.

In China, however, American diplomacy and the human rights movement operated in a state of natural contention. American leaders, up until Tiananmen, had seen China as a special case—an exception—in part because the Mao era had been so repressive, and Deng, whatever his shortcomings, was so much more tolerant a leader.

For Roy, the first American ambassador in the post-Tiananmen and post–Cold War era, the main diplomatic task was the rehabilitation of U.S.-China relations. That would require an acceptance of China for what it was. Roy could not change Deng's vision or plan for China's modernization; he could only maneuver on the margins, he could only trade day by day and month by month American incentives and concessions for a lessening of the repression and the release of political prisoners. In all of this, the underlying assumption was that Deng was taking the country in the right direction and that the economic revolution was spinning off other benefits that improved the lives of the Chinese people. In this meat grinder, Roy seemed hindered by the human rights movement, whose task was to highlight the repression that still existed in Chinese society, thus causing endless diplomatic tension. There was no agreement on which approach was more correct or effective, and getting the balance right was an unfinished work in American foreign policy.

WINSTON LORD WAS rewarded for his defection from the Bush camp with the job of supervising China policy as assistant secretary of state, confirming Beijing's worst suspicion that the Democratic administration was going to take a hard line on China. Lord's voice had been among the most strident, even emotional, in condemning the Chinese leadership after Tiananmen and in predicting that Deng and the other "butchers" would be swept from power by the rising tide of democracy. As a Republican in a Democratic administration, he brought credibility to the hard-line policy. Few people who had worked with Lord under Kissinger recognized his new evangelism on human rights; some assumed that it was a reflection of Bette Bao Lord's zeal or that Lord was repositioning himself for a new political incarnation.

Roy tried to ease Beijing's anxiety. He had worked closely with Lord in the Reagan and Bush years. Roy had even defended Lord when the Bush White House turned against him over the Fang Lizhi dinner invitation. Lord's post-Tiananmen tirades made Roy as nervous as they made a lot of people, but he was certain that he could work with Lord—that once back in government, Lord would settle down to the practical task.

Roy told Chinese officials that *any* new assistant secretary was going to come on strong on human rights because that was the message that had come out of the campaign and because Clinton had appointed Warren Christopher as secretary of state. Christopher's commitment to a strong human rights policy dated back to the Carter administration, where its foundations had been laid.

Roy also reminded the Chinese that Lord had been involved in China policy from the beginning. He was a Kissinger protégé, so his knowledge and experience would be an asset even if he carried a tougher message on human rights. But Chinese anxieties went far beyond Lord's appointment. The Republicans had been in power for twelve years. A whole new cast of characters was taking control in Washington, many of them openly hostile to China.

As the first post–Cold War president, Clinton ushered in a spring blizzard of policy reforms, but he seemed least prepared—or even disinclined—to step into Bush's shoes as a foreign policy president. His entire political career was that of a southern governor devoted to domestic policy, and it was soon apparent that he would take no personal role in converting the foreign policy messages of his campaign into any coherent new strategy. As soon as he entered the White House, Clinton made clear that his style of governing would be to leave the day-to-day management of foreign policy to the team that had advised him during the campaign—Lake, Christopher, and Les Aspin, the activist congressman from Wisconsin whom Clinton had named secretary of defense.

Clinton did not intend to meet with his foreign policy team frequently, as Bush had. Rather, he preferred that the "principals" and their deputies make recommendations to him. In the Clinton White House, it was soon apparent that nothing would come down from the top to initiate or guide foreign policy development. And getting a decision could take months, during which there would be conspicuous silence from the Oval Office. Most of the so-called policy wonks running the White House did not look beyond the water's edge. When they did, it was through the lens of domestic politics.

The first interagency reviews to formulate foreign policy objectives promoted tough new initiatives on counterproliferation, counterterrorism, and counternarcotics. The Clinton team thus hoped to address the emerging, transnational threats that could harm American interests, and the bureaucracy busied itself filling out this new architecture of national security. For some, China loomed as a "rogue" state that repressed its own people and spread dangerous weapons to unstable parts of the world. Lake had lumped China in with the so-called backlash states, arguing that by hitting China with sanctions for its missile exports, by creating Radio Free Asia, and by threatening to withdraw China's trading privileges over human rights, the Clinton administration intended to "seek a stronger relationship with China that reflects both our values and our interests."[6]

While Americans were absorbed with the presidential campaign, the CIA's Non-Proliferation Center had detected a new surge of Chinese proliferation in late 1992. The center had been set up to funnel raw intelligence from diverse sources to a group of specialists in nuclear, chemical, and biological weapons and the means to deliver them. Satellite images had tracked the shipment of large crates to Pakistan, and the analysts believed that M-11 missiles or missile parts were inside. The shipment, if verified, would prove that China had violated its pledge of November 1991 to Baker not to ship such missiles.* Moreover, if the president determined that there was convincing proof of new missile shipments by China, he was obliged by law to impose sanctions.†

Lord had embraced all the new concerns about China and had campaigned for a high-level policy job by arguing that the best way to get results from China was to get tough.** The Chinese would always cave if you hit them hard, he advised. Senator Jesse Helms, who in the Reagan era had held up Lord's nomination as ambassador to China, this time declared himself enthusiastically in favor of Lord's confirmation because he seemed willing to take all the tough steps against China that Bush had avoided or deferred. Most importantly, Lord was willing to attach strict conditions on the renewal of China's most-favored-nation trade status. Lord had thus aligned himself with the coalition of conservative Republicans and liberal Democrats who were ready to consider tough new sanctions against China if Beijing did not moderate its internal repression, its weapons proliferation, and its trade surplus with the United States, which had reached $20 billion.

---

*The Chinese would later imply that Bush's decision to sell the F-16 to Taiwan, and thus violate American pledges made in the August 1982 communiqué, was grounds for China to violate its pledge to halt missile sales to its ally, Pakistan. Some Chinese officials subsequently tried to link any discussion of Beijing's "proliferation" to Pakistan with Washington's "proliferation" to Taiwan.
†In the fall of 1990, William C. Triplett II of Senator Jesse Helm's staff was behind a successful effort to attach an automatic sanctions amendment to the Defense Authorization Act of 1991. In other circumstances, Bush might have vetoed such a measure, but since the act also carried funding for Operation Desert Storm, it was impossible for the White House to consider a veto without risking a delay in launching the war against Iraq.
**On the day Lord went to the Senate for his confirmation hearing, *The Washington Post* carried a review of Chinese military developments entitled "As China Builds Arsenal and Bases, Asians Fear a Rogue in the Region."

"In recent years, China has opened up to the world," Lord told the senators, "moved toward a market economy, and enjoyed the fastest growth rate in the world."[7] But at the same time, he added, "its leaders cling to an outdated authoritarian system." Americans, Lord said, would never be able to forget Tiananmen Square, and, therefore, the United States would conduct a "nuanced policy" toward Beijing—one that "seeks cooperation on a range of issues" but that would go little further "until a more humane system emerges."

"We need both to condemn repression and preserve links with progressive forces which are the foundations for our longer-term ties," he said.

It was a deeply conflicted prescription, founded on the notion that the Clinton administration could ignore the dominant faction of the Chinese leadership that remained in power under the eighty-eight-year-old Deng. The Lord formula seemed to assume that national leadership could be disaggregated, that Washington could somehow ignore the hard-liners who had all the power in the regime and deal instead with the progressives, who had little or no power.

As soon as Lord was confirmed by the Senate, he sent instructions to Roy to inform the Chinese leadership that the Clinton administration was laying down a set of fourteen principles that would have to be addressed in order for the relationship to get on the right track. These demands covered the whole agenda of human rights, proliferation, and trade, and they were written with the same kind of tough-sounding rhetoric that played well in Congress. Then Lord flew to Beijing to gauge the Chinese reaction, which, predictably, was a blast of anger, indignation, and defiance. No senior leader would meet with him.[8] Foreign Ministry officials warned Lord that any attempt to "impose one's will" on China would fail. Lord said he needed concessions that would help him strike a deal with Congress to avoid placing conditions on the renewal of China's most-favored-nation status. But the Chinese were skeptical and suspicious.

Lord returned to Washington and, with Clinton's blessing and after consultation with Senator George Mitchell, presided over the drafting of a set of human rights conditions that China would have to meet in twelve months or lose its most-favored-nation status. Clinton put the conditions in an executive order and signed it, starting the clock ticking on a twelve-month deadline. China would have to make "overall significant progress" in human rights, allowing the free emigration of dissidents, preventing prison labor exports to America, accounting for political prisoners, and releasing as many such prisoners as possible. If Beijing failed to meet Clinton's standard, catastrophic trade penalties would be imposed, increasing the cost of Chinese products on American shelves by a third or more, thus bankrupting thousands of Chinese factories and devastating many businesses in China and Hong Kong.

As a compromise between Congress and the executive branch, the Lord initiative was a model of cooperation. But it was also absurd, because the two parties making the agreement (Congress and the White House) had no agreement with the party that was expected to perform—China. But more, in their effort to court all sides of the issue, Lord and his legislative allies, including Representative Nancy Pelosi, publicly asserted that no one wanted to see China's most-favored-nation trade privileges revoked. That would cost American consumers billions of dollars, they admitted, because consumers benefited from the inexpensive Chinese-made goods that were filling the shelves of every American retail chain from Wal-Mart to the Gap. The Chinese understood that it was a colossal, unpredictable game of chicken, but it was being played in an era in which both sides considered trade stability an integral part of national security. Looking at what Washington had wrought, the Chinese saw that Clinton had in fact painted himself into a corner, trusting in Lord's assurance that China would cave and thereby show him the way out. But, if anything, the Chinese are endlessly pragmatic, and they respected the power of a new president's mandate, and so they began to consider what minimal steps they might take to avoid the calamity of a trade war.

B Y THE SPRING OF 1993, the United States and China were two ships passing in a fog of recrimination and denunciation. European and Asian countries already were moving toward putting their relations with Beijing back on a stable footing, but Bush's loss to Clinton had reversed the trend to recovery in the United States.

China, at the same time, was in the midst of a profound leadership struggle as well as an economic crisis. Provincial administrations were building luxury hotels, golf courses, racetracks, and condominiums with loans from local government–run banks that had insufficient capital to support them and no collateral against their failure. By early 1993, the speculative bubble had driven inflation over 25 percent in the construction trades, where prices for concrete, steel, and wood products were soaring. At the CIA, analysts were beginning to express concern that the Chinese economy might spiral out of control,[9] but in China, Jiang Zemin, Li Peng, and the rest of the politburo could not rein in the runaway engines of growth without appearing to challenge Deng. Some analysts believed that the collective leadership would let the inflationary crisis build and build until even Deng would see the threat from the superheated bubble. But until that moment, it was risky for any junior leader to challenge the growth crusade.

At least one top leader, Li Peng, seemed to dive for cover. In April, the premier suddenly dropped out of sight. It was first reported that he had a cold, but then his office revealed that he had suffered a mild heart attack. As the leader of the hard-line faction that had opposed many of Deng's reforms, Li was most at risk. For him to stomp on the brakes and bring the economy under control would have looked like a coup of sorts against the Deng line. The convenient illness removed Li from the line of fire.

Now on his own, Jiang Zemin was paralyzed. He was no economist and was otherwise simply unequipped to take action. As a result, he dallied for months before finally turning to Zhu Rongji, the vice premier and former Shanghai mayor. Zhu seized control of the central bank and imposed a punishing, sixteen-point austerity program on the whole country to get inflation under control. He bullied and threatened provincial leaders to cancel speculative projects, and he called in all loans that exceeded the credit limits of the central bank, while reassuring foreigners that their investments and joint ventures were safe. Zhu became an instant hero among international bankers and economic leaders. Someone, they said, was finally in charge in China.

As Zhu grappled with the economy, the Communist Party leadership took bolder steps to lift the country out of its post-Tiananmen isolation, launching a major campaign to host the 2000 Summer Olympics in Beijing. The campaign galvanized the country's youth, diverting them from the aftermath of June 4th. Even student leader Wang Dan, who had been released from prison, urged the International Olympic Committee to anoint Beijing, not because human rights conditions had improved but because holding the summer games in China "would accelerate China's opening to the rest of the world."[10] China's Olympic campaign—like nothing before it—bound the Chinese together at home and abroad in the shared national pride of offering Beijing, the capital of Chinese civilization for thousands of years, as the host city. It lifted the pride of China's youth and deflected their animosity—once directed exclusively at the government—to other targets, particularly the United States. There, many in Congress opposed China's bid. And in some ingenious way that the Chinese leaders may not have intended, the Olympic campaign also gradually created an incentive to reduce the level of repression. In the space of a few months, the authorities released more Tiananmen Square leaders, underground Catholic clerics, and even several leading stalwarts of the Democracy Wall movement.

INSTEAD OF CONNECTING with or even recognizing the extraordinary forces that were churning inside China, the Clinton administration remained a scatter of competing constituencies. The trade constituency was going after both China and Japan for their big trade surpluses and closed markets; the counterproliferation constituency was going after China for the illicit leakage of weapons technology; and the human rights constituency was going after China for its internal repression. In meetings with senior Defense and State Department officials, Lake openly disparaged China as a "discredited human rights violator"[11] that the Clinton administration intended to hold at arms length.

In July, Lynn E. Davis, the undersecretary of state for international security affairs, arrived in Beijing and confronted the Chinese with the inescapable fact that they were facing sanctions.[12] Beijing could either confess that its military industries had shipped M-11 missiles to Pakistan, she said, or face the legally mandated sanctions.

Not only did the Chinese refuse to even discuss what they might or might not have shipped to Pakistan, they told Davis that they would only discuss U.S. concerns about Chinese "proliferation" if the United States was willing to discuss Chinese concerns about American "proliferation" to Taiwan.

Davis replied that Taiwan was not her department. She was trying to carry out a policy to stabilize the arms race in South Asia. The State Department was putting pressure on Russia to end its support for India's Prithvi missile program, and she was trying to do the same to shut down the M-11 program between China and Pakistan. When Davis returned to Washington, shaking her head about Chinese intransigence, she started drawing up sanctions.

And, while these were being drafted, the CIA's Non-Proliferation Center obtained a new piece of intelligence that only threw gasoline onto the flames. A Chinese military company was—at that moment—preparing to ship dangerous chemical agents to Iran. The compounds were key ingredients in the manufacture of chemical weapons. The cargo manifest of the Chinese ship carrying the goods had fallen into the CIA's hands, and Gordon Oehler, the head of the Non-Proliferation Center, told the White House that, for an intelligence professional, it just didn't get any better than this. The manifest was proof.

The container vessel, the *Yinhe* (pronounced Eeen huh), was registered to the China Ocean Shipping Company, China's state-owned shipping monopoly. It was getting ready to sail from a pier at the port of Dalian in northeastern China. The document indicated that the ship was going to deliver a large consignment of thiodiglycol and thionyl chloride to the Iranian port of Bandar Abbas.[13] The first chemical is the base for mustard gas and the second a building block for sarin, the nerve gas.

An "immediate action" cable flashed to the embassy in Beijing instructing Roy to inform the Chinese at a high level of the intelligence report and to ask for an investigation and clarification. When Roy got to the Foreign Ministry on July 23, the *Yinhe* was already en route to its first stop in Singapore, and the Chinese were still seething over Lynn Davis's "threat" to impose sanctions if China did not come clean on the missile transfers to Pakistan. A senior official told Roy that he would look into the *Yinhe* allegation, denying as usual that China engaged in proliferation.

In Washington, pressure mounted to act. The ship stopped in Singapore, and the CIA station chief there confirmed that no chemical containers had been off-loaded. They were still on the ship, which soon was on its way across the Indian Ocean toward the Arabian Sea.

In late July, Lake called the president's national security advisers to the White House, and they unanimously agreed that Washington should show its resolve. They recommended that the president approve an aggressive program of naval surveillance combined with urgent diplomatic demands that the ship be subjected to search. General Colin Powell, the chairman of the Joint Chiefs of Staff, relayed the "execute" orders from the president to the Seventh Fleet, and a contingent of warships converged on the *Yinhe*, stalking the Chinese vessel and its suspect cargo.*

On August 4, Roy was summoned back to the Foreign Ministry, where Assistant Foreign Minister Qin Huasun told him that the Chinese government had thoroughly investigated the allegation that the *Yinhe* was carrying illicit chemical agents to Iran and had determined that no such chemicals were on the ship.

Roy's cable relaying the Chinese denial was hooted down by the CIA. The rest of the bureaucracy followed suit. The common refrain was that the Chinese always lied about proliferation. The Pacific Fleet continued to bear down on the ship.

Roy was instructed to return to the Chinese and demand that the ship heave to for a search. The Chinese got their backs up further but agreed in principle to a search by a neutral authority. Roy could see the collision coming.

In Washington, a few voices in the bureaucracy made the point that the United States was risking a full-blown confrontation with China over a single piece of evidence, a manifest. Couldn't the CIA come up with some confirmation? After all, a manifest was just a list of cargoes that were scheduled

---

*As in the case of U.S. counternarcotics strategy, the Pentagon's lawyers had drafted legal arguments to support boarding non-U.S. vessels on the high seas to protect American interests, since American forces in the Persian Gulf, it could be argued, might become the target of Iranian chemical weapons. But there were powerful counterarguments, most prominently the consequences for state-to-state relations, since such boarding could constitute an act of war.

to be loaded before a sailing date. Hadn't anyone at the CIA ever ordered something in the mail that didn't arrive? But the Non-Proliferation Center was adamant. The manifest *was* the confirmation.

The Chinese leadership decided to go public on August 8, accusing the United States of harassing its cargo vessel.[14]

"The ship was forced to be adrift on the high seas, subject to such extraordinary activities of interruption and coercion, including the pursuit and photography by U.S. warships and military aircraft on the high seas," the statement read.

The official Chinese news agency attacked the "utterly unjustifiable bullying" by the United States. Qin Huasun said publicly that despite Chinese reassurances about the *Yinhe*'s cargo, the United states "chose to cling to its unfounded information in an attempt to sow discord in the friendly relations between China and other countries concerned."

As soon as the Chinese went public with these statements, Roy knew that the chemicals were not on the ship. Washington had allowed itself to be stampeded by the CIA. But now that the confrontation was out in the open, attitudes hardened on both sides. The U.S. Navy tracked the vessel day by day as Roy received instructions to negotiate the details of an inspection.

On August 18, Roy accompanied a congressional delegation headed by Senator Chuck Robb of Virginia to the Great Hall for what was to be a routine courtesy call on President Jiang Zemin. During the session, Jiang made a point of speaking directly to Roy about the *Yinhe* crisis.

"I have personally looked into this matter," Jiang said, adding that he was sure that there were no chemicals on the ship. He wanted the American ambassador to know that the controversy had reached the top level. He was speaking as the President of China. There were no chemicals on the ship.

Roy instinctively believed him. No president of China would put his own prestige on the line unless he was sure. But more importantly for Roy, once Jiang had spoken, the American response would speak volumes. The Chinese were now testing the new administration by asking what kind of relationship Clinton wanted with China. Did he want a relationship in which Washington assumed that no Chinese leader could be trusted to speak the truth? Did he want confrontation?

Roy warned Washington that, in his opinion, Jiang's statement meant that the chemicals were likely not on the ship, and therefore Washington had better tone down its rhetoric. But Roy's arguments were dismissed. The CIA denigrated Jiang's assurances, arguing that the Chinese president was not reliable and that Roy had acquired no information through clandestine channels to back up his statement, whereas the CIA still had a high degree of confidence in its own assessment. It had the manifest. Roy had nothing.

The White House was beyond the point of no return and feared a blow-back from Congress if it failed to force an inspection of the Chinese ship. If the *Yinhe* landed at Bandar Abbas and a satellite spotted the chemicals being off-loaded, there would be hell to pay because the news would surely leak and Clinton would be savaged for allowing the butchers of Beijing to sucker him. Lake's attitude was that Clinton could not afford *not* to go ahead. He had to go after the ship.

Some intelligence professionals worried that the CIA's Non-Proliferation Center had injected itself too deeply into policymaking by using "hot" intelligence items to stampede the bureaucracy. There was too much focus on generating "actionable intelligence"—the tendency of a CIA analyst to evaluate the quality of intelligence information on the basis of whether policymakers would take action on it. In addition, some of the center's officers were advocating specific courses of action in interagency meetings, saying that China had to be disciplined or that it was violating treaties. It was not the CIA's role to advocate policy—only to gather facts and to present them, neutrally, to policymakers.*

In the middle of the *Yinhe* crisis, Clinton announced that he was imposing sanctions on China over the suspected transfer of M-11 missiles or missile parts to Pakistan.[15] The decision was driven by counterproliferation bureaucrats implementing an automatic legislative mandate to act on the evidence of proliferation. The sanctions froze $1 billion in high-technology sales from American aerospace and computer corporations to Chinese firms.

At the end of August, Saudi Arabia offered to host an inspection of the *Yinhe*, and China agreed, provided no Americans boarded the ship. The CIA flew its experts to Saudi Arabia to supervise the inspection. And after a week of searching every container on the ship's deck and in its hold, the exercise proved to everyone's satisfaction that no chemicals were onboard.[16]

The Chinese declared victory. The vaunted instruments of U.S. intelligence had lied, they said. Beijing launched a propaganda campaign, demanding compensation for the harassment of the *Yinhe* and its crew. Qian Qichen, speaking at the annual session of the UN General Assembly, attacked "the hegemonic conduct of a self-styled world cop who tramples on international law and norms of international relations."[17]

In Washington, Lake, Christopher, and Aspin were furious at the CIA. In-

---

*The intelligence community was still divided on the question of China's evolving attitudes regarding proliferation. In less than a decade, China's leaders had gone from believing that the more nuclear weapons states there were, the better, to rethinking the consequences of proliferation. China had joined the International Atomic Energy Agency and, in 1992, signed the Nuclear Non-Proliferation Treaty. In the 1990s, China's proliferation of weapons and technology had greatly diminished, and when it still occurred it was more difficult to determine who was behind it, whether the top leaders or individual organizations within the military desperate to find new markets.

stead of acknowledging the error, the Non-Proliferation Center spread the story that the Chinese had somehow dumped the chemicals along the way, as if a container ship could have accomplished such a feat while under intensive surveillance. When the CIA was forced to submit to an official after-action inquiry, the flaws in its agents' analytical judgments emerged. The Non-Proliferation Center had placed too much stock in the manifest. The chemicals probably never got on the ship.

The fiasco mobilized a political reaction. Alexander Haig, in Beijing that fall to introduce the new president of United Technologies Corporation to the Chinese leadership, scalded Clinton's approach to China.[18]

"How dare we go around telling the rest of the world" that it must live up to American standards on human rights? "I think the time has come to take a different tack here. And Tiananmen is a long way behind us."[19]

Kenneth Lieberthal, a China scholar at the University of Michigan, declared more pointedly than anyone yet had, "The United States should stop punishing China for the massacre of demonstrators in Tiananmen Square in 1989. China is too important to make this the pivot of our policy."[20]

Lake and Lord decided to conduct a snap policy review in September. Unwilling to make any fundamental adjustments, they did agree that the administration had better get the lines of communication open. They set up a series of cabinet-level and subcabinet-level visits to China and nailed down arrangements for a presidential meeting between Clinton and Jiang during the November summit of Asia-Pacific leaders in Seattle. The Pentagon was allowed to open military-to-military contacts for the first time since 1989.[21] Lord called the whole shift a process of "enhanced engagement."

On September 25, Lake called the Chinese ambassador, Li Daoyu, to the White House and told him that it was time both sides tried to reverse the downward spiral. Lake described how the White House already was looking for a way to waive part or all of the sanctions that had just been imposed on high-tech sales.[22] And Clinton wanted to meet with Jiang Zemin.

But the larger collision on human rights still loomed.

Christopher held to the tough line that Clinton would pull down the temple at the twelve-month deadline for human rights compliance. Meeting with senior business executives at the State Department on October 20, the secretary of state seemed almost fatalistic. "I have to say, I don't believe we can sustain the position beyond next June unless we see continued improvement, improvements in the human rights field by the Chinese, as well as reforms in connection with trade practices and progress in the non-proliferation front."[23] Separately, John Shattuck, the assistant secretary for human rights, warned Chinese officials that time was running out.

Clinton and Jiang met face-to-face for the first time in Seattle. Clinton came away appalled by the stiff and sterile encounter. During their meeting, Jiang had read from note cards and refused Clinton's efforts to draw him into a more freewheeling conversation about human rights and other issues of common concern. Jiang treated Clinton to a fifteen-minute monologue on the importance of noninterference in the affairs of other countries.[24] He never left his script. The two men might as well have exchanged diplomatic texts.

Nevertheless, the two sides took pains to reduce the level of tension. Just before the summit, China had announced that for the first time ever it would give "positive consideration" to inviting a delegation from the International Committee of the Red Cross to discuss humanitarian visits to political prisoners.[25] And in his meeting with Jiang, Clinton tried to induce further Chinese concessions by approving the sale of an $8 million Cray supercomputer for use in Beijing's weather forecasting. These increments showed that Washington and Beijing were interested in heading off a train wreck. But the climate of suspicion remained pervasive, with both leaders seeming to cower before powerful domestic constituencies.

At the end of Clinton's first year in office, American China policy was still in the hands of Lord, but almost no one in the administration was satisfied. Lord was leading Christopher and the White House toward the precipice of total breakdown on the basis of his inner confidence that the Chinese would buckle under U.S. pressure. During the fall and winter of 1993, Lord called large meetings of his China steering committee, and he would express surprise that it was difficult to reach a consensus among thirty-five participants. Lord showed great skill in laying out a variety of options, but in the face of warring constituencies, he often pronounced himself "agnostic" about what course of action to press on the White House.

Most human rights partisans in the administration wanted to use the annual most-favored-nation renewal as permanent leverage over Beijing, setting conditions year after year under threat of revocation and higher tariffs. Others wanted the president to break the link between human rights and trade if China made good progress on issues that were clearly defined.

In Beijing, Roy could get no guidance from Washington as to what steps, exactly, the Clinton administration wanted China to take to meet the "overall, significant progress" standard. And there was no commitment on what Clinton would do if China took such specific steps. Without goalposts, China would not play, Roy believed. He argued in cables back to Christopher and Lord that the only way the administration was going to get progress with China was to enter a bargaining process, which meant putting something on the table. Roy favored making a commitment to break the link between human rights and trade if Beijing made sufficient progress in human rights compliance that year. Otherwise, Clinton had no card to play short of a potentially catastrophic trade war.

But Christopher and Lord refused to enter any bargaining process with Beijing. Both feared that the human rights community would attack them for making concessions or for setting terms that might look like a compromise of human rights principles. They preferred to stand at a distance, refusing to say how much progress would constitute "overall significant progress." It was going to be like pornography—they would know it when they saw it.

At the end of the year, the *New York Times* correspondent in China* requested that Roy give an on-the-record interview to address the question of how much or how little progress China had made so far on human rights, given that there was less than six months to go. Sitting in a reception alcove at the ambassador's residence, Roy laid out the arguments he had been making privately. He talked about the transformation that was under way in China and how important it was.[26] "If you look at the 150 years since the Opium Wars, then you can't avoid the conclusion that the last 15 years are the best 15 years in China's modern history," he said, "and of those 15 years, the last 2 years are the best in terms of prosperity, individual choice, access to outside sources of information, freedom of movement within the country, and stable domestic conditions."[27]

Roy refused to predict whether China would satisfy the standard of "overall, significant progress" on human rights. "I can't answer those questions, because the Administration is going to have to define what it views as significant progress."

It was true there were continuing abuses of human rights in China, Roy said, but he maintained that the dramatic changes under way in Chinese society ought to be taken into account in any evaluation of China's progress.

The interview set off a storm within the administration. Roy seemed to be saying that human rights conditions in China had dramatically improved, whereas Christopher's position was that there had been scant progress. Shattuck and his deputies in the human rights bureau privately attacked Roy, saying that the administration could not have its ambassador in Beijing undercutting policy. Christopher was angry; Roy's comments would only encourage the "business" side of the administration—Commerce, Treasury, and the National Economic Council—to break ranks. Peter Tarnoff, the undersecretary for political affairs, got Roy on the phone. Washington wanted a transcript of the interview. There was going to be a review.

As this review got under way, Roy accompanied a congressional delegation to a meeting with Li Peng, who startled the ambassador by telling the

---

*The author.

group, "If you want to know about human rights in China, talk to the American ambassador, he can tell you what it is about."

Roy was deeply embarrassed. Li was using him to excuse China's repression. Roy sent a full transcript of the conversation back to Washington and waited. Christopher also saw what Li Peng was doing and asked Tarnoff and Lord whether they ought to recall Roy. How could they stand by while Li Peng turned the American ambassador's statements into an endorsement of Beijing's human rights record?

But no one wanted to put Roy through the humiliation. He was respected in the department, and calling him home would just draw more attention to the story. Roy had already received dozens of congratulatory messages from all over the world—including from Clinton cabinet secretaries—applauding him for giving a more balanced view of China. But in their own comments to the press in Washington, the human rights bureau kept up the attack on the ambassador's loyalty. After nearly a week of twisting in the wind, the State Department spokesman was still telling reporters that Roy was under investigation. An angry Roy telephoned Lord.

"Win, you either have the department spokesman endorse me or take me out of here." Roy and Lord had had hundreds of long-distance phone conversations over the years, but Lord had never heard as much intensity from the diplomat as he was now hearing.

"You have my transcript," Roy continued. "You know exactly what I said. If you are not prepared to endorse me, get me out of here because I will not defend the administration's policy if the administration leaves me dangling like this."[28]

The next day, the department spokesman expressed full confidence in America's ambassador in Beijing. But Christopher was not going to let that be the last word. He let two weeks pass before repudiating Roy's views, without mentioning the ambassador by name.

"I would say, from our standpoint, the progress they've made on their economy, while laudable, does not excuse the failure to make progress on the human rights record," Christopher said in a January 16 television appearance. "A number of people have said, 'Look, they're doing so well on the economy, you ought to forget about the human rights record.' That's not my position. It's not the president's position."[29]

But even as Christopher fought to ensure that the administration spoke with one voice on China, there were major defections. At a breakfast meeting with journalists on January 29, Robert E. Rubin, the chairman of the National Economic Council and one of Clinton's closest advisers, said that he would like to see the administration end the link between trade and human rights. "There is no question that absent some unexpected event, China will be the largest economy in the world not too far into the next century," he said, "it is imperative that we have an economic relationship with it."[30]

Also striking was China's pragmatism, on the one hand taking a tough stand against American interference but on the other trying to make incremental moves on human rights that would signal its desire to accommodate Clinton without appearing to surrender. To every American delegation that came to China that winter, Jiang Zemin said that China was "going to make an effort" to meet Clinton's concerns. And, in January, China hosted its first-ever meeting with representatives of the International Committee of the Red Cross to discuss whether it might be possible for Red Cross workers to visit the thousands of political detainees languishing in Chinese prisons.

Also in January, Treasury secretary Lloyd Bentsen arrived in Beijing to revive the long-dormant "joint economic commission" that had been established during the Carter administration to promote trade and investment in China. The Bentsen trip was another vehicle to convey the message that Clinton wanted to get past the May deadline to a new era of relations, but could only do so by showing that China had made real progress on human rights.

House Democratic majority leader Dick Gephardt followed up with a large delegation from Congress to reinforce the same message. Clinton was serious in his threat to revoke most-favored-nation status, and Congress would back him up.

In a gesture to Bentsen, the Chinese signed a memorandum of understanding allowing U.S. customs officers to investigate reports of prison labor used in the manufacture of Chinese goods exported to the United States. The agreement was a key requirement of Clinton's executive order.

But the surface unity of the Clinton administration was a mirage. Back in Washington, Rubin; Commerce secretary Ronald H. Brown; Bentsen's undersecretary, Lawrence S. Summers; and W. Bowman Carter, the deputy assistant to the president for economic policy, had begun a quiet campaign to undermine the State Department's narrow focus on human rights. They were among those who had privately cheered Roy's public comments to *The New York Times* that China's economic revolution had to be taken into account in evaluating the country's human rights progress.

They had important allies. Major corporations—many of them contributors to the Clinton campaign—had huge interests in Asia, especially China, and believed that the revocation of China's most-favored-nation status would be a disaster for both the Asian and the American economy. George Bush and Brent Scowcroft also traveled to Beijing in January 1994 and gave an extensive private presentation to the Chinese leadership on the politics of the

Clinton administration—an analysis that inescapably would have conveyed to the Chinese that both Congress and the administration were divided.

With Deng's health fading, the Chinese leadership was also split.

On February 9, Deng appeared on national television during the Chinese New Year's ceremony in Shanghai, and the footage showed his dramatic physical decline. He had to be propped up on both sides by his daughters. His gaze was blank and insentient. Family members whispered to American friends that he was suffering from advanced Parkinson's disease.

The U.S. intelligence community sounded an alarm that Deng might not be strong enough to impose order on the leadership in Beijing or to force through the concessions necessary for Clinton to renew China's trade privileges. Jiang Zemin certainly would not be able to force a consensus and could take few risks with Deng's health in such a perilous state. In this volatile political climate, North Korea's persistent drive to complete its secret nuclear weapons complex was building toward a military crisis, in which Clinton would have to consider a preemptive military strike to knock the facility out. China might be the only power in the region capable of bringing the reclusive and fanatical North Korean leaders back from the brink.

These factors weighed heavily on Christopher's decision to make his first visit to Beijing. And they also contributed to Christopher's realization that the only way he could induce China to make the needed concessions was to offer the possibility that Washington would then break the link between trade and human rights.

Other pressures were building that neither side seemed able to control.

Wei Jingsheng, the fiery Democracy Wall leader, out of jail after fourteen years, was conducting a one-man free speech movement, galvanizing the tattered ranks of China's dissident community. His bold testing of the government's limits was inciting others to speak out. For Wei, Clinton's May deadline for human rights progress represented real leverage to force the release of more political prisoners.

In February, Wei sent a secret emissary to meet with an American diplomat[31] and arrange a meeting with John Shattuck, who was due in Beijing at the end of the month to continue the campaign for human rights improvements. Roy had to make the decision whether he would let the embassy get involved in arranging a clandestine rendezvous that—if discovered—would enrage the Chinese. It was political dynamite, but given the influence of the human rights bureau within the Clinton State Department, Roy suppressed his instinct to challenge the wisdom of the meeting. The odds of heading off an assistant secretary were slim, anyway.

Shattuck was oblivious to how his meeting might disrupt Christopher's trip, which was just ten days away, and he made no attempt to clear his plans with the secretary. He didn't think that anyone could criticize him for meeting Chinese dissidents and thus upholding the administration's commitment to the struggle for freedom of expression in China.

With admirable stealth, Shattuck and Wei evaded Chinese detection. The two men openly sat down in the lobby of one of Beijing's most prominent hotels for a searching conversation. The plainclothes secret police assigned to keep Shattuck under constant surveillance did not recognize Wei. And the squad of secret police assigned to Wei failed to recognize Shattuck. And so the meeting proceeded unmolested under the gaze of up to a dozen state security officers hovering nearby.

Shattuck was deeply impressed by Wei, whose nearly fifteen years of suffering in prison had drawn comparisons to South Africa's Nelson Mandela. For Shattuck, the clandestine meeting was an expression of American solidarity with China's democratic underground, and he accepted Wei's message to Clinton: Sustained pressure is the only strategy that leads to the release of political prisoners in China.

The meeting had taken place on the day of Shattuck's arrival. He then conducted a full two days of public consultations with the Chinese. But his meeting with Wei was not destined to stay secret. Wei's secretary telephoned *The New York Times* and recounted Wei's message to Clinton. The Chinese learned of the meeting the next day when Liu Huaqiu, the vice foreign minister, was briefing Western reporters on an unrelated matter. He was asked about China's reaction to the meeting.

"I did not know that Wei Jingsheng had met with John Shattuck!" he said.

Roy was summoned to the Foreign Ministry, where explanations were demanded. Shattuck's meeting was seized upon by hard-liners as evidence that the United States was not as interested in engaging Beijing in a new dialogue as it was in encouraging the overthrow of Communist Party rule by consorting with the dissident underground, personified by Wei. After all, Wei had publicly stated that the Communist regime was irredeemable, like an "old wolf" that never tired of devouring the people.[32]

Of course, Shattuck had not been fomenting insurrection. If anything, he merely wished to sample a wide variety of government and nongovernment views during his trip. If he had formally requested a meeting with Wei, the Chinese leadership would have refused him. His deception was a modest one, although most certainly self-interested and in furtherance of the moral crusade that Jimmy Carter had institutionalized by creating a State Department bureau dedicated to becoming a bully pulpit for human rights. To the Chinese regime, Wei was a criminal, released from prison on terms that precluded any political activity on his part. Shattuck, in their view, had suborned

Wei to violate his parole, and the incident poisoned the atmosphere as Christopher prepared to make his entrance into China.

Even without the Shattuck uproar, Christopher's timing was terrible. He was to arrive just as the party was convening the annual session of the National People's Congress. The leadership would be distracted by the huge gathering of party leaders from across the country. Security would be tight. Dissidents would be rounded up or placed under house arrest, and that would put Christopher under greater pressure from Congress to extract concessions.

True to form, the Chinese security services arrested Wei Jingsheng on March 4, prompting both Clinton and Christopher to make public statements deploring the act.*

Four days later, as Christopher made his way toward Asia, there were more arrests in Shanghai and Beijing. Panicked by Lord and his other senior aides, Christopher telephoned key members of Congress, including Mitchell and Pelosi, seeking their advice on whether he should cancel his trip.

In Hawaii, Christopher said publicly, "It would be hard to overstate the strong distaste that we all feel over the recent detentions and the hostile measures taken by the Chinese. Certainly these actions will have a negative effect on my trip to China as well as on the subsequent review within the United States of the favored nation trade question."[33]

Christopher's public warnings escalated. He expressed hope that "China will not force us" to revoke most-favored-nation status, and, from Canberra, Australia, he said, "I'm concerned that China seems to be going in the wrong direction."[34]

The tension in China and on Christopher's plane was palpable, and when he landed in Beijing on March 11, it was as if he was coming ashore at Omaha Beach. Li Peng unleashed a torrent of invective against American interference in China's internal politics that was so ferocious that the Americans wondered whether they ought to get up and walk out of the room. Li assailed American sanctimony over human rights, claiming that the Los Angeles riots of 1991 showed that human rights conditions in America were worse than in China.[35] Who was America to preach and make demands? he asked. Li violently jabbed and slashed with his hands; he pounded the arm of his chair. China, he said, was fully prepared for Clinton to revoke Beijing's most-favored-nation privileges. America would suffer, too. China would not accept

---

*Wei was released within days, but forced to leave Beijing while Christopher was in the country. When Wei tried to return to the capital on April 1, he was arrested by seven carloads of secret police; he then disappeared for a year before being charged with plotting to overthrow the state and sentenced to another thirteen years in prison. He was effectively exiled in November 1997 when he was released on medical parole on the condition that he leave the country.

pressure. And, personalizing his attack, Li said that it had taken men like Nixon and Kissinger to have the vision to open relations with China, but Clinton and Christopher had no such vision. They would be blamed for "losing" China.*

Frank G. Wisner, the Pentagon's undersecretary for policy, who was accompanying Christopher, was awestruck by Li's performance. Wisner simply could not fathom why the Chinese would treat the American secretary of state to such a humiliating reception. After they had filed out of the Great Hall, Wisner told his colleagues that it was the worst diplomatic meeting he had attended in thirty years as a foreign service officer.

Christopher sent an initial reporting cable to Clinton saying that his reception was "rough, somber, sometimes bordering on the insolent." The artillery had been so heavy that he might have to consider cutting his trip short.[36]

But, like at Normandy, getting onto the beach was the worst part of the battle. Jiang Zemin welcomed Christopher the next day with his customary affability and abstraction. The Chinese president dismissed the fireworks, saying: "In order to become friends, we have to clash."

Turning to Clinton's demand that China make great progress in human rights compliance in a twelve-month period, Jiang said, "You can't become a fat man with one big meal."[37] He meant: The Chinese must proceed step-by-step toward human rights reform, and no amount of force-feeding could speed up the process. As ever, Jiang was up in the clouds, exuding a goodwill that conveyed China's desire to find a solution.

On the final day of the visit, Roy accompanied Christopher and Lord to the Foreign Ministry, where Qian Qichen offered the first real concessions the Americans had heard.

China, he said, would agree to release Wang Juntao, sentenced in 1991 to thirteen years in prison for his role as one of the "black hands" behind the Tiananmen uprising. At the same time, Qian said that China would begin discussing in detail the Red Cross's interest in getting access to Chinese prisons. And he agreed to a meeting of technical experts to discuss allegations that China was jamming broadcasts of the Voice of America.

These concessions offered on the last day of Christopher's visit were significant. They might not be enough to provide Clinton with the cover he needed to abandon the destructive policy his administration had undertaken,

---

*It is likely that Li Peng invoked the "losing China" argument because he understood how powerful it was in American domestic politics. After so many years of dealing with American officeholders, and then having them return to China after their terms of office as highly paid consultants, Chinese leaders had learned many of the American pressure points.

but there were still two months to go before the president had to make that decision.

Roy was hopeful, and that's why it was so disturbing to see Christopher intent on declaring failure, as if he were following some script that destined his trip to be a political disaster. There was something almost fatalistic about Christopher and his trip to China; perhaps he was reliving that terrifying journey to Taiwan in 1978, when the crowd had pummeled his car and given him what he later told friends was a near-death experience.

In any case, his return to Washington was funereal. Christopher's attempt to condition most-favored-nation renewal as a means of winning fundamental changes in human rights practices in China was finished. The president was reported to be upset. Rubin and the other economic advisers blamed Christopher's unskillful megaphone diplomacy, charging as he did across the Pacific and wagging his finger at the Chinese from every stop. Three former secretaries of state—Kissinger, Eagleburger, and Vance—pronounced the Christopher-Lord policy to be a failure at a Council on Foreign Relations forum, with Vance saying that the United States "should not make one interest determinative" in the relationship.[38]

On March 17, three days after he returned to Washington, Christopher found that attitudes in Congress had also shifted. Representative Jim Kolbe, an Arizona Republican, likened the Clinton policy to "a train headed for a cliff and I don't see that the brakes have been turned on." He wanted to know whether Christopher agreed with his assessment that the administration's "failure to resolve this, to engage the third-largest economy in the world, would be absolutely devastating."

Christopher was too much the gentleman to show anger. But in times of stress, his face went to war with itself, reflecting his inner turmoil. His craggy features would tense and contort around pursed lips and a creased brow. He would fix his gaze at some middle distance, and, as he spoke, his head would rock and tilt as if his gyros were beginning to wobble. The overall impression was of a straining to control a wicked psychic shimmy.

"I felt good about being in China, carrying out the president's policy and carrying out a policy that was overwhelmingly supported here in Congress," he replied to his critics. But Christopher was defending a doomed notion.

One of his aides was sure that the "radio silence" from the White House meant that the president was deliberately letting Christopher twist in the wind; this was Clinton's way of conveying his desire that the secretary take the fall and recommend abandoning the policy. Rubin and Bentsen were privately advising the president to abandon the human rights–trade linkage as they publicly disparaged the narrow focus of a human rights–based policy.

Clinton's only public comments were that China was a huge and important country and that the United States could not afford to isolate it. Then he would say he was waiting for Christopher's recommendation.

Seeing the open revolt, Christopher called a "principals" meeting in the Roosevelt Room of the White House in late March. Lake sat beside Christopher, but the secretary spoke, addressing Bentsen, Rubin, and the others.

"We can't have an Administration at war in the newspapers,"[39] he told them.

He admitted that the policy was a failure. They were not going to make it to the mileposts defined by the executive order before the deadline.

"I know in the end where we are going to end up, but we have to do it honestly," he said. That meant no disingenuous claims that the standard of "overall, significant progress" had been met. And revoking China's most-favored-nation privileges was not acceptable as a solution. Showing as much anger as he ever had, the secretary told them that he did not want to be undermined while he prepared his recommendation.

After the meeting in the Roosevelt Room, it was an open secret in the administration that Clinton was going to dump the policy that so epitomized the moralism of his campaign. The only question was how to manage it. Lord, still a captive of the congressional constituencies he had courted, floated trial balloons suggesting that Clinton revoke *some* Chinese trade privileges, for instance targeting military firms and state-owned factories. But Lord had by now lost all credibility in the White House. Indeed, the State Department's stock was so low that Lake, without even consulting Christopher and Lord, set up a committee chaired by Sandy Berger, the deputy national security adviser, to map out how the White House would break the linkage. The committee members were drawn exclusively from the economic agencies.

As each day passed, China seemed more confident that the tide in Washington was turning in its favor. A week after Christopher's visit, Qian Qichen met with Howell Raines, the editorial page editor of *The New York Times*, and raised in public the notion that Clinton was "losing" China.

"For 23 years before President Nixon opened the door of relations between China and the United States, there was no trade whatsoever between China and the United States," Qian said. Then he added dryly, "I think you lived quite well. And so did we."[40]

Christopher decided that if he was going to recommend abandonment, he should try to squeeze another 5 percent out of the Chinese. He telephoned Michael Armacost, the former deputy secretary of state and veteran Asia hand in both Democratic and Republican administrations, and asked him if he would undertake a secret mission to Beijing to press Jiang for a little more.

Armacost was a man of measured words, and in his no-nonsense baritone he told Christopher that he was not inclined to help unless there was a consensus that the human rights linkage was going to be jettisoned. He was soon satisfied. Lake and Berger told him that the policy was already dead, and the only question was how to bury the corpse. Armacost wanted to see the president before leaving for Beijing, because that would allow him to speak with greater authority in seeking last-minute concessions. And so, on May 6, Armacost walked into the West Wing of the White House, where Berger intercepted him, and together they entered the Oval Office. There, they encountered a strange sight. A half dozen people hovered around Clinton's desk, all reading from documents and carrying on an intense conversation in lowered tones. Armacost thought that perhaps they were Asian experts come to attend his session, but he recognized none of them, which only added to his confusion.

Clinton looked across the room, distractedly taking note of the arrival of his secret envoy to China. Berger held Armacost near the doorway. The group of men around Clinton's desk made no move to disperse. Armacost was puzzled. He had envisioned fifteen to twenty minutes of serious conversation about China. Now, it seemed, he would not be invited to even sit down.

After the embarrassing interlude, Clinton strode over to Armacost and locked onto his envoy with a handshake and a focused expression of interest. The president said he really wanted to get his China policy straightened out and was grateful to Armacost for undertaking such an important mission on short notice. Just that afternoon, Clinton had said publicly in a television interview, "If we were to withdraw the most-favored-nation status from China, it would undermine what I hope to see in terms of our relationship."

In a few minutes it was over, and Armacost was out the door guided by Berger back down the hall toward the exit.

"What was that all about?" Armacost asked.

"You'll find out soon enough," Berger replied.

The next morning, as Armacost prepared to fly to Beijing, the newspapers answered his question. In Little Rock, Arkansas, a former state employee named Paula Corbin Jones had filed a lawsuit against the president. She alleged that while he was still governor in 1991, he had summoned her to a meeting in a Little Rock hotel room and exposed himself to her.

ON APRIL 23, China released Wang Juntao from prison and sent him into exile in the United States. On May 13, just after Armacost returned from China believing that his mission had garnered little besides more heated rhetoric, Chen Ziming was released to his home in Beijing. These two political prisoners were perhaps the most high-profile detainees being held in China under long prison terms. For Roy, and for other China specialists, the release of these so-called black hands of Tiananmen was a significant victory. China also cleared the decks of immigration cases, allowing dissidents who had previously been denied permission to leave the country to go.

Yu Haocheng, a cheery and bespectacled essayist who had championed the rule of law over the party, was informed that he would be allowed to leave so he could attend Columbia University. And Chai Ling, the Tiananmen student leader, received word that her father would be able to travel to America. For Roy, these were important steps that raised the question whether the administration was rushing too quickly to declare failure. The ambassador began to argue that the administration could jettison its hard line on human rights by declaring partial success, thereby extending some credit to Beijing for the steps it had taken.

But Clinton already had pulled the plug by turning the issue over to his economic advisers. On May 27, he declared that the policy of linking China's human rights performance to the annual renewal of its most-favored-nation trade privileges was over.

China had made progress in "important areas," Clinton allowed, but it was not enough to claim that the policy had succeeded. And, though China had failed to meet the standard of his executive order, he was not willing to launch a catastrophic trade war, because that was not the best way to build a long-term relationship with China.

In a nod to the human rights community, Clinton said that, due to China's continuing and "very serious human rights abuses," he was extending the sanctions imposed after the 1989 Tiananmen massacres and increasing support for the Voice of America and Radio Free Asia to further promote the ideals of human rights and democracy among the Chinese people.

Breaking the post-Tiananmen knot was a milestone in American foreign policy, and Clinton never looked back, another indication of how tactical his moralism during the campaign had been.

Commerce, Treasury, and other business-oriented departments and agencies rejoiced that their vision of American priorities in Asia had prevailed. And a newly strengthened centrist coalition in Congress was determined to measure the totality of American interests in China, even if that meant that political prisoners would continue to be imprisoned.

At the end of the summer, Nancy Pelosi attempted a show of strength in the House of Representatives by introducing legislation to place steep tariffs on Chinese exports from military factories. It failed 270–158, a sign of how much the political landscape had shifted.

Inside the State Department, Lord wrote a self-serving memo to Christopher suggesting that the administration's Asia policy had led to a state of confrontation that was driving Japan and China closer together. It was rumored that Kissinger had taken Lord "to the woodshed" to make just this point. Lord distributed the memo widely, reading it aloud at academic meetings, until it leaked to the press. Many of his contemporaries took the implied criticism of Christopher's management of foreign policy as another reflection of Lord's ever-shifting loyalties.

The Chinese showed no public elation at their victory. America, in their view, had simply and finally come to its senses. They even chastised Clinton for failing to drop the remaining Tiananmen sanctions.

China viewed the relationship very much through the lens of its own domestic struggle. Jiang Zemin, as the "core" of a collective leadership, was trying to consolidate his position as first among equals. He badly wanted his Foreign Ministry to convince the Clinton White House that it was time for a state visit. Such a visit would build up Jiang's image as the heir to Deng, who was slipping fast. Relationships in the politburo during this time of transition were extremely fragile.

But Washington was in no mood to see Jiang. From the White House perspective, China had done nothing to show its gratitude for the political risks Clinton had taken in breaking the linkage. If anything, China had regressed. It froze its dialogue with the Red Cross, broke off technical discussions with the Voice of America, and increased the pace of arrests of religious and political dissidents. Chen Ziming, who had earlier been released from prison, was held under virtual house arrest in his own tiny apartment, with a squad of two dozen secret police encamped in the elevator lobby and around the building. Each morning they rang his doorbell to verify his presence.

Still, business continued. Commerce secretary Ron Brown led a large delegation of American CEOs to Beijing and promoted the notion that a new era of business development and cooperation was under way.

Qian Qichen, in a meeting with Christopher on October 4 in Washington, pledged for the first time that Beijing would not export M-11 ground-to-ground missiles, thus closing the loophole by which China had earlier claimed that it could sell the M-11 to Pakistan and other countries because it allegedly fell outside the definitions established by the Missile Technology Control Regime.

The October agreement allowed Clinton to lift the sanctions he had imposed in August 1993, freeing American corporations to resume the sale of telecommunications satellites and other high-tech systems to China.

But these sales took place against a backdrop of diplomatic warfare. At the White House, Lake and Christopher had resolved that the United States would take its human rights campaign against China to a higher plane. They laid plans for the United States and European countries to press more forcefully for a vote at the UN Commission on Human Rights in Geneva to seek an investigation of human rights abuses in China. American diplomats, encouraged by Lake, began privately waging a highly contentious battle against China in the corridors of the United Nations and in the capitals of more than fifty countries represented at the Commission on Human Rights.

At the same time, Lake and Lord worked to complete a "Taiwan Policy Review" that called for a symbolic upgrading of Taiwan's status in Washington. Ostensibly, the review was a way to reward Taiwan for the democratic reforms it had undertaken and for its considerable economic weight in Asia. But Beijing regarded the exercise with deep suspicion.

Then, in May 1994, Taiwanese president Lee Teng-hui orchestrated a dramatic diplomatic incident. On a stopover in Hawaii on his way to Central America, Lee tried and failed to get State Department permission to stay overnight and play a round of golf. Lord had refused, allowing only a refueling stop. During the layover, Lee stayed on board, claiming to the international news media that the State Department had humiliated him by refusing him permission to get off the plane. Congress, always well-watered with Taiwanese lobbying favors, expressed outrage at the treatment.

Then the congressional elections of 1994 ushered in a revival of conservative Republicanism.

In February 1995, at Lord's first appearance before the House subcommittee on Asia policy, nearly every Republican member hammered away at the administration's refusal to allow Lee Teng-hui to visit the United States. A Democratic staff member on the committee, Richard Bush, soon thereafter told Robert Suettinger, a China specialist at the White House, that Taiwan's lobbying organization, fueled with partisan Republican energy, was rolling down Pennsylvania Avenue like a tidal wave. "You want to lose early and graceful or you want to lose ugly and late?" Bush asked Suettinger.

Days later, the Senate Foreign Relations Committee voted legislation declaring that Tibet was "an occupied, sovereign country" and calling on Clinton to name a U.S. envoy to Tibet.

China wasn't making it easy, either.

In March, Vice President Al Gore and Li Peng had met during a UN conference in Copenhagen and clashed so vehemently over human rights that both men took it personally.* In retaliation, Clinton rebuffed China's

---

*Days earlier, China had narrowly defeated the joint American-European attempt to bring up a resolution before the UN Commission on Human Rights that would effectively condemn human rights abuses in China.

attempt to arrange a summit meeting between Jiang and Clinton in Moscow, where they both would attend the fiftieth anniversary of the allied victory in World War II.

Despite the warning signs in Congress, few in the administration imagined that Clinton would cave in to Republican pressure so swiftly, least of all Roy, sitting in Beijing and believing that Christopher and Lord—and Clinton—were surefooted on the ramparts.

The problem was that Lee had been invited to visit his alma mater, Cornell University, and he wanted badly to go to score political points against the mainland. In April, Christopher met with Qian Qichen and assured the foreign minister that no visa would be granted, but Christopher also tried to convey his own uncertainty about the future of Washington's China policy. He told Qian that the entire U.S. Congress disagreed with the administration's position on the visa.

On May 19, Roy called the Beijing press corps into his living room. A reporter asked about the visa issue, and Roy became animated, unable to suppress his frustration. He already suspected which way the decision was going to go.

"If China loses this one," he said, "it doesn't know whether we want a strong and prosperous China, or a weak and divided one. It interprets our actions on Taiwan as a reflection of the latter, in part because it doesn't see enough coherence in the way we are dealing with the region." His sudden vehemence puzzled the journalists.

"At a time when we need strategic cooperation on North Korea," Roy continued, "we're in a trade war with Japan and we may permit Lee Teng-hui to visit the United States; we are talking about theater missile defenses [for Asia] which raise questions of what our longer-term views of China are. Where are the Chinese left in the wake of the Lee Teng-hui visit in assessing whether the U.S. has a foreign policy?"

After Clinton issued the visa, Roy could see the storm coming. He had already told Washington that he would be leaving Beijing. He had given four years and had secured an onward assignment to Jakarta, and he was anxious to get started there. There was no need to delay his departure any longer. He was never much for farewell calls, and they would be impossible to arrange now anyway.

Although Roy had previously told colleagues that the Clinton administration regarded China as too important to leave unattended by an ambassador, he made plans in early June 1995 to slip out of town unnoticed. The battle over the visa had changed everything. Roy believed that it was the job of the president to use his office to shape opinion, to withstand the gales that arise from domestic politics. Clinton had not even tried. He had seen the non-binding votes in the new Republican Congress calling for Lee to get a visa, and he had folded his tent without a fight.

Representative Dennis Hastert, the deputy Republican whip, showed up in Beijing the week after the visa was issued and claimed to Roy that no one in the White House had made a case against it, least of all Clinton. He implied that the votes could have been turned around if Clinton had made the case.

Roy was incredulous.

One of the last people to see Roy before he slipped out of Beijing for the last time as ambassador was John Kamm, an American businessman from Hong Kong who had been carrying on a longstanding dialogue with Chinese officials on human rights. Roy told him that the American ambassador had become a pariah and there was no sense in staying on. "Why have an ambassador?" asked Roy, his tone conveying a personal sense of betrayal.

TRANSITION:

. . . IT BEGINS AGAIN

THE NIGHT OF FEBRUARY 19, 1997, I was detained by a squad of Chinese policemen in a small town on China's border with Kazakhstan, about as far away as you can get from Beijing and still be in the country. I had crossed into China from the territory of its western neighbor and was trying to reach the remote city of Yining, where Chinese Muslims had rioted during the holy month of Ramadan. The region is hauntingly beautiful, framed on the north and south by the snowy Mountains of Heaven, which overlook the plain where Chinese and Russian forces clashed during the Sino-Soviet border crisis of 1969.

Traveling as a journalist in China can be difficult, especially without official permission or required escort. To reach a trouble spot like the Muslim communities of the Far West, it is necessary to circumvent the rules that are designed to prevent you from ever getting there. In this case, I had flown to the Kazakh capital, Almaty, and planned to return unescorted to Beijing via a long overland route passing directly through the area of turmoil. If challenged, I could claim that I was merely in transit back to Beijing.

As soon as I entered China, however, where my passport bore the stamp of a foreign journalist, the Chinese border police conducted a four-hour investigation of my luggage and placed me in a small hotel under surveillance. They then notified the State Security Bureau in Urumqi, the provincial capital, to arrange my "escort" back to Beijing. I was shown to my room, and the front door of the hotel was locked with a tractor chain and padlock. I was thus ensconced as a "guest" of the local Public Security Bureau when my colleague in Beijing, Seth Faison, managed to get a telephone circuit through to tell me that China's official news agency had reported the death of Deng Xiaoping.

Deng was dead. After a hundred false alarms, he had finally succumbed to advanced Parkinson's disease. In the last years of decline, he had lain like an emperor behind the curtain, his power still pulsing even as his organs seized up and his mind slipped into a state of insentience. Now the power was extinguished and, again, the world paused, this time to consider China without the man for whom the title "paramount leader" had been invented.

I had to break out of the hotel and run for two miles through the darkened countryside to hitch a ride to Urumqi—eight hours across the desert by car—and catch the last plane flying east that afternoon.

While sitting on that Russian-made airliner traversing the whole of China on the day that the Deng era passed into history, I was overcome with curiosity about the Chinese with whom I was traveling. What were they thinking? And so I walked the aisle for the next two hours, introducing myself and asking people about the future.

What I learned profoundly impressed me about the pragmatism of the Chinese.

The prevailing view was that Deng Xiaoping had so personified the reform era that his death was less a source of mourning than it was of deep concern that what he had started might come to an end; that China might go backward. Deng was the last of the revolutionary leaders of Mao's generation strong enough to overthrow Mao's conventions. Deng's reforms, modest as they were, sparked China's economic revolution. Over the next two decades, Deng was the last line of defense in protecting the reform process as the pendulum swung from go-go periods of expansion into troughs of retrenchment; between political tolerance and intolerance. Deng had kept the country moving forward and, as a consequence, hundreds of millions of Chinese had bettered their circumstances.

Most of the Chinese traveling with me, a number of them party members, worried that Deng's death would weaken the party's commitment to the "socialist market economy" that Deng had enshrined at the Fourteenth Party Congress in 1992. They were afraid that the new generation of leaders, with President Jiang Zemin at the center of an unwieldy collective, would not be able to uphold the reform line if faced with economic downturn, political upheaval, or a determined assault from hard-liners; that China would lapse back into the chaotic politics of the past.

With these sentiments, these few dozen Chinese, strapped into their seats inside a Russian airframe that was hurtling across the Gobi and Tenger Deserts, saw the fate of Deng's reform era intimately connected with their own lives.

America was almost the last thing on their minds, but, of course, America was inextricably connected with China's fate. In the 1990s, America had become China's most important export market, its most powerful engine of growth. By the end of the decade, the annual revenues flowing back to Beijing, Shanghai, Guangzhou, and Hong Kong from China's trade with the

United States had surpassed the $50 billion mark and the "Made in China" label had become ubiquitous from Wal-Mart to the Gap. U.S. sales to the huge China market lagged far behind, and while the trade imbalance was another source of tension, the reality was that the unquenchable demand in the American market was helping to lift China to a higher plane of development. American technology was transforming Chinese industries. Tens of thousands of Chinese students were enrolled in American universities, and Chinese communities in every major American city had become the pillars of a new cultural bridge across the Pacific.

Many Americans certainly wondered that night what would become of China after Deng. To many of them, Deng was as connected to the bloodshed at Tiananmen as he was to the economic revolution he had fostered. Many hoped or expected that his death would pave the way for a democratic revolution. But this was the remotest of possibilities, since the party had been preparing for Deng's passing with heightened security procedures throughout the country.

Still, these two sets of expectations—one Chinese and one American—showed a great contrast in outlook in the two societies.

A FTER THE AMERICAN aircraft carriers had receded over the horizon following the Taiwan crisis of 1996, Clinton sought to calm the China front. It was, after all, a presidential election year, and the last thing Clinton wanted was another military confrontation. He sent Tony Lake to Beijing in July 1996 with a message that the president was ready to exchange state visits with Jiang Zemin and thereby elevate, once again, the strategic dialogue to the highest plane.

Privately, Lake asked the Chinese to smooth the way for summitry by making a series of gestures on human rights, such as signing two United Nations covenants: the International Covenant on Civil and Political Rights and the International Covenant on Economic, Social, and Cultural Rights. He also asked China to resume its negotiations with the International Committee of the Red Cross in Geneva to establish a program of accounting for political and religious detainees languishing in Chinese prisons. And he asked that Beijing release a nominal group of seven well-known detainees. If China was forthcoming on this agenda, Lake indicated, the United States would be prepared to abandon its annual effort at the United Nations to condemn China's human rights record.

This was welcome news in Beijing. Over the next two years, China agreed to sign both UN covenants, although it continued to refuse Red Cross representatives access to its prisons. China also released, or sent into exile, all the political prisoners on Lake's list, including Wei Jingsheng, who arrived in the United States in November 1997, and Wang Dan, who arrived in April 1998.

Four months after Deng's death, Jiang Zemin presided over the mammoth celebration marking the July 1, 1997, return of Hong Kong to Chinese sovereignty; that fall, he stood before the Fifteenth Party Congress and reaffirmed that, despite Deng's absence, China would stay on the road to building a market-based economy.

Jiang strengthened his own position and, in early 1998, presided over the appointment of a new and more pragmatic prime minister, Zhu Rongji, replacing the hard-liner Li Peng, who was shunted off to the chairmanship of the National People's Congress. These were no small accomplishments for a government that had no constitutional process of succession beyond whatever consensus the ruling party could reach.

Immediately following the Party Congress, Jiang flew to Washington for a state visit. It was clear that China and the United States were still in the midst of a tortuous process of recovery. Clinton and Jiang spoke past each other on human rights and other points of conflict. Then it was Clinton's turn, traveling to Beijing in June 1998 as the domestic political storm gathered for his impeachment.

Major issues between Washington and Beijing were unresolved:

- Taiwan. In June 1998 in Shanghai, Clinton publicly reiterated an American commitment not to support an independent future for Taiwan, or Taiwan's entry into any international body reserved for sovereign states. And he pledged that Washington would not pursue any policy that would lead to separatism. Yet American arms sales to Taiwan were continuing at higher levels than ever, certainly higher than those established by the August 1982 communiqué, which committed the United States to a gradual reduction. In the fall of 1998, Beijing and Taiwan agreed to resume their cross-strait political dialogue, but these superficial discussions were overshadowed by a far more robust level of military planning and by Lee Teng-hui's provocative campaign in the summer of 1999, to reject the principle of one China as a means to further assert Taiwan's independence from the mainland.

- Theater missile defense. By 1999, China's opposition to the deployment of a U.S. theater missile defense system in Asia had become a top diplomatic priority for Beijing. The Chinese military saw the system as a threat to the integrity of its own strategic nuclear missile force. The missile defense system now held the potential to draw Japan, Taiwan, and the United States together in de facto alliance against China (although the ostensible threat was the North Korean missile program). Senior Chinese officials warned: "Should the United States bring Taiwan into its proposed anti-missile scheme, Sino-U.S. relations would suffer a setback unprecedented since the normalization of bilateral ties." One Chinese official called theater missile defense an "extension of efforts to contain China militarily."[1]

- World Trade Organization (WTO) membership. China's trade barriers are among the most formidable in the world, and they protect a landscape of national industries that would lose huge portions of their markets at home if subjected to open competition from foreign manufacturers. The collapse of those industries under the free trade requirements of the WTO could send millions of Chinese factory workers into unemployment, touching off a wave of labor unrest. Unwilling to dismantle its monopolies or open its markets, China has not been able to meet the criteria for entry into the WTO. In 1994, Chinese leaders began a campaign to pressure the United States to sponsor China's entry irrespective of its market barriers. They called on Clinton to make a political, not an economic, decision. No world body, Chinese leaders asserted, could claim to represent the globe without the participation of China. But the WTO's members have held firm, not wishing to institutionalize China's market barriers. A compromise calling for a phased-out reduction of China's market barriers has long been possible. In early 1999, Zhu Rongji made clear in private discussions in Beijing with Alan Greenspan, the U.S. Federal Reserve Board chairman, that China was ready to open its markets even if that meant risking unpredictable consequences. And Premier Zhu arrived in Washington in April 1999 with significant concessions, but Clinton balked, stricken by the congenital indecision that had marked his presidency. He feared that a bold stroke on China would draw a strong reaction from Congress, where China remained unpopular and under constant assault.

- Proliferation and technology transfer. After signing the Nuclear Non-Proliferation Treaty in 1992, China seemed to be on the road to improving its proliferation record, but George Bush's sale of the F-16 to Taiwan marked a significant setback. China had promised James Baker in November 1991 that it would not transfer the M-11 missile to Pakistan, but after the F-16 sale, China shipped dozens of crates containing missiles or missile parts to Pakistan. As long as the United States continues to violate its commitment to gradually reduce arms sales to

Taiwan, China is unlikely to commit itself to a full partnership with Washington in stemming the flow of dangerous military technologies to unstable parts of the world.

This was the menu of contention. The danger was that without the clarity of the Cold War, without an urgent common threat to drive America and China together, China's emergence as an Asian power would clash with a long tradition of American dominance in Asia, causing the points of contention to overwhelm the tally of common interests between them.

A huge factor was China itself, which, after Deng, was still a work in progress. Deng's successors were all in their seventies, and although they could remain in power for another decade, they were nonetheless a transitional leadership trying to complete the most difficult task of economic reform—transforming China's moribund state industries with their mountainous legacy of debt, which threatened to undermine the banking system. They also had to find a way to provide some kind of future for the hundreds of millions of new Chinese workers who are expected to swell the labor pool in the coming decades. The obstacles to China's orderly growth in the new century are formidable, and managing growth in a population that will reach 1.6 billion by 2030 will be the greatest challenge.

Voices in the Republican Party in 1996 and again in 1999 called for an aggressive foreign policy campaign targeting China as a threat to American interests in Asia—as an enemy that needed to be contained. Evidence of a China threat was marshaled in Congress, whose members received testimony from a prominent Democratic party fundraiser that China's chief of military intelligence, General Xiong Guangkai, and perhaps others in the PLA high command, had succeeded in funneling cash into Democratic political campaigns in hopes of purchasing influence in the White House and Congress. The Justice Department and several congressional committees also were investigating whether China had extracted too many militarily useful secrets from its access to the U.S. space launch market, where American missile and satellite manufacturers at times shared insights with Chinese partners on how to improve the reliability of rocket boosters that also power China's strategic nuclear missiles.

On December 30, 1998, a select committee of the House of Representatives chaired by Christopher Cox, a Republican from California, completed a classified study of Chinese espionage in the United States, and an unclassified version was released publicly in May 1999. The study concluded that over the previous two decades, China had acquired a range of sensitive American technologies, including information on the design of the American neutron bomb and the W-88 thermonuclear warhead, which sits atop the Trident II missile in the belly of American strategic submarines.[2] Though some of the findings that emerged were startling, it was clear that much of the espionage occurred in the 1980s and had not resulted in any militarily significant Chinese advancements that might endanger U.S. armed forces in Asia, or American security more broadly. China's chronic weakness in strategic and conventional military forces could not be ameliorated by a silver bullet stolen from a more sophisticated arsenal. The fact remained that Beijing commanded a few hundred warheads at most and only a few dozen of those warheads were mounted on intercontinental ballistic missiles (ICBMs) capable of reaching American cities. In contrast, the United States and Russia at the end of the century each possessed as many as 10,000 nuclear weapons. The balance of power was simply overwhelming. In the American arsenal, as many as 6,000 nuclear weapons could be programmed to strike Chinese targets, including the twenty or so silos where China stores its ICBMs capable of reaching the United States. Most profoundly, for the last thirty years, the Pentagon's strategic planners were confident that China's ICBMs could simply be eliminated with preemptive strikes in any period of hostilities where nuclear war seemed likely. In other words, all of China's ICBM's could be destroyed in their caves or silos to prevent them from ever coming into play in a crisis.

The reality is that China, from the outset of the nuclear era, struggled against great odds to join the nuclear club because Mao insisted that China not be subjected to blackmail by the superpowers.

The history of China as a nuclear power* tells us that the People's Republic did not become the nuclear rogue that Brezhnev had feared. China has not resorted to nuclear blackmail in its foreign relations nor has it activated its nuclear forces in any crisis. Instead, China has consistently maintained a small deterrent force under a no-first-use policy and it has joined the Comprehensive Test Ban Treaty.

China hopes to deploy more survivable, mobile missiles in the future with smaller and more reliable warheads, but these would be incremental improvements long anticipated in the Pentagon and U.S. intelligence community. Greater survivability will simply ensure that China's small deterrent force will remain viable in the next century. It will not make China's nuclear posture more threatening, as the Cox committee asserted.

Almost as soon as the Cox committee report emerged, it was challenged by a wide variety of scientists and intelligence professionals with access to the

---

*China exploded its first atomic bombs in October 1964 at the Lop Nor nuclear test range. It exploded its first hydrogen bomb two years later.

same data.* Though it seemed a valuable wake-up call to improve security at U.S. nuclear laboratories, the Cox committee report was too seriously flawed by an ideological tone and technical inaccuracies to stand as any objective assessment of China's military aims.

And, of course, it was almost absurd to think that nuclear war with China was even remotely likely. In the worst case scenario of a military crisis over Taiwan, most analysts could envision a long war of attrition, even devastating clashes along China's coast, but no serious analyst of international affairs has postulated that Beijing's leaders would be willing to risk the annihilation that would result from launching a nuclear war against the United States and its overwhelming nuclear forces. Despite their differences, China and the United States both were promoting the growth of world trade, the expansion of markets, and the spread of information technologies that were breaking down many of the old barriers. No calculation of the differences between Washington and Beijing rose to the level of global competition that marked the Cold War with the Soviet Union, or joined the question of nuclear war. To view China from this frame of reference was simply a muddled nostalgia for a global rival. For four decades, American presidents had ridden the tiger of global rivalry with the Soviet Union. The annual debate over the size of the defense budget and the birth of each new weapon system had been attended like rites of a national religion. Generations of national security analysts had been trained for a competition that, in the end, simply collapsed. While the nostalgia was not surprising, it contributed little to understanding the new era. Geostrategy had moved on to other measures of national power. Economic strength and the global integration of markets were far more important to the lives of hundreds of millions of Chinese and Americans who will live and work and do business with each other in the new century.

China's espionage, though potentially a serious penetration of American nuclear laboratories, was not a provocation of war or a pretext for isolating or containing the People's Republic. To be sure, one of the reasons Congress was learning so much about Chinese espionage was that American intelligence agencies—the CIA, DIA, and NSA—had so effectively penetrated or detected many Chinese intelligence operations. The congressional uproar over the security lapses at American nuclear laboratories during the Reagan, Bush, and Clinton administrations, reflected the intense partisanship that was the most prominent feature of the impeachment drama of 1998 and 1999, and that permeated the foreign policy debate in advance of the 2000 presidential election season. (Clinton had played the same partisan game in

---

*A member of the Cox committee, Representative John Spratt, a Democrat from South Carolina, issued a sharp dissent asserting that Cox committee staffers had drawn many conclusions that simply could not be supported by the intelligence.

1992 when he attacked Bush for "coddling tyrants" from Baghdad to Beijing.) The intensity of the American political climate was not lost on the Chinese, either. China's Premier Zhu, prior to arriving in the United States in the spring of 1999, wondered aloud whether a new McCarthy Era, "where everyone was afraid of being accused by everyone else," was gathering on the American political landscape.[3] And when American bombers mistakenly attacked the Chinese embassy in Belgrade during NATO's Balkan campaign, the reaction in China was a police-supervised riot of rock throwing students pelting American diplomatic compounds as a transparent response calculated to convey Beijing's frustration with the anti-Chinese sentiments being expressed in the U.S. Congress, but also with American interventionism. For China's leaders, worried that just as Americans and Europeans saw an urgent need to violate Yugoslav sovereignty to prevent further massacres in Kosovo, they might see a similar cause in Tibet or the Taiwan Strait should instabiliy erupt there. Indeed, Beijing's party bosses had begun to fear that the new century would not see a decline in American power, but the reverse and, therefore, any precedent for American interventionism—on moral grounds or otherwise—was regarded as potentially dangerous in Beijing, whose leaders could easily imagine that China might face a severe challenge from any future American administration that embraced the China-threat rhetoric coursing through both political parties.

In Beijing, Jiang Zemin faced his own domestic challenges—the tenth anniversary of the Tiananmen massacres (June 4, 1999), and fresh appeals from prominent Chinese intellectuals for national reconciliation and a call for justice against those hard-liners still in power who ordered the military assault on unarmed students. But in preparation for the fiftieth anniversary of the founding of the People's Republic of China on October 1, 1999, Jiang demonstrated once again that the Communist Party leadership has zero tolerance for political dissent. He pronounced that the party's absolute leadership could not be challenged and that any attempt to do so would be "annihilated." When Democracy Wall veteran Xu Wenli and a group of like-minded cohorts sought to organize a pro-democracy party during the summer and fall of 1998, Jiang crushed it, rounding up its leaders and throwing them in prison.

Clinton admonished China for its hypersensitivity to political challenge. Stability, he said, should not have to come at the expense of liberty. But although Clinton reaffirmed his commitment to a long process of engagement with China, his two terms in office had done little more than postpone and defer the big issues, which awaited the next president.

Clinton's view was that Jiang Zemin's generation was not the future of China, but that some younger and more progressive set of leaders would

emerge with the courage to do what Jiang and the party elders had long refused to do—express some regret over the Tiananmen massacres and, with
that bold stroke, begin a new era of political reform. "I think it's just inevitable just as, inevitably, the Berlin Wall fell,"[4] Clinton had said. But Clinton's call for courage in the Chinese leadership drew attention to how little
courage he himself had shown in managing China policy. After all, this was a
president more driven by polls and congressional pressure than most of his
predecessors. Halfway through his second term in office, Clinton banned
television coverage of his first major speech on China because he and his political advisers feared too much exposure on a subject that incited congressional thunder. Yet, in that low-profile presidential speech, he said:

> At the dawn of the new century, China stands at a crossroads. The direc-
> tion China takes toward cooperation or conflict will profoundly affect Asia,
> America, and the world for decades. The emergence of a China as a power
> that is stable, open, and non-aggressive, that embraces free markets, politi-
> cal pluralism, and the rule of law, that works with us to build a secure inter-
> national order—that kind of China, rather than a China turned inward and
> confrontational, is deeply in the interests of the American people.[5]

But it could also be said that America stands at a crossroads. The direction
America takes toward conflict or cooperation with China will profoundly affect the future of Asia. An America that turns inward or becomes more confrontational is profoundly against the interest of a stable international order.

No president has done less than Bill Clinton to prepare the American people for a new era in foreign policy. Clinton might blame Congress for his
lackluster performance, but history has proven often enough that when a
president makes a compelling case—when a president is engaged in foreign
policy management and its presentation to the American people—Congress
follows. In this regard, how lamentable it seems that in 1999, Zhu Rongji—
the man once called China's Gorbachev due to his pragmatic and open style
of governance—would visit the United States ready for compromise and
concession on major trade issues only to find Clinton indecisive, cowed by
Congress, and distracted by his Balkan military campaign.

Nothing is so emblematic of Clinton's shortcomings as a foreign policy
president as his failure to go to Congress in 1995 and work out a compromise
over the visit of Taiwanese president Lee Teng-hui to America, or his long-
standing trepidation about speaking to the nation directly on American policy toward the People's Republic, or his unseemly dash to China in June 1998
that was designed to upstage through pageantry the corrosive politics of the
Paula Jones Corbin sex scandal at home. For Clinton, China was good for a

tactical photo opportunity, but otherwise was a subject to be avoided. As a consequence, the president took no time to develop a relationship with Premier Zhu and was inattentive to the opportunities that developed in early 1999 to break down the final barriers holding back China's entry to the World Trade Organization. It was as if Clinton had looked at the Chinese leadership with a glancing eye and seen a complex problem that would require time and political investment. Unwilling to give either, he walked away. If he makes a recovery in his final year in office, it would be a laudable act of learning for a president who has already missed so many opportunities.

Thus, the next president will face the same circumstances Clinton faced coming into office—an authoritarian China struggling to reform and develop its economy while remaining ever paranoid about attempts to topple Communist Party rule through democracy and human rights movements; a China determined to recover Taiwan through peaceful means, but fearful that America will seek to thwart its national aspirations by indulging in an arms race in the Taiwan Strait and thereby increasing the risk of war.

So, it will begin again.

A new president will confront the complexity of China and will make the decision that each of the preceding presidents has made: whether or not to run against China—in other words to exploit for domestic political gain the unresolved issues of Taiwan, Tibet, proliferation, espionage, trade, religious freedom, and human rights, or whether to run on the principle that China, like Russia, presents a multi-faceted challenge for American diplomacy that cannot be exempted from politics, but which needs to be protected so an incoming president has the greatest latitude to formulate a constructive foreign policy. The preceding history demonstrates that American leaders are capable of both approaches, but that the burden on the relationship was increasing, as the presidential campaign in 1992 had shown. But ever since the Nixon opening, each president, to some extent, had exploited the China relationship, even those who most piously insisted that they had only a long-term strategic vision in mind. With the fading of the Cold War, China was an easy target for domestic critics—it remained a repressive state under monolithic, one-party rule with a leadership heavily influenced by a military establishment hypersensitive to any challenge to Chinese sovereignty over Taiwan and Tibet.

And while some Americans may be tempted to indulge the old anti-Soviet reflex and turn China into an increasingly hostile adversary, what a tragedy it would be for such a diversion to blind Americans to the reality of China's transformation. On the day that Deng Xiaoping died, those Chinese flying across the country were not nurturing their ambition to bury America in the next century, rather they were seized with a desire to continue the economic revolution that Deng Xiaoping had started, to keep the process of development moving forward. Whether that economic revolution engenders political reform that eliminates repression is a matter of concern for Chinese and Americans alike. But a confrontational posture toward China would eliminate the potential for American participation in, and contribution to, reform in China.

Americans are great missionaries, and the modern missionary agenda in China includes the advocacy of greater adherence to universal principles of human rights; the development of democratic institutions; peaceful negotiation over the future of Taiwan; the control of dangerous weapons technologies; and free trade. This agenda supports the overarching strategic objective of making room for—and assisting—the rise of China as a developed country with a constructive outlook of its own. It would be both a tragedy and a travesty of American national interests for the United States to turn hostile toward China and the 1.2 billion Chinese, most of whom admire the nation that, in Chinese, is called 美 国, or Beautiful Country.

What does this mean for China policy in the new century? Politicians and diplomats like to use the word "engagement," as if that were a magical prescription. Engagement may be essential, but if neither side is willing to make the compromises necessary to jointly enhance the security of Northeast Asia, or find a formula for China's entry into the WTO, or practice restraint in the arms buildup in the Taiwan Strait, or ensure the inalienable human rights of the Chinese, engagement will never be enough. The compromises are there to be made, but leaders will have to lead, and the more transparent the leadership, the better. The essential ingredients of American foreign policy have long been innate economic strength and enlightened moral precepts backed by global military power. But these strengths add up to little without a strong American president who is capable of articulating and then managing a forward-looking foreign policy, who is willing to defend this policy in Congress, and who is committed to building support for it among Americans.

WHETHER OR NOT A Chinese Gorbachev materializes in the future, the country may well remain an authoritarian state for decades, but it is also likely that the rule of law will take greater hold because the Chinese themselves are demanding it, that police and security forces will become more accountable for repressive acts because most Chinese abhor police abuse, that local elections will gain popularity and expand out of the villages and into the county and township governments, and that China's parliament will play a greater role in expressing the will of the Chinese people to the Communist Party leadership. The party leadership itself will undergo a transformation that is impossible to predict. The next leader of China may be a politburo member relatively unknown outside of China, such as Hu Jintao; no one knows how he will react when the Chinese people project their hopes, anxieties, and expectations on him in the new century.

No matter who the coming leader is, Deng Xiaoping's prediction will likely prevail: that China's reform and opening-up process will continue for one hundred years, and any leader who tries to overthrow reform will be toppled. America should bet on Deng's forecast, and, with magnanimity, support it. That will mean taking risks and making compromises when the polling numbers suggest a safer course. The Chinese want to move forward, and China's leaders and people alike will continue to hope that America will play the role of benevolent partner in Chinese nation building, and not become a churlish or hostile impediment.

For now, China's relations with America are up in the air, still poised between conflict and cooperation, still awaiting leaders who will take the next steps.

China's rise need not be threatening to the United States or its interests. As the preeminent military power in Asia, the United States, by its very presence, will continue to provide the most powerful deterrent to aggression in the region. Therefore, America can afford a policy of restraint and dialogue on the question of Taiwan. American restraint will force the Chinese on both sides of the Taiwan Strait to talk to each other instead of acting out their security concerns—and demands—before an American audience. (As Lee Teng-hui appeared to be doing by abandoning the one China doctrine in the summer of 1999.) American restraint is more likely to promote the realization that neither side can resolve the Chinese civil war through unilateral actions, that any settlement will have to be the product of negotiation and compromise among the Chinese. An arms race only poisons this process.

China also will have to show restraint, in the Taiwan Strait, in Tibet and among the Chinese more broadly. Nothing has undermined international support for reform and opening up in China more than the rigid and repressive policies that have prevailed in Beijing since the Tiananmen crackdown. China's experiments with village elections have shown that democracy does not lead to chaos, as some hard-liners asserted, and the time was long overdue for Beijing to extend the democratic experiment to township and county governments and, eventually, to the National People's Congress, which remains a slave to the dictates of the Communist Party Central Committee and its seven-member politburo led by Jiang.

Americans will have to work hard to avoid confrontation with China in the coming decades and to accommodate China's inevitable rise as a powerhouse in Asia, one that will have its own national interests—some of them distinctly different from America's. No one can predict whether China will, on its own, turn hostile in the future. Nothing is preordained, but it would be foolish to presume that hostility is inevitable and to act on that presumption. Better that the United States work for the best outcome, than contribute to the worst.

NOTES

T HE MANY CLASSIFIED documents referenced below were obtained through Freedom of Information Act requests, most of them filed by the National Security Archive, a private foundation dedicated to openness in government. At the archive, Thomas Blanton, William Burr, and Jeffrey Richelson generously shared an extraordinary collection of 15,000 pages of newly declassified documents almost as quickly as they received them. The collection is now available to the public. The Nixon, Ford, and Carter presidential libraries also provided timely assistance, although a large archive of classified material on U.S.-China relations remains locked up by outdated secrecy protocols. Not referenced below were some extensive oral histories provided to the author on the condition that they not be specifically named. Where I have relied on the diaries of H. R. Haldeman, I have used dates instead of page numbers for citations since the most extensive edition of the diaries is on CD-ROM and organized by date. The diary of Dwight L. Chapin, referenced below, is not yet publicly available, but was generously shared for this reconstruction by Mr. Chapin. Most of the interviews cited below were conducted on a "background basis" in the interest of promoting greater candor and with permission to cite the interviews in a general listing of references; hence the absence of precise attributions in the interview category.

PROLOGUE: THE RISK OF WAR . . .

1. Richard F. Grimmett, *Conventional Arms Transfers to Developing Nations, 1990–1997*, Congressional Research Service, July 31, 1998, pp. 52, 63–64.
2. For a full discussion of Chinese military capabilities, see James R. Lilley and Chuck Downs, eds., *Crisis in the Taiwan Strait* (Washington, D.C.: National Defense University/AEI, 1997); Hans Binnendijk and Ronald N. Montaperto, eds., *Strategic Trends in China* (National Defense University, 1998); Bernard D. Cole and Paul H. B. Godwin, *Advanced Technology and the PLA: Priorities and Capabilities for the Twenty-First Century* (Washington, D.C.: National War College, 1998); Michael Pillsbury, ed., *Chinese Views of Future Warfare* (National Defense University, 1997); Michael D. Swaine, *The Role of the Chinese Military in National Security Policymaking* (Santa Monica, Calif.: RAND Corporation, 1996); and Major Mark A. Stokes, *China's Strategic Moderniza-*

tion: Implications for U.S. National Security, rev. ed. (U.S. Air Force Institute for National Security Studies, October 1997, revised July 1998).

3. Zhou was not addressing the Taiwan question in his remarks to Henry Kissinger on February 18, 1973, but his observation is revealing: "The objective fact of the largeness of the Chinese nation and Chinese area easily creates a tendency to nationalistic sentiments and big nation chauvinism. If there are too strong nationalist feelings, then one will cease to learn from others; one will seal oneself in and believe one is the best or will cease to learn from the strong points of others." Zhou Enlai, interview by James Reston, *New York Times*, August 10, 1971.

4. Henry Kissinger, Memorandum of Conversation with Mao Zedong (Top Secret), Chairman Mao's residence, November 12, 1973, 5:40–8:25 P.M., p. 11.

5. Department of Defense, *Selected Military Capabilities of the People's Republic of China*, Report to Congress, Pursuant to Section 1305 of the FY 1997 National Defense Authorization Act, April 8, 1997, p. 3.

6. Richard Bernstein and Ross H. Munro, *The Coming Conflict with China* (New York: Alfred A. Knopf, 1997), p. 3.

THE TAIWAN CRISIS

1. This reconstruction of the March 1996 crisis is based on interviews with Anthony Lake, Warren Christopher, William Perry, John Shalikashvili, Winston Lord, Jeffrey Bader, Robert Suettinger, Peter Tarnoff, Kurt Campbell, Chas. W. Freeman Jr., Scott Hallford, J. Stapleton Roy, Richard Solomon, and Tom Donilon.

2. Hau Pei-tsun and other Nationalist Party officials, interviews by author; Hau is a former Republic of China premier.

3. Senior Clinton administration official, interview by author.

4. Ibid.

5. See Jason DeParle's profile of Lake, *New York Times Magazine*, August 20, 1995.

6. Anthony Lake, "From Containment to Enlargement" (address presented at the Johns Hopkins School of Advanced International Studies, Washington, D.C., September 21, 1993).

7. For a complete discussion of covert American planning vis-à-vis Chinese nuclear capabilities during the Kennedy and Johnson administrations, see Gordon Chang, "JFK, China, and the Bomb," *Journal of American History* 74, no. 4 (March 1988); *Foreign Relations of the United States*, vol. 30, 1964–1968; and National Security Archive collection on China.

8. Maxwell Taylor, Memorandum (Top Secret), Joint Chiefs of Staff, November 18, 1963, re: Chinese Nuclear Development.

9. Walt W. Rostow, Memorandum for the President (Secret), April 17, 1964, re: The Implications of a Chinese Communist Nuclear Capability.

10. McGeorge Bundy, Memorandum for the Record (Top Secret), September 15, 1964.

11. McGeorge Bundy, Memorandum of Conversation with Ambassador Dobrynin, September 25, 1964, re: China; reprinted in *Foreign Relations of the United States*, vol. 30, 1964–1968, pp. 104–105.

12. For an account of the plot on Zhou's life, see Humphrey Trevelyan, *Living with the Communists: China 1953–1955, Soviet Union 1962–1965* (London: Gambit, 1971); and *New York Times*, April 12–14, 1955.

13. See Richard Madsen's study of mythology in U.S.-China relations, *China and the American Dream* (Berkeley: University of California Press, 1995), pp. 77–82.

14. CIA analysts in the Directorate of Intelligence, interviews by author.

15. Max Frankel, interview by author; see also Frankel's memoir, *The Times of My Life* (New York: Random House, 1998), pp. 295–296.

THE SINO-SOVIET BORDER: 1969

1. Among those interviewed on the Sino-Soviet crisis of 1969 were: Henry Kissinger; Robert Gates, then a young analyst of Soviet affairs at the CIA; Arthur Cohen, an analyst of Chinese affairs at the CIA; William Hyland, also a CIA analyst, on the staff of the National Security Council; Harry Gelman, an analyst of Soviet affairs at the CIA; Richard Helms, CIA director; John Huizenga, chairman of the Board of National Estimates at the CIA; Melvin Laird, secretary of defense; and the following National Security Council staffers: Helmut Sonnenfeldt, Alexander Haig Jr., Anthony Lake, Morton Halperin, David Aaron, Winston Lord, Lawrence Eagleburger, Peter Rodman, and John Holdridge.

   Also interviewed were Allen Whiting of the University of Michigan; at the State Department, Secretary William Rogers, Marshall Green, William Bundy, William Gleysteen Jr., William Stearman, and Paul Kreisberg; and Richard Solomon, James Schlesinger, James Lilley, Admiral (Ret.) Thomas Moorer, Morton Abramowitz, A. Doak Barnett, and Ji Chaozhu of the Chinese Ministry of Foreign Affairs. Other confidential Chinese sources were interviewed as well.

2. Accounts of the Sino-Soviet border crisis can be found in the following publications: Harry Gelman, *The Soviet Far East Buildup and Soviet Risk-Taking Against China* (Santa Monica, Calif.: RAND Corporation, 1982); and Arthur A. Cohen, "The Sino-Soviet Border Crisis of 1969," in *Avoiding War: Problems of Crisis Management,* ed. Alexander L. George (Boulder: Westview Press, 1991), pp. 269–296. Both Cohen and Gelman worked under W. P. "Bud" Southard at the CIA's Research Department. See also Thomas W. Robinson, "The Sino-Soviet Border Conflict," in *Diplomacy of Power: Soviet Armed Forces As a Political Instrument* (Washington, D.C.: Brookings Institution, 1981), pp. 265–313; Christian F. Ostermann, "New Evidence on the Sino-Soviet Border Dispute, 1969–1971," in a special issue, "The Cold War in Asia," of *Cold War International History Project Bulletin* (Winter 1995–1996): 186–193; and *The Cambridge History of China,* vol. 15, *The People's Republic* (Cambridge: Cambridge University Press), pp. 254–275.

3. Robert M. Gates, *From the Shadows: The Ultimate Insider's Story of Five Presidents and How They Won the Cold War* (New York: Simon & Schuster, 1997), p. 36; and CIA officials, interviews by author.

4. Henry Kissinger, *The White House Years* (Boston: Little, Brown, 1979), p. 172.

5. Richard Nixon, *RN: The Memoirs of Richard Nixon* (New York: Grosset and Dunlap, 1978), pp. 371–373.

6. Esau was the elder son of Isaac in the Old Testament (Gen. 27). Esau's younger brother, Jacob, contrived with his mother, Rebecca, to steal Esau's birthright by approaching the elderly and blind Isaac with lamb's wool on his arms to make them seem hairy like Esau's. The story of the competing sons became a metaphor for the Sino-Soviet dispute, as it had been termed a "family quarrel" over the "birthright" of leadership in the socialist camp.

7. Robert Ellsworth, interview by author; and Anatoly F. Dobrynin, *In Confidence: Moscow's Ambassador to America's Six Cold War Presidents (1962–1986)* (New York: Times Books, 1995), pp. 191–192.

8. CIA and State Department intelligence analysts, interviews by author.

9. Henry Kissinger, William Rogers, Alexander Haig Jr., Richard Allen, and Marshall Green, interviews by author; see also H. R. Haldeman, *The Haldeman Diaries,* for March 1969 (Star Press Multimedia, CD-ROM Edition, 1996).

10. Seymour M. Hersh, *The Price of Power* (New York: Summit Books, 1983), pp. 11–14; and Walter Isaacson, *Kissinger: A Biography* (New York: Simon & Schuster, 1992), pp. 129–134.

11. *The Haldeman Diaries,* March 8, 1969.

12. Department of Defense, *Review of the International Situation As of 20 January 1969* (Washington, D.C., 1969), response to National Security Study Memorandum 9, vol.

2, re: Communist China. This study was ordered on January 23, 1969, by Kissinger on behalf of Nixon as an "inventory" of the international situation.

13. Marshall Green, interview by author.

14. Donald M. Anderson, Memorandum of Conversation with unnamed Polish diplomat (Confidential), Department of State, January 14, 1969.

15. Kissinger, *White House Years*, p. 169.

16. As part of a general review of foreign policy at the outset of the Nixon administration, Kissinger issued, on February 5, 1969, National Security Study Memorandum 14, directing the State Department to review U.S.-China policy. Responses were to be supplied to the National Security Council's Interdepartmental Group for East Asia by March 10, 1969.

17. United Press International, dispatch from Hong Kong, March 1, 1969.

18. H. R. Haldeman with Joseph DiMona, *The Ends of Power* (New York: Times Books, 1978), p. 91.

19. Department of State, telegram from U.S. Embassy Warsaw (Secret), February 18, 1969.

20. Kissinger, *White House Years*, p. 169.

21. Christian F. Ostermann, trans., "Soviet Report to German Democratic Republic Leadership on 2 March 1969 Sino-Soviet Border Clashes," *Cold War International History Project Bulletin: The Cold War in Asia* (March 8, 1969).

22. Kissinger, *White House Years*, p. 172.

23. Richard Nixon, presidential news conference, March 14, 1969.

24. *New York Times*, March 21, 1969.

25. See John Wilson Lewis and Hua Di, "China's Ballistic Missile Programs," *International Security* (Fall 1992).

26. Kissinger, *White House Years*, p. 173.

27. Nixon, *RN*, p. 566.

28. Cohen, "Sino-Soviet Border Crisis," p. 282.

29. *New York Times*, March 21, 1969; and Radio Moscow, Mandarin Service, March 17, 1969, quoted in Gelman, *Soviet Far East Buildup*, p. 37.

30. Roderick MacFarquhar, ed., *The Cambridge History of China*, vol. 15, *The People's Republic* (Cambridge: Cambridge University Press, 1991), 305–311; and Frederick C. Teiwes and Warren Sun, *The Tragedy of Lin Biao* (Honolulu: University of Hawaii Press, 1996), pp. 104–111.

31. Cohen, "Sino-Soviet Border Crisis," pp. 280–281.

32. Ibid., p. 283.

33. Arkady N. Shevchenko, *Breaking with Moscow* (New York: Alfred A. Knopf, 1985), pp. 165–166.

34. Robinson, *Cambridge History of China*, p. 291.

35. Kissinger, *White House Years*, p. 179.

36. Melvin R. Laird, interviews by author.

37. Henry Kissinger, National Security Study Memorandum 69, National Security Council, July 14, 1969, re: U.S. Nuclear Policy in Asia.

38. Kissinger, *White House Years*, p. 179.

39. *New York Times*, August 1, 1969; and *New York Times*, August 8, 1969.

40. Department of State, telegram from U.S. Embassy Warsaw (Secret), August 18, 1969.

41. Marshall Green, Memorandum to the Undersecretary, Department of State (Secret/Nodis), October 6, 1969, re: Next Steps in China Policy.

42. General Graham's exaggerated predictions of a Soviet attack on China sparked a strong reaction from other parts of the intelligence community. One former DIA director, General Sam Wilson, characterized Graham's estimates as "hyperbolic—he had a penchant for reasoning beyond his data" and for reaching "extreme" conclusions. A number of CIA analysts at the time shared the view that Graham's predictions were not based on sound analysis. The CIA's Office of Current Intelligence consistently argued that there was a low probability that the Soviet Union would attack

China's nuclear weapons complex because Soviet forces could not preclude the possibility that China would be able to hide a sufficient number of weapons to mount a retaliatory strike on Vladivostok or some other Soviet city in the Far East within range of China's first-generation nuclear missiles.

43. William G. Hyland, *Mortal Rivals: Superpower Relations from Nixon to Reagan* (New York: Random House, 1987), pp. 25–26.

44. Henry Kissinger, William Stearman, William Rogers, Marshall Green, Robert Gates, and Arthur Cohen, interviews by author; see also Kissinger, *White House Years*, p. 183.

45. Colonel (Ret.) Robert S. Hopkins II, interview by author (Colonel Hopkins was with the 744th Bomber Squadron, Beale Air Force Base); and personal account of Robert S. Hopkins III, son of Colonel Hopkins. The colonel's account emerged from the research of Scott Sagan, codirector of the Center for International Security and Cooperation at Stanford University, who generously shared it.

46. Richard Helms, Robert Gates, Arthur Cohen, Harry Gelman, and other CIA officials, interviews by author. Helms told CIA officers that his briefing of Washington correspondents in late August 1969 was the only time in his career that he was directed by Nixon to give a "backgrounder" to the press. This signified to Helms the president's urgent desire to signal Moscow that Washington was deeply concerned about reports that Soviet forces were preparing to attack China.

47. CIA officials, interviews by author.

48. *New York Times*, August 29, 1969.

49. Kissinger, *White House Years*, p. 183; and CIA official, interview by author.

50. One CIA official recollected that Huizenga, the head of the Board of Estimates, was chairing a meeting of CIA analysts when a messenger arrived with a flash directive from the White House to examine the impact of a massive Soviet nuclear strike on China. The consensus was that such an attack was the remotest of possibilities.

51. *New York Times*, September 6, 1969.

52. Hyland, *Mortal Rivals*, p. 27.

53. Kissinger, *White House Years*, p. 186.

54. Isaacson, *Kissinger*, p. 335.

55. Mark H. Doctoroff, trans., "Information About A. N. Kosygin's Conversation with Zhou Enlai on 11 September 1969," *Cold War International History Project Bulletin: The Cold War in Asia*.

56. Cohen, "Sino-Soviet Border Crisis," p. 288; Gelman, *Soviet Far East Buildup*, p. 37; and Kissinger, *White House Years*, p. 185.

57. Xiong Xianghui, "Dakai Zhong Mei guanxi de qianzou," *Zhonggong dangshi ziliao*, no. 42. Xiong was an aide to Zhou Enlai and a participant in the meetings.

58. Ibid.

59. Ibid.

60. Ibid.

61. John Wilson Lewis and Xue Litai, *China Builds the Bomb* (Stanford: Stanford University Press, 1988), p. 244. The ninth and tenth Chinese tests were conducted on September 23 and 29, 1969.

62. Sun Tzu, *The Art of War*, trans. Samuel B. Griffith (Oxford: Oxford University Press, 1963), p. 77.

63. Marshall Green, interview by author.

64. Marshall Green, Memorandum to the Undersecretary (Secret/Nodis), Department of State, October 6, 1969, re: Next Steps in China Policy.

65. Kissinger, *White House Years*, p. 187.

66. Department of State, telegram from U.S. Embassy Warsaw (Secret), December 3, 1969.

67. Department of State, telegram from U.S. Embassy Warsaw (Secret), December 7, 1969.

68. Department of State, telegram from U.S. Embassy Warsaw (Secret), December 11, 1969.

69. Department of State, *Draft Instruction to Warsaw for Meeting with Chinese*, January 12, 1970; Memorandum to the President, January 20, 1970, re: Guidance for Sino-U.S. Ambassadorial Meeting; Department of State, telegram to U.S. Embassy Warsaw (Secret), January 17, 1970; Department of State, telegram from U.S. Embassy Warsaw (Secret), January 20, 1970; and Department of State, transcription of 135th meeting, Stoessel-Lei talks, January 20, 1970 (transmitted January 24, 1970).

70. Department of State, transcription of 136th meeting (Secret), Stoessel-Lei talks, February 20, 1970 (transmitted February 21, 1970).

71. William Rogers, Memorandum for the President (Secret), March 10, 1970, re: A Higher-Level Meeting with the Chinese.

72. Nixon, *RN*, pp. 405–406.

73. Kissinger, *White House Years*, p. 690.

74. Ibid., p. 691.

75. James C. H. Shen, *The U.S. and Free China: How the U.S. Sold Out Its Ally* (Lakewood, Colo.: Acropolis Books, 1983), p. 51.

76. Ibid.

77. Ibid., p. 53.

78. William Rogers, Memorandum for the President (Secret), May 12, 1970.

79. Richard H. Solomon, "US-PRC Political Negotiations, 1967–1984: An Annotated Chronology" (Santa Monica, Calif.: RAND Corporation). An unpublished chronology prepared by the RAND Corporation under contract to the CIA, which was declassified in part in 1995 and released under the Freedom of Information Act.

80. *New York Times*, May 21, 1970.

81. Kissinger, *White House Years*, p. 696.

82. CIA official, interview by author.

83. *New York Times*, July 10, 1970.

84. Solomon, "Annotated Chronology."

85. Edgar R. Snow, *Red Star over China* (New York: Grove Press/Atlantic, Inc., 1968), p. 90.

86. Li Zhisui, *The Private Life of Chairman Mao: The Memoir of Mao's Personal Physician* (New York: Random House, 1994), p. 566.

87. Solomon, "Chinese Political Negotiating Behavior: An Interpretive Assessment, 1967–1984" (Santa Monica, Calif.: RAND Corporation, 1985), pp. 42–43.

88. Edgar R. Snow, "Notes of Chairman Mao's Talk," December 18, 1970, Edgar Snow Collection, University of Missouri at Kansas City. By permission of Lois Wheeler Snow.

89. Lois Wheeler Snow, personal correspondence to author.

90. Ibid.

91. Kissinger, *White House Years*, p. 796.

92. Nixon, *RN*, p. 485.

93. Hyland, *Mortal Rivals*, pp. 31–33.

94. Kissinger, *White House Years*, p. 701.

95. Nixon, *RN*, p. 546.

96. *Haldeman Diaries*, December 12, 1970.

97. Kissinger, *White House Years*, 702; and Solomon, "Chinese Political Negotiating Behavior."

98. *New York Times*, January 25, 1971; see also *New York Times*, February 5, 1971.

99. Nixon, *RN*, p. 548; and Kissinger, *White House Years*, p. 707.

100. Nixon, *RN*, p. 548.

101. William Safire, *Before the Fall: An Inside View of the Pre-Watergate White House* (Garden City, New York: Doubleday & Co., Inc., 1975), p. 393.

102. *New York Times*, March 10, 1971.

103. Shen, *U.S. and Free China*, p. 5.

104. Li, *Private Life of Chairman Mao*, p. 558.

105. *New York Times*, April 8, 1971.

106. Li, *Private Life of Chairman Mao*, p. 558.
107. *Haldeman Diaries*, April 17, 1971.
108. Ibid.
109. *New York Times*, April 20, 1971.
110. *Haldeman Diaries*, April 20, 1971.
111. *New York Times*, April 27, 1971.
112. Nixon, *RN*, pp. 549–550; and Kissinger, *White House Years*, p. 714.
113. *Haldeman Diaries*, May 10, 1971.
114. Ibid., June 2, 1971.
115. Charles M. Colson, *Born Again* (Grand Rapids, Mich.: Fleming H. Revell, 1977), p. 43.
116. Kissinger, *White House Years*, pp. 726–727; and Solomon, "US-PRC Political Negotiations: An Annotated Chronology."
117. *Haldeman Diaries*, June 28, 1971; and Isaacson, *Kissinger*, pp. 331–334.
118. James Reston, *Deadline: A Memoir* (New York: Random House, 1991), pp. 381–387; and Kissinger, *White House Years*, p. 737.
119. Marshall Green, Melvin Laird, and William Rogers, interviews by author.
120. Chinese Foreign Ministry officials, interviews by author. The interviewed officials had participated in debriefing sessions with Mao during the visits of Kissinger, Haig, and Nixon.
121. Solomon, "Chinese Political Negotiating Behavior," p. 11.
122. Ibid., p. 2.
123. John H. Holdridge, *Crossing the Divide* (Lanham, Maryland: Rowman & Littlefield Publishers, Inc., 1997), p. 57; Solomon, "Chinese Political Negotiating Behavior"; and Kissinger, *White House Years*, p. 746.
124. Solomon, "Chinese Political Negotiating Behavior," p. 9.
125. Ibid., p. 81; and Solomon, "US-PRC Political Negotiations: An Annotated Chronology."
126. Solomon, "An Interpretive Assessment," p. 20.
127. Kissinger, *White House Years*, p. 750; and Solomon, "US-PRC Political Negotiations: An Annotated Chronology."
128. Department of State, *Private Statements Made by PRC Leaders to Secretary Kissinger or President Nixon Regarding the Peaceful Liberation of Taiwan* (Top Secret) (Washington, D.C.). The document covers the years 1971–1974.
129. Solomon, "Chinese Political Negotiating Behavior," p. 57.
130. Kissinger, *White House Years*, pp. 754–755; Nixon, *RN*, p. 554.
131. Zhou Enlai, interview by James Reston, *New York Times*, August 10, 1971.

NIXON: THE OPENING . . .

1. H. R. Haldeman, *The Haldeman Diaries: Inside the Nixon White House* (Star Press Multimedia, CD-ROM Edition, 1996), July 13, 1971.
2. Ibid., July 15, 1971.
3. Ibid.; see also Henry Kissinger, *The White House Years* (Boston: Little, Brown, 1979), p. 756.
4. Anatoly F. Dobrynin, *In Confidence: Moscow's Ambassador to America's Six Cold War Presidents (1962–1986)* (New York: Times Books, 1995), pp. 226–227; and Kissinger, *White House Years*, p. 760, 766.
5. *Haldeman Diaries*, July 13, 1971.
6. A month after the July 15 announcement of Nixon's journey to China, Kissinger and General Vernon Walters met secretly with Huang Zhen, the Chinese ambassador to France. In the meeting, Kissinger revealed that the United States had received its first proposal from Moscow for a U.S.-Soviet "Agreement on the Prevention of Nuclear War," which would, in effect, allow either superpower to attack China with impunity.

Kissinger said that the United States had rejected the Soviet proposal, but would be prepared to sign a similar agreement with the People's Republic. He also pledged that Nixon would not meet with any Soviet leader before coming to China. These secret assurances by Kissinger indicate that, at the outset of this new era of triangular diplomacy, Kissinger was seeking to create and wield leverage within the relationship like a blunt instrument, most certainly hoping to sober Moscow over its continuing support for Hanoi. See Richard H. Solomon, "US-PRC Political Negotiations, 1967–1984: An Annotated Chronology" (Santa Monica, Calif.: RAND Corporation), August 16, 1971. An unpublished chronology prepared by the RAND Corporation under contract to the CIA, which was declassified in part in 1995 and released under the Freedom of Information Act.

7. Dobrynin, *In Confidence*, pp. 227–228.
8. The Quadripartite Agreement on Berlin was signed on September 3, 1971, by the Soviet Union, the United States, Great Britain, and France. See Dobrynin, *In Confidence*, p. 233 for a discussion of the significance of this agreement to the Soviet leadership; see also Robert M. Gates, *From the Shadows: The Ultimate Insider's Story of Five Presidents and How They Won the Cold War* (New York: Simon & Schuster, 1997), p. 44.
9. Harry Gelman, *The Soviet Far East Buildup and Soviet Risk-Taking Against China* (Santa Monica, Calif.: RAND Corporation, 1982), p. 59; and Kissinger, *White House Years*, pp. 768–769.
10. The search for the truth in the Lin Biao affair has consumed Chinese and Western scholars over the decades. A reliable accounting of events is far from settled. A study by Frederick C. Teiwes and Warren Sun, *The Tragedy of Lin Biao* (Honolulu: University of Hawaii Press, 1996), suggests that the traditional portrait of Lin Biao as a scheming and power-hungry general bent on overthrowing Mao is not supported by the still incomplete record. Teiwes and Sun argue that "Lin not only did not engage in a power struggle with Mao, but in fact had little interest in politics in general and in being Mao's successor in particular." Instead, they argue, the sickly and reclusive Lin—after supporting Mao's purge of party leaders during the Cultural Revolution and after marshaling the military to tame the subsequent chaos that swept China from 1966 to 1969—simply fell out of favor with Mao as Lin and his military colleagues sought to run the country. Whether or not there was a well-developed plot to kill Mao remains a matter of debate, but what is clear is that members of Lin's family, feeling that he had been targeted by Mao for removal from office, organized a sudden and unsuccessful escape by air, ending in the Mongolia crash.
11. James C. H. Shen, *The U.S. and Free China: How the U.S. Sold Out Its Ally* (Lakewood, Colo.: Acropolis Books, 1983), p. 76.
12. *Haldeman Diaries*, October 11, 13–15, 1971.
13. Dwight L. Chapin, *First Advance Trip to the People's Republic of China* (unpublished diary), p. 7.
14. *Haldeman Diaries*, July 13, 1971.
15. Shen, *U.S. and Free China*, pp. 76–77.
16. Chapin, *First Advance Trip*, p. 15.
17. Ibid., pp. 20–24.
18. Ibid.
19. Kissinger, *White House Years*, p. 778.
20. Chapin, *First Advance Trip*, p. 54.
21. Department of State, *Private Statements Made by PRC Leaders to Secretary Kissinger or President Nixon Regarding the Peaceful Liberation of Taiwan* (Top Secret) (Washington, D.C.). The document covers the years 1971–1974.
22. Ibid.
23. Ibid.
24. Chapin, *First Advance Trip*, p. 86.
25. George Bush with Victor Gold, *Looking Forward* (New York: Doubleday, 1987).
26. Ibid.

27. *Haldeman Diaries*, October 26, 1971; and Kissinger, *White House Years*, p. 785.

28. Kissinger, *White House Years*, p. 785.

29. *Haldeman Diaries*, November 22, 1971.

30. Richard Nixon, *RN: The Memoirs of Richard Nixon* (New York: Grosset and Dunlap, 1978), p. 527.

31. Gelman, *Soviet Far East Buildup*, p. 60.

32. Ibid. Haldeman's diary entries for late November and December reflect a consensus in the White House that Kissinger had poorly managed the crisis machinery over the India-Pakistan conflict and knew it. Haldeman described the Washington Special Action Group (WSAG) as being in "open rebellion" against Kissinger. Aside from the political pressure of protecting Nixon's trip to China, Kissinger appeared to be in a manic state over his status in the Nixon administration.

33. Henry Kissinger, Memorandum of Conversation with Huang Hua (Top Secret), November 23, 1971.

34. Ibid.

35. Howe, Lord, and Colonel Robert McFarlane provided intelligence briefings for Chinese officials at the Chinese Mission to the United Nations in New York during Kissinger's tenure. The intelligence information related to the disposition of Soviet forces along the Chinese border as well as the location of Soviet nuclear forces in the Far East. These "order of battle" briefings were believed to be useful to the Chinese, who received the information without comment and without reciprocity. One of the briefers asserted in an interview that Kissinger had instructed them to emphasize Soviet superiority and the threat of Soviet attack.

36. Kissinger, Memorandum of Conversation with Huang Hua, November 23.

37. *Haldeman Diaries*, December 7, 1971.

38. Dwight L. Chapin, *Second Advance Trip to the People's Republic of China*, p. 6.

39. Henry Kissinger, Memorandum of Conversation with Huang Hua (Top Secret), December 10, 1971.

40. Ibid.

41. Ibid.

42. Henry Kissinger, Memorandum for the President, re: My December 10 Meeting with the Chinese in New York. That Kissinger was acting with Nixon's approval is evident in his three-page report to the president. "The main objective of the meeting," he told Nixon, "was to inform Peking fully about our various moves concerning South Asia and to indicate our approval of Chinese support for Pakistan, including diversionary troop movements." Kissinger also told Nixon how he had baited the Chinese with an offer of satellite intelligence on Soviet troop movements; he added, "With all this background, I got to the main point: It was of course up to the PRC [People's Republic of China] to decide its own course of action in this situation, but you wanted it to know that 'if the People's Republic were to consider the situation on the Indian subcontinent a threat to its security, and if it took measures to protect its security, the United States would oppose efforts of others to interfere with the People's Republic.'" At the conclusion of this memorandum, Kissinger states that on December 11, "we received our first hard news that Chinese troops were moving toward India's Northeast Frontier area. While this decision clearly was taken before Zhou could have known of our New York meeting, this session could only help to reinforce Chinese penchant for action." Kissinger's reliance on a fragmentary intelligence report that later proved to be incorrect was another indication of his zeal to provoke a confrontation.

43. Kissinger, Memorandum of Conversation with Huang Hua, December 10.

44. Henry Kissinger, Memorandum to R. T. Kennedy, White House (Top Secret), December 12, 1971.

45. Alexander Haig, Memorandum of Conversation with Huang Hua, New York City, East Side, December 12, 1971, 3:50 P.M.–4:20 P.M.

46. On December 12, 1971, the White House issued the following statement: "With East Pakistan virtually occupied with Indian troops a continuation of the war would take on

increasingly the character of armed attack on the very existence of a member state of the United Nations. All permanent members of the Security Council have an obligation to end this threat to world peace on the most urgent basis. The United States will fully cooperate in this effort."

47. Gelman, *Soviet Far East Buildup,* p. 63.

48. Although Brezhnev could certainly make this claim, the fact was that scarcely more than seven years later, Deng Xiaoping ordered the Chinese army to attack in the south against Vietnam. Soviet forces on China's northern border failed to deter Deng's southward aggression in that instance.

49. Richard Nixon, White House document with notation "Handed to General Walters 17 Dec. 71 for delivery Dec. 18," n.d., 3 pp. For an assortment of analyses of the event and its geostrategic significance, see Nixon, *RN,* pp. 530–531; Dobrynin, *In Confidence,* pp. 235–237; Gelman, *Soviet Far East Buildup,* pp. 53, 64; and Kissinger, *White House Years,* pp. 913, 918.

50. *Haldeman Diaries,* December 21, 1971; Haldeman refers to several of Anderson's columns.

51. *New York Times,* December 26, 1971.

52. Chapin, *Second Advance Trip,* pp. 46–47.

53. *New York Times,* December 28, 1971.

54. Solomon, "US-PRC Political Negotiations: An Annotated Chronology"; and Robert S. Ross, *Negotiating Cooperation: The United States and China, 1969–1989* (Stanford: Stanford University Press, 1995), p. 49.

55. Solomon, "Chinese Political Negotiating Behavior" Rand Chronology, January 30, 1972.

56. Ibid., February 6, 1972.

57. Ibid., February 11, 1972; also February 16, 1972.

58. Shen, *U.S. and Free China,* p. 83.

59. *New York Times,* February 20, 1972.

60. As a gesture in advance of Nixon's trip, the Chinese released forty-three-year-old Richard G. Fecteau, a CIA officer whose C-47 plane (equipped with a nose scoop for extracting a person from the ground without landing by employing an elevated tether) had been shot down over Manchuria in November 1952. Fecteau had served nineteen years of a twenty-year sentence; he had been on a mission with John T. Downey, another CIA officer, to extract a team of agents spying behind Chinese lines during the Korean War. One of the agents betrayed the operation. Two CIA contract pilots were killed, and Downey and Fecteau were captured. Downey remained in detention until 1973.

61. Nixon, *RN,* p. 559.

62. Dwight L. Chapin, *The President's Trip to the People's Republic of China (diary),* p. 2.

63. Ibid., pp. 3–4.

64. Both Nixon and Kissinger, in their memoirs, deal extensively with the presidential visit to China, but a more candid account of the behind-the-scenes tension and maneuvering can be found in *The Haldeman Diaries.* The Chapin diary provides additional information, as does John H. Holdridge's *Crossing the Divide: An Insider's Account of Normalization of U.S. — China Relations* (Lanham, Maryland: Rowman & Littlefield, 1997), pp. 81–96. In addition, several participants, including Holdridge, Green, and Chas. W. Freeman Jr., have recorded oral accounts of the visit, which are stored with the Foreign Service Association in Roslyn, Virginia. Among those interviewed about the visit were Kissinger, Rogers, Green, Chapin, Patrick Buchanan, and Zhang Hanzhi of the Chinese Foreign Ministry.

65. For an extensive account of Mao's medical history, see Li Zhisui, *The Private Life of Chairman Mao: The Memoir of Mao's Personal Physician* (New York: Random House, 1994), pp. 544–568. Dr. Li, Mao's private physician, wrote this history in Chinese and, after he emigrated to the United States, had it translated into English and augmented with the assistance of China scholar Anne F. Thurston.

66. From the accounts of Haldeman and Chapin, it seems likely that Kissinger had assured Nixon that, in accordance with his instructions, the president would meet alone with Mao later in the week. In this manner, Kissinger manipulated events to get himself included in the first meeting with Mao. By the end of the week, neither side considered a second meeting crucial to the success of the visit.

67. Richard Nixon, Memorandum of Conversation with Mao Zedong (Top Secret), Chairman Mao's Residence, February 21, 1972, 2:50–3:55 P.M.

68. Ibid.

69. Ibid.

70. Ibid.

71. Ibid.

72. Nixon's attempt to deceive the Chinese leaders on Soviet military deployments was a puzzling tactic, given that China had access to a great deal of information on Soviet forces. Solomon, in his interpretive assessment of U.S.-Chinese negotiating behavior, suggests that Mao and Zhou were not fooled by such statements and, in their internal speeches and communications, assured China's top cadres that the Soviets were only "feinting toward the East to attack in the West." Over time, Kissinger's persistent exaggerations in his personal statements and in the intelligence briefings he offered the Chinese on the Soviet military threat contributed to the erosion of his credibility with the Chinese leadership. In 1975, Deng Xiaoping bluntly declined Kissinger's offer to provide further intelligence briefings.

73. Nixon, Memorandum of Conversation with Mao Zedong, February 21.

74. Ibid.

75. See Max Frankel's account of the "Minimal Greeting," *New York Times*, February 21, 1972.

76. Chapin, *President's Trip (diary)*, p. 32.

77. Nixon, *RN*, pp. 567–568.

78. Ibid., p. 568.

79. Nixon had tried a similar argument on the Soviets. On October 20, 1970, Nixon told Dobrynin that within ten years, China would be a nuclear power capable of terrorizing other countries. Therefore, time was running out for the Soviet Union and the United States to build a different kind of world. "The only beneficiary of U.S.-Soviet disagreement over Vietnam is China," Nixon said, "and therefore this is the last opportunity to settle these disputes." Nixon, *RN*, p. 406.

80. Ibid.

81. Department of State, *Private Statements Made by PRC Leaders*.

82. Ibid.

83. Ibid.

84. Li, *Private Life of Chairman Mao*, p. 551.

85. Nixon, *RN*, pp. 571–572.

86. Ibid., pp. 569–570.

87. *Haldeman Diaries*, February 22, 1972.

88. Patrick J. Buchanan, interview by author.

89. Henry Kissinger, William Rogers, and Marshall Green, interviews by author. See also *Haldeman Diaries*, February 23–27, 1972; Kissinger, *White House Years*, 1077–1084; and Solomon, "US-PRC Political Negotiations: An Annotated Chronology," February 23–27, 1972.

90. Marshall Green, interview by author.

91. Ibid.

92. Henry Kissinger and Marshall Green, Press Briefing (Shanghai), *New York Times*, February 28, 1972.

93. Holdridge, *Crossing the Divide*, p. 95.

94. Kissinger and Green, Press Briefing.

95. Patrick J. Buchanan, interview by author; and Chapin, *President's Trip (diary)*, p. 52.

96. Chapin, *President's Trip (diary)*, p. 52.

97. Patrick J. Buchanan, interview by author; Kissinger, *White House Years; Haldeman Diaries*; and Chapin, *President's Trip (diary)*.

98. Shen, *U.S. and Free China*, p. 92.

99. Ibid., p. 95.

100. Ibid., p. 113.

101. Chiang Kai-shek, statement, Republic of China on Taiwan Government, February 28, 1972.

102. William F. Buckley Jr., quoted in the *Washington Star*, February 29, 1972. Buckley's remarks were made in Manchester, New Hampshire, on February 28, 1972.

103. Nixon, *RN*, p. 565.

104. Zhou Enlai, quoted in Solomon, "Chinese Political Negotiating Behavior: Interpretive Assessment," p. 19.

105. Gates, *From the Shadows*, p. 80.

106. Solomon, "US-PRC Political Negotiations: An Annotated Chronology"; and Henry Kissinger, *Years of Upheaval*, p. 55.

107. Such an agreement was first mentioned to the U.S. delegation at the SALT I negotiations in Vienna in July 1970, and then against in August 1971 (as reported by Kissinger to Chinese ambassador Huang Zhen in Paris). But the Soviets did not put the proposal in writing until May 1972, when a draft agreement was presented to Nixon's delegation in Moscow on May 12 by Ambassador Dobrynin. The second paragraph of the treaty stated that the United States and the Soviet Union "shall prevent" situations in which third countries might cause or provoke nuclear war. Nixon and Kissinger read this paragraph as an attempt by Moscow to gain a free hand in attacking China on the pretext that the growth of China's nuclear arsenal, together with Beijing's anti-Soviet diplomacy, constituted a threat to the Soviet Union.

108. Dobrynin, *In Confidence*, p. 259.

109. Henry Kissinger, Memorandum of Conversation with Huang Hua, August 4, 1972, quoted in Solomon, "US-PRC Political Negotiations: An Annotated Chronology."

110. Li, *Private Life of Chairman Mao*, pp. 572–573.

111. Solomon, "Chinese Political Negotiating Behavior," pp. 46–47.

112. Raymond Price, *With Nixon* (New York: Viking, 1977), pp. 109–115.

113. Ibid.

114. Ibid.

115. Henry Kissinger, Memorandum of Conversation with Huang Hua, November 13, 1972, quoted in Solomon, "US-PRC Political Negotiations: An Annotated Chronology."

116. Henry Kissinger, Memorandum of Conversation with Huang Hua, January 3, 1973, quoted in Solomon, "US-PRC Political Negotiations: An Annotated Chronology."

117. Message from Zhou Enlai to Nixon delivered through the PRC Mission to the UN, January 6, 1972. Solomon, "US-PRC Political Negotiations: An Annotated Chronology." Zhou's message was delivered via the Chinese Mission to the United Nations on January 6, 1972.

118. Ibid., November 18–19, 1972.

119. *Haldeman Diaries*, November 20, 1972.

120. Henry Kissinger, Memorandum for the President (Top Secret), March 2, 1973, re: Atmospherics of My Trip to Beijing.

121. Ibid., p. 3.

122. Henry Kissinger, Memorandum of Conversation with Zhou Enlai, February 15, 1973, quoted in Solomon, "US-PRC Political Negotiations: An Annotated Chronology."

123. Henry Kissinger, Memorandum of Conversation with Mao Zedong (Top Secret), Chairman Mao's residence, February 17–18, 1973, p. 5.

124. Ibid., p. 21.

125. Ibid., p. 22.

126. Ibid., p. 13.

127. Ibid., p. 4.

128. The presence of the marines proved to be a source of diplomatic friction in the early years, as the young leathernecks set up their "Red-Ass Saloon" for after-hours drinking and socializing. It was harmless fun, but it also attracted a crowd from among the fun-starved expatriate residents of Beijing's diplomatic quarter. Radicals in the Chinese leadership used every opportunity to criticize Zhou and the Foreign Ministry for condoning such a rowdy "foreign" military presence in Beijing.

129. Vaclav Smil, in *China's Environmental Crisis: An Inquiry into the Limits of National Development* (Armonk, N.Y.: M. E. Sharpe, 1993), states that the total length of China's railways was 53,000 kilometers in 1990, corresponding to the total U.S. rail network in 1863.

130. Nixon granted Boeing an export license for ten Boeing 707 jets in a deal valued at $150 million. See *New York Times*, July 6, 1972. Nixon had earlier authorized the sale of an RCA satellite ground station to China in February 1972. It was used to transmit the live television pictures of Nixon's trip to China.

131. Shi Lin, ed. *Dangdai Zhongguo de duiwai jingji hezuo* (Contemporary Chinese foreign economic cooperation) (Beijing: Chinese Academy of Social Sciences Publishing House, 1989), p. 320; and Ross, *Negotiating Cooperation*, p. 73.

132. Xiao Rong, interview by author. Xiao is Deng's youngest daughter.

133. Lucian W. Pye, "Deng Xiaoping and China's Political Culture," *China Quarterly* (September 1993): 417.

134. Biographies of Deng include: Deng Maomao, *My Father Deng Xiaoping* (New York: Basic Books, 1995); Ruan Ming, *Deng Xiaoping: Chronicle of an Empire* (Boulder: Westview Press, 1992); Uli Franz, *Deng Xiaoping* (New York: Harcourt, Brace, Jovanovich, 1988); Richard Evans, *Deng Xiaoping and the Making of Modern China* (New York: Penguin Books, 1993); and articles in *China Quarterly*, special issue: "Deng Xiaoping: An Assessment" (September 1993).

135. Xiao Rong, interview by author.

136. Kissinger, Memorandum of Conversation with Mao Zedong, February 17–18.

137. PRC note delivered to the US government, September 26, 1972, Solomon, "US-PRC Political Negotiations: An Annotated Chronology"; and Henry Kissinger, Memorandum of Conversation with Huang Hua, New York City, October 3, 1972, 8:30 P.M.–9:20 P.M., quoted in Solomon, "Chinese Political Negotiating Behavior."

138. Henry Kissinger, Memorandum of Conversation with Huang Hua (Top Secret), UN Mission, PRC, April 16, 1973, 5:40 P.M.–7:55 P.M., p. 15. Neither Nixon nor Kissinger, in their memoirs, mention making a commitment "to the integrity of China" as a "fundamental element" of American policy.

139. Ibid.

140. See Kissinger's account of the Zavidovo session in *Years of Upheaval*, pp. 232–233.

141. Kissinger staffers Helmut Sonnenfeldt, William Hyland, and Peter Rodman, interviews by author; see also William G. Hyland, *Mortal Rivals: Superpower Relations from Nixon to Reagan* (New York: Random House, 1987), p. 64.

142. Henry Kissinger, Memorandum of Conversation with Han Xu, White House, Map Room, May 15, 1973, 10:20 A.M.–11:00 A.M. In this conversation, held in the White House, Kissinger recounted to the Chinese diplomat Brezhnev's comments and provided him with a copy of the Agreement on the Prevention of Nuclear War, annotated with Kissinger's commentary on the meaning of various provisions.

143. Ibid.

144. Kissinger, *Years of Upheaval*, p. 232.

145. Kissinger, Memorandum of Conversation with Han Xu, May 15.

146. Kissinger, *Years of Upheaval*, p. 282.

147. Kissinger staff member, interview by author.

148. Henry Kissinger, Memorandum of Conversation with Huang Zhen, May 29, 1973, quoted in Solomon, "US-PRC Political Negotiations: An Annotated Chronology."

149. In the course of that contingency planning, the White House ordered the first studies on how the United States might come to China's rescue in the event of an all-out

military attack by the Soviet Union. A panel of nuclear weapons analysts examined how, in a crisis, the United States might arm China with nuclear weapons or send American forces equipped with nuclear weapons into China. It would be a complex task. The Joint Chiefs of Staff were in the midst of rewriting the basic assumptions from which America's nuclear war plan, the Single Integrated Operating Plan (SIOP), was drawn. Since the early 1960s, the SIOP had been based on three objectives: (1) "to destroy the Soviet and PRC nuclear offensive capability"; (2) "to destroy the Soviet and PRC military target system"; and (3) "to cause heavy damage to the enemy's industrial base supporting the war effort and its urban-industrial centers." See White House, *Analytical Summary: DOD Targeting Study Results and Proposals* (Washington, D.C., 1973). The shortcomings of this strategy were obvious. In the event of war, an American president could not attack the Soviet Union without also attacking China. Nixon insisted that he have better options to limit nuclear war and control escalation. As a result, on December 26, 1972, Defense secretary Melvin Laird forwarded to Nixon the results of the Defense Department's Strategic Target Attack Policy Study, conducted by a panel chaired by Johnny Foster. Laird also forwarded a new draft, "Nuclear Weapons Employment Policy," and a number of recommendations, including a detailed set of limited nuclear attack options that treated the Soviet Union and China separately. Under the new policy emphasizing the need to control escalation, three attack options against: (1) "PRC nuclear threats"; (2) "PRC national civilian and military controls"; and (3) "PRC conventional threat to U.S. forces and allies," were formulated.

150. See Kissinger's account of the Zavidovo session in *Years of Upheaval*, pp. 232–233; and Henry Kissinger, interview by author.

151. Kissinger, Memorandum of Conversation with Mao Zedong, February 17–18.

152. Nixon, *RN*, p. 882; Hyland, *Mortal Rivals*, pp. 60–63; Dobrynin, *In Confidence*, pp. 277, 282; and William Hyland, Helmut Sonnenfeldt, Winston Lord, Peter Rodman, Richard Solomon, and Henry Kissinger, interviews by author.

153. Nixon, *RN*, p. 882.

154. Henry Kissinger, Memorandum of Conversation with Huang Zhen, July 6, 1973.

155. Ibid.

156. Ibid.

157. Phil Odeen, Memorandum for Dr. Kissinger (Top Secret), June 8, 1973, re: National Security Study Memorandum (NSSM) 169: Nuclear Policy.

158. Ibid.

159. Ibid.

160. Kissinger, Memorandum of Conversation with Huang Zhen, July 6.

161. People's Republic of China, untitled statement, n.d., received June 14, 1973, by the White House.

162. Kissinger, Memorandum of Conversation with Huang Zhen, July 6.

163. Stanley I. Kutler, *Abuse of Power: The New Nixon Tapes* (New York: The Free Press, 1997), pp. 635–636.

164. Solomon, "US-PRC Political Negotiations: An Annotated Chronology."

165. Gates, *From the Shadows*, p. 43.

166. Extract from a Henry Kissinger Memorandum of Conversation with Qiao Guanhua, October 3, 1973, quoted in Solomon, "US-PRC Political Negotiations: An Annotated Chronology."

167. Henry Kissinger, Memorandum of Conversation with Zhou Enlai, Great Hall of the People, November 11, 1973, 3:15 P.M.–7:00 P.M., pp. 5–7.

168. Ibid., pp. 7–8.

169. Henry Kissinger, Memorandum of Conversation with Zhou Enlai, guesthouse villa, Beijing, November 12, 1973, 3:00 P.M.–5:30 P.M., pp. 4–5.

170. Ibid.

171. Members of Kissinger's delegation, interviews by author.

172. Kissinger, Memorandum of Conversation with Zhou Enlai, November 12, pp. 3–4.

173. Henry Kissinger, Memorandum of Conversation with Zhou Enlai, Great Hall of the People, November 13, 1973, 10:00 P.M.–12:30 P.M.

174. Ibid.

175. Chinese officials, interviews by author.

176. Henry Kissinger, Memorandum of Conversation with Zhou Enlai, guesthouse villa, Beijing, November 14, 1973, 7:35 A.M.–8:25 A.M.

177. Chinese officials, interviews by author.

178. Henry Kissinger, Memorandum of Conversation with Mao Zedong, Chairman Mao's residence, November 12, 1973, 5:40 P.M.–8:25 P.M., p. 10.

179. Ibid., p. 5.

180. Ibid., p. 12.

181. Ibid., p. 29.

182. Interviews with Kissinger, Lord, and members of Kissinger's staff indicate that U.S. intelligence never learned of Mao's attack on Zhou following the latter's November 1973 presentation on a military alliance.

183. Jia Ennan, *Mao Zedong renji jiaowang shilu* (True record of Mao Zedong's interpersonal contacts) (Nanjing: Jiangsu Wenyi Chubanshe, 1990).

184. Henry Kissinger, Memorandum for the President (Top Secret), November 19, 1973, re: My Visit to China.

185. *New York Times*, November 15, 1973.

186. Arthur Hummel Jr., Winston Lord, and Richard Solomon, Action Memorandum (Top Secret), Washington, D.C., May 24, 1974. The memo emphasized that while relations with Mao and Zhou were increasingly strained, "Taiwan on the other hand has been buoyed by recent events, feeling that it has a new lease on life." It also pointed out that "the relatively easy steps of the first phase of the opening to Peking are over, and the harder choices of how to modify our relations with the ROC [Taiwan] are before us." It further warned that Taiwan had put in a string of new requests for military sales, including for the F-4 Phantom jet, and that pro-Taiwan lobbyists were fully mobilized in Congress, taking many congressional members and their staffs on free trips to Taiwan. If the administration had any hope of turning the situation around, "we must have an overall strategy tailored to the goals of the Administration's China policy."

187. Central Intelligence Agency, Biographical Data Sheet on Deng Xiaoping, April 4, 1974.

188. Richard H. Solomon, Memorandum for Secretary Kissinger (Top Secret), April 12, 1974, re: The PRC's Domestic Political Situation and Foreign Policy As a Context for Your Meeting with Deng Xiaoping and Qiao Guanhua.

189. Henry Kissinger, Memorandum of Conversation with Deng Xiaoping (Top Secret), April 14, 1974, 8:05 P.M.–11:00 P.M., p. 26.

190. Ibid.

191. Members of Kissinger's staff, interviews by author.

192. See Hyland's account of this meeting in *Mortal Rivals*, pp. 62–65.

FORD: ESTRANGEMENT

1. Henry Kissinger, White House communication (1607 Z[ulu]), Situation Room Flash to Ambassador David Bruce, U.S. liaison office, Beijing, August 9, 1974.

2. Henry Kissinger, Memorandum of Conversation with Huang Zhen, 4:50 P.M.–5:20 P.M., August 9, 1974, p. 3.

3. White House Document (Top Secret), "Peoples Republic of China," August 14, 1974, handwritten notation: Briefing Paper for President.

4. Ibid., p. 9.

5. Ibid. p. 10.

6. Ibid.

7. Gerald R. Ford, interview by author.

8. Ibid.
9. Fulbright Congressional Delegation, Memorandum of Conversation with Qiao Guanhua, September 3, 1974.
10. Ibid.
11. Ibid.
12. Richard H. Solomon, "Chinese Political Negotiating Behavior: An Interpretive Assessment, 1967–1984," p. 87.
13. Unsigned memorandum (Top Secret), October 3, 1974, re: Your Dinner Conversation with the Chinese. This memorandum was possibly from Solomon to Kissinger.
14. Henry Kissinger, Memorandum of Conversation with Qiao Guanhua (Top Secret), October 2, 1974, 8:15 P.M.–11:35 P.M., Secretary's Suite, Waldorf Towers, New York City, p. 14.
15. Chinese officials and others in Mao's circle, interviews by author.
16. Kissinger, Memorandum of Conversation with Qiao Guanhua, October 2, p. 17.
17. Ibid., p. 18.
18. Ibid., p. 21.
19. Unsigned Memorandum (possibly from Solomon to Kissinger) entitled "Your Dinner Conversation with the Chinese (Top Secret), October 3, p. 3.
20. Henry Kissinger, National Security Study Memorandum 212 (Top Secret), to Secretary of Defense, Secretary of State, and Director of Central Intelligence (with copy to Chairman of the Joint Chiefs of Staff), re: U.S. Security Assistance to the Republic of China. The memorandum stated: "The President has directed a study of U.S. policy on the transfer of American military equipment to the Republic of China over the next three to five years." The study assumed that normalization of U.S.-China relations would continue, that there would be no radical change in the Sino-Soviet conflict, and that the defense commitment to Taiwan would remain in effect. Given these assumptions, the memo, signed by Kissinger, asked what was "the threat to the security of Taiwan over this period" and what roles would U.S. and Taiwanese forces play in "deterring and defending against a possible PRC attack on Taiwan and the Pescadores."
21. Kissinger, National Security Study Memorandum 212 (Top Secret), November 12, 1974.
22. Ibid.
23. Henry Kissinger, discussion with Philip Habib, William Gleysteen Jr., Arthur Hummel Jr., Harry E. T. Thayer, Herbert Horowitz, Oscar Armstrong, and Winston Lord, October 29, 1976, transcript.
24. Li Zhisui, *The Private Life of Chairman Mao: The Memoir of Mao's Personal Physician* (New York: Random House, 1994), pp. 581, 592.
25. Department of State, Bureau of Intelligence and Research, "The Chinese Leadership After the National People's Congress" (Secret), by D. W. Keyser (Washington, D.C., February 13, 1975).
26. Li, *Private Life of Chairman Mao*, p. 582.
27. Ibid., p. 583.
28. Ibid., p. 578.
29. Wang Ruoshui and other Chinese officials, interviews by author. Wang was a former deputy editor of the *People's Daily* and a member of the pro-Zhou Enlai faction during the Cultural Revolution.
30. Li, *Private Life of Chairman Mao*, pp. 578–579.
31. Zhongguo Gongchandang lishi dashiji, p. 309; Jia Ennan, *Mao Zedong renji jiaowang shilu* (True record of Mao Zedong's personal relations) (Nanjing: Jiangsu Wenyi Chubanshe, 1990); Robert S. Ross, *Negotiating Cooperation: The United States and China, 1969–1989* (Stanford: Stanford University Press, 1995), p. 62; and Lin Qing, *Zhou Enlai zaixiang shengya* (The career of Premier Zhou Enlai) (Hong Kong: Changcheng Wenhua Chubanshe, 1991).
32. Li, *Private Life of Chairman Mao*, p. 587.
33. Kissinger's strategy and preparation for the November 1974 trip to China is described

in various staff documents, including Winston Lord, Arthur Hummel Jr., and Richard Solomon, Memorandum for Secretary Kissinger (Top Secret), November 9, 1974, re: Briefing the President on your Forthcoming Trip to Peking; *Scope Analysis: U.S.-PRC Normalization at the Turning Point* (Top Secret); *Normalization of U.S.-PRC Relations and the Future of Taiwan* (Top Secret); and Kissinger, National Security Study Memorandum 212, November 12.

34. Gerald Ford, Henry Kissinger, Robert Hartmann, Ron Nessen, William Gleysteen Jr., John Holdridge, Richard Solomon, Winston Lord, and Arthur Hummel Jr., interviews by author.

35. Kissinger threw around pejoratives easily, a reflection of his own insecurities. In the case of Deng, Kissinger used flattery and inducements to try to build a close relationship, and he indeed developed a certain respect for Deng over time, but he often confided to aides, as he did in October 1976, that "[China's] foreign policy has not been subtle since Zhou."

36. Henry Kissinger, Memorandum of Conversation with Deng Xiaoping (Top Secret), Great Hall of the People, November 26, 1974, 10:20–11:02 A.M.

37. Ibid., p. 7.

38. Ibid., p. 8.

39. Henry Kissinger, Memorandum of Conversation with Deng Xiaoping (Top Secret), Great Hall of the People, November 26, 1974, 3:45–5:00 P.M.

40. Ibid., p. 5.

41. Ibid., p. 6.

42. Ibid., p. 7.

43. Ibid., p. 8.

44. Ibid.

45. Ibid., p. 10.

46. Ibid., p. 14.

47. Brent Scowcroft, Memorandum for the President (Secret), November 27, 1974, re: Secretary Kissinger Asked That I Pass You the Following Report.

48. Henry Kissinger, Memorandum of Conversation with Deng Xiaoping (Top Secret), 4:00 P.M.–6:15 P.M., Great Hall of the People, November 28, 1974.

49. Henry Kissinger, Memorandum of Conversation with Qiao Guanhua (Top Secret), October 8, 1976, p. 17.

50. Department of State, telegram from American Consul General Hong Kong (Secret), December 27, 1974.

51. Department of State, telegram to U.S. Liaison Office Beijing (Secret), December 26, 1974.

52. See Richard H. Solomon, "US-PRC Political Negotiations, 1967–1984: An Annotated Chronology" (Santa Monica, Calif.: RAND Corporation), August 16, 1971; and Philip Habib, Memorandum to the Secretary of State, March 26, 1975. Habib's memorandum conveyed the decision to postpone indefinitely the U.S. tour of the Performing Arts Troupe of China.

53. Robert Ingersoll, Memorandum of Conversation with Huang Hua, May 12, 1975, quoted in Solomon, "US-PRC Political Negotiations: An Annotated Chronology." Ingersoll was the deputy secretary of state.

54. Henry Kissinger, Memorandum of Conversation with Huang Zhen, 5:35 P.M.–6:40 P.M., May 9, 1975.

55. National Security Council, *Peoples Republic of China* (Top Secret), July 1975. This document is a summary of intelligence drawn from wiretaps or intercepts.

56. *Washington Post*, April 15, 1975.

57. Gerald Ford, interview by author; see also *New York Times*, May 8, 1975.

58. Ford staffer members, interviews by author; see also Robert M. Gates, *From the Shadows: The Ultimate Insider's Story of Five Presidents and How They Won the Cold War* (New York: Simon & Schuster, 1997), p. 87.

59. Ross, *Negotiating Cooperation*, p. 80.

60. *New York Times*, October 16, 1975.
61. Gates, *From the Shadows*, pp. 65–69; see also John Stockwell, *In Search of Enemies: A CIA Story* (New York: W. W. Norton, 1978), pp. 53–54.
62. Gates, *From the Shadows*, p. 66.
63. Department of State, telegram from Brent Scowcroft (Top Secret), CIA Voyager Channel, July 13, 1975.
64. Henry Kissinger, Memorandum of Conversation with Qiao Guanhua (Top Secret), 8:10 P.M.–11:55 P.M., Suite of the Secretary of State, Waldorf Towers, New York, p. 28.
65. Ibid., p. 29.
66. Kissinger staff members, interviews by author.
67. Henry Kissinger, Memorandum of Conversation with Deng Xiaoping (Top Secret), Great Hall of the People, October 20, 1975, 10:00–11:40 A.M., p. 17.
68. Henry Kissinger, Memorandum of Conversation with Deng Xiaoping (Top Secret), Great Hall of the People, October 20, 1975, 4:15–6:35 P.M., p. 3.
69. Ibid., p. 7.
70. Ibid., p. 9.
71. Ibid., p. 12.
72. Ibid., p. 13.
73. Ibid., p. 14.
74. Ibid., p. 16.
75. Henry Kissinger, Memorandum of Conversation with Mao Zedong (Top Secret), Chairman Mao's residence, October 21, 1975, 6:25–8:05 P.M., p. 2.
76. Ibid., p. 3.
77. Ibid., p. 4.
78. Ibid.
79. Ibid., p. 10.
80. Ibid., p. 16.
81. Arthur W. Hummel Jr., oral history interview, Foreign Service Institute and Georgetown University, Washington, D.C., April 13, 1994, p. 46; see also Henry Kissinger, Memorandum of Conversation with Senior Staff Members (Secret), October 29, 1976.
82. Brent Scowcroft, Memorandum for the President (Top Secret), October 23, 1975, re: Secretary's Talks with Chinese Officials," p. 3.
83. Kissinger staff members, interviews by author.
84. Scowcroft, Memorandum for the President, October 23, p. 2.
85. *New York Times*, December 4, 1975.
86. Gerald Ford and Robert Hartmann, interviews by author.
87. Herbert Horowitz, Memorandum to William Gleysteen (Secret), with attachment by C. J. Szymanski, "China in 1975," November 26, 1975, re: Memoranda in Support of the President's Trip to China. Kissinger's briefing book for Ford included summary memorandums on the history of U.S.-China relations; see Henry Kissinger, Memorandum for the President, November 20, 1975, re: Your Trip to the People's Republic of China: A Scope Analysis for Your Discussions with Chinese Leaders; Henry Kissinger, Memorandum for the President, re: Our Future Relationship with the People's Republic of China, undated; Henry Kissinger, Memorandum for the President, November 28, 1975, re: Your Meeting with Chairman Mao; and White House, *Mao Tse-Tung's Personal Style and Political Views*, undated.
88. *New York Times*, December 2, 1975.
89. Ibid.
90. Gerald Ford, Memorandum of Conversation with Deng Xiaoping (Secret), Great Hall of the People, December 2, 1975, 10:10 A.M.–12:30 P.M., p. 14.
91. Ibid., p. 15.
92. Gerald Ford, interview by author.
93. Gerald Ford, Memorandum of Conversation with Mao Zedong (Secret), Chairman Mao's residence, December 2, 1975, 4:10 P.M.–6:00 P.M., p. 2.

94. Ibid., p. 3.
95. Ibid., p. 14.
96. Gerald Ford, Memorandum of Conversation with Deng Xiaoping (Secret), guest-house villa, Beijing, December 3, 1975, 9:25 A.M.–11:55 A.M., p. 19.
97. Gerald Ford, Memorandum of Conversation with Deng Xiaoping (Secret), Great Hall of the People, December 4, 1975, 10:05 A.M.–11:47 A.M., p. 3.
98. Ibid., p. 5.
99. Winston Lord, Memorandum of Conversation with Han Xu, January 30, 1976, quoted in Solomon, "US-PRC Political Negotiations: An Annotated Chronology."
100. Gerald Ford, interview by author.
101. *New York Times*, March 7, 1976.
102. James A. Baker III with Thomas DeFrank, *The Politics of Diplomacy* (New York: G.P. Putnam's Sons, 1995), p. 22.
103. Li, *Private Life of Chairman Mao*, p. 614.
104. Hugh Scott, Memorandum of Conversation with Zhang Chunqiao, quoted in Solomon, "US-PRC Political Negotiations: An Annotated Chronology."
105. Richard Nixon, Memorandum to Dr. Henry Kissinger (Eyes Only), March 12, 1976, p. 49.
106. Liu Chuanzhen, interview by author. Liu was a resident of Tangshan.
107. Li, *Private Life of Chairman Mao*, p. 624.
108. James Schlesinger, interview by author.
109. Henry Kissinger, Memorandum of Conversation with Qiao Guanhua (Secret), October 8, 1976.
110. Ibid., p. 11.
111. Ibid., p. 22.
112. Ibid., p. 20.
113. Henry Kissinger, Memorandum of Conversation with Senior Staff Members (Secret), October 29, 1976.
114. Ibid.

CARTER: FULFILLMENT

1. Among those interviewed on the Carter administration's China policy were: President Jimmy Carter, President Gerald Ford, Henry Kissinger, Brent Scowcroft, Vice President Walter Mondale, Zbigniew Brzezinski, Warren Christopher, David Aaron, Marshall Shulman, Peter Tarnoff, Richard Holbrooke, Gerald Rafshoon, Michel Oksenberg, Harry Thayer, Chas. W. Freeman Jr., William Gleysteen Jr., Roger Sullivan, Leonard Woodcock, J. Stapleton Roy, Alan Romberg, James Lilley, William Hyland, and Richard Solomon.
2. Jimmy Carter, *Keeping Faith* (New York: Bantam Books, 1982), p. 186.
3. Ibid., p. 188; and Jimmy Carter, interview by author. The president-elect hosted a large group of foreign policy experts in Plains, Georgia, after the election.
4. R. W. Apple Jr., interview by author.
5. Averell Harriman, Memorandum for the Record, August 31, 1976, re: WAH's Talk with Governor Carter.
6. Ibid.
7. Carter aides, interviews by author; and Cyrus Vance, *Hard Choices* (New York: Simon and Schuster, 1983), p. 29.
8. Zbigniew Brzezinski, *Power and Principle: Memoir of the National Security Advisory, 1977–1981* (New York: Farrar, Straus & Giroux, 1985), p. 5.
9. Vance, *Hard Choices*, p. 30.
10. Averell Harriman, Memorandum of Conversation with Leonid Brezhnev, Kremlin, September 20, 1976.
11. Averell Harriman, Memorandum of Conversation with Jimmy Carter, November 29,

1976; Averell Harriman, Memorandum of Conversation with Anatoly Dobrynin, December 1, 1976; and Averell Harriman, Memorandum of Conversation with Anatoly Dobrynin, December 8, 1976.

12. Jimmy Carter, Zbigniew Brzezinski, Richard Holbrooke, Peter Tarnoff, and other Carter aides, interviews by author.

13. Ibid.

14. *Washington Post*, February 27, 1977.

15. Cyrus Vance, *Face the Nation*, Columbia Broadcasting System, February 27, 1977, transcript.

16. Richard Holbrooke, Michel Oksenberg, Zbigniew Brzezinski, Roger Sullivan, Peter Tarnoff, Harry Thayer, and William Gleysteen Jr., interviews by author.

17. *New York Times*, April 11, 1977; quoting "key officials" in the Carter administration, *The Times* reported that Nixon had pledged to China that he strongly desired to normalize relations in his second term. *The Times* said that the Nixon pledge was "unknown until now."

18. Jimmy Carter, Zbigniew Brzezinski, David Aaron, Michael Armacost, Michel Oksenberg, and Leonard Woodcock, interviews by author.

19. Brzezinski refers to Carter's reaction to the secret U.S.-China record in *Power and Principle*, p. 200; the president admonished Brzezinski that in dealing with Beijing, we "should not ass-kiss them the way Nixon and Kissinger did, and also be careful not to antagonize domestic constituencies."

20. Brzezinski, *Power and Principle*, p. 64.

21. Jimmy Carter, Leonard Woodcock, Walter Mondale, Richard Holbrooke, Michel Oksenberg, and Gerald Rafshoon, interviews by author.

22. Robert M. Gates, *From the Shadows: The Ultimate Insider's Story of Five Presidents and How They Won the Cold War* (New York: Simon & Schuster, 1997), p. 88.

23. Cyrus Vance, Memorandum of Conversation with Huang Zhen, April 11, 1977, quoted in Richard H. Solomon, "US-PRC Political Negotiations, 1967–1984: An Annotated Chronology" (Santa Monica, Calif.: RAND Corporation).

24. Brzezinski, *Power and Principle*, pp. 199–200; Harry Harding, *A Fragile Relationship* (Washington, D.C.: Brookings Institution, 1992), pp. 71–73; Robert S. Ross, *Negotiating Cooperation: The United States and China, 1969–1989* (Stanford: Stanford University Press, 1995), pp. 104–105, 116–117; Michel Oksenberg, "A Decade of Sino-American Relations," *Foreign Affairs* (Fall 1982); and Jimmy Carter, speech delivered at the University of Notre Dame, Notre Dame, Ind., May 1977.

25. *Washington Post*, April 28, 1977.

26. This meeting occurred on July 30, 1977, and was attended by Carter, Vance, Brzezinski, Brown, Holbrooke, and Oksenberg.

27. Oksenberg, "Decade of Sino-American Relations," 182; and Brzezinski, *Power and Principle*, p. 201.

28. Jimmy Carter, interview by author.

29. Carter, *Keeping Faith*, pp. 190–191.

30. *New York Times*, August 27, 1977. Goldwater told a gathering in Lake Tahoe, Nevada, on August 26: "I can state with assurance that no president has ever, in our entire history, unilaterally abrogated a treaty with any foreign government in violation of that treaty and without cause from the other party. He [Carter] may have the power to recognize, but he cannot terminate a treaty without the approval of the Senate or Congress. Failure to conform with this requirement would be grounds for impeachment."

31. Richard Holbrooke, Michel Oksenberg, William Gleysteen Jr., James Lilley, Richard Solomon, and Roger Sullivan, interviews by author.

32. U.S. liaison office staff members, interviews by author.

33. Cyrus Vance, Memorandum of Conversation with Deng Xiaoping, August 23–24, 1977, quoted in Solomon, "US-PRC Political Negotiations: An Annotated Chronology."

34. Ibid.

35. Vance, *Hard Choices*, pp. 82–83; and Leonard Woodcock, Michel Oksenberg, Richard Holbrooke, William Gleysteen Jr., and Roger Sullivan, interviews by author.

36. A summary of Deng's statements, by agreement without direct quotations, was carried by the Associated Press on September 7, 1977. The State Department declined to comment on the report.

37. Leonard Woodcock, William Gleysteen Jr., and Michel Oksenberg, interviews by author.

38. Zbigniew Brzezinski, Michel Oksenberg, and Michael Armacost, interviews by author.

39. Zbigniew Brzezinski, Richard Holbrooke, Michel Oksenberg, William Gleysteen Jr., and Harry Thayer, interviews by author.

40. David Broder, "Skillful Prod on China," *Washington Post*, February 1, 1978.

41. U.S. liaison office staff members, interviews by author.

42. *Washington Post*, February 2, 1978; and *New York Times*, February 3, 1978.

43. Leonard Woodcock, Michel Oksenberg, Richard Holbrooke, and William Gleysteen Jr., interviews by author.

44. Jimmy Carter, Walter Mondale, Leonard Woodcock, and Michel Oksenberg, interviews by author.

45. Cyrus Vance, Harold Brown, and Zbigniew Brzezinski, Memorandum for the President (Secret), May 5, 1978, re: Normalizing U.S.-China Relations.

46. Brzezinski, *Power and Principle*, pp. 208, 459.

47. Zbigniew Brzezinski, Leonard Woodcock, Richard Holbrooke, Michel Oksenberg, and William Gleysteen Jr., interviews by author.

48. Ibid.

49. Solomon, "US-PRC Political Negotiations: An Annotated Chronology," p. 16; and Brzezinski, *Power and Principle*, pp. 213–215.

50. Brzezinski, *Power and Principle*, p. 214.

51. Solomon, "US-PRC Political Negotiations: An Annotated Chronology," p. 16

52. *Washington Post*, May 24, 1978.

53. Leonard Woodcock, Sharon Tuohy, Michel Oksenberg, and Zbigniew Brzezinski, interviews by author.

54. Leonard Woodcock, Michel Oksenberg, Richard Holbrooke, and William Gleysteen Jr., interviews by author.

55. Jimmy Carter, Zbigniew Brzezinski, Warren Christopher, Richard Holbrooke, and Leonard Woodcock, interviews by author.

56. Ibid.

57. Leonard Woodcock, Michel Oksenberg, Warren Christopher, Richard Holbrooke, William Gleysteen Jr., and J. Stapleton Roy, interviews by author.

58. Solomon, "US-PRC Political Negotiations: An Annotated Chronology"; and Leonard Woodcock, Michel Oksenberg, and William Gleysteen Jr., interviews by author.

59. Deng Xiaoping, "Emancipate the Mind, Seek Truth from Facts, and United As One in Looking to the Future," *The Selected Works of Deng Xiaoping*, vol. 2, 1975–1982, pp. 175–158. This speech was delivered on December 13, 1978.

60. *Guangming Ribao*, November 15, 1978.

61. Solomon, "US-PRC Political Negotiations: An Annotated Chronology."

62. Michel Oksenberg, Zbigniew Brzezinski, and Leonard Woodcock, interviews by author; Zbigniew Brzezinski, Memorandum of Conversation with Chai Zemin, December 11, 1978, quoted in Solomon, "US-PRC Political Negotiations: An Annotated Chronology"; and Brzezinski, *Power and Principle*, p. 230.

63. Leonard Woodcock, Zbigniew Brzezinski, Michel Oksenberg, Richard Holbrooke, Roger Sullivan, and William Gleysteen Jr., interviews by author.

64. Michel Oksenberg, Zbigniew Brzezinski, Warren Christopher, Richard Holbrooke, and Roger Sullivan, interviews by author.

65. Ibid.

66. Ibid.
67. Ibid.
68. Ibid.
69. Ibid.
70. Ibid.
71. Jimmy Carter, Leonard Woodcock, J. Stapleton Roy, Ji Chaozhu, Michel Oksenberg, Zbigniew Brzezinski, Warren Christopher, Richard Holbrooke, and Roger Sullivan, interviews by author.
72. Ibid.
73. One reconstruction of events by Martin Tolchin of *The New York Times* (December 18, 1978) indicated that Brzezinski was awakened at 2 A.M. on December 15 (3 P.M. Beijing time on the same day) and told that the normalization agreement was unraveling over the Taiwan arms sales question. According to this account, based on statements made by senior administration officials to Tolchin, Brzezinski telephoned Chai Zemin in the predawn hours of December 15 and urged him to accept the formulation that the two sides should agree to disagree on the arms sales question (see note 76 below for references to similar accounts). Tolchin's account further states that Brzezinski did not inform President Carter of the last-minute crisis, instead moving ahead with the ad hoc formulation that Woodcock had urged on Deng—that the two sides agree to normalize relations despite the serious disagreement over the arms sales question. The importance of these contemporaneous accounts is that they contradict later assertions by Brzezinski and other senior members of the Carter administration that the United States clearly and unequivocally reserved the right to continue selling arms to Taiwan throughout the negotiating process. The record suggests the reverse was true.
74. Zbigniew Brzezinski, Memorandum of Conversation with Chai Zemin, December 15, 1978, quoted in Solomon, "US-PRC Political Negotiations: An Annotated Chronology." "Zbigniew Brzezinski says public discussion of Taiwan arms sales after normalization cannot be avoided; U.S. Government will state on an "if asked" basis that Taiwan arms sales will continue after normalization, that the PRC does not endorse the U.S. actions, but both sides have nevertheless agreed to normalize, Deng should be quickly informed of this position to avoid public U.S.-PRC controversy just after normalization is announced."
75. Warren Christopher, Michael Armacost, Richard Holbrooke, Michel Oksenberg, Roger Sullivan, Peter Tarnoff, and Leonard Unger, interviews by author.
76. *Washington Post*, December 28, 1978; *New York Times*, December 28, 1978; *Time*, January 8, 1979; and *Newsweek*, January 8, 1979.
77. *Washington Post*, December 24, 1978.
78. White House aides, interviews by author.
79. One senior Chinese official said he believed that Deng misunderstood the American offer to terminate the Mutual Defense Treaty over twelve months. Deng believed that this was an offer to phase out arms sales, after which they would end. When Woodcock clarified the American position on December 15, telling Deng that it was Washington's intention to continue selling arms, Deng was angry but decided to go forward with normalization for strategic reasons, as Chinese military forces were poised to strike Vietnam, and the vice premier was concerned about Soviet retaliation. As a result, Deng stated that he reserved the right to return to the arms sales question and expected Carter to reenter negotiations in the future.
80. Carter, *Keeping Faith*, p. 208.
81. Jimmy Carter, Leonard Woodcock, Zbigniew Brzezinski, Michel Oksenberg, and Robert Gates, interviews by author.
82. Carter, *Keeping Faith*, p. 209; Brzezinski, *Power and Principle*, pp. 406–407; and Leonard Woodcock and Michel Oksenberg, interviews by author.
83. Brzezinski, *Power and Principle*, pp. 408–410; and Carter, *Keeping Faith*, p. 206.
84. Jimmy Carter and Zbigniew Brzezinski, interviews by author.

85. Jimmy Carter, Memorandum of Conversation with Deng Xiaoping, January 30, 1979, quoted in Solomon, "US-PRC Political Negotiations: An Annotated Chronology."

86. Jimmy Carter, Zbigniew Brzezinski, Michel Oksenberg, and Leonard Woodcock, interviews by author.

87. Zbigniew Brzezinski, Michel Oksenberg, Leonard Woodcock, and Roger Sullivan, interviews by author; Harding, *Fragile Relationship*, p. 90; Brzezinski, *Power and Principle*, pp. 412–413; Gates, *From the Shadows*, pp. 121–122; John H. Holdridge, *Crossing the Divide* (Lanham, Maryland: Rowman & Littlefield, 1997), p. 188; and Anatoly F. Dobrynin, *In Confidence: Moscow's Ambassador to America's Six Cold War Presidents (1962–1986)* (New York: Times Books, 1995), p. 421.

88. Jimmy Carter, interview by author.

89. *New York Times*, February 28, 1979.

90. Zbigniew Brzezinski, Leonard Woodcock, Michel Oksenberg, Robert Gates, and Kenneth Allen, interviews by author; Kenneth Allen, *People's Republic of China: People's Liberation Army Air Force* (Washington, D.C.: Defense Intelligence Agency, 1991); and Allen, Krumel, and Pollack, *China's Air Force Enters the Twenty-First Century* (Santa Monica, Calif.: RAND, 1995), pp. 87–96.

91. Dobrynin, *In Confidence*, p. 418.

92. *New York Times*, March 3, 1979; and Banning N. Garret, "The China Card and Its Origin" (Ph.D. Diss., Brandeis University, 1983), p. 157.

93. *New York Times*, March 3, 1979.

94. For a comprehensive account of the intellectual awakening in China during the Deng era, see Merle Goldman, *Sowing the Seeds of Democracy in China: Political Reform in the Deng Xiaoping Era* (Cambridge: Harvard University Press, 1994).

95. Leonard Woodcock, Michel Oksenberg, J. Stapleton Roy, Roger Sullivan, Wei Jingsheng, and Xu Wenli, interviews by author.

96. Patricia Derian, Leonard Woodcock, Michel Oksenberg, and Richard Holbrooke, interviews by author.

97. Jimmy Carter, Zbigniew Brzezinski, Walter Mondale, Leonard Woodcock, Michel Oksenberg, Robert Gates, David Gries, James Lilley, John Holdridge, and confidential sources, interviews by author.

98. Ibid.

REAGAN: . . . AND TAIWAN

1. *New York Times*, February 13, 1976. Reagan's letter to M. Stanton Evans was reprinted in a volume of Reagan correspondence edited by his longtime aide, Helene Van Damm.

2. Ibid.

3. Michael K. Deaver with Mickey Hershowitz, *Behind the Scenes* (New York: William Morrow, 1987), p. 129.

4. Richard Allen, Raymond Price, Robert Ellsworth, James Lilley, Alexander Haig Jr., William Rope, James Baker III, and John Holdridge, interviews by author.

5. *New York Times*, January 31, 1976. In a dispatch from Melbourne, Florida, *Times* correspondent Wayne King reported that Reagan said he would tie formal diplomatic recognition to a pledge from China to recognize the right of South Korea and Taiwan to independence.

6. Harry Harding, *A Fragile Relationship* (Washington, D.C.: Brookings Institution, 1992), p. 109; and *New York Times*, August 17, 1980.

7. Leonard Woodcock, J. Stapleton Roy, Michel Oksenberg, Roger Sullivan, and James Lilley, interviews by author.

8. Richard Allen, James Lilley, and other Reagan aides, interviews by author.

9. *New York Times*, August 17, 1980.

10. Bush aides, interviews by author.

11. Richard Allen, James Lilley, and other American officials, interviews by author.
12. Ibid.
13. Kissinger, in a July 6, 1975, meeting with his senior China staff, had stated his assessment of U.S.-China relations bluntly: "In my view, the relationship is based on their fear of the Russians."
14. Richard Allen, James Lilley, Leonard Woodcock, and other American officials, interviews by author.
15. *New York Times*, August 22, 23, 1980.
16. Richard Allen, James Lilley, and other Reagan aides, interviews by author.
17. Ibid.
18. *New York Times*, August 25, 1980.
19. Leonard Woodcock and other Carter aides, interviews by author; and *New York Times*, August 27, 1980.
20. Alexander Haig Jr., Richard Allen, John Holdridge, William Rope, and James Lilley, interviews by author; and Alexander Haig Jr., *Caveat: Realism, Reagan, and Foreign Policy* (New York: Macmillan, 1984), pp. 194–200.
21. See John Holdridge, Memorandum to the Secretary, re: Scope Paper for Your Visit to China, undated. Holdridge defines "strategic association" as "a new conceptual basis for a more durable U.S.-Chinese relationship built upon strategic association, under which the U.S. will treat China as a friendly non-allied country, and to demonstrate this by modifying restrictive legislation and regulations on export controls."
22. Alexander Haig Jr. with Charles McCarry, *Inner Circles: How America Changed the World* (New York: Warner Books, 1992), pp. 32–33.
23. Chas. Freeman, William Rope, Alexander Haig Jr., John Holdridge, Richard Allen, and James Lilley, interviews by author.
24. White House official, interview by author.
25. White House, Memorandum for Vice President, Secretary of State, et al., June 6, 1981, re: Presidential Decisions (U.S. Policy Toward China).
26. Alexander Haig Jr., Memorandum of Conversation with Huang Hua, June 15, 1981, quoted in Richard H. Solomon, "US-PRC Political Negotiations, 1967–1984: An Annotated Chronology" (Santa Monica, Calif.: RAND Corporation); Haig, *Caveat*, p. 207; and John Holdridge, Scott Hallford, and William Rope, interviews by author.
27. Department of State, "Secretary's Talking Points on Taiwan," undated, p. 3; and Alexander Haig Jr., Memorandum of Conversation with Huang Hua, June 17, 1981.
28. Department of State, "Secretary's Talking Points on Taiwan," undated, p. 3.
29. Alexander Haig Jr., John Holdridge, William Rope, Scott Hallford, and Richard Burt, interviews by author.
30. Alexander Haig Jr., Memorandum of Conversation with Geng Biao, quoted in Solomon, "US-PRC Political Negotiations: An Annotated Chronology."
31. Interviews with Haig aides; also, *New York Times*, June 17, 1981; also, *Washington Post*, June 17, 1981; also, US Embassy Beijing, Transcript of Secretary Haig's June 16 Beijing Press Conference, June 17, 1981; also, Transcript of President Reagan's News Conference, June 17, 1981(via *New York Times*).
32. Alexander Haig Jr., John Holdridge, James Lilley, Richard Burt, and Don Oberdorfer, interviews by author.
33. Bush aides, interviews by author.
34. Deaver, *Behind the Scenes*.
35. Haig, *Inner Circles*, pp. 189–209.
36. Ibid., p. 53.
37. Ibid., p. 65.
38. Ibid., p. 36.
39. Haig, *Caveat*, p. 92.
40. Richard Allen, James Lilley, John Holdridge, William Rope, and other Reagan aides, interviews by author.
41. Ibid.

42. Ibid.
43. Deaver, *Behind the Scenes*, p. 129.
44. Haig, *Caveat*, p. 200.
45. Richard Allen, James Lilley, John Holdridge, William Rope, and other Reagan aides, interviews by author.
46. Haig aides, interviews by author.
47. John H. Holdridge, *Crossing the Divide: An Insider's Account of Normalization of U.S.—China Relations* (Lanham, Maryland: Rowman & Littlefield, 1997), p. 212.
48. Richard Allen, James Lilley, William Rope, Scott Hallford, and John Holdridge, interviews by author.
49. Haig, *Caveat*, p. 208.
50. Robert S. Ross, *Negotiating Cooperation: The United States and China, 1969–1989* (Stanford: Stanford University Press, 1995), p. 184; see also Deng Xiaoping, interview by Louis Cha, *Ming Pao*, quoted in *South China Morning Post*, August 26, 1981. Deng elaborated, "Even if relations deteriorate to a level below that of 1972, China will not collapse. We didn't collapse then and we certainly won't collapse now." Later, he said, "The Chinese are proud. They will never bow, kneel, or beg."
51. Haig, *Caveat*, pp. 208–209; and Haig aides, interview by author.
52. *Dangdai Zhongguo Waijiao* (Contemporary Chinese diplomacy) (Beijing, 1987), p. 236.
53. Solomon, "US-PRC Political Negotiations: An Annotated Chronology"; and Haig aides, interviews by author.
54. Haig aides, interviews by author.
55. Ibid.
56. Ronald Reagan, Memorandum of Conversation with Zhou Ziyang, quoted in Solomon, "US-PRC Political Negotiations: An Annotated Chronology."
57. Alexander Haig Jr., Memorandum of Conversation with Huang Hua, 8:00 P.M., quoted in Solomon, "US-PRC Political Negotiations: An Annotated Chronology."
58. Haig, *Caveat*, p. 210; Holdridge, *Crossing the Divide*, p. 213; Alexander Haig Jr., Memorandum of Conversation with Huang Hua, quoted in Solomon, "US-PRC Political Negotiations: An Annotated Chronology"; and Haig aides, interviews by author.
59. Haig, *Caveat*, p. 210.
60. Solomon, "US-PRC Political Negotiations: An Annotated Chronology," p. 81; and Walter Mondale, Memorandum of Conversation with Zhang Wenjin.
61. Haig, *Caveat*, pp. 211–212.
62. Harding, *Fragile Relationship*, pp. 114–115.
63. Haig aides, interviews by author.
64. John Holdridge, William Rope, Scott Hallford, and James Lilley, interviews by author; and Holdridge, *Crossing the Divide*, pp. 215–219.
65. John Holdridge, William Rope, and Arthur Hummel, interviews by author.
66. Holdridge aide, interview by author.
67. Haig, *Caveat*, pp. 213–214.
68. Holdridge, *Crossing the Divide*, p. 226; Ross, *Negotiating Cooperation*, p. 194; and *New York Times*, May 10, 1982.
69. Reagan administration official, interview by author.
70. See Haig's own account of his departure in *Caveat*, pp. 214–215.
71. George Shultz, *Turmoil and Triumph: My Years as Secretary of State* (New York: Scribner's, 1993), pp. 5–6, 14, 381–384.
72. Haig, *Caveat*, p. 213; and *Washington Post*, March 5, 1982.
73. United States–China Joint Communiqué on United States Arms Sales to Taiwan, August 17, 1982.
74. Arthur Hummel and William Rope, interviews by author.
75. During the Ford administration, a policy review conducted under Kissinger considered and rejected proposals to transfer fighter aircraft manufacturing technology to China. See Henry Kissinger, discussion with Philip Habib, Arthur Hummel, William Gleysteen Jr., and Oscar Armstrong, October 29, 1976, transcript.

76. Richard Baum, *Burying Mao: Chinese Politics in the Age of Deng Xiaoping* (Princeton: Princeton University Press, 1994), p. 143; and Harding, *Fragile Relationship*, pp. 123–124.

77. Tokuma Utsunomiya, remarks to Japanese reporters, Associated Press dispatch, November 10, 1982. Tokuma was a member of the Japanese Diet.

78. Shultz, *Turmoil and Triumph*, pp. 385–386.

79. *New York Times*, January 30, 1983.

80. *New York Times*, February 2, 1983.

81. Paul Wolfowitz, Memorandum to the Secretary (Secret), January 26, 1983, re: Your Visit to China.

82. George Shultz, Memorandum of Conversation with Zhang Aiping, quoted in Solomon, "US-PRC Political Negotiations: An Annotated Chronology." This memorandum refers to the establishment of a working-level meeting to discuss U.S.-China defense cooperation. See also Paul Wolfowitz, Memorandum to the Secretary, January 26, 1983, p. 5; and Paul Wolfowitz, Memorandum to the Secretary (Secret), January 27, 1983, re: Your Meeting with Chinese Premier Zhao Ziyang. Wolfowitz's January 26 memorandum refers to licenses approved "over the past year" for sales presentations "on wide variety of equipment which could help China against USSR. Recently approved licenses for sales presentations of anti-armor missiles, helicopter-mounted close support weapons systems, and sophisticated photo reconnaissance equipment."

83. *New York Times*, September 28, 1983.

84. *The Selected Works of Deng Xiaoping*, vol. 3, *1982–1992*, p. 105.

BUSH: . . . AND TIANANMEN

1. James Lilley, interview by author.

2. For a detailed discussion of White House strategy in U.S.-China relations, see George Bush and Brent Scowcroft, *A World Transformed* (New York: Alfred A. Knopf, 1998), pp. 86–111.

3. Brent Scowcroft, James Lilley, James Baker, and Winston Lord, interviews by author.

4. Ibid.

5. Perry Link, *Evening Chats in Beijing* (New York: W. W. Norton, 1992), pp. 29–33. Link, a China scholar at Princeton University, accompanied Fang and his wife, Li Shuxian, as they attempted to attend the Bush banquet.

6. Lord, his deputy, Peter Tomsen, and J. Stapleton Roy, who was coordinating the trip in the State Department, all assert that Lord gave sufficient warning to the White House that the embassy was inviting several dissidents, including Fang. Therefore, they insist, Lord should not have been blamed. Another group of officials in the State Department and the White House believe that the explosive Chinese reaction to the invitation was predictable and that Lord should have insisted to the State Department that the matter be vetted at a higher level before he issued the invitation, especially because Fang had personally targeted Deng Xiaoping with his criticism. Lord might instead have offered to arrange a separate meeting between Bush and Fang. Had Lord done so, the Chinese reaction might have been the same, but the decision would have been reserved for the president.

7. See Apple's account of the backgrounder by a "senior White House official," *New York Times*, March 3, 1989; and Hoffman's account, *Washington Post*, March 3, 1989.

8. Henry Kissinger, Lawrence Eagleburger, Winston Lord, James Baker, James Lilley, Robert Kimmitt, Brent Scowcroft, Peter Tomsen, Douglas Paal, J. Stapleton Roy, Jeffrey Bader, and Donald Keyser, interviews by author.

9. The most complete accounts of the events of April–June 1989 can be found in Michael Fathers and Andrew Higgins, edited by Robert Cottrell, *Tiananmen: The Rape of Peking* (New York: Doubleday, 1989); see also Richard Gordon and Carma Hinton, *The Gate of Heavenly Peace*, Long Bow Group, 1996, documentary film; Orville Schell, *Mandate of Heaven: In China, A New Generation of Entrepreneurs, Dissidents, Bohemians,*

and Technocrats Lays Claim to China's Future (New York: Simon & Schuster, 1994), pp. 33–184; and George Black and Robin Munro, *Black Hands of Beijing: Lives of Defiance in China's Democracy Movement* (New York: John Wiley, 1993).

10. DIA officials, interviews by author.

11. Jack Leide, Kenneth Allen, James Lilley, James Huskey, and other American officials, interviews by author.

12. James A. Baker, III with Thomas M. DeFrank, *The Politics of Diplomacy: Revolution, War, and Peace, 1989–1992* (New York: G.P. Putnam's Sons, 1995), p. 102.

13. Chai Ling, Li Lu, Philip Cunningham, Robin Munro, Carma Hinton, Dai Qing, Liu Xiaobo, and Chen Xiaoping, interviews by author.

14. Ibid.

15. Chai Ling, video recording by Philip Cunningham, translated by Carma Hinton. Courtesy of Carma Hinton.

16. Chai Ling challenged the translation from the Chinese of the word *qidai*, which is usually translated as "expecting"; the passage would then be rendered "what we were actually expecting was bloodshed" instead of "what we actually are hoping for is bloodshed." Carma Hinton, the translator, insists that in the context of Chai's remarks, with her open profession that her goal was to "provoke" the government to violence, the proper translation of *qidai* in this context is "hoping for." Several prominent Chinese, including Ruan Ming, entered the fray over the translation dispute, arguing narrowly about the translation of a single word without addressing Chai's overall message. Thus, the original Hinton translation is left unchanged here for the simple reason that even if *qidai* were changed in the first reference, the context of Chai's remarks in seeking to provoke the Chinese government to violence is unmistakable.

17. James Huskey, interview by author. In August 1998, Huskey, his wife, and two daughters all were present at the U.S. embassy in Nairobi, Kenya, when a terrorist bomb devastated the building. Huskey was attending a meeting in one part of the embassy while his wife and daughters were on their way into the building for a dental appointment, approaching through an underground tunnel from the parking garage. After the detonation, Huskey remembered the dental appointment and realized that his family was probably in the building at that time. He pulled himself out of the rubble of the meeting room and raced outside, to the rear of the building, where he saw the face of one of his daughters through the smoke and fire. All of Huskey's family members were uninjured.

18. Bette Bao Lord, *New York Times,* Op-Ed article, June 4, 1989.

19. Bush and Scowcroft, *A World Transformed,* p. 98.

20. Ibid.

21. James Baker, Robert Kimmitt, Margaret Tutwiler, and other State Department officials, interviews by author.

22. DIA officials, Jack Leide, James Lilley, Kenneth Allen, and other embassy staff members, interviews by author.

23. Ibid.

24. Bush and Scowcroft, *A World Transformed,* pp. 100–102.

25. Ibid., p. 109.

26. Ibid., p. 111.

27. *The Selected Works of Deng Xiaoping,* vol. 3, *1982–1992,* p. 321.

28. Brent Scowcroft, Lawrence Eagleburger, Winston Lord, and Douglas Paal, interviews by author.

29. Winston Lord, "Misguided Mission," *Washington Post,* December 19, 1989.

30. Ibid.

31. *Selected Works of Deng Xiaoping,* vol. 3, p. 315.

32. *New York Times,* May 25, 1990.

33. Shirley A. Kan, *Chinese Proliferation of Weapons of Mass Destruction: Background and Analysis* (Washington, D.C.: Congressional Research Service, 1996, updated January 1998); and Baker, *Politics of Diplomacy,* p. 589.

34. Baker, *Politics of Diplomacy*, p. 590.
35. *New York Times*, February 1, 1992.
36. *Selected Works of Deng Xiaoping*, vol. 3, p. 360.
37. Ibid., p. 361.
38. Nixon confided this assessment of Bush's political dilemma in an off-the-record session in Washington, D.C., with a group of *New York Times* reporters and editors, including the author.
39. *Far Eastern Economic Review*, August 20, 1992.
40. Brent Scowcroft, Douglas Paal, James Lilley, and other senior Bush aides, interviews by author.
41. In saying privately that he hoped to "make it up" to the Chinese, Bush did not explain what he meant.
42. Brent Scowcroft, Douglas Paal, James Lilley, J. Stapleton Roy, and other Bush administration officials, interviews by author.
43. George Bush, personal correspondence to author (response to written questions).

CLINTON: THE BUTCHERS OF BEIJING . . .

1. Pieter Bottelier, interview by author. Bottelier was the World Bank director in China from 1993 to 1997.
2. Ezra F. Vogel, introduction to *The Rise of China*, by William H. Overholt (New York: W. W. Norton, 1993), pp. 19–20.
3. Ibid.
4. Among those interviewed on the development of Clinton's foreign policy were Anthony Lake, Warren Christopher, Peter Tarnoff, Winston Lord, Peter Tomsen, J. Stapleton Roy, Thomas Donilon, Michel Oksenberg, Richard Bush, Alan Romberg, Jeffrey Bader, and Chas. Freeman Jr.
5. J. Stapleton Roy, Scott Hallford, John Aloisi, Chris Szymanski, and other members of the U.S. embassy staff in Beijing, interviews by author
6. Anthony Lake, "From Containment to Enlargement" (address presented at the Johns Hopkins School of Advanced International Studies, Washington, D.C., September 21, 1993).
7. Senate Foreign Relations Committee, Confirmation Hearing of Winston Lord, opening statement by Lord, March 31, 1993.
8. *New York Times*, May 13, 1993.
9. Central Intelligence Agency, Directorate of Intelligence, Report to Joint Economic Committee, July 1993; and *New York Times*, August 1, 1993.
10. *New York Times*, September 23, 1993.
11. Clinton administration officials, interviews by author.
12. Lynn Davis, Anthony Lake, Winston Lord, Peter Tarnoff, J. Stapleton Roy, Jeffrey Bader, Ezra Vogel, and other administration officials, interviews by author.
13. Among those interviewed about the *Yinhe* incident were Anthony Lake, Warren Christopher, Thomas Donilon, Peter Tarnoff, James Woolsey, Winston Lord, Peter Tomsen, Jeffrey Bader, Lynn Davis, Robert Suettinger, Ezra Vogel, J. Stapleton Roy, Donald Keyser, and Chas. Freeman Jr.
14. *New York Times*, August 9, 1993.
15. *New York Times*, August 26, 1993.
16. *New York Times*, September 3, 1993; and *New York Times*, September 6, 1993.
17. *New York Times*, October 1, 1993.
18. Alexander Haig Jr., interview by author, October 1993. Haig's demeanor during the interview, which was requested by him through a public relations firm that was representing United Technologies, was scolding; he carried a strong tone of rebuke for the Clinton administration, which he accused of living in a "cultural cocoon."
19. *New York Times*, October 28, 1993.
20. *New York Times*, July 14, 1993.

21. At the Pentagon, Chas. W. Freeman Jr., then an assistant secretary of defense, pressed for a resumption of military-to-military contacts with China, in part because he felt that the State Department was driving U.S.-China policy to an overly contentious state.

22. *New York Times*, October 2, 1993.

23. *New York Times*, October 21, 1993.

24. *New York Times*, November 20, 1993.

25. China's announcement that it would consider visits by Red Cross personnel was made by Foreign Minister Qian Qichen in a meeting on November 9, 1993, with American correspondents at the Great Hall of the People. It was clearly timed as a gesture to Clinton in advance of his meeting with Jiang at the Seattle summit.

26. Roy was scrupulously loyal to the administration's position, but he was also clearly engaged in a conspiracy of sorts to get a broader debate going. Before the interview, he had met with Frank Qing, a columnist in Hong Kong who had covered China for many years. Both Qing and Roy had marveled at how much the life of the average Chinese had changed during the previous decade, particularly in the area of personal freedoms, even freedom to criticize the government as long as it was not done publicly. Roy and Qing wondered why this expanding zone of freedom for individual Chinese was not a factor in the debate over human rights progress. Qing returned to Hong Kong and pointed out this apparent policy shortcoming in a column in the *Far Eastern Economic Review*. In Roy's interview with Beijing's *New York Times* correspondent, the ambassador decided that he would make the same point while fundamentally adhering to the State Department line, that the Chinese would have to make "overall, significant progress" under the terms of the executive order.

27. *New York Times*, January 1, 1994.

28. Warren Christopher, Peter Tarnoff, Winston Lord, J. Stapleton Roy, and other State Department officials, interviews by author.

29. Warren Christopher, *Meet the Press*, National Broadcasting Company, January 16, 1994, transcript.

30. *New York Times*, January 30, 1994.

31. Wei's emissary was Tong Yi, his secretary, who met with Deborah Kingsland, a second secretary in the political section of the U.S. embassy.

32. Wei Jingsheng, "The Wolf and the Lamb," *New York Times*, November 18, 1993.

33. Department of State, press briefing by Warren Christopher, March 8, 1994, transcript.

34. Department of State, press conference by Warren Christopher with Australian Minister for Foreign Affairs Gareth Evans, March 9, 1994, transcript.

35. Warren Christopher, *In the Stream of History: Shaping Foreign Policy for a New Era* (Stanford: Stanford University Press, 1998), p. 155.

36. Christopher, *In the Stream of History*, pp. 153–154.

37. These quotations were disseminated by Christopher's aides in the briefing that followed the secretary's meeting with Jiang Zemin.

38. *New York Times*, March 18, 1994.

39. Warren Christopher, Tom Donilon, Winston Lord, Jeffrey Bader, Robert Suettinger, and other administration officials, interviews by author.

40. *New York Times*, March 21, 1994.

TRANSITION: . . . IT BEGINS AGAIN

1. Reuters, quoting *China Daily*, January 27, 1999.

2. *New York Times*, *Washington Post*, and *Los Angeles Times*, December 31, 1998.

3. *New York Times*, March 16, 1999.

4. Bill Clinton, presidential news conference, January 28, 1997.

5. Bill Clinton, "Address on China and the National Interest," speech delivered at the Voice of America, Washington, D.C., October 24, 1997.

PHOTOGRAPH CREDITS

3 PROLOGUE: THE RISK OF WAR. . .

Chinese warplanes during exercises near Taiwan. (AFP/Bettmann photo by CNS, Agence France Presse/CORBIS/Bettmann-UPI©)

19 THE TAIWAN CRISIS

Chinese soldiers and tanks enact a mock assault on an enemy position near the Taiwan Strait during joint land, sea, and air military exercises organized by the Nanjing Military Command, March 18–25, 1996. (AP/Wide World Photos)

45 THE SINO-SOVIET BORDER: 1969

Chinese soldiers during a "provocation" at Damansky Island on the Russian/Chinese border, January 1969. (New China Pictures/Eastfoto)

105 NIXON: THE OPENING. . .

Mao Zedong and Richard Nixon, February 1972. Courtesy of The Richard Nixon Library.

181 FORD: ESTRANGEMENT — "I SMILE BITTERLY. . . "

Mao Zedong met on December 2, 1975 with Gerald Ford. (Xinhua News Agency, CORBIS/Bettmann-UPI©)

227 CARTER: FULFILLMENT — "THE PRESIDENT HAS MADE UP HIS MIND. . . "

Deng Xiaoping spoke on January 29, 1979 during a welcoming ceremony as Jimmy Carter looks on. (CORBIS/Bettmann-UPI©)

287 REAGAN: . . . AND TAIWAN

Zhao Ziyang with Ronald Reagan and Alexander Haig at the Opening Session of the Economic Summit in Cancun, Mexico, October 22, 1981. (CORBIS/Bettmann-UPI©)

341 BUSH: . . . AND TIANANMEN

Pro-democracy demonstrations in Beijing in 1989 (© 1990 Kenneth Jarecke/Contact Press Images)

381 CLINTON: THE BUTCHERS OF BEIJING. . .

Bill Clinton with Jiang Zemin at a joint press conference at the White House in 1997. (© 1997 David Burnett/Contact Press Images)

ACKNOWLEDGMENTS

NEWSPAPER BOSSES GRANT book leaves grudgingly. The only defense, therefore, is to write a book of sufficient interest to engender pride of sponsorship. This also helps ameliorate the pain of lost services. Luckily for me, Joseph Lelyveld, the executive editor of *The New York Times*, without whose patience and support this book would not have been written, was a China correspondent himself in the 1970s. He bore witness to the China of Mao and Zhou long before any newspaper was allowed to open a bureau there. He was growled at by Henry Kissinger, and he encountered Deng Xiaoping before anyone knew that Deng would become China's most phenomenal modern leader. Along with Max Frankel and Howell Raines, Joe was instrumental in my joining *The Times* nearly a decade ago, and I am grateful for his leadership and patronage. I am also indebted to Robert L. Bernstein, one of the great humanitarians of our time, who took on my book project as agent and booster—a minor sideline to his real work as fundraiser and spiritual adviser to major institutions advancing the cause of human rights. His wisdom about the publishing business seems wholly secondary to his wisdom about life.

This book is being published by a unique enterprise called PublicAffairs, founded by Peter Osnos and dedicated to building creative partnerships to finance book projects on serious topics for a broad audience. To any writer, this is grounds for sainthood. At PublicAffairs, senior editor Geoff Shandler brought an innovative mind to the editing process, along with managing editor Robert Kimzey. The group's partner is the Century Foundation, whose president, Richard C. Leone, has done as much as any private institution head in America to support a rich and well-informed debate on public policy issues. Crucially, Stanford University and its Center for International Security and Cooperation provided the support of its world-class research facilities and the collegiality of its extraordinary faculty, especially John W. Lewis, cofounder of the center and respected China scholar.

Many hands made this work a collaboration; chief among them were

Patrik Nylund, my research assistant at Stanford, and Benjamin L. Read, a doctoral candidate at Harvard University, who over four years helped me shape the concept for the book and then contributed trenchant criticism to each draft. I am also grateful to Chen Xiaoping and his wife, Zhang Xiaoru, who shared with me a life's worth of insights about the people of China. Many careful readers reviewed the manuscript, but none were more insightful or prolific than William G. Hyland, one of the leading foreign policy analysts of the Cold War, and Seth Faison, my great friend and colleague in covering China for *The Times*. Finally, my warmest thanks to all those who opened their guestrooms to me during long months of travel and interviewing, and most of all, to Linda Tyler for all these years of love, joy, and shared adventures.

INDEX

456th Bomber Wing, 67–68

ABM system. *See* Antiballistic missile system
Acheson, Dean, 139
Afghanistan, 16, 285, 297, 330
Africa, 204–205
Agnew, Spiro T., 92
Agreement on the Prevention of Nuclear War, 146, 158–161, 166, 207, 437–438(n6), 442(n107)
Allen, Ken, 353
Allen, Richard V., 290–294, 304–305, 308, 318
Almond, Edward M., 302–303
Alsop, Joe, 155
American Institute in Taiwan, 290, 291
American Socialist Party, 240
Amur River, 61
Anderson, Jack, 125
Andropov, Yuri, 331, 335, 336
Angola, 204–205, 217–219, 224, 241, 253
Antiballistic missile system (ABM), 58, 59, 88
Apple, R.W., Jr., 231, 346
April Fifth Forum, 283
Arkhipov, Ivan V., 335
Armacost, Michael, 248, 410–412
Armitage, Richard, 301, 307, 321
Arms control, 178, 242, 260, 278
Arms race, 209, 231–232
Arms sales. *See also* Arms sales to Taiwan; Nuclear weapons programs; Weapons
  to China, 298–301, 306, 331, 455(n75), 456(n82)
  France and, 377, 378–379
  to Middle East, 337, 396, 399, 421
Arms sales to Taiwan, 446(n20). *See also* Mutual Defense Treaty; Weapons
  Carter administration and, 257–258, 263, 265–270, 274, 277, 452(n73)
  cutoff date, 315–316, 324–326
  FX fighter issue, 300, 306–316, 321–322
  Reagan administration and, 292, 299–301, 312–320, 332–333
  spare parts issue, 319, 323
  U.S.-China joint communiqué, 326–327
  U.S. economy and, 376–378

Ashbrook, John, 144
Asian Development Bank, 333, 343, 363
Aspin, Les, 28, 391, 399

B-52s, 67–68, 163
Baker, James A., III, 220, 302, 347, 352(n6), 353, 361, 368, 373
  F-16 sales and, 376, 378
Balkans, 7, 425
Bandar Bin Sultan, 337
Bao, Bette (Lord), 79, 80, 346, 359, 390
Barnett, A. Doak, 42
Beg, M.F.H., 96
Begin, Menachem, 256–257
Beijing Radio, 57, 362
Beijing University students, 346, 349
Bentsen, Lloyd, 30, 404, 409
Berger, Sandy, 22–23, 410, 411
Berlin Wall, 365
Blackhawk helicopters, 336
Blockade, 26–27
Blue Ridge, 345, 351–352
Blumenthal, Michael, 279
Boeing 757 jets, 365
Boggs, Hale, 185
Boggs, Lindy, 185
Bourne, Peter, 231
Brandt, Willy, 87
Brezhnev, Leonid, 61–62, 96, 322, 344
  Carter administration and, 240–241, 261–262
  on China, 159–160, 161–162
  death of, 328
  Nixon, meeting with, 177–179
  Nixon administration and, 124, 145, 146, 158
  nuclear strategy, 159–161
  Vietnam and, 280
Brezhnev Doctrine, 42, 56, 109, 322
Britain, 164
British intelligence, 155–156
Brown, Harold, 230, 284
Brown, Ronald H., 30, 404, 413
Brownell, Herbert, 258
Bruce, David K.E., 157–158, 164, 177, 183

Brzezinski, Muska, 255
Brzezinski, Zbigniew, 452(n73)
  ambition, 232–233, 248, 255, 261–262,
    264–265, 281
  Harriman and, 232–235
  Holbrooke and, 252–253, 255–256, 265
  invitation to China, 248–249, 250, 251
  Soviet Union, view of, 241
  Vance and, 237–239, 246
  visit to China, 253–255
Buchanan, Patrick, 137–138, 142–143
Buckley, James, 117, 312
Buckley, William F., Jr., 117, 144
Bunker, Ellsworth, 242
Bunker Hill, 33, 34
Burghardt, Raymond, 362
Burkhalter, Holly, 372
Burt, Rick, 313, 320
Bush, Barbara, 347
Bush, George, 7, 16, 29, 273, 339, 404
  Chinese leaders, view of, 368–369
  Deng, meetings with, 292–293, 323–324, 344
  Ford administration and, 188, 214
  Haig and, 302
  India-Pakistan conflict and, 118, 119, 121
  letter to Deng, 363
  liaison office position, 193, 201, 291
  Nixon administration and, 112, 116, 117
  Reagan campaign and, 291–292, 294, 295,
    304–305
  technology and, 333
  Tiananmen Square and, 352(n6), 359–364,
    368–369, 386
Bush, Richard, 414
Butz, Earl, 202

Caesar study, 51
Cambodia, 28, 78, 80, 190, 201–202
Camp H.M. Smith, 7
Canada, 83
Cannon, Lou, 202
Capitalist roaders, 84, 111, 153–154
Carlucci, Frank, 337
Carter, Jimmy, 229, 406
  cabinet, 233–235
  campaign, 230, 239–240
  Deng, meetings with, 276–277
  FX fighter and, 308
  on Kissinger, 237
  Soviet policy, 240–241
Carter, W. Bowman, 404
Casey, William, 296
Castro, Fidel, 204–205
Ceauşescu, Elena, 371
Ceauşescu, Nicolae, 64, 371
Central Committee, 60, 165
Central Intelligence Agency (CIA), 9, 16,
    154–155, 284–285, 328, 373. *See also* In-
    telligence
  China Operations Division, 156
  Far East Division, 157

National Intelligence Estimate, 166
Non-Proliferation Center, 396, 399–400
Sino-Soviet relations and, 65
Central Military Commission, 192, 336
Chai Ling, 349–350, 353, 354–356, 362, 412,
    457(n16)
Chai Zemin, 257, 258, 261, 263, 267, 270
  Reagan administration and, 298, 304–305
Chapin, Dwight, 112, 127, 143
Chemical weapons, 396–397
Cheney, Dick, 378
Chennault, Anna, 304, 305
Chennault, Claire, 304
Chen Yi, 71, 73, 118, 129, 147
Chen Yun, 259
Chen Ziming, 412, 413
Chernenko, Constantin, 336
Cherokee discussions, 59
Chestnut bases, 278, 284–285, 297
Chiang Ching-kuo, 24, 76, 77–78, 190, 263,
    269, 271, 273
Chiang Kai-shek, 5, 8–9, 14, 40, 56, 90,
    109(n1)
  death of, 202
  Mao on, 131
  nuclear program and, 190
  Reagan and, 290
Chiang Yan-shih, 305–306
Chien, Frederick, 271–272
Chin, Larry Wu-Tai, 187(n1)
China. *See also* Nuclear weapons programs;
    Sino-Soviet relations
  domestic struggles, 337–338, 345–346, 369,
    374, 413, 425
  economy, 30, 262, 333–334, 338, 374–376,
    383–385
  founding of People's Republic, 9, 425
  future prospects, 427–429
  infrastructure, 152
  most-favored-nation trade status, 30, 371
  nature of people, 11, 387–389
  as regional hegemon, 385–386
  suspension of relations with U.S., 175–177
  United Nations General Assembly and, 27,
    30, 40, 88, 92, 101, 112, 116–117, 196
China Desk, 307, 309, 312, 313, 320, 352
China Ocean Shipping Company, 396
China Operations Division (CIA), 156
China-Taiwan relations
  as internal issue, 198, 219, 242(n3), 247
  invasion preparations, 215
  nine-point plan, 310, 314
  non-peaceful transition, 172, 186–187, 189,
    198, 219, 221
Chinese Academy of Social Sciences, 354
Chinese embassy (Belgrade), 7, 12
Chinese Foreign Affairs Ministry, 96, 343,
    360–361, 393, 413
Christopher, Warren, 22, 24, 26, 30, 31, 33, 35
  Carter administration and, 265–266,
    271–273

Clinton administration and, 391, 399, 400,
 401, 403, 405, 413–415
  Lord initiative failure and, 409–411
  visit to China, 407–409
  visit to Taiwan, 271–273
CIA. *See* Central Intelligence Agency
Clark, William, 311–312
Clemins, Archie, 27
Cline, Ray, 158, 293
Clinton, Bill, 9–10, 15, 16, 21, 30, 378, 411,
 414–415. *See also* Human rights
  anti-China statements, 386–387, 389
  foreign policy failures, 12, 425–427
  Jiang, meeting with, 400–401, 420–421
  Lee visa and, 22, 24–25, 28, 31
  missile exercises and, 35
CNN, 366, 367
Colby, William, 156, 214
Cold War, 8, 9, 16, 284
Colson, Charles, 94
Committee of One Million, 40
Communiqués. *See also* Shanghai Communiqué
  Carter administration and, 252, 258
  Ford administration and, 206, 213–214
  Kissinger and, 115–116
  U.S.-China Joint Communiqué, 326–327
  Woodcock and, 264–265
Communist Manifesto (Marx), 338
Communist Party, 334, 338, 385, 395
  Central Committee, 60, 165
  future prospects, 429
  leadership style, 309–310
  specialists on America, 36–37
  Taiwan and, 10
  Tiananmen Square demonstrations and, 348
Congress, 165, 196
  Carter administration and, 268, 273–274
  conservative view, 201–203, 258, 290, 325,
   333
  F-16 sale and, 376, 378
  Ford and, 186
  hostility toward China, 12, 15, 373, 422
  Lee visit and, 414, 426
  military buildup and, 7–8
  pro-Taiwan lobby, 11, 15–16, 24, 196, 414,
   426
  Tiananmen Square and, 365–366
Connally, John, 92
Corruption, 338
Council on Foreign Relations, 409
Coup attempt, 110–112, 114, 131–132, 149,
 438(n10)
Cowan, Glenn, 90
Cox, Archibald, 166
Cox, Christopher, 422
  and committee, 422–426
Cranston, Alan, 335
Cross, Charles, 305
Cuba, 87, 204–205, 253
Cultural Revolution, 41, 60, 71, 84–85, 90, 111,
 118, 153-154, 155, 259

Deng's view of, 389–390
Culver, John, 16
Cunningham, Phil, 354–356
Czechoslovakia, 42

Dalai Lama, 125
Damansky Island incident, 47–51, 57–60
Davies, John, 320–321
Davis, Lynn E., 396, 397
Davis, Nathaniel, 205
Davydov, Boris, 67
"Day in the Life of the President, A," 120
Détente, 146, 164, 198, 202, 207–208, 216
Dean, John, 166
Deaver, Michael, 290, 298, 302
Defend Tiananmen Headquarters, 354
Defense Authorization Act, 392(n2)
Defense Intelligence Agency (DIA), 13, 16, 65,
 67, 308, 353, 359
Democracy Wall movement, 259, 282–283,
 345, 389, 425
Democratic National Committee, 147
Democratic National Convention, 386
Democratic Progressive Party, 14–15
Democrats, 58–59, 91–92, 131, 242, 372, 422
  Bush and, 376
  China policy, 229–230
Deng Pufang, 154
Deng Xiaoping, 165
  Brzezinski and, 254–255
  Bush, meetings with, 292–293, 323–324, 344
  Carter, meetings with, 276–277
  character of, 194, 207, 262–263, 292
  on détente, 207–208
  death of, 417–418, 427
  defense policy and, 336–337
  democracy, view of, 389–390
  democracy movement and, 282–283
  Gorbachev visit and, 351
  illness, 405, 413
  invitation to Schlesinger, 198–199
  Kissinger, meetings with, 194–200,
   206–210, 213
  leadership, 259–260, 262, 275–276
  Mao's distrust of, 111, 152–154, 172,
   192–193, 214, 220-221
  Mutual Defense Treaty and, 262–264,
   266–270, 274,452(n79)
  press and, 260–261
  Reagan administration and, 299–300
  reemergence of, 243–244, 259
  as reformer, 259–260, 274–275, 282, 334,
   374–375, 383,418, 428–429
  Soviet threat, view of, 206–208, 216
  Taiwan issue and, 176–177, 187, 218–219,
   308–310, 315
  Tiananmen Square demonstrations and,
   348–349, 351, 353–354, 360, 362–364,
   369–370
  on Tiananmen Square massacres, 364–365,
   369–370

Deng Xiaoping *(cont.)*
U.S. visit, 176–177, 187, 275–278
Vance, meeting with, 245–246
on Vietnam, 276, 277
Woodcock, meetings with, 262–264, 266–270
Deng Yingchao, 215
Derian, Patricia M., 283–284
DIA. *See* Defense Intelligence Agency
Diaoyutai, 97
Ding Zilin, 362
Diplomacy, 12, 300
Dobrynin, Anatoly, 39, 51–52, 234
Angola and, 224
Kissinger and, 57–59, 66, 69, 87, 108, 110, 160
Vietnam and, 280
Dole, Bob, 147
Downey, John T., 154–155, 158, 440(n60)
Dual Representation formula, 90
Dulles, John Foster, 11, 40, 97, 144, 155

Eagleburger, Lawrence, 79, 332, 363–367, 369, 409
Earthquake, 221–222
East Asia Bureau, 307, 309, 312, 313, 320, 388
East Europe, 203, 320
East Germany, 87
Economy, China, 418–419
Clinton administration and, 403–404
human rights conditions and, 393–394
inflation, 394–395
Egypt, 256–257
Ehrlichman, John, 164
Eisenhower, Dwight D., 8, 139
Ellsberg, Daniel, 95
Ellsworth, Robert, 51–52
Engagement, 26–27, 400, 428
Enlightenment, 338
Enterprise, 122
Esau study, 51
Evans, M. Stanton, 289
Evans, Rowland, 260
Exclusion zone, 33
Exploration, 282
Export-Import Bank, 370

F-4 Phantom jets, 167
F-5E fighters, 169–170, 308, 310, 312–313, 315, 320–322, 324, 326, 377
F-8 fighter, 366
F-8 fighters, 338, 366
F-16 fighters, 7, 32, 376–378, 392(n2), 421
F-104 fighters, 377
Face the Nation, 235
Faison, Seth, 417
Fallaci, Oriana, 149
Fang Lizhi, 346, 347, 362, 366, 371, 391, 456(n6)
Fang Zheng, 359(n9)
Far East, 344

Fecteau, Richard, 154–155, 158, 440(n60)
Federal Reserve Board, 421
"Fifth Modernization, The" (Wei Jingsheng), 282
Five assurances, 167
Flying Tigers, 304
FNLA. *See* National Front for the Liberation of Angola
Fong, Hiram L., 186
Ford, Betty, 185
Ford, Gerald
candidacy, 203
communiqué proposal, 206, 213–214
conservatives and, 201, 202
letter to Mao, 183
Mao, meeting with, 217
presidential primary campaign, 220
Taiwan, position on, 201–206, 273
visit to China, 215–219
Zhou, meeting with, 185
Ford, Susan, 215, 217
Foreign Affairs, 41, 42–43, 62
Foreign Relations Committee (Senate), 414
Four Modernizations, 259
Fourteen principles, 393
France, 50–51, 164
arms sales, 377, 378–379
Frankel, Max, 41, 127
Freeman, Chas. W., Jr., 335
Friendship Treaty, 281
Fulbright, J. William, 186
Fuller, Keith, 246
Fu Yuehua, 282
FX fighter issue, 300, 306–316, 321–322

Gandhi, Indira, 118, 119, 121–124
Gang of Four, 193, 221, 223, 243. *See also* Jiang Qing
Garten, Jeffrey, 30
Gates, Thomas, 240
Gaulle, Charles de, 50–51, 58, 103, 135
Gelb, Leslie H., 330
General Dynamics, 376, 378
Geneva Conference, 11
Geng Biao, 300
Gephardt, Richard, 404
Germany, 145–146
Glenn, John, 335
Gleysteen, William H., Jr., 190, 225, 247, 252, 256
Goddess of Democracy, 356
Godwin, Paul, 17
Goldwater, Barry, 117, 202, 204, 232, 243, 258, 273, 325, 450(n30)
Gorbachev, Mikhail, 343–345, 349–351, 371
Gore, Al, 414
Graham, Daniel O., 65, 434(n42)
Graham, Katharine, 246
Great Leap Forward, 39–40, 259
Great Wall, 40
Grechko, Andrei, 61

Green, Marshall, 55, 64, 74, 76–78, 87–88, 96, 118, 268
  visit to China, 138–141
Greenspan, Alan, 421
Gromyko, Andrei, 70, 256, 280, 328
Grumman, 366
Guam Doctrine, 64
Guangming, 259

Habib, Phil, 200–201, 247, 249
Haig, Alexander M., Jr., 79, 96, 113, 143
  arms sales and, 298–301, 306–307, 310, 312–317, 319–320
  India-Pakistan crisis and, 120, 123
  military career, 302–303
  Reagan administration and, 296–300, 305, 323–325
  Tiananmen Square massacres and, 366
  Vietnam and, 125–126
  on *Yinhe* incident, 400
Haldeman, H.R., 54, 57, 88, 91, 92, 95, 107, 114, 120
  Nixon's China visit and, 128, 137, 139
  Watergate and, 164
Hallford, Scott, 309, 318
Halperin, Morton, 79
Hannaford, Peter, 290
Han Nialong, 261
Han Xu, 200–201, 202, 219
Harriman, W. Averell, 38, 58, 231–234
Hastert, Dennis, 416
Helms, Jesse, 337, 359
Helms, Richard, 63, 65, 66, 68, 435(n46)
Helsinki Accords, 367, 390
Helsinki Conference on Security and Cooperation in Europe, 203, 207, 224
Hilaly, 93
Hinton, Carma, 457(n16)
Hirohito, Emperor, 344
Ho Chi Minh, 39, 52, 70
Hoffman, David, 346
Holbrooke, Richard, 231, 233–235, 247, 248, 249
  Brzezinski and, 252–253, 255–256, 265
  FX fighter and, 311–312, 313
  review of China policy and, 236–237
Holdridge, John H., 97, 99
  Nixon administration and, 305, 306–307, 312–313, 320–322, 329
Hong Kong, 13, 15, 155–156, 354, 388, 420
Hopkins, Robert S., II, 67–68
House Foreign Affairs Committee, 186
Howe, Jonathan T., 119
Hua Guofeng, 220, 221, 222, 243, 244, 259
Huang Hua, 97, 328
  Carter administration and, 244, 246, 248, 256–258, 261
  Nixon administration and, 102, 119, 121–124, 146, 159
  Reagan administration and, 299, 314–317, 322

Huang Zhen, 184, 201–202, 235, 437(n6)
  on Angola, 241
  Nixon administration and, 162, 164, 176
Huff, Billy, 356, 357
Huguang Railway bonds, 333
Huizenga, John, 65
Hu Jintao, 428
Human rights, 30, 39–40. *See also* Tiananmen Square
  Bush administration and, 337–338, 346–347, 367, 372, 374
  Carter administration and, 243, 283–284
  economy and, 393–394
  Lord initiative, 393–394, 410
  moralism and, 389–390, 406, 410, 412
  most-favored-nation status and, 393–394, 401, 404, 407–410
  political prisoners and, 401, 404, 411–412
  significant progress standard, 393, 401–402, 408–409
  trade issues and, 403–404, 412–414
Human Rights Watch, 372
Human-wave attacks, 38
Hummel, Arthur, Jr., 175, 316, 318–319, 322, 323, 325, 326, 333
Hummel, Betty Lou, 322
Hu Na, 333
Huskey, James L., 357–358, 457(n17)
Hussein, Saddam, 372, 386, 387
Hu Yaobang, 259, 328, 334, 338, 347, 348
Hyland, William G., 59, 65, 69

ICBMs. *See* Intercontinental ballistic missiles
Ideology, 15, 113
Ilichev, Leonid F., 327–328
Independence, 27, 33, 34, 35
India, 117–125, 148, 331–332, 344
India-Pakistan crisis, 117–125, 150, 208, 210, 439(n42), 439–440(n46)
Indigenous Fighters, 7
Indochina conference (Geneva), 56
Intelligence. *See also* Central Intelligence Agency
  British intelligence, 155–156
  Chinese espionage in U.S., 328–329, 422–424
  India-Pakistan crisis and, 119–123
  Iranian revolution and, 277–278
  national security wiretaps, 202
  Sino-Soviet relations and, 51, 54–56, 65, 333, 356, 439(n35), 441(n72)
Intercontinental ballistic missiles (ICBMs), 163, 178, 336, 423
International Atomic Energy Agency, 335
International Committee of the Red Cross, 401, 419–420
International Conference of Communist Parties, 61
International Covenant on Civil and Political Rights, 419

International Covenant on Economic, Social, and Cultural Rights, 419
Iran, 26–27, 277–278, 280, 337
  arms sales to, 396–397
  hostage crisis, 285
  nuclear weapons program, 373
Iraq, 26–27, 34, 372
Israel, 256–257

Jackson, Henry "Scoop," 194, 196, 198, 203, 232
Japan, 10, 32, 148, 300, 301, 344, 384, 387, 413
  theater missile defense and, 420–421
Japan formula, 167, 196, 241
Jiang Qing, 97, 129, 136–137, 165, 188, 192–193, 223
  Deng and, 192–193, 214, 221, 375
  as general secretary, 374
Jiang Zemin, 28, 36, 363, 370, 425
  Clinton, meeting with, 400–401, 420–421
  Clinton administration and, 394, 395, 398, 403, 405, 409, 413, 420
Ji Chaozhu, 97, 297–298
Ji Pengfei, 125, 172
Joffe, Ellis, 17
Johnson, Lyndon B., 41, 54
Joint Chiefs of Staff, 21, 33, 38, 303, 318, 444(n149)
Joint economic commission, 404
Jones, Paula Corbin, 411, 426
Jones, Tom, 308
Jordan, 87
Jordan, Hamilton, 230
Judd, Walter, 40
Judiciary Committee, 177
June Fourth, 375. *See also* Tiananmen Square demonstrations
Justice Department, 422

Kamm, John, 416
Kang Sheng, 147
Kennedy, Edward M., 58–59
Kennedy, John F., 38, 54, 209, 231, 239
Kennedy, Ted, 239, 249
KGB, 67
Khabarovsk military region, 47
Khan, Sher Ali, 74
Khan, Yahya, 64, 83, 87, 117–118
Khrushchev, Nikita, 14, 38, 58, 344
Kim Il-Sung, 98
Kissinger, Henry, 8, 28–29
  ambition of, 120–121, 149, 199, 202, 237
  Brezhnev, meeting with, 159–160
  Carter administration and, 235–237
  Cherokee discussions and, 59–60
  CIA and, 156–158
  Deng, meetings with, 194–200, 206–210, 213
  diversion strategy, 62, 123–124, 150, 170–172, 207–210

Dobrynin and, 57–59, 66, 69, 87, 108, 110, 160
  five assurances and, 167
  Ford, relationship with, 203
  India-Pakistan crisis and, 118–119
  intelligence reports and, 62–63, 69–70, 441(n72)
  Lord and, 79–80
  Lord initiative and, 409, 413
  on Mao, 213
  Mao, meetings with, 130–133, 150–151, 210–213
  on Munich policy, 208
  on Mutual Defense Treaty and, 115, 139–140, 184–185, 195–196
  Nixon, relationship with, 80, 95, 164–165
  Pentagon Papers and, 94–95
  ping-pong diplomacy and, 92
  political advancement of, 52–53
  Qiao, meeting with, 188–189, 223–224
  as secretary of state, 165, 183
  on Soviet power, 208–209
  State Department and, 78
  on support for China, 158–159
  Tiananmen Square massacres and, 366, 369
  two-China plan and, 167–169, 174–175, 195–196
  UN General Assembly seat and, 101, 112–113, 116–117
  on Vietnam, 148–149
  visits to China, 93–103, 113–117, 127–145, 149–150
Kolbe, Jim, 409
Korea. *See* North Korea; South Korea
Korean War, 9, 38, 74, 154, 388
Kosygin, Alexei, 60, 70–71, 145
Kraft, Joe, 235
Kraslow, David, 141
Krug, Fred, 361
Kuo, Shirley, 343
Kuwait, 372

Laird, Melvin R., 62, 63, 66, 163, 444(n149)
Lake, Anthony, 22, 26, 28–31, 79
  on Carter administration, 231
  Clinton administration and, 386–387, 391, 395, 396, 399, 400, 410, 411, 413–414, 419
Lake, Kirsopp, 29
Laxalt, Paul, 275
Le Duc Tho, 126
Lee, T.D., 369–370
Lee Kuan Yew, 248
Lee Teng-hui, 6, 22, 23–25, 28, 31, 414, 415–416, 420, 429
Leide, Jack, 352–353, 356–357, 360
Lei Yang, 75–76, 78
Liaison offices, 152, 154, 157, 173, 175
  American Institute in Taiwan, 290, 291
  Bush and, 193, 201, 291
  Taiwan proposal, 196, 198, 245, 246, 247

Libya, 373
Li Daoyu, 400
Lieberthal, Kenneth, 400
Li Lu, 354
Lilley, Frank, 154
Lilley, James R., 17, 154–158
    Bush administration and, 343–345, 369
    F-16 sale and, 377–378
    Reagan administration and, 291, 292, 294,
        301, 304, 305, 320
    Tiananmen Square and, 347–348, 350–352,
        354, 357–358, 361–362, 378
Lin Biao, 60, 97, 110–112, 114, 132, 149,
    438(n10)
Lin Liguo, 111
Linowitz, Sol, 242
Li Peng, 31, 35, 36, 420
    Clinton administration and, 394, 403,
        407–408, 414–415
    Deng and, 375
    Tiananmen Square and, 348, 352, 360, 364,
        367, 370, 371, 375
    United Nations summit and, 374
Li Shuxian, 362
Liu Binyan, 338
Liu Bocheng, 153
Liu Chuanzhen, 222
Liu Huaqing, 300, 306, 310
Liu Huaqiu, 30–32, 361, 406
Liu Qing, 283
Liu Shaoqi, 85, 111, 154
Li Zhisui, 129
Lodge, Henry Cabot, 92, 93, 231
Long March, 82, 153
Lon Nol, 201
Lop Nor, 71, (n)423
Lord, Bette. *See* Bao, Bette
Lord, Mary Pillsbury, 79
Lord, Oswald B., 79
Lord, Winston, 24, 29–30, 35, 79–80, 119, 175,
    332, 337, 456(n6)
    Bush administration and, 346–347, 367–368
    Clinton administration and, 390–391,
        392–394, 400–402, 413
    human rights initiative, 393–394, 409–411,
        413
Los Angeles Times, 141
Louis, Victor, 71
Luke Air Force Base, 7
Luo Ruiqing, 215
Lynn, James T., 215

M-9 missile, 337
M-11 missiles, 373, 396, 399, 413
Macao, 13
MacArthur, Douglas, 303
Macke, Richard, 27
Manifest Destiny, 10
Mansfield, Mike, 63, 72, 77, 91–92, 200
Mao Yuanxin, 214
Mao Zedong, 8–9
    on Angola, 217–218
    Cambodia and, 80–81
    on coup attempt, 131–132
    coup attempt and, 110–112
    death of, 222–223
    Deng, distrust of, 111, 152–154, 172,
        192–193, 214, 221
    Ford, meeting with, 217
    human rights abuses, 39–40
    illness, 129, 184, 191–192, 193, 210, 221
    India-Pakistan crisis and, 124
    Kissinger, meetings with, 130–133,
        150–151, 210–213
    long-term viewpoint, 10–11, 172–173, 177,
        187, 198, 210-211
    Nixon, meeting with, 130–134
    ping-pong players and, 90–91
    Sino-Soviet relations and, 60, 150–151
    Snow and, 83–85
    on Soviet Union, 173–174, 210–211
    on spying, 156
    Taiwan, attack on, 172–173
    warmonger image of, 11, 73, 174
    Zhou, distrust of, 152, 172, 174, 192,
        445(n186)
Marcos, Imelda, 191
Marshall, George C., 9
Marx, Karl, 338
Matsu, 10, 21, 23
Mauz, Henry H., Jr., 345, 352
Mayaguez, 201
May Fourth Movement, 345
McCone, John, 39
McCurry, Mike, 26
McGovern, George S., 88–89, 90, 148
McNamara, Robert, 39
Meeker, Leonard, 81
Meese, Ed, 294, 295, 298
Middle Kingdom, 6
MIG-19 fighters, 81
MIG-21 fighters, 338
Military-to-military exchanges, 12, 400
Mirage 2000-5 fighter-bombers, 7, 377
Missile exercises, 21, 25–27, 31–36
Missiles, 7–8, 373–374
    intercontinental ballistic missiles (ICBMs),
        163, 178, 336, 422–423
    Pakistan and, 396, 399, 421
    Silkworm missiles, 337
    theater missile defense, 420–421
    Trident II, 422–423
Missile Technology Control Regime, 373–374,
    413
Mitchell, George, 372, 376, 393
Mitchell, John, 117
Mondale, Walter, 242, 284, 317
Moorer, Thomas, 63(n5), 80, 166
Moralism, 27–28, 37–38, 387, 389, 406, 410,
    412
Most-favored-nation trade status, 371–372,
    376. *See also* Trade issues

Most-favored-nation trade status (*cont.*)
  human rights and, 30, 393–394, 401, 404,
    407–410
MPLA. *See* Popular Movement for the Libera-
  tion of Angola
Murphy, Robert, 90
Muskie, Edmund, 285
Muslims, 417
Mutual Defense Treaty (1955), 307, 452(n79)
  Carter administration and, 241–243, 252,
    258, 262–270, 274
  Ford administration and, 184, 195–196
  Nixon administration and, 115, 139, 140,
    167

National Committee on Sports (China), 90
National Economic Council, 403–404
National Front for the Liberation of Angola
  (FNLA), 204, 205
National Intelligence Estimate (CIA), 166
Nationalist Party, 25
Nationalists, 8–9, 13–15, 23, 25, 40, 190–191,
  229
National Military Command Center, 26, 353
National People's Congress, 60, 111, 351, 407,
  420, 429
National Security Agency (NSA), 9, 68, 353
National Security Council (NSC), 38, 54, 66,
  67, 90. *See also* Brzezinski, Zbigniew;
  Kissinger, Henry; Lake, Anthony; Scow-
  croft, Brent
  Carter administration and, 236, 238
  Nixon administration and, 118, 125
  Reagan administration and, 320
National Union for the Total Independence of
  Angola (UNITA), 204–205
NATO. *See* North Atlantic Treaty Organiza-
  tion
Neto, Agostinho, 204
New China News Agency, 25, 83, 155–156,
  293
Newhauser, Charles, 236
New York Times, 41, 64, 94, 110, 246, 346, 402,
  404
Nguyen Van Thieu, 125
Nie Rongzhen, 71
Nimitz, 34, 35
Nine-point plan, 310, 314
Nitze, Paul, 178
Nixon, Pat, 37, 127
Nixon, Richard, 8, 13, 14, 16, 37–38, 41–42,
  212. *See also* Shanghai Communiqué;
  Watergate
  Brezhnev, meeting with, 177–179
  Chian Ching-kuo and, 77
  Damansky Island incident and, 49–50
  Foreign Affairs essay, 41, 42–43, 62
  global diplomacy and, 108–109
  Kissinger on, 212
  letter to Mao, 158–159
  Mao, meeting with, 130–134

Mao on, 85–86
pardon, 186
ping-pong diplomacy and, 91
public relations and, 112, 128, 147
reelection concerns, 88, 94, 100, 117
on Sino-Soviet relations, 135, 147–148,
  441(n79)
State of the World speech, 89
Tiananmen Square and, 359, 366
view of China, 55–57
visits to China, 37–38, 127–145, 220
on Watergate, 164–165
Zhou Enlai and, 128, 134–136
Zhou Enlai on, 99–100, 103
Nofziger, Lyn, 294
Non-Proliferation Center (CIA), 396, 399–400
Normalization, three principles of, 199–200
North Atlantic Treaty Organization (NATO),
  7, 425
Northern Expedition, 319
North Korea, 387, 405, 415, 421
Northrop Corporation, 307, 308, 314, 321
North-South Summit, 314
Novak, Robert, 260
NSA. *See* National Security Agency
NSC. *See* National Security Council
Nuclear energy program, 334–336
Nuclear Non-Proliferation Treaty, 335, 374,
  421
Nuclear war planners, 162–163
Nuclear weapons program, China, 61, 63, 329,
  373–374
  espionage and, 422–424
  Soviet Union and, 38–39, 67–71, 73,
    159–161, 160
Nuclear weapons programs. *See also* Agreement
  on the Prevention of Nuclear War
  Iran, 373
  Pakistan, 331–332, 335, 373
  Taiwan, 190
  thermonuclear warheads, 422–423

Oberdorfer, Don, 235–236
Oehler, Gordon, 396
Ogarkov, Andrei, 61
Oksenberg, Michel, 236–237, 248, 249, 252,
  256, 257, 264, 279
Olympics, 224, 395
One-China principle, 13–15, 27, 28, 98–99,
  116, 167, 168, 175, 186, 197, 324
One-country-two-systems guarantee, 15
Operation Desert Storm, 372
Opium Wars, 48
Outer Mongolia, 344

Paal, Douglas, 377
Pacific Fleet, 27
Pakistan, 74, 76–77, 83, 148, 392(n2)
  India, conflict with, 117–125
  missile sales to, 396, 399, 421
  nuclear weapons progam, 331–332, 335, 373

Palestinian Liberation Organization (PLO), 87
Panama Canal zone, 242–243, 251
Panmunjom armistice talks, 97
Paris peace accord, 149
Party Congresses
  Ninth National People's Congress, 60
  Tenth Party Congress, 165
  Eleventh Party Congress, 244, 262
  Twelfth Party Congress, 328
  Fourteenth Party Congress, 418
  Fifteenth Party Congress, 420
Peasant border incidents, 60–61
Pelosi, Nancy, 394, 412
Peng Zhen, 259
Pentagon Papers, The, 94–95, 231
People's Daily, 89, 203, 283, 338, 348–349, 375
People's Liberation Army (PLA), 7, 10, 21, 36,
  111, 149, 189–191. *See also* Military
  modernization of, 12–13, 163–164, 331–333
  Tiananmen Square demonstrations and,
    352, 357, 358–359
  Vietnam and, 279–280
People's Republic of China. *See* China
Perle, Richard, 302, 307
Perry, William J., 22, 26, 31–32, 33–35, 284,
  285
Persian Gulf War, 26–27, 34, 386
Pillsbury, Michael, 17
Ping-Pong diplomacy, 37, 90–92, 132–133
PLA. *See* People's Liberation Army
PNUT. *See* Possible nuclear underground test
  facility
Poland, 318, 320, 321
Polo study, 51, 96–97
Pompidou, Georges, 123
Popular Movement for the Liberation of An-
  gola (MPLA), 204, 205, 218
Population control program, 337
Portugal, 204
Possible nuclear underground test facility
  (PNUT), 206
Powell, Colin, 397
Presidential Review Memorandum No. 24, 241
Princelings, 338, 358
Prithvi missile, 396
Provisional Students' Federation of Capital
  Universities, 348
Prueher, Joseph W., 7, 27

Qaddafi, Muammar, 373
Qian Dayong, 362
Qian Qichen, 327–328, 350, 364, 371
  Clinton administration and, 399, 408, 410,
    413, 415
  visit to U.S., 372–373
Qiao Guanhua
  Ford administration and, 186–187, 200
  Ford communiqué proposal and, 206, 213,
    214
  Nixon administration and, 130, 140,
    148–149, 166, 171, 176–177

UN General Assembly session and, 187–188
U.S. visit, 223–224
Qingdao, 48
Qing Dynasty, 48
Qinghua University, 192
Qin Huasun, 397, 398
Quadripartite Agreement on Berlin, 145–146,
  438(n8)
Quemoy, 10, 21, 23

Radio Free Asia, 392, 412
Rafshoon, Gerald, 275
Raines, Howell, 410
Rather, Dan, 350, 359
Reagan, Nancy, 302, 318
Reagan, Ronald, 109(n1), 232
  assassination attempt, 298
  campaign, 203–204, 214–215, 220, 273,
    290–291
  on Nixon's policy, 117, 289
  political education of, 297–298
  visit to China, 334–335
Reagan-Bush Inaugural Committee, 304
Red Cross, 401, 404, 413, 419–420, 459(n25)
Red Detachment of Women, The, 136
Red Guard, 71, 84, 154
Red Star over China (Snow), 82
Regan, Donald, 317
Ren Wanding, 282
Republicans, 24–25, 41, 92, 137–138, 142–143,
  422
Republic of China. *See* Taiwan
Reston, James "Scotty," 96, 102–103, 155
Review of the International Situation, 54
Richardson, Elliot L., 69, 74, 166
Robb, Chuck, 398
Roberto, Holden, 204
Rockefeller, Nelson, 113(n3), 202
Rogers, William P., 50, 52–54, 63–64, 66, 68,
  76–78, 81, 87–88, 96
  Kissinger and, 107–108, 120
  Pentagon Papers and, 95
  UN General Assembly seat and, 112, 113,
    116, 117
  visit to China, 114, 134, 138–140
Romance of the Three Kingdoms, 216
Romania, 371
Romberg, Alan, 322
Rope, William F., 307–313, 318, 319–320,
  329
Rostow, Walt W., 38
Roy, J. Stapleton, 28, 262, 268, 269–270, 292,
  459(n26)
  Clinton administration and, 387–390,
    391, 397–398, 401, 402–403, 409,
    415–416
  F-16 sales and, 377, 378
Rubin, Robert E., 30, 403, 409
Rumsfeld, Donald, 193, 214
Rusk, Dean, 38, 39, 74, 232
Russell, McKinney, 362

Sadat, Anwar, 256–257
Safire, William, 89
Sakharov, Andrei, 241, 283
SALT I. *See* Strategic Arms Limitation Treaty
Saudi Arabia, 337, 399
Savimbi, Jonas, 204–205, 217
Sawyer, Diane, 265
Scali, John, 139–141
Schlesinger, James R., 214, 230, 232
    Carter administration and, 230
    invitation to China, 196–197, 212
    Nixon administration and, 156, 164, 166,
        178
    visit to China, 222–223
Scott, Hugh, 221
Scowcroft, Brent, 157, 404
    Bush administration and, 344, 346–347,
        363–369
    F-16 sales and, 376, 378
    Ford administration and, 199, 205–206,
        214, 220, 236
Scranton, 224–225
Second Artillery Corps (China), 26
Senate Foreign Relations Committee, 414
Sequoia, 94
Seventh Fleet, 7, 9, 10, 35, 74, 172, 191, 345,
    397
Shackley, Ted, 155, 157
Shalikashvili, John, 21, 22, 26, 27, 33–35
Shanghai, 345, 350–352
Shanghai Communiqué, 13, 27, 137–142, 268,
    318, 322
    Ford administration and, 184, 189
    Nixon administration and, 167, 175, 177
    principles, 142–143
    Taiwan's response, 143–144
Shattuck, John, 402, 405–407
Shaw, Bernard, 352
Shen, James, 111–113, 126, 143–144
Shenzhen, 375
Shevardnadze, Edouard, 373
Shi Yanhua, 263–264
Shriver, Sargent, 231
Shulman, Marshall, 233
Shultz, George, 324, 329–332, 333
Sicherman, Harvey, 324
Silkworm missiles, 337
Simons, Thomas, 75
Sinai Peninsula, 256–257
Single Integrated Operating Plan (SIOP),
    67–68, 444(n149)
Sino-Soviet relations, 109–110, 145,
    434–435(n42), 443–444(n149). *See also*
        Agreement on the Prevention of Nuclear
        War; China; Soviet Union
    Cambodia and, 80–81
    Chinese mobilization, 149–150
    collective security proposal, 61–62
    Damansky Island incident, 47–51, 57–60
    improvement in, 331–336, 343–344
    India-Pakistan crisis and, 117–125

intelligence reports, 51, 54–56, 65, 71–73,
    333, 356, 439(n35), 441(n72)
    Lin Biao incident and, 111–112
    MIG incident, 81
    Nixon on, 135, 147–148, 441(n79)
    nuclear attack proposal, 62–63
    Pakistani connection, 74, 76–77, 83
    peasant incidents, 60–61
    rapprochement talks, 327–328
    Soviet attack plans, 64–70
    Taiwan and, 87–88, 90, 98–101, 126
    trade agreement, 371
    trade embargo and, 63–64, 90
    U.S-China talks, 74–76
    Xinjiang Province attack, 65
SIOP. *See* Single Integrated Operating Plan
Snow, Edgar, 81–87, 127(n8), 130
Snow, Lois, 83, 88–89
Socialist Call, 240
Solarz, Steven J., 359
Solomon, Richard, 157, 175
Solzhenitsyn, Aleksandr I., 203
Song Ching-ling, 82, 127(n8)
Sonnenfeldt, Hal, 160, 178
South Africa, 217–218
Southard, W. P. "Bud," 51
South China Sea, 377
South Korea, 387
Soviet Union, 16. *See also* Sino-Soviet relations
    Angola and, 204–205, 224
    arms control, 178, 242
    arms race, 209, 231–232
    China, view of, 58
    Chinese nuclear weapons program and,
        38–39, 69–71, 73, 159–161
    Chinese view of, 331, 332–333
    East Europe and, 203
    military strength, 166, 209
    Vietnam and, 51–52, 58, 110, 259–260,
        276–281, 284
Spratly Islands, 377
Spratt, John, 424
State Department, 29, 30, 55, 156, 332, 414
    Carter administration and, 237–238, 249,
        250, 253, 255-256, 258, 265–266, 268
    Nixon's visit to China and, 134, 138–140
    Sino-Soviet relations and, 78, 86, 96
State Security Bureau, 417
Stearman, William L., 66–67
Stevens, George, 275
Stilwell, Joseph, 154
Stoessel, Walter J., Jr., 74–76, 312
Strategic ambiguity, 35
Strategic Arms Limitation Treaty (SALT I), 93,
    94, 145–146, 178, 179, 205
    Carter administration and, 256, 261, 265
Strategic association, 298, 300–301, 321, 331
Strategic passivity, 204, 205
Strelnikov, Ivan, 47–49
SU-27, 377
Suettinger, Robert, 414

Sullivan, Roger, 265
Sulzberger, Arthur O., 246
Summers, Lawrence S., 404
Sun Tzu, 73
Swaine, Michael, 17
Symbolism, 34
Syria, 87, 337, 373

Tacksman bases, 278
Taipei, 6
Taiwan. *See also* Arms sales to Taiwan; Mutual
      Defense Treaty; Shanghai Communiqué;
      Taiwan Relations Act; U.S.-China Joint
      Communiqué
   Bush administration and, 376–377
   Chinese missile exercises and, 21, 25–27,
      31–36
   Clinton administration and, 414, 420
   Congress and, 11, 15–16, 24, 414, 426
   conservative U.S. view, 201–203, 258, 290,
      325, 333
   elections, 25
   military buildup, 6–8, 13, 166, 169–170
   missile crisis and, 6–7, 31–36, 221, 419
   Nationalists, 8–9, 13–15, 23, 40, 190–191,
      229
   nuclear programs, 190
   political support network, 15–16
   pro-independence faction, 11, 14–15, 23, 36
   response to missiles, 32
   Sino-Soviet relations and, 87–88, 90,
      98–101, 126
   theater missile defense and, 420–421
   United Nations seat, 40, 112, 116–117
   U.S.-China talks and, 77
   withdrawal of U.S. troops, 14, 196–197
Taiwan-China relations. *See* China-Taiwan re-
      lations
Taiwan Enabling Act, 274
Taiwan Relations Act, 6(n1), 31, 274
   Reagan administration and, 292–301, 304,
      307, 326, 327
Taiwan Strait, 9, 32–35, 74, 221
Tang, Nancy, 83, 84, 97, 131, 168, 169, 191,
      212, 245
Tanker War, 26
Tarnoff, Peter, 23, 238, 402, 403
Taylor, Maxwell, 38
Telecommunications, 337, 370
Thayer, Harry, 264
Theater missile defense, 420–421
"Theory Conference," 283
Think tanks, 16–17
Thirty-eighth Army, 357
Thurmond, Strom, 325
Tiananmen Square demonstrations, 16, 29,
      220–221, 259, 343, 347–349, 387, 425
   arrests and executions, 362–363
   diplomatic quarter, attack on, 360–362
   hunger strike, 349–350, 351, 353
   massacres, 357–359

   media coverage, 350
   reopening of Square, 370–371
   sanctions, 362–363, 365–366
   student leaders, 349–350
Tibet, 36–37, 39, 125, 376, 414, 425
Tolstikov, Vasily, 260
Trade issues, 63–64, 74, 81, 90, 317, 333–334,
      371–372. *See also* Most-favored-nation
      trade status
   human rights and, 403–404, 412–414
Treaty of Bjorko, 178
Trident II missile, 423
Trilateral Commission, 232
Triplett, William C., II, 392(n2)
Trudeau, Pierre Elliot, 83
Truman, Harry, 9, 139
Turner, Stansfield, 238, 328
Tutweiler, Margaret, 359–360, 368
Two-China plan, 92, 167–169, 174–175,
      195–196, 293

U-2 spy planes, 167
UN Commission on Human Rights, 414
Unconventional Warfare Program BRAVO, 38
Unger, Leonard, 176, 271, 272
UNITA. *See* National Union for the Total In-
      dependence of Angola
United Nations General Assembly, 24, 27, 30,
      40, 88, 92, 101, 112, 116–117, 196, 373
United Nations Security Council, 27, 387
United States Information Agency, 125
United Technologies Corporation, 400
U.S.-China Joint Communiqué on United
      States Arms Sales to Taiwan, 326–327
U.S. embassy (Beijing), 7
Ussuri River, 47

Vance, Cyrus, 230, 233, 235–236, 237–239,
      250, 409
   SALT and, 256, 265
   visit to China, 242, 244–246
Vietnam, 16, 28, 39, 89, 94–95, 101, 116, 231,
      344
   Chinese attack on, 11, 279–282, 440(n48)
   Deng on, 276, 277
   Kissinger on, 148–149
   Saigon, fall of, 201
   Soviet Union and, 51–52, 58, 62, 110,
      259–260, 276–281, 284
   Zhou Enlai and, 125, 126, 135, 149
Vietnam Desk, 66–67
Vladivostock summit, 194
Vogel, Ezra F., 385
Voice of America, 412, 413
Voyager channel, 183

W-88 thermonuclear warhead, 422–423
Walsh, James Edward, 81
Walters, Vernon A., 78
Wang Dan, 349, 350, 354, 362, 395, 420
Wang Dongxing, 223

Wang Hairong, 91
Wang Jisi, 36
Wang Juntao, 408, 411
Wang Ruoshui, 338
Wan Li, 351, 353
Warsaw meetings, 56, 57, 72, 74–75, 78
Warsaw Pact, 384
Washington Post, 14, 241, 246, 255, 273, 335, 346, 367
Washington Special Action Group (WSAG), 349(n32)
Watergate, 149, 162–163, 166, 173, 177, 178, 212
Weapons. *See also* Arms sales
  chemical weapons, 396–397
  F-5E fighters, 32, 169–170, 308, 310, 312–313, 315, 320–322, 321, 324, 326
  F-8 fighters, 338, 366
  F-16 fighters, 7, 376–378, 392(n2), 421
  FX fighter issue, 300, 306–316, 321–322
  M-9 missiles, 373
  M-11 missiles, 373, 396, 399, 413
  MIG-19 fighters, 81
  MIG-21 fighters, 338
  Mirage 2000-5 fighter-bombers, 7, 377
  missile control, 373–374
  Prithvi missile, 396
  W-88 thermonuclear warhead, 422–423
Wei Jingsheng, 282–283, 345, 389, 405–407, 420
Weinberger, Caspar, 302, 306, 307, 319, 337
Wells, Bill, 155
Whiting, Allen, 86
Wisner, Frank J., 408
Wolfowitz, Paul D., 329, 330–331
Woodcock, Leonard, 239–248, 257–258, 260–261, 285
  Carter, meeting with, 250–251
  communiqué and, 264–265
  Deng, meetings with, 262–264, 266–270
  Reagan administration and, 290, 292, 294, 295–296
  UAW speech, 249–250
Woodcock, Sharon, 255
Woods, Rose Mary, 137, 143
Woolsey, R. James, 28
World Table Tennis Championship, 90
World Trade Organization (WTO), 421, 427
WSAG. *See* Washington Special Action Group
WTO. *See* World Trade Organization
Wuer Kaixi, 362
Wu Xueqian, 331, 362, 364

Xinjiang Province, 65
Xiong Guangkai, 356–357, 422
Xu Wenli, 282, 425
Xu Xiangqian, 71

Yang Shangkun, 259, 364, 366, 374
Yao Wenyuan, 165, 223
Ye Jianying, 71, 97, 129, 170, 192, 193, 223, 243
  nine-point plan, 310, 314
Yinhe incident, 396–398
Yom Kippur War, 166
Yu Haocheng, 412

Zablocki, Clement J., 186
Zaire, 204
Zhang Aiping, 331
Zhang Chunqiao, 221, 223
Zhang Hanzhi, 188
Zhang Wenjin, 301, 310–312, 313, 322, 332
Zhao Ziyang, 312, 314, 322, 325, 331, 334, 344
  on nuclear proliferation, 335
  Tiananmen Square demonstrations and, 348, 351, 363, 365
Zhenbao Island, 48. *See also* Damansky Island incident
Zhongguo, 6
Zhongnanhai, 83–84
Zhongshan Institute, 190
Zhou Enlai, 8, 10, 11, 39, 70–71, 87, 150
  death of, 220, 222
  Ford, meeting with, 185
  illness, 147, 152, 169, 172, 184, 191–192, 194, 215
  Jiang Qing and, 136–137, 192
  joint communiqué and, 115–116
  Kissinger and, 97–99, 114–116, 167–172
  Mao's distrust of, 152, 172, 174, 192, 445(n186)
  on nationalism, 432(n3)
  on Nixon, 99–100, 103
  Nixon and, 128, 134–136
  ping-pong players and, 90–91
  on Taiwan, 135–136
  Vietnam and, 125, 126, 135, 149
Zhuang Zedong, 90
Zhu De, 222
Zhuo Lin, 153
Zhu Qizhen, 378
Zhu Rongji, 370, 395, 420, 421, 425, 426
Ziegler, Ron, 134, 139

PublicAffairs is a new nonfiction publishing house and a tribute to the standards, values, and flair of three persons who have served as mentors to countless reporters, writers, editors, and book people of all kinds, including me.

I. F. Stone, proprietor of *I. F. Stone's Weekly*, combined a commitment to the First Amendment with entrepreneurial zeal and reporting skill and became one of the great independent journalists in American history. At the age of eighty, Izzy published *The Trial of Socrates*, which was a national bestseller. He wrote the book after he taught himself ancient Greek.

Benjamin C. Bradlee was for nearly thirty years the charismatic editorial leader of *The Washington Post*. It was Ben who gave the *Post* the range and courage to pursue such historic issues as Watergate. He supported his reporters with a tenacity that made them fearless, and it is no accident that so many became authors of influential, best-selling books.

Robert L. Bernstein, the chief executive of Random House for more than a quarter century, guided one of the nation's premier publishing houses. Bob was personally responsible for many books of political dissent and argument that challenged tyranny around the globe. He is also the founder and was the longtime chair of Human Rights Watch, one of the most respected human rights organizations in the world.

·   ·   ·

For fifty years, the banner of Public Affairs Press was carried by its owner Morris B. Schnapper, who published Gandhi, Nasser, Toynbee, Truman, and about 1,500 other authors. In 1983 Schnapper was described by *The Washington Post* as "a redoubtable gadfly." His legacy will endure in the books to come.

Peter Osnos, *Publisher*

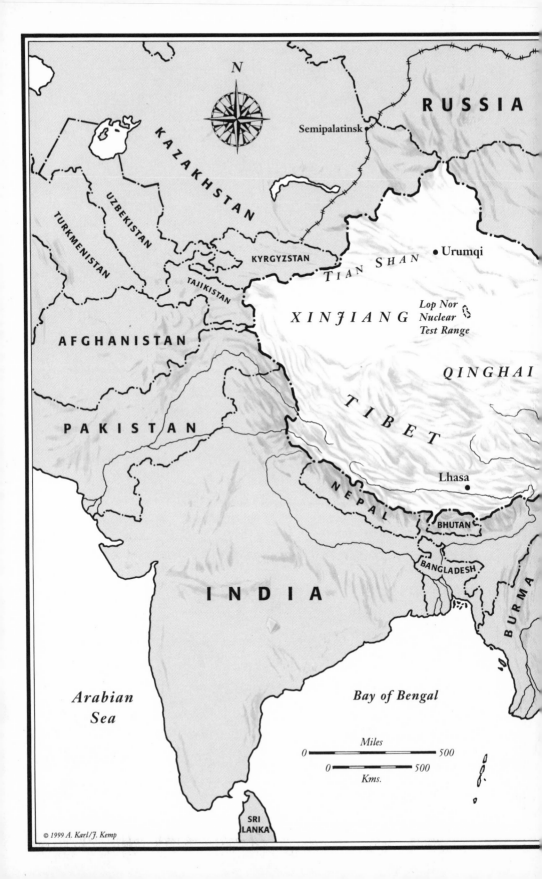